Happy 18th Birthday Sam

with love

& best wishes

from

John Alexandra Daisy & Freds

xxxx   July 2005

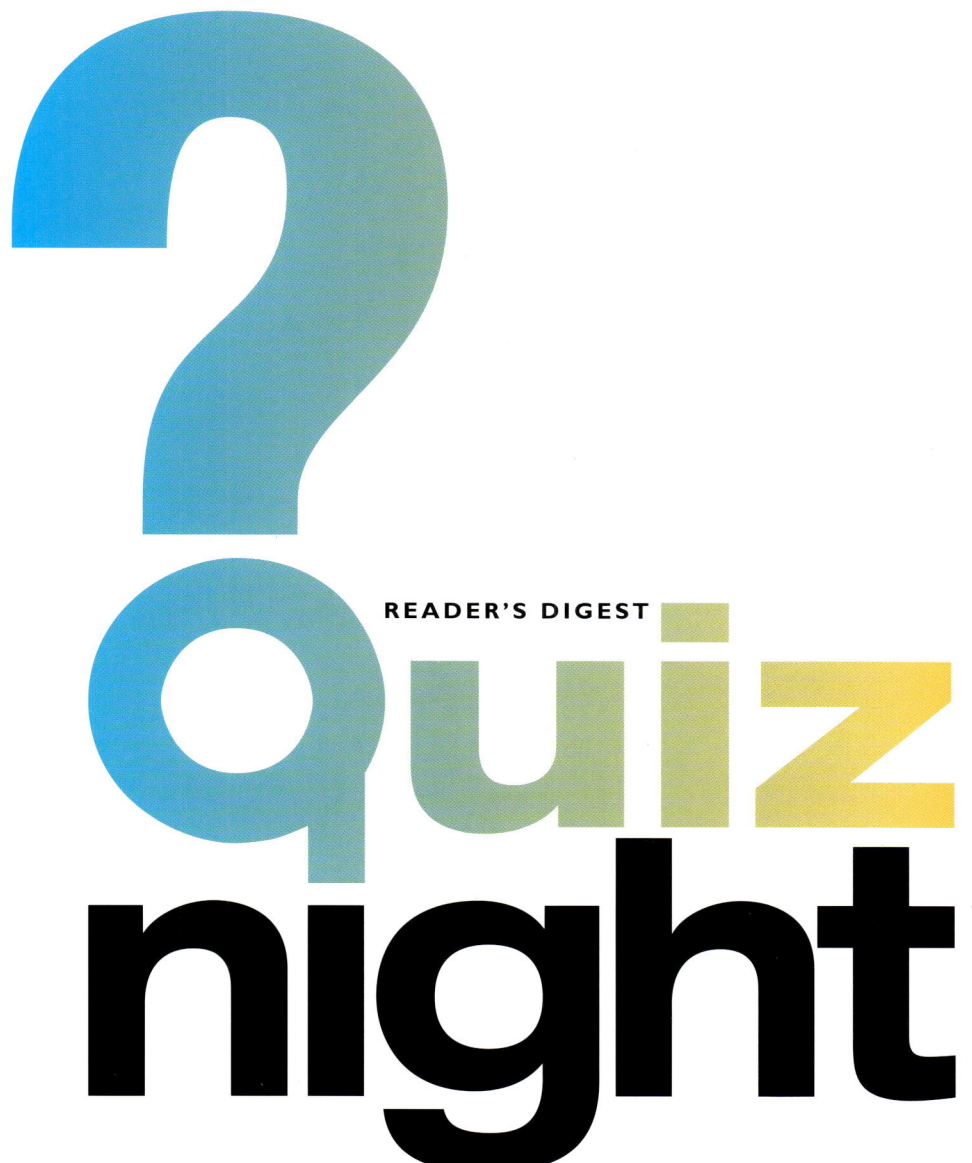

READER'S DIGEST

quiz
night

READER'S DIGEST

quiz
night

Contents

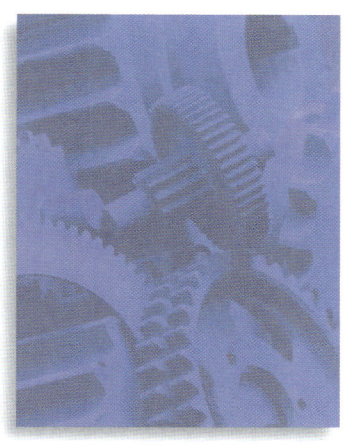

Introduction

There is something deeply satisfying about getting a quiz question right. It is not just that you knew the name of the Duke of Wellington's horse, it is also that you were able to riffle through the card-index of your mind and extract that very snippet in double-quick time. Good quizzing is about mental agility as well as about book knowledge – and fortune does not always favour the brainy.

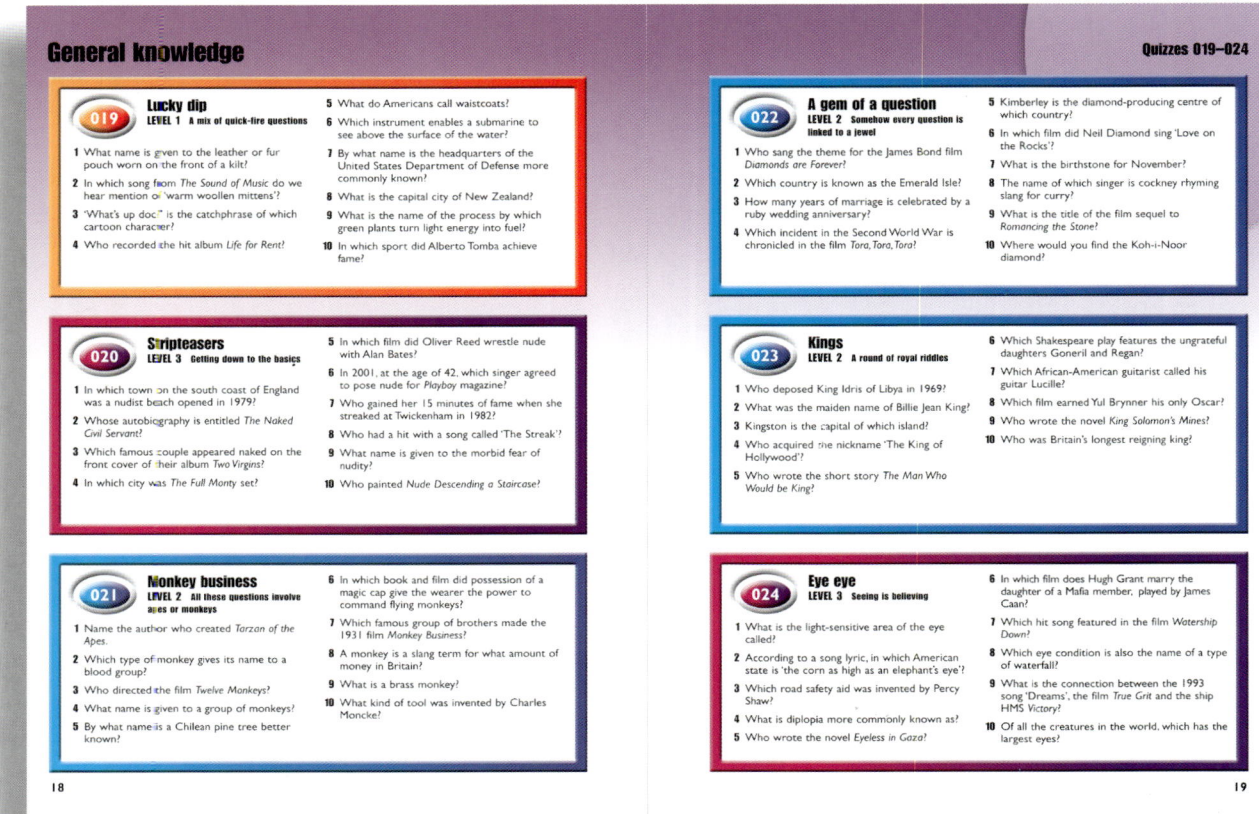

019 Lucky dip
LEVEL 1 A mix of quick-fire questions

1 What name is given to the leather or fur pouch worn on the front of a kilt?
2 In which song from *The Sound of Music* do we hear mention of 'warm woollen mittens'?
3 'What's up doc?' is the catchphrase of which cartoon character?
4 Who recorded the hit album *Life for Rent*?
5 What do Americans call waistcoats?
6 Which instrument enables a submarine to see above the surface of the water?
7 By what name is the headquarters of the United States Department of Defense more commonly known?
8 What is the capital city of New Zealand?
9 What is the name of the process by which green plants turn light energy into fuel?
10 In which sport did Alberto Tomba achieve fame?

020 Stripteasers
LEVEL 3 Getting down to the basics

1 In which town on the south coast of England was a nudist beach opened in 1979?
2 Whose autobiography is entitled *The Naked Civil Servant*?
3 Which famous couple appeared naked on the front cover of their album *Two Virgins*?
4 In which city was *The Full Monty* set?
5 In which film did Oliver Reed wrestle nude with Alan Bates?
6 In 2001, at the age of 42, which singer agreed to pose nude for *Playboy* magazine?
7 Who gained her 15 minutes of fame when she streaked at Twickenham in 1982?
8 Who had a hit with a song called 'The Streak'?
9 What name is given to the morbid fear of nudity?
10 Who painted *Nude Descending a Staircase*?

021 Monkey business
LEVEL 2 All these questions involve apes or monkeys

1 Name the author who created *Tarzan of the Apes*.
2 Which type of monkey gives its name to a blood group?
3 Who directed the film *Twelve Monkeys*?
4 What name is given to a group of monkeys?
5 By what name is a Chilean pine tree better known?
6 In which book and film did possession of a magic cap give the wearer the power to command flying monkeys?
7 Which famous group of brothers made the 1931 film *Monkey Business*?
8 A monkey is a slang term for what amount of money in Britain?
9 What is a brass monkey?
10 What kind of tool was invented by Charles Moncke?

022 A gem of a question
LEVEL 2 Somehow every question is linked to a jewel

1 Who sang the theme for the James Bond film *Diamonds are Forever*?
2 Which country is known as the Emerald Isle?
3 How many years of marriage is celebrated by a ruby wedding anniversary?
4 Which incident in the Second World War is chronicled in the film *Tora, Tora, Tora*?
5 Kimberley is the diamond-producing centre of which country?
6 In which film did Neil Diamond sing 'Love on the Rocks'?
7 What is the birthstone for November?
8 The name of which singer is cockney rhyming slang for curry?
9 What is the title of the film sequel to *Romancing the Stone*?
10 Where would you find the Koh-i-Noor diamond?

023 Kings
LEVEL 2 A round of royal riddles

1 Who deposed King Idris of Libya in 1969?
2 What was the maiden name of Billie Jean King?
3 Kingston is the capital of which island?
4 Who acquired the nickname 'The King of Hollywood'?
5 Who wrote the short story *The Man Who Would be King*?
6 Which Shakespeare play features the ungrateful daughters Goneril and Regan?
7 Which African-American guitarist called his guitar Lucille?
8 Which film earned Yul Brynner his only Oscar?
9 Who wrote the novel *King Solomon's Mines*?
10 Who was Britain's longest reigning king?

024 Eye eye
LEVEL 3 Seeing is believing

1 What is the light-sensitive area of the eye called?
2 According to a song lyric, in which American state is 'the corn as high as an elephant's eye'?
3 Which road safety aid was invented by Percy Shaw?
4 What is diplopia more commonly known as?
5 Who wrote the novel *Eyeless in Gaza*?
6 In which film does Hugh Grant marry the daughter of a Mafia member, played by James Caan?
7 Which hit song featured in the film *Watership Down*?
8 Which eye condition is also the name of a type of waterfall?
9 What is the connection between the 1993 song 'Dreams', the film *True Grit* and the ship HMS *Victory*?
10 Of all the creatures in the world, which has the largest eyes?

18

19

Quiz Night contains more than 10,000 questions in eight main sections. Each chapter covers a different field of knowledge from Film and Television to Natural History. If you choose one round from each section you will have a well-balanced quiz, but of course you can have a quiz entirely about sport if that is what suits your audience. Each round is graded for difficulty: level 1 is the easiest and level 3 the hardest. A good quiz will have some simple rounds and some harder ones. Each set of ten questions has its own number which will guide you to the corresponding set of answers in the back of the book.

If as quizmaster you want to read the questions straight from the book, you may find it helpful to flag the pages with sticky labels or pieces of paper. For a bigger, more formal quiz it makes sense to photocopy the rounds you are using onto separate sheets. You are welcome to photocopy as many pages as you need, as often as you wish: there are no copyright restrictions.

A few rules

The last thing you want in a quiz is a dispute, so lay down a few simple rules before you start. Each correct answer earns one point (no half-points for nearly-rights!); no taking back answer sheets after they have been handed in; and no arguing with the quizmaster. If your quiz ends in a draw, use the tie breakers on page 396. Give tied teams a fixed amount of time – two minutes is good – to write down as many items as they can in the chosen category. The team with the most correct items carries the day.

Jokers

Using jokers is a way of introducing an element of luck and judgment into your quiz. Each team or individual plays their joker before the round in which they think they will do best, and are awarded double points for that round. A well-played joker can transform a team's fortunes – so use it well. A joker that can be photocopied is provided at the front of *Quiz Night*. Alternatively you might invite each team to make its own joker and award a prize for the best one.

Scorecard and answer cards

Quiz Night comes with a scorecard and an answer card, both of which can be found at the back of the book. You can photocopy these for each quiz that you do. You will need one answer

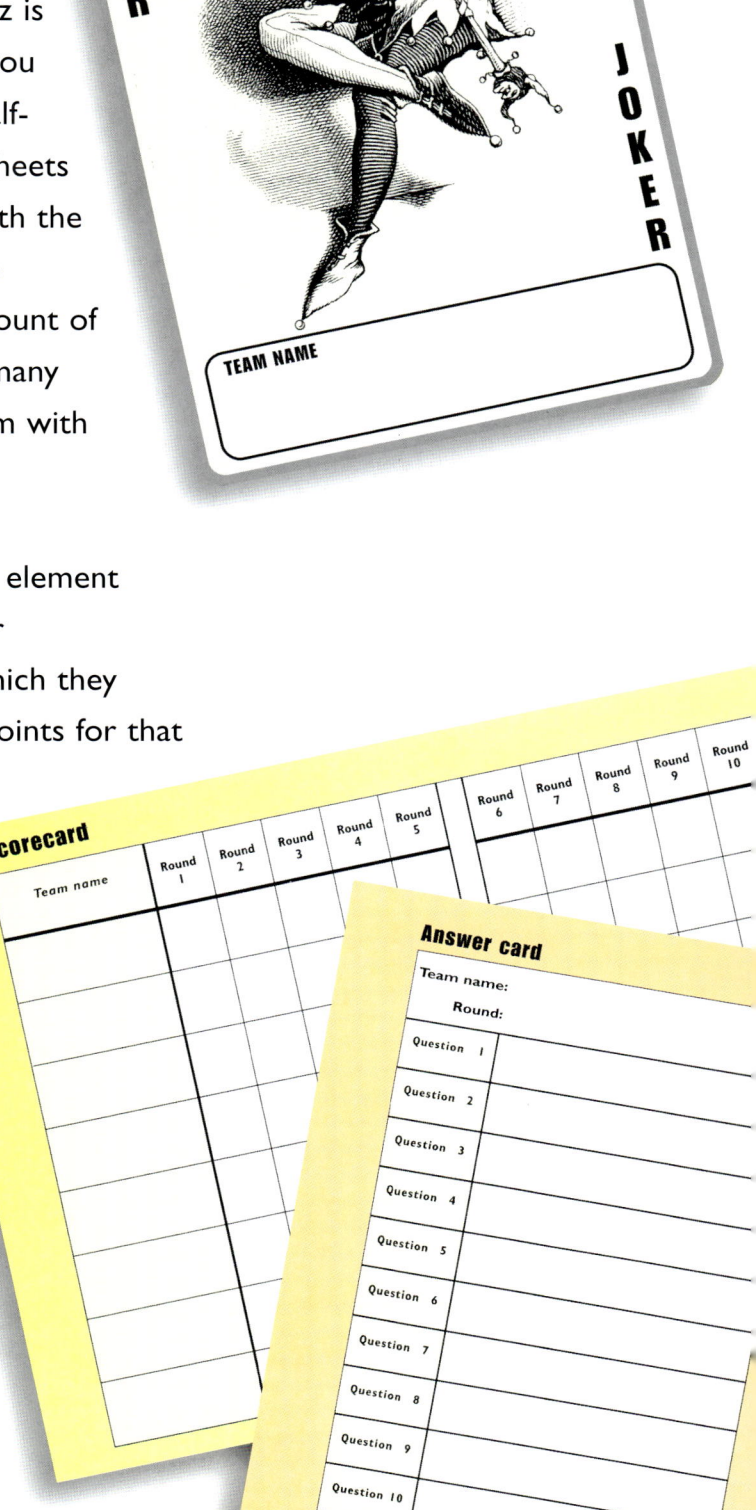

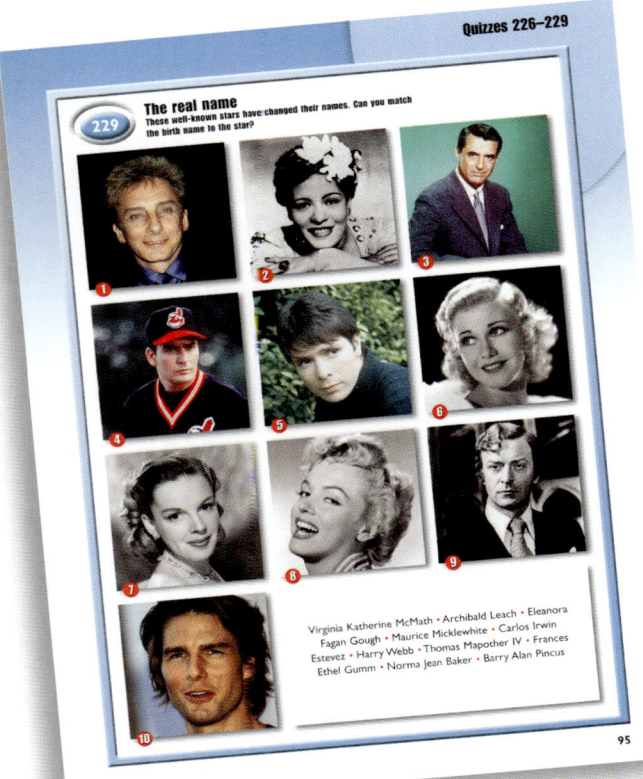

229 The real name
These well-known stars have changed their names. Can you match the birth name to the star?

Virginia Katherine McMath • Archibald Leach • Eleanora Fagan Gough • Maurice Micklewhite • Carlos Irwin Estevez • Harry Webb • Thomas Mapother IV • Frances Ethel Gumm • Norma Jean Baker • Barry Alan Pincus

95

card per team per round of your quiz. So if, for example, there are six teams involved in your quiz and you have seven rounds planned, you need to make 42 copies of the answer card. You only need one copy of the scorecard, though it makes sense to run off a few spares — just in case the person in charge of adding up the scores makes a mistake.

Picture posers
There are a number of visual quizzes in the book. These quizzes work best as 'table rounds', something for the teams to be working on while they settle down before the formal start of the quiz. They will look best if they are photocopied in colour (one copy for each player or team), but they will also reproduce perfectly well on a standard black-and-white photocopy machine.

Go off on a quest
In each section of *Quiz Night* you will find some rounds that are entitled 'Quest'. These are super-difficult rounds that demand a little creative thinking, a knack for following a hunch, or even some book research. You will find that most quest questions are too devious or difficult to answer off the top of your head (so they are not suitable for a standard quiz). They are a different kind of quiz — designed to be played over the course of a weekend or even a week — say, in the long evenings during a winter holiday. So don't give up too easily on a quest: you never know when a brilliant flash of inspiration will strike.

678 Nature quest

These questions are tougher than the others and you may need to do some research

1 What do the following animals have in common: the blue antelope, the Falklands fox, the Bali tiger, the Badlands bighorn sheep?

2 In Malay this animal's name means 'man of the forest'. What is it?

3 In Old Afrikaans this animal is 'earth pig'. What is it?

4 Which animal would you associate with a 'Nantucket sleighride'?

5 Where the bee sucks, there sucks who?

6 What is the link between the glowworm, the koala bear and the Tasmanian tiger?

7 Cambrian, Ordovician, Silurian: what next?

8 Which Wilde animal is uneatable?

9 'The unicorn is a passing ugly beast to look upon,' wrote a disappointed Marco Polo in the 14th century, "Tis altogether different from what we imagined.' What was it he had seen, in fact?

10 Hibernation means sleeping through the winter — but what is the word for sleeping through the summer?

11 Collared, dusky, superb fruit. Which bird?

12 Sea, tumble, giant hog. All types of what?

13 'In their queer, inimitable, vegetative gracefulness … a family of rare, long-stemmed speckled gigantic flowers slowly advancing.' Which animals are being described here?

14 Rumen, abomasum, omasum, reticulum. The four parts of what?

15 After what animal are the Canary Isles named?

A clue to question 6

265

Quick quizzes

On pages 360 to 395 you will find rounds of 'Quick Quizzes'. Within this section of the book you can use a dice to make the selection of questions asked more random. This is a good way to conduct an informal quickfire quiz – and it allows everybody to join in because there is no need for a quizmaster to act as guardian of the answers. Quick quizzes are also an ideal way to play alone.

The first step is to pick a number from 1 to 36. Find the Quick Quiz that corresponds to that number. Now you can either answer all the questions on the page, or roll the dice to go to a numbered panel on that page. Again, you have the choice of answering all the questions in that panel or you can throw the dice again and get a random question. Answer the question or questions, then the go passes along: the next player can take their pick of any of more than a thousand questions.

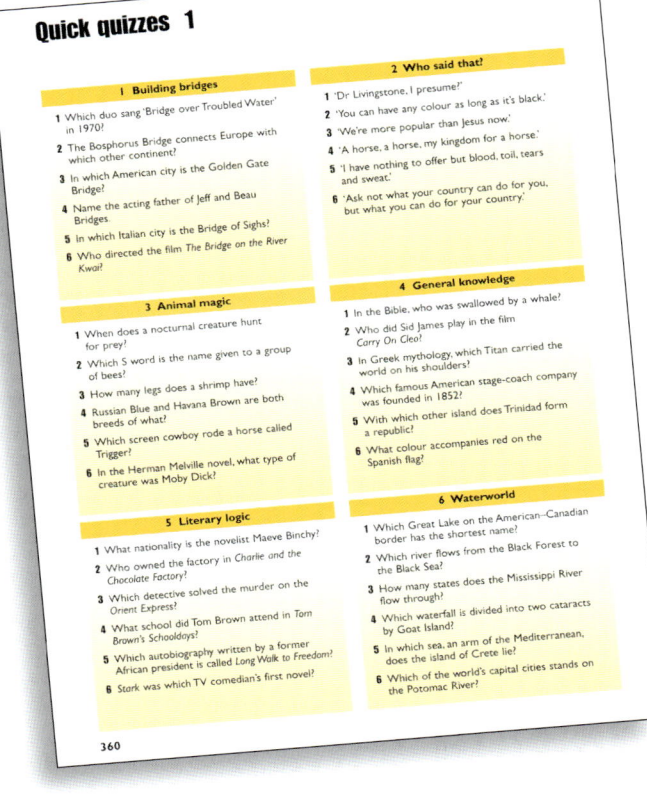

Young quizzlets

Each section of the book has some questions designed specially for children. These too have levels of difficulty based on age: 7–11 and 12–14. All keen quizzers are naturally free to try questions aimed at older children – and there's nothing to stop children of any age tackling the grown-up questions.

In this section of *Quiz Night* – as in every other part of the book – there is really only one rule: do your best, and have lots of fun.

Quizzes

001–201

GENERAL KNOWLEDGE

General knowledge

Lucky dip
001

LEVEL 1   Test your knowledge

1 Arch, girder, suspension and cantilever are all types of what?

2 What is the chemical formula for liquid ice?

3 Which member of the British royal family saw active service during the Falklands War?

4 Which Hollywood actor set up a research foundation to investigate Parkinson's disease, a condition from which he suffers?

5 What was the nationality of the writer Hans Christian Andersen?

6 For what did Suffragettes campaign?

7 In which 1956 film did Yul Brynner play the ruler of Siam?

8 Which is the most abundant gas in the Earth's atmosphere?

9 In which European country is the Prado art gallery?

10 What connects the man who discovered penicillin with the creator of James Bond?

Witchy Worries
002

LEVEL 1   Which question is witch?

1 What name is given to a group of witches?

2 Which Shakespeare play featured a trio of witches?

3 What is another name for *Hamamelis virginiana*, a small winter-flowering tree used to treat skin conditions?

4 What was the name of the cat in *Sabrina the Teenage Witch*?

5 What name is given to a male witch?

6 What was the name of the magical land in *The Lion, the Witch and the Wardrobe*?

7 In which film did the wicked witch write the words 'Surrender Dorothy' in the sky with smoke from her broomstick?

8 On screen, Susan Sarandon, Michelle Pfeiffer and Cher played 'The Witches' of what town?

9 In the 1960s sitcom *Bewitched*, how did Samantha the witch cast her magic?

10 Which 1999 film told the story of a documentary about a local witch?

Alias Smith and Jones
003

LEVEL 2   All the questions relate to someone called either Smith or Jones

1 Mandy Smith was briefly married to Bill Wyman, a member of which famous rock band?

2 Where is Davy Jones's locker?

3 Who directed the 1997 comedy film *Bean*?

4 Who swivelled his hips while singing 'It's Not Unusual'?

5 Who ruled Rhodesia from 1964 to 1979?

6 Which model and singer played the character of Mayday in the Bond film, *A View to a Kill*?

7 Who starred in the films *Independence Day* and *Wild Wild West*?

8 Which all-action hero did Harrison Ford play on film in 1981, 1984 and 1989?

9 Name the actress who, on screen, has played a Mother Superior, one of Harry Potter's teachers and a Greek goddess.

10 Who was the infamous leader of 'The People's Temple', a religious cult that committed mass suicide in 1978?

Something fishy

004

LEVEL 2   You may have to work hard to find the fish or sea connection

1 What name is given to a dish of pickled herring that is traditionally served with an onion or a gherkin?

2 What is the first name of Private Pike in the television series *Dad's Army*?

3 Who wears 'The Fisherman's Ring'?

4 Which actor played the character of Otto in the film *A Fish Called Wanda*?

5 What kind of animal was Beatrix Potter's Jeremy Fisher?

6 What was Monstro, the giant animal that swallowed *Pinocchio* and his father?

7 According to the Bible, Jesus fed the 5000 with five loaves and how many fishes?

8 Which actor played Captain Quint in the film *Jaws*?

9 By what other name is the literary character William Fisher known?

10 Fish was the lead singer of which pop group, who had a hit with the song 'Kayleigh'?

Give us a kiss!

005

LEVEL 2   Romantic clinchers

1 On which vessel did Horatio Nelson allegedly say: 'Kiss me Hardy'?

2 Which Disney animation featured the song 'Kiss the Girl'?

3 In The Drifters' song, where was the kissing taking place?

4 Who sculpted *The Kiss*?

5 Which nursery rhyme character 'kissed the girls and made them cry'?

6 Under which plant do you traditionally kiss at Christmas?

7 What do the initials SWALK stand for on a Valentine's envelope?

8 Who caused a scandal by being photographed having her toes kissed?

9 On which Shakespeare play was the film *Kiss Me Kate* based?

10 Who is reported to have said, but denies saying it: 'Kissing Marilyn Monroe was like kissing Hitler'?

Leaders of the gang

006

LEVEL 3   Questions about the people who are in charge

1 Which peace-keeping organisation was founded in the USA by Curtis Sliwa?

2 Name the American President who was responsible for introducing Prohibition.

3 Who is the only British Prime Minister to have married a divorcee?

4 Peter Cetera was the lead singer of which pop group?

5 What name is given to the spiritual leader of a Jewish congregation?

6 Which politician founded the British Union of Fascists?

7 Who was the ruler of Argentina at the time of the Falklands conflict?

8 Who is the only American President to have been a bachelor?

9 Ammon is the chief god in which civilisation's mythology?

10 Who played the leader of the gang in the classic comedy film *The Lavender Hill Mob*?

General knowledge

Time for bed
007
LEVEL 1 A round of questions that won't put you to sleep

1 In which 1993 film did Tom Hanks meet Meg Ryan at the top of the Empire State Building?

2 What is a somnambulist?

3 What do the initials REM stand for with regard to dream patterns?

4 What type of rodent fell asleep inside the teapot at the Mad Hatter's tea party in *Alice in Wonderland*?

5 Which actress engaged in pillow talk with Rock Hudson in a 1959 film?

6 Which female songstress hit the charts in 1978 with a song called 'Talking in your Sleep'?

7 In which field of entertainment is Wayne Sleep a famous name?

8 Who committed the murders in the film *A Nightmare on Elm Street*?

9 Which detective made his literary debut in *The Big Sleep*?

10 Who ended each TV episode of *The Magic Roundabout* with the words: 'Time for bed'?

Games and pastimes
008
LEVEL 1 Don't play up, just play the game

1 What name is given to the Japanese art of paper folding?

2 In the London version of Monopoly, which is the cheapest property?

3 How many points are scored with a try in rugby union?

4 A 'royal flush' is the top hand in which game?

5 With how many pieces does each player begin in the game of backgammon?

6 What do Americans call the game of draughts?

7 In which city were the 1992 Summer Olympic Games held?

8 In which game would you play a 'rubber'?

9 In which card game would you meet 'Mr Bun the Baker'?

10 In the Nintendo game, what was Mario's trade?

Say it with flowers
009
LEVEL 2 Every question is related somehow to a flower

1 Which flower shares its name with the coloured part of the eye?

2 Which pop group had a 1960s hit with the song 'Build me up Buttercup'?

3 According to Shakespeare, what 'by any other name would smell as sweet'?

4 Which flower was named after a mythological character who fell in love with his reflection?

5 Who wrote the novel *The Name of the Rose*?

6 What is the national flower of Japan?

7 Which flowery hit of 1967 begins with the line: 'Woke up one morning half asleep with all my blankets in a heap'?

8 Which part of a flower contains the pollen?

9 What is the name of the Indian Princess in *Peter Pan*?

10 Who looked 'sweet upon the seat of a bicycle made for two'?

010 Vive la France
LEVEL 2   Questions about France and all things French

1 Which French heroine was burnt at the stake in Rouen?

2 What is the common name of the oldest university in France?

3 Which Parisian nightclub became famous for its cancan?

4 In which building is the famed Hall of Mirrors?

5 Which singer was 'Lost in France' in 1976?

6 Who captained France to victory in the 1998 football World Cup?

7 Which city provided the French connection in the film of the same name?

8 What name is given to the national flag of France?

9 During the Second World War, Marshal Philippe Pétain ruled over unoccupied France. By what name was his regime known?

10 Which mountain range separates France from Spain?

011 Lucky dip
LEVEL 2   Mixed bag of posers to get you guessing

1 What sort of building derives its name from the Greek for 'seat'?

2 Which musical instrument is the largest member of the tuba family?

3 In the ranking of the aristocracy, what comes between a Baron and an Earl?

4 Which Andrew Lloyd Webber musical was performed on roller skates?

5 In which European country did Punch and Judy shows originate?

6 Which Brazilian dance became popular throughout Europe in 1989?

7 In the E.M. Forster novel *A Room with a View*, which city provided the view?

8 Which fashion designer created 'The New Look' in the 1950s?

9 What is made from a mixture of linseed oil and powdered chalk?

10 What is the capital city of Norway?

012 Lucky dip
LEVEL 3   You may have to dig deep to solve these questions

1 Who has been played on screen by Kurt Russell, Henry Fonda, James Stewart and Kevin Costner?

2 Who was shot and killed on November 24, 1963, on live television?

3 What is the connection between Chester Gould and Warren Beatty?

4 If you had a 'Cambridge Rival' in your mouth, what would you be eating?

5 Whose portrait appears on a United States $100 bill?

6 What is the Index Librorum Prohibitorum?

7 What kind of race is the Atlantic City marathon?

8 Who is the Greek god of sleep?

9 'Galvayne's groove' can be used to determine the age of what?

10 The foreign minister for which European country died after being stabbed in September 2003?

General knowledge

The letter A

013

LEVEL 1   All 10 answers begin with the letter A

1 What is the eleventh sign of the zodiac?

2 What name is given to the smallest indivisible particle of an element?

3 By what other name is a German shepherd dog commonly known?

4 What is the name of God in Islam?

5 Which seven-letter word means to withhold one's vote from an election?

6 For what crime was Anne Boleyn executed in 1536?

7 What name is given to a substance that is taken to counteract a poison?

8 What is the name of the largest dam on the River Nile?

9 Of which region in southern Spain is Seville the central city?

10 What was the name of the first US space programme that put a man on the Moon?

The letter A

014

LEVEL 2   All 10 answers begin with the letter A

1 What is the middle name of the inventor Thomas Edison?

2 What ten-letter word is the name given to the long staff used by mountain climbers?

3 What flavour is ouzo, the national drink of Greece?

4 What name is given to the fear of heights?

5 What name was given to the outpost held by Texan fighters for 13 days against the Mexican army in 1836?

6 Which film featured a spacecraft called *The Nostromo*?

7 In the Bible, who was married to Sarah, Hagar and Keturah?

8 What is the collective name for a group of frogs?

9 Who won football's World Cup in 1978?

10 In which country is the Pashtu language spoken?

The letter A

015

LEVEL 3   All 10 answers begin with the letter A

1 Globe and Jerusalem are both varieties of what?

2 In the church hierarchy, what rank is immediately below a Bishop?

3 What is the name of the wax-like substance obtained from sperm whales and used in perfumes?

4 What is the birthstone for March?

5 Little Rock is the state capital of which American state?

6 What was the surname of the first woman MP?

7 In mythology, who was the beautiful youth loved by Venus?

8 What is the name of the world's driest desert?

9 The axilla is the technical term for which part of the body?

10 What is the name of the princess in *Sleeping Beauty*?

The letter B

016

LEVEL 1 All 10 answers begin with the letter B

1 In boxing weights, what comes between flyweight and featherweight?

2 What name is given to the crime of marrying for the second time while a first marriage is still valid?

3 Who said: 'I shall hear in heaven'?

4 In which city are the headquarters of the European Union?

5 What kind of grass provides the staple diet of a panda?

6 In which TV show did Pamela Anderson play C.J. Parker?

7 With which London market would you associate fish?

8 What name is given to a male rabbit?

9 Which war was fought in South Africa between 1899 and 1902?

10 What is the study of the science of plants known as?

The letter B

017

LEVEL 2 All 10 answers begin with the letter B

1 What is the national sport of Malaysia?

2 Who captained England to win a 1988 Rugby Union grand slam?

3 What breed of dog is Disney's Pluto?

4 What is the name of the shrew-like marsupial, native to Australia?

5 What was the surname of the central family in the drama series *Upstairs, Downstairs*?

6 Which fluid is secreted by the liver and stored in the gall bladder?

7 What was the official designation of the American Second World War bomber the *Flying Fortress*?

8 What is the more common name for the Tower of London's Yeomen of the Guard?

9 Which singing voice comes between a tenor and a bass?

10 What plant is often known as the butterfly bush?

The letter C

018

LEVEL 1 All 10 answers begin with the letter C

1 In which bar did the TV character Sam Malone work?

2 What name is given to the approximately 5m-long tree trunk tossed in Scotland's Highland Games?

3 Which American state has the highest population?

4 What is the name of the British Prime Minister's official country residence?

5 What name is given to a young male horse?

6 What is the name of the building in which the American Congress meets?

7 Which fabled creature was half man, half horse?

8 What type of animal tried in vain to catch the roadrunner in the Warner Brothers' cartoons?

9 What is an alternative name for a puma?

10 Which reptile is noted for its ability to change colour?

General knowledge

019 Lucky dip
LEVEL 1   A mix of quick-fire questions

1 What name is given to the leather or fur pouch worn on the front of a kilt?

2 In which song from *The Sound of Music* do we hear mention of 'warm woollen mittens'?

3 'What's up doc?' is the catchphrase of which cartoon character?

4 Who recorded the hit album *Life for Rent*?

5 What do Americans call waistcoats?

6 Which instrument enables a submarine to see above the surface of the water?

7 By what name is the headquarters of the United States Department of Defense more commonly known?

8 What is the capital city of New Zealand?

9 What is the name of the process by which green plants turn light energy into fuel?

10 In which sport did Alberto Tomba achieve fame?

020 Stripteasers
LEVEL 3   Getting down to the basics

1 In which town on the south coast of England was a nudist beach opened in 1979?

2 Whose autobiography is entitled *The Naked Civil Servant*?

3 Which famous couple appeared naked on the front cover of their album *Two Virgins*?

4 In which city was *The Full Monty* set?

5 In which film did Oliver Reed wrestle nude with Alan Bates?

6 In 2001, at the age of 42, which singer agreed to pose nude for *Playboy* magazine?

7 Who gained her 15 minutes of fame when she streaked at Twickenham in 1982?

8 Who had a hit with a song called 'The Streak'?

9 What name is given to the morbid fear of nudity?

10 Who painted *Nude Descending a Staircase*?

021 Monkey business
LEVEL 2   All these questions involve apes or monkeys

1 Name the author who created *Tarzan of the Apes*.

2 Which type of monkey gives its name to a blood group?

3 Who directed the film *Twelve Monkeys*?

4 What name is given to a group of monkeys?

5 By what name is a Chilean pine tree better known?

6 In which book and film did possession of a magic cap give the wearer the power to command flying monkeys?

7 Which famous group of brothers made the 1931 film *Monkey Business*?

8 A monkey is a slang term for what amount of money in Britain?

9 What is a brass monkey?

10 What kind of tool was invented by Charles Moncke?

 **022**

A gem of a question
LEVEL 2   Somehow every question is linked to a jewel

1 Who sang the theme for the James Bond film *Diamonds are Forever*?

2 Which country is known as the Emerald Isle?

3 How many years of marriage is celebrated by a ruby wedding anniversary?

4 Which incident in the Second World War is chronicled in the film *Tora, Tora, Tora*?

5 Kimberley is the diamond-producing centre of which country?

6 In which film did Neil Diamond sing 'Love on the Rocks'?

7 What is the birthstone for November?

8 The name of which singer is cockney rhyming slang for curry?

9 What is the title of the film sequel to *Romancing the Stone*?

10 Where would you find the Koh-i-Noor diamond?

 **023**

Kings
LEVEL 2   A round of royal riddles

1 Who deposed King Idris of Libya in 1969?

2 What was the maiden name of Billie Jean King?

3 Kingston is the capital of which island?

4 Who acquired the nickname 'The King of Hollywood'?

5 Who wrote the short story *The Man Who Would be King*?

6 Which Shakespeare play features the ungrateful daughters Goneril and Regan?

7 Which African-American guitarist called his guitar Lucille?

8 Which film earned Yul Brynner his only Oscar?

9 Who wrote the novel *King Solomon's Mines*?

10 Who was Britain's longest reigning king?

 **024**

Eye eye
LEVEL 3   Seeing is believing

1 What is the light-sensitive area of the eye called?

2 According to a song lyric, in which American state is 'the corn as high as an elephant's eye'?

3 Which road safety aid was invented by Percy Shaw?

4 What is diplopia more commonly known as?

5 Who wrote the novel *Eyeless in Gaza*?

6 In which film does Hugh Grant marry the daughter of a Mafia member, played by James Caan?

7 Which hit song featured in the film *Watership Down*?

8 Which eye condition is also the name of a type of waterfall?

9 What is the connection between the 1993 song 'Dreams', the film *True Grit* and the ship HMS *Victory*?

10 Of all the creatures in the world, which has the largest eyes?

General knowledge

The letter B

025

LEVEL 3 All 10 answers begin with the letter B

1 What type of confectionery has a name that literally means 'baked twice'?

2 What is a tower jutting out over the gate of a castle called?

3 What name is given to the bottle of champagne that holds 16 ordinary bottles?

4 Norman Dagley was a former world champion in which sport?

5 What name is given to the box in which a ship's compass is stored?

6 Which 1988 film told the story of a 1963 crime?

7 According to Islam, what was the name of the mythical horse-like creature that carried Muhammad to heaven?

8 The name of which element is derived from the Greek for 'stench'?

9 What was the full surname of Biggles, the literary creation of W.E. Johns?

10 What is the form of torture whereby the soles of the feet are beaten with a stick?

The letter C

026

LEVEL 2 All 10 answers begin with the letter C

1 What word is the name given to a Bishop's staff?

2 What is the opposite of convex?

3 In which country was Robert Maxwell born?

4 Which word for a pyramid of stones is also the name of a breed of terrier?

5 A lych gate is an entrance to a what?

6 In the Roman Catholic church, what festival is celebrated on February 2 each year?

7 What name was given to a tradesman who made or traded knives?

8 What is the name of America's first space shuttle, launched in 1981?

9 What name is given to a yacht with two hulls?

10 In the Star Wars films, what is the name of Han Solo's hairy friend?

The letter C

027

LEVEL 2 All 10 answers begin with the letter C

1 What does a cryptologist study?

2 The TV programme *The Six Million Dollar Man* was based upon which novel?

3 What five-letter word is the name given to the outer covering or cup of a flower?

4 In which sport would you start at the south stake?

5 What is the name of the scarlet dye obtained from the dried bodies of beetles?

6 What is the uppermost layer of a forest called?

7 Calligraphy is the art of beautiful handwriting. What is bad writing called?

8 A Candiot is a native of which island?

9 What sort of musical instrument was used to play the theme to *Coronation Street*?

10 What was the name of Jacques Cousteau's research ship?

028 Knowledge quest

These questions are tougher than the others and you may need to do some research

1 What links the career paths of Sting, Mark Knopfler, Bryan Ferry and Ian Dury?

2 What connects dwarf, shift and Leicester?

3 What is the literal meaning of the word Beelzebub?

4 What word links: marker, lantern, mountain (fictional)?

5 UDTQCS . . . next?

6 What connects John, Jack and Jim (where one is a pedestrian, one a lion-tamer and the third on a ship)?

7 What connects Muhammed Ali, John Lennon and Boris Pasternak?

8 Which cartoon character has a statue erected in his honour in Crystal City, Texas?

9 Where was the inventor of the dynamo replaced by the composer of *The Dream of Gerontius*?

10 What connects the Hanging Gardens of Babylon, Tom Selleck and a wise man?

11 What is the family connection between Margaret Thatcher, Mel Gibson and William Shakespeare?

12 If you went north from the Land of Enchantment until you reached Big Sky Country, then turned east and travelled to the town of Bismark, what country would be to the north of you?

13 If the Pogues are Tuesday and the Undertones are Wednesday, what day are Blondie?

14 How did Yaron Cohen achieve fame and notoriety in 1998?

15 Designed to accommodate a French farmer, his pig and his bowler hat. What?

A clue to question 9

General knowledge

Ticklish allsorts

029

LEVEL 3   Wide-ranging trivia

1 Which TV series was spawned by the 1949 film *The Blue Lamp*?

2 What was Eric the Red's colourful lie (first told in 985 and repeated ever since)?

3 Which football team does novelist Nick Hornby support?

4 Who resigned as Director General of the BBC following the 2003 Hutton Inquiry?

5 Do bananas have seeds?

6 Which science-fiction film contains a sequence in which a panorama is depicted to the strains of Strauss's *Blue Danube*?

7 What is the perfect score in a game of ten-pin bowling?

8 Who won her first Grammy award in 1999 after 16 years in the pop business?

9 Whose favourite food is cow pie?

10 What connects Boris Pasternak, the most expensive painting in the world, a song with the line: 'Don't pay money just to see yourself...' and the bizarre practice of talking to the animals?

Alphabet soup

030

LEVEL 1   All 10 answers begin with the letter D

1 What is the city where John F. Kennedy was assassinated?

2 What is the title of a book made in 1086 recording the extent, value and ownership of all land in England?

3 What is a feeling of having already experienced a present situation?

4 What is the capital city of the Republic of Ireland?

5 Who was the female star of *Pillow Talk*?

6 What was the name of the medieval Italian poet who wrote *The Divine Comedy*?

7 What D is a cake of sweetened yeast pastry with fruit or nuts?

8 What D is (in theory) a system of government by the whole people, usually through elected representatives?

9 What D is a kind of light-brown cane sugar originating in Guyana?

10 What D is a Scottish town famous for marmalade and a type of fruit cake?

Just desserts

031

LEVEL 2   A basinful of questions for the sweet-toothed

1 Of which type of fruit is a Jonathan?

2 What is the literal meaning of the Italian 'tiramisu' pudding?

3 What is Chunky Monkey?

4 A loganberry is a cross between a raspberry and what?

5 Apart from milk and sugar, what is the main ingredient of crème caramel?

6 What type of pastry is used to make profiteroles?

7 In what country might you eat a trifle called 'whim wham'?

8 Is barley an ingredient of barley sugar?

9 What sweet was advertised as 'just enough to give your kids a treat'?

10 What are the three elements of baked Alaska?

Stars and their eyes

032

Can you identify these famous people from their eyes alone?

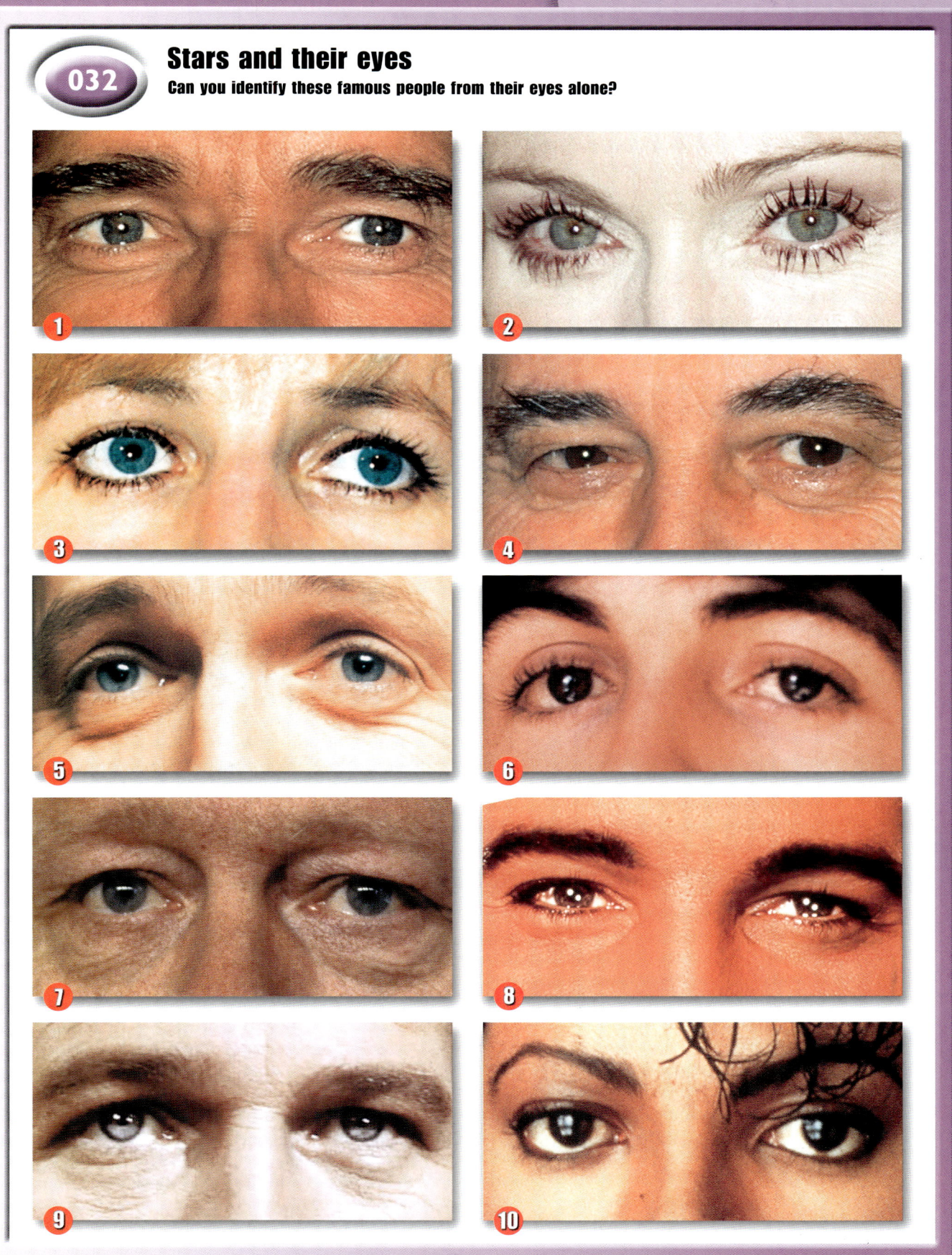

1

2

3

4

5

6

7

8

9

10

General knowledge

033 The letter D
LEVEL 1 All 10 answers begin with the letter D

1 What language is spoken in the Netherlands?

2 What is the surname of Wendy, John and Michael in *Peter Pan*?

3 What is the state capital of Colorado?

4 What is the alternative name for a crane fly?

5 What type of headgear is favoured by Arthur Conan Doyle's *Sherlock Holmes*?

6 By what name is a male honey bee known?

7 In which series of films did Charles Bronson play the vigilante Paul Kersey?

8 What name is given to a camel with one hump?

9 What word describes a score of forty-all in tennis?

10 What is the highest, non-royal rank of British nobility?

034 The letter D
LEVEL 2 All 10 answers begin with the letter D

1 What gaming devices are nicknamed Devil's Bones?

2 On which river does the English city of Sheffield stand?

3 What name is given to the fin on a fish's back?

4 What is the technical term for word blindness?

5 By what name was the Second World War Operation Overlord more commonly known?

6 In which film was Michael Douglas sexually harassed by his boss, Demi Moore?

7 What is the oldest state in the USA?

8 What is the name of the wife of Shakespeare's Othello?

9 What does the d stand for in the name of the singer kd lang?

10 Who is the Roman goddess of hunting?

035 The letter D
LEVEL 2 All 10 answers begin with the letter D

1 If you possess terpsichorean talents, what are you good at?

2 Which district of Cuba gave its name to a cocktail of rum and lime juice?

3 What does a mysophobic person fear?

4 When a cow is crossbred with a yak, what name is given to the male offspring?

5 What name is given to the long loincloth worn by men in India?

6 The Rogun Tajikistan is the world's highest what?

7 Which musical direction means 'getting gradually softer'?

8 In which TV series of yesteryear did Patrick McGoohan play the character of John Drake?

9 What name is given to the loose hanging skin under the throat of a chicken?

10 What name is given to the science of dating by counting tree rings?

No smoke without fire

036

LEVEL 2   An incendiary round, in a manner of speaking

1 Which adversary of Muhammad Ali was nicknamed Smokin' Joe?

2 In the 1977 film *Smokey and the Bandit*, who played the Bandit?

3 What is the significance of white smoke being released from the Vatican?

4 Which pop group hit the charts in 1959 with the song 'Smoke Gets in Your Eyes'?

5 In what year was cigarette advertising banned from British television?

6 What type of smoked sausage took its name from a German city?

7 Harold Wilson, James Galway and Freddie Trueman are all past winners of which award?

8 Which singer had hits with 'Tracks of my Tears' and 'I Second that Emotion'?

9 Name the author of *Kim*, who said: 'A woman is just a woman, but a cigar is a good smoke.'

10 Who played the fire chief in the 1974 film *The Towering Inferno*?

A land down under

037

LEVEL 2   Questions about, or related to, Australia

1 Which Australian outlaw did Mick Jagger portray in a 1970 film?

2 What is the capital of Tasmania?

3 Which animal indigenous to Australia has a name that means 'no drink'?

4 By what Aboriginal name is Ayers Rock now known?

5 Which Australian film was advertised with the line 'Dirty Dancing Down Under'?

6 What is the name of the famous musical venue that was designed by Jorn Utzon?

7 Which former Australian Wimbledon champion was nicknamed 'the Rockhampton rocket'?

8 What is the name of the street where the TV *Neighbours* live?

9 How many players are in each team in an Australian Rules football match?

10 Which Australian pop group had hits with 'The Carnival is Over' and 'World of our Own'?

Speak up!

038

LEVEL 3   A round related to speech and talking

1 What did Oscar Wilde describe as: 'the unspeakable in full pursuit of the uneatable'?

2 Whose autobiography is entitled *Can We Talk*?

3 In *The Hitchhiker's Guide to the Galaxy*, what type of fish is put in the ear in order to make all the spoken languages of the galaxy understandable?

4 What nine-letter word is the name given to a solo speech in a play?

5 Who said: 'I married beneath me, all women do'?

6 In which British building is the Whispering Gallery?

7 Who painted *The Scream*?

8 Which is the only English-speaking country in South America?

9 Who wrote the novel *The Horse Whisperer*?

10 Which TV character owned a talking horse called Mr Ed?

General knowledge

039

Rings on their fingers
LEVEL 1   Your fingers will point to the answers in this round

1 What kind of animals are central to the plot in the novel *Ring of Bright Water*?

2 Johnny Fingers was the pianist for which punk rock band?

3 In which 1981 film did Jack Nicholson enjoy an encounter on a kitchen table with Jessica Lange?

4 Which word beginning with P is the medical term for the fingers?

5 Who composed a four-opera cycle entitled *The Ring*?

6 Which Queen of England had an extra finger?

7 Which famous novel was set in Middle Earth?

8 Which American TV comedy series of the 1960s often pointed 'the fickle finger of fate'?

9 Who hit the charts in 1979 with the song 'Ring my Bell'?

10 By what name was the diminutive Charles Sherwood Stratton better known?

040

Peak practices
LEVEL 2   Climb every mountain or hill or gentle slope

1 Which fictional character fell asleep in the Catskill Mountains for 20 years?

2 What is the highest mountain in North America?

3 Which peak is nicknamed 'the meanest mountain on Earth'?

4 What was the only tune that 'Tom, Tom the piper's son' could play?

5 Which 1993 film sees Sylvester Stallone battling in the mountains against John Lithgow?

6 From which mountain did Moses descend with the Ten Commandments?

7 Which is the highest mountain in England?

8 Near which city did Julie Andrews sing: 'The hills are alive with the sound of music'?

9 In which country are the Taurus Mountains?

10 According to Laurel and Hardy, where is the trail of the lonesome pine?

041

5 for silver, 5 for gold
LEVEL 3   Ten for a secret never to be told

1 What do the initials EPNS stand for?

2 Which ex-Yardbird enjoyed a solo hit with 'Hi Ho Silver Lining'?

3 Who played an unlikely town sheriff in the 1985 western, *Silverado*?

4 Which American rock star is backed by the Silver Bullet band?

5 What was the title of the sixth novel in *The Chronicles of Narnia*?

6 Which film villain drove a car with the registration plate that read AU 1?

7 What is the more common name for iron pyrites?

8 In which city was the American sitcom *The Golden Girls* set?

9 In archery, how many points does the gold section of the target score?

10 Which country was formerly known as The Gold Coast?

Money, money, money

042

LEVEL 1   A bundle of questions about the green stuff

1 Which President features on a United States $1 bill?

2 According to the song 'Penny Lane', what photographs does the barber sell?

3 Which pop group hit the charts with the song 'Money for Nothing'?

4 What did Judas receive for betraying Jesus?

5 Which country and western singer was nicknamed 'the man in black'?

6 *The Color of Money* starring Paul Newman was a belated sequel to which film?

7 What is Russia's currency called?

8 Who played the man with no name in the film *A Fistful of Dollars*?

9 On which street does the Bank of England stand?

10 Judith Keppel was the first British person to win £1million on which game show?

A round of drinks

043

LEVEL 2   It's your turn to get the answers in

1 Which fruit is used to flavour the liqueur Southern Comfort?

2 What three-letter word is Chinese for tea?

3 Who composed the musical work *The Water Music*?

4 Vinho Verde is a white wine from which European country?

5 Who played Compo in the British sitcom, *Last of the Summer Wine*?

6 Who wrote the novel *Cider with Rosie*?

7 What brand of lager was advertised on TV by the actor Paul Hogan?

8 From which country does the drink tequila originate?

9 From which fruit is the drink perry distilled?

10 What is the title of the poem that contains the line: 'Water, water everywhere nor any drop to drink'?

Water, water everywhere

044

LEVEL 3   A round about the sea, rivers or water just to drink

1 Which is the world's busiest ship canal?

2 Which literary villain disappeared over the Reichenbach Falls?

3 What is a tsunami?

4 Who starred in the 1953 film classic *The Cruel Sea*?

5 In which country is the River Kwai?

6 Which singer had a No. I hit in the UK with 'Orinoco Flow'?

7 Which is the world's least salty sea?

8 Which song by a famous duo starts with the line: 'When you're weary, feeling small'?

9 What is the name of the stretch of water that separates the Isle of Wight from mainland Britain?

10 Of all the rivers in the world, which contains the greatest amount of water?

General knowledge

045 — Thicker than water

LEVEL 1 A gruesome collection of blood and gore

1 Who played Prince Vlad Dracula in the 1992 film, *Bram Stoker's Dracula*?

2 What C word is the name given to the smallest blood vessels in the body?

3 What is the medical term for an obstruction of a blood vessel by a clot or an air bubble?

4 Which organisation's motto is 'Blood and Fire'?

5 What name is given to the liquid part of the blood?

6 Which rocker wrote the song 'Only Women Bleed'?

7 What colour is Mr Spock's blood?

8 Which military leader acquired the nickname of 'old blood and guts'?

9 Which swashbuckling actor played Dr Peter Blood in the 1935 film *Captain Blood*?

10 Who was the first member of the British royal family to donate blood?

046 — Sun, Moon and stars

LEVEL 3 The answers are in the stars in this astrological round

1 What is the name of the Egyptian God of the Sun?

2 Which rock musical featured the song 'Good Morning Starshine'?

3 In the third of the *Star Wars* films, *Return of the Jedi*, which monstrous villain was choked to death by Princess Leia?

4 How many men have walked on the Moon?

5 Which country has a symbol called 'The Sun of May' at the centre of its flag?

6 In Greek mythology whose wings melted when he flew too close to the Sun?

7 Who wrote the novel *The Moon and Sixpence*?

8 Which song opens with the line: 'Starry, starry night paint your palettes blue and grey'?

9 Kenny Jones replaced Keith Moon in which pop group?

10 Who is the leader of the Unification Church?

047 — Let's dance

LEVEL 2 A top 10 for dancing the night away

1 By what popular name is The Royal Ballet Company known?

2 What was the full name of the character played by John Travolta in the film *Saturday Night Fever*?

3 What is the name of the ceremonial dance performed by the New Zealand All Blacks rugby union team?

4 Which film told the story of Lieutenant John Dunbar?

5 Which dancer's last words were: 'Get my swan costume ready'?

6 What is the name of the national dance of Poland?

7 Fred Astaire described Tula Ellice Finklea as 'beautiful dynamite'. What was her stage name?

8 In which musical did a dance called 'The Lambeth Walk' first appear?

9 Which biblical character performed the dance of the seven veils?

10 What is the name of the court dance made popular by Marie Antoinette?

048 Titled trivia
LEVEL 1 Royalty, lords and ladies

1 What is the favourite colour of the pop star Prince?

2 What name is given to the wife of a Sultan?

3 Which Hollywood star, known for his portrayal of western characters, was known as 'The Duke'?

4 Carrie Fisher played which royal character in the *Star Wars* films?

5 Which king said on his deathbed: 'Let not poor Nelly starve'?

6 In the British nobility, which is more senior, a Viscount or Baron?

7 Who on TV drove a car called General Lee?

8 Who disappeared after he allegedly murdered his family's nanny Sandra Rivett?

9 Who won his only best actor Oscar for his role in the film *The African Queen*?

10 What have you joined if you have taken the Queen's (or King's) shilling?

049 A weather report
LEVEL 2 Sun, snow, wind and rain: a round about the weather

1 Which former world snooker champion was nicknamed 'The Hurricane'?

2 Which cartoon character owns a dog called Snowy?

3 Which Disney film features the song 'Little April Showers'?

4 Who played Scarlett O'Hara in the film *Gone with the Wind*?

5 Which former Spice Girl had a UK Top 20 hit with 'It's raining men'?

6 Which former presenter of *Tomorrow's World* is famous for his election-night swingometer?

7 Who played Dustin Hoffman's brother in the film *Rain Man*?

8 Who created the police detective Jack Frost, played on TV by David Jason?

9 Which Gulf War general was nicknamed 'stormin' Norman'?

10 Which 1966 children's TV series featured the character Windy Miller?

050 You're in the army now
LEVEL 2 Questions about wars and the armed forces

1 Big Willy and Little Willy were the first types of what kind of war machine?

2 At which battle did the Charge of the Light Brigade take place?

3 Which is more senior, a lieutenant general or a major general?

4 Which country's soldiers were the first to enter Berlin at the end of the Second World War?

5 What Eastern European military alliance, which took its name from the Polish capital, was formed in 1955 and disbanded in July 1991?

6 Name the war memorial in Whitehall, London.

7 What name was given to the 1878 organisation founded by General William Booth?

8 The Second World War Home Volunteer Force was better known as what?

9 With which branch of the army are maroon berets associated?

10 What is the highest award for bravery in the American armed forces?

General knowledge

Birds of a feather
051
LEVEL 1   Strictly for the birds

1 Which Eagles hit begins with the line: 'On a dark desert highway, cool wind in my hair'?

2 What name is given to a baby pigeon?

3 Who created the character, Woody Woodpecker?

4 Which species of bird was considered sacred by Ancient Egyptians?

5 What bird has the largest wingspan?

6 What colour are budgerigars in the wild?

7 What is the alternative name for the butcher bird?

8 Who wrote the novel *Swallows and Amazons*?

9 Who directed the 1963 classic film *The Birds*?

10 What is the name of the world's smallest bird?

Wild west
052
LEVEL 1   Cowboys and Indians

1 What are cowboys called in Argentina?

2 What was the name of the ranch where the Cartwright family lived in the TV series *Bonanza*?

3 Henry Longfellow wrote a famous poem about which Native American?

4 Which Native American woman fell in love with a British settler called Captain Smith?

5 In which 1988 film did Emilio Estevez play Billy the Kid?

6 What was the name of Tonto's horse?

7 In the 1960s TV series, who played 'The Rifleman'?

8 James Fenimore Cooper wrote about the last of which tribe of Native Americans?

9 What was the name of the gang led by Butch Cassidy?

10 In which film did Dustin Hoffman play Jack Crabb, a man from the old west who allegedly lived until the ripe old age of 121?

Gospel musings
053
LEVEL 3   Questions about Matthew, Mark, Luke and John

1 In Treasure Island who marks out Billy Bones by passing to him the Black Spot which so terrifies him he dies of a heart attack?

2 Which novel by John Steinbeck told the story of the Joad family?

3 Who was the manager of Manchester United football team at the time of the 1958 Munich air crash?

4 Name the patron saint of butchers.

5 Who won an Oscar playing a character called Dragline in the film *Cool Hand Luke*?

6 Which British soap character has been played by both David Scarboro and Todd Carty?

7 In 1977, which Luke was played for the first time by a Mark?

8 Who was the first actor to play John Boy in *The Waltons*?

9 What is an Honest John?

10 Which actor starred in the films *Pacific Heights* and *Cutthroat Island*?

The letter E
054

LEVEL 1   All 10 answers begin with the letter E

1 From what are black piano keys traditionally made?

2 At which race course is the English Derby run?

3 What is the national flower of Austria?

4 In which part of the human body would you find the smallest bones?

5 Which Christian festival is celebrated on January 6?

6 What is the second book of the Old Testament?

7 The intensity of what are measured on the Richter Scale?

8 By what name are the Ancient Greek carvings, owned by Britain but demanded back by Greece, better known?

9 Who phoned home in a 1982 film?

10 What is the name of the European single currency?

The letter E
055

LEVEL 1   All 10 answers begin with the letter E

1 Which river ran through the ancient city of Babylon?

2 What sort of oil is obtained from the Australian gum tree?

3 Julius Caesar, Vincent Van Gogh and Edward Lear all suffered from which disease?

4 In which Jane Austen novel did Henry Knightley marry Miss Woodhouse?

5 What was Che Guevara's real first name?

6 What name is given to a person who carries out the instructions of a will?

7 By what acronym is the random number generator that selects winning Premium Bond numbers known?

8 What is the name of the main river running through Hamburg?

9 In which city was Alexander Graham Bell, the inventor of the telephone, born?

10 Which English king was murdered in 1327?

The letter E
056

LEVEL 3   All 10 answers begin with the letter E

1 In a medieval castle what name was given to an opening in the wall from which cannons were fired?

2 In the Old Testament, who was described as a cunning hunter?

3 What is cerumen more commonly known as?

4 Who was Orpheus attempting to rescue when he travelled down to Hades?

5 What name is given to a group of larks?

6 What is the alternative name for Beethoven's 3rd Symphony?

7 Nuno Bettencourt was an essential part of which 1990s pop group?

8 What title is shared by a Keats poem and a novel by Benjamin Disraeli?

9 Sea urchins and starfish both belong to which marine animal group?

10 With which pop group was Eddy Grant performing when he sang 'Baby Come Back' in 1968?

General knowledge

057 The letter F
LEVEL 1 All 10 answers begin with the letter F

1 What distance is defined as one-eighth of a mile?

2 What F was a hat worn by Tommy Cooper?

3 What name is given to the elected spokesperson of a jury?

4 Which car company has a badge in the form of a prancing horse?

5 What was the name of the skunk in Walt Disney's *Bambi*?

6 In a game of poker, what name is given to a hand where all the cards belong to the same suit?

7 What name is given to the part of a horse's leg just above the hoof?

8 What is the name of the *Addams Family*'s uncle?

9 What name is given to the pivot on which a lever moves?

10 What is stored in a camel's hump?

058 The letter F
LEVEL 2 All 10 answers begin with the letter F

1 What does a palaeontologist study?

2 Which musical term means 'very loud'?

3 What name was given to a market or meeting place in ancient Rome?

4 Viti Levu is the main island in which island group?

5 Which tubes connect the ovaries to the uterus?

6 In which Italian city is the Uffizi Gallery?

7 What is the longest bone in the human body?

8 What is the name of the famous cave found on the Scottish island of Staffa?

9 What name is given to the under-structure petticoats worn by women in the 16th and 17th centuries?

10 What was the name of the Suffolk mill that became the subject of a famous painting by John Constable?

059 The letter F
LEVEL 3 All 10 answers begin with the letter F

1 In which 1990 film did Julia Roberts, Kevin Bacon and Kiefer Sutherland play medical students?

2 In cookery, what name is given to a dish that has spinach as a main ingredient?

3 'Thunder and lightning' and 'Greenwell's glory' are both types of what?

4 What unit of measurement is equivalent to nine gallons?

5 What name is given to goods that are washed overboard from a shipwreck?

6 What is scorpion grass also known as?

7 What name is given to the crime of killing one's brother?

8 In which city was the treaty signed that saw the end of the Franco-Prussian War?

9 The unit of capacitance was named after which British scientist?

10 In which 1972 Hitchcock thriller did Barry Foster play a necktie murderer?

Losers
060
LEVEL 2   Get the answer right to be a winner

1 Which nursery rhyme character 'lost her pocket'?

2 Who is generally held to have caused the collapse of Barings Bank?

3 Who commanded the losing side at the Battle of the Little Big Horn?

4 Who were the losing finalists when Manchester United won the European Champions' League in 1999?

5 Which 1960s sci-fi TV series was adapted into a film in 1998, starring Matt LeBlanc?

6 The 2003 film *Lost in Translation* starring Bill Murray was set in which city?

7 What is the name of the mythical land that features in the novel *Lost Horizon*?

8 Which former World Cup winning goalkeeper for England lost an eye in a car crash?

9 What do you lose if you desquemate?

10 Which duo sang 'You've Lost that Loving Feeling'?

Paint your wagon
061
LEVEL 1   A rainbow of colourful questions

1 Which London football club sang: 'Blue is the colour'?

2 What is the equivalent of the Red Cross in Muslim countries?

3 In which country is the Yellow River?

4 What colour belt is worn by the highest grades in judo and karate?

5 Which Protestant organisation holds an annual march in Northern Ireland to commemorate the Battle of the Boyne?

6 What US army medal is awarded for wounds received by enemy action whilst on service?

7 What colour is associated with death in Islam?

8 By what nickname are the Royal Military Police known?

9 In TV's *Captain Scarlet*, which member of Spectrum was a Mysteron agent?

10 Violet Elizabeth Bott appeared in which series of books written by Richmal Crompton?

Bean bonanza
062
LEVEL 1   All questions are somehow related to beans

1 Who plays the comic character Mr Bean?

2 What sort of beans are a chief ingredient of chilli con carne?

3 What was the name of the cow in *Jack and the Beanstalk*?

4 What name is given to a French-style dish that is garnished with beans?

5 Judge Roy Bean was played by which actor in the 1972 film of the same name?

6 In which James Bond film did Sean Bean play the character 006?

7 What soft toy range devised by H Ty Warner included characters such as Flash the Dolphin, Splash the Whale and Patti the Platypus?

8 What is the name of the bear in the *Beano* comic?

9 Which film villain ate a census-taker's liver with: 'some fava beans and a nice Chianti'?

10 In the 1950s TV series, what did Billy Bean build?

General knowledge

063 A walk in the park
LEVEL 2 Parks and parking questions

1 In which African country is Serengeti National Park?

2 Where does Yogi Bear live?

3 What are the names of the cheese-eating bachelor and his dog in the animated films by Nick Park?

4 What is the name of the lake in Hyde Park?

5 Which creatures roam in *Jurassic Park*?

6 What play, later a film starring Robert Redford and Jane Fonda, was written by Neil Simon?

7 Which actor had a hit with the song 'MacArthur Park' in 1968?

8 What is the name of the house that the Queen bought for Princess Anne as a wedding present?

9 Who provides the voice of Chef in *South Park*?

10 Which American park has the largest active geyser-field in the world?

064 Green issues
LEVEL 3 Not just ecology, or even the colour

1 What name is given to the green colouring in plants?

2 Who wrote the novel *Anne of Green Gables*?

3 What is a greengage?

4 In British politics, what was the former name of The Green Party?

5 Which pop group had an instrumental hit with the song 'Green Onions'?

6 What is the name of the cape located at the southern tip of Greenland?

7 What is the title of the 1999 film, starring Tom Hanks as a prison guard on death row?

8 In which conflict was the Battle of Goose Green fought?

9 What was the title of Norman Greenbaum's only hit record?

10 In which country is the Richard Llewellyn novel *How Green was my Valley* set?

065 Island info
LEVEL 3 A round about places surrounded by sea

1 Rhodes is the largest of which group of Greek islands?

2 Which film told the story of the incarceration of Henri Charrière on Devil's Island?

3 Which entrepreneur owns Neckar Island?

4 Fort de France is the capital of which island?

5 Whose real-life experiences are portrayed by Amanda Donohoe in the film *Castaway*?

6 Which popular island holiday destination derives its name from the Portuguese for 'bearded'?

7 Who wrote the novel *Coral Island*?

8 In October 1983, General Hudson Austin led forces to take control of which island?

9 Who founded Island Records?

10 Which song ends with the line: 'and an island never cries'?

Well-known birthdays
066

LEVEL 1   When do these famous people blow out their candles?

1 She was born on June 12, 1929, died while a teenager, and wrote a diary that has been read the world over. Who was she?

2 Which leading lady was born on July 6, 1921 and went on to become a First Lady?

3 Who was born on July 18, 1918 and spent 27 years in prison on Robben Island?

4 What impressive age did the Queen Mother reach in 2001?

5 With a singer for a mother, and an England football captain for a father, who was born on March 4, 1999?

6 She was born a lady on July 1, 1961 and died a princess on August 31, 1997. Who was she?

7 Who was born on August 11, 2000, with a pop icon for a mother and a director for a father?

8 Which famous train robber was born in 1929?

9 Who was born in Austria on April 20, 1889 and in 1936 opened the Olympic Games?

10 Who was born on August 7, 1960 and became famous for playing a Fox on TV?

Congratulations
067

LEVEL 1   Match the famous singers with their birthdays

1 Which singer was born in the USA on September 23, 1949?

2 Who was born on August 9, 1963 and had her body guarded by Kevin Costner on film?

3 Name the singer born on June 25, 1945 who sang 'Nobody Does it Better', the Bond theme for *The Spy Who Loved Me*?

4 Which Traveling Wilbury was born on April 23, 1936 and died on December 6, 1988?

5 She was born on November 26, 1939 and sang: 'What's love got to do with it?' Who was she?

6 Born February 25, 1943 and died November 30, 2001, which one of the Fab Four wrote 'While my Guitar Gently Weeps'?

7 Who was born in Cuba on September 1, 1957 and went on to front The Miami Sound Machine?

8 Name the Pop Idol born on January 20, 1979.

9 Who was born on June 20, 1953 and claimed: 'Girls just want to have fun'?

10 Who was born on May 16, 1966 and duetted with her brother on 'Scream'?

Make a wish
068

LEVEL 2   Identify these famous people by their birth dates

1 Who was born in London on October 16, 1925 and starred in *Death on the Nile* and *Bedknobs and Broomsticks*?

2 Who was born on February 10, 1894 and once said: 'You've never had it so good'?

3 Who was born on December 16, 1775 and wrote the classic novel *Pride and Prejudice*?

4 Which British Prime Minister was born on May 6, 1953?

5 Who was born on July 30, 1866 and created the character of Mrs Tiggywinkle.

6 Who was born on December 26, 1893 and wrote his thoughts in a little red book?

7 Which 1984 Nobel peace prize recipient was born on October 7, 1931?

8 Who was born on January 8, 1935 and died in 1977 at his Gracelands home?

9 Who was born on February 8, 1931 and died in a car crash on September 30, 1955?

10 Which founder member of *Monty Python* was born on October 27, 1939?

General knowledge

Another year older
069
LEVEL 1 Whose name is it on the birthday cake?

1 Who was born in Albania on August 26, 1910 and won the 1979 Nobel peace prize?

2 Which former England football manager was born on February 18, 1933?

3 Who was born on August 8, 1928, and said: 'In the future everybody will be world famous for 15 minutes'?

4 Which of *The Goons*, born on January 26, 1922, had a Peruvian father?

5 Which American President, who brought about the emancipation of the slaves, was born on February 12, 1809?

6 Born March 25, 1947, he sang 'Goodbye England's Rose'. Who is he?

7 Name the 'funny girl' born on April 24, 1942.

8 Who was born March 9, 1934 and became the first man in space?

9 Which writer was born January 18, 1882 and set his stories in 100 Aker Wood?

10 Born on October 23, 1940, how is footballer Edson Arantes do Nascimento better known?

A star is born
070
LEVEL 2 Which famous thespians were born on these days?

1 Famous for his portrayal of the little tramp, this star was born on 16 April, 1889. Who was he?

2 Name the child actor who shares his July 31 birthday with the author of the bestselling book turned film that made him famous?

3 Which actor, famous for playing a wheelchair-bound detective, was born on May 21, 1917?

4 Who was born on October 14, 1927 and went on to play James Bond?

5 Which actor, who played a Fort Baxter sergeant, was born on May 11, 1911?

6 Who was born on December 28, 1954 and was acclaimed for his portrayal of Malcolm X?

7 Born September 15, 1946, he won an Oscar for his role in *The Fugitive*. Who is he?

8 Name the husband of Lucille Ball who was born on March 2, 1917.

9 Name the actor born July 26, 1959 who played the international criminal Keyser Soze?

10 Who was born on April 3, 1924 and made her screen debut in *Romance on the High Seas*?

Party time
071
LEVEL 3 Who would celebrate on a day like this?

1 Who was born on December 30, 1865 and wrote *Barrack Room Ballads*?

2 Who was born on January 15, 1929 and became the youngest Nobel laureate?

3 Who was born on October 2, 1921 and became the 102nd Archbishop of Canterbury?

4 Who was born on February 7, 1478 and was the subject of the film *A Man for all Seasons*?

5 Who was born in Verano di Costa on July 29, 1883 and was executed 62 years later?

6 Who was born on May 6, 1856 and in 1924 was granted the freedom of the city in Vienna?

7 Who was born on October 2, 1452 and became the subject of a Shakespeare play?

8 What birthday would Marilyn Monroe have celebrated if she had been alive in 2000?

9 What painter was born in Malaga on October 25, 1881, with the middle name of Ruiz?

10 Who was born on August 9, 1757 and was nicknamed 'the Colossus of Roads'?

072 Lucky dip
LEVEL 1   Take your pick

1 What is the capital of Thailand?

2 A pug is what kind of animal?

3 According to the Bible, who were the sons of Adam and Eve?

4 Who founded the National Viewers and Listeners Association, campaigning against sex and violence on TV?

5 Where do Jews go to pray?

6 What was Madonna's first UK No. 1 hit?

7 Who coined the phrase 'big brother'?

8 Which country was awarded the George Cross in 1942?

9 In military terms, what do the initials SAS stand for?

10 Which novelist wrote *Tinker, Tailor, Soldier, Spy*?

073 Lucky dip
LEVEL 2   A mixed bag of questions

1 Which German chancellor was nicknamed the 'iron chancellor'?

2 What is a kipper?

3 New Amsterdam was the first name of which American city?

4 With which 1999 film did writer Richard Curtis follow the success of *Four Weddings and a Funeral*?

5 What was the capital of the Austro-Hungarian Empire?

6 How many states are there in Australia?

7 What is a chiropodist?

8 Name the computer software giant founded by Bill Gates.

9 What colour is lobster blood?

10 In computing terms, how did the word 'bit' originate?

074 What a creep
LEVEL 2   Creepy crawlies

1 By what name is the pop singer Stuart Goddard better known?

2 What was the nickname given to the 1934 home-built wooden aeroplane typically powered by a motorcycle engine?

3 What name is given to the study of insects?

4 What is the secret identity of *Spiderman*?

5 What name is given to the morbid fear of spiders?

6 What sort of acid is secreted by ant stings?

7 What is the name of the world's heaviest insect?

8 Who played the title role in the film *Beetlejuice*?

9 In which TV series did Master Po call Cain 'grasshopper'?

10 What is the alternative name for a white ant?

General knowledge

Marks out of ten
075
LEVEL 1   How well will you do with these random questions?

1 Which famous film star took over as Governor of California in November 2003?

2 In November 1997, All Saints had their first No. 1 hit with which song?

3 What colour are the seats in the House of Commons?

4 What two words are inscribed on a Victoria Cross?

5 Which is the world's largest city by population?

6 What does the abbreviation OED stand for?

7 With a top speed of 55km/h, what is the fastest swimming mammal?

8 What is the main ingredient of sauerkraut?

9 What is the more popular name for Britain's Secret Intelligence Service?

10 The M1 links London to which city?

Out of the bath
076
LEVEL 2   Take a lucky dip with this round

1 Which daily national British newspaper prints on pink paper?

2 With which sport do you associate the shock-haired Don King?

3 From what is a rhinoceros's horn made?

4 What form of transport is a junk?

5 Who came to the throne on the death of Queen Victoria?

6 How many time zones does China cross?

7 In football, is Tranmere's league team a rovers, a town or a united?

8 According to the Bible, how many plagues of Egypt were there?

9 In which city would you find the airport with the international code LAX?

10 Which country has a parliament called the Knesset?

Brainteasers
077
LEVEL 3   Test yourself with these tough questions

1 How many letters of the alphabet can be signalled in semaphore using only one flag?

2 Who was the first footballer to be knighted, in the 1965 New Year's honours?

3 In which year did the British sixpence cease to be legal tender?

4 How many points is the letter K worth in Scrabble?

5 Who wrote *The Barchester Chronicles*?

6 For what did Olivia Newton-John's grandfather win a Nobel prize in 1954?

7 Who was the last British Governor of Hong Kong?

8 Titan is a satellite of which planet?

9 What does the acronym SARS stand for?

10 In which sport are you not allowed to play left-handed?

078 Knowledge quest

These questions are tougher than the others and you may need to do some research

1 'I saw the dull, yellow eye of the creature open'. Where did these words first appear in 1818?

2 What moved to the capital of Wales in 2001 after being held in the capital of England for 77 years?

3 In which film did Robert Redford play Henry Longbaugh?

4 What is the connection between Dr Kildare, 1984 and a pop group called *The Ugly Rumours*?

5 What is the lovely connection between the Aga Khan, Picasso, Sacha Distel and Marlene Dietrich?

6 What is the connection between the Princess Royal, Dr Benjamin Spock and Errol Flynn?

7 Southampton, Holland, France, Paris, Seine, Gibraltar, Spain and Paris. According to Lennon, where was next?

8 Which villain first appeared on the big screen in 1960, and reappeared in sequels in 1983, 1986, 1990 and 1991?

9 What is the first name of Gulliver in the novel *Gulliver's Travels*?

10 What first was achieved by *Wings* in 1928?

11 A reverberation, a dance, a ball sport, a building, a country. Which girl's name comes next?

12 What connects a dramatic symphony by Berlioz, a five-act opera by Gounod, an overture by Tchaikovsky and a ballet by Prokofiev?

13 How are Mike, Carol, Jan, Cindy, Marcia, Greg, Peter and Bobby collectively known?

14 What is the connection between Wells, Barry, Welles and Wayne?

15 To what dessert did Helen Porter Mitchell give her name?

A clue to question 15

General knowledge

The bear essentials

079   **LEVEL 2**   A round of questions about bears

1 What is the name of the bear who lives in Nutwood?

2 What name is given to a female bear?

3 Which animated bear was voiced by Phil Harris in the film *The Jungle Book*?

4 After whom is the teddy bear named?

5 What is the name of Yogi Bear's girlfriend?

6 What name is given to the headdress worn by soldiers of the Guards Division?

7 Who created the character of Paddington Bear?

8 What species of bear is named after an island in the Gulf of Alaska?

9 Who played the title role in the 1993 film *Jack the Bear*?

10 Who was the author of *Winnie the Pooh*?

Simply the best

080   **LEVEL 3**   Be the best you can

1 What is advertised in Britain with the slogan: 'Probably the best lager in the world'?

2 Who won a best actor Oscar for the film *Kiss of the Spiderwoman*?

3 What item of furniture did William Shakespeare leave to his wife in his will?

4 Whose autobiography is entitled *The Good, the Bad and the Bubbly*?

5 Which poem contains the line: 'the best laid schemes o'mice an' men'?

6 According to a Bryan Adams song, when were: 'the best days of our lives'?

7 Which film first featured the song 'I Will Always Love You'?

8 Who had a hit in 1975 with the song 'Best Thing That Ever Happened to Me'?

9 Which sport featured in the 1986 film *Best Shot*, starring Gene Hackman?

10 What name is given to the best man at a royal wedding?

The letter G

081   **LEVEL 1**   All 10 answers begin with the letter G

1 Count Dracula can be repelled with what plant?

2 What is the birthstone for January?

3 What group of people speak a language known as Romany?

4 What is four quarts equivalent to?

5 Of what dish did Oliver Twist want more?

6 Which river is considered sacred in India?

7 From which animal is cashmere obtained?

8 Which instrument of execution was used extensively during the French Revolution?

9 What is the name of a bird's second stomach?

10 What is the name of the field marked with parallel lines upon which American Football is played?

The letter G
082

LEVEL 2 All 10 answers begin with the letter G

1 In Japan, what name is given to a woman who acts as a professional hostess and entertainer?

2 What is defined as 'the deliberate extermination of a race of people'?

3 What is the procedure called whereby iron is electrically coated with zinc to avoid rusting?

4 Which branch of medicine deals with the diseases and care of old people?

5 Which fabled creature has the body and legs of a lion and the head and wings of an eagle?

6 Which was the first African colony to gain independence from Britain?

7 What name is given to the rotating device that is used to keep navigational instruments steady?

8 What does the G stand for in GM food?

9 What is the much shorter name for the wildebeest?

10 What was the main currency of the Netherlands before the single European currency?

The letter G
083

LEVEL 3 All 10 answers begin with the letter G

1 What was the name of the US space probe launched towards Jupiter in 1989?

2 What is the name of *Dr Who*'s home planet?

3 What name is given to the practice of arranging boundaries of a constituency in order to gain an unfair electoral advantage?

4 Which disease is caused by an excess of uric acid in the blood?

5 What is the more common name for aphids?

6 Which Turkish peninsula provided the title of a 1981 film starring Mel Gibson?

7 Who was the last reigning British monarch to lead his troops on a battlefield?

8 In France, what name is given to a soldier employed to carry out police duties?

9 What is the metal rod in the centre of a sundial called?

10 Who was the wife of King Arthur?

The letter H
084

LEVEL 1 All 10 answers begin with the letter H

1 Which mythological hero had to perform 12 labours, including capturing the Cretan bull?

2 Which famous novel by Johanna Spyri was set in Switzerland?

3 What name is given to the ring of light around an angel's head?

4 Along with the sickle, what was the emblem of the former USSR?

5 Which king led the English troops at the Battle of Agincourt?

6 What nationality was the inventor of the biro pen?

7 Which American university was founded in 1636?

8 What name is given to New Year's Eve in Scotland?

9 What type of cigar shares its name with the capital of Cuba?

10 Name the traditional Scottish dish that comprises sheep's stomach filled with offal.

How to write questions

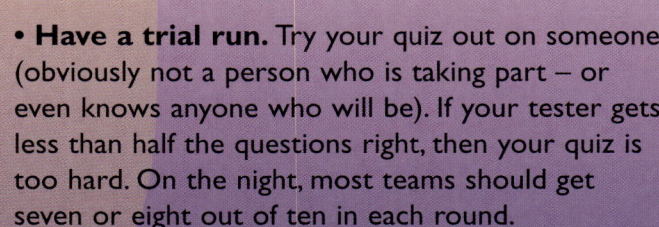

Writing your own questions can be a lot of fun, and it allows you to tailor your quiz precisely to your audience. But it takes time and thought to compile a good set of questions: each one has to be unambiguous, intriguing – and guessable by the don't-knows.

The golden rule of writing questions is: don't make them too difficult. The fun of a quiz is getting the answers right. They have to be challenging, but they mustn't be so hard they put people off. Nothing is more boring and dispiriting than a quiz in which everyone scores zero.

Not too hard

The right level of difficulty is a hard thing for a quiz writer to judge. But there are some things that you can do to make sure that the questions are pitched right. Here are some tips:

• **Avoid your own favourite subjects.** You may know everything about Wagner's Ring Cycle, but the chances are most of your audience couldn't name a single opera.
• **An interesting fact does not always make a good question.** It is interesting to know that Louis Bleriot, the first man to fly across the Channel, financed his passion for planes with a fortune made from car headlamps. But 'What kind of business financed Louis Bleriot's passion for planes?' is not clear or at all intriguing.
• **Try to write a clue into the question.** A history question such as 'What is a *gladius*?' is dull. Better to say 'What essential piece of Empire-building kit was known to the Romans as a *gladius*?' Put like that, a good guess might lead to the right answer: that it is a sword.

• **Have a trial run.** Try your quiz out on someone (obviously not a person who is taking part – or even knows anyone who will be). If your tester gets less than half the questions right, then your quiz is too hard. On the night, most teams should get seven or eight out of ten in each round.
• **On the other hand, don't make the questions too easy.** By all means include a few real stinkers. One or two tough ones per round is enough to separate the men from the boys.

Do your research

The best single source of questions is a decent general encyclopedia. Almost any hard fact can be turned into a question. Your task as writer is to make sure there is only one possible answer, and that it is not too obscure. Say, for example, that you happen upon the fact that the Prussians occupied Paris in 1871 at the conclusion of the Franco-Prussian war. A reasonable question is: 'In which decade of the 19th century was the Franco-Prussian war fought?' Much tougher is: 'In what year did the Franco-Prussian war end?' But a question that reads: 'In what year was the Franco-Prussian war fought?' is badly researched, because it started in 1870. And: 'When did German soldiers occupy Paris?' is a bad question, because it's happened more than once.

Ring the changes

Your quiz should be as wide-ranging as possible. Whatever the occasion, you should not have a quiz that is limited to one subject. Even if you are holding the quiz for your local football club, you should resist the temptation to have a quiz that concentrates entirely on sport. You might allow yourself one highly specialised round on, say, the history of the FA Cup – but more than that and you risk alienating your audience which, after all, may consist in part of partners, friends and guests who have no interest in the core business of the club. Always aim to base at least half the rounds in the quiz on general knowledge.

Keep it light and witty

A little humour and inventiveness can go a long way to generating a good atmosphere on the night. General knowledge rounds, for example, are more fun if they have some spurious theme: why not have a whole round called 'Good as Gold', which could cover the Californian Gold Rush, the film *Goldfinger*, Israeli prime minister Golda Meir, the sitcom *Golden Girls*, Olympic gold medallists – and so on.

Check your facts

Beware of questions based on facts that may have gone out of date: world record holders and sports statistics change often. Even seemingly immutable facts are subject to change: the capital city of Kazakhstan is now Astana, not Almaty.

Beware of contentious facts, such as the true inventor of television (some say Logie Baird, others say he doesn't count because his system is not the one now in use). And always make sure you have confirmation of your answer from two separate and reliable sources. You may even like to keep a note of your source – just in case of arguments.

Essential bookmarks

Here is a list of some useful web sites for quiz-setters:

www.google.com The best search engine. Very fast and very thorough.

www.imdb.com A huge movie database with information on films, cast lists and trivia.

www.Britannica.com You have to pay to use the site, but it is worth the subscription if you set lots of quizzes.

www.bartleby.com/65 The Columbia Encyclopaedia. Not as comprehensive as Britannica, but free.

www.cia.gov/cia/publications/factbook/ The CIA world fact book.

www.biography.com An excellent source of biographical data.

www.s9.com/biography A searchable biographical dictionary.

www.bookbrowser.com Exhaustive site on anything to do with books.

www.allmusic.com Thorough listings of music by genre, artist, and so on.

www.flags.net The world flag database.

www.webelements.com Excellent information on the periodic table.

www.xrefer.com Search a broad-based collection of reference books on one searchable site.

Using the Internet

The Internet is a rich resource both for questions ideas and for checking answers. But much of the information on the Internet is produced by amateurs or by people with a particular viewpoint that they want to promote, and so may be factually inaccurate. To be on the safe side, stick to sites that are connected to official or to well established institutions. Anything with the suffix .gov is a government site and so can usually be trusted for matters of official fact. The web site www.whitehouse.gov, for example, is the definitive source for information on US presidents.

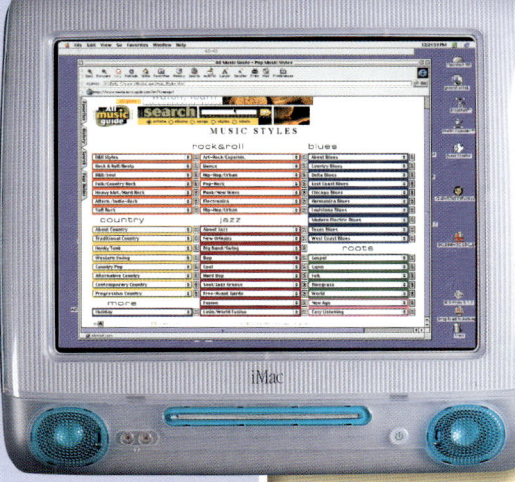

General knowledge

085

The letter H
LEVEL 2 All 10 answers begin with the letter H

1 What sort of creature is Bilbo Baggins?
2 Which film company was founded by George Harrison?
3 What is the name of a female salmon?
4 What type of poison did Socrates use to kill himself?
5 Which Greek physician is known as 'the father of Medicine'?
6 Whose diaries were forged by Konrad Kajau?
7 For which 1948 film did Laurence Olivier win a best actor Oscar?
8 What is the capital of Zimbabwe?
9 What is the name of the reddish-brown dye obtained from the Egyptian privet?
10 Which unit of measurement is equivalent to $100m^2$?

086

The letter H
LEVEL 3 All 10 answers begin with the letter H

1 Which mythological creature has the wings and feet of a vulture and the body and head of a woman?
2 What is measured by a hygrometer?
3 In Roman times, what name was given to the arena in which chariots were raced?
4 What is an 'alaskan malamute'?
5 Who was nicknamed 'the swan of Meander'?
6 What is the capital of Bermuda?
7 What name is given to a person who displays a needless anxiety over their health?
8 What does the H stand for in the name of D.H. Lawrence?
9 What was the name of the comet that could be seen in daylight in 1997?
10 In a Christian church, what is the name of the cushion that is kneeled on when praying?

087

Hair today...
LEVEL 1 Some hair-raising questions

1 Which pop group recorded the song 'Dreadlock Holiday'?
2 Who played the bald detective Kojak?
3 In 2001, who became the first footballer to captain England with a Mohican haircut?
4 What was the name of the completely bald singer in the band Hot Chocolate?
5 Which song opens with the line: 'Take the ribbon from your hair'?
6 Which 1980s pop star was known as 'the singing haircut'?
7 By what nickname was the pirate Edward Teach better known?
8 What is a 'Mexican hairless'?
9 Which actress had her hair plaited into beads in the film *10*?
10 Which biblical character lost his strength when his hair was cut off?

088 A magical mystery tour
LEVEL 1 A round of intrigue and the unexplained

1 What is the name of King Arthur's magician?

2 Covered by Take That, who originally charted with the song 'Could it be Magic'?

3 Which supermodel was once engaged to the magician David Copperfield?

4 What is the name of the Headteacher at Hogwarts School for Witches and Wizards?

5 By what name is the former US basketball player Earvin Johnson better known?

6 For which film did Queen provide the soundtrack, and later release an album called *It's a Kind of Magic*?

7 Which Hollywood director started a company called Industrial Light and Magic that provided special effects for the *Star Wars* films?

8 Who 'lived by the sea and frolicked in the autumn mists'?

9 What is the name of the cow in *The Magic Roundabout*?

10 In which year did The Beatles release their *Magical Mystery Tour* EP?

089 Nicknames
LEVEL 3 By what other names are these people and places known?

1 Which Middle Eastern city is nicknamed 'the pearl of the desert'?

2 What was the real name of the murderer who was nicknamed 'the Boston strangler'?

3 Which composer was nicknamed 'the March king'?

4 Which boxer was nicknamed 'the Manassa mauler'?

5 Which American President was nicknamed 'old hickory'?

6 Which pop star is nicknamed 'the groover from Vancouver'?

7 What sort of bird has acquired the nickname of 'the laughing jackass'?

8 Which singer and actress was nicknamed 'the professional virgin'?

9 Which legendary American sports star was nicknamed 'The Sultan of Swat'?

10 Name the British king who was known as 'the wisest fool in Christendom'?

090 Higher or lower
LEVEL 2 Play your cards right for a winning hand

1 In which film did Paul Newman and Robert Shaw play poker aboard a train?

2 In a deck of cards, which card is the 'suicide king'?

3 Which credit card features a centurion's head as its symbol?

4 What is divided into the minor and the major arcana?

5 Which star of the film *Doctor Zhivago* is an accomplished bridge player?

6 Who stole the Queen of Hearts' tarts?

7 Who played the politician Francis Urquhart in the British TV drama *House of Cards*?

8 How many cards does each player start with in a game of gin rummy?

9 In *Alice in Wonderland*, who shouted: 'Off with her head'?

10 Which rock group recorded the song 'Ace of Spades'?

General knowledge

091   Mr and Mrs
LEVEL 2   Not just stories about happy couples

1 Roger Hargreaves created which famous series of children's books?

2 How are Mrs Ford and Mrs Page otherwise known in the title of a Shakespeare play?

3 Which children's character lived at 52 Festive Road?

4 In which 1997 film did Judi Dench play Queen Victoria?

5 Which Dickens novel features the character of Mr Micawber?

6 Which baseball star is mentioned in the lyrics of the song 'Mrs Robinson'?

7 Who created the detective Mr Moto?

8 Which short-sighted millionaire was played by Leslie Nielsen in a 1997 film?

9 What is the name of the postmistress in Greendale?

10 Who played Robin Williams' estranged wife in the film *Mrs Doubtfire*?

092   Very inventive
LEVEL 3   Test your ingenuity with these inventions questions

1 Which famous Swede, better associated with peace, invented dynamite?

2 Who, on seeing his invention tested for the first time, said: 'I have become death, the destroyer of worlds'?

3 What did Blaise Pascal invent while researching the theories of perpetual motion?

4 What invention by Wallace Carothers was named after New York and London?

5 Who played the inventor Thomas Alva Edison, in the 1940 film *Edison the Man*?

6 And who played the young Edison in the 1940 film *Young Tom Edison*?

7 David Brewster invented which visual toy?

8 What nationality was the inventor of the Rubik's Cube?

9 Who played Barnes Wallis, inventor of the bouncing bomb, in the film *The Dam Busters*?

10 Which 1940s Hollywood star is credited with inventing part of the technology behind mobile phones?

093   Family matters
LEVEL 1   Keep it in the family

1 Which author created the literary character of Brother Cadfael?

2 Which actress is the sister of Warren Beatty?

3 What is the home state of the Osmond Brothers?

4 In Russia, which member of the family is called a babushka?

5 Which Hollywood icon's fourth wife was Lauren Bacall?

6 Who wrote *Uncle Tom's Cabin*?

7 What is the name of Sherlock Holmes' brother?

8 Name the actor who played Big Daddy in a 1999 film.

9 Who wrote *My Family and Other Animals*?

10 Which female group claimed: 'We are family'?

 **094**

Still waters run deep
LEVEL 1   A round to test your knowledge of lakes

1 According to legend, what did the Lady of the Lake give to King Arthur?

2 Which 1995 film about a monster, and starring Ted Danson, was set in Scotland?

3 Which African lake was named after a British queen?

4 What was the title of Greg Lake's 1975 Christmas hit record?

5 Which is the world's largest lake by surface area?

6 Which biblical sea is also known as Lake Tiberias?

7 On which lake was Donald Campbell killed?

8 Toronto stands on which lake?

9 What event was held at Lake Placid in 1980?

10 What giant animal terrorised Bill Pullman and Bridget Fonda in the film *Lake Placid*?

 **095**

Chased by the law
LEVEL 3   Cops and robbers

1 What was the name of the character played by Angie Dickinson in the TV series *Police Woman*?

2 What was stolen by Vincenzo Perrugia in 1911?

3 Who played the drums in the pop group the Police?

4 Which debonair actor played the jewel thief in the original *Pink Panther* film?

5 What is the title of the novel by Colin Dexter, that ends with the death of Inspector Morse?

6 According to the proverb, what is 'the thief of time'?

7 Who composed the theme music for the crime-fighting series *Miami Vice*?

8 What was the name of the 1950 film starring Jack Warner, which spawned the long-running *Dixon of Dock Green* TV series?

9 Who played Mel Gibson's long-suffering partner in the *Lethal Weapon* films?

10 Who was known as 'Texas' beloved bandit' and 'Robin Hood on a Fast Horse'?

 **096**

Out of Africa
LEVEL 2   Questions from the 'dark continent'

1 The Oscar-winning film *Out of Africa* tells the life story of which woman?

2 Which is the largest country in Africa?

3 In which country is Timbuktu?

4 Who wrote the novel *The African Queen*?

5 Which American pop group had a hit with a song entitled 'Africa' in 1983?

6 Which African country was invaded by Italy on October 3, 1935?

7 On which African island was Freddie Mercury born?

8 Name the most highly populated city in Africa?

9 In 1992, Abuja replaced Lagos as the capital of which country?

10 Which southern African country, beginning with B, was known as Bechuanaland before gaining independence from Britain in 1966?

General knowledge

All rounders

097

LEVEL 1   Questions to test your general knowledge

1 What title did Edward Anthony Richard Louis Windsor acquire in 1999?

2 CH is the international car plate for which country?

3 In 2003, which country accepted responsibility for the Lockerbie plane crash of 1988?

4 Which gravel voiced singer had a No 1 hit with 'Wandrin' Star'?

5 What do the initials plc after a company name stand for?

6 Morrissey was the lead singer of which band?

7 In the Police Service, which is more senior, a chief superintendent or a chief inspector?

8 On what date is the patron saint of England celebrated?

9 In which country is the *Süddeutsche Zeitung* a major newspaper?

10 What is the largest species of bird?

Ten for starters

098

LEVEL 2   A round of mixed questions

1 After the two species of elephant, what is the next largest land mammal?

2 In tennis, what name is given to winning the four major tournaments in a season?

3 What is the Royal Air Force equivalent rank to a Royal Marine colonel?

4 In the Bible, how many tribes of Israel are there?

5 In email 'netiquette', what would you type to express happiness?

6 Belgrade was the capital of which country?

7 In Morse Code, how is the letter 'E' transmitted?

8 John Keats described which season as the 'Season of mists and mellow fruitfulness'?

9 Which is the largest of the states that make up the United Arab Emirates?

10 What part of the body does the Yashmak cover?

Hard lines

099

LEVEL 3   When the going gets tough

1 Which football chairman said: 'I believe in Frankenstein, aliens, flying saucers and the Hand of God. But most of all I believe in on-loan goalkeepers from Swindon scoring in the 95th minute'?

2 Into which semi-autonomous province was the peacekeeping force KFOR deployed in 1999?

3 Whom did President Clinton defeat in 1996 to win his second term in office?

4 In mythology, who ferried the dead across the Styx to Hades?

5 Where would you find the inscription 'DG REG FD'?

6 The Lek is the currency of which country?

7 How should the youngest daughter of a Viscount be addressed?

8 Which was the only pop group to appear in the charts in every year of the 1970s?

9 What is the lightest class of weight in boxing?

10 What unique distinction did 70-year-old Lorna Johnstone achieve in the 1972 Olympic games?

100 Knowledge quest

These questions are tougher than the others and you may need to do some research

1 What connects an opera by Alban Berg, a Scottish singer whose real name is Marie McDonald McLaughlin and the silent film actress Louise Brooks?

2 What do you get if you add together tin, oxygen and tungsten?

3 What runs from Chicago to LA?

4 What connects a gun-slinging android, the Ewings' ranch, Josey Wales and arms to the Contras?

5 What is Idlewild Airport now called?

6 The word 'bistro' came into French from Russian – what does it mean in Russian?

7 What connects Luke Skywalker, King Arthur, Jesus Christ and Tarzan?

8 What begins with a clock striking 13?

9 What is the astronomical connection between Debussy, Beethoven and Creedance Clearwater Revival?

10 What connects Chelsea, Bath and Dundee?

11 What connects racing, winter and Shepherd's Bush?

12 What connects *The Third Man*, *Some Like It Hot*, William and Mary and a yellow porcelain from Kyushu?

13 The sales contract of which world-networked TV programme specifies that it may never be interrupted by commercials?

14 D R M ? S L T D

15 What connects Mahler, *The Planets* and the Eiffel Tower?

A clue to question 4

General knowledge

101 Boney brain busters
LEVEL 2   A quiz about, or related to, bones

1 Which emperor was known as 'Boney'?

2 Which character in Shakespeare's *Hamlet* appears only as a skull?

3 Which disease of the bones is caused by a deficiency of Vitamin D?

4 To the nearest ten, how many bones does a normal adult have?

5 Whose arch enemy is called Skeletor?

6 What is the medical term for the shoulder blade?

7 Which movie monster was discovered on Skull Island?

8 Which famous song by Queen features the line: 'sent shivers down my spine'?

9 Who played Dr 'Bones' McCoy in the TV series *Star Trek*?

10 What is the more common name for the clavicle?

102 A shapely round
LEVEL 3   See how you shape up to these questions

1 What name is given to a triangle with sides all of differing lengths?

2 How many sides has a icosahedron?

3 What is the name of the wizard in *The Lord of the Rings*?

4 Which female singer hit the charts in 1988 with a song called 'Circle in the Sand'?

5 Who designed London's Marble Arch?

6 In which film did Marilyn Monroe sing: 'Diamonds are a girl's best friend'?

7 What name is given to a ring-shaped coral island?

8 Which South American city was designed in the shape of an aeroplane?

9 Which model played a shape shifter in the film *Star Trek VI: The Undiscovered Country*?

10 There are two American states that are rectangular in shape. Wyoming is one. Name the other.

103 The letter I
LEVEL 1   All 10 answers begin with the letter I

1 What name is given to the front teeth between the canines?

2 What colour falls between blue and violet in the spectrum?

3 In which sport is the Stanley Cup a major competition?

4 What is the medical term for sleeplessness?

5 The *Koran* is the holy book of which religion?

6 Which country has a shamrock as its national emblem?

7 Which country won eight Olympic gold medals in the 20th century for men's hockey?

8 Diabetes is caused by a lack of what?

9 Springfield is the state capital of which American state?

10 What is the Russian equivalent for the name John?

The letter I
104
LEVEL 2 All 10 answers begin with the letter I

1 What is dyspepsia more commonly known as?

2 What is Spain's national airline called?

3 What does the first I stand for in the company name ICI?

4 What name is given to a large heated box for hatching eggs?

5 What is the capital city of Pakistan?

6 What is the title of the poem by Rudyard Kipling that ends: 'And, what is more, you'll be a man, my son'?

7 Who was created by Sir Walter Scott and played on TV by a young Roger Moore?

8 Which race of people worshipped the rain god Apu Ilapu?

9 What is the fourth most densely populated country in the world?

10 What seven-letter word is the name given to a legendary demon that descends on women while they are sleeping?

The letter I
105
LEVEL 3 All 10 answers begin with the letter I

1 What is the name given to a scientist who studies fish?

2 Which 1987 film starring Dustin Hoffman and Warren Beatty was a major box-office flop?

3 What is entomophobia the morbid fear of?

4 Who was the only survivor of the shipwrecked Pequod, in the novel *Moby Dick*?

5 If 25 equals silver and 50 equals gold, what does 14 equal?

6 What was the title of the painting that was sold at Sotheby's New York for $49 million on November 11, 1987?

7 On which river does the city of Mandalay stand?

8 What is the name of the last part of the small intestine?

9 The Majlis is the parliament of which country?

10 What name is given to the Japanese art of flower-arranging?

The letter J
106
LEVEL 1 All 10 answers begin with the letter J

1 What sort of projectile was thrown by the athlete Tessa Sanderson?

2 What is Paul McCartney's first name?

3 Levi Strauss is credited with inventing what?

4 According to Shakespeare, which young girl marries a Montague against her father's wishes and eventually kills herself?

5 Which piece of clothing worn by horse riders is named after an Indian town?

6 Which is the world's oldest known walled town?

7 Which condition causes the skin to turn yellow?

8 Which biblical character was renowned for his patience?

9 What name is given to the small target ball in the game of crown green bowls?

10 Which poem by Lewis Carroll shares its title with a film starring Michael Palin?

General knowledge

The letter K

107

LEVEL 1 *All 10 answers begin with the letter K*

1 Which organs are affected by Bright's disease?

2 What name was given to the leader of imperial Germany until November 1918?

3 What name was given to the United Nations' first war, taking place in Southeast Asia between June 1950 and July 1953?

4 What type of police officer was Arnold Schwarzenegger in a 1990 film?

5 What is the more common name for the patella?

6 What name is given to the god of love in Indian mythology?

7 What is the name of the *Dandy* comic's cat?

8 Meaning 'divine wind', what word was given to the Japanese suicide attacks of the Second World War?

9 What was the name of the crazy police force created by Mack Sennett?

10 What K is the seat of the Russian government?

The letter K

108

LEVEL 2 *All 10 answers begin with the letter K*

1 What name is given to the Anglo-Indian dish that comprises smoked haddock, rice and eggs?

2 What is the name given to a communal settlement in Israel?

3 The song 'Stranger in Paradise' features in which musical?

4 What in the Greek alphabet is equivalent to the letter K?

5 What English word is derived from the Hebrew for proper?

6 Which male name is derived from the Gaelic for handsome?

7 The Mammoth Caves can be found in which American state?

8 Which disputed region of northern India was famous for its luxurious houseboats on lakes Dal and Nageen?

9 In which 1971 film did Jane Fonda play a prostitute?

10 What is a young beaver called?

Who said it?

109

LEVEL 3 *Some famous quotations, but who said them?*

1 'Mankind must put an end to war or war will put an end to mankind.'

2 'Men seldom make passes at girls who wear glasses.'

3 'To jaw-jaw is always better than to war-war.'

4 'I never forget a face, but in your case I will make an exception.'

5 'Political power grows out of the barrel of a gun.'

6 'It is necessary only for the good man to do nothing for evil to triumph.'

7 'A foolish consistency is the hobgoblin of little minds.'

8 'Only two things are infinite, the universe and human stupidity, and I'm not sure about the former.'

9 'A man can't be too careful in the choice of his enemies.'

10 'There never was a good war, or a bad peace.'

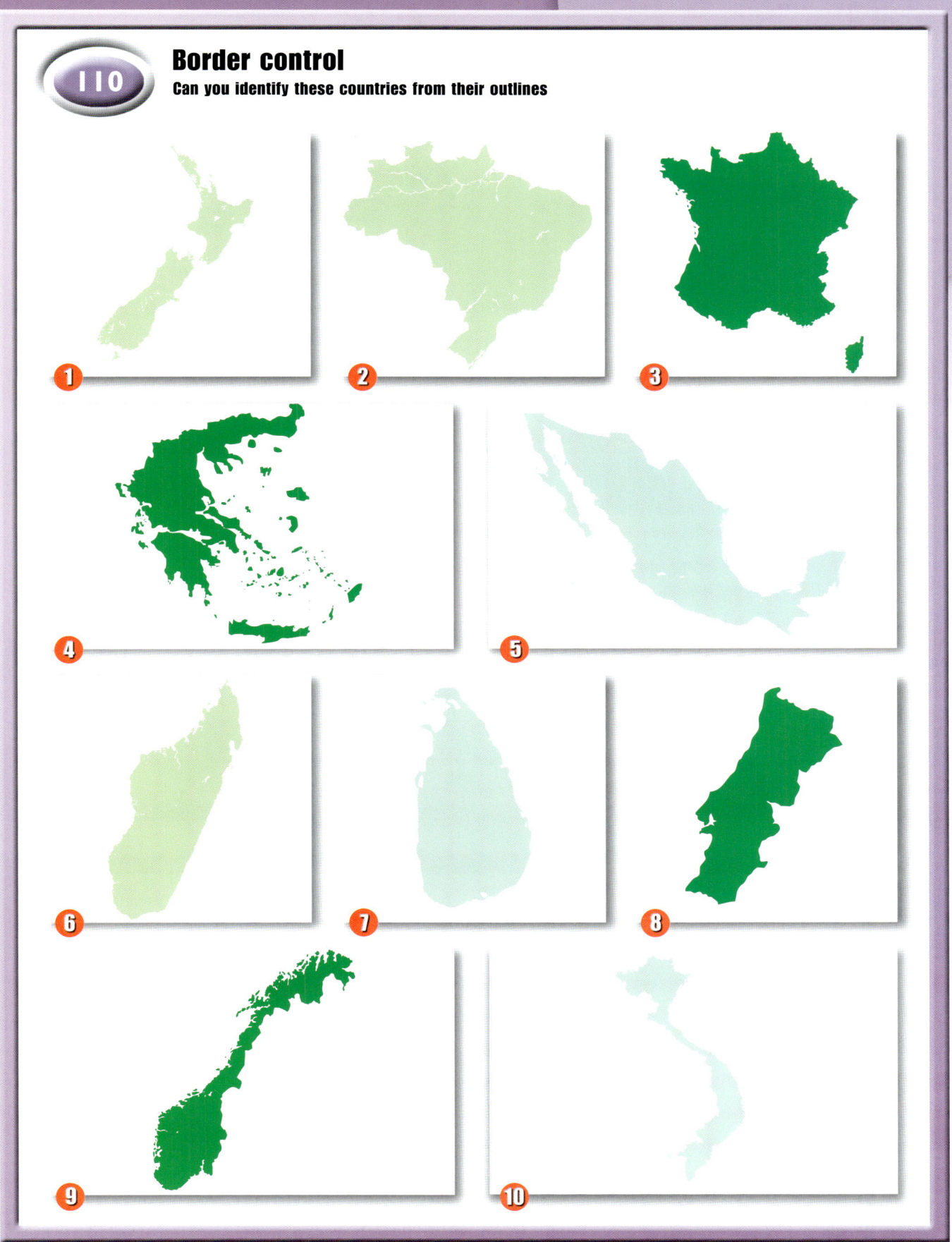

110 Border control
Can you identify these countries from their outlines

1

2

3

4

5

6

7

8

9

10

General knowledge

Force the issue
LEVEL 1 Questions about armies, navies and air forces

1 What was the name of the German air force during the Second World War?

2 Whose private army is called 'the Swiss Guard'?

3 Which pop group had a hit in 1979 with a song called 'In the Navy'?

4 In which 1997 film did Demi Moore join the US Navy Seals?

5 Set in the army, what was the title of the first *Carry On* film?

6 Who said: 'An army marches on its stomach'?

7 What is the motto of the SAS?

8 What did Paul Hardcastle claim was the average age of a soldier in the Vietnam War?

9 Which military organisation did Laurel and Hardy join in the film *Beau Hunks*?

10 Which of the three services is known as 'the senior service'?

Childish pursuits
LEVEL 3 Some questions about – but not for – children

1 Who said: 'Anyone who hates dogs and children can't be all bad'?

2 Who painted *The Blue Boy*?

3 Who in 1976 had a UK Christmas hit with the song 'When a Child is Born'?

4 Which children's hospital benefits from the royalties on the novel *Peter Pan*?

5 What name is given to a doctor who specialises in diseases affecting children?

6 Who wrote the novel *The Children of the New Forest*?

7 Monday's child is fair of face, but what is Friday's child?

8 Who wrote *The Common Sense Book of Baby and Child Care*?

9 One interpretation of the nursery rhyme character Humpty Dumpty is said to represent which 15th century English king?

10 Which child performer won a best supporting actress Oscar for the 1993 film *The Piano*?

Uncle Sam
LEVEL 2 All about America

1 Which city was the capital of the United States from 1790 to 1800, before Washington DC?

2 Which city in West Virginia gave its name to a type of dance?

3 In which city was the Motown record label founded?

4 What is the smallest state in the USA?

5 What is the state capital of Arizona?

6 Who lives at 1600 Pennsylvania Avenue?

7 Which is the only American city to be named after a British Prime Minister?

8 What was the name of the first permanent British settlement in the United States?

9 Which is the most southerly state in the United States?

10 Which city is known as the home of country and western music?

On the run

114

LEVEL 2   A round of questions to race through

1 In which English city did Roger Bannister run the first sub-four-minute mile?

2 The 1987 film *The Running Man* starring Arnold Schwarzenegger was based on a story by which horror writer?

3 How was the confectionery bar 'Marathon' renamed?

4 Which British Olympic medal-winner and MP failed to help William Hague's run for office?

5 Who did the singer Dion advise you to stay away from?

6 Who wrote the novel *The Loneliness of the Long Distance Runner*?

7 Name the lead vocalist of Dexy's Midnight Runners.

8 Which gold medal-winner did Ben Cross portray in the film *Chariots of Fire*?

9 How many runs has a cricket batsman scored if he has notched up a 'nelson'?

10 Which legendary athlete was nicknamed 'the ebony express'?

Murder most foul

115

LEVEL 3   Some 'who dunnits' from history

1 In Shakespeare's *Macbeth*, which king was murdered by Macbeth?

2 Which infamous killer prowled the streets of Whitechapel?

3 Who was nicknamed 'the acid bath murderer'?

4 Which Italian Prime Minister was assassinated by the Red Brigade in 1978?

5 Which actress was murdered by the Manson family in 1969?

6 Name the girlfriend that punk rocker Sid Vicious was accused of murdering?

7 In the Bible, where was Cain banished to after murdering Abel?

8 In January 2001, Laurent Kabila was murdered by one of his bodyguards. Of which republic was he the President?

9 Who did Andrew Cunanan murder in 1997?

10 Name the Mafia boss who was jailed in April 1992 after being found guilty of murder.

Pachyderm posers

116

LEVEL 1   A round of huge questions

1 Who played the Elephant Man in the 1980 film of the same name?

2 Who collaborated with Paul McCartney on the song 'Ebony and Ivory'?

3 What name is given to a male elephant?

4 What is the name of the rodent who is Dumbo's best friend?

5 Which American political party has an elephant as its symbol?

6 Which H word is the name given to a seat on the back of an elephant or camel?

7 Which literary elephant married his cousin Celeste?

8 What was the name of the elephant that was the major attraction at Barnum and Bailey's Circus?

9 Who wrote the *Just So* story, *The Elephant's Child*, which told how it got its long trunk?

10 The Order of the Elephant is the name of the highest honour that can be awarded to a person in which European country?

General knowledge

Jack the lad

117

LEVEL 2 All these people share a name, but that's all

1 Who played a retired astronaut in the film *Terms of Endearment*?

2 Who won a World Cup medal in 1966, alongside his brother Bobby?

3 Who sang the theme tune for the TV series *The Love Boat*?

4 In Dickens' *Oliver*, what was the real name of the Artful Dodger?

5 Which sports star is sometimes known as 'the golden bear'?

6 Which actor was born Chan Kwong Sang?

7 Which former world motor racing champion was also a champion at clay pigeon shooting?

8 Which singer had hits with 'Reet Petite' and 'I get the Sweetest Feeling'?

9 Who wrote the novel *The Call of the Wild*?

10 Who starred as Curly Washburn in the film *City Slickers*?

Weaponry

118

LEVEL 1 A round on rounds, as it were

1 In the 1974 film, who played Scaramanga, *The Man with the Golden Gun*?

2 In medieval times, what did a fletcher make for a living?

3 Name the lead singer of the rock group Guns n' Roses.

4 In which First World War battle were tanks first used?

5 What type of bullet was named after an arsenal near the Indian city of Calcutta?

6 In which musical is the villain called 'Mac the Knife'?

7 Who is credited with the invention of the revolver?

8 What make of gun is favoured by *Dirty Harry*?

9 Who wrote the book *The Guns of Navarone* that became a 1961 film?

10 What is an assegai?

Planet posers

119

LEVEL 2 A planetary quiz

1 Which planet is named after the Roman god of the sea?

2 Which is the hottest planet in our Solar System?

3 Which 'new romantic' pop group first hit the charts in 1981 with the song 'Planet Earth'?

4 In the Superman series, in which city are *The Daily Planet* offices located?

5 Which planet's moons are named mainly after characters from Shakespeare plays?

6 On which planet was the film *Total Recall* predominantly set?

7 The film *The Forbidden Planet* is based on which Shakespeare play?

8 Who composed the *Planets Suite*?

9 Who directed the 2001 remake of *The Planet of the Apes*?

10 Which is the second largest planet in our Solar System?

A million to one
120

LEVEL 2 A round of number questions for you to figure out

1 In which 1966 film did Raquel Welch play a cave woman?

2 Which singer had a hit with 'The Night has a Thousand Eyes'?

3 What three-figure number is the American equivalent for the British emergency telephone number 999?

4 Which FA Cup-winner played a car thief in the film *Gone in 60 Seconds*?

5 How many thieves did Ali Baba face?

6 What is the minimum age requirement for an American President?

7 If you suffer from triskaidekaphobia, of what are you afraid?

8 Who directed the 1956 film *The Ten Commandments*?

9 Who composed the violin concerto *The Four Seasons*?

10 Which film featured a motorcycle gang called 'The Black Rebels'?

Human consumption
121

LEVEL 3 Tasty trivia

1 Which fruit is a cross between a grapefruit and a tangerine?

2 What is noble rot?

3 From which language does the word 'alcohol' originate?

4 Which drink is made from the roots of the smilax plant?

5 Which is the only type of cheese that merits a mention in the Domesday Book?

6 Which Spanish town gives its name to the alcoholic drink sherry?

7 What is the name of the tract that carries food through the body's digestive system?

8 What is the much shorter name of Feast of the Presentation of Christ in the Temple?

9 What Japanese delicacy is considered to be the world's most dangerous food?

10 Which Asian country is the world's largest producer of cashew nuts?

The letter L
122

LEVEL 1 All 10 answers begin with the letter L

1 What is a wolf's home called?

2 Which name for Satan is also the name for a type of match?

3 Which species of monkey is native to Madagascar?

4 What name is given to a noosed rope used for catching cattle?

5 What name is given to a Tibetan Buddhist monk?

6 What is a reading desk in a church called?

7 In the signs of the zodiac, which animal comes between a crab and a virgin?

8 What is a group of puppies called?

9 What name is given to the international insurance market in the City of London?

10 In *Gulliver's Travels*, what is the name of the land of the little people?

General knowledge

The letter L
123   LEVEL 2   All 10 answers begin with the letter L

1 What is the name of the fluid secreted by a rubber tree?

2 What breed of dog is a cross between a collie and a greyhound?

3 The Anna Livia Fountain is in Dublin. Which river is Anna Livia the spirit of?

4 Which acid is present in milk?

5 In the Bible, what was the name of the man Jesus brought back to life?

6 What was Casanova's occupation at the time of his death?

7 In ancient Rome, ten cohorts made up one what?

8 Which city hosted the 1948 Olympic Games?

9 What sort of paper is turned red by acids and blue by alkalis?

10 Which song by Derek and the Dominoes was inspired by Patti Boyd?

The letter L
124   LEVEL 3   All 10 answers begin with the letter L

1 Which glands of the body make white blood cells?

2 What name is given to a collector of butterflies and moths?

3 Which leguminous tree has yellow flowers and poisonous seeds?

4 What is the name of the harvest festival, celebrated on August 1?

5 Which musical instrument shares its name with an Australian bird?

6 What is the capital city of Angola?

7 Humbert Humbert is the lead male character in which Vladimir Nabokov novel?

8 What name is given to a sauce made with onions and white wine?

9 What does a limnologist study?

10 What name is given to the text of an opera?

The letter M
125   LEVEL 1   All 10 answers begin with the letter M

1 What cocktail of whisky and vermouth is named after one of the five boroughs of New York?

2 What name is given to a race run over 26 miles, 385 yards?

3 Who was the Roman god of war?

4 What name is given to animals that carry their young in a pouch?

5 Which breakfast food consists of mixed cereals, nuts and dried fruit?

6 What is the male equivalent of a mermaid?

7 Towards which city do Muslims face when they pray?

8 What sort of implement is used to strike the ball in croquet?

9 Which alcoholic drink is made from fermented honey and water?

10 Which three-letter prefix means 'son of' in Scottish surnames?

The letter M

126 LEVEL 2   All 10 answers begin with the letter M

1 What name is given to molten rock within the Earth's crust?

2 Which game of Chinese origin is played with 144 rectangular tiles?

3 What was the name of the pop singer Smokey Robinson's backing group?

4 What name is given to the staff carried by the Speaker of the House of Commons?

5 Which six-letter word is the name of a trader who sells silk and woollen cloth?

6 Which device is used to keep time in music?

7 What name is shared by a small orange and a Chinese official?

8 What is the name of the viral disease that is fatal to rabbits?

9 What name is given to a political party's declaration of policies?

10 Which song written by Lennon and McCartney was a UK No. 1 for The Overlanders?

The letter M

127 LEVEL 3   All 10 answers begin with the letter M

1 What name is given to the Sun's position at noon?

2 Which Royal Navy rank comes between cadet and sub-lieutenant?

3 What is the medical name for the lower jaw bone?

4 What is a tall tower on top of a mosque called?

5 What is the female equivalent of a marquis?

6 What name is given to the lace veil worn over the head or shoulders by Spanish women?

7 Which word is the name of a fine white clay that is used to make tobacco pipes?

8 Which singing voice comes between soprano and contralto?

9 Which mythological beast was killed by Theseus?

10 Which religious movement follows the teachings of John Wesley?

The letter N

128 LEVEL 1   All 10 answers begin with the letter N

1 Who is the Greek winged goddess of victory who shares her name with a brand of sports footwear?

2 In which TV series did Jason Donovan play Scott Robinson?

3 What is the largest city in Kenya?

4 In mythology, what was the drink of the gods?

5 Who is the patron saint of children?

6 To where did Wendy, John and Michael travel with *Peter Pan*?

7 What name is given to the US army's part-time military force that is called out in times of emergency?

8 What is the longest river in the world?

9 On which city was an atom bomb dropped on August 9, 1945?

10 The Earth's major unit of force is named after which scientist?

General knowledge

The letter N
129 LEVEL 2 All 10 answers begin with the letter N

1 Of which city is a Neapolitan a citizen?

2 What name is given to the central part of a church?

3 Where was Bianca Jagger born?

4 What is the name of Captain Nemo's submarine?

5 Which hard, aromatic seed of the East Indian tree is used as a spice?

6 According to the Bible, who was the first person to get drunk?

7 What name is given to the fur of the coypu?

8 What is the name of the three chalk pinnacles that lie off the coast of the Isle of Wight?

9 Which six-letter word is the official title of an ambassador to the Pope?

10 Which grunge group released a bestselling album entitled *Nevermind*?

The letter N
130 LEVEL 3 All 10 answers begin with the letter N

1 What was the venue of the 1998 Winter Olympics?

2 In the novel *1984*, what is the name of the language the authorities are trying to introduce?

3 What name is given to a person who collects coins or medals?

4 Which is the only sea creature to have an ivory tusk?

5 What is the name of the major desert that lies in Sudan?

6 From which compound are mothballs made?

7 What name is given to a morbid fear of the dark?

8 In maths, what name is given to the number above the line of a vulgar fraction?

9 What was Bob Marley's middle name?

10 By what name is the dramatic 'flesh-eating bug' more properly known?

The letter O
131 LEVEL 1 All 10 answers begin with the letter O

1 Liam Gallagher is the lead singer of which pop group?

2 By what name is the Central Criminal Court of the City of London more usually known?

3 What nickname is given to the gold-plated figurines awarded annually by the American Academy of Motion Picture Arts?

4 Which is the only bird from which leather can be obtained?

5 What sort of branch symbolises peace?

6 What name is given to the elliptical course of a planet?

7 What kind of angle is between 90° and 180°?

8 Which four-letter word is the name of a semi-precious stone characterised by striped layers?

9 What name is given to a brief biography for a person who has died?

10 Which three-letter word is the name of the unit for electrical resistance?

The letter O
132
LEVEL 2   All 10 answers begin with the letter O

1 What do coin collectors call the head side of a coin?

2 Which mountain was the home of the Greek gods?

3 Which six-letter word means the opposite of transparent?

4 Which sport involves the use of a map and a compass?

5 What name is given to the study of birds?

6 What name is given to the piece of music that opens an opera?

7 Which animal has a name that, in Malay, literally means 'old man of the woods'?

8 Which animal is the only marsupial native to the Americas?

9 What is the last letter of the Greek alphabet?

10 Which four-letter word is the name of a kiln in which hops are dried?

The letter O
133
LEVEL 3   All 10 answers begin with the letter O

1 What word with musical associations is the singular of the Latin word *opera*?

2 Which character was played by Maud Adams in a 1983 James Bond film?

3 What name is given to an infection of the ear?

4 What name is given to the parliamentary official appointed to investigate maladministration?

5 What name is given to the study of eggs?

6 Which historical empire shares its name with a cushioned, backless seat?

7 Which nine-letter word is the name of a secret dungeon, to which entrance can be gained from a trapdoor above?

8 Which seven-letter word is the name given to a member of Oxford University?

9 What name is given to a scientist who studies diseases of the eye?

10 Which classical figure unwittingly murdered his father and married his mother, Jocasta?

Bats and balls
134
LEVEL 1   Some questions to bat at each other

1 Whose bestselling album is *Bat out of Hell*?

2 How many players are there in a Rugby Union football team?

3 Which city does Batman watch over?

4 Who was the youngest member of England's 1966 football World Cup winning team?

5 In sport, what sort of bat can be held employing the pencil holder grip or the shake hands grip?

6 What trade is associated with the sign of three golden balls?

7 Who was the first cricket batsman to hit six consecutive sixes off one over?

8 What name is traditionally given to an army officer's valet?

9 Nora Batty is a character in which long-running British TV series?

10 Who was the engine driver of the Cannonball Express?

General knowledge

X marks the spot
135 **LEVEL 2** All 10 answers contain the letter X

1 Which hero did Mel Gibson play in three films, the first of which appeared in 1979?

2 Who is Superman's arch-enemy?

3 What is the alternative name for the flight recorder in an aeroplane?

4 Austin is the capital of which American state?

5 From which plant is linen obtained?

6 With whom did Cyrano de Bergerac fall in love?

7 Marc Bolan was the lead singer of which glam rock group?

8 Who created *The Three Musketeers*?

9 In which film did Robert de Niro play the character of Travis Bickle?

10 What is the more common name for the disease varicella?

Old, new, borrowed, blue
136 **LEVEL 2** Charms for a bride, but will they help with the answers?

1 Which song by The Who contains the line: 'Hope I die before I get old'?

2 Who played Superman in the TV series *The New Adventures of Superman*?

3 What is the name of the diminutive central character in the Dickens novel *The Old Curiosity Shop*?

4 In which 1966 film did George Peppard play a German First World War pilot?

5 Which boy band that had a hit with 'Candy Girl' included Bobby Brown in their line up?

6 Which royal wrote a story about 'the old man of Lochnagar'?

7 Which American President introduced 'the New Deal'?

8 What colour comes before blue in a rainbow?

9 Which pop group sang: 'I'd like to teach the world to sing'?

10 What name was given to the Second World War military assistance programme in which Britain borrowed equipment from the USA?

Good and bad
137 **LEVEL 2** Can you tell them apart?

1 What is the name of the cape at the southernmost point of South Africa's Cape Peninsula?

2 Who played the coach in the film *The Bad News Bears*?

3 *Good Wives* was the sequel to which novel?

4 Which disco diva charted with the song 'Bad Girls'?

5 Who directed the film *The Good, the Bad and the Ugly*?

6 Buster Bloodvessel was the lead singer of which pop group?

7 Who played a gangster called Harold Shand in the film *The Long Good Friday*?

8 In which year did Michael Jackson release the album *Bad*?

9 Who wrote the novel *Goodbye Mr Chips*?

10 Who said: 'When I'm good, I'm very good but when I'm bad, I'm better'?

A European tour
LEVEL 2   A grand tour on a small scale

1 What is the official language of Liechtenstein?

2 Cape Wrath is a headland at the north western tip of which country?

3 What sort of animal featured on the Spanish 25 peseta coin?

4 Which city is served by Marco Polo airport?

5 Which country is called Suomi by its inhabitants?

6 What did Italy abolish in a 1946 referendum?

7 Which country was invaded by the Soviet Union in 1956?

8 In which country is the source of the River Rhine?

9 In which city was Christopher Columbus born?

10 From which country did Bulgaria gain independence in 1908?

The good book
LEVEL 3   How well do you know your Bible?

1 Which peak was the final resting place of Noah's Ark?

2 Which was the only miracle performed by Jesus to be mentioned in all four Gospels?

3 Which two books of the Bible are also women's names?

4 Who was the first person to see Jesus after his resurrection?

5 Who replaced Judas as one of the 12 apostles?

6 What collective name is given to the first five books of the Bible?

7 Which two words make up the shortest verse in the Bible?

8 What is the Decalogue otherwise known as?

9 Which book of the Bible tells us that the number of the beast is 666?

10 In which garden was Jesus betrayed by Judas?

Sci-fi trivia
LEVEL 1   Space, the final frontier

1 In Hollywood, who is known as 'Mr Star Wars'?

2 Where are the letters and numbers NCC 1701 to be found?

3 Who did the actor Gil Gerard portray in the 25th Century?

4 Who wrote the novel *The Sentinel* on which the film *2001:A Space Odyssey* was based?

5 Which animated, space-age family owned a dog called Astro?

6 Which *A-Team* actor also played Lieutenant Starbuck in *Battlestar Galactica*?

7 Who wrote *The Hitchhiker's Guide to the Galaxy*?

8 Who directed the 1979 film *Alien*?

9 Who plays Captain Jean Luc Picard in *Star Trek: The Next Generation*?

10 Who wrote the sci-fi novel *Dune*?

General knowledge

141 Hot and cold
LEVEL 2 Some questions that may make you sweat

1 Who played Hot Lips Hoolihan in the TV series *M*A*S*H*?

2 Which C word is the name given to the study of low temperatures?

3 Who directed the film *Some Like It Hot*?

4 What is the coldest planet in our Solar System?

5 Maggie Pollitt is the central character in which Tennessee Williams play?

6 By what name is *herpes simplex* more commonly known?

7 Who won a best actor Oscar for his role in the film *In the Heat of the Night*?

8 Which soup served cold is the national soup of Spain?

9 What was the surname of the French brothers who invented the hot air balloon?

10 What is the more common name for solid carbon dioxide?

142 Ding dong bell
LEVEL 2 Some questions that may ring a few bells

1 What is the name of the world's largest bell?

2 Robert Jordan is the central character in which novel?

3 Who played the headmistress in the film *The Belles of St Trinians*?

4 Which pop duo consists of Vince Clarke and Andy Bell?

5 Which C word is the technical term for bell ringing?

6 Which literary bell ringer fell in love with Esmerelda?

7 Which female artist had a disco smash in 1979 with the song 'Ring my Bell'?

8 Who played Tinkerbell in the 1991 film *Hook*?

9 The dong is a unit of currency in which Asian country?

10 Who is generally credited with inventing the telephone?

143 Love and marriage
LEVEL 1 The quiz of true love

1 According to Frank Sinatra, love and marriage go together like what?

2 Which tennis star married Steffi Graf?

3 Who wrote the novel *Love Story*?

4 Who played Carrie in the film *Four Weddings and a Funeral*?

5 How many years of marriage are celebrated for a tin anniversary?

6 Who sang 'All you need is Love'?

7 Which rocker married Bianca and Jerry and had an affair with Luciana?

8 Who did Jacqueline Kennedy marry after the death of her husband, John F. Kennedy?

9 Who wrote the novel *Sons and Lovers*?

10 What is a 'love apple' more commonly known as?

What the Dickens?
144 LEVEL 2   How well do you know your Dickens?

1 Which Dickens novel was set in London and Paris?

2 What was Dickens' three-letter pen name?

3 Which Dickens character has been played on film by Alec Guinness and Ron Moody?

4 In which prison was Amy Dorrit born in *Little Dorrit*?

5 Philip Pirrip is the central character in which novel?

6 Which novel featured the Jarndyce court case?

7 'God bless us everyone' is the last line in which seasonal novel?

8 Who married Madeline Bray?

9 Which Dickens novel is set against the Gordon Riots?

10 Which novel was left unfinished when Charles Dickens died?

Creature comforts
145 LEVEL 3   A round of questions on zoology

1 What is the world's largest lizard?

2 Who rode an eight-legged horse called Sleipner?

3 What is the name of Long John Silver's parrot in *Treasure Island*?

4 What has an octopus got three of, that humans have only one?

5 Which common household pet is descended from the wild cavy?

6 Which mythical beast became part of the Royal Coat of Arms for the first time in 1603?

7 What name is given to a female ferret?

8 Which species of snake is also called the hamadryad?

9 What is the young of an otter called?

10 Which mammals belong to the chiroptera order of mammals?

Capital punishment
146 LEVEL 2   'C' here

Listed below are capital cities of countries that all begin with the letter C. Name the ten countries from their capital cities.

1 Zagreb

2 Santiago

3 Bogotá

4 San José

5 N'Djamena

6 Ottawa

7 Havana

8 Nicosia

9 Phnom Penh

10 Yaoundé

General knowledge

Crime and punishment
147 LEVEL 2 **Let the answer fit the question**

1 In which building was Thomas Becket murdered in 1170?

2 What name is given to the written form of slander?

3 Which aviator's son was kidnapped and murdered in 1932?

4 In which city was Bobby Kennedy assassinated in 1968?

5 In what year was Nelson Mandela sentenced to life imprisonment?

6 In the world of cricket, which Pakistan batsman was banned for life in 2000 after being found guilty of match fixing?

7 Whom did John Wilkes Booth assassinate in 1865?

8 Who was found not guilty of the murders of his wife Nicole and her friend Ronald Goldman?

9 In which capital city is Lubyanka prison?

10 What nickname was acquired by the multiple murderer David Berkowitz?

Novel occupations
148 LEVEL 3 **There's a book in each of us**

Who wrote the following novels, all of which have occupations in the title?

1 *The Mayor of Casterbridge*

2 *The Vicar of Wakefield*

3 *Doctor Jekyll and Mr Hyde*

4 *The Little Drummer Girl*

5 *The Sailor who fell from Grace from the Sea*

6 *Dr Faustus*

7 *The Virgin Soldiers*

8 *The Postman always Rings Twice*

9 *The Ambassadors*

10 *A Portrait of the Artist as a Young Man*

Transport trivia
149 LEVEL 2 **Questions on getting around**

1 From which country did Saab cars originate?

2 What is the underground system in Paris called?

3 What name is given to the powered water buses on the canals in Venice?

4 To where did Gladys Knight and the Pips take a midnight train?

5 What was the name of the oil tanker that sank off the coast of Brittany in 1978?

6 Which model of car did Henry Ford name after his son?

7 What is the name of the biggest plane built in Britain?

8 Which city is served by Santa Cruz airport?

9 What went down in 1545 and was raised in 1982?

10 Which famous train ran from Cincinnati to New Orleans?

Name the language

Can you identify the languages below from the snapshots shown?

1 اللوى بين الدخول فحوملر حبيب ومنزلِ بسقط قفا نبكِ من ذكرى

2 半月將影, 羌須及等。

3 קפוצ'ינו ואספרסו? קפוצ'ינו מהם

4 Она была одновременно за няньку и за прислугу

5 Γιατί οι βάρβαροι θα φθάσουν σήμερα· και τέτοια ποάγματα θαμπονουν τους βαρβαρους.

6 Việc sang-ták chữ quóc-ngữ chắc là một cong-cuộc chung của ñhièu ngư`

7 Eis aqui um povo, que não tem senão uma mesma linguagem.

8 Tá an bás ag cur seaca ar bheatha anseo, Aige tá manaigh ar aimsir,

9 नित्यः सर्वगतः स्थाणुरचलो ऽयं सनातनः ॥

10 Ok er Snorri var kváñgaðr pá fór Guðriðr úfan ok gekk suðr ok kom út aptr bús

Hindi • Irish Gaelic • Icelandic
Modern Greek • Arabic • Modern Hebrew
Portuguese • Russian • Vietnamese • Chinese

General knowledge

151 And the winner is...

LEVEL 2 Solve these posers to reveal the answers

1 Who was the first black man to win a best actor Oscar?

2 In which sport is the North Sea Cup won?

3 Which veteran rocker won a clutch of Grammies for his 2000 album *Supernatural*?

4 In what field is the Kate Greenaway Medal awarded?

5 Which British Prime Minister won a Nobel prize for literature?

6 Which Dutch footballer dedicated his 1987 European Footballer of the Year award to Nelson Mandela?

7 Who was the first person to win a Grammy, an Oscar, a Tony and have a No. 1 hit in the UK and the USA?

8 Who refused his best actor Oscar, for a performance in *The Godfather*, in protest at the treatment of Native Americans?

9 Who was the first actor to win a posthumous best actor Oscar?

10 At the Cannes Film Festival, which award is given to the best film?

152 Around South America

LEVEL 3 Questions from the southern Americas

1 Which country was ruled by Bernardo O'Higgins in the early 19th century?

2 In 1999, parts of which South American country were devastated by mud landslides?

3 In which South American country is Dutch the official language?

4 Which capital city has a name meaning 'I see the mountain'?

5 In which country was Che Guevara born?

6 In which city is the Maracana football stadium?

7 In which country is the Itaipu Dam?

8 Which Peruvian lake is the world's highest?

9 What is the main currency unit of Ecuador?

10 Which South American country is the supposed site of El Dorado, the lost city of gold?

153 The Christmas quiz

LEVEL 1 A round of festive questions

1 Which six-letter A word is the name given to the preparatory season for Christmas?

2 Which Dr Seuss character stole Christmas?

3 What is the name of the business partner of Scrooge in *A Christmas Carol*?

4 What would be the star sign of someone born on Christmas Day?

5 According to the carol, which is the only tree 'That bears the crown'?

6 In the USA what is nicknamed 'tinsel town'?

7 Which Shakespeare play might you associate with January 6?

8 In which ocean is Christmas Island?

9 Which of Santa's reindeers is also the name of the Roman god of love?

10 Name the scientist who discovered gravity, who was born on Christmas Day 1642?

Christmas songs

LEVEL 1   Festive songs, carols and traditional hymns

1 Who co-wrote 'Do they know it's Christmas' with Bob Geldof?

2 Who duetted with David Bowie on the Christmas hit 'Little Drummer Boy'?

3 Which seasonal hit song contains the line: 'Another year over, a new one just begun'?

4 Which glam rock group recorded 'I Wish it Could be Christmas Everyday'?

5 Who had a Christmas chart-topper with 'Mistletoe and Wine'?

6 On the eighth day of Christmas, what did my true love give to me?

7 Who wrote the song 'White Christmas'?

8 In the 1950s, who had a hit with the song 'A Christmas Alphabet'?

9 In a Christmas carol, which four words precede: 'no crib for a bed'?

10 Name the singer nicknamed 'The King of Calypso' who had a Christmas hit with 'Mary's Boy Child'.

Turkey and tinsel

LEVEL 2   A round of teasers for the festive season

1 In 1931 which drinks company popularised the traditional image of a red-cloaked Father Christmas that we accept today?

2 The Christmas tree in London's Trafalgar Square is an annual gift from which European capital?

3 What is another name for a snow grouse?

4 By what name are the pantomime characters Anastasia and Drizella otherwise known?

5 Who wrote the book *The Snowman*?

6 Which song contains the line: 'Sleigh bells ring are you listening'?

7 Which Lord Mayor of London, who is known as a famous pantomime character, married Alice Fitzwarren?

8 Which saint's day is celebrated on Boxing Day?

9 In 1932, which king gave the first ever Christmas Day broadcast?

10 Which country was invaded by China on Christmas Day 1950?

Christmas everyday

LEVEL 1   A Yuletide challenge

1 Which nursery-rhyme character sat in a corner eating a Christmas pie?

2 Which seven-letter C word is an alternative name for a reindeer?

3 Which comedy group were 'Walking Backwards for Christmas'?

4 Who were Caspar, Balthazar and Melchior?

5 According to the Bible, who were the first people to pay homage to the infant Jesus?

6 What infuriating puzzle was the bestselling toy of 1982?

7 What unusual event took place between some British and German troops on Christmas Day 1914, despite the war?

8 In which European city is Wenceslas Square?

9 'It's Gonna be a Cold Cold Christmas' was a 1975 hit for which Irish presidential candidate?

10 Which Soviet leader resigned on Christmas Day 1991?

General knowledge

The Christmas movie
157
LEVEL 2   Films about or involving Christmas

1 Who played Scrooge in the 1988 film *Scrooged*?

2 Who played Santa in the 1994 film *Miracle on 34th Street*?

3 In which 1946 film did James Stewart attempt to commit suicide at Christmas?

4 Which Bond film features Dr Christmas Jones?

5 Which film sees Arnold Schwarzenegger attempting to buy a Turbo Man doll for his son's Christmas present?

6 Who played Scrooge in *A Muppet's Christmas Carol*?

7 In which 1998 film does Michael Keaton play a deceased father who comes back to life as a snowman?

8 The 1982 animated film *The Snowman* featured which boy soprano singing: 'We're walking in the air'?

9 Which wrestler played the title role in the 1996 film *Santa with Muscles*?

10 Who played Mr Lawrence in the 1983 film *Merry Christmas Mr Lawrence*?

Ask the family
158
LEVEL 3   Give your brain a yuletide workout

1 What name is given to a young turkey?

2 In which language does 'God Jul' mean Happy Christmas?

3 Who wrote the poem 'Twas the Night before Christmas'?

4 In which city were the Summer Olympics held in December?

5 Who sang: 'All I want for Christmas is a Beatle'?

6 Good 'King' Wenceslas was the Duke of where?

7 On which group of islands do turtle doves live in the wild?

8 Which horse won the Epsom Derby in 1964?

9 What was the first film to feature the song 'White Christmas'?

10 Who composed *The Christmas Oratario*?

The letter P
159
LEVEL 1   All 10 answers begin with the letter P

1 What is the name given to a field in which rice is grown?

2 Which canal shares its name with a type of hat?

3 Which bird can hold more in its beak than it can in its stomach?

4 What is the name for a stamp collector?

5 Which mythical bird rose from its own ashes?

6 Which saint is the patron saint of Ireland and is celebrated on March 17 every year?

7 Which process destroys bacteria in milk?

8 Which type of nut has an edible green kernel?

9 What is the name of the red pepper that is used to flavour goulash?

10 What name is given to a word that spells the same forwards as it does backwards?

The letter P
160 LEVEL 2   All 10 answers begin with the letter P

1 Which town was completely buried when Mount Vesuvius erupted in AD 79?

2 What name is given to the movement whereby a ballerina spins around on one foot?

3 What name is given to the vast, treeless plains of South America?

4 What is a simple story with a moral known as?

5 Which Jewish festival is celebrated 50 days after Passover?

6 What name is given to the study of drugs?

7 What word describes a horse with black and white patches?

8 What is the female organ of a flower called?

9 What name is given to a person who is bringing an action in a court of law?

10 Which radioactive metallic element is used in nuclear reactors?

The letter P
161 LEVEL 3   All 10 answers begin with the letter P

1 What is the astronomical name for the North Star?

2 What name is given to an instrument that is used to measure walking distances?

3 The lapwing is also known as the peewit. Which other 'p' is the bird family to which it belongs?

4 Which musical term means 'very softly'?

5 What name is given to any animal that has flippers?

6 What name is given to the study of fossils?

7 Who is the Greek God of flocks and shepherds?

8 Which three-letter word is the name of the vessel in which Holy Communion bread is kept?

9 What adjective means 'pertaining to the lungs'?

10 Which six-letter word is the name given to the outer joint of a bird's wing?

The letter Q
162 LEVEL 1   All 10 answers begin with the letter Q

1 What is half a crotchet equivalent to?

2 In what fictional game are teams made of seekers, beaters, chasers and keepers?

3 Twenty-four sheets of paper make one what?

4 By what name is the Society of Friends also known?

5 What name is given to a container for holding arrows?

6 Which game involves the throwing of iron rings at a peg?

7 Which pop group released the album *Sheer Heart Attack*?

8 In the army, what name is given to the officer responsible for attending to the troops' provisions and lodgings?

9 In which Canadian province are the Plains of Abraham?

10 What is the most widely spoken Indian language in South America?

General knowledge

The letter R
163
LEVEL 2   All 10 answers begin with the letter R

1 What is the other common name for the mountain ash?

2 What name is given to a meeting for boat or yacht races?

3 What name is given to the nesting site of a penguin?

4 Which synthetic fibre is made from cellulose?

5 What disease is characterised by a morbid fear of water?

6 Which period of art came between the 14th and 16th centuries?

7 What was England's smallest county until it was amalgamated with Leicestershire in 1974?

8 From which cereal is whisky distilled?

9 What name is given to the study of X-rays?

10 What is the main unit of currency in Russia?

The letter R
164
LEVEL 3   All 10 answers begin with the letter R

1 What is the spiked wheel on a cowboy's spur called?

2 What name is given to any animal that chews cud?

3 What is the crime of killing a king called?

4 What was the first name of the wife of former Soviet leader Mikhail Gorbachev?

5 Which seven-letter word is the name of an oar rest on the side of a boat?

6 In which land was the novel *The Prisoner of Zenda* set?

7 Which Swedish pop duo enjoyed a 'Joyride'?

8 Who was Hitler's foreign minister who signed a non-aggressionist treaty with the Soviet Union?

9 In heraldry, what word describes a lion standing on its hind legs with its front paws in the air?

10 Which Daphne du Maurier novel featured a housekeeper called Mrs Danvers?

The letter S
165
LEVEL 1   All 10 answers begin with the letter S

1 What name is given to a group of bees led by a queen?

2 Which musical featured the song 'Ol Man River'?

3 What name is given to a poem of 14 lines?

4 What is the national symbol of Ireland?

5 Which wordy board game was invented by James Brunot?

6 Which cocktail comprises vodka and fresh orange juice?

7 Which seven-letter word is the name given to a surgeon's small knife?

8 How many sides has a heptagon?

9 Tiger and thresher are both species of what?

10 By what abbreviation was the black-uniformed elite corps of the German Nazi Party known?

The letter S
LEVEL 2 All 10 answers begin with the letter S

1 On which river does the city of Brussels stand?

2 What is the name of the ancient and sacred language of the Hindus?

3 Which city hosted the 1984 Winter Olympics?

4 Which 1960 film directed by Stanley Kubrick was based on a novel by Howard Fast?

5 What name is given to a musical composition in several movements for a full orchestra?

6 On which hill was the Battle of Hastings fought?

7 In music, what do four crotchets make?

8 Which famous volcano, that has erupted every day for 2000 years, can be found in the Aeolian archipelago?

9 What is the medical term for the breastbone?

10 In a court of law what name is given to the person who records the proceedings in shorthand?

The letter S
LEVEL 3 All 10 answers begin with the letter S

1 What is the state capital of California?

2 What five-letter word is the name given to loose rocks on a mountainside?

3 What is the heraldic name for the colour black?

4 What five-letter word is the name given to a Buddhist burial mound?

5 What is Islam's code of law known as?

6 What name is given to the study of the meanings of words?

7 In harness racing, what is the name of the vehicle that is pulled by the horse?

8 What is the Wednesday before Good Friday sometimes called?

9 What name is given to a score of three over par in golf?

10 What does the S stand for in the name of the author C.S. Lewis?

The letter T
LEVEL 1 All 10 answers begin with the letter T

1 What name is given to the line marking the edge of the field of play in a soccer pitch?

2 Which Michael Jackson album contained the track 'Billie Jean'?

3 Which is the most northerly country in Africa?

4 What name is given to the study of God and religion?

5 What is the frilly skirt of a ballet dancer called?

6 What name is given to the three-pronged fork as carried by Neptune, god of the sea?

7 Which 1960s pop group recorded the song 'Wild Thing'?

8 What collective name was given to the English sovereigns from Henry VII to Elizabeth I?

9 What T word is the name given to criminal societies in China?

10 Which species of fly transmits the disease sleeping sickness?

General knowledge

The letter T

169 **LEVEL 2** All 10 answers begin with the letter T

1 What was the name of the singer Frankie Lymon's backing band?

2 By what name is lockjaw otherwise known?

3 What name is given to the art of ornamental tree-shaping?

4 In which 1984 film did Linda Hamilton play the character of Sarah Connor?

5 Which dessert is prepared from the roots of the cassava plant?

6 In which film did Tina Turner play 'the Acid Queen'?

7 Which alcoholic drink is distilled from the agave plant?

8 Which 11-letter adjective means 'of the earth'?

9 What name is given to a horse of pure breed?

10 What is TNT short for?

The letter T

170 **LEVEL 3** All 10 answers begin with the letter T

1 Who is the wife of Oberon, king of the fairies?

2 At which British golf course is there a hole called 'the postage stamp'?

3 What is the name of the spice used to colour curry yellow?

4 What layer comes between the Earth's surface and the stratosphere?

5 What is the scientific name for the study of hair?

6 What name is given to a Russian carriage pulled by three horses abreast?

7 From which language does the word 'yoghurt' originate?

8 Which novel by George du Maurier is also the name of a type of headgear?

9 In which sport would a competitor perform moves called randolphs and rudolphs?

10 Which eight-letter word is the name given to a rail around the stern of a ship?

All the world's a stage

171 **LEVEL 2** Actors and theatrical questions

1 Kathleen Turner, Jerry Hall, Anne Archer, Amanda Donohoe and Linda Gray have all appeared naked on the West End stage, playing which character?

2 Which brothers composed *Porgy and Bess*?

3 Who has been played on stage by Philip Schofield, Jason Donovan, Donny Osmond and Aled Jones?

4 Which musical features the song 'Getting to Know You'?

5 Which play is referred to as 'the Scottish play'?

6 On whose poetry was the stage musical *Cats* based?

7 In which country is the play *Miss Saigon* set?

8 Which street is the home of New York theatre?

9 Which musical is based on the legend of King Arthur?

10 The musical *Theatre of Dreams*, tells the story of which English football club?

Know your onions
172 **LEVEL 2   Test your knowledge of fruit and vegetables**

1 To which fruit family does the kumquat belong?

2 In cockney rhyming slang, what are 'apples and pears'?

3 What is the alternative name for a Chinese gooseberry?

4 Which American state is nicknamed 'the potato state'?

5 Who wrote the play *The Cherry Orchard*?

6 According to the saying: 'smooth words butter no . . .'. What is the missing word?

7 Which fruity song is on the flip side of the Beatles hit 'Penny Lane'?

8 Who painted a picture called *The Potato Eaters*?

9 Which vegetable has a French name that means 'eat all'?

10 Which variety of berry was named after an American judge?

Collectively known as
173 **LEVEL 3   A group of questions about groups**

1 What is the name for a group of toads?

2 Martinique, Grenada, Dominica, St Lucia and St Vincent are collectively known as what?

3 In mythology, who are Aglaia, Euphrosyne and Thalia?

4 Name two of the four countries that collectively made up' the Barbary Coast?

5 In pop music, by what name are John Maus, Gary Leeds and Scott Engels known?

6 What is the term for a group of ferrets?

7 How are Burne-Jones, Holman Hunt, Rossetti, Millais and William Morris collectively known in the art world?

8 How are the trio of Yarrow, Stookey and Travers better known in the world of pop music?

9 How are Blondie, Angel Eyes and Tuko otherwise known in the title of a film?

10 How are Leonard, Adolph, Milton, Julius and Herbert collectively known?

The letter U
174 **LEVEL 1   All 10 answers begin with the letter U**

1 What does the U stand for in the abbreviation UFO?

2 Which African nation was ruthlessly led by Idi Amin?

3 Which mythical beast was a horse with a horn on its head?

4 Which actress, her first name beginning with U, co-starred in *Pulp Fiction*?

5 What is the milk-secreting organ of a cow called?

6 Which five-letter word means pertaining to a town?

7 Which group of crime fighters were led by Eliot Ness?

8 What does the UX stand for in the initials UXB?

9 What is the medical name for the womb?

10 What name was given to German submarines during the Second World War?

General knowledge

The letter U
175 LEVEL 2   All 10 answers begin with the letter U

1 In which country is the meat-producing area Fray Bentos found?

2 Which mythological hero was played in a 1954 film by Kirk Douglas?

3 What is cosmology the study of?

4 Which bone lies next to the radius?

5 Which 1992 film earned Clint Eastwood a best director Oscar?

6 Salt Lake City is the capital of which American state?

7 Which nine-letter word means a final offer of terms?

8 Robin and Ali Campbell founded which pop group?

9 Which grey, radioactive metallic element is used to fuel reactors and nuclear bombs?

10 Fergal Sharkey was the lead singer of which punk rock band?

The letter U
176 LEVEL 3   All 10 answers begin with the letter U

1 In mythology, Rhea is the daughter of whom?

2 What name was given to Schubert's *Symphony No 8 in B Minor*?

3 What was Shylock's occupation in *The Merchant of Venice*?

4 If cat equals feline, what word equals bear?

5 What name is given to the underground railway system in Berlin?

6 What name is given to the two dots placed over a letter in the German language to indicate the pronunciation of a word?

7 What name is given to animals with hooves?

8 What five-letter word is the name given to the shadow of the Earth on the Moon?

9 What was the title of the first film that featured the song 'Unchained Melody'?

10 Tashkent is the capital of which country?

The letter V
177 LEVEL 1   All 10 answers begin with the letter V

1 What is Britain's highest award for gallantry?

2 Which mythical creatures cast no reflection and are destroyed by sunlight?

3 In the *Star Wars* series of films, what did Anakin Skywalker change his last name to?

4 Which style of black magic originated in Haiti?

5 What name is given to the meat of a deer?

6 What name is given to a stadium in which cycle races are held?

7 Who was Britain's longest-reigning monarch?

8 In which city is the Rialto Bridge?

9 What sort of entertainer 'throws' his voice into a dummy?

10 What does a virologist study?

The letter V
178 LEVEL 2 All 10 answers begin with the letter V

1 What is the third largest city in Spain?

2 What is the full name of a cello?

3 Phlebitis is a disease affecting the what?

4 In which Hitchcock thriller did James Stewart have a morbid fear of heights?

5 The last day of the Second World War is known as what?

6 What name is given to a scientist who studies volcanoes?

7 Which No. 1 hit for Madonna is also the name of a world-famous magazine?

8 Montpelier is the capital of which American state?

9 What name is given to a car built between the years of 1917 and 1931?

10 Which musical instruments are seated closest to the conductor in a symphony orchestra?

The letter V
179 LEVEL 3 All 10 answers begin with the letter V

1 On which river does the city of Warsaw stand?

2 By what six-letter name is the drug diazepam also known?

3 Which manufacturing company takes its name from the Latin meaning 'I roll'?

4 What was the name of the ship in which Ferdinand Magellan sailed around the world?

5 What were the handmaidens of Odin called?

6 The name of which type of pasta literally means 'little worms'?

7 If a bee lives in an apiary, in what does a wasp live?

8 What are the two large chambers of the heart called?

9 What name is given to the fine parchment, originally made from calf's skin?

10 In Hinduism, what name is given to Lord Vishnu's heavenly abode?

The letter W
180 LEVEL 1 All 10 answers begin with the letter W

1 Which boys' name is also the name of a rabbit's home?

2 Which long-running annual almanac is known as 'the bible of cricket'?

3 'Land of my Fathers' is the title of the national anthem of which country?

4 What type of salad, named after a hotel, contains walnuts and apples?

5 What name is given to the ridge between the shoulder blades of a horse?

6 Which medieval kingdom was ruled by Alfred the Great?

7 Where in the body would you find the carpals?

8 In which sport do competitors clean and jerk?

9 What is known as the 'universal solvent'?

10 In which American state is the majority of Yellowstone National Park?

General knowledge

The letter W
181
LEVEL 2 All 10 answers begin with the letter W

1 What is Ronald Reagan's middle name?

2 Which question was asked in a song title by Donny Osmond and Anthony Newley?

3 Which was the first ever Western pop group to tour China?

4 What name is given to the headdress worn by a nun?

5 What is the most southerly capital city in the world?

6 What is the name of Honolulu's main beach?

7 Which town did the chart-topping group Slade hail from?

8 Which 1995 film starred Kevin Costner as the hero and Dennis Hopper as the villain?

9 What is the alternative name for a glutton in the animal world?

10 In which 1971 film did Jenny Agutter play a schoolgirl lost in the Australian outback?

The letter X
182
LEVEL 3 All 10 answers begin with the letter X

1 Into which tribe was Nelson Mandela born?

2 A mammogram is a type of what?

3 Which object derives its name from the Greek words for wood and sound?

4 Which element beginning with X is one of the inert gases?

5 Which warrior princess was played on TV by Lucy Lawless?

6 What were the Royal Navy's midget submarines used in the sinking of the *Tirpitz* known as?

7 Which X is one of the middle names of the politician Michael Portillo?

8 Andy Partridge was the lead singer of which British pop group?

9 What was the name of the wife of the Greek philosopher Socrates?

10 Which 1980 film co-starred Gene Kelly and Olivia Newton John?

Behind bars
183
LEVEL 2 Prepare for questioning with this round about jail birds

1 Lester Piggott, Sophia Loren and Al Capone have all served jail sentences for which crime?

2 In which field is Elizabeth Fry a famous name?

3 Which novel was written by John Bunyan while serving a prison sentence?

4 By what name was Robert F. Stroud, the inmate of a notorious American prison, more popularly known?

5 Which Australian TV drama series was set at the Wentworth Detention Centre?

6 Which type of institution for young offenders derived its name from a town in Kent?

7 In the 1960s, who played 'the Prisoner' on TV?

8 Which bank robber was played on film by the lead singer of The Who in 1980?

9 Who wrote the novel *The Prisoner of Zenda*?

10 Which soul star was given a six-year jail sentence in December 1989 for assault and firearms charges?

Location location location
184
LEVEL 1 All 10 answers are towns and cities beginning with C

1 Which German city gave its name to a perfume?

2 What is the capital of Venezuela?

3 Which city changed its name to Istanbul?

4 Which university competes against Oxford in Varsity matches?

5 Which American city is nicknamed 'the Windy City'?

6 Which capital city is located in the Australian Capital Territory?

7 The Tivoli Gardens can be found in which European city?

8 Which city is home to the Welsh Rugby Union national stadium?

9 What Middle Eastern city is home to the Sphinx?

10 In which Asian city was the notorious 'black hole'?

The letter Y
185
LEVEL 1 All 10 answers begin with the letter Y

1 Which song contains the line: 'Suddenly, I'm not half the man I used to be'?

2 What is Fred Flintstone's catchphrase?

3 Which mammal lives at the highest altitude?

4 Which stringed toy was originally used as a weapon by native tribes of the Philippines?

5 What is the main unit of currency in Japan?

6 Which cartoon character claims that he is smarter than the average bear?

7 What type of singing, originating in Switzerland, was popularised by the singer Frank Ifield?

8 What name is given to the veil worn by Muslim women that covers the face below the eyes?

9 By what other name is the 'abominable snowman of the Himalayas' known?

10 Which English city was called *Eboracum* by the Romans?

The letter Z
186
LEVEL 3 All 10 answers begin with the letter Z

1 Which 1960s model of Ford car is also the name of a mild gentle breeze?

2 On what type of musical instrument was the film theme for *The Third Man* performed?

3 What name is given to a cell formed from the union of two gametes?

4 Colin Blunstone was the lead singer of which 1960s pop group?

5 The Avesta is the sacred book of which religion?

6 In India, what name is given to a room where women live?

7 What name was given to French foot soldiers wearing Arab dress?

8 Which 1964 film was narrated by Richard Burton and featured Michael Caine and Jack Hawkins?

9 What is the title of the penultimate book of the Old Testament?

10 Alphabetically, what is the last element?

General knowledge

Cranial challenge

Kids 12–14 Get all these right to go to the top of the class

1 In scrabble, what is the value of the blank tile?

2 Which Premiership football team plays at White Hart Lane?

3 Which island is off the northwestern tip of Wales?

4 In the Royal Navy, who is more senior: a commander or a lieutenant?

5 What does the C stand for in BBC?

6 What is the name of the pirate played by Johnny Depp in the film *Pirates of the Caribbean*?

7 The name of Busted's album is *A Present For* who?

8 Which bank holiday comes immediately before Easter Day?

9 What does it mean when a cricket umpire raises his finger above his head?

10 Who won the last football World Cup of the 20th century?

Back to basics

Kids 7–11 Delve into these easy questions to see who's brainiest

1 On a monopoly board, what colour is Old Kent Road?

2 Of which country is Moscow the capital city?

3 Who told the Queen that Snow White was: 'the fairest of them all'?

4 With which pop group did Rachel Stevens sing?

5 Who scored a hat trick playing football against Germany in Britain's 5–1 victory in 2001?

6 How many actors speak in a monologue?

7 What did David throw from his sling to kill the giant Goliath?

8 How many rings are there in the Olympic Games symbol?

9 In which American city would you find Central Park?

10 There are two black suits in a pack of cards. Spades is one, what is the other?

Test your friends

Kids 12–14 Who gets the highest score?

1 In the initials for the animal welfare organisation RSPCA, what does the P stand for?

2 What is the French word for yes?

3 Which Roman governor presided over the trial of Jesus?

4 How many British kings have been called Charles?

5 On which row of the computer keyboard is the letter M?

6 Is Princess Anne's son a Prince, a duke or just plain mister?

7 What is the motto of the SAS?

8 What would you store in the MP3 format on your computer?

9 What would you do with mulligatawny: wear it, plant it or drink it?

10 What is the capital of Germany?

190 Test your brain power
Kids 7–11 Lucky dip

1 What is the French word for mister?

2 Name one of the three primary colours.

3 In which country is Sumo wrestling the national sport?

4 What is the connection between a horseshoe, a rabbit's foot and a sprig of heather?

5 What name is given to the seeds of apples or oranges?

6 Which black-and-white animal, native to Africa, belongs to the horse family?

7 How many pockets does a snooker table have?

8 The Sahara and the Gobi are both names of what?

9 On which date is Boxing Day?

10 In which town does Noddy live?

191 Know-it-all
Kids 12–14 A round for those who think they know best

1 Purr is the favourite pet food of which comic strip cat?

2 What is popularly believed, although not proven, to have killed King Harold at the Battle of Hastings?

3 In which country did kung fu originate?

4 Which European country is known as Deutschland by its own citizens?

5 Who played the action hero John McClane in the *Die Hard* series of films?

6 If an object is diminishing, is it getting larger or smaller?

7 In which country is the Taj Mahal?

8 In which country would you find the monument the Sphinx?

9 What is a penny farthing?

10 Which C word is another name for the centigrade scale on a thermometer?

192 Get it right
Kids 7–11 On a winning streak

1 In which garden did Adam and Eve live?

2 What is the name of Queen Elizabeth II's only daughter?

3 Who is the patron saint of England?

4 With what sort of animal did Hannibal cross the Alps?

5 What was the nationality of the first man in space?

6 What is a referee in a game of tennis called?

7 Which famous highwayman rode a horse called Black Bess?

8 Which legendary king turned everything he touched into gold?

9 In which country of the world are you most likely to see a wallaby?

10 Who led a band of men called 'The Argonauts'?

General knowledge

Questions, questions
Kids 12–14   Got any answers?

1 What is the name of Tony Blair's wife?

2 Reg Dwight is the real name of which singer?

3 How is the rap artist Marshall Mathers better known?

4 Which scientist is associated with the equation $E=mc^2$?

5 Which country did Adolf Hitler rule during the Second World War?

6 Which town in Nevada is famous for its casinos?

7 In which decade did man first land on the Moon?

8 Name the daughter of Elvis Presley who married Michael Jackson?

9 Who directed the films *ET* and *Jurassic Park*?

10 Who is third in line to the English throne?

Lessons in life
Kids 7–11   Have you done your homework?

1 What is the national animal of Australia?

2 How many people perform a solo song?

3 How many cents are in an American dollar?

4 What name is given to a male cat?

5 How many strings does a violin have?

6 Which character in *Alice in Wonderland* disappears leaving just a smile?

7 Flamenco, rumba and samba are all types of what?

8 In which forest did Robin Hood live?

9 What relation is the brother of your father to you?

10 Which weapon is thrown after a pin is pulled out?

So many questions
Kids 12–14   All mixed up

1 Who is the oldest of the seven dwarfs?

2 Which word means thank you in French?

3 The players of which country's national rugby team are known as the All Blacks?

4 Which doctor assists Sherlock Holmes?

5 What is the more common name for sodium chloride?

6 Which P word is the name given to a painting of a person?

7 Which continent is sometimes known as the 'dark continent'?

8 The island of Malta is in which sea?

9 How many days are there in a leap year?

10 On the human body, where is the nape?

Think carefully now
196 Kids 7–11   Lucky dip

1 What name is given to a young sheep?

2 With whom was the English folk hero Robin Hood in love?

3 Name the type of animal that lives in a sty?

4 How many wheels does a tricycle have?

5 What name is given to a leather seat that is put on a horse's back before it is ridden?

6 Who met three bears in a well-known fairytale?

7 What is a boa constrictor?

8 Where on the body would you wear a bowler?

9 In which sport did Mike Tyson face Lennox Lewis?

10 Which of the following is not a disease: mumps, marbles or measles?

It's not all in the mind
197 Kids 12–14   Body matters

1 How many legs has an octopus?

2 The jugular is one of the body's main what?

3 What name is given to the bones that make up the spine?

4 What is lost when suffering from amnesia?

5 Which part of Achilles' body was vulnerable?

6 Which part of the body is divided into hemispheres?

7 Roughly what percentage of the human brain is water (to the nearest five per cent)?

8 Which part of the body is treated by a chiropodist?

9 What is the most common blood group?

10 Which is the only animal that has four knees?

Youthful knowledge
198 Kids 7–11   Easy peasy

1 What is an almond?

2 Which land animal has the longest neck?

3 What is the sixth month of the year?

4 How many eyes does a Cyclops have?

5 Does a car's accelerator make it go faster or slower?

6 What name is given to the small pieces of coloured paper thrown at weddings?

7 In *Cinderella*, what was changed into a glass coach by the Fairy Godmother?

8 In which country did spaghetti originate?

9 What is the name of the thin stick used by witches to cast spells?

10 Which letter of the alphabet represents the number ten in Roman numerals?

General knowledge

A monumental round
Kids 12–14   Building blocks

Name the cities in which the following buildings and monuments are found.

1 The Eiffel Tower

2 St Paul's Cathedral

3 The Statue of Liberty

4 The White House

5 The Kremlin

6 Disneyland, Florida

7 The Vatican

8 The Acropolis

9 Sears Tower

10 The Little Mermaid statue

Brain box
Kids 7–11   Lucky dip

1 How many people make up a quartet?

2 Which swimming stroke shares its name with a type of insect?

3 What A word is the name given to a large mass of snow and ice when it slides down a mountain?

4 Which D word is a type of book that tells us the meaning of words?

5 What is it called when the Moon blocks out the light from the Sun?

6 How would someone be feeling if they were suffering from fatigue?

7 How many seconds are there in two minutes?

8 What kind of cards are sent on February 14?

9 What is the opposite of feminine?

10 Which M word are a ship's sails attached to?

Expand your mind
Kids 12–14   General knowledge

1 If there's 'something strange in your neighbourhood', 'who ya gonna call'?

2 How old must you be to hold a full driving licence in Britain?

3 What happens to a person who stares into the eyes of a Gorgon?

4 Which M word is the name given to a Spanish bullfighter?

5 If someone gave you an *hors d'oeuvre*, would you sit on it, eat it or play a tune on it?

6 Sycamore and spruce are both types of what?

7 Nimbus and cumulus are both types of what?

8 What type of sweet is also a place where coins are made?

9 In which country is the city of Toronto?

10 Which gas has the chemical symbol H?

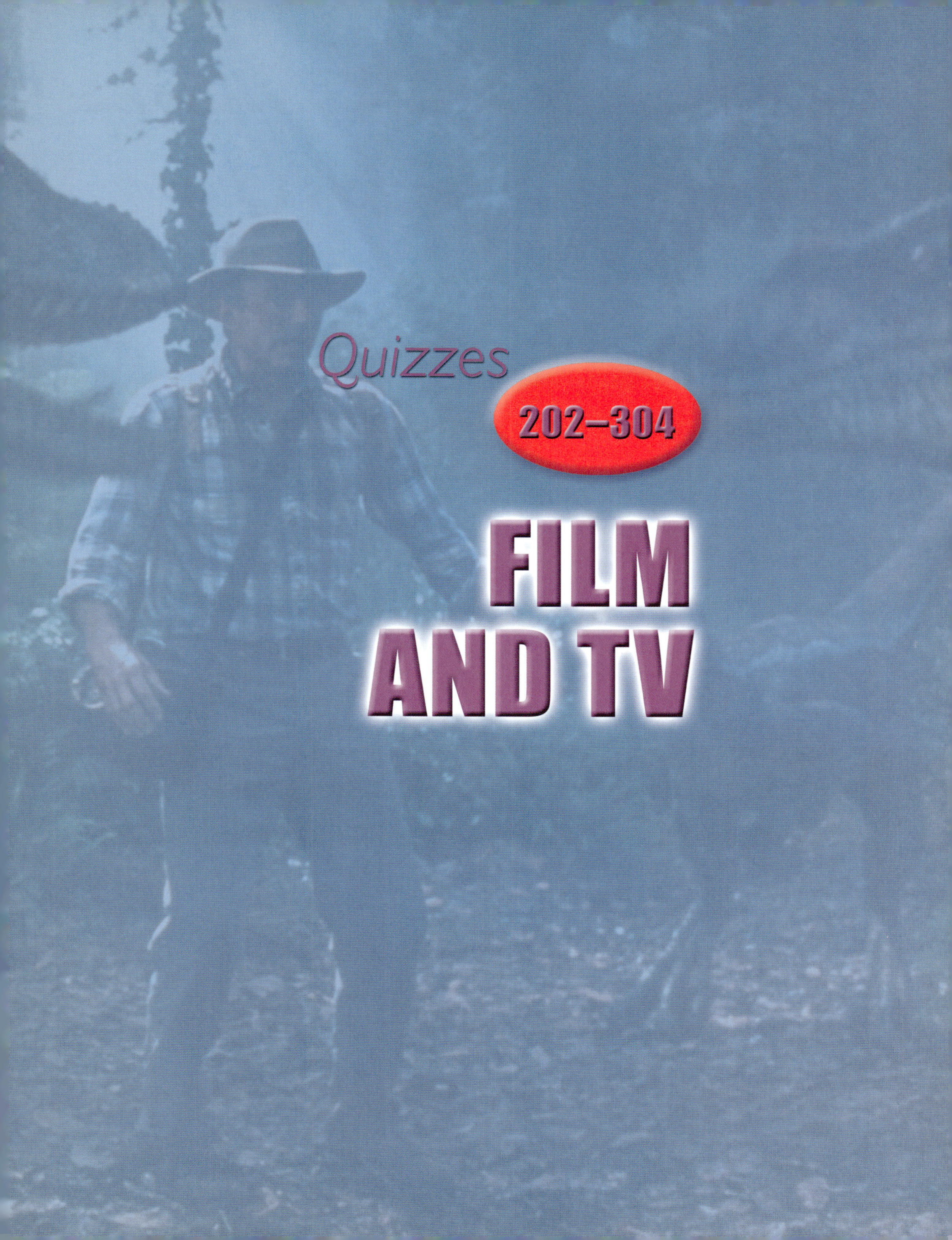

Quizzes

202–304

FILM
AND TV

Film and TV

Screen play
202

LEVEL 1   Take the credit for this film round

1 In 1982, Ben Kingsley won an Oscar for playing which non-violent character?

2 Who played James Bond on just two occasions – in *The Living Daylights* and *Licence to Kill*?

3 *Lock, Stock and Two Smoking Barrels* features a former Wimbledon footballer. Who is he?

4 In 2000, which British actress signed a pre-nuptial agreement with Michael Douglas?

5 Who did Rick Moranis play on the big screen in *The Flintstones*?

6 Which member of The Who played Tommy in the 1975 film of the same name?

7 How were Jim Carrey and Jeff Daniels known in the title of a 1994 film?

8 Who played Catwoman in *Batman Returns*?

9 In the 1993 film *Indecent Proposal*, how much money did Robert Redford offer Demi Moore to sleep with him?

10 Who directed *The Passion of the Christ* and was the voice of Rocky Rhodes in *Chicken Run*?

On the box
203

LEVEL 1   Your starter for ten: a TV round

1 Fox and Dana were the lead characters in which long-running American TV series?

2 Which of the TV detectives in *Cagney and Lacey* was married?

3 What is the name of Homer Simpson's son?

4 Who created *Thunderbirds*?

5 Who became an international superstar after landing the role of J.R. Ewing?

6 Hannibal Smith was the leader of which gang of renegade soldiers?

7 Who made his name playing the scruffy detective Colombo?

8 In which city is the US medical drama *ER* set?

9 Which ecological pioneers live on Wimbledon Common?

10 Which city was policed by Sonny Crockett and Ricardo Tubbs?

Ask the family
204

LEVEL 1   There's something for everyone in these film and TV questions

1 Which stage musical, film and TV series features Coco and Leroy at a New York school?

2 What was the favoured headgear of Frank Spencer in *Some Mothers do 'Ave 'Em*?

3 Which actress played C.J. in *Baywatch*?

4 In which TV series did Cybill Shepherd and Bruce Willis play Maddie and David?

5 Who played The Saint on TV and James Bond on film?

6 In which country is the TV drama series *Ballykissangel* set?

7 Mike Myers, Cameron Diaz and Eddie Murphy were in one of the biggest hits of 2001, but were never seen on screen. In which film did they star?

8 In which 1993 film did Tom Hanks play an AIDS sufferer?

9 *The Firm*, *The Pelican Brief* and *The Chamber* are all films based on books by which bestselling author?

10 Who played Dr Ross in *ER* and Bruce Wayne in *Batman and Robin*?

205 Star gazing
LEVEL 2   A round for movie buffs and channel hoppers

1 Who co-starred with John Belushi as a 'Blues Brother'?

2 Frances McDormand won an Oscar for her portrayal as a pregnant police chief in which Coen brothers' 1996 hit?

3 In which 1997 film did Nicolas Cage swap faces with John Travolta?

4 Christopher Walken won a best supporting actor Oscar for his role in which war film?

5 Which 1976 film, starring Robert Redford and Dustin Hoffman, told the story of the fall of US President Richard Nixon?

6 Which controversial Irish writer did Stephen Fry portray in a 1997 film?

7 Which star of the sitcom *Happy Days* directed the film *Apollo 13*?

8 Debbie Reynolds' daughter achieved fame in the 1977 film *Star Wars*. Who is she?

9 Who played Felix Unger in two film versions of *The Odd Couple*?

10 Who was nicknamed 'Hollywood's Mermaid'?

206 Universally challenging
LEVEL 3   A set of real TV testers

1 Which of the Teletubbies has a triangular antenna?

2 On whose novel was the drama series *Brideshead Revisited* based?

3 Which Joe Cocker hit was used as the TV theme for *The Wonder Years*?

4 Which *Coronation Street* actress was Cherie Blair's stepmother?

5 Ed Asner played the editor of the *LA Tribune* in which TV series?

6 On which singer's TV show did the Osmond Brothers make their TV debut?

7 What is the name of Frasier Crane's brother?

8 Which TV series featured a Pontiac Transam Firebird car?

9 Who was the Wombles' cook?

10 Sabrina Duncan, Jill Monroe and Kelly Garrett were the original characters in which TV series?

207 Tough guys
LEVEL 3   You'll kick yourself when you hear the answers

1 Who did frame Roger Rabbit?

2 Of which city was Jerry Springer once mayor?

3 Herve Villechaize played the manservant Tattoo in which American TV series?

4 In which TV series did Neil Patrick Harris play a boy genius?

5 Which film saw the death of a racehorse called *Khartoum*?

6 Who did Clark Gable play in the film *Mutiny on the Bounty*?

7 In which film did Eddie Murphy play Prince Akeem of Zamunda?

8 Which brothers, who also directed *Dumb and Dumber*, directed *There's Something about Mary*?

9 Which King of England did Sir Alec Guinness play in the 1977 film *Cromwell*?

10 Which actor married Barbra Streisand in 1998?

Film and TV

21st century flicks

208

LEVEL 1   How well do you know the films that saw in the millennium?

1 Julianne Moore played FBI agent Clarice Starling in which film?

2 Renée Zellweger starred with Colin Firth and Hugh Grant in the adaptation of which novel?

3 Angelina Jolie brought which computer game heroine to life in the 2001 film *Tomb Raider*?

4 Who did Lucy Liu, Cameron Diaz and Drew Barrymore play in 2000?

5 What was the 2000 sequel to *101 Dalmatians*?

6 In which film does Mel Gibson play an advertising executive who can read women's minds?

7 Which Oscar-winning film, starring Russell Crow, was Oliver Reed making when he died?

8 Who played the father in the 2000 comedy *Meet the Parents*?

9 In which 2000 film did Clint Eastwood play a retired astronaut?

10 Which Ang Lee martial arts film won four Oscars in 2001 including best foreign language film?

Films of the 1990s

209

LEVEL 1   It seems like only yesterday these films were on the silver screen

1 Name Jim Carrey's pet detective.

2 Who stars in the 1993 film *Sister Act II: Back in the Habit*?

3 Which 1991 Spielberg film is based on a book by J.M. Barrie?

4 In which film does Cher fall in love with Bob Hoskins?

5 The 1992 film *Death Becomes Her* stars Goldie Hawn and which other leading actress?

6 Which late actor, best known for playing Sir Humphrey Appleby in *Yes, Prime Minister*, played the king in *The Madness of King George*?

7 In which 1996 film does Tom Cruise play the character of Ethan Hunt?

8 In which 1999 film does Julia Roberts suffer from an aversion to weddings?

9 Gwyneth Paltrow and Joseph Fiennes star as lovers in which 1998 Elizabethan film?

10 In the 1991 film *Backdraft*, what job does Kurt Russell's character have?

Films of the 1980s

210

LEVEL 3   The decade when 'greed is good', according to Gordon Gekko

1 Arnold Schwarzenegger fell pregnant in which film?

2 In which 1986 film was Bette Midler married to Richard Dreyfuss?

3 What sort of shop can be found at 84 Charing Cross Road?

4 Which 1985 film sees Jack Nicholson and Kathleen Turner play Mafia contract killers?

5 Who directed the 1984 film *Amadeus*?

6 In which 1986 film did Sean Connery state: 'There can be only one'?

7 Brian de Palma directed Robert de Niro and Kevin Costner in which 1987 film, set in prohibition Chicago?

8 What was the title of the 1987 film in which Sylvester Stallone played a truck-driving arm wrestler?

9 The 1987 film *Roxanne* was an adaptation of which classic story by Edmond Rostand?

10 In which 1983 film did Matthew Broderick play a computer hacker who almost triggered World War III?

211 Films of the 1970s

LEVEL 2 A decade that saw some great, and not so great, films

1 Which British director directed the 1974 film *Death Wish*?

2 In which 1977 Spielberg film did Devil's Tower in Wyoming play a significant part?

3 For which 1977 film starring Diane Keaton did Woody Allen win a best director Oscar?

4 Who composed the music for the film *Jaws*?

5 What was the 'silver streak' in the title of the 1976 film?

6 Who was the director of the 1973 film *American Graffiti,* made four years before he directed an all-time box-office smash hit?

7 Which character went on a killing spree in the 1978 film *Halloween*?

8 Whose last film as director was the 1976 film *Family Plot*?

9 Who was the intended target of the assassin in *The Day of the Jackal*?

10 Which highly controversial drama set in ancient Rome co-starred Malcolm McDowell and Peter O'Toole?

212 Films of the 1960s

LEVEL 2 Films that shaped an entire generation

1 In 1963 who played Billy Liar on the big screen?

2 What was the title of The Beatles' first film?

3 Who played the Sundance Kid's girlfriend in the 1969 film *Butch Cassidy and the Sundance Kid*?

4 What was the name of Dick Van Dyke's sweep in *Mary Poppins*?

5 Which actress plays Mrs Robinson in the 1967 film *The Graduate*?

6 Which actor almost escaped on a motorbike in the film *The Great Escape*?

7 In which film did Tony Curtis play serial killer Albert de Salvo?

8 Which 1969 film earned Glenda Jackson a best actress Oscar?

9 In 1963 who played *The Nutty Professor*?

10 Which 1965 comedy was sub-titled *Or How I Flew from London to Paris in 25 Hours and 11 Minutes*?

213 Films of the 1950s

LEVEL 3 The world shakes off its post-war austerity

1 Who died in 1957, one half of a great screen pair? His last film was *Robinson Crusoeland*.

2 Who won his first Academy Award in 1953 and had his first No. 1 hit single the following year?

3 Which 1952 John Wayne film was set in the Irish village of Innisfree?

4 Name the 1950s actor who starred in the films *Storm Warning* and *Law and Order* and later achieved high political office?

5 In 1959, which film won 11 Oscars, including best actor, best picture, and best director?

6 In which 1955 film did Spencer Tracy play a mysterious one-armed stranger?

7 Name the actress who was born with the surname Kappelhoff and starred in 21 films.

8 Who was nominated for an Oscar for his role in the 1951 film *A Streetcar Named Desire*?

9 *Cuban Rebel Girls* was the last film of which swash-buckling Hollywood legend?

10 In which 1954 film of a Jules Verne novel did Kirk Douglas do battle with a giant octopus?

Film and TV

Movie menagerie

214

LEVEL 1 Every question or answer has something to do with an animal

1 In the 1989 film *Turner and Hooch*, what type of animal was Tom Hanks' slobbery partner?

2 Which 1963 film told the true story of two dogs and a cat that travelled 250 miles to be reunited with their owners?

3 What type of fish is Nemo?

4 Thomas Harris' novel became a 1991 box-office smash for Jodie Foster and Sir Anthony Hopkins. What was the film?

5 'Just when you thought it was safe to go back in the water' was the catchphrase for which film sequel?

6 Clyde the orang-utan shares the screen with which lead actor in *Every Which Way but Loose*?

7 By what name was the Australian Mick Dundee, played by Paul Hogan, better known?

8 What is the panther's name in *The Jungle Book*?

9 Which 1966 film recounted the true story of a lioness called Elsa?

10 Simba, Mufasa, Timon and Pumbaa were all stars of which 1994 Disney animation?

Tasty TV trivia

215

LEVEL 1 Questions and answers that have something to do with food

1 In which English city was the sitcom *Bread* set?

2 In which series is a coffee bar called Central Perk a favourite meeting place?

3 What is the name of the toddler in the *Popeye* cartoons?

4 What is the favourite food of the *Teenage Mutant Ninja Turtles*?

5 Which New York detective of the 1970s had a penchant for lollipops?

6 Bingo and Snork were two members of which 1970s fruity TV quartet?

7 For which soft drinks company was Michael Jackson filming an advert when he set his hair on fire?

8 In which British sitcom is Norman Stanley Fletcher confined to Slade Prison?

9 Harry Enfield's 1980s comic character 'Stavros' sold what kind of food?

10 Which 1970s children's animated series narrated by Richard Briers featured a green dog and a pink cat?

Streets ahead

216

LEVEL 3 Don't get lost in this round about addresses

1 Who played Captain Frank Furillo in *Hill Street Blues*?

2 Which family lived at 698 Sycamore Road, San Pueblo, California?

3 Who played Lieutentant Mike Stone in *The Streets of San Francisco*?

4 Della Street was which TV character's secretary?

5 Which TV family lived on Crestview Drive?

6 In which year did *Coronation Street* celebrate its 40th anniversary?

7 Which 1960s and 1970s TV duo lived on Oil Drum Lane with Hercules?

8 Which gruesome family lived on Mockingbird Lane?

9 'Avenues and Alleyways' was the theme song for which 1970s TV series starring Robert Vaughan?

10 On which Bedrock thoroughfare did the Flintstones live?

Technicolour trivia
217 LEVEL 2 A colourful round

1 During which war was the 1968 film *The Green Berets* set?

2 Which Quentin Tarantino film features the characters: Mr Orange, Mr Pink and Mr White?

3 In which 1990 film did Sean Connery play a defecting Soviet submarine commander?

4 Who played Dr Mark Greene in *ER*?

5 Which Gerry Anderson character was described as indestructible?

6 In which 1968 animated feature film were the villains called the Blue Meanies?

7 Dennis Franz plays Andy Sipowicz in which US police series?

8 Which 1986 film features Eddie Murphy as the bodyguard to an infant with supernatural powers?

9 The TV series *Black Beauty* was based on a novel by which author?

10 Which 1939 epic was the first colour film to win a best film Oscar?

Days like these
218 LEVEL 2 It's just one of those days

1 Which film saw Arnold Schwarzenegger battling against Satan in the shape of Gabriel Byrne?

2 In which film did the Marx Brothers assist a young girl who owned a sanatorium and a racehorse?

3 In which 1990 film did Tom Cruise play a stock car driver?

4 Which 1962 film is based on John Wyndham's book about giant plants taking over the world?

5 Which 1973 film shared its title with a 1957 hit for Buddy Holly and the Crickets?

6 In which 1969 film did Richard Burton play Henry VIII in pursuit of his second wife?

7 What was the 1998 film in which Harrison Ford crash-landed a plane on a deserted island?

8 George Clooney fell in love with Michelle Pfeiffer in which 1996 film?

9 In which film did Sir Anthony Hopkins play a butler called Stevens?

10 In which 1996 film does Will Smith play a US Air Force pilot battling against alien invaders?

Muppet mania
219 LEVEL 1 It's time to play the music, and light the lights

1 What is the name of the stand-up comic bear?

2 Which Muppet doctor is assisted by Beaker?

3 What is the name of the Muppets' patriotic eagle?

4 Which hook-nosed character is nicknamed 'the great'?

5 Who did Tim Curry play in the film *The Muppets Treasure Island*?

6 Which *Muppet Show* heckler takes his name from a famous hotel?

7 In the *Muppet Show*, what were the sketches that were a spoof on *Star Trek* called?

8 What is the name of the piano-playing dog?

9 What is the nationality of the chef?

10 In which Muppet film adaptation of a Dickens novel did Robin the frog play Tiny Tim?

TV sitcoms

220

LEVEL 1   A round of questions on some of TV's great comedy shows

1 Who played Sybil Fawlty in *Fawlty Towers*?

2 In which city is *Frasier* set?

3 What is the name of the manservant in *The Addams Family*?

4 In which American series did Michael J. Fox play the Deputy Mayor of New York?

5 Which comedy series was introduced with the words: 'These are the Tates and these are the Campbells'?

6 Who played Dan in *Roseanne*?

7 In which city was *Happy Days* set?

8 In which early sitcom was Phil Silvers based at Fort Baxter?

9 Who played the title role in the sitcom *Ellen*?

10 How are Dorothy, Blanche, Rose and Sophia collectively known?

Soap suds

221

LEVEL 1   A round on popular programmes

1 In which city was *Dynasty* set?

2 Who played Pam, wife of Bobby, in the 1980s series *Dallas*?

3 Anna Friel got her break playing which character in *Brookside*?

4 Who appeared in *EastEnders* and was a member of the pop group Spandau Ballet?

5 In which soap do the cast dine in Summer Bay's 'Beachside Diner'?

6 Which Hollywood superstar played Jason Colby in *The Colbys*?

7 Which spin-off from *Dallas* featured the character of Gary Ewing?

8 Which *Coronation Street* character was jailed for 18 months for credit card fraud?

9 Which British soap is set in a suburb of Chester?

10 In which American state was *Northern Exposure* set?

In the lead

222

LEVEL 1   A round about leading ladies and leading men

This round challenges you to dig deep into your memory to discover who played the title roles in the TV series and films listed below.

1 TV: *The Equaliser*

2 TV: *A Man called Ironside*

3 TV: *The Bionic Woman*

4 TV: *Wonder Woman*

5 TV: *Inspector Morse*

6 Film: *Superman* (1978)

7 Film: *The Cable Guy*

8 Film: *Robin Hood, Prince of Thieves*

9 Film: *Jerry Maguire*

10 Film: *Erin Brockovich*

Plane crazy

223

LEVEL 2   This round features questions linked to aircraft

1 Who starred in Hitchcock's 1959 film *North by Northwest*?

2 George Peppard and James Mason starred in which 1966 film about German pilots?

3 In which 1997 film did Nicolas Cage share a plane with criminals led by John Malkovich?

4 Which film duo appeared in *Flying Down to Rio*?

5 The 1956 film *Reach for the Sky* told the story of which British Second World War ace?

6 Which film starring Steve Martin ended with Paul Young's hit 'Every Time you go Away'?

7 A novel by Arthur Hailey was made into which 1970 blockbuster featuring Burt Lancaster, Jacqueline Bisset and George Kennedy?

8 Which famous aviator's life story was chronicled in the film *The Spirit of St Louis*?

9 Who was nicknamed 'the Baron of beefcake' and made his debut in the 1948 film *Fighter Squadron*.

10 The last line of which 1933 classic film was: 'It wasn't the planes, it was beauty that killed the beast'?

Classic TV

224

LEVEL 2   Great TV programmes of a previous age

1 In which 1960s soap did Ryan O'Neal play Rodney Harrington?

2 Who sang the theme for the TV western *Rawhide*?

3 In the 1970s, William Conrad played which portly US private investigator?

4 Who played Peter 'Tucker' Jenkins in *Grange Hill* from 1978 to 1982?

5 Which actor first stepped out of the tardis?

6 The TV company Desilu was formed by a husband and wife team. Desi Arnez was the husband. Who was the wife?

7 Which member of The Monkees starred in the TV series *Circus Boy* as a child actor?

8 In which 1970s series did Roger Moore play Lord Brett Sinclair?

9 In which state capital was *Hawaii 5-0* set?

10 What piece of classical music was used for the theme for *The Lone Ranger*?

TV music box

225

LEVEL 3   How well do you remember these musical moments from TV?

1 Which US sitcom uses the song 'Love and Marriage' sung by Frank Sinatra as its theme?

2 Which DJ hosted the first-ever edition of *Top of the Pops*?

3 The Rembrandts recorded the song 'I'll be there for you' as the theme for which hit TV series?

4 Which comedy star sang the theme for the British sitcom *One Foot in the Grave*?

5 Who wrote the theme for the Australian soap *Neighbours*?

6 Al Jarreau had a hit with the TV theme for which 1980s TV series?

7 'Eye Level', a No.1 hit in 1973, was the theme tune to which TV detective series?

8 Which singer played Sonny Crockett's wife in *Miami Vice*?

9 What is the name of the saxophonist in the *Muppet Show* band?

10 Which 1970s UK drama told the story of a female pop group called The Little Ladies?

Film and TV

226 The boxer beat
LEVEL 2 A round about films that go for rounds

1 In which year was the first *Rocky* film made?

2 Which famous heavyweight champion played a black slave in the film *Freedom Road*?

3 In which 1956 film did Paul Newman play the boxer Rocky Graziano?

4 In the 1980 film *Raging Bull*, which told the true story of Jake La Motta, who played the lead role?

5 Who played Apollo Creed in the *Rocky* films?

6 Which Belgian-born actor, nicknamed 'the muscles from Brussels', played the title role in the film *Kickboxer*?

7 Which famous singer played the boxer Kid Galahad in a 1962 film?

8 In which 1979 weepie did Jon Voight play the boxing father of Ricky Schroder?

9 In which 1999 film did Denzel Washington play the boxer Rubin Carter?

10 Who played Ivan Drago in *Rocky IV*?

227 Compass points
LEVEL 1 A round of questions that could go in any direction

1 Which 1958 musical featured classics such as 'There is nothin' like a Dame'?

2 In which 1973 film did Yul Brynner play a robotic gunslinger?

3 Cary Grant was pursued by a crop duster in which Hitchcock thriller?

4 In which building is the American TV drama series *The West Wing* set?

5 Caleb Trask, played by James Dean, appears in which 1955 film?

6 Uncle Remus recounts the tales of Brer Rabbit in which film?

7 After which actress was a life jacket nicknamed?

8 Which San Francisco cop was played by Clint Eastwood in five films?

9 Which TV series featured a dog called Diefenbaker?

10 The cartoon series *South Park* is set in which US state?

228 The name is James
LEVEL 3 But not simply about Bond, James Bond

1 *James and the Giant Peach* was a 1996 film adaptation of which author's book?

2 Who played Sonny Corleone in *The Godfather*?

3 In which 1950 film did Jimmy Stewart play a down-and-out with an invisible rabbit for a friend?

4 Which character was played from 1967 to 1973 by Peter Graves in the TV series *Mission Impossible*?

5 In which classic film did James Cagney co-star with the Dead End Kids?

6 Name the Scottish actor who played the character of Sir Lancelot Spratt in the *Doctor* series of British comedy films?

7 Captain James T. Kirk commanded the *Starship Enterprise*. But what did the T stand for?

8 Which British actor died in 1984 shortly after starring in the film *The Shooting Party*?

9 How often was Roger Moore James Bond?

10 Who played the title role in the TV western *The Virginian*?

229

The real name
These well-known stars have changed their names. Can you match the birth name to the star?

Virginia Katherine McMath • Archibald Leach • Eleanora Fagan Gough • Maurice Micklewhite • Carlos Irwin Estevez • Harry Webb • Thomas Mapother IV • Frances Ethel Gumm • Norma Jean Baker • Barry Alan Pincus

Film and TV

Heaven and hell

230

LEVEL 2   A celestial – or diabolical – round of questions

1 In which 1978 high-school film does Frankie Avalon descend from heaven to sing 'Beauty School Dropout'?

2 At the end of which 1990 film does Patrick Swayze ascend to heaven?

3 Who was Ronald Reagan's leading lady in the 1957 film *Hellcats of the Navy*?

4 In which TV series did Michael Landon play an angel on Earth?

5 In Frank Cappa's 1946 film *It's a Wonderful Life*, what happens when an angel wins its wings?

6 Which series of horror flicks featured a fearsome-looking character called Pinhead?

7 Which 1978 film featured Warren Beatty as a wrongfully killed quarterback?

8 Which Rodgers and Hammerstein musical features a man returning from heaven?

9 In the 1999 film *Dogma*, which supreme role was Alanis Morissette cast into?

10 In *High Plains Drifter*, Clint Eastwood painted the town red and signposted it what?

War films

231

LEVEL 2   A round of questions to fight battles over

1 In which country did Tom Hanks attempt to save Private Ryan?

2 The character of Major Reisman was the leader of which group of 12 misfits?

3 Which controversial 1989 Vietnam war film co-starred Michael J. Fox and Sean Penn?

4 Who did Rod Steiger play in the 1971 film *Waterloo*?

5 Which 1977 film tells the story of the 1944 Battle of Arnhem?

6 Which British war hero was portrayed by Richard Todd in the film *The Dam Busters*?

7 *All Quiet on the Western Front* was set during which war?

8 The actor Martin Sheen suffered a heart attack while making which war film in 1979?

9 According to the title of a Vietnam war film, when was Tom Cruise born?

10 Which 1964 film told the story of the Battle of Rourke's Drift?

Travelling rough

232

LEVEL 3   All these questions relate to journeys of some kind

1 What title is shared by a James Mason film, a Jules Verne novel and a Rick Wakeman album?

2 Who played Columbus in the film *1492: Conquest of Paradise*?

3 Alex Winter co-starred alongside whom in the film *Bill and Ted's Bogus Journey*?

4 What was the name of the submarine in the 1960s TV series, *Voyage to the Bottom of the Sea*?

5 Which actress won an Academy Award for her role in the film *A Passage to India*?

6 What was the title of the last 'road' film co-starring Bob Hope and Bing Crosby?

7 Which writer was portrayed by John Thaw in the TV drama *A Year in Provence*?

8 Which 1971 action film starred Gene Hackman and a stunning chase sequence?

9 Geraldine Page won a best actress Oscar for which 1985 film?

10 Which 1949 Ealing comedy co-starred Stanley Holloway and Margaret Rutherford?

Connections

233

LEVEL 2   Find the missing link in each of these questions

1 Who connects *T.J. Hooker* and *Star Trek*?

2 What connects the films *Enter the Dragon*, *The Curse of Frankenstein* and *Malcolm X*?

3 Peter Sellers, Alan Arkin and Roberto Benigni are connected by which film role?

4 Who connects the films *The Doors*, *JFK* and *Natural Born Killers*?

5 The films *Private Benjamin*, *Bird on a Wire* and *The First Wives Club* are connected by whom?

6 Who connects *Léon* to *Star Wars Episode 1: The Phantom Menace*?

7 What connects Olive Oyl to the film *The French Connection*?

8 Which 1963 film connects James Garner, James Coburn and Charles Bronson?

9 What connects a female deer and a drink with jam and bread?

10 What surname connects the thespians Gordon, Glenda and Samuel L.?

Watching the detectives

234

LEVEL 1   Some arresting questions to try you

1 Who played Detective Dave Starsky's partner, Ken 'Hutch' Hutchinson, in the 1970s series *Starsky and Hutch*?

2 Who played Sherlock Holmes on TV to Edward Hardwicke's Dr Watson?

3 Which opera-lover was assisted by Sergeant Lewis?

4 Who played Hercule Poirot in the 1974 film *Murder on the Orient Express*?

5 Which detective has been played by both Richard Roundtree and Samuel L. Jackson?

6 Who played Sherlock Holmes on film to Nigel Bruce's Dr Watson?

7 The TV series *The Bill* is centred around which fictional police station?

8 Which TV detective played by James Garner lived on a trailer park?

9 Which 1960s TV series featured Detective Sergeant Barlow and Detective Inspector Watt?

10 Who wrote the TV drama series *The Singing Detective*?

Musical moments

235

LEVEL 1   A round to make you sing

1 Which 1968 Mel Brooks film was about a musical that featured the song 'Spring time for Hitler and Germany'?

2 How many Von Trapp children were there in *The Sound of Music*?

3 Who played the Artful Dodger in the 1969 musical *Oliver*?

4 Which song from *Dr Dolittle* won a best song Oscar in 1968?

5 On which George Bernard Shaw play was the musical *My Fair Lady* based?

6 In which 1956 film did Grace Kelly play Tracy Samantha Lord?

7 In the 1983 film *Flashdance*, which actress was a welder by day and a dancer by night?

8 Alan Parker directed which famous pop star in the title role of the 1996 film *Evita*?

9 In which 1952 film did Gene Kelly sing 'What a glorious feeling, I'm happy again'?

10 What song did John Travolta sing while leaping off a car in a 1978 film?

Film and TV

236 Strike up the band
LEVEL 2   A round of teasers about great musicals

1 Which was the first musical to win ten Oscars?

2 Which Oscar-winning 1972 musical film was set in pre-war Berlin at the Kit Kat Club?

3 In which musical did we first meet the character of Fanny Brice?

4 Which 1969 musical had Clint Eastwood singing 'They call the wind Mariah'?

5 What were Rodgers and Hammerstein's first names?

6 Where, according to the title of the 1944 musical starring Judy Garland, were you to meet?

7 Which actress was *Dirty Dancing* with Patrick Swayze in 1987?

8 Judy Garland and James Mason both won Oscar nominations for their roles in which 1954 musical directed by George Cukor?

9 With which cartoon character did Gene Kelly dance in the film *Anchors Aweigh*?

10 Whereabouts was Gene Kelly an American, according to the title of the 1951 film directed by Vincente Minnelli?

237 Maybe baby
LEVEL 2   Some very childish questions

1 In which 1968 film did Mia Farrow give birth to the son of Satan?

2 Which *Star Trek* actor directed the film *Three Men and a Baby*?

3 What sort of animal was Baby in the film *Bringing up Baby*, starring Cary Grant?

4 Name the 1987 film in which Diane Keaton played an executive who acquires a baby.

5 Which actor–director named his son Satchel?

6 The life of which sporting legend was chronicled in the 1992 film *The Babe*?

7 What was the title of the 1998 sequel to the 1995 film *Babe*?

8 Who starred alongside Holly Hunter in the 1987 film *Raising Arizona*?

9 Which comedy duo assisted Santa Claus in the 1934 film *Babes in Toyland*?

10 In which film sequel did Rick Moranis inadvertently expose his two-year-old son to a ray that made him grow excessively?

238 Science-fiction facts
LEVEL 2   A round of questions from outer space

1 Who plays the part of Ripley in the *Alien* films?

2 Which 1995 film starring Tom Hanks told the true story of a failed Moon mission?

3 In which 1977 film did Richard Dreyfuss attempt to mould a sculpture from mashed potatoes?

4 Which cult sci-fi film starring Harrison Ford was based on the novel *Do Androids Dream of Electric Sheep*?

5 Which ex-Monty Python member directed the 1995 film *Twelve Monkeys* starring Bruce Willis?

6 Which 1927 film directed by Fritz Lang is regarded as the first great science-fiction film?

7 Who wrote the book from which Stanley Kubrick made the film *2001: A Space Odyssey*?

8 In which sequel did Arnold Schwarzenegger appear as a destructor in 1991?

9 Which film, made in 1956 with Kevin McCarthy, was remade in 1978 starring Donald Sutherland?

10 Who played the British Prime Minister in the film *Mars Attacks*?

What's up doc?

239

LEVEL 1 All these questions have a medical theme

1 In which film did Harrison Ford play Dr Richard Kimble?

2 Which Bond villain was played by Joseph Wiseman in a 1962 film?

3 Who played *Dr Who* on film in 1965 and 1966?

4 In which film about John Merrick did Sir Anthony Hopkins play Dr Frederick Treves?

5 Jack Nicholson played a patient in a mental institute in which 1975 film?

6 In the 1978 film *The Boys from Brazil*, Gregory Peck plays which infamous Nazi doctor?

7 Who wrote the novel on which the 1965 film *Doctor Zhivago* was based?

8 Who played Matron in the 1972 film *Carry on Matron*?

9 In which film did Robin Williams play a psychiatrist who treated a coma patient played by Robert de Niro?

10 Who played Dr Simon Sparrow in the *Doctor* series of films?

Title trivia

240

LEVEL 2 All these questions are about people's titles

1 Who played the Fresh Prince of Bel Air?

2 Which actor played CIA deputy director James Greer in adaptations of Tom Clancy novels?

3 When Robert de Niro played the monster, which English actor played Baron Victor Frankenstein?

4 Who made a fleeting appearance as King Richard at the end of the film *Robin Hood: Prince of Thieves*?

5 Who played the lead in the 1991 film *King Ralph*?

6 Who wrote the novel on which Stanley Kubrick's 1980 film *The Shining* was based?

7 Which actor played Tom Wingo, who fell in love with Barbra Streisand's Susan Lowenstein in the 1991 film *The Prince of Tides*?

8 Peter O'Toole played which English king in the films *Becket* and *The Lion in Winter*?

9 Who provides the adult Simba's voice in the Disney animated film *The Lion King*?

10 In the 1970s drama Gemma Jones played 'the Duchess' of which street?

Metallic movies

241

LEVEL 3 Some heavy-metal questions

1 Who played Private Joker in the 1987 film *Full Metal Jacket*?

2 In which 1989 film did Julia Roberts suffer from diabetes?

3 For which film did Jeremy Irons win a best actor Oscar for his portrayal of Claus von Bülow?

4 In the 1999 comedy starring John Cusack, *Pushing Tin*, to what does the title refer?

5 Name the actor famous for playing Tarzan on TV who played *Doc Savage, Man of Bronze* on film.

6 Who played the leader of the Grimethorpe Colliery Brass Band in the film *Brassed Off*?

7 In which 1976 film did Gene Wilder witness a murder on a trans-continental train?

8 Which 1998 version of an Alexander Dumas novel starred Leonardo DiCaprio?

9 Name the 1987 film in which Richard Dreyfuss and Danny DeVito played two feuding salesmen.

10 The 1999 animated film *The Iron Giant* was based on a book by which English poet?

Film and TV

242 Action!
LEVEL 2 Which films open with the following memorable lines?

1 'I never knew the old Vienna before the war, with its Strauss music, its glamour and easy charm.'

2 'Saigon…'

3 'Henslowe, do you know what happens to a man who doesn't pay his debts? His boots catch fire!'

4 'I beg your pardon, but aren't you Guy Haines?'

5 'Last night, I dreamt I went to Manderley again.'

6 'So this is the world and there are almost 6 billion people on it. When I was a kid there were three. It's hard to keep up.'

7 'The white zone is for immediate loading and unloading of passengers only.'

8 'It is I, Arthur, son of Uther Pendragon from the Castle of Camelot. King of the Britons, Defeater of the Saxons, Sovereign of all England!'

9 'Chapter One. He adored New York City. He idolised it all out of proportion.'

10 'I believe in America. America has made my fortune.'

243 Memorable quotes
LEVEL 2 From which films are the following lines taken?

1 'I'm sorry, honey, but you know … toys don't last forever.'

2 'Chuck! Chuck! It's Marvin, your cousin, Marvin BERRY. You know that new sound you're looking for? Well, listen to this!'

3 'It's from the Talmud. It says, "Whoever saves one life, saves the world entire".'

4 'The greatest trick the devil ever pulled was to convince the world he didn't exist.'

5 'I love the smell of Napalm in the morning.'

6 'Prison life consists of routine, and then more routine.'

7 'For God's sake, Mrs Robinson, here we are, you got me into your house … and tell me your husband won't be home for hours…'

8 'I've watched you your whole life … I know you better than you know yourself …'

9 'I enjoyed the movie very much … did you ever consider having more horses in it?'

10 'I'd want to here more about Sam, Samwise the brave.'

244 Roll the credits
LEVEL 2 Which films close with the following memorable lines?

1 'Sir, if any of my circuits or gears will help, I'll gladly donate them.' 'He'll be all right.'

2 'Thank God for that. For a moment there I thought we were in trouble.'

3 'I do wish we could talk longer, but I'm having an old friend for dinner.'

4 'Atta boy. Clarence.'

5 'Well, nobody's perfect.'

6 'Louis, I think this is the beginning of a beautiful friendship.'

7 'All right, Mr DeMille, I'm ready for my close-up.'

8 'Made it Ma. Top of the world.'

9 'I think it would be fun to run a newspaper.'

10 'This is Ripley, last survivor of *The Nostromo*, signing off.'

245 Screen quest

These questions are tougher than the others and you may need to do some research

1 Which role connects Audrey Hepburn in a 1976 film and Mary Elizabeth Mastrantonio in a 1991 film?

2 What is the connection between the films *Easy Rider*, *The China Syndrome* and *My Darling Clementine*?

3 What is the connection between the TV programme *ER* and the films *Jurassic Park* and *Congo*?

4 Who connects the films *El Cid*, *Major Dundee* and *The Omega Man*?

5 What is the connection between the films *Ghost*, *Octopussy* and *10*?

6 Which actor connects the TV programmes *Charlie's Angels* and *Dynasty*?

7 What connects the films *The Forbidden Planet*, *West Side Story* and *Kiss Me Kate*?

8 What is the connection between Rita Coolidge, Nancy Sinatra and Sheryl Crow?

9 What is the connection between the films *Three Men and a Baby*, *Natural Born Killers* and *Look Who's Talking*?

10 What was the name of the cruise ship in the TV series *The Love Boat*?

11 In the Gerry Anderson puppet series, who invented Supercar?

12 Who is Erique Claudin, played on film by Herbert Lom, Claude Rains and Lon Chaney?

13 Who is the only actor to have received Oscar nominations in the 1950s, 1960s, 1970s and 1980s?

14 Which film opens with the line 'No man's life can be encompassed in one telling'?

15 Her real name is Tula Finklea and she co-starred with Fred Astaire in the 1953 film *The Band Wagon*. What is her stage name?

A clue to question 5

How to be a quiz master

A good quiz master is like the conductor of an orchestra. It is his job to pace the evening, to make the most of the raw material, and all the while to keep a firm, authoritative grip on the participants. To achieve this the quiz master must be prepared – and be able to handle the unexpected.

The quizmaster should be the first person at the venue. You need to turn up a good hour before everybody else. Get some helpers to to arrange tables, and distribute answer sheets and pens. You should have a technical expert on hand to set up equipment such as the overhead projectors spreadsheets for scoring, and the sound system.

Speak up

Ideally you should use a microphone even in a small room. Speaking over a noisy roomful of players is very tiring, and an amplified voice grabs the attention of the participants much more effectively than a raised voice. Check that the mike works at the right volume, and that there is no feedback. Test your tape machine or CD player. It is a good idea to get someone to stand at the back of the room to ensure your voice is audible.

Now check that you have all the questions arranged in the order that you will be reading them out. Be sure that the answers are in order too. It is much better to keep the answers on separate sheets: in the heat of the moment it is all too easy to ruin a question by blurting out the answer along with it.

Tips for top quiz masters

What to do

- Advertise the event at least two weeks ahead of time.
- Put a limit on the size of teams – no more than eight.
- Arrive early and check the equipment thoroughly.
- Make sure that everyone can see and hear you clearly.
- Read each question twice with a gap of 30 seconds or so.
- Use a microphone – even in a small room.

What not to do

- Don't rush the questions: give contestants time to talk over the answers
- Don't mumble: speak clearly and loudly
- Don't be too authoritarian: it's only a game, after all.
- Don't improvise; planning is the key to a good night.
- Don't stand for disputes: if a player contests an answer, assert your authority.

The quiz master's helpers

It is almost impossible to run a quiz on your own: you must have a team of helpers. Dole out the jobs ahead of time. You need one arithmetically confident person to tot up the scores and put them on the board. You also need two or three fast workers to mark the answer sheets. Keep your technical person close at hand in case of mishaps with the mike or the sound system.

Round one, question one

Make sure you strike a friendly note right at the outset. Once all the teams are settled, say a word of welcome to your guests, then state the rules of the competition. These are important, but they should be short and to the point: you don't want it all to sound too serious. Here are the basic rules:

1 Don't shout out the answers

2 Don't trade answers with other teams

3 Jokers must be played promptly, before the start of the round

4 The quiz master's decision is final

Managing your audience

It is a good idea to practise reading the questions out loud before the night. This will give you prior warning of any tongue-twisting turns of phrase. It will also give you the chance to check the pronunciation of tricky words such as 'Hanukah' 'cardiomyopathy' and 'Azerbaijani'.

Read each question twice with a gap of 30 seconds or so between readings. For the players, the fevered discussion over the right answer is the meat of the quiz, so don't be in a big hurry to get through the questions. But do offer to repeat any questions at the end of the round.

Bear in mind that people are there to have fun, so don't be too dictatorial. But at the same time, players must keep to the rules, so don't tolerate cheating. And don't be swayed by the odd heckler or know-all. In any quiz at least one answer will almost certainly be disputed. If you have written your own questions and checked them, or if you have taken them from an impeccable source, then stick to your guns. You are in charge, remember, and your decision is final.

And the winner is...

It adds to the fun of a quiz if there is some form of prize to play for. Trophies can be bought in most high streets – why not have the name of the winning team engraved on it for posterity?

Make a bit of a show of awarding the trophy to the captain of the winning team (make sure someone takes a photograph of the triumphal moment). This makes a neat climax to the evening. For a quiz when perhaps people have paid an entry fee, you could award a cash prize or a bottle of wine for each member of the winning team.

For the losers a wooden spoon or a lemon is the traditional consolation prize.

On the other hand, if everyone agrees that an answer is wrong, consider declaring it void so that no points are scored. Apologise graciously, and point out that nullifying the question is the most equitable way to deal with it.

What to wear

There is nothing wrong with over-dressing as quiz master. A dinner jacket might be a bit over the top for the average pub night, it will leave no one in any doubt about who is in charge. Dressing smartly might boost your confidence and lend that all-important air of authority.

Using a celebrity quiz master

Fundraiser events might require a celebrity, but 'celebrity' could mean a local face, say, the head master at a PTA quiz. If you want to use a big-name celebrity, then follow some basic rules to make the evening go smoothly. Liaise with the celebrity's agent as early as possible to find out what special requests he or she might have. Some may insist on transport to and from the quiz. Some may not want to ask questions on certain subjects, so it is a good idea to send the questions to your celebrity well in advance.

On the night, designate someone to meet your celebrity and act as host. You will need to provide refreshments and changing facilities. When the quiz is over, by all means invite your celeb to stay on, but don't be surprised if they want to go straight away. The first rule of fame (like the first rule of quiz-mastery) is leave the punters wanting more.

Film and TV

B movies
246
LEVEL 2   All 10 answers are films beginning with the letter B

1 In which 1956 film did Marilyn Monroe play a café singer?

2 In which 1955 classic did Glenn Ford play a school teacher in an inner-city school?

3 In which 1998 Disney film did Kevin Spacey provide the voice for Hopper?

4 What was the title of the 1975 film in which John Wayne played a Chicago policeman sent to London to arrest a gangster?

5 Which 1987 film, directed by Blake Edwards, co-starred Bruce Willis and Kim Basinger?

6 The song 'Be our Guest' was sung by a candlestick in which Disney film?

7 Which Oscar-winning film of 1995 told the story of William Wallace?

8 Which 1968 film starring Jane Fonda and set in the 41st century featured a blind angel?

9 Which 1976 film, set among New York gangsters in 1929, starred a teenage Jodie Foster?

10 In which 1992 film co-starring Sharon Stone did Michael Douglas investigate a murder?

Beasts on the box
247
LEVEL 2   A quiz about famous TV animals

1 Which TV drama of the 1960s featured Clarence the cross-eyed lion?

2 Who described himself as: 'the fastest mouse in all Mexico'?

3 What was the name of Manuel's pet rat in *Fawlty Towers*?

4 In the 1950s adventure series, what was the name of the wonder horse?

5 Name *Doctor Who*'s robotic dog.

6 Which marsupial was Sonny Hammond's best friend?

7 Who played Robin to Adam West's *Batman*?

8 What is the name of Martin Crane's dog in *Frasier*?

9 Which porpoise was Sandy and Bud Ricks' best friend?

10 What sort of creature was Aristotle, the Addams family's pet?

Blue movies
248
LEVEL 3   Not what it might seem. All the questions are linked to the colour

1 Which 1990 film comedy co-starred Steve Martin and Rick Moranis?

2 In which 1990 film did Jamie Lee Curtis play a rookie cop hunting a serial killer?

3 What was Blue Thunder in a 1983 film?

4 Angela Lansbury played the mother of Elvis Presley in which 1961 film?

5 Which 1986 film shared its title with a hit record by Bobby Vinton?

6 Which 1949 film starred Jean Simmons in a role that was reprised by Brooke Shields in a 1980 remake?

7 Which film told the story of the jazz legend Billie Holliday?

8 Which film featured the songs 'Sweet home Chicago' and 'Minnie the Moocher'?

9 What was the title of the 1988 film in which Matthew Broderick played a raw army recruit?

10 What was the *Blue Angel* in the 1930 film of the same name starring Marlene Dietrich?

Great children's films

249

LEVEL 1 Children's films but not childishly simple questions

1 Who played the title role in the 1971 film adaptation of Roald Dahl's *Willy Wonka and the Chocolate Factory*?

2 In the film *The Wizard of Oz*, what colour are Dorothy's slippers?

3 R. Lee Ermey, who starred in *Full Metal Jacket*, plays what part in Disney's 1995 *Toy Story*?

4 Which author, more famous for writing spy novels, wrote *Chitty Chitty Bang Bang*?

5 Which eight-time married actress starred in the 1944 film *National Velvet*?

6 Which sailing novel, the first of a series by Arthur Ransome, was adapted into a 1974 film?

7 Which child star was 'home alone' in 1990?

8 Angela Lansbury played a trainee witch who helped repel a German invasion of Britain in which 1971 children's film?

9 Who provides the voice for Mushu, the Demoted One in Disney's 1998 *Mulan*?

10 Which 1999 children's film was advertised with the slogan: 'the Little family just got bigger'?

Family affairs

250

LEVEL 1 Ask the family these questions

1 In which US state was *The Waltons* set?

2 Which TV family lived at The Skypad Apartments?

3 What is the surname of the central family in the sitcom *Roseanne*?

4 The Hood was the arch-enemy of which TV family?

5 What is the surname of Del and Rodney in the TV sitcom *Only Fools and Horses*?

6 Which TV family had a hit record with the 1970 song 'I think I love you'?

7 In *Happy Days*, with which TV family does 'the Fonz' lodge?

8 What is the surname of the central family in *The Cosby Show*?

9 *The Swiss Family Robinson* was adapted and set in space as a 1960s TV series and 1998 film. What was the film called?

10 What is the surname of the family who live next door to the Simpsons in the TV series of the same name?

Island info

251

LEVEL 3 No man is an island, but all these questions are

1 Who played Long John Silver in the 1950 film *Treasure Island*?

2 John Mills played the patriarch of which shipwrecked family in a 1960 film?

3 Which 1963 film, based on a novel by William Golding, told the story of a group of schoolboys stranded on a desert island?

4 In *Jason and the Argonauts*, to which island did Jason sail in his quest for the golden fleece?

5 In which TV series did Ricardo Montalban play the owner of an island where visitors paid $10,000 to make their dreams come true?

6 On which island are the film and the novel *Catch 22* set?

7 On which island was the actor Errol Flynn born?

8 The film *The Island of Dr Moreau* was based on whose novel?

9 On which island is the film *Zorba the Greek* set?

10 Which Oscar-winning actor was born on Sakhalin Island?

Film and TV

252 Robotic riddles
LEVEL 2 A round to test your robot knowledge

1 Which *Star Wars* character made C-3PO?

2 What was the name of the robot in the 1956 film *Forbidden Planet*?

3 Skaro was the home of which robotic villains in *Doctor Who*?

4 Which 1986 comedy film told the story of a military robot called Number 5?

5 Who played the title role in the 1987 film *Robocop*?

6 Which ex-member of The Monkees produced the TV series *Metal Mickey*?

7 What is the name of the android played by Brent Spiner in *Star Trek: The Next Generation*?

8 In which 1999 film did Robin Williams play a domestic android?

9 Which character, played on film by Linda Hamilton, was the Terminator trying to kill?

10 Which 2001 film by Steven Spielberg features a child android?

253 What a carry on
LEVEL 2 Ooh matron . . . and other classic British comedies

1 Who played the title role in *Carry On Columbus*?

2 Which *Carry On* actor was born in South Africa in 1913 and died on stage in 1976?

3 In which film did Barbara Windsor make her *Carry On* debut?

4 In which horror spoof did Kenneth Williams play a character inspired by Baron Frankenstein?

5 In which year was the first *Carry On* film released?

6 Phil Silvers appeared as a Foreign Legionnaire, Sergeant Nocker, in which *Carry On* film?

7 Which of the *Carry On* films was set against the French Revolution?

8 Who played the Khasi of Kalabar in *Carry on up the Khyber*?

9 Which *Carry On* film featured the exploits of a highwayman?

10 Who was the director of the majority of the *Carry On* films?

254 Spooks and spectres
LEVEL 3 A round to chill your bones

1 Who played Cole Sear, the boy who could see dead people in *The Sixth Sense*?

2 Who directed the 1982 film *Poltergeist*?

3 Who played the possessed Regan MacNeil in the 1973 horror classic *The Exorcist*?

4 Name the 1947 film, starring Rex Harrison, that told the story of a widow's love for a ghost?

5 Who played the ghostly Marty Hopkirk in the original series of *Randall and Hopkirk Deceased*?

6 What is the first name of Demi Moore's character in the film *Ghost*?

7 Which 1983 film, based on a Stephen King novel, told the story of a haunted car?

8 In which 1989 Spielberg film did Richard Dreyfuss play a ghost watching over his girlfriend?

9 Who directed the 1973 supernatural thriller *Don't Look Now*, starring Donald Sutherland and Julie Christie?

10 Who wrote the play on which the film *Blithe Spirit* was based?

On the beach

255

LEVEL 1 Life is a beach, and so are these questions

1 In which 1953 film did Burt Lancaster embrace Deborah Kerr on the beach?

2 What is the full name of the character played by David Hasselhoff in *Baywatch*?

3 The beaches of Amity Island were terrorised by a shark in which series of films?

4 The first 20 minutes of which 1998 box office smash depicts the bloody storming of Omaha beach in the Second World War?

5 Who starred in the 1988 film *Beaches*?

6 Which 1962 film memorably saw Ursula Andress walking from the sea onto the beach in a white bikini?

7 The film *Quadrophenia* featured a seaside battle at which British resort?

8 In which 1968 film did Charlton Heston sink to his knees when discovering the Statue of Liberty buried in the sand?

9 In which country is Alex Garland's *The Beach* set?

10 In which 1970s sitcom did Leonard Rossiter fake his own suicide by walking into the sea?

Hey good looking

256

LEVEL 1 Some great looking questions

1 Who played pretty woman, Vivian Ward, on film?

2 In the Disney version of *Beauty and the Beast*, what was the name of Beauty?

3 Which famous actress won the Miss Hungary title in 1936?

4 The song 'I Feel Pretty' features in which musical?

5 Which *Carry On* film centres around the exploits of a seaside beauty contest?

6 Which Scottish hero was played by David Niven in a 1948 film?

7 In a 1986 film, which colour was the actress Molly Ringwald pretty in?

8 Who won a best actor Oscar for his role in the 1999 film *American Beauty*?

9 Which French sex symbol married the film director Roger Vadim?

10 Which Disney film featured the song 'Once Upon a Dream'?

Man to man

257

LEVEL 3 All these questions or answers have a man in them

1 Which explosive 1993 film starred Sylvester Stallone pitted against Wesley Snipes?

2 What was the title of the 1976 film featuring Sir Laurence Olivier as a vicious Nazi dentist?

3 Who played the title role in the 1960s TV drama *Danger Man*?

4 In which 1980 film did Peter O'Toole play a manic film director?

5 Which film first featured the song 'Que Sera, Sera'?

6 Which TV hero worked for the Office of Scientific Intelligence?

7 Who played Liberty Valance in the film *The Man who Shot Liberty Valance*?

8 What was Mark Harris' underwater alter ego?

9 Who played the title role in the 1992 film *The Lawnmower Man*?

10 Which musical features the song '76 Trombones'?

Film and TV

Birds of a feather

258

LEVEL 2 Questions that are related in some way to birds

1 Which brothers starred in the film *Duck Soup*?

2 What sort of bird accompanied a cat in the title of a 1939 Bob Hope film?

3 What was the name of the parrot that taught Dr Dolittle to talk to the animals?

4 In which 1978 film did Richard Burton lead a troop of mercenaries?

5 Which 1969 film, starring Clint Eastwood, was based on a novel by Alistair Maclean?

6 What was the name of the character played by John Wayne in the film *True Grit*?

7 Which 1969 British film explored a boy's relationship with a kestrel?

8 On whose poem was the 1963 horror film *The Raven* based?

9 In which film did Kris Kristofferson play Rubber Duck?

10 What was Anthony Edwards' call-sign in the 1986 film *Top Gun*?

Driving tests

259

LEVEL 2 These questions should put you in a spin

1 Which actress drove a bus with a bomb on board in the film *Speed*?

2 In which 1968 film did Steve McQueen drive a Ford Mustang?

3 What was the title of the 1984 film in which Eddie Murphy drove a tank?

4 What was the 1993 film in which Michael Douglas played a motorist stuck in a traffic jam who eventually cracked under the pressure?

5 Which 1969 film featured Dennis Hopper driving a chopper motorcycle?

6 In which 1971 film did Steve McQueen compete in a famous 24-hour race?

7 Which 1965 film, co-starring Jack Lemmon and Tony Curtis, was set in 1908?

8 At the end of which 1991 film did Geena Davis drive a car into the Canyonlands, Utah?

9 Name the actor who played the chauffeur in the film *Driving Miss Daisy*?

10 Which 1971 Spielberg film featured a commuter terrorised by an evil truck driver?

Body matters

260

LEVEL 3 Some anatomically challenging questions

1 Which gothic horror film features Johnny Depp hunting a headless horseman?

2 Which spy was played by Michael Caine in the film *Billion Dollar Brain*?

3 What was Major Hoolihan's nickname in *M*A*S*H*?

4 In which film did Shirley Temple sing 'On the Good Ship Lollipop'?

5 Which 1946 horror film featured a demonic severed hand?

6 Who was nicknamed 'the man of a thousand faces'?

7 Which actress was known as 'the girl with the million dollar legs'?

8 Who played the creator of *Edward Scissorhands*?

9 Which pop group starred in a 1968 film called *Head*?

10 Of what did Steve Martin have two in the title of a 1983 film?

Child stars

261

LEVEL 1 They have stars in their young eyes

1 Which actor, married eight times, once said: 'I was a 14-year-old boy for 30 years'?

2 In which city was Kevin McCallister home alone, in a 1992 film?

3 Who was the youngest-ever person to receive an Oscar in the 20th century?

4 Who played Elliot's sister in *ET*?

5 Jamie Bell starred in which British film about ballet, made in 2000?

6 Which Dickens character was played by Mark Lester in a 1968 film?

7 How old was Justin Henry, the boy in *Kramer versus Kramer*, when he was nominated for an Oscar?

8 In which film series did Christina Ricci play the daughter Wednesday?

9 Which Hollywood star, who drowned in 1981, first came to light in the 1947 *Miracle on 34th Street*?

10 Who co-starred with her father Ryan in the film *Nickelodeon*?

Time for action

262

LEVEL 1 When the going gets tough

1 Which 1998 swashbuckler co-starred Catherine Zeta Jones and Antonio Banderas?

2 In which 1996 film were the cast chasing tornadoes?

3 Name the 1992 film in which Jean Claude van Damme played a computerised soldier?

4 Who played the lead villain in the films *Mission Impossible* and *Enemy of the State*?

5 What was Rambo's first name?

6 Who played CIA agent Jack Ryan in *Clear and Present Danger* and *Patriot Games*?

7 In the 1995 film *Crimson Tide*, Denzel Washington plays the ambitious 1st Officer Hunter. But who plays the captain of the nuclear missile submarine?

8 Who plays the tough lead in Ridley Scott's 1997 film *GI Jane*?

9 John McClane was the hero in which series of action movies?

10 Dustin Hoffman was battling against a killer virus in which 1995 film?

Cartoon capers

263

LEVEL 1 Can you identify these animated greats?

1 What is the name of Fred Flintstone's wife?

2 Which cartoon series features a married couple called Hank and Peggy Hill?

3 Which canine cartoon character was continually harassed by Musky Muskrat?

4 Which female cartoon character was censored by the US movie censorship board, the Hays Office, in the 1930s on grounds of immorality?

5 'My Darling Clementine' was often sung by which animated hound?

6 What was Hong Kong Phooey's alter ego?

7 What is the name of the red-bearded hombre, an arch-enemy of Bugs Bunny?

8 Who was the best friend of Scooby Doo, voiced by Casey Kasem?

9 Cut Throat Jake was the arch-enemy of which seafaring children's cartoon character?

10 Which great soul singer plays Chef in the animated series *South Park*?

Film and TV

Just for laughs
264
LEVEL 2   A round of ticklish teasers

1 On film, which duo met the Mummy, Frankenstein and the Wolfman amongst others?

2 Which 1940 film, starring one of the greats of silent cinema, was a satire on Nazi Germany?

3 Who played Inspector Dreyfus in the *Pink Panther* films?

4 In the film *Four Weddings and a Funeral*, who played the part for whom the funeral was held?

5 Which, now dead, member of the Monty Python team played the title role in *The Life of Brian*?

6 Which 1964 black comedy about the Cold War had Peter Sellers playing three different roles?

7 In which 1990 film did Eric Idle and Robbie Coltrane both wear wimples?

8 Which woman was portrayed by the actor Arthur Lucan in 15 films?

9 In which 2000 film did Adam Sandler play the third son of the devil?

10 What was the title of the 1990 sequel to *Three Men and a Baby*?

A night at the Oscars
265
LEVEL 2   The world's greatest film awards

1 In which decade were the Oscars first awarded?

2 Who won an Academy Award for the film *On Golden Pond*? The Oscar was collected by his daughter as he was too ill to attend the ceremony.

3 Which 1981 Oscar-winning film reached its climax in 1924 in Paris?

4 Who won consecutive best actor Oscars in 1994 and 1995?

5 Which Oscar-winning film of the 1980s told the story of Karen Blixen?

6 The film adaptation of which Stephen King novel earned Kathy Bates an Oscar?

7 Which film won Oscars in 1991 for best picture, direction, actress, actor and screenplay?

8 How many Oscars did *The Lord of the Rings: The Return of the King* win in 2004?

9 For which 1997 film did Kim Basinger win an Oscar?

10 Which was the first-ever sequel to win a best film Oscar?

A winning performance
266
LEVEL 3   A hard round on the world's greatest film awards

1 Which film shares, with *Titanic,* the most number of Oscar nominations in the 20th century?

2 Which 1980 film earned Robert Redford an Oscar for best director?

3 For which film did George C. Scott refuse his Oscar?

4 How old was Jessica Tandy, the oldest actress to win an Oscar, in *Driving Miss Daisy*?

5 On what does an Oscar statuette stand?

6 Which Oscar-winning film of 1956 was based on a novel by Jules Verne?

7 How was Pu Yi known in the title of a film that won nine oscars?

8 Who was the first-ever actor to win best actor Oscars in two consecutive years?

9 What was the title of the first best film Oscar winner to contain a capital city in the title of the film?

10 Which was the first non-Hollywood film to win an Oscar for best film?

267

Showtime

Are you a telly addict? Identify the TV show from the scenes shown here

1

2

3

4

5

6

7

8

9

10

Film and TV

Friend or foe

268   **LEVEL 1**   Can you tell the good from the bad?

1 Who played Rachel in the TV sitcom *Friends*?

2 What is the name of the arch-enemy of Flash Gordon?

3 Who played Peter in the 1992 British film *Peter's Friends*?

4 In the film *Batman Forever*, who played Batman's foe the Riddler?

5 What is Flicka in the film *My Friend Flicka*, based on the novel by Mary O'Hara?

6 Which of James Bond's arch-enemies has been played by Donald Pleasence, Telly Savalas and Charles Gray?

7 Which controversial film director directed Twiggy in the film *The Boy Friend*?

8 Dr Evil is the arch-enemy of which international man of mystery?

9 Which 1997 film about marriage co-starred Julia Roberts, Cameron Diaz and Rupert Everett?

10 Which 2001 film starring Jude Law has two snipers playing a game of cat-and-mouse during the Battle of Stalingrad?

Around the houses

269   **LEVEL 1**   All questions or answers are about houses

1 Where was the *Little House on the Prairie* set?

2 Which 1996 film featured a giant spaceship that destroyed The White House?

3 In which film did Pauline Collins play a bored housewife holidaying on a Greek island?

4 Name the star of the 1978 film *National Lampoon's Animal House* who died in 1982?

5 Which classic 1981 TV drama was filmed in Castle Howard?

6 Tara was the name of a house in which epic film of 1939?

7 Jack Lemmon won his only Oscar for his role in which 1960 Billy Wilder film?

8 In which 1990s TV drama was the lead character often heard to remark: 'You might say that, I couldn't possibly comment'?

9 The sitcoms *Robin's Nest* and *George and Mildred* were spin-offs from which British sitcom?

10 Which TV series starring Sid James as a father coping with two teenagers was one of the longest-running sitcoms on British TV?

Nationalities

270   **LEVEL 3**   A global round of questions

1 Who wrote the novel on which the film *The English Patient* is based?

2 Who directed the film *The French Connection*?

3 In which film did Michael Caine exclaim: 'You were only supposed to blow the bloody doors off'?

4 In what country was Ursula Andress born?

5 Which sport featured in the 1985 film *American Flyers*?

6 Which 1941 film told the story of the search for a sculpture of a bird?

7 In 1995 who played *The Englishman who went up a hill but came down a Mountain*?

8 What is the title of the 1995 film in which Kevin Kline plays a thief who falls in love with Meg Ryan?

9 Who played the President in the 1995 film *The American President*?

10 In which Bond film did an Israeli actor play a Greek smuggler?

271 Snakes alive
LEVEL 2   Some rather slippery questions

1 In which 1963 film was Elizabeth Taylor bitten by an asp?

2 Which highly controversial 1994 Oliver Stone film featured Woody Harrelson and Juliette Lewis wading through venomous rattlesnakes?

3 Name the actor who played Baldrick in the British TV series *Blackadder*.

4 Which film hero who appeared on the big screen in the 1980s had a fear of snakes?

5 In which 1997 film was Jon Voight swallowed by a giant snake?

6 What was the title of the 1998 film in which Nicolas Cage played a corrupt policeman?

7 Name the snake in *The Jungle Book*.

8 In which 1986 film did Sylvester Stallone play a ruthless city policeman?

9 Which Monty Python film told of the legend of King Arthur?

10 In which Bond film did Roger Moore save Jane Seymour from being bitten by a snake in a voodoo ceremony?

272 Disney delights
LEVEL 2   Questions about the great animator

1 Which was the first Disney film to be nominated for a best picture Oscar?

2 Name the whale in *Pinocchio*.

3 Which was the first Disney film to be made with stereo soundtrack?

4 Which Disney film featured a character called Thomas O'Malley?

5 What were the names of the canine parents in *101 Dalmatians*?

6 In the Disney animation *Robin Hood*, what sort of animal was Little John?

7 What is the name of the skunk in *Bambi*?

8 Which was the first animated Disney film to tell the story of a real person?

9 Which 1994 Disney film has a soundtrack written by Tim Rice and Elton John?

10 Which was the first of Disney's full-length animated films to have a sequel?

273 Husbands and wives
LEVEL 3   Some famous on and off screen couples

1 Name the actress who played Mrs Rocky Balboa.

2 Who played the wife of Michael Douglas in *Fatal Attraction*?

3 In which film did Michael Douglas and Kathleen Turner play an unhappily married couple?

4 Which husband and wife co-starred in the 1953 film *Houdini*?

5 Who married the actress Anne Bancroft in 1964?

6 Who was married to fellow thespian Lynne Frederick at the time of his death in 1980?

7 Which wife of Orson Welles was born Margarita Carmen Cansino?

8 The husband starred in *Evita* and the wife starred in *Working Girl*. Who are they?

9 Name the wife of Clark Gable who died in a plane crash.

10 Which *Carry On* actress was married to John Le Mesurier?

Film and TV

Sport on the screen
274
LEVEL 2 A collection of sporting challenges

1 What sport was featured in the 1977 film *Slap Shot*, in which Paul Newman played the coach?

2 In which film did Tom Cruise play the sports agent of Cuba Gooding Jr?

3 Which Second World War film had roles played by Pelé, Osvaldo Ardiles and Bobby Moore?

4 *Bull Durham*, starring Kevin Costner, was a 1988 film about which sport?

5 Who directed *Chariots of Fire*?

6 James Caan starred in which 1975 film that featured a brutal and ultra-violent sport?

7 The film *Fever Pitch*, which followed the fortunes of Arsenal Football Club, was based on a novel by which author?

8 Who played the lead, 'fast' Eddie Felson, in the 1961 snooker film *The Hustler*?

9 For which 1976 film did Sylvester Stallone receive an Oscar nomination?

10 Which 2000 film stars Will Smith as a mystical caddy helping Matt Damon to regain his golf swing?

Relative values
275
LEVEL 1 Questions to keep in the family

1 Who played Brother Cadfael in the 1990s British TV drama of the same name?

2 In which 1989 film did Macaulay Culkin play the nephew of John Candy?

3 *O Brother, Where Art Thou?* was a 2000 hit film starring which Hollywood heart throb?

4 In *The Godfather*, who plays Santino 'Sonny' Corleone?

5 If Pugsley is the son and Gomez the father, who is the mother?

6 Which actress played the title role in the film *My Stepmother is an Alien*?

7 Who did Robert Vaughn play in *The Man from UNCLE*?

8 What was the 1992 film that starred Whoopi Goldberg pretending to be a nun?

9 Dermot Morgan played the title role in which Irish sitcom?

10 What do the films *The Parent Trap* and *Dead Ringers* have in common?

Vampires
276
LEVEL 2 A round of questions to give you a pain in the neck

1 *Dracula: Dead and Loving it* was a spoof vampire film starring which US comedian?

2 *Interview with a Vampire* starred Brad Pitt and which other lead actor as bloodsuckers?

3 Who wrote the novel on which the *Dracula* films are based?

4 Which German actor, father of Nastassja, played Dracula in the 1979 film *Nosferatu: The Vampyre*?

5 On TV, who played *Buffy the Vampire Slayer*?

6 When Gary Oldman played Dracula, who played Van Helsing?

7 George Clooney, Harvey Keitel and Quentin Tarantino featured in which 1996 film about Mexican vampires?

8 Which British actor, whose name is synonymous with the role of Dracula, first played the vampire in 1958?

9 Who starred as the vampire in the comedy film *Love at First Bite*?

10 Which Romanian-born actor played Dracula on numerous occasions between 1931 and his death in 1956?

277 The A team
LEVEL 2 All 10 answers are people whose surnames begins with A

1 Who starred in the films *Desperately Seeking Susan* and *Pulp Fiction*?

2 Who starred as Pinkie Brown in *Brighton Rock* and as John Hammond in *Jurassic Park*?

3 Of whom did Christopher Plummer say: 'Working with her is like being hit over the head with a Valentine's card'?

4 Name the actress famous for playing Hilda Ogden in *Coronation Street*.

5 Who won an Academy Award for his role as a rejuvenated senior citizen in the film *Cocoon*?

6 Who traded places with Eddie Murphy in a 1983 film?

7 Who played Dana Scully in the cult series *The X-Files*?

8 Who starred in the film *California Suite* and the TV series *M*A*S*H**?

9 How is Allen Stewart Konigsberg better known?

10 Name the actress, born in 1952, who sprang to fame after playing one of the 'Railway Children' on film?

278 Court cases
LEVEL 2 Some challenging questions to try you

1 Who wrote the stories on which the British TV series *Rumpole of the Bailey* is based?

2 Name the actor who was best known for playing Perry Mason on TV.

3 Which 1992 military courtroom drama starred Jack Nicholson, Tom Cruise, Demi Moore and Kevin Bacon?

4 Judge John Deed is played on TV by which actor?

5 In which film was Harrison Ford accused of the murder of Greta Scacchi?

6 Corbin Bernsen played the amorous attorney Arnold Becker in which TV drama?

7 Which QC was portrayed by John Thaw in the British TV drama series?

8 Name the 1957 film in which Henry Fonda played an idealistic member of a jury?

9 In which 1985 film did Glenn Close defend Jeff Bridges against an accusation of murder?

10 Which actress played the lawyer of Jodie Foster in the film *The Accused*?

279 Think of a number
LEVEL 1 All these questions are about numbers

1 According to a 1966 film starring Raquel Welch, when were humans walking the Earth?

2 The Eurythmics performed the theme 'Sex Crime' for which film?

3 The 1969 film *Anne of a Thousand Days* told the story of which wife of Henry VIII?

4 In which film did Nick Nolte spring Eddie Murphy from jail to help him catch a pair of criminals?

5 Name the 1985 film that saw Richard Pryor inheriting a vast amount of money?

6 In the film *The Omen*, what is the number of the beast?

7 Jane Fonda, Lily Tomlin and Dolly Parton played office colleagues in which 1980 film?

8 How are Curly-Joe, Larry and Mo collectively known?

9 According to the title of a 1986 film, how long was Kim Basinger's and Mickey Rourke's affair?

10 In which film did Charlton Heston play Moses?

Film and TV

Leading ladies
280

LEVEL 1 Some of the great stars of the silver screen

1 Whom did Bruce Willis marry in 1987?

2 What was the title of the 1998 film in which Meg Ryan played the leading lady to Tom Hanks for the third time?

3 Which actress defended Daniel Day Lewis in the film *In the Name of the Father*?

4 Who played the mother of *Forrest Gump*?

5 Which English actress played *Billy Elliot's* ballet instructor?

6 Which Hollywood great leading lady was nominated for a record 12 Oscars, winning four of them?

7 Who played Olive Oyl to Robin Williams' Popeye in the film *Popeye*?

8 Who played the title role in the film *Private Benjamin*?

9 Name the actress who played the Wicked Lady in a 1983 film remake of the same name.

10 Which actress walked through a pair of sliding doors on screen in 1998?

Catchphrases
281

LEVEL 1 Phrases you have heard a dozen times, but who said them?

1 Which TV game show has spawned several catchphrases including: 'Is that your final answer'?

2 Which catchphrase was used for the title of the first Monty Python film?

3 Which Dame greets 'her' audience with the words: 'Hello possums'?

4 Who, as Steve McGarrett, often said: 'Book 'em Danno' in *Hawaii 5-0*?

5 In which game show does the host yell: 'Come on down'?

6 Which cartoon character stammers: 'That's all folks' at the end of Warner Brothers' cartoons?

7 In which film did Arnold Schwarzenegger first utter the line: 'I'll be back'?

8 'Who loves ya baby?' was the catchphrase of which TV cop?

9 Name the cartoon villain who was often heard cursing: 'Drat and double drat'.

10 Name the lady that you would associate with the words: 'You are the weakest link, goodbye'.

What a disaster!
282

LEVEL 1 A group of films featuring disasters: man-made or otherwise

1 Which 1974 film featuring a host of stars had Steve McQueen playing Fire Chief Michael O'Hallorhan?

2 Name the 1972 film in which Shelley Winters and Gene Hackman perished at sea.

3 Who played the President of the USA in the disaster film *Deep Impact*?

4 Which British actress was cast into the spotlight after taking the lead in *Titanic*?

5 In which 1998 space film did Bruce Willis play oil driller Harry Stamper who saves the world?

6 Which 1975 film told the true story of a 1937 disaster involving an airship?

7 Which 2000 film saw George Clooney battling against the elements of the sea?

8 Who played the volcano expert in the 1997 film *Dante's Peak*?

9 In which 1979 film did Jack Lemmon and Jane Fonda avert a nuclear power plant disaster?

10 Who played the computer genius in the film *Independence Day*?

Magnificent sevens

283 **LEVEL 2** All the questions are linked to the lucky number

1 In how many James Bond films did Sean Connery play 007?

2 Who played the leader of *The Magnificent Seven* in the original film?

3 In which 1995 thriller were Morgan Freeman and Brad Pitt chasing Kevin Spacey?

4 Which famous literary sleuth was lured to Vienna to cure his cocaine addiction in the film *The Seven Per Cent Solution*?

5 Which 1954 film musical featured the song 'Bless your Beautiful Hide'?

6 Name the film in which Marilyn Monroe's skirt was blown upwards by air from a grating.

7 In the 1964 film *Robin and the Seven Hoods*, who sang 'My Kind of Town'?

8 In which year was the first full-length animated film *Snow White and the Seven Dwarfs* released?

9 Where did Brad Pitt spend seven years according to the title of a 1997 film?

10 Who directed the film *The Seven Samurai*, on which *The Magnificent Seven* was based?

Spin-offs

284 **LEVEL 2** Great TV series can create many new programmes in their wake

1 Which spin-off from *Buffy the Vampire Slayer* features a vampire cursed with a conscience?

2 *The Men from Shiloh* was a spin-off from which TV western?

3 *Laverne and Shirley*, *Mork and Mindy* and *Chachi Loves Joanie* were spin-offs from which TV show?

4 What was the title of the spin-off from *The Cosby Show* that told of the college life of Denise Huxtable?

5 Which *Star Trek* spin-off features Captain Kathryn Janeway as a ship's commander?

6 Which period drama produced the spin-off series *Thomas and Sarah*?

7 Name the 1970s spin-off police series starring Stratford Johns as Chief Inspector Barlow.

8 *Stop the Pigeon* was a spin-off from which cartoon series?

9 *Richie Brockleman Private Eye*, was a spin-off from which American TV series?

10 What is the connection between the TV shows *Rhoda*, *Lou Grant*, *The Love Boat* and *Phyllis*?

Time for romance

285 **LEVEL 3** Questions about some of cinema's most passionate moments

1 In which 1997 film does Jack Nicholson find love with a waitress played by Helen Hunt?

2 Who played Ryan O'Neal's father in *Love Story*?

3 Diana Ross and Lionel Richie sang the theme for which 1981 film starring Brooke Shields?

4 'They're young, they're in love and they kill people' was the blurb for which 1967 film?

5 Name the wife Steven Spielberg met whilst directing *Indiana Jones and the Temple of Doom*.

6 In *Brief Encounter*, name the fictional station where Celia Johnson and Trevor Howard met.

7 Which film characters shared spaghetti while being serenaded with the song 'La Bella Notte'?

8 The film *You're in the Army Now* featured the longest-ever screen kiss but with which actress?

9 In which film did Lauren Bacall utter: 'You know how to whistle, don't you, Steve. You just put your lips together . . . and blow'?

10 Which was the first film to star the legendary Spencer Tracy and Katharine Hepburn screen team?

Film and TV

TV transport trivia
286
LEVEL 2 Tricky questions about planes, trains, automobiles, etc.

1 In the TV series *Dallas*, in what was Jock Ewing travelling when he was killed?

2 What type of car does British sitcom character Del Boy use for his business?

3 What vehicle did Doctor Who use to transport himself through time and space?

4 How did the British TV chefs the Two Fat Ladies get around?

5 Which man of the cloth created *Thomas the Tank Engine*?

6 In which TV series did Jan Michel Vincent pilot a military helicopter?

7 What was the model of red and white Ford car driven by Starsky in *Starsky and Hutch*?

8 In the *Wacky Races*, who drove a car called 'the Turbo Terrific'?

9 Who played motorcycle cop Frank Poncherella in *CHIPS*?

10 Christopher Pike was the first captain of which vessel?

The final curtain
287
LEVEL 2 Name the film stars from their final screen appearances

1 *I Could Go On Singing* (1963)

2 *The Shootist* (1976)

3 *Avalanche Express* (1979)

4 *The Carpetbaggers* (1964)

5 *Brainstorm* (1983)

6 *Cannonball Run II* (1983)

7 *Harry Potter and the Chamber of Secrets* (2002)

8 *The Hunter* (1980)

9 *Wicked Stepmother* (1989)

10 *Soylent Green* (1973)

Movie mindbenders
288
LEVEL 3 More challenging questions about the cinema

1 Which film stopped *Citizen Kane* winning best picture Oscar?

2 Who directed *Spartacus*?

3 What connects a Nobel laureate, Anthony Quinn and the Sunday after Easter?

4 Which 1995 film was promoted with the line: 'Five criminals. One line up. No coincidence'?

5 Who did William Boyd play in 66 films?

6 Who directed *Flatliners*?

7 Who died of a cardiac arrest on November 9, 1991, shortly after his screen character died of a cardiac arrest?

8 Who starred in the Hollywood remake of *A Bout de Souffle*?

9 Who won the best actor Oscar the year after Jeremy Irons and before Al Pacino?

10 Who played James Bond in *The Man With the Golden Gun*?

 **Screen quest**

These questions are tougher than the others and you may need to do some research

1 What is the Christian name of Inspector Morse?

2 Which actress was adopted as the official mascot of the Chilean Navy on the orders of President Alessandri?

3 About whom did Lucille Ball say, 'She wasn't really stand-offish. She ignored everyone equally'?

4 Who is the only Oscar-winning actress to have two Oscar-winning parents?

5 What does the acronym UNCLE stand for in the TV series *The Man From UNCLE*?

6 Who is the only Oscar to have won an Oscar?

7 What do the initials CJ stand for in the character of CJ Parker from Baywatch?

8 Linguistically, what is unique about the 1965 film *Incubus*, starring William Shatner?

9 Which 1934 film resulted in a decline in the sale of vests?

10 Anthony Daniels and Kenny Baker appeared in five films together, although they were never actually seen in the flesh. Who did they play?

11 What connects Batman with *The Game of Love* and the Duke?

12 Albert, Harry, Sam and Jack all had a keen interest in Bugs Bunny. Why?

13 What was the name of the ragdoll on *Playschool*?

14 'If you build it, he will come.' The pivotal promise of which movie?

15 What is the name of Rigsby's cat?

A clue to question 14

Film and TV

290 Down under
LEVEL 1   Questions from the other side of the globe

1 Which country played host to most of the filming for the *Lord of the Rings* trilogy?

2 Which rock star took the title role in the 1970 film *Ned Kelly* about the Australian outlaw?

3 Which school do the pupils in the Australian soap *Neighbours* attend?

4 Donald Fisher was a headmaster in which soap?

5 Which medical TV drama was set in the town of Cooper's Crossing?

6 What was the title of the series in which Kylie Minogue made her soap debut?

7 Name the 1970 film in which Jenny Agutter got lost in the Australian outback.

8 What is the name of the Australian Cultural Attaché to the Court of St James as portrayed by Barry Humphries?

9 Which Australian actor played the title role in the 2000 film *Gladiator*?

10 The music of which European group was featured in the Australian film *Muriel's Wedding*?

291 Screen villains
LEVEL 1   A round of questions about the people we love to hate

1 In *Star Trek: The Next Generation*, what name is given to the hive-like entity which assimilates all that it encounters?

2 Which actor played the lead villain in the films *Die Hard* and *Robin Hood, Prince of Thieves*?

3 By what name was the intergalactic villain Anakin Skywalker better known?

4 Whom did Sherlock Holmes describe as 'the Napoleon of crime'?

5 Who played Bill Sikes in the musical *Oliver*?

6 In *Toy Story*, who is Buzz Lightyear's sworn enemy?

7 In *From Russia with Love*, what was the name of the Soviet agent armed with a pair of shoes fitted with poison-tipped blades?

8 What was Dr Hannibal Lecter's field of medical expertise?

9 Martin Sheen is sent to assassinate Colonel Kurtz in which 1979 Vietnam War movie?

10 Who played the part of Lex Luthor, Superman's arch-enemy in the 1978 film *Superman*?

292 Novel ideas
LEVEL 3   The quiz of the film of the book

1 Which 1991 film was based on a novel by Anthony Powell?

2 Who did Sir Anthony Hopkins play in *Shadowlands*?

3 On whose book was the film *The Name of the Rose* based?

4 Who wrote the novel *The Godfather*, on which the Mafia films were based?

5 The book *Enemy Coast Ahead* was adapted into which war film?

6 Whose true story was adapted into the 1987 film *Castaway*, starring Oliver Reed?

7 Who wrote the novel on which the TV mini-series *Rich Man Poor Man* was based?

8 Dustin Hoffman starred as *The Graduate*. Who wrote the novel?

9 Which novel by Kazuo Ishiguro became a 1993 film starring Emma Thompson and Sir Anthony Hopkins?

10 Which Thomas Hardy character was played by Nastassja Kinski in a 1979 film?

Pop stars on film
293
LEVEL 2   Stars who can not only sing but can act

1 Which rocker, famous for his lips, had a starring role in the 1992 sci-fi thriller *Freejack*?

2 Who played Jim Morrison in the film *The Doors*?

3 In the 1983 film *Merry Christmas, Mr Lawrence*, who played the part of Major Jack 'Strafer' Celliers?

4 The film *La Bamba* told of the brief life of which pop star?

5 Who starred in the film *Shanghai Surprise* with her then husband Sean Penn?

6 In the 1998 film *Out of Sight*, which female pop singer co-starred with George Clooney?

7 Laurence Fishburne played which pop star in the 1993 film *What's love got to do with it*?

8 Who played Elvis Presley in the 1979 TV movie *Elvis*?

9 Which British singer had a cameo role as a police detective in the Spielberg movie *Hook*?

10 Which 1980s rocker played a teacher in the 1985 film *Back to the Future*?

Film sequels
294
LEVEL 2   Films so good they made another – and sometimes another

1 Who directed the film *Staying Alive*, the sequel to *Saturday Night Fever*?

2 *The Spy Who Shagged Me* was the second in a series of films. What was the name of the first?

3 How many *Police Academy* films were made between 1984 and 1994?

4 Which British actor played the character Zod in *Superman II*?

5 In which film sequel did Michelle Pfeiffer play a 'pink lady'?

6 What was the sub-title of *Star Trek II*?

7 Which series of horror films, featuring the malevolent Jason, has stretched to a total of eleven films?

8 Who played the Penguin in the film *Batman Returns*?

9 *The Final Conflict* was the third in which series of films?

10 What was the title of the third *Star Wars* film to be made, although it is sixth in the series?

I spy
295
LEVEL 3   Do you know your CIA from your KGB?

1 Who played the title role in the 1965 film *The Spy who Came in from the Cold*?

2 Who played Bill Cosby's partner in *I Spy*?

3 Who played Reilly in the 1983 TV series *Reilly, Ace of Spies*?

4 Who recorded the theme song for the 1985 film *Spies Like Us*?

5 What was the first film in which Michael Caine played the spy Harry Palmer?

6 Which 1977 film featured an outsized villain with metal teeth?

7 Who starred as the bookish CIA agent Joe Turner in the 1975 film *Three Days of the Condor*?

8 Which 1964 film featured an evil organisation known by the acronym STENCH?

9 What was the title of the 1996 film in which Michelle Trachtenberg played an 11-year-old who spied on her friends and neighbours?

10 What breed of dog was *The Spy with a Cold Nose* in a 1966 film?

Bits and pieces

296

Kids 7–11 A round of film and TV trivia

1 Where did Toad live in *The Wind in the Willows*?

2 What is the name of Woody's horse in *Toy Story 2*?

3 What kind of bird is the cartoon character Daffy?

4 What name is given to Batman's car?

5 In which film does Mickey Mouse conduct the orchestra?

6 Which cartoon character often said: 'I tawt I taw a puddy tat'?

7 Which evil character was assisted by Horace and Jasper?

8 What colour is the teletubby Po?

9 What is the name of the pub in *EastEnders*?

10 What kind of animal is Garfield?

Couch potatoes

297

Kids 12–14 Test your knowledge of the screen

1 In the *Lord of the Rings* films, what is the name of the dwarf who joins the fellowship of the Ring?

2 In *Star Trek*, what is Mr Spock's home planet?

3 What is the name of the Flintstones' baby?

4 In *The Lion King*, what is the name of Simba's wicked uncle?

5 What is the name of Doctor Who's time machine?

6 What is the name of the butler in *The Addams Family*?

7 Which animated film featured a bird called Zazu?

8 Which school is attended by Buffy the Vampire Slayer?

9 Who does David Schwimmer play in *Friends*?

10 Who is the star of the film *The Last Samurai*?

Allsorts

298

Kids 7–11 A lucky dip of TV and film questions

1 In *Thomas the Tank Engine*, what is the number of Gordon the big green tender engine?

2 In the cartoon series, what is the first name of the secret agent whose surname is Possible?

3 The villain of the first Spiderman film is The Green what?

4 In *The Lord of the Rings*, what is the surname of the hobbit called Meriadoc?

5 What is The Incredible Hulk's real name?

6 In *Rugrats*, what is Tommy's surname?

7 In the cartoon series, what is the name of the little girl whose parents make wildlife documentaries and who can talk to animals?

8 What are the names of The Cat in the Hat's two helpers?

9 How many Power Puff Girls are there?

10 In *Scooby Doo*, what is the name of the only member of Mystery Inc. who wears glasses?

The Simpsons
Kids 12–14 A round about Springfield's favourite family

1 Who is Homer Simpson's boss?

2 What nationality is Willie, the school caretaker?

3 What is the name of the bar where Homer does most of his drinking?

4 What is the name of Bart Simpson's bespectacled best friend?

5 What is the name of the principal in Springfield's school?

6 Which violent cartoon series is often watched by Lisa and Bart?

7 What is the last name of Barney, Homer's drinking buddy?

8 On what is Bart seen writing at the start of every episode?

9 What is the name of the clown, Bart's hero?

10 Which evil character was briefly married to Bart's aunt?

Screen test
Kids 7–11 A random round of riddles

1 What was the scarecrow lacking in *The Wizard of Oz*?

2 What colour is The Incredible Hulk?

3 What does Spiderman shoot from his wrists to capture criminals?

4 According to Mary Poppins, what helps the medicine go down?

5 What is the name of Tarzan's female companion?

6 In *Monsters, Inc.*, what is the name of Sulley's little green one-eyed friend?

7 What is Bugs Bunny's favourite food?

8 What is the name of the bear in *The Jungle Book*?

9 What is the name of the 'friendly ghost' who lives with his three ghostly uncles?

10 In the film *Lady and the Tramp*, is Lady a poodle or a cocker spaniel?

Potter mania
Kids 12–14 How well do you know Harry Potter and the Philosopher's Stone?

1 Which Scottish actor plays Gatekeeper Rubeus Hagrid on screen?

2 Which wizard is discovered to be playing host to: 'He who must not be named'?

3 The Sorting Hat places Harry into Gryffindor, but which other house did Harry nearly get put into?

4 Who is the potions professor at Hogwarts?

5 Although not named in the film, what is Harry's owl called?

6 In what form does Professor McGonagall first appear?

7 How does Hagrid's beard catch fire?

8 Which instrument is used to pacify Fluffy, the three-headed guard dog?

9 What gives Harry's wand its magical powers?

10 Where does Ron appear as both head boy and Quidditch captain?

Film clips

302

Kids 7–11   Test your knowledge of film and TV

1 Which vegetable gives Popeye his strength?

2 In *Toy Story*, what is the name of the pizza restaurant to which Woody and Buzz are driven?

3 What kind of animal is the cartoon character Silvester?

4 Is James the Tank Engine green, red or blue?

5 Dot, Heimlich, Tuck and Roll are all characters in which Disney film?

6 What kind of creature is Pingu?

7 What is the name of the wizard that featured in the Disney film *The Sword in the Stone*?

8 What is the name of the cowgirl in *Toy Story 2*?

9 What kind of animal is Captain Hook scared of in *Peter Pan*?

10 In the cartoon series, where does Dexter spend most of his time: in the laboratory, in the bathroom, or in the swimming pool?

May the force be with you

303

Kids 12–14   From a galaxy far, far away

1 Who was Princess Leia's brother?

2 What was the title of the sequel to *Star Wars* released in 1980?

3 What is the favoured weapon of a Jedi Knight?

4 Endor was the home planet of which furry creatures?

5 What are the white-clad soldiers of the Imperial Army called?

6 Which *Star Wars* character did Princess Leia describe as 'a walking carpet'?

7 What is the name of the black-and-orange faced villain in *Episode 1: The Phantom Menace*?

8 In *The Empire Strikes Back*, who teaches Luke the ways of a Jedi knight?

9 Which character has been played by Ewan McGregor and Sir Alec Guinness?

10 Who played Han Solo in the 1977 film *Star Wars*?

Disney delights

304

Kids 7–11   A round about cartoon favourites

1 Which part of Pinocchio got larger when he told lies?

2 What is the name of Disney's flying elephant?

3 Which group of miners shared a house with Snow White?

4 What is Winnie the Pooh's favourite food?

5 Which flying horse featured in the Disney animation *Hercules*?

6 What is the name of Mickey Mouse's dog?

7 Which character was voiced by Robin Williams in the film *Aladdin*?

8 In *Toy Story 2*, who turns out to be Buzz Lightyear's father?

9 What is the name of the Little Mermaid?

10 What sort of creatures are *The Rescuers*?

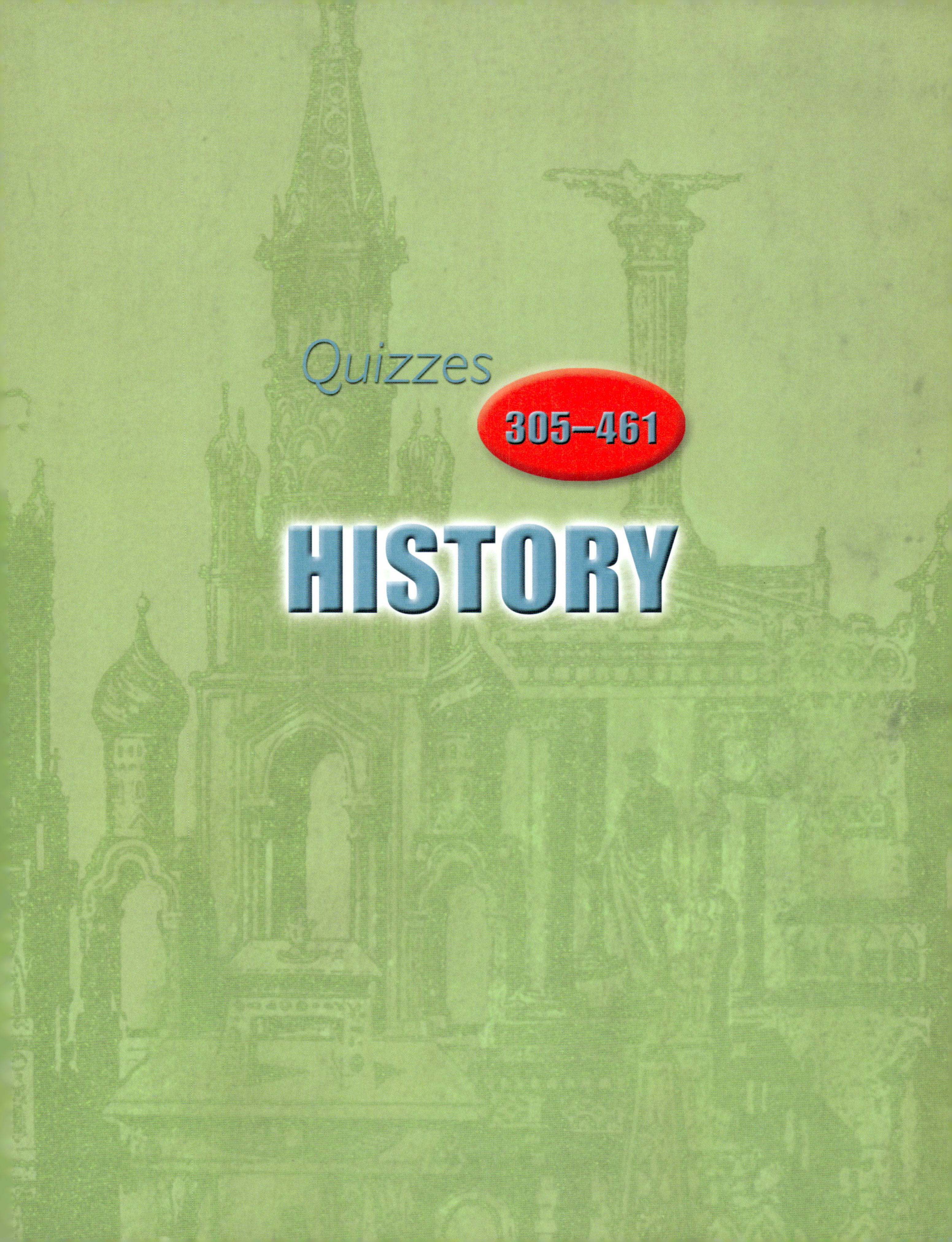

Quizzes

305–461

HISTORY

History

305

A round of As
LEVEL 1   Every answer begins with the letter A

1 Who is the only English king to be known as 'the Great'?

2 Name the hill in Athens on which the Greeks built the Parthenon temple.

3 Which Norwegian explorer led the expedition to the South Pole in 1911?

4 Who was the King of the Huns, who almost captured Rome in 452?

5 What do the initials ANC stand for?

6 Which Egyptian city, named after a Greek conqueror, had the greatest library in the Ancient World?

7 Which South American country was led by General Galtieri between 1976 and 1983?

8 Who was the second person to walk on the Moon, in July 1969?

9 Against which country did the US launch Operation Enduring Freedom in 2001 to destroy the Al Qaeda network?

10 By what other name was Mustafa Kemal, the founder of modern Turkey, known?

306

Risings and revolutions
LEVEL 1   Great movements in history

1 A popular uprising across Eastern Europe led to what momentous event in Berlin in November 1989?

2 How is the overthrow, between 1688 and 1689, of the Catholic King James II that brought William of Orange to the British throne, known?

3 Which gladiator led a rising against Rome?

4 Which flag was first flown in 1777 aboard a ship leaving Portsmouth, New Hampshire?

5 In which European city was a violent student protest held in 1968?

6 In which city did the Easter Rising break out in 1916?

7 Against which conquering force did Hereward the Wake lead a fenland revolt?

8 Which warrior race fought the British during an uprising in New Zealand in 1845?

9 In 1381, which uprising of English paupers was led by Wat Tyler and John Ball?

10 Who led the 1917 Communist revolution in Russia?

307

Know your enemy
LEVEL 2   Who was on the other side?

1 Who led the Afrika Corps that was defeated by General Montgomery in the Second World War?

2 Who was the infamous leader of the Khmer Rouge in Cambodia between 1975 and 1979?

3 What was the South Vietnamese insurgent force, supported by the North Vietnamese Army, against whom America fought?

4 Who was the leader of Imperial Germany during the First World War?

5 In 1982, Britain defended the Falkland Islands after they were invaded by which country?

6 Against which country did Britain fight the Battle of Crécy during the Hundred Years War?

7 Who headed the Communist Party in the Soviet Union from 1964 to 1982?

8 Who was the American commander-in-chief during the American War of Independence?

9 Who was the president of Yugoslavia during Nato's 1999 Kosovo campaign?

10 Who commanded the Luftwaffe during the Battle of Britain in 1940?

Red letter dates

308

LEVEL 1   A round of great events and eventful years

1 The 1789 revolution ended the *ancien regime* in which European country?

2 At the 11th hour of the 11th day of the 11th month of 1918, what came to an end?

3 What 1776 event do Americans commemorate?

4 Which empire's legions came ashore in Britain in the year AD 43?

5 In 1492, who 'sailed the ocean blue' – the Atlantic – to reach America?

6 October 1917 marked the overthrow of the Tsar in which country?

7 In 1991, the Gulf War brought Iraq's invasion of which country to an end?

8 In 1963 the assassination of which US president took place?

9 In 1969, someone famously declared: 'That's one small step for a man, one giant leap for mankind'. Where were these words said?

10 In 1945, what new type of bomb was dropped on to two Japanese cities, bringing about the end of the Second World War?

The shortest month

309

LEVEL 2   All these questions relate to events that took place in February

1 What public, male-only, facility was opened in London's Fleet Street in February, 1852?

2 Name the Mediterranean island that gained independence from Britain in 1960?

3 In what Texan town did a fatal stand-off between the FBI and the Branch Davidians sect start in February, 1993?

4 What fate befell the USS *Maine* in Spanish-owned Havana in 1898?

5 Which English king died of apoplexy in 1685?

6 In February of which year did Britain adopt decimal currency?

7 Which precious piece of ancient pottery was smashed in the British Museum in 1845?

8 Which famous navigator was stabbed to death in the Sandwich Islands (now Hawaii) in 1779?

9 The massacre of the MacDonalds by the Campbells in Scotland in February,1692, is known by what name?

10 From which country did the United States purchase Miami in 1819?

War in the Pacific

310

LEVEL 3   A round about the closing stages of the Second World War

1 Which British-held territory did Lieutenant General A.E. Percival surrender to Japan in February 1942?

2 What name was given to the first US air raid on Tokyo in 1942?

3 Which British base in Ceylon was attacked from the air on Easter Sunday, 1942?

4 What airborne weapons did the Japanese send to attack the United States in November 1944?

5 Who led the Chindits until a fatal plane crash?

6 Which naval battle of October 1944 opened the way for the US recapture of the Philippines?

7 Why did Allied naval crews scan the skies for Bettys and Nells?

8 What was the name of the plane flown by Colonel Paul W. Tibbets on August 8, 1945?

9 Which Japanese island was taken by the Americans in June 1945 after 83 days of fighting?

10 Which US cruiser was sunk in the Philippines, her last mission having been to carry materials for the atomic bomb to the US base at Guam?

History

311 Lost at sea

LEVEL 2 Questions about great naval battles

1 What fleet of 130 ships tried, unsuccessfully, to launch an invasion of England in 1588?

2 Which German battleship was chased into the River Plate and then scuttled in Montevideo harbour in 1939?

3 Which British troopship in the Falklands War was known as the 'great white whale'?

4 How was the *Lusitania* lost, claiming 1198 lives, during the First World War?

5 What kind of ships fought their last great sea battle in Europe in 1571, at the Battle of Lepanto?

6 What significant ceremony took place aboard the USS *Missouri* on September 2, 1945?

7 Aboard which ship did Admiral Nelson die?

8 Name the only major sea battle of the First World War.

9 During which naval battle of 1942 was the USS *Lexington* sunk, but 2735 men rescued?

10 What were Silkworms, downed by Sea Darts, in the 1991 Gulf War?

312 A touch of the blarney

LEVEL 1 Questions about Irish history

1 Which famous saint is supposed to have sent the snakes packing from Ireland?

2 How is the shooting of 13 people, in Derry in 1972 by the Parachute Regiment, known?

3 Who became First Minister of Northern Ireland in December 1999, following the Good Friday peace accords?

4 Who was the first woman to be elected President of the Irish Republic, in 1990?

5 Which little people are first mentioned in a 14th-century retelling of an old story?

6 Which 17th-century English leader laid waste to Ireland with his parliamentary army?

7 Which battle fought on July 1, 1690 is still a cause of contention today?

8 Name the IRA hunger-striker who was elected MP for Fermanagh-South Tyrone in 1981.

9 Which university, founded in Dublin in 1592, is Ireland's oldest?

10 Who was the first Irish prime minister known officially as the Taoiseach (ti-shach), in 1937?

313 Old news stories

LEVEL 3 Front-page news in the 1970s, but has memory faded?

1 On January 27, 1973, peace talks in which city finally ended the Vietnam War?

2 What were Ling-Ling and Hsing-Hsing, presents from China to the United States in 1972?

3 Which emperor first stepped outside his imperial islands as head of state in 1971?

4 For which newspaper did Carl Bernstein and Bob Woodward work while uncovering the Watergate scandal?

5 Which US president wobbled at the knees having run too far in Maryland in 1979?

6 On January 16, 1979 the Shah of Iran fled, leaving which Islamic fundamentalist in power?

7 Aged 11, at which game did Nigel prove to be a prodigy in the 1977 British championships?

8 Of which country did Zulfikar Ali Bhutto become president in 1972?

9 Where did Deke move from one craft to shake hands with Alexei in another in 1975?

10 Which princess made a London balcony appearance with her new husband in 1973?

314 Famous inventions

Match these inventions to the list of inventors and the year of invention

1

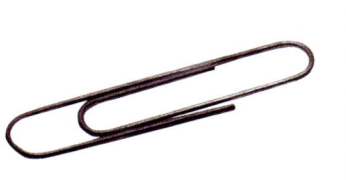
2

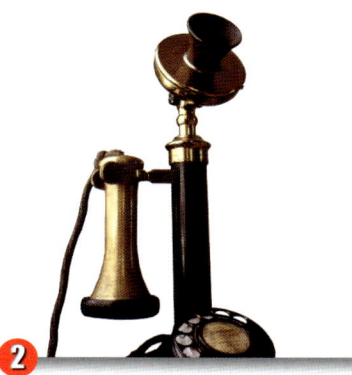
3

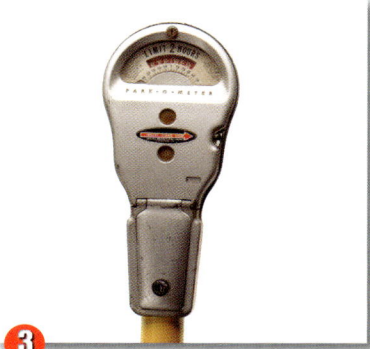
4

5

6

7

8

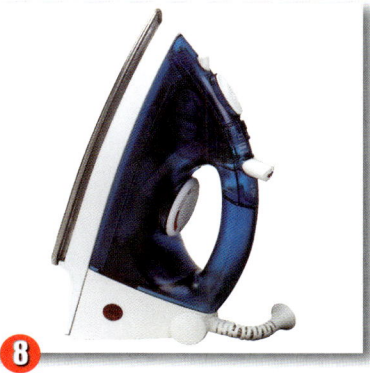
9

10

Josephine Garis Cochran, 1886 • Johan Vaaler, 1899
Edwin R. Davis, 1890 • Alexander Graham Bell, 1876
Carl Magee, 1932 • Henry Seeley, 1882
Baron Karl von Sauerbronn, 1817 • Craven Walker, 1963
Charles Babbage, 1822 • Christopher Cockerell, 1956

History

Founding fathers
315   **LEVEL 2**   **Who founded what?**

1 Who founded the Five Cent Store at Utica, New York, in 1879?

2 Brothers William and George founded what well known Charing Cross Road bookshop?

3 What fast-food chain did Ray Kroc found in 1965 in Des Plaines, Chicago?

4 What shopping revolution was heralded by Clarence Saunders' Piggly Wiggly store in 1916?

5 In 1602, which country opened the world's first stock exchange?

6 Which Japanese magnate used army surplus parts to start his business in 1948?

7 Captain Bailey founded what form of fare-paying transport in London's Strand in 1625?

8 On which industrial product was the wealth of Andrew Carnegie founded?

9 Who turned the Electric Suction Sweeper Company of 1908 into a household name?

10 Which religious organisation was founded by William Booth in 1865?

Governing bodies
316   **LEVEL 2**   **Questions about the leaders**

1 In which ancient city did citizens practise ostracism, voting to expel politicians they disliked?

2 Whose national parliament from 1906 to 1917 was known as the Duma?

3 In which European country was there both a Long and a Rump parliament?

4 Which is Europe's oldest law-making body, dating from 930?

5 Which communist leader addressed the UN for over four hours in 1960?

6 Which two European nations have the longest continuous treaty of friendship, signed in 1373?

7 Which Pacific kingdom claimed in 1976 to have had the heaviest monarch at 33st (210kg)?

8 Which country has the oldest written constitution?

9 England's briefest parliament was called by Edward I in 1306. How long did it last?

10 Which modern multinational executive body was headed by Jacques Delors until 1995?

Who said it?
317   **LEVEL 3**   **Famous historical quotations, but who said them?**

1 'Great Britain has lost an empire and not yet found a role.'

2 'I have not become the King's first minister in order to preside over the liquidation of the British Empire.'

3 'I have a dream that my four little children will live in a nation where they will not be judged on the colour of their skin . . .'

4 'Little local difficulties . . .'

5 'I don't know what effect these men have upon the enemy, but, by God, they terrify me.'

6 'A statesman is a politician who has been dead 10 or 15 years.'

7 'I have the happiness to command a band of brothers.'

8 'As President I have no eyes but constitutional eyes; I cannot see you.'

9 'I don't mind how much my ministers talk, as long as they do what I say.'

10 'There can be no whitewash at the White House.'

Famous firsts

318

LEVEL 1   Who got there first?

1 In which country was the motor car invented?

2 Which country played host to the first modern Olympic Games in 1896?

3 What first did Sir Edmund Hillary and Sherpa Norgay Tensing make in 1953?

4 What breakfast food was first served at the Battle Creek Sanatorium, Michigan, in 1894?

5 Who was the first monarch to live at Buckingham Palace?

6 Who was the first person to swim the English Channel?

7 Which tattooed people did British sailors first meet in 1769 at a place they called Poverty Bay?

8 Which game came into being when William Webb Ellis picked up the ball and ran with it in 1823?

9 Who packed off his first tourists to Paris in 1861, starting a holiday revolution?

10 What was the nickname of Ivan, the first Tsar of Russia?

Charlies

319

LEVEL 1   A round about people called Charles, Charlie, Carlos or even Karl

1 Which British king was known as 'the merry monarch'?

2 Which British-born film comedian and actor was banned from re-entering the United States in 1952 for being 'un-American'?

3 Who became Duke of Cornwall in 1952?

4 Charles the Bad, Charles the Fat, Charles the Simple, Charles the Greedy. Which one of these was not a real-life king of France?

5 Who, along with Frederick Engels, wrote the *Manifesto of the Communist Party*?

6 *On the Origin of Species* was published by which Charles in 1859?

7 Which Charles said 'non' to Britain joining the European Union?

8 In which country did Charles Haughey become leader in the Dail?

9 Which Scottish battle in 1745 sent young Charlie away with his hopes dashed?

10 By what other name was Charles the Great, King of the Franks, known?

Avenues and alleyways

320

LEVEL 3   Questions at street level

1 To which 19th-century reformer is Eros, in London's Piccadilly Circus, a monument?

2 The prime minister of which country resides at 24 Sussex Drive?

3 In which city did Temple Bar bar royal progress?

4 What collective nickname, originating in the 18th century, is given to impoverished writers?

5 In which area of Dublin was Lord Frederick Cavendish murdered in 1882?

6 Along which American street do presidents travel on Inauguration Day?

7 In what square did Mathias Rust, a 19-year-old German, land his small aircraft in May 1987 after penetrating one of the world's most advanced air defence networks?

8 Which Canadian street is credited with being the longest street in the world?

9 Which London street has been associated with law enforcement since 17th-century detectives nicknamed 'robin redbreasts' worked there?

10 In which British city were protesting workers in St Peter's Fields quashed by the cavalry?

History

Long-lost lovers
LEVEL 2   Famous paramours of history

1 In the 1670s, which actress bore Charles II two sons, named Charles Beauclerk and James?

2 An ambassador's wife fell in love with a visiting admiral in 1793. Who was she?

3 Which divorcee's relationship with the Prince of Wales cost him the crown in 1936?

4 Who was Hitler's lover, who died alongside him in the Berlin Bunker on April 30, 1945?

5 Who abandoned Rome for an Egyptian queen?

6 Whose 12-volume autobiography, published between 1826 and 1838, established his reputation as one of the world's greatest lovers?

7 Which medieval teacher's affair with Héloïse had a painful ending?

8 Which of Queen Victoria's sons was a notorious philanderer?

9 Which Hebrew king allegedly put his lover's husband in the front line to be rid of him?

10 Which Italian poet's unrequited love for Beatrice was the inspiration for his work, *Divine Comedy*?

Conquerors
LEVEL 2   History is written by the victors

1 Which warrior-chief became leader of the Mongols in 1206 before conquering Asia?

2 Which leader of the Ancient World conquered most of the known world by the age of 24?

3 What new religion swept through the Persian Empire in the 7th century?

4 Who sacked Rome in 410?

5 What Andean empire did King Pachacuti extend in the 1400s?

6 According to Marshal Ney, which 'general' prevented Napoleon's conquest of Russia?

7 In which country was the Sudetenland, which Hitler declared part of Germany in March 1939 in the first move towards the Second World War?

8 In which continent did the British and the Ashanti fight each other in the late 19th century?

9 Which African tribe of well-trained regiments, overran Natal in the 1820s?

10 Which Asian country raised its flag over its conquered neighbour, Korea, in 1906?

A time for giving?
LEVEL 3   A round about events connected with Yuletide

1 Who began leading his men across the Delaware River on Christmas Day 1776?

2 What was significant about the air raid on Dover on Christmas Eve 1914?

3 Which historic Scottish stone was stolen from Westminster Abbey on Christmas Day 1950?

4 Who marched into Hong Kong in 1941?

5 What annual event first took place at the Serpentine in London on Christmas Day 1864?

6 Which Portuguese explorer named Natal in South Africa, having arrived there en route to India on Christmas Day 1487?

7 Which mathematical genius, famous for his work on optics, was born at Woolsthorpe in Lincolnshire on Christmas Day 1642?

8 Born on Christmas day in 1906, by what name did Lewis Winogradsky gain fame in Britain?

9 Born on Christmas Day 1821 in Massachusetts and known as 'the angel of the battlefield', who founded the American Red Cross?

10 What popular song was code for the evacuation of Saigon in April 1975?

Monumental task
324
LEVEL 1   Built for the moment, made to last

1 In which country is Yad Vashem a memorial to the six million Jews killed during the Holocaust?

2 Which arch in Paris bears the names of 386 of Napoleon's generals?

3 Who is commemorated by the statue at the top of the column in London's Trafalgar Square?

4 In which country do the Colossi of Memnon stand as reminders of the pharaohs?

5 In which American city is the Lincoln Memorial?

6 Which mountain in the USA is carved with the 18m (60ft)-high likenesses of Washington, Jefferson, Lincoln and Roosevelt?

7 Which US president's memorial is in England at Runnymede, where the Magna Carta was signed?

8 In which UK city does a monument to Sir Walter Scott overlook Princes Street?

9 The Menin Gate, where Belgian firemen sound *The Last Post* every night, is a monument to the fallen of which war?

10 What incendiary event does the Monument, in London, commemorate?

Where there's a Will
325
LEVEL 1   Every question or answer has a William, Will, Bill, or Billy in it

1 Which 19th-century American frontier scout and hunter took his famous Wild West Show to Europe?

2 Which Bill was the 41st President of the United States?

3 Which William founded the aircraft manufacturer that builds B52s and 747s?

4 Which William, an English politician, campaigned to end the slave trade?

5 Which future leader of the Conservative Party addressed its 1977 annual conference as a 16-year-old boy?

6 Where did Kaiser Bill rule, for a while?

7 Which Conservative elder statesman was Mrs Thatcher's favourite Willy?

8 Which Norman king of England died in 1087 after falling from his horse?

9 Who was Britain's youngest-ever prime minister, in 1783?

10 In 1813, what was known as 'puffing Billy'?

Roaring twenties
326
LEVEL 2   A round about the decade of jazz and flappers

1 Whose death in New York in August 1926 caused hysteria among film fans?

2 Which royal played doubles at Wimbledon in 1926?

3 What Olympic event was inaugurated in France in 1924?

4 Which Fascist leader did the Honourable Violet Gibson try to kill in 1926, wounding him on the nose?

5 What made the 1927 film *The Jazz Singer* unique in cinematic history?

6 Which dancer died in 1927 when her scarf became entangled in the wheel of a car?

7 Which dance, named after a city in South Carolina, was the smash hit of 1925?

8 Who raced across Pendine Sands at over 200mph (322km/h) in 1928?

9 What crashed on October 24, 1929?

10 Where did Howard Carter see 'many wonderful things'?

History

327   A dainty dish
LEVEL 2   A visit to the history kitchen

1 The Incas of the Andes used maize to make a drink called chicha – what was chicha?

2 What drink was first served in Venice after 1683, with the opening of the Caffé Florian?

3 What did medieval diners do with the wassail bowl?

4 Samuel Pepys wrote in 1667 that he had enjoyed 'sparrow grass' with a little bit of salmon. What would we call sparrow grass?

5 What kind of fish proved fatal for England's King Henry I?

6 In the Middle Ages, poor people in England caught and ate coneys. What were coneys?

7 Why did Captain Cook make his sailors eat pickled cabbage?

8 Dr John S. Pemberton claimed to have invented a popular soft drink in 1886. What was it?

9 Swiss confectioner, Daniel Peter, transformed the chocolate market in 1875 with what invention?

10 What modern holiday began in 1621 with a supper including clams, wild plums and turkeys?

328   Pharaohs and pyramids
LEVEL 2   All about ancient Egypt

1 From what was the paperlike material made that the ancient Egyptians wrote on?

2 Name the valley in Upper Egypt that contains many pharaoh tombs, including those of Tutankhamun and Rameses the Great.

3 What name is given to the temple of Rameses II that was moved up the hillside between 1963 and 1968 because of the Aswan High Dam?

4 What creature guards the pyramids at Giza?

5 Who was the Egyptian god of the underworld?

6 The god Anubis had the head of which animal?

7 On what was a solemn ceremony called 'opening the mouth' performed, to ensure a dead person would live again in the next world?

8 How many wheels did an Egyptian war chariot have?

9 Imhotep built the first one at Sakkara over 4000 years ago. What was it?

10 In what year did people queue for hours to visit the Tutankhamun exhibition at the British Museum?

329   The year 1900
LEVEL 3   The turn of the 20th century was a momentous time

1 Why did Brigham Roberts' marital state bar him from sitting in the American House of Representatives?

2 Which future world leader published an adventure novel entitled *Savrola*?

3 Where was King Umberto I shot dead by an anarchist?

4 Why, in April, did soccer fans head for Crystal Palace to watch Bury play Southampton?

5 What was London's new 'tuppenny tube'?

6 What was 'the cakewalk', all the rage in America?

7 Huge celebrations were held for the relief of which Boer War town?

8 Why were 12-year-old boys no longer to be found underground in Britain?

9 Who did nationalist leader John Redmond call upon to rise up against the British?

10 Where was the *Deutschland* setting new speed records?

Macs factor
330
LEVEL 2 A round about people whose names have Mac or Mc in them

1 For whose independence did Simon Maccabee fight in 142 BC?

2 Which US senator led an anti-Communist witch-hunt in the 1950s?

3 By what name was Scottish clan-chief and cattle-rustler Robert Macgregor known?

4 Author of *The Prince*, which Italian political writer's surname is a byword for duplicity?

5 Which British journalist, held hostage for five and a half years in Beirut, was released in 1991?

6 After which US president, shot dead in 1901, is North America's highest mountain named?

7 Who rejected his family book business to lead the British government from 1957 to 1963?

8 Which tough-talking Mac was US secretary of defense from 1961 to 1968?

9 Which general was fired in 1951 by President Truman as commander of forces in Korea?

10 Which Canadian university was founded in 1821 by a Scottish-born businessman?

Mothers and daughters
331
LEVEL 1 Behind every great woman is another one

1 For what cause did Mrs Pankhurst and her daughter Sylvia march?

2 Which British queen, when her eldest daughter married the Crown Prince of Prussia, sobbed: 'It is like taking a poor lamb to be sacrificed'?

3 Who was the first British queen to have a living centenarian mother?

4 Which queen of the ancient Britons went to war when her daughters were abused?

5 Irène Curie and her mother both won a Nobel prize. Who was her mother?

6 Which authoress was the stepmother of Diana, Princess of Wales?

7 Her mother wrote *A Vindication of the Rights of Woman*. She wrote *Frankenstein*. Who is she?

8 Who is the mother of British journalist Carol, and an influential politician of the 20th century?

9 Who is the mother of Chelsea and the first ex-President's wife to become a US senator?

10 Kamala Kaul and Jawaharlal Nehru's daughter became famous in India. Who is she?

When in Rome
332
LEVEL 1 Do as the Romans did

1 What kind of racing vehicles wheeled around the Circus Maximus in Rome?

2 What was the Roman name for ordinary working people?

3 Who was murdered in the Capitol in 44 BC?

4 To what new religion did Emperor Constantine subscribe in 312?

5 What was the main battle unit of the Roman army called?

6 In a Roman city, what was the basilica?

7 Who was the king of the Roman gods?

8 What kind of weapon was a ballista?

9 For what purpose did the Romans install a hypocaust in their houses?

10 The Pantheon in Rome was a unique building in its time. What shape was it?

History

British prime ministers

333

LEVEL 2 How well do you know Britain's leaders?

1 Hester Grenville was the 18th-century wife of one prime minister and the mother of another. Who were the two prime ministers?

2 Who was the 20th-century's tallest British prime minister?

3 Who was the last prime minister to sit in the House of Lords before the Commons?

4 How did the Earl of Bute break an English monopoly in 1762?

5 Which British prime minister joined a rock band called The Ugly Rumours while a student?

6 Who was the first prime minister to head a Labour government?

7 Which prime minister resigned over the Suez crisis?

8 What other government position has every prime minister since the 18th century taken?

9 Who was the first prime minister to be elected in the 20th century?

10 Who is credited with being, in 1721, Britain's first prime minister?

Women on top

334

LEVEL 2 Notorious or famous women from history

1 Which American girl was tried, in 1893, on charges of killing her father and stepmother with an axe, but acquitted?

2 In Renaissance Italy, who was the notorious Alexander and Cesare Borgia's sister?

3 Who was the real-life crackshot Annie whose life inspired the musical *Annie Get Your Gun*?

4 For who did Lady Caroline Lamb fall, though he was 'mad, bad and dangerous to know'?

5 What unusual profession (for a woman) did Mary Bonney take up beneath a black flag?

6 Aung San Suu Kyi won the 1991 Nobel peace prize for heading the opposition to the brutal regime in which Southeast Asian country?

7 Which 12th-century queen was the wife of a king of France and of a king of England?

8 Of which ancient land was Nefertiti queen?

9 In which imperial city did Agrippina, mother of Nero, marry Claudius but was later murdered?

10 Of which country was Golda Meir the first prime minister from 1969 to 1974?

Who said that?

335

LEVEL 3 Quotations from history

1 Who declared in 1919 that: 'History is bunk'?

2 Who experimented 'but did not inhale'?

3 Who, on hearing of the death of US President Coolidge in 1933, replied: 'How could they tell'?

4 On seeing his bride, which British monarch said: 'I am not well, pray get me a brandy'?

5 Which wartime leader said: 'Democracy is the worst form of government except all those other forms that have been tried . . .'?

6 Which US politician described the American way as one of 'rugged individualism'?

7 Who allegedly said she had: 'the body of a weak and feeble woman, but the heart and stomach of a king'?

8 Which US president's last words were: 'That's good. Read me some more'?

9 Who said after coming home from Moscow: 'There is only one step from the sublime to the ridiculous'?

10 Which British politician, speaking in 1918, said: 'What is our task? To make Britain a fit country for heroes to live in.'?

First names
LEVEL 1   What's in a name?

1 What was the first name of Britain's Lord Protector?

2 By what name was Argentina's Eva Peron popularly known?

3 What was President de Gaulle's first name?

4 Which country's recent prime ministers have included a Gough, a Bob and a Paul?

5 Which country has had 19 kings named Louis?

6 What was President Eisenhower's first name?

7 What name did the first Roman Emperor, Octavian, choose for himself and in so doing give us a summer month?

8 What was the first name of the Egyptian president who made peace with Israel but was assassinated in 1981?

9 What first name was shared by the American inventor of Morse Code and the compiler of the first English dictionary?

10 What was the first name of Russia's first president after the collapse of the Soviet Union?

Mind your Ps and Qs
LEVEL 1   All answers have a P or Q in them

1 What Q was China's last imperial dynasty, also known as the Manchu dynasty?

2 Which Spanish king ordered the Armada to attack England?

3 How are the wars between Carthage and Rome known?

4 What name is more commonly given to the 3rd Battle of Ypres in 1917, which resulted in 310,000 British Expeditionary Force casualties?

5 Who said in 1770: 'Unlimited power is apt to corrupt the minds of those that possess it'?

6 Which British spy escaped to the Soviet Union along with Donald Maclean in 1963?

7 By what title were ancient Egyptian kings known in Tutankhamun's day?

8 Which Muslim Asian country came into being in August 1947?

9 Which is the oldest airline in the English-speaking world?

10 Which fashion designer opened a shop called Bazaar on London's King's Road in 1957?

Sightseeing
LEVEL 2   Sights and sites from history

1 Who said on looking at the battlefield after defeating the Romans at Asculum in 279 BC: 'One more such victory and we are lost'?

2 In which great English cathedral can visitors see the relics of the 7th-century St Cuthbert?

3 In which US city was the Liberty Bell rung?

4 In which European city is the Brandenburg Gate?

5 Which sights of London and New York arrived by sea from Egypt in the 1870s?

6 Which British cathedral, built near the site of the ruins of its bombed predecessor, houses works by Graham Sutherland, John Piper, Jacob Epstein and Elizabeth Frink?

7 Which first couple played host at Mount Vernon?

8 Overlooking which city was a 30m (98ft) figure, known as the Corcovado Christ, completed in 1931?

9 Which goddess did the Greeks come to worship at the Parthenon in Athens?

10 In which country would you find a 2000-year-old terracotta army numbering some 8000 warriors?

History

Flights of fancy
339
LEVEL 2   Questions about fleeing and flying, sometimes literally

1 Baroness Raymonde de la Roche of France received ticket No. 36 on March 8, 1910 making her the first what?

2 Which Nazi landed in Scotland in 1941, offering a peace deal, but ended up in jail for life?

3 From which city did *Concorde 203* take off on its fateful journey on July 25, 2000?

4 Which prince hid in a beanfield and an oak tree, but was then restored to the British throne?

5 In which country did 11,000 prisoners of the Shah flee jail during the 1979 Islamic revolution?

6 How did 'barnstormers' entertain crowds in the 1920s?

7 Over what did American aviator Richard Byrd make a first flight in 1926?

8 What unique feat did Jacqueline Cochrane achieve for female jet pilots, in 1953?

9 Eliza Garnerin floated safely to Earth beneath her father's 1797 invention. What was it?

10 According to the Bible, who lead the Israelites on their flight from Egypt?

Royal wives
340
LEVEL 2   Can you name these regal spouses or their kingly partners?

1 Which Leonine king of England was married to Berengaria of Navarre?

2 Queen Sonja is the wife of which northern European reigning monarch?

3 According to popular history, who was told 'not tonight' by her imperial husband?

4 Which British king, who was married to Henrietta Maria, lost his head?

5 Which Spanish queen, with her husband Ferdinand, was patron of Columbus's expedition to America?

6 Who married King William IV and had the capital of South Australia named after her?

7 How did Princess Sophia of Greece come to be Queen of Spain?

8 Which English king defeated the French in 1415, then married their king's daughter?

9 Which American film star became a Mediterranean princess in 1956?

10 Who did Elizabeth Bowes-Lyon marry in 1923?

Great Greeks
341
LEVEL 3   The founders of modern society

1 Which ancient people were famous for training children for outdoor life from an early age?

2 Which king died a hero's death fighting the Persians at Thermopylae in 480 BC?

3 Which Greek teacher lectured at the Academy in Athens?

4 What kind of architectural features did Greek builders design which are known as Doric, Ionian or Corinthian?

5 Who in ancient Greece would have carried a sarissa?

6 In which city did Pericles hold the floor as leader?

7 Which author is known as both the father of history and the father of lies?

8 Which Athenian general wrote the first definitive account of the Peloponnesian War?

9 Where was the most famous oracle in all Greece?

10 Which Greek philosopher, accused of impiety, drank poison and killed himself?

Lost and found

342

LEVEL 1 Delve into the lost property box of history

1 Which sporting trophy was lost and then found by a dog in 1966?

2 Which king of England is said to have lost the royal jewels in the Wash?

3 What was found at Sutter's Mill on the American River in 1848?

4 Who, according to the ancient Greeks, found his way out of a labyrinth using a ball of thread?

5 What kind of unusual craft was found on dry land at Sutton Hoo in Suffolk, England?

6 Who lost his cavalry at the Little Big Horn?

7 What had RAF pilot Douglas Bader lost when taken prisoner by the Germans in 1941?

8 Which climber's frozen body was uncovered more than 75 years after he was lost on Everest in 1924?

9 Which 'lost princess' from a murdered Russian royal family did Anna Anderson claim to be?

10 What were the *Eurydice*, lost in 1970, and the *Kursk*, lost in 2000?

The eighties

343

LEVEL 1 The age of Thatcher and Reagan

1 In which former country did Chernenko follow Andropov as leader in February 1984?

2 Which newly-weds waved from the balcony of Buckingham Palace in 1986?

3 Where did workers join Solidarity in protest at the Communist government?

4 In which city was Terry Waite kidnapped in 1987, while trying to negotiate the release of Middle East hostages?

5 Which fictional oil man's on-screen shooting made headlines in 1980?

6 Into which town did sabotaged Pan Am Flight 103 crash in 1988?

7 Who resigned from the British government in 1988 after saying most eggs were unsafe to eat?

8 In 1983 President Reagan ordered troops to quash a coup on which Caribbean island?

9 From which hotel did Mrs Thatcher and her colleagues make a lucky escape in 1984?

10 Of which country was Olof Palme prime minister when he was killed in Stockholm?

Sheer extravagance

344

LEVEL 3 A generous round about profligate expenditure

1 Who had the expensive Spandau Prison to himself from 1966 to his death in 1987?

2 Which English cardinal built Hampton Court Palace, so grand that King Henry VIII annexed it?

3 Name the building commissioned by the Indian ruler Shah Jahan as a mausoleum for his wife.

4 Jean-Bédel Bokassa ruled which African state where he appointed himself emperor in a lavish ceremony in 1977, costing over US$20 million?

5 What was unusually cold about the winter palace built in Russia for the Empress Anna?

6 Which Roman emperor allegedly played the fiddle inside his Golden House?

7 Which Victorian edifice entailed 80 glaziers fitting up to 18,000 panes of glass a week?

8 In which Asian country was a palace completed in 1984 with 1788 rooms?

9 Which newspaper tycoon funded films in the 1930s starring his lover, Marion Davies?

10 In which Russian city is the Winter Palace, built between 1754 and 1762 by Rastrelli?

History

Enigmatic initials

345 **LEVEL 2** **What were the names behind these historical figures' real names?**

1 Which South African politician was known as 'F.W.'?

2 What does the W stand for in George W. Bush's middle name?

3 Prime minister Churchill signed himself Winston S. Churchill – the S standing for what?

4 L.B.J. was a US president in the 1960s. What did the initials stand for?

5 What did the E stand for in Robert E. Lee?

6 Prime Minister Harold Wilson's initials were J. H. In 1976 he was succeeded by another J. In both cases, what did the J stand for?

7 President John F. Kennedy's middle name had an Irish ring to it. What did the F stand for?

8 Which British politician of the 1940s and 1950s was often referred to by his initials, 'Rab'?

9 Richard M. Nixon's middle name was his mother's maiden name. What was it?

10 What did the first initial of the Gulf War commander H. Norman Schwarzkopf stand for?

Losing their heads

346 **LEVEL 2** **Everyone in this round lost their head somehow**

1 What was significant about Lord Lovat's execution at Tower Hill in 1747?

2 Above the gateway of which bridge on the Thames were the heads of traitors gruesomely fixed on iron spikes for the citizens to see?

3 Which Scottish monarch was beheaded in 1587 for allegedly plotting against Elizabeth I?

4 Which execution device, much used in France, was first known as the Louisette?

5 Which king wore two shirts for his beheading, so that he did not shiver or appear frightened?

6 How many of Henry VIII's wives were beheaded on his orders?

7 How did the Countess of Salisbury disrupt her execution, declaring she was: 'no traitor'?

8 Which husband and wife lost their heads in front of the Paris mob on January 21, 1793?

9 'His body was dug up and his head stuck on a pole by his restored enemies.' Who met this fate?

10 Which conquering king is said to have introduced beheading to England?

Rogues' gallery

347 **LEVEL 3** **Villains throughout time**

1 Tyrannical Austrian governor Gessler was killed by a Swiss bowman. Who was the marksman?

2 Which actress was charged with indecency following her show *Sex on Broadway* in 1927?

3 Which illusive Chicago gangster was eventually imprisoned for tax evasion?

4 Fugitives 'Mr Robinson and son' were caught with the aid of what new communications invention in 1910?

5 Which former heavyweight boxer ruled Uganda from 1971 until his overthrow in 1979?

6 How was media baron Jan Ludvik Hoch, who fell off his boat in 1992, better known?

7 Which Nazi war criminal was hanged in Israel for crimes committed 20 years earlier?

8 Which media tycoon's daughter, kidnapped in 1974, became an armed robber?

9 Lucky disappeared in November 1974 leaving an unsolved murder mystery; who was Lucky?

10 How were the four conspirators, jailed in China in 1976 for plotting a coup, known?

Battles

LEVEL 1 Fighting for their place in history

1 During which war did the Battle of Goose Green take place on a South Atlantic island?

2 At which 1942 desert battle did Montgomery's Desert Rats defeat the Afrika Korps?

3 At which snowbound city did a German army surrender to the Russians in 1943, after a long and bitter battle?

4 During which battle of the Crimean War did the Light Brigade charge gallantly into disaster?

5 In which war was the Battle of Yorktown in 1783 the final blow to British hopes?

6 What great naval battle took place between Britain and Germany in 1916 off the coast of Denmark?

7 What battle in 1815 was the final defeat for Napoleon?

8 In which ocean was the Battle of Midway fought?

9 What 1863 US Civil War battle dealt Robert E. Lee and the Confederates a crushing blow?

10 During which war were the bloody battles of Verdun and Marne?

Nicknames

LEVEL 1 By what names were these famous historical figures known?

1 Which 20th-century politician was known as 'the iron lady'?

2 Which Soviet dictator was known as 'uncle Joe'?

3 'Bluff king Hal' was which king of England?

4 Which country's soldiers were known to their enemies as 'the Boche', 'the Hun', or 'Jerries'?

5 The name 'Teflon president' was given to two American presidents, who were they?

6 People in the Navy began talking about 'flat-tops' in the 1920s. What were these new ships?

7 Which Second World War general was nicknamed 'the desert fox'?

8 Supermac said people had never had it so good. Which leader was caricatured as Supermac?

9 Which great wartime leader was nicknamed 'Winnie'?

10 The 'little corporal' marched across Europe. Who was he?

Canada quiz

LEVEL 3 The British North American territories

1 Which French explorer named his settlement Quebec in 1608?

2 What did the French call their territory in Canada?

3 What name was given to American colonists loyal to Britain who moved to Canada after the Americans declared independence?

4 Which prime minister put troops on the streets during the Quebec crisis in 1960?

5 Which two parts of British-ruled Canada were united by the Act of Union in 1840?

6 Which important cross-Canada transport link was completed in 1885?

7 When did Canada become an independent nation, by a Statute of Westminster?

8 Who was the Canadian prime minister during the Second World War?

9 Which leaf appeared on flagstaffs for the first time on February 16, 1965?

10 Who was Canada's first female prime minister, in 1993?

141

History

South of the border
351   **LEVEL 3**   **Down Mexico way**

1 Which South American soldier-statesman became known as 'the liberator' and has a country named after him?

2 Which people did Tupac Amara lead in revolt against their Spanish rulers in 1780?

3 In which island did Toussaint l'Ouverture try to imitate the French Revolution and create a new order among slaves?

4 Which country ruled Havana in 1899?

5 In which modern country did the Chavin culture flourish some 2500 years ago?

6 Which Caribbean island did England take from Spain in 1655 to create a buccaneers' haven?

7 Which two countries agreed to share the New World between them in 1494?

8 Which country defeated Peru and Bolivia in the 1879 War of the Pacific?

9 In which country did President Vargas take power in 1930?

10 Where was Somoza removed by the Sandinistas in 1979?

Australian challenge
352   **LEVEL 3**   **Questions from a land down under**

1 Which service did John Flynn and Alfred Traeger found in 1928?

2 Name the mother who claimed her daughter Azaria was killed by a dingo in August 1980.

3 Whose gang took over Glenrowan, Victoria, in 1880?

4 Who was the longest-serving Australian prime minister of the 20th century, over two terms in 1939–41 and 1949–66?

5 What great sporting event did Australia win in 1983, so ending a US run of 132 years?

6 What were the men on the Ballarat Field digging for in the 1850s?

7 For which song is Banjo Paterson credited with writing the lyrics?

8 Which New South Wales politician earned the title 'Father of Federation'?

9 Who was replaced as prime minister of Australia after the 1975 constitutional crisis?

10 After which botanist, who arrived with Cook in 1770, is the Banksia plant group named?

R you sure
353   **LEVEL 3**   **The letter R is the clue in this round**

1 In 1898, who led the rough riders up San Juan Hill?

2 Who became Congress Party leader in India after the death of Rajiv Gandhi, and was prime minister from 1991 to 1996?

3 Which Egyptian king claimed a win at the Battle of Kadesh in 1285 BC?

4 Who founded the British base of Singapore in 1819?

5 Which black US singer, actor and activist | had his passport seized in 1950 for alleged 'un-American activities'?

6 Known as 'the mad monk', who calculated his way into the affections of a Russian empress?

7 In America where did the 'lost colony' get lost?

8 How was Armand Jean du Plessis, who took power in France from 1624 to 1642, known?

9 What area of Europe was illegally re-occupied by German troops in March 1936?

10 Which international organisation was founded in 1863 by Henri Dunant?

Discoveries
LEVEL 1   They led the way

1 In which oriental country did people first make paper, and use it for money?

2 Who explored the Land of Punt in reed boats?

3 Which Nordic sailors travelled in longships to Iceland, Greenland, England and North America?

4 Which explorer is credited as the first to bring tobacco and potatoes from the New World?

5 Whose mission was: 'to explore strange new worlds, to seek out new . . . civilisations'?

6 Which continent did Dutch sailors 'discover' around 1605, to find Aborigines already there?

7 European sailors had to sail around which African cape to reach the Indian Ocean?

8 In 1858, which great lake in Africa did the explorer John Hanning Speke name after Britain's queen?

9 Which newly discovered continent was named after an Italian explorer called Amerigo Vespucci?

10 Who was the first explorer to circumnavigate the globe, proving it was not flat?

The wild west
LEVEL 1   Where men were men

1 What did mountain men catch for a living, when they weren't guiding wagon trains?

2 What did cowboys keep in the chuck wagon?

3 Which gunslinging marshal was shot dead while playing cards in Deadwood?

4 Sounds like a wild pony, but this Sioux leader won a famous victory in 1876. Who was he?

5 Where did a cowboy wear his chaps?

6 Which Indian tribe was led by Geronimo, who surrendered to the US Army in 1886 and died in 1909?

7 What material was used to cover Indian tepee poles, and so keep the people inside dry?

8 In which US state did 'the rangers' keep the peace?

9 Which frontiersman gave his name to a knife, specially adapted so that he didn't lose his grip on the handle?

10 What did Henry Derringer invent for gamblers to keep hidden in their coat pockets?

The American colonies
LEVEL 2   A history of America

1 Which was the first permanent English colony in North America, named after England's Scottish king in 1607?

2 Which English Quaker made a treaty with the Indians in 1682?

3 Which state joined the Union on January 3rd, 1959?

4 Who were put on trial at Salem, Massachusetts on March 5, 1770?

5 Which colony did 'the pilgrims' found in 1620?

6 Which college, later one of America's great universities, was first founded in the colonies?

7 How is the killing by British troops of five colonists in Massachusetts, in 1770, known?

8 Which was the last of the 13 English colonies to be founded in 1733?

9 With which European nation did America conclude the 'Louisiana purchase' by buying nearly 600 million acres for US$15 million?

10 What notable first did the *Boston News-Letter* achieve in 1704?

History

357 **Flypast**
LEVEL 2 Take to the skies

1 Who crossed the ocean in *The Spirit of St Louis* in 1927?

2 Where did two Douglas World cruisers fly in 1924?

3 In which American state did the Wright brothers make their historic first flights on December 17, 1903?

4 Name the two RAF men who first crossed the Atlantic Ocean non-stop in 1919.

5 In which country was Qantas founded in 1920?

6 Where was London's first civil air terminal, opened in 1920?

7 What kind of craft was the *R-101*, which crashed in France in 1930 en route to India?

8 What notable feat did the *Heinkel He 178* achieve on August 24, 1939?

9 Which airport opened in 1946 with the landing of a *Constellation* from across the Atlantic?

10 How was communication speeded by the departure of a Pan Am *Yankee Clipper* on May 20, 1939 from New York?

358 **General knowledge**
LEVEL 2 Military top brass

1 Which British general entered Jerusalem in 1917 and has a bridge named after him linking Israel and Jordan?

2 Which general commanded all British forces in the Middle East during the 1991 Gulf War?

3 Which general took command of Britain's Eighth Army in August 1942?

4 Which British field marshal was lost at sea, when HMS *Hampshire* went down in 1916?

5 Which American Civil War general has an ancient Californian tree named in his honour?

6 Which American general and president has a tomb overlooking the Hudson River?

7 Which American general inspired the US aid plan for shattered post-war European states?

8 Which 18th-century English commander was known as 'the butcher' to his Scottish foes?

9 What was remarkable about the career of Field Marshal Sir William Robertston?

10 Which French general said: 'My centre is giving way, my right is in retreat; situation excellent'?

359 **The forties**
LEVEL 2 Britain's darkest, but maybe finest, hours

1 Which new system of income-tax assessment began in the UK in April 1944?

2 Which duke died in a plane crash in 1942?

3 Which hilltop monastery in Italy was the scene of bitter fighting in 1944?

4 Which American bandleader disappeared over the English Channel in 1944?

5 In which 1948 conflict did Jews shoot at Spitfires?

6 Where did the sun set on the Raj in 1947?

7 What revolution in the health of the nation was introduced by Aneurin Bevan in 1948?

8 Which female newspaper comic strip character was known affectionately as 'the soldiers' favourite strip'?

9 Which orchestral conductor died suddenly in 1944 at one of the concerts he had helped to found?

10 In what was there a New Look in 1947?

366 History quest

These questions are tougher than the others and you may need to do some research

1 Who is the odd one out in this list: Duke of Newcastle, Duke of Grafton, Duke of Norfolk, Duke of Wellington?

2 The Fat, the Bold, the Fair, the Pock-Marked: which epithet was not applied to a medieval French king?

3 Which king met his death on 2 Pluviose 1?

4 What spread from Mainz in 1456, to Basle by 1466, Rome in 1467, and reached Westminster in 1476?

5 Sophia Dorothea, Wilhelmina Caroline and Charlotte. What do they have in common?

6 If Eden went as Avon, who went as Stockton?

7 1865, 1881, 1901… What year comes next?

8 What is the connection between William III, William the Conqueror and Roy Kinnear?

9 How were Castor, Pollux, Orpheus and 46 others collectively known?

10 Of whom was it said: 'If he was not a great man, he was, at least, a great poster.'

11 To what was General Pierre Bosquet referring to when he said: 'It is magnificent, but it is not war'?

12 On February 21, 1963, what was missing from the new British £5 note?

13 Willy, Willy, Harry, Steve – who are the next four?

14 What connects the American Civil War, James Joyce and the Cyclops?

15 What connects the Dominicans, the West Midlands and Lloyds Bank?

A clue to question 14

History

Ancient Britons
367
LEVEL 2   The land the Romans found, and left

1 Who was the last, self-proclaimed Prince of Wales to attempt to overthrow English rule?

2 The son of King Cunobelinus, he led the Britons against the invading Romans until taken prisoner in AD 51. Who was he?

3 Which city was the Celtic capital, and a key target for the Roman invaders 2000 years ago?

4 Who, according to legend, were Hengist and Horsa?

5 Which famous monastery was pillaged by Vikings in 787?

6 Which city was called Eboracum by the Romans and Jorvik by the Vikings?

7 Who is alleged to have won the battle of Mount Badon in 503?

8 Which Welsh county name means 'land of the Welsh Prince Morgan'?

9 Which 8th-century English king built a wall of earth to keep out the Welsh?

10 Which kingdom did Kenneth McAlpin found in 843?

Warships
368
LEVEL 2   The ironclad warriors of the sea

1 Which was the first Royal Navy ship to be sunk in action after the Second World War?

2 Which aircraft carrier, bearer of a Royal Navy name, was sunk by an Italian torpedo in 1941?

3 Which famous Second World War battleship saw action during the 1991 Gulf War?

4 What kind of warships were biremes and triremes?

5 Which is the oldest surviving ship in the US Navy, veteran of a fight against HMS *Guerriere*?

6 Which battleship was destroyed in 1945 while on a one-way suicide mission to Okinawa?

7 What was new about the French warship *La Gloire* of 1858?

8 PT boats were used during the Second World War. What did the initials PT stand for?

9 Which 45,000-ton German battleship spent much of the Second World War in a Norwegian fjord?

10 What distinction does the USS *Enterprise*, hold?

Rivers
369
LEVEL 3   A cruise down the world's great waterways

1 On which river were the ancient cities of Elephantine and Abydos?

2 Which river did Cartier explore in 1535?

3 Which British river was first bridged by the Romans in about AD 50?

4 Which Roman crossed the Rubicon?

5 Which legendary river did the Ancient Greeks believe would dissolve any cup save one made from a horse's hoof?

6 On which river did Horatius defend the bridge against an army?

7 Which Asian river was the setting for a 1949 confrontation involving the British warship HMS *Amethyst*?

8 In which river did Cornelius Drebbel of Holland row himself underwater in the 1620s?

9 Over which river was the rail bridge at Remagen captured by American troops in March 1945?

10 Who crossed the Indus in 326 BC with an army beginning to weary of conquests so far from home?

Family fortunes
370

LEVEL 1 We're in the money . . .

1 Which US family has produced two presidents?

2 From what business did John D. Rockefeller make his first millions in the 1860s and 1870s?

3 On what business was the Rothschild fortune founded in the late 1700s?

4 Which prominent US political dynasty was founded by ambassador Joe and his wife Rose?

5 Which British family changed its name from Battenberg to avoid anti-German feeling?

6 Which family emerged victorious from England's Wars of the Roses, in the person of King Henry VII?

7 Which ancient empire was ruled by the Safayid dynasty?

8 Which ruling dynasty's empire governed Austria, Hungary, Bohemia, Dalmatia, Croatia and many areas of Italy, Yugoslavia, Poland, Romania and the Ukraine?

9 Which heiress of the Tesco empire was once the controversial leader of Westminster Council?

10 In which country were the Ming removed by the Manchu in 1648?

Wagons west
371

LEVEL 1 There's gold in them thar hills

1 What kind of vehicle was a conestoga?

2 By what popular name was the gunman James Butler Hickok known?

3 On the trail or on a cattle drive, what did the wrangler look after?

4 Which famous wagon trail, which began in Independence, Missouri, wound all the way to the northwest?

5 What did the settlers do with a bit of jerky?

6 In western towns, what was a circuit rider?

7 Which hills in South Dakota were thick with gold hunters in 1874?

8 What popular name was given to the mail service between St Joseph, Missouri, and San Francisco, California, in April 1860 to November 1861?

9 In which town did the gunfight at the OK Corral take place?

10 What was a longhorn?

Vikings and Saxons
372

LEVEL 3 A round about Britain's early conquerors

1 What did the Vikings use their knorrs for?

2 In which part of Europe did Rollo the Viking settle in 911?

3 In Saxon England what was a witan?

4 Which king bought peace with 36,000 pounds of silver – but not for long?

5 Which Viking is credited with discovering the New World around 1000?

6 Sweyn landed in England in 1003. What was this Viking king's nickname?

7 Which Earl of Wessex ruled England in all but name in the mid-1000s?

8 Whose daughter was Aethelflaed, known as the Lady of the Mercians?

9 What position did Dunstan hold in the 900s?

10 Which Essex riverside battle of 991 between the English and the Vikings was immortalised in an English poem?

History

Kings English
373
LEVEL 2 A round on England's rulers

1 Which Protestant king of Britain was born in The Hague, in 1650?

2 Who was the first king to be King of both England and Scotland?

3 Which king was mockingly called Lackland?

4 Who was the first king of Britain to be made Emperor of India?

5 Which Saxon king hurried north to win one battle, then hurried south, but lost the next?

6 Which British king was the son of Albert and Victoria?

7 Which king died (of thrombosis) in his native Hanover in 1727?

8 Who was on the British throne during the First World War?

9 Which English king ordered the *Domesday Book* to be made?

10 Which British king's taxation policies led to the American War of Independence?

Historical Henries
374
LEVEL 2 Every question is about a Henry – or possibly a Harry

1 From which country did Henry 'the navigator' originate?

2 With what useful invention is America's Joseph Henry, first director of the Smithsonian Institution, associated?

3 Which Henry developed the first process for manufacturing steel inexpensively in 1856?

4 Which royal Henry is supposed to have asked: 'Who will rid me of this turbulent priest?'

5 By what name was the Hungarian-born escapologist Erik Weisz better known?

6 King Henry I of England was the 3rd son of which previous king?

7 Which Henry got rid of a cardinal, a saint and a senior courtier in quick succession?

8 Which president led America through the final stages of the Second World War?

9 Which American lawyer declared in 1775: 'Give me liberty or give me death'?

10 Which Henry founded a food chain built on beans?

Gods and goddesses
375
LEVEL 3 By heavens, some tough questions

1 Which Norse god gave his name to Wednesday?

2 Whose brother was Pluto, king of the underworld?

3 Which Greek goddess was deadly with her bow?

4 Who was the son of the Egyptian couple Osiris and Isis?

5 Who in Norse mythology was always playing tricks on the gods?

6 Which people of the Americas worshipped a god named Tezcatlipoca?

7 Where in the Far East did an ancient people pray to a Sun god called Tankun?

8 In which religion was Agni, god of fire, portrayed with three legs and a thousand eyes?

9 Who was the Roman goddess of love?

10 Which Roman god was literally two-faced and is remembered in the first month of the year?

Playing the part
376
LEVEL 1   A round about recreating history on screen

1 *The Longest Day* was the 1962 dramatisation of what major event of the Second World War?

2 The film *Braveheart*, directed by Mel Gibson, portrays which 13th century rebel.

3 David O. Selznick's 1939 fictional epic *Gone With the Wind* was set against which war?

4 Which US cavalry leader did Errol Flynn play in the film *They Died with Their Boots On*?

5 Who directed *Bridge over the River Kwai*?

6 Which actor played both wartime bandleader Glenn Miller and pioneer aviator Charles Lindbergh in films?

7 Which American actor played Napoleon, facing Christopher Plummer as Wellington?

8 Which Steven Spielberg film told of one man's attempt to save Jews from the Holocaust?

9 Who played the part of Oliver Cromwell on film, and stood by while Alec Guinness went to the block?

10 Simon Ward starred in the 1972 film exploring the early life of which great 20th-century prime minister?

The fifties
377
LEVEL 1   Questions on the post-war decade

1 The nationalisation of what by Egypt caused an invasion by Britain and France?

2 The first regal ceremony to be shown on British TV was on June 2, 1953. What was it?

3 In which country was Janos Kadar installed as a Soviet puppet after the crushing of democracy?

4 What name was given to the group of people who wore drainpipe trousers, knee-length jackets and thick soled brothel-creeper shoes?

5 What was detonated at Eniwetok Atoll in the Pacific in 1952?

6 In 1953, Edmund Hillary and Tenzing Norgay were the first people to climb which mountain?

7 Which American-built jet airliner went into commercial operation in 1954?

8 Which athlete broke the four-minute mile in May 1954 at Iffley Road in Oxford?

9 Why was Calder Hall hailed as the start of a new age of cheap power in 1956?

10 What did the Soviet spacecraft *Luna 2* achieve in 1959?

Noble Romans
378
LEVEL 2   The greatest empire of classical times

1 Which emperor's constructions included a wall that can still be seen in northern England?

2 Who saw off Antony's challenge, and became first emperor?

3 Which Roman emperor visiting Britain reputedly rode through Colchester with elephants?

4 Who was the second emperor of Rome who ruled from AD 14 to AD 37?

5 Which emperor, who regarded himself as the greatest artist who had ever lived, murdered both his mother and his first wife?

6 Who conspired with Brutus to murder Julius Caesar and was said in a Shakespeare play to have 'a lean and hungry look'?

7 Which emperor made his horse a consul?

8 Which Roman wrote *A History of Rome*?

9 Who restored law and order after the turmoil of Nero's reign?

10 Romulus Augustus was the last of a long line of what?

Quiz night at home

You only have to switch on the television to see how popular quizzes are. But instead of watching, why not play one yourselves? Using this book, you can organise a quiz for almost any occasion, from a quiet family night in, to a big annual get-together.

At its most simple, a quiz need be nothing more than you and your family or a few friends picking a few rounds from the book for fun. But if you want to make an evening of it, a little planning will go a long way.

Know your audience

Sitting through round after round of really tough questions to which no one knows the answers isn't fun for anyone. So get everyone involved with a range of questions for all the family. If Uncle Jim always wins, then choose areas he is not so good at to give other people a chance. And don't forget the children. Think about including a round just for them to answer.

Quizzes work just as well with teams as individual players. If it is a big family occasion, like Christmas, group people together, spreading out the family experts, and splitting up couples if you think they will squabble! To spice up the competition, you could give the winners a small prize, such as a box of chocolates or a bottle of wine.

Do remember, though, that holding a quiz is all about enjoyment. Make a rule before you start that the quiz master's word is final and don't allow any disputes to get out of hand.

Bring family ghosts back to life

Give your quiz a personal touch with some family-only questions. Trawl through the old photograph albums and compile a picture quiz about summer holidays or family weddings. Ask people to identify the year of the wedding, the location of the holiday, the name of the landlady at that B&B in Bridlington. Nostalgia is an inexhaustible source of questions.

Play the game

Make your quiz as formal or informal as you like. You could each pick rounds from the book for one another, tailoring them to people's strengths – or their weaknesses! – or nominate a quiz master to select the rounds in advance and to ask all the questions.

Making it a family affair

Use these suggestions to give you inspiration for a tailor-made family quiz. Just be careful not to cause offence or upset – or open any old feuds.

Name the baby
Ask everyone to bring along a picture of themselves as a baby. Mount them on card, or scan and print them in advance if you have a computer and scanner. Either hold them up so people only have a few minutes to answer, or use the cards as a table round (see pages 344–345).

Family history
Delve into the archives for some probing personal questions.
Where did Billy break his leg?
In what regiment did Great Grandad serve in the Second World War?
What was the name of Aunt Joan's pet cat that died in 1986?
In which restaurant did Mum and Dad meet?

Who's who?
Ask the family to identify relatives or friends from clues that you have put together.
Which cousin was born on July 12, 1943, and became a maths teacher?

On the street where you live
Test your quizzers' knowledge of your local area. Take close-up photographs of landmarks, such as a distinctive gravestone from the churchyard, a chimney, or a shop sign and ask them to identify and locate the feature. Another teasing idea is to ask really obvious questions that everyone should know the answer to. *What colour is next door's front door? What time does the corner shop shut? What is the name of the church on Sutton Street?*

Organising the evening

The golden rule when planning an evening of quizzing is not to make it last too long. Five or six rounds with a good mix of questions is more than enough.

- Think about the time of day when planning the quiz and how long it will take. Are children involved? Will people have far to travel home?

- Are you going to play after dinner or serve food and drinks during the quiz?

- If there will be several teams, work out a seating plan so that players can confer without the others overhearing.

- Don't forget to provide pens and answer sheets. An answer card to photocopy comes with this book.

- Who is going to mark the answers? If you are among friends and family, you could ask everyone to mark each other's.

Fun for all ages

Every section in the book has a selection of kids' rounds at the end for ages 7–11 and 12–14. Unless there are a lot of children in your group no more than one round should be kids-only, but you could include a children's question in each round if you prefer.

Make it even more fun by writing your own questions linked to school activities, favourite TV shows or books and comics.

History

Party time

379

LEVEL 2 A round about politics and celebrations

1 The motto of which party, founded in Shanghai in 1921, is 'Seeking truth from the facts'?

2 For which event were street parties much in evidence in Britain during June 1977?

3 To which party did David Lloyd George belong, the party's last prime minister?

4 Where did the Falangists fight for power in the 1930s?

5 Who became leader of the German National Socialist Party in the 1920s?

6 Where did Sinn Fein lead a nationalist rising in 1919?

7 To which political party did W.E. Gladstone belong?

8 By what name was the 1773 protest in Boston, against the East India Company, popularly known?

9 Which party was purged by Stalin in the 1930s?

10 Which British party celebrated the war's end in 1945 with election victory?

Fire, flood and quake

380

LEVEL 2 Terrible disasters through the ages

1 In what year was Britain's only recorded earthquake fatality – when a man was hit by falling stones from a church in London?

2 Which European city was devastated by an earthquake in 1755?

3 What name is given to the night when, in Nazi Germany, more than 1000 synagogues were burned to the ground?

4 From what did Samuel Pepys escape in 1666?

5 In which South American country were 2500 people reportedly burned to death inside a church in 1863?

6 Which American city was hit by a fire in 1871?

7 In which country did the Yellow River flood in 1887, killing some 900,000 people?

8 What double-disaster hit San Francisco in April 1906?

9 Which city established the first paid fire department in the American Colonies in 1679?

10 Which ancient imperial city went up in flames in AD 64?

Japan

381

LEVEL 3 Land of the rising sun

1 Which title was Yoritomo the first to assume in Japan in 1192?

2 Who was Jimmu Temmo?

3 In the 1500s, which European country's traders were allowed into Nagasaki but no further?

4 What religious sect released nerve gas into the Tokyo subway in March 1995?

5 Whose arrival in 1853 startled the Japanese, who had never seen such ships before?

6 Which emperor gave his name to the period of westernisation that began in 1868?

7 Which fleet did the Japanese defeat at Tshushima in 1905?

8 Which neighbouring Asian state did the Japanese conquer in 1931 and rename Manchukuo?

9 What natural disaster devastated Tokyo-Yokohama in 1923?

10 Which emperor succeeded Hirohito in 1989?

382 The bug that never was
LEVEL 1   A round about events from the year 2000

1 Which former leader of Yugoslavia appeared at the UN International Criminal tribunal charged with war crimes?

2 Which politician, who became mayor of London, was expelled from his own party in February 2000?

3 Whose running mate was Joseph Lieberman?

4 Of what did General Joseph Ralston take command?

5 Why did 60 small ships set out to cross the English Channel in June 2000?

6 Which swaying bridge was closed for repairs only days after it was opened?

7 What was the Steel Dragon, opened in Japan in August 2000?

8 What took off for the 100th time in October?

9 Which country decided to bring back their old anthem but with new words?

10 Which aerospace consortium announced plans for a super-jumbo, able to seat 555 passengers?

383 Mary, Mary
LEVEL 2   Here the names to watch for are Mary, Maria, Marie . . .

1 Who was queen alongside her husband William in 1688?

2 Mary of Teck married the brother of the prince to whom she was first engaged in 1891. He later became king of England. Who was he?

3 How did Marie Taglione's twinkling feet entrance audiences in the 1800s?

4 Which Marie allegedly said: 'Let them eat cake' on being told the people had no bread?

5 Who founded the museum in central London housing wax works of famous figures?

6 Which Mary, mother of the author of Frankenstein, was a leading suffragette?

7 Who was married to King Henry IV of France and from 1610 to 1614 ruled as regent?

8 Of which empire was Maria Theresa empress in the 1700s?

9 Which Scottish Mary was born in Linlithgow Palace in 1542 and died at Fotheringhay Castle in 1587?

10 Whose unhappy wife was Mary of Modena?

384 Civil rights
LEVEL 3   People righting the wrongs of the world

1 Whose 1791 book *Rights of Man*, a defence of the French revolution, caused uproar?

2 Who put his seal to the Magna Carta in 1215?

3 Why was Rosa Parks arrested during a bus ride in Montgomery, Alabama, in 1955?

4 What did Emily Davison do for the suffragette cause at the 1913 Derby?

5 What was Marcus Garvey's 1920s solution to racial discrimination in the USA?

6 In which Southern US city did the Central High School become a flashpoint in 1957 over the issue of student segregation?

7 In which country did the Chartists march to demand electoral changes in the 1840s?

8 How did Thurgood Marshall break through a legal barrier in 1967?

9 What name was given by Louis Farrakhan to the Nation of Islam march in Washington DC in October 1995?

10 Which civil rights leader spoke to 200,000 people in Washington in 1963?

History

385 That sinking feeling
LEVEL 2   Will you be lost at sea with this round?

1 Where did the *Vasa* go down in 1628?

2 What kind of boat was the *Surcouf*, sunk after being hit by an American freighter in 1942?

3 Which king of England watched in dismay as his finest ship rolled over in 1545?

4 Which British battleship was sunk by a U-boat in Scapa Flow in October 1939?

5 Which Argentine warship was sunk by HMS *Conqueror* in the 1982 Falklands War?

6 What was HMS *Edinburgh* carrying when sunk in 1942 – the cargo was recovered almost 40 years later?

7 Which Russian submarine sank in the Barents Sea in 2000, with the loss of 118 lives?

8 What record is held by the bathyscaphe *Trieste* after its 1960 dive?

9 What was historic about the USS *Nautilus*'s first voyage in 1955?

10 What record does the 71,890-ton Japanese aircraft carrier *Shinano* hold, sunk in 1944 by a torpedo from the USS *Archerfish*?

386 Accidents of war
LEVEL 2   Test your mettle with a round of warfare

1 At which battle was General James Wolfe killed in 1759?

2 How did the *Merrimack* and *Monitor* make history in 1862?

3 For what purpose did medieval soldiers use bombards outside the castle wall?

4 Which country's embassy in Belgrade was accidentally bombed by the US during the 1999 Kosovo campaign?

5 A sniper's bullet fatally wounded which admiral at the moment of his victory in 1805?

6 By what common name was President Kennedy's abortive attempt to overthrow the Cuban government in 1961 known?

7 What new type of aerial observation device did the French use at Fleurus in 1794?

8 Which were the first two British warships to be destroyed by the Japanese airforce in 1941?

9 Which new weapons did Japanese warriors of the 1500s despise as 'cowards' weapons'?

10 Which king lost his life at Bosworth in 1485?

387 Saints and sinners
LEVEL 3   The blessed and the damned

1 After which saint is the oldest permanent European settlement in the United States, founded in Florida in 1565, named?

2 In which city was the first public striptease show performed in 1894?

3 Who clashed at Cape Saint Vincent in 1797?

4 Which French fashion designer was assistant to Christian Dior and in 1957 took over from him?

5 How did Edith Cavell meet her death in 1915?

6 Which leader spoke of 'the evil empire' but later shook hands with it?

7 Which pope created the greatest number of saints?

8 Which saint prayed that he might be chaste, but not yet?

9 Who toured the streets of 19th-century London, rescuing street boys and housing them?

10 Who, in 1840, brought about a ban on using small boys to sweep chimneys?

388 Crisis, what crisis?
LEVEL 1 Tense moments in history

1 Over which Caribbean island did the US and the Soviet Union come close to war in 1962?

2 Which American divorcée caused a constitutional crisis in Britain in 1936?

3 Which European city was sustained by a massive airlift in 1949?

4 What crisis came to a head when a South Georgia whaling station was claimed by Argentina in 1982?

5 The invasion of which country on September 1, 1939 led to world war?

6 How did the Prague spring come to a crushing end in 1968?

7 Who came to power after climbing on a tank during the 1991 attempted coup in the USSR?

8 Which British prime minister was famously misquoted as saying: 'Crisis, what Crisis?'

9 Which 1857 Indian crisis was blamed on cartridge grease containing pig and beef fat?

10 In which Balkan city was Archduke Ferdinand shot, so triggering the First World War?

389 1066 and all that
LEVEL 1 How much do you know about England's battles of that year?

1 At the first battle in 1066 Tostig deserted his brother to fight for the other side and was killed. Who was Tostig's brother?

2 What is the link between a London football club and the first 1066 battle the English fought?

3 Which famous piece of needlework tells the tale of the Battle of Hastings?

4 Who wrote the book *1066 and all That*, a humorous guide to British history?

5 Why did Norman knights take care of their *destriers*?

6 What was the most feared weapon wielded by the Saxon soldiers?

7 In which historic church was William the Conqueror crowned King of England?

8 Where can visitors stand where, it is believed, the English king fell during the battle?

9 How does the shape of a Norman shield remind one of flying?

10 Why were many Norman soldiers able to look down on the English they were fighting?

390 Going to law
LEVEL 3 A round for the lawyers

1 Who was the first person to be executed in America following the reinstatement of the death penalty in 1976?

2 Who was the last person to be executed for treason in Britain, in 1946?

3 Which judge presided over England's so-called 'bloody assizes' of 1685?

4 Which notorious 19th-century wild west judge fined a corpse for carrying a concealed weapon?

5 Who did Arthur Orton claim to be in 1865, leading to a 1000-day 'impersonation' case?

6 How old was Missouri judge Albert R. Alexander when he retired in 1965?

7 In which country were 15,617 demonstrators arrested at one time during unrest in 1988?

8 Which country imprisoned Elizabeth Bathory for murdering 612 girls between 1560-1615?

9 What gruesome job did Albert Pierrepoint hold until 1956?

10 Which British husband and wife serial killers are believed to have murdered 13 people?

History

The Second World War
391
LEVEL 2   The last global conflict

1 What material made up the bulk of the Mosquito aircraft used by the RAF during the war?

2 What building housed Britain's successful code-breaking operations?

3 What were Thunderbolts and Lightnings?

4 In June 1944 what was a Mulberry?

5 What did the British refer to as doodlebugs?

6 What was Operation Sealion, which never took place, designed to achieve?

7 On which Japanese island did US troops raise the flag in February 1945?

8 Where did Marshal Badoglio become leader in 1943 and switch allegiance?

9 Where did the British Fourteenth Army, the 'forgotten army' fight?

10 What name was given to the German counter attack through the Ardennes in winter 1944?

Symbols and signs
392
LEVEL 2   Decoding the symbols of history

1 What distinctive symbol did Christian soldiers of the Crusades wear on their chests?

2 What did a bunch of grapes hanging outside a Roman shop signify?

3 Which profession adopted the red-and-white striped pole as its trademark?

4 The English pub sign of the White Hart refers to a particular king's badge. Which king was that?

5 What colour were the first flags carried by Muhammad's Muslim armies?

6 Which army's cavalry galloped into battle with a *vexillum*?

7 Of which European country did the harp become a symbol?

8 Which lunar symbol did the Turks adopt around 1250 which became commonplace throughout Islam?

9 Which bird did the Roman legions guard?

10 Which country's heraldic arms features three gold crowns on blue?

Shoot to kill
393
LEVEL 3   Assassins and their victims

1 Whom did Sara Jane Moore shoot at in San Francisco in 1975?

2 Who was shot by fellow gang member Robert Ford in 1882?

3 What accident did the USS *Vincennes* cause in July 1988 with the loss of 290 lives?

4 Who ordered an SS soldier to shoot him and his wife on May 1, 1945, after he had poisoned his six children?

5 Which propagater of non-violence was shot dead in India in 1948?

6 Who was taken off an alleged 'shoot to kill' policy inquiry in Northern Ireland in 1986?

7 Which aristocratic flying ace died when his triplane was shot down in 1918?

8 In the investigation of whose shooting did film taken by Abraham Zapruder play a vital part?

9 Which king of England died in 1199 in France after a crossbow wound turned gangrenous?

10 Which British government minister fought a duel with George Canning in 1809?

394 Medieval medley
LEVEL 1 Questions from one of history's more colourful periods

1 What did castle guards shoot through loopholes?

2 Which medieval cathedral has the tallest spire of any English cathedral?

3 Who wrote *The Canterbury Tales*?

4 What kind of hooved and horned animals pulled medieval farmers' ploughs?

5 Which farm animal was most important to England's economy in 1300?

6 What was a troubadour's job?

7 Which Italian city adopted the lion of St Mark as its symbol?

8 What name was given to the series of holy wars launched by the Christian states against the Saracens, starting in 1095?

9 What was the name of the young men who helped a knight put on his armour and carried his weapons for him?

10 In medieval illuminated manuscripts, what were the illuminations?

395 The year 2001
LEVEL 1 It seems like only the other day . . .

1 From whom did Iain Duncan Smith take over as leader of the Conservative Party in September?

2 Where did Denis Tito travel to on a trip costing more than US $20million?

3 Who was executed in June for bombing the Alfred P. Murrah building in Oklahoma City?

4 Into which borough of New York did American Airline flight 587 crash, killing 265 people?

5 Craig Evans made an impact on John Prescott at an election rally in Rhyl. How?

6 Who was the disgraced author found guilty of perjury and jailed for four years?

7 How did a virus of the *picornaviridae* family cause disaster to British livestock?

8 Who did 16-year-old Alina Lebedyver slap in Latvia in protest at the Afghanistan War?

9 What was the Northern Alliance?

10 What did a Scottish court sitting in the Netherlands decide Abdelbaset al Megrahi was guilty of?

396 Black America
LEVEL 3 A round about Afro-American history

1 Who did Harriet Tubman help to escape to freedom?

2 Which Dodger became the first black professional to hit his way into what had been an all-white game, in 1947?

3 In which fight did Crispus Attucks die for the revolution?

4 Which black explorer was at Peary's side when he reached the North Pole in 1909?

5 Which singer was barred from singing at Washington's Constitution Hall in 1939 even though one of America's greatest opera stars?

6 Which US congressman, sent to the UN by Jimmy Carter, later became Mayor of Atlanta?

7 Which black tennis star is remembered in a renamed US stadium?

8 Which radical party was led in the 1960s by Huey Newton and Bobby Seale?

9 In 1839, which slave ship had a mutiny?

10 Which Harriet Beecher Stowe novel made people aware of the slavery issue in the US?

History

397 In good Queen Bess's day
LEVEL 2   The first Queen Elizabeth

1 Who did Queen Elizabeth knight on his return home in 1580?

2 Who was Elizabeth's half-sister, from whom she inherited the throne?

3 If a nobleman was 'attained' what happened to him?

4 What was a virginal?

5 Which soldier-poet's death in battle at Zutphen in 1586 sent Elizabeth's court into mourning?

6 What position was held by Paul IV on the accession of Elizabeth in 1558?

7 Who was Elizabeth's principal secretary, often considered to be her spymaster?

8 Which nobleman did the Queen call lovingly her 'sweet Robin'?

9 What profession was practised by the Lord Chamberlain's Men?

10 In which Elizabethan London landmark did people live above rushing water?

398 Iron and steel
LEVEL 2   History with some metal in it

1 Who was known as 'the iron duke'?

2 Which commander's soldiers were known as 'ironsides'?

3 Which English ironmaster perfected the smelting of iron using coke in the early 1700s?

4 Which Spanish city was renowned for its steel and its swords?

5 Which British Liberal leader was the first presiding officer of the Scottish Parliament?

6 What name is given to the period in pre-history beginning in the Middle East and southeastern Europe around 1200 BC?

7 Which dictator, whose real name was Iosif Dzhugashvili, adopted a name that meant 'the man of steel'?

8 What Nazi award, designed by Karl Friederich Schinkel, was given to soldiers for bravery in the face of the enemy?

9 Who popularised the phrase 'iron curtain'?

10 In which country was there a 1930s Fascist grouping known as the Iron Guard?

399 Memorable meetings
LEVEL 2   Who met who, where, when and why?

1 Whom did Henry Morton Stanley meet in 1871 beside Lake Tanganyika?

2 Who was the US president who met Stalin and Churchill at Yalta in February 1945?

3 Which Egyptian president was the first Arab leader to give an address to the Israeli parliament?

4 On which island did President Reagan shake hands with the USSR's architect of 'glasnost'?

5 Who did crowds of Tahitians meet on April 13, 1769 as his ship *Endeavour* dropped anchor?

6 Who returned to London from Munich in 1938 with a piece of paper 'signed by Herr Hitler'?

7 Which English king met his French counterpart at the Field of the Cloth of Gold in 1520?

8 Which Greek student arrived in Athens in 367 BC, and became as respected as Plato?

9 Which European traveller made a three-year journey to be greeted by Kublai Khan in 1274?

10 In 1519, which South American ruler welcomed the Spanish soldier Cortés, as a god?

400   Kings and queens
LEVEL 1   A right royal round

1 What is the name of Queen Elizabeth II's youngest child?

2 How many kings of Great Britain have been called George?

3 Which country had a king known as 'the Sun king'?

4 Who was crowned king of Spain in 1975?

5 In which Southeast Asian country did King Bhumibol Adulyadej (Rama IX) accede to the throne in June 1946?

6 Who was the only British monarch to abdicate?

7 Which Catherine was Henry VIII's last wife?

8 What is the most frequently used name for kings who have ruled in England?

9 Which English queen shares her nickname with a vodka and tomato juice cocktail?

10 In which European country did Albert II accede after the death of Baudouin?

401   Battle stations
LEVEL 1   Bloody battles and the men who fought them

1 Which battle marked the end of the Napoleonic Wars and provided the title of a winning song in the Eurovision Song Contest?

2 What type of headgear was named after a Crimean War battle on October 25, 1854?

3 Which Second World War battle was the largest tank confrontation of the entire war?

4 In 1429, who was defeated at Orleans by an English army?

5 At the site of which Montana river did Sitting Bull and Crazy Horse defeat General Custer?

6 What war was triggered by the attack on Fort Sumter on April 12, 1861, in the United States?

7 At which battle did Admiral Nelson die?

8 How was the 1991 operation 'desert storm' known?

9 To what was Winston Churchill referring when he said: 'Never in the field of human conflict, was so much owed by so many to so few'?

10 Which city, known as 'the jewel of the Adriatic', was damaged during the 1990s Bosnian conflict?

402   Russian roulette
LEVEL 3   A round about Russia

1 To which Scandinavian raiders did Rurik, the legendary name provider of Russia, belong?

2 In 1773, which Russian ruler crushed a revolt led by Pugachev?

3 Who was the last leader of the USSR?

4 Which 16th-century tsar of Russia married five wives in nine years and killed his oldest son?

5 What was the family name of Michael, first of his line, who became Tsar of Russia in 1613?

6 How many states were formed on the break up of the USSR in 1991?

7 During which 19th-century war did Russian troops fire on the British?

8 Which Russian ruler became Tsar in 1598 and later had an opera by Mussorgsky written about him?

9 Which Russian city was renamed Petrograd in 1914 and Leningrad in 1924?

10 Which Soviet leader got so angry he banged his shoe on the desk while addressing the UN?

History

Young at heart

403

LEVEL 2   Not everyone in history is old

1 Who was the youngest elected president of America?

2 Which US astronaut, who landed on the Moon in 1972, made more flights than any other?

3 Which Mormon leader spent two years as a missionary in Britain from 1839 to 1841?

4 In which country was the group of reformers called the Young Turks founded in 1865?

5 Who was Britain's youngest prime minister of the 20th century?

6 In 1844, what new organisation for young men was led by George Williams?

7 How old was Nelson when he joined the British Navy in 1771?

8 How old was Charles Kennedy when he was elected, making him Britain's youngest MP?

9 The writings on which ancient stone were decoded by Thomas Young?

10 Which 20th-century cartoon strip was created by Chic Young?

Springtime

404

LEVEL 2   All these events took place in March, April or May

1 Which European war was ended by the Treaty of Paris in March 1856?

2 Which department store opened in London's Oxford Street in March 1909?

3 From which Mediterranean island base did the British Navy pull out in March 1979?

4 What appeared in the pages of *The Times*, for the first time in April 1875?

5 What did the RFC and RNAS merge to form in the spring of 1918?

6 What was *Early Bird*, flying high in April 1965?

7 The author of *Daffodils* became Poet Laureate in April 1843. Who was he?

8 Why could New Yorkers celebrate May Day 1931 from 102 floors up?

9 What great show did Queen Victoria open on May 1, 1851?

10 Who went up in *Freedom 7* on May 5, 1961 only to splash down again?

War in the Gulf

405

LEVEL 3   How much do you remember about the 1991 Gulf War

1 Who was the Iraqi foreign minister during the Gulf War?

2 Who commanded Britain's 'desert rats', despatched to the Gulf in October 1990?

3 The hostilities against Iraq began with the announcement: 'The liberation of Kuwait has begun'. Who said it?

4 Who was the British prime minister at the end of the Gulf War?

5 Which CNN journalist was famous for broadcasting from Baghdad?

6 What is a scud?

7 What was the name of *The Observer* journalist accused by Iraq of spying, and executed in 1990?

8 Name the bestselling book by SAS soldier Andy McNab, about his capture by the Iraqis.

9 What name was given to Saddam Hussein's elite military force, used as his personal guard?

10 The *F117A* aircraft was used to attack targets in Baghdad. How is this unique aircraft popularly known?

Assassinations

406

LEVEL 1   A round about people who met an untimely end – or nearly did

1 Who said: 'Honey, I forgot to duck', after a failed assassination attempt outside the Washington Hilton hotel in March, 1981?

2 Yitzhak Rabin, assassinated in 1995, was prime minister of which country?

3 Which co-author of the *Guinness Book of Records* was assassinated by the IRA in 1975?

4 Which Indian prime minister was assassinated in 1984 by her own bodyguards?

5 Elton John was comforted by Diana, Princess of Wales at whose funeral?

6 Who was the first president of the USA to be assassinated in the 20th century?

7 Who was accused of assassinating President John F. Kennedy in Dallas, Texas, in 1963?

8 Who was watching the play, *Our American Cousin*, when he was assassinated?

9 Martin Luther King and Robert Kennedy both fell victim to an assassin's bullet in which year?

10 Which Earl was killed by the IRA on August 27, 1979?

Testing times

407

LEVEL 1   Some dates to test you

1 In which year did Mother Teresa receive a Nobel peace prize and the USSR invade Afghanistan?

2 Which year followed 1 BC?

3 In which century did Isaac Newton discover gravity, Samuel Pepys write his diary and 'the Gunpowder Plot' take place?

4 Which year provided the title of a George Orwell novel, first published in 1949?

5 For how many years did the Hundred Years War last?

6 How many years separated the assassinations of John F. Kennedy and his brother Robert?

7 In which decade did Charles Dickens write *A Christmas Carol*, David Livingstone discover the Victoria Falls and Florence Nightingale nurse injured soldiers in the Crimean War?

8 In which year did the First World War start?

9 Which European country was unified in 1861?

10 In what year was George Bush Snr inaugurated as President of the USA?

American history

408

LEVEL 1   A trip around the land of the free

1 Which former US president's wife is associated with clinics for alcoholics?

2 In which American state did Davy Crockett, Colonel Travis and Jim Bowie perish while defending the Alamo?

3 How was William Bonney better known in America's wild west?

4 In 1620, what was the name of the flagship on which the pilgrim fathers sailed to America?

5 Which US president declared: 'Ich bin ein Berliner'?

6 The White House has been the home for every American president, except for whom?

7 Which animal is associated with William Frederick Cody, who was born in 1846 and died in 1917?

8 Who was America's longest serving president?

9 Which letter of the alphabet did Malcolm Little adopt as his surname in 1952?

10 Which child actress of the 1930s became the American ambassador to Ghana?

History

Historic houses
409
LEVEL 2   Homes of the rich and famous

1 Which US president designed his own house, called Monticello, in Virginia?

2 In which city is Holyrood House?

3 Where was Princess Elizabeth staying when she heard news of her father, George VI's death?

4 Which famous architect wanted to rebuild Hampton Court Palace in the 1600s, but never got the chance?

5 Who lived in a chalet at Obersalzberg above Berchtesgaden?

6 In medieval times, poor people built houses from wattle and daub – what was daub?

7 Which country house in Hertfordshire, England, was owned by the Cecil family?

8 Chevening is the official residence of which British cabinet post?

9 Which British royal residence is in Norfolk?

10 In which French palace was the treaty that officially ended the First World War signed?

On the rails
410
LEVEL 2   Get your ticket for this railway round

1 Which country's surrender was taken by Adolf Hitler in Marshal Foch's historic railway coach?

2 Which Cornish engineer developed the world's first practical steam-carriage, in 1804?

3 Which two coasts were linked when workers knocked in the golden spike at Promontory, Utah, in 1869?

4 What left London's Waterloo station at 08.23 on November 14, 1994?

5 What distinction is held by the Swansea and Mumbles railway?

6 What was the link between standard gauge rail track and a horse and cart?

7 Which US inventor spent part of his boyhood selling newspapers and snacks on the Grand Trunk Railway from Port Huron to Detroit?

8 Name the world's longest continuous railway, across tundra and taiga, completed in 1916.

9 What did George Pullman and Ben Field invent?

10 Which British train holds the world record for being the fastest steam locomotive?

Winston Churchill
411
LEVEL 3   Britain's greatest wartime leader

1 What is the link between Churchill and a European battle, fought in 1704?

2 Speaking at Missouri in 1946, what did Churchill say had descended across Europe 'from Stettin in the Baltic to Trieste in the Adriatic'?

3 Of which famous soldier-ancestor did Churchill write a biography?

4 To which school did Churchill's parents send him to improve his health?

5 In which country was the young Churchill taken prisoner by farmers?

6 Who did Churchill succeed as Britain's prime minister in 1940?

7 To which potential ally did Churchill say: 'Give us the tools and we'll finish the job'?

8 How was Churchill honoured for his writing achievements in 1953?

9 Of which country did Churchill become an honorary citizen in 1963?

10 What unique honour did the US Navy bestow on Churchill's memory in 2001?

412

The living years
Can you identify these famous faces and name one year in which each of them lived?

1 Wrote *Für Elise*

2 Sailed the ocean blue

3 Sometimes known as Boz

4 She saved the life of Captain Smith

5 First head of the Church of England

6 Populated the Globe

7 Did OK at the Corral

8 Tried by the Inquisition

9 Discovered radium

10 Master of self-portrait

History

Women of substance
413
LEVEL 1   Leading female figures from the past

1 Who was known as 'the maid of Orleans'?

2 Name the Dutch-Jewish girl who compiled a famous diary during the Second World War.

3 What first did the British MP Margaret Grace Bondfield achieve for female politicians in 1929?

4 Which South American leader was played by Madonna in a 1996 Alan Parker film?

5 What was Margaret Thatcher's maiden name?

6 By what name was Martha Jane Canary more popularly known in the wild west?

7 What was the name of Adolf Hitler's mistress, who he married in 1945?

8 By what married name was Jacqueline Bouvier known to the world?

9 Which film star did Prince Rainier of Monaco marry in 1956?

10 The name of which famous clown also provided the nickname of the French fashion designer Gabrielle Chanel?

Historical films
414
LEVEL 1   History as seen through the lens

1 In which 1969 film did Paul Newman play the outlaw Robert Leroy Parker?

2 Who committed suicide after the Battle of Actium and was played by Richard Burton in the film *Cleopatra*?

3 Who played the title role in the 1982 film *Gandhi*?

4 Who played Henry VIII in the film *Carry on Henry*?

5 Which crime lord was played on film by Robert de Niro in *The Untouchables*?

6 Which biblical strongman was portrayed by Victor Mature in a 1949 film?

7 Which heroic figure, played in a 1962 film by Peter O'Toole, was killed in a motorcycle crash?

8 The film *Reach for the Sky*, chronicled the life of which Second World War pilot?

9 Which 11th-century hero was played by Charlton Heston in a 1961 film?

10 Which King who lost his sanity was played in a 1995 film by Sir Nigel Hawthorne?

Around the world
415
LEVEL 1   A global picture of our past

1 In which African capital city was General Gordon killed in 1885?

2 To which country did governance of Hong Kong revert in 1997, after 99 years of British rule?

3 Who founded and gave his name to the country of Rhodesia (now Zimbabwe) in 1895?

4 Which ancient South American civilisation worshipped Tialoc, the rain god?

5 In which country in 1980 was Desert One the scene of a bungled rescue operation?

6 From the late 12th century, which country was ruled by the Shoguns?

7 Which Asian country was known as 'the jewel of the British Empire'?

8 What was Marco Polo's home city?

9 In 1975, which city was renamed Ho Chi Minh City?

10 Omaha, Gold, Juno, Sword and Utah were D-day beachheads in which part of northern France?

Star turns

416

LEVEL 2   Earning a place in the heavens

1 Which 16th-century Polish astronomer upset the established order by putting the Sun in its rightful place?

2 What was the Star Chamber?

3 Which was the most famous of the White Star Line's passenger ships?

4 What name was popularly given to the American government's Strategic Defense Initiative of 1983?

5 What did King Charles II set up in 1675 to study the heavens?

6 Which star appeared on the flag raised by the Israelis over their newly created state in 1948?

7 Which jewel did J.P. Morgan present to the American Museum of Natural History?

8 In which country are the remains of a Stone Age settlement, known as Star Carr?

9 How many stars were there on the first American flag?

10 Which American state became known as 'the lone star state'?

The sixties

417

LEVEL 2   Can you remember these front-page news stories?

1 What New York-based position did U Thant of Burma take in 1961?

2 Which British prime minister celebrated England's football World Cup victory in 1966?

3 In which country were ZANU and ZAPU campaigning?

4 Who was the first professional tennis player to win the Wimbledon men's singles title in 1968?

5 Which country did Biafra fight to break away from between 1967 and 1970?

6 Which world statesman died on January 25, 1965 at the age of 90?

7 In whose car was Mary Jo Kopechne when she drowned in 1969 on Chappaquiddick Island?

8 What was the name of the Liberian oil tanker wrecked in 1967 off the Scilly Isles?

9 Who became leader of the Palestine Liberation Organisation in 1969?

10 Who or what was the white and cuddly Pipaluk, on show in London in 1967?

Getting the vote

418

LEVEL 3   People power through the ages

1 Which US state kept the American people guessing during the 2000 presidential elections?

2 Which was the first English-speaking country to give women the vote?

3 In which year did a British government vow to make an enemy pay 'until the pips squeak'?

4 Where did a bishop named Abel Muzorewa become his country's first black prime minister after an election in 1979?

5 Which 'third way' coalition won 25 per cent of the vote in the 1983 British general election?

6 Who campaigned for a 'new deal' in the 1932 American election?

7 Who defeated George McGovern in a 1972 landslide victory to become US president?

8 Which Australian prime minister was sacked by the governor-general in 1975?

9 In which country are the world's biggest democratic elections held?

10 In which country did Corazon Aquino win the leadership in 1986?

History

Politically correct
419
LEVEL 1   Key political figures from around the world

1 Prior to Bill Clinton, who was the last Democrat president of the USA?

2 *Love is on the Air* and *The Killers* were the first and last films of which future US leader?

3 In which country was the Dear Leader followed by the Great Leader?

4 Who worked as an electrician in a Gdansk shipyard before becoming the president of Poland?

5 Who was the colonel at the centre of the 1987 Iran-Contra scandal?

6 Which Pakistani politician was previously a world-class cricket player?

7 Which British prime minister said: 'There is no such thing as society'?

8 In which country did Baby Doc succeed Papa Doc?

9 Who narrowly missed becoming president of the USA in the 2001 general election?

10 Which British political party was founded in 1900?

The world at war
420
LEVEL 1   A simple round about conflict

1 Who were Great Britain's opponents in the Opium Wars?

2 Which war was fought between 1775 and 1783?

3 Which ancient war was triggered by the kidnapping of Helen?

4 Who or what were 'Pershing's doughboys'?

5 Which Guy led the 'dambusters' raid?

6 Which country opposed England in the Hundred Years War?

7 Which war lasted 100 hours?

8 Which major event of the Second World War took place in Hawaii on December 7, 1941?

9 The only Nobel peace prize issued during the First World War was awarded to which organisation?

10 In which country did Australian and New Zealand troops fight at Gallipoli?

A variety of folk
421
LEVEL 1   Do you know these people well?

1 Who was the first leader of a unified Germany?

2 Innocent, Gregory, Pius and Benedict have held which high office?

3 Which 20th-century artist was famed for his 'blue' and 'rose' periods?

4 What day did a Catholic priest, killed on February 14, 270, reputedly give his name to?

5 In which country did Colonel Gadaffi seize power in the 1960s?

6 Of which country was Thabo Mbeki elected president in 1999?

7 In 1206, who became the leader of the Mongol tribes?

8 In 1829, members of the London Metropolitan Police became known as Bobbies, after whom?

9 Which future president of France commanded the 'free French forces' during the Second World War?

10 Who was Marie Curie's scientist husband?

The British Empire

422

LEVEL 2   The greatest empire the world has ever seen

1 In which part of the British Empire did Robert Clive make his name?

2 Which part of Britain's Empire was first settled by the convicts who landed from the First Fleet in 1788?

3 In which country is a bay named after the explorer Henry Hudson?

4 Which British monarch was proclaimed Empress of India in 1876?

5 What was abolished in the British Empire in 1833, but not in the USA for another 32 years?

6 With which country did Britain go to war in 1839 to preserve the rights of opium-smokers?

7 From where did Lady Sarah Wilson say: 'Breakfast … horse sausage. Lunch … curried locust.'?

8 What organisation in Canada proudly boasted that they would 'always get their man'?

9 During which uprising of 1857 did the Rani of Jhansi lead an army against the British?

10 Where in 1840 did explorer Edward John Eyre discover a lake that is usually dry?

Faith founders

423

LEVEL 3   These people were responsible for changing lives

1 French theologian Jean Chauvin took the Protestant Reformation to Geneva, Switzerland in the 1500s and changed his name. To what?

2 What movement was founded by Mary Baker Eddy?

3 Who got on his horse in the 1700s to bring a new method to Christianity in Britain?

4 According to Jewish teaching, who made the covenant with God?

5 Which city was founded by Brigham Young's Mormons in 1847?

6 Who was the first Sikh guru, born in 1469?

7 Which branch of Islam followed the leadership of the first caliph, Abu Bakr?

8 Which Christian saint was captured by pirates aged 16, and said he was called in a dream to preach to the Irish?

9 Which world religion evolved from the ancient writings called the Rig-Veda?

10 Which spiritualist's conception was foretold by his mother's dream of a white elephant?

Mysteries of history

424

LEVEL 2   Spooky facts from the past

1 Where did George Mallory and Andrew Irvine vanish into the clouds in 1924?

2 How many people were left on board the *Mary Celeste*, found drifting in the Atlantic in 1872?

3 What mysterious objects were reported by Kenneth Arnold in Washington in June 1947?

4 According to legend, what was Atlantis?

5 What is the name for the North American yeti, a forest 'ape-man' who eludes identification?

6 How is the area in which six US Navy planes disappeared off Florida in 1945 known?

7 Where is an Irish monk alleged to have voyaged in an oxhide boat in the 6th century?

8 Conspiracy theorists suggest what landed secretly in Area 51?

9 What mysterious Scottish water-beast was allegedly filmed in 1975, convincing some naturalists that it might be a prehistoric plesiosaur?

10 Which legendary king is traditionally associated with Cadbury Hill in Somerset, England?

History

C for yourself

425

LEVEL 1 A round in which all the answers begin with the letter C

1 Which Labour minister of the 1960s published his controversial diaries giving the inside account of the Wilson era?

2 By what name is the compulsory call-up of men to fight in wars known?

3 Which Mediterranean island was invaded by Turkey in 1974 and is now divided in two?

4 Which anti-nuclear weapons group campaigned from the 1960s to the 1990s?

5 Who was the first English book publisher?

6 What city was known as Deva by the Romans?

7 Which glass conservatory, designed to house the 1851 Great Exhibition, burned down in 1936?

8 What name was given to people who refused to fight during the world wars for moral and religious reasons?

9 What name was given to the 12th-century military expeditions authorised by the Pope?

10 What name was given to the period of tension from the mid-1940s to the 1990s between the Eastern Bloc and the West?

Who had it first?

426

LEVEL 2 Can you identify the innovators from these clues

1 Which ancient people can claim to have had the first adhesive bandages, to have used cannabis as an anaesthetic and honey as an antiseptic?

2 Which ancient people left the first descriptions of tug of war, leapfrog and blind man's buff?

3 Who invented the crane and the guidebook?

4 Which people invented the non-lethal mousetrap and first distilled alcohol?

5 Stirrups for horses, sugar for tea: which country had them first?

6 Which country pioneered the picture postcard, the pocket watch, and the diesel engine?

7 These traders, from what later became known as the Levant, gave us an alphabet and also false teeth. Who were they?

8 Ice cream, kites and toilet paper – all have their place, but which place had them first?

9 The 'beamlight', probably the world's first pinball machine, was invented where, in 1938?

10 Which country invented margarine in 1869?

Historical oddities

427

LEVEL 3 How much do you know about these curious historical facts

1 Through which continent was Harold Macmillan's 'wind of change' blowing in 1960?

2 In 1855, Britain had 11,744 of these, Germany 7826 and France only 1588 – what were they?

3 Match these 20th-century dictators to their countries: Admiral Horthy, General Primo de Rivera, Marshal Pilsudski.

4 Which surname links the editor of *Poor Richard's Almanac* to a British explorer?

5 Over which empire did Suleiman the Magnificent rule during the 16th century?

6 Which ancient Egyptian leader donned a beard to persuade officials to accept her authority?

7 If George was first, and John was second, who was third?

8 What unsavoury distinction is shared by the Legion of Saint George, the Charlemagne Division and the Langemarck Division?

9 Which famous scientist became master of the mint in 1699?

10 What colour were Nazi storm troopers' shirts?

 # History quest

These questions are tougher than the others and you may need to do some research

1 What connects Captain Jenkins, Pinocchio and the Watergate source?

2 What connects red, white, black and pale?

3 Who is the only person to have won both a Nobel prize and an Oscar?

4 What were the names of the four monarchs of Cair Paravel?

5 What connects the 1944 Education Act, Erewhon, *On the Buses* and Jeeves?

6 The Apostle Paul, Alastair Cooke, Carrie Fisher, Screwtape. Which is the odd-one-out?

7 What connects *The Memoirs of a Lady of Pleasure*, the inventor of the Penny Post and Fats Domino?

8 Tintin's dog was called Snowy in English; what was he called in French?

9 What global organisation was founded by Ray Kroc in San Bernadino, California, in 1954?

10 What single event links Vaughan Williams' 'All people that on the earth do dwell', Parry's 'I was glad...', Wesley's 'Thou wilt keep him in perfect peace', and Handel's *Zadok the Priest*?

11 September 11, 1752, was a pretty uneventful day in Britain. Why?

12 Where do the following people appear together? Tony Curtis, Marlon Brando, Oliver Hardy, Stan Laurel, Fred Astaire, Albert Einstein, Oscar Wilde, Karl Marx, W.C. Fields, Edgar Allan Poe and Shirley Temple.

13 What was first classified in 1900 according to the Galton-Henry System?

14 For what did Pheidippides provide the inspiration in 490 BC?

15 What links Alexander the Great, Vladimir Lenin and Lord Nelson?

A clue to question 14

History

429 First choices
LEVEL 1   Who got there first?

1 In 1969, the US *Mariner* beamed back to Earth the first pictures of which planet?

2 In 1934, the first-ever what was opened in Fort Worth, Texas. Was it a laundrette, a library or a disco?

3 In 1807, which became the first-ever city in the world to be lit by gas light: Paris, London or New York?

4 Name America's first black secretary of state.

5 In 1885, Dr Williams West Grant of Iowa performed the first-ever what?

6 In 1892, the first recorded game of which sport took place in Massachusetts?

7 In 1796, Edward Jenner administered the first successful vaccination against which disease?

8 In 1850, the first-ever what was seen in Britain as an exhibit in London Zoo?

9 What did the King Kullen Grocery Company open the first of in 1930?

10 What was published for the first time in London on January 15, 1880?

430 Biblical times
LEVEL 1   History according to the Good Book

1 Who was the Roman governor who ordered the crucifixion of Jesus Christ?

2 Which book of the Bible tells the story of the creation of the world?

3 Who was the oldest son of Adam and Eve?

4 Goliath, slain by David, belonged to which tribe of people?

5 What was the first task God gave to Adam?

6 Name the archangel who announced to Mary that she was to be the mother of Jesus.

7 How many people ate at the last supper?

8 Which day in the calendar year is celebrated by Christians as the anniversary of Christ's crucifixion?

9 In the Bible, who is named as 'the father of the Jewish race': Moses, Abraham or Solomon?

10 Which disciple was known as 'doubting' after he questioned the resurrection of Jesus?

431 US presidents
LEVEL 2   How much do you know about the most powerful man on Earth?

1 Who was the only US president to belong to no official political party?

2 Which 20th-century president was 73 years old when elected for his second term?

3 John Tyler had 15 of them, more than any other US president. What were they?

4 Presidential papers are housed in presidential libraries. Whose presidential library was moved to Little Rock, Arkansas?

5 Which president took the oath of office on board an aircraft in 1963?

6 Which president was the first to travel overseas as president?

7 Presidents Lincoln, Garfield, McKinley and Kennedy shared a common fate. What was it?

8 Which uniquely long-serving US president was the last to die in office of natural causes?

9 Who was the only US president to face a vote of impeachment in Congress?

10 Who was the only president to achieve office under the 25th Amendment?

African answers

432   **LEVEL 3**   Questions about a continent with a long and varied history

1 What name did Nyasaland take on independence from Britain in 1964?

2 What name did the Gold Coast adopt on becoming independent in 1957?

3 Which ancient African kingdom, located south of Egypt, had its capital at Meroe?

4 Which kingdom in West Africa became famous for its bronze-casting, many pieces surviving from the 15th and 16th centuries?

5 In which country was the Sharpeville massacre?

6 Of which country did former schoolteacher Kenneth Kaunda become president in 1964?

7 Which European country seized colonies in Africa in the 19th century because it wanted 'a place in the sun'?

8 Which state, founded in 1822 by former slaves, became known for registering oil tankers?

9 In which African country did the FLN fight the French for independence, achieved in 1962?

10 Which island joined mainland Tanganyika to form the independent state of Tanzania?

French without tears

433   **LEVEL 2**   What do you know about your next-door neighbour?

1 Which type of building did the Musée d'Orsay, in Paris used to be?

2 Which great event in French history did Robespierre and Danton help bring about?

3 What is the name of the French National anthem?

4 What rank in the church did the 17th century French leaders Richelieu and Mazarin each hold?

5 Which symbol of France later became the badge of the Scouts?

6 Which general led the Free French in London during the Second World War?

7 Which French town was the last English possession in France?

8 What was the Maginot Line?

9 Which engineering project, first suggested in the 19th century, was dismissed because Britain feared an underground invasion from France?

10 In which senior position did Edith Cresson break a male monopoly in 1991?

Spies and plotters

434   **LEVEL 3**   Undercover agents and devious villains through the ages

1 Which Old Testament lawgiver is said to have sent the first spies mentioned in history on a mission into Canaan?

2 Against which queen was the so-called Ridolfi Plot of 1570 aimed?

3 Which English naval base was the setting for a 1960s spy ring involving Gordon Lonsdale?

4 What kind of plane was US pilot Gary Powers flying over the Soviet Union in 1960?

5 In which country was Mata Hari born?

6 Which famous plot was led by Robert Catesby in 1605?

7 Which security and intelligence-gathering organisation is based in Langley, Virginia?

8 Put to death in 1945, which pair were the first Americans executed for wartime spying?

9 Who was named as the 'third man' in the Burgess and Maclean spy scandal?

10 Which country hanged John André for spying during a revolutionary war?

History

Be prepared
435
LEVEL 1 All answers start with the letter B

1 What was the first plastic, invented by Alexander Parkes in 1860?

2 Which new game were YMCA students playing in the USA in 1891?

3 Who drove the first petrol-driven car in 1885?

4 Who founded the Boy Scout movement?

5 Which revolutionary group seized power in Russia in 1917?

6 In 1877, which city in Massachusetts had the world's first telephones?

7 Which retiring British prime minister chose to become Earl of Bewdley in 1937?

8 Which US president ordered Operation Desert Storm in 1991?

9 Who became the first woman Speaker of the House of Commons?

10 Whose 1963 report recommended the closure of large swathes of the British railway network?

The nineties
436
LEVEL 1 The last decade of the second millennium

1 Where did officials order all chickens to be destroyed in 1997 to wipe out a fowl disease?

2 In which US city did film of policemen beating a black motorist cause outrage in 1991?

3 Which treaty organisation celebrated 50 years in 1999?

4 Where did Vladimir Putin take over the reins of power in 1999?

5 Who described 1992 as an 'annus horribilis'?

6 In which American country did Jean Chrétien become prime minister in 1993?

7 Who said, during an American election campaign in 1992, that she could have 'stayed home and baked cookies rather than follow her own legal career'?

8 Who, in 1997, became the first Labour Party prime minister of Great Britain since 1979?

9 In which country did Albert take over as king in 1993, from his brother Baudouin?

10 Which royal castle burst into flames in November 1992?

Sibling rivalry
437
LEVEL 1 Questions about brothers and sisters

1 Which Italian saint saw all living things as his brothers?

2 Which murdered US president's brother was assassinated by the gunman Sirhan Sirhan?

3 What was the name of a man in striped trousers and top hat that replaced Brother Jonathan as an early American symbol?

4 Which US president had an embarrassing brother named Billy?

5 Which 16th-century English queen died childless, and was succeeded by her half-sister?

6 Ronnie or 'the Colonel' was said to be the dominant twin of which infamous gangster pair?

7 Who took their airplane to Kitty Hawk?

8 When Sanjay died, his brother Rajiv became next in line for which senior position in 1984?

9 After England's Prince Arthur died, his Spanish bride married his brother. Who was he?

10 Whose sister was Margaret Rose, a princess who could have married a Battle of Britain pilot but instead married a photographer?

Legendary landings

438

LEVEL 2   What landed in the history books where and when?

1 Where did a Surveyor land on June 2, 1966?

2 What was unique about the 1979 English Channel crossing by the extremely light aircraft, the *Gossamer Albatross*?

3 Who landed in October 1492, on an island he named San Salvador?

4 Which explorer landed at Sting Rays Harbour in 1770, and then, on seeing the plant life, renamed it Botany Bay?

5 Which French flier made a historic first landing near Dover on July 25, 1909?

6 During which 20th-century war did General MacArthur make the daring Inchon landings?

7 Who took off from Roosevelt Field on May 20, 1927 and landed 33 hours later at Le Bourget, making the first solo transatlantic flight?

8 Who or what fell from the skies above Holland during Operation Market Garden in 1944?

9 Which Roman landed in England in 55 BC?

10 Which Wright brother made the first-ever aeroplane landing on December 17, 1903?

Feminine endings

439

LEVEL 1   Mourning the death of a lady

1 Which long-reigning British queen died in 1603?

2 Which Queen requested a white funeral and got a snowy day in 1901?

3 What fate befell the First World War spy Mata Hari?

4 Which princess died in a car crash in 1982?

5 What was historic about the death of Ruth Ellis in 1955?

6 Which queen made her last voyage in 1968?

7 Whose marriage ended in 1809 because her emperor-husband wanted a son and heir?

8 Who was told by her colleagues in 1990 that after the poll tax it was time to go?

9 Whose attempt to fly around the world ended with a mysterious disappearance in 1937?

10 Who was killed in a car crash in Paris in August 1997 while being chased by paparazzi?

Historic animals

440

LEVEL 3   Furry friends from the past

1 What kind of birds – the world's largest flightless – did Egyptian kings like to chase?

2 If the lion was the symbol of Britain, and the eagle of America, what country was the bear?

3 The last of these in mainland Britain was shot around 1743. What kind of wild animal was it?

4 Which birds sat on the god Odin's shoulder?

5 Which animal was described by medieval writers in Europe as a 'cameleopard'?

6 What kind of animal was the aurochs, which once lived in Britain and could still be seen in Poland until 1627?

7 What animals appeared on the royal coat of arms after the union of England and Scotland in 1603?

8 What animal caused the death of Queen Cleopatra?

9 This Hindu god, son of Shiva and Parvati, takes the form of a man with which animal's head?

10 What kind of animal was *Dash*, a favourite of Queen Victoria?

History

The 18th century
441

LEVEL 1 The beginning of the modern age

1 Noted for its barbary apes, what was captured from the Spanish by a British fleet in 1704?

2 What did Thomas Chippendale design?

3 In which city was the 'black hole' where as many as 123 British soldiers and civilians died?

4 What was seen in the skies in 1758 after previously being seen in 1682?

5 The 1739 'War of Jenkin's Ear' was between Britain and which other European power?

6 Which two countries were joined by the 1707 Act of Union?

7 In 1746, what type of textile pattern was banned in Scotland?

8 In 1714, the German-speaking Elector of Hanover became king of England. What was his royal title?

9 In 1788, what were transported to Australia for the first time, finally landing at Botany Bay?

10 In 1795, the Royal Navy adopted the compulsory use of lime juice as an antidote to which disease?

The 19th century
442

LEVEL 1 Victorian Britain at its most powerful

1 What was abolished throughout the British Empire in 1833?

2 In 1896, the Klondyke gold rush took place in which country?

3 What is the name of the high-kicking dance associated with the Moulin Rouge?

4 In 1884, a book known by the initials OED, was first published. What do the initials stand for?

5 What was patented by Samuel Colt in 1835?

6 What calamity between 1845 and 1852 was caused by the fungus *Phytophthora infestans*, and led to the death of millions in Ireland?

7 Which famous building was completed in 1889, to become the world's tallest at that time?

8 What name was given to the series of 19th-century government acts that gave many more people the vote?

9 What was the name of the brother of the 19th-century outlaw Jesse James?

10 What name was given to the organised band of craftsmen who rioted for the destruction of the textile machinery that was displacing them?

2003
443

LEVEL 1 All 10 questions relate to events in 2003

1 Which space shuttle disintegrated in February on re-entering earth's atmosphere killing all 7 astronauts on board?

2 Which British royal celebrated his 21st birthday on 21 June?

3 Who won the 2003 European Champions League?

4 Who won the Ladies' Singles Finals at Wimbledon?

5 In which country did the England cricket team refuse to play during the 2003 World Cup?

6 Which record producer, who worked with The Beatles, was charged with murder in February?

7 President Charles Taylor was forced from power in which African country in August?

8 Which craft was taken out of commercial service after 27 years?

9 A robot called Spirit left earth to investigate what in June?

10 On whose head did President George W. Bush place a £15 million bounty?

Beginnings
444   LEVEL 2   It started like this

1 How did a new era in British funerals begin at Woking in 1885?

2 Which mail service began with a rider galloping out of St Louis in 1860?

3 Who began keeping a record of his life in shorthand in 1660?

4 What was seen for the first time around the *New York Times* building in Times Square, New York City on November 6, 1928?

5 How is the period from the collapse of Roman civilisation to the Renaissance known?

6 Which form of advertising began in the USA, promoting the Bulova Watch and Clock Co.?

7 What new deterrent was introduced in Britain in May 1983 to deter illegal parking?

8 Which royal dynasty began after the battle of Bosworth Field?

9 What left Greece for the first time in 1936 and was taken to Berlin?

10 What anti-drink-driving measure was introduced in Britain in 1967?

The thirties
445   LEVEL 2   All about a decade when there was trouble brewing

1 What war was fought in Spain between 1936 and 1939?

2 What did the British Empire become by statute in 1931?

3 Where did Farouk become king in 1936?

4 Who found himself swept out of office by FDR in 1932?

5 What name was given to the period of economic slump in America in the 1930s?

6 Of which European state did Eduard Benes become president in 1935, before it was occupied three years later?

7 The death in 1934 of President Paul von Hindenburg allowed which dictator to sweep to power?

8 In which gentlemanly game did 'bodyline' become a dirty word?

9 Who or what was *Phar Lap*?

10 In 1936, what new position in the BBC was occupied by Leslie Mitchell?

Alias Smith and Jones
446   LEVEL 3   Every question is about one or the other

1 Who was elected the Liberal MP for Rochdale in 1972?

2 How did Keith and Ross Smith from Adelaide earn fame, and knighthoods, in the early 1900s?

3 Which 17th-century Jones designed masques and palaces?

4 Which trade-union boss, born in 1913 in Liverpool, became a campaigner for pensioners' rights in Britain after he retired in 1978?

5 In 1776, which Scottish economist published the influential book *The Wealth of Nations*?

6 According to his own book, who was saved from death by a chieftain's daughter 1607?

7 By what nickname did US railroad engineer John Luther Jones go down in history?

8 What British astronomical post did Harold Spencer Jones take up in 1933?

9 Which mountains did Jedediah Smith cross by way of the South Pass in 1826?

10 Who was leader of Britain's Labour Party prior to Tony Blair?

It's a date

447

Kids 7–11   How well do you know your history?

1 In which city was there a great fire in 1666?

2 Where, in 1969, was astronaut Neil Armstrong the very first to make footprints?

3 Which war began with the invasion of Poland in 1939?

4 What event of 1605 is remembered every year on Guy Fawkes night?

5 From which country did William the Conqueror come in 1066?

6 Which ocean liner sank after hitting an iceberg in 1912?

7 What terrible event happened in New York on September 11, 2001?

8 What popular name was given to the outbreak of disease in England in 1348 that killed thousands?

9 Remembrance Day is traditionally the 11th of November. Which war ended on that date?

10 To where did Vasco da Gama sail in 1498?

True or false?

448

Kids 12–14   Can you spot the howlers here?

1 The last counter attack made by the Germans in the Second World War was called the Battle of the Bulge.

2 Napoleon was exiled for the last six years of his life, on Corsica.

3 Sir Francis Drake commanded the British forces at Trafalgar.

4 Martin Luther was required to attend the Diet of Frogs in 1521.

5 Until the building of the Eiffel Tower, the Great Pyramid in Egypt was the world's tallest building.

6 The last execution of a witch in England took place in 1712.

7 A trireme is a type of ancient Greek chariot.

8 Tax on windows was abolished in 1851.

9 President Kennedy was assassinated in 1865 while at the theatre.

10 New Zealand was the first country to give women the vote.

Your majesty

449

Kids 7–11   A round of royal riddles

1 Which queen of England never married?

2 Which king of England had six wives?

3 Who was the first British monarch to travel by train?

4 Who was crowned queen in 1953 live on TV?

5 Who lost the Battle of Hastings in 1066?

6 Which crusading king was said to have 'the heart of a lion'?

7 In which country have there been 18 kings called Louis?

8 Who was the queen in Ancient Britain who fought against the Romans?

9 What is the name of Queen Elizabeth II's husband?

10 What is the name of the palace in London where the British royal family now lives?

Random round

450

Kids 12–14 A mixed round of history questions

1 Revolutionaries stormed the Bastille in Paris in 1789, but what was the Bastille?

2 In 1914 the Panama Canal linked which oceans?

3 What did Cornishman Richard Trevithick invent in 1803 which transformed transport?

4 Against which country did Britain and her allies go to war in the Crimea in 1854?

5 Where was de Valera President of the Dail?

6 What name was given to the Protestant people who favoured plain styles of dress and led lives of strict morality?

7 What was the uprising by agricultural workers led by Wat Tyler in June 1381?

8 In what year was the last Viking attack on Britain: 874, 903, 1066?

9 What important document was signed in Runnymede in the 13th century?

10 What nickname was given to the soldiers who fought for the parliamentary side in the English Civil War?

Villains

451

Kids 7–11 Criminals through the ages

1 What kind of villain was Dick Turpin, who, the story goes, rode his horse from London to York to escape the law?

2 In which country did Ned Kelly live with a gang of outlaws in the bush?

3 Which outlaw, according to legend, lived in Sherwood Forest?

4 In the wild west, what did rustlers steal?

5 Whose effigy is burnt on the 5th of November when remembering the 'Gunpowder Plot'?

6 In the wild west, who ended up in Boot Hill?

7 What grim flag did pirates fly?

8 In which country were Jesse James and Billy the Kid wanted men?

9 What valuables did Captain Blood try to steal from the Tower of London in 1671?

10 In which US city did the Capone gang rule in the 1920s?

Britain's rulers

452

Kids 12–14 The people who were at the top

1 Who was Britain's last Catholic monarch?

2 Which king of England was beheaded in 1649?

3 Which ruler of England called himself the Lord Protector?

4 Who was the father of Queen Mary and Queen Elizabeth I?

5 Who was the only British king to abdicate?

6 Which tapestry depicts the events surrounding William the Conqueror's invasion of England?

7 Which queen of England ruled for just nine days in 1553?

8 What king of England was also the first to be king of Scotland too?

9 Which king could speak almost no English, only German, on taking the throne?

10 Who was the last Tudor monarch?

History

The Romans
453
Kids 7–11   How much do you know about ancient Rome?

1 How were soldiers of the Roman army commonly known?

2 Who was the first Roman emperor?

3 What language did the Romans speak?

4 Where is Hadrian's wall?

5 How many cohorts were there in a Roman legion?

6 In roman numerals, what does M stand for?

7 Where did Hannibal come from?

8 Was a scutum a shield, a sword, or a lance?

9 What did the Romans call Britain?

10 Of what was Saturn the god?

Four at a time
454
Kids 12–14   All the answers are four-letter words

1 Which canal, completed in 1869, links the Mediterranean Sea to the Red Sea?

2 In the Gulf War, what kind of weapons were *Abrams*, *Challenger* and *T-55s*?

3 Ayatollah Khomeini was the spiritual leader of which Middle Eastern state?

4 What does the A stand for in 'A Bomb'?

5 Which South African settlers did Britain fight?

6 By what name did the Romans call the region comprising modern-day France and parts of Belgium, western Germany, and northern Italy?

7 Which African army attacked the British in 1879 at Isandhlwana, killing 800 British soldiers?

8 Egbert, who died in 839, is generally agreed to be England's first what?

9 Which part of the divided Germany was ruled by the Communist Party until 1990?

10 Which currency became official tender in 12 countries of Europe on January 1, 2002?

Animal antics
455
Kids 7–11   History that wasn't made by humans

1 With what animals did Hannibal cross the Alps?

2 Which mythical animal was the symbol of ancient Wessex, Wales and China?

3 Which ancient people mummified their cats?

4 Which rodent is blamed for spreading the black death throughout Europe?

5 Which hopping animal astonished Captain Cook and his crew when they saw them?

6 Which country adopted the Bald Eagle as its national symbol?

7 One of the treasures in Tutankhamun's tomb shows the Egyptian king hunting large flightless birds in the desert. What birds were they?

8 In the Middle Ages, what kind of animals were only kings allowed to hunt?

9 What kind of animals did the cavalry ride into war?

10 What sort of dog was used by Captain Scott on his ill-fated polar expedition?

Battles

456

Kids 12-14 **A round all about combat**

1 The years 1775 to 1781 saw which British colony win its independence?

2 Which Southeast Asian war was fought between 1964 and 1975?

3 What colour rose did the Yorkists wear during England's War of the Roses?

4 By what name was the quiet period that immediately followed the declaration of war in 1939 known?

5 Who did Gavrilo Princip assassinate in Sarajevo in 1914, so triggering the First World War?

6 What war did Britain fight against South African settlers between 1899 and 1902?

7 In which war were British and Allied servicemen rescued from Dunkirk beaches?

8 Which country was wracked by civil war between 1861 and 1865?

9 What awesome weapon was used twice to bring the Second World War to a close?

10 In which war did the Battle of Tannenberg take place?

Recent events

457

Kids 7-11 **History, but only just**

1 What war was fought between 1914 and 1918, mainly in Europe?

2 Who was the leader of Nazi Germany, who led the country to war in 1939?

3 Who preceded Tony Blair as prime minister of Britain?

4 With which country did Britain go to war over the Falkland Islands?

5 What did John Logie Baird give the first demonstration of in 1926?

6 How was the heavy German bombing of British cities during the Second World War known?

7 Which European monarch celebrated her Golden Jubilee in 2002?

8 Who was the leader of Iraq during the 1991 Gulf War?

9 How many female prime ministers did Britain have in the 20th century?

10 In which war were *V1* and *V2* flying rockets used?

ABC of history

458

Kids 12-14 **Every answer begins with either A, B or C**

1 What name is given to the government department that controls the British Navy?

2 What name is given to the study of objects dug up from the past?

3 What name was given to the fleet of ships sent by Spain to defeat the British Navy under Elizabeth I?

4 Which British general founded the Girl Guide movement?

5 What popular name was given to the medieval plague epidemics?

6 What name was given to Sunday January 30, 1972, when 13 Catholics were killed by the British Army in Derry, Northern Ireland?

7 During which 1940 battle did *Hurricanes* and *Spitfires* pursue *Me109s* and *Dorniers*?

8 Which country's capital is Ottawa?

9 What name is given to the ceremony involving the crowning of a king or queen?

10 Who was the king at the time of the English Civil War?

History

459 Mixed bag
Kids 7–11 A lucky dip of history questions

1 Which came first: the Iron Age or the Bronze Age?

2 On which river was Rome built?

3 Which king was killed at the Battle of Hastings?

4 In which war was the Battle of the Somme?

5 Who was married to Queen Victoria?

6 How many female presidents of the United States were there during the 20th century?

7 Who flies in *Air Force One*?

8 What was a Penny Black?

9 Which volcano erupted destroying the Roman town of Pompeii?

10 Who invented dynamite?

460 World leaders
Kids 12–14 Presidents, kings and despots

1 Who was the wartime Fascist leader of Italy who was executed and hanged upside down?

2 Who was the first prime minister and, later president, of Zimbabwe when the country gained independence in 1980?

3 Mao Zedong ruled which Communist country from 1949 until his death in 1976?

4 Who was the leader of the Soviet Union at the end of the Second World War?

5 Who was Britain's prime minister from 1940 to the end of the Second World War?

6 Who was the first black president of South Africa?

7 Who was president of the United States before Bill Clinton?

8 Who was the first president of the United States of America?

9 Helmut Köhl was the first leader of which reunified country?

10 Who became president of Russia on the resignation of Boris Yeltsin in 1999?

461 All in the past
Kids 7–11 An assortment of questions from history

1 Which nurse of the Crimean War was known as 'the lady of the lamp'?

2 Which king of England founded the Church of England?

3 Who brought back tobacco from the New World in the 16th century?

4 Which British engineer designed the Clifton suspension bridge in Bristol as well as the SS *Great Britain* and SS *Great Eastern*?

5 Which British religious figure, known as the venerable, was born in Northumbria, in 672?

6 Which country used aircraft called Zero in the Second World War?

7 According to the legend, which historical figure 'burned the cakes'?

8 On what material, beginning with P, did the ancient Egyptians write?

9 During the Second World War, what kind of military vehicle were Shermans and Tigers?

10 Which mythical British king held his court at Camelot?

Quizzes

462–564

MUSIC

Music

Top of the pops
462
LEVEL 1   An easy round of mixed music questions

1 In which film did Robert Carlyle strip to the sound of Hot Chocolate's 'You Sexy Thing'?

2 Name Tina Turner's first husband.

3 George Michael had his first No. 1 hit as a member of which group?

4 Who was the only member of The Monkees to be born in Britain?

5 Which Aberdeen-born singer was lead vocalist in The Eurythmics?

6 According to Benny Hill, who was the fastest milkman in the West?

7 Which band, fronted by Boy George, had a No. 1 hit with the song 'Karma Chameleon'?

8 Who is the only female singer to be managed by Brian Epstein and who became a TV presenter on *Blind Date* and *Surprise Surprise*?

9 Who wrote the lyrics for the stage musicals, *Evita* and *Jesus Christ Superstar*?

10 Which country and western singer's autobiography is entitled *The Rhinestone Cowboy*?

Sing something simple
463
LEVEL 1   Keeping it easy

1 Which former front man for The Police married Trudie Styler in 1992?

2 The Cliff Richard stage musical *Heathcliff* was based on which novel?

3 Under what name did Yusef Islam sing 'Morning has Broken' in 1972?

4 What character did Val Kilmer play in the 1991 film *The Doors*?

5 Errol Browne was which group's lead singer?

6 Which instrumental album by Mike Oldfield made Richard Branson his first million?

7 Noddy Holder was the lead singer of which rock group?

8 To which leading composer of popular musicals was Sarah Brightman once married?

9 In which country was heart-throb singer Sacha Distel born?

10 What was the 1950s singing star Johnny Ray famous for doing on stage?

Musical connections
464
LEVEL 1   Easy links

1 Boyzone had a hit with 'Love Me for a Reason'. Which boy band had a hit with it in 1974?

2 Crispian Mills, once the singer in the group Kula Shaker, is the son of which actress?

3 What colour precedes Hot Chili Peppers and follows Simply to make the names of two groups?

4 Which Birmingham group's name is often abbreviated to ELO?

5 How many Spice Girls remained following the departure of Geri Halliwell?

6 Who performed three James Bond themes, including *Goldfinger*?

7 On what was Otis Redding sitting in the 1968 charts?

8 Name the David Bowie song that contains the line 'Ground control to Major Tom'.

9 What surname is shared by singers called Howard, Grace, Aled, Quincy, Paul and Tom?

10 Name the guitarist who connects the groups The Faces and The Rolling Stones.

Pop classics

465

LEVEL 1   Questions on essential pop

1 From which city did the two male members of Abba hail?

2 Name the group that Lionel Richie left to pursue a solo career.

3 Which new kids were the first to score eight UK top ten entries in a year?

4 Which group was formed by Mark Knopfler in 1977?

5 Name the country and western star who founded the group First Edition in 1967.

6 Who is the lead singer of REM?

7 Which rock group's career was revived when it collaborated with rappers Run DMC on the 1986 song 'Walk this Way'?

8 Who formed Public Image Ltd after the break up of The Sex Pistols?

9 Susanna Hoffs fronted which all-girl group?

10 Which organisation provided The Shadows with a February 1961 hit single?

Names and tunes

466

LEVEL 1   Well-known people from the world of music

1 Which supermodel appeared in the video for the Billy Joel hit 'Uptown Girl'?

2 Name the writer of the song 'Blue Suede Shoes' who died in 1998.

3 For whom did Neil Sedaka write the song 'Oh Carol'?

4 Which rocker caused a scandal when he married his 13-year-old cousin in 1957?

5 Who wrote the song 'Nothing Compares 2 U', a hit for Sinead O'Connor?

6 Which member of The Eagles charted with the song 'The Boys of Summer' in 1985?

7 Who took a walk on the wild side in 1973?

8 What was the title of the bestselling debut album of Alanis Morissette?

9 Which surname connects The Monkees, The Clash and The Rolling Stones?

10 What is the connection between a Red Indian, an American policeman, a construction worker, a cowboy, a GI and a biker?

Music challenge

467

LEVEL 3   Tough fun for pop afficionados

1 Which song was a hit in the 1960s for The Ronettes and in the 1980s for The Ramones?

2 Who was nicknamed 'the king of skiffle'?

3 What do the initials EMI stand for?

4 Which song from *Joseph and the Technicolor Dreamcoat* was a UK No. 1 hit for Jason Donovan?

5 Who is Kurt Cobain's widow?

6 Which famous all-girl group were originally called The Primettes?

7 What song was released by The Rolling Stones as a tribute to the ex-wife of David Bowie?

8 Which 1973 hit for Elton John shares its name with a book of the Bible?

9 In which year did Freddie Mercury die?

10 Which Scottish band was fronted by Jim Kerr?

Music

Mix 'n' match
468

LEVEL 1   A medley of music questions

1 Which all girl group had a hit in 1989 with 'Eternal Flame'?

2 What nationality is the singer Demis Roussos?

3 In which decade did cassette tapes first go on sale?

4 Who, nicknamed 'king of the crooners', died on a Spanish golf course in 1977?

5 Who provided lead vocals for The Who?

6 Who left The Equals to have solo hits with 'Electric Avenue' and 'I Don't Wanna Dance'?

7 According to Rolf Harris, two little boys had two little toys. Each had a wooden what?

8 Which cartoon family had a 1991 hit with 'Do the Bartman'?

9 Which seafaring song, a huge hit for Rod Stewart in 1975, was written by Gavin Sutherland?

10 In the Paul Simon song '50 Ways to Leave your Lover', who didn't need to be coy?

Family favourites
469

LEVEL 1   Questions for all ages

1 In the song 'Twelve Days of Christmas', which birds are swimming?

2 For which country did Johnny Logan twice win the Eurovision Song Contest?

3 'Seven little girls sitting on the back seat, hugging and kissing with' who?

4 How many valves does a trumpet have?

5 Robert Plant was the lead singer with which group that recorded 'Stairway to Heaven'?

6 Who did Ron Moody play in the film musical *Oliver*?

7 What name is given to half a quaver?

8 Who was backed by The Blockheads when singing 'Hit Me With Your Rhythm Stick'?

9 What river did Gerry and the Pacemakers take the ferry across?

10 Who played Professor Higgins in the film musical *My Fair Lady* when Audrey Hepburn played Eliza Dolittle?

Pop posers
470

LEVEL 3   Put your music knowledge to the test

1 Which French composer released the album *Oxygène* in 1976?

2 What is the connection between the singer Tom Jones and the TV programme *The Equaliser*?

3 The REM hit 'Man on the Moon' was inspired by which actor and comedian?

4 What was Abba's only No. 1 hit in the USA?

5 What was Ray Charles' only UK No. 1?

6 Sting's hit 'An Englishman in New York' was a song about whom?

7 Who was the first artist to have a posthumous No. 1 hit in the UK?

8 Which group took their name from the Gaelic word for 'family'?

9 Which famous soul singer won the American amateur Golden Gloves welterweight boxing title in 1950?

10 Who is the only singer to have recorded No. 1 hit singles in the UK over five different decades?

Colour my world

471

LEVEL 2   Every question is linked to a colour

1 Which singer released an album, a single and starred in a film called *Purple Rain*?

2 Tony Iommi, Geezer Butler, Bill Ward and Ozzy Osbourne were founder members of which heavy metal group?

3 Which Pink Floyd album cover featured an illustration of a prism?

4 What did Priscilla White change her name to?

5 Which anti-drugs song was released in 1984 by Grandmaster Flash, Melle Mel and the Furious Five?

6 Which rocker had a hit with 'Purple Haze' in 1967?

7 In 1953, who charted with the song 'She Wore Red Feathers'?

8 Which deep-voiced soul icon acquired the nickname of the 'walrus of love'?

9 Jack Bruce, Eric Clapton and Ginger Baker formed which group?

10 Who invented medicinal compound?

Country roads

472

LEVEL 2   Both sorts of music: country and western

1 Which country singer starred in the films *9 to 5* and *Steel Magnolias*?

2 Which country star had hits with 'Welcome to my World' and 'I Love you Because'?

3 Who played country singer Loretta Lynn in the film *Coal Miner's Daughter*?

4 Whose autobiography is entitled *Stand By Your Man*?

5 Who sang about a boy named Sue?

6 'Coward of the County' was a transatlantic hit for which country legend?

7 Who recorded the bestselling album *Come On Over* in 1997?

8 Who wrote the song 'Crazy', a hit for Patsy Cline?

9 Which country and western star appeared alongside John Wayne in the film *True Grit*?

10 Who wrote the song 'Take me Home Country Roads'?

Sounds of the seventies

473

LEVEL 2   Remember flares the first time around?

1 Whose first UK No. 1 as a solo artist was entitled 'I'm Still Waiting'?

2 Who duetted with Elton John on the 1976 hit 'Don't go Breaking my Heart'?

3 Which 1977 hit contains the line 'Four hungry children and a crop in the field'?

4 Which Scottish comedian enjoyed a 1975 hit with a cover version of the Tammy Wynette song 'D.I.V.O.R.C.E.'?

5 Which pop trio were 'Walking on the Moon' in 1979?

6 Name the Canadian singer who enjoyed a worldwide hit with the song 'Seasons in the Sun' in 1974.

7 Who managed The Sex Pistols?

8 What was the first No. 1 to feature bagpipes?

9 Brian Connolly was the lead singer with which glam rock group?

10 Name the French singer who released the song 'She' in 1974.

Music

Girls, girls, girls
474
LEVEL 1   Singers and their songs

1 Which singer was born Mary O'Brien in 1939 and died of cancer in 1999?

2 Which disco diva sang 'I Feel Love' in 1977?

3 Who is the female lead vocalist with The Pretenders?

4 Which singer, born in St Kitts in the West Indies, released an album entitled *Me, Myself, I* in 1980?

5 Who duetted with Kenny Rogers on the song 'Islands in the Stream'?

6 Which Spice Girl collaborated with Bryan Adams on the song 'When you're Gone'?

7 Which singer was born in 1898 in the Lancashire town of Rochdale and died in 1979 on the island of Capri?

8 Cerys Matthews led which Welsh band?

9 For which singer did Bacharach and David write the song 'Do you Know the Way to San José'?

10 Which sister of Kylie sang 'This is it' in 1993?

Classical music quiz
475
LEVEL 1   How well do you know the classics?

1 Which of the following was composed by Aram Khachaturian: 'The Foil Dance', 'The Sabre Dance' or 'The Epée Dance'?

2 Who was known as 'the waltz king'?

3 What year provides the title of the overture composed by Tchaikovsky to commemorate the defeat of Napoleon?

4 Does the musical term *forte* mean loud or soft?

5 Which symphony by Beethoven was used in the Second World War because its opening four notes are similar to the Morse code for V?

6 Was Mozart born in Vienna or Salzburg?

7 Stradivarius is a famous maker of which musical instrument?

8 What is the highest singing female voice?

9 Which orchestra is sometimes referred to by the initials N.Y.P.O.?

10 What name is given to the principal female singer in an opera?

Duos
476
LEVEL 3   It takes two

1 Which actor duetted with Barbra Streisand on the 1988 hit 'Till I Loved You'?

2 Which duo split up in 1973 and got back together for a Royal Albert Hall concert on September 23, 1983?

3 Who originally recorded under the name of Tom and Jerry?

4 Which duo accompanied Cher on her 1994 re-release of 'I got you Babe'?

5 Who has sung duets on hit records with Elton John, Aretha Franklin and Toby Bourke?

6 Which father and daughter sang 'Somethin' Stupid' in 1967?

7 What was the nationality of Esther and Abi Ofarim who, in 1968, sang 'Cinderella Rockefella'?

8 Who collaborated with Marvin Gaye on the 1969 hit 'The Onion Song'?

9 Which 1981 film theme was a hit for Diana Ross and Lionel Richie?

10 What did Jennifer Warnes and Joe Cocker sing for the film *An Officer and a Gentleman*?

477 Opening lines
LEVEL 2   Which pop songs begin with the following lyrics?

1 'There is a house in New Orleans'

2 'We don't need no education, we don't need no thought control'

3 'You can tell by the way I use my walk, I'm a woman's man'

4 'Your Momma says that through the week you can't go out with me'

5 'A long long time ago when I can still remember how that music used to make me smile'

6 'We're caught in a trap, I can't walk out'

7 'Why do birds suddenly appear every time you are near'

8 'In the town where I was born, lived a man who sailed to sea'

9 'I feel it in my fingers, I feel it in my toes'

10 'The minute you walked in the joint, I could see you were a man of distinction'

478 The fab four
LEVEL 2   The Beatles – who else?

1 Who was the first of The Beatles to become a grandfather?

2 On which record label did The Beatles have their first hit?

3 Who was the first Beatle to have a solo No. 1 hit single?

4 Which American city is mentioned in the first line of the hit 'Back in the USSR'?

5 What was the title of The Beatles debut album?

6 Which Beatles song starts with the line 'Picture yourself in a boat on a river'?

7 The front cover of which Beatles album features the group walking across a zebra crossing?

8 What is the first name of John Lennon's first wife?

9 Who did Ringo Starr replace as drummer?

10 In what year did The Beatles manager Brian Epstein die?

479 Classical capers
LEVEL 3   Questions for the music buffs

1 Who composed the opera *Don Giovanni*?

2 How is Dvorak's *Symphony No. 9* better known?

3 Who composed the classical music on which the pop song 'A Whiter Shade of Pale' was based?

4 The Duke of Mantua is a character from which opera?

5 Which opera is set aboard the HMS *Indomitable*?

6 Who composed the *Peer Gynt Suites*?

7 What is the title of Beethoven's only opera?

8 Who composed *The Blue Danube Waltz*?

9 What is the alternative name for Bach's *Air from Suite No. 3*?

10 What does the musical direction *rallentando* signify?

Music

480 The royal family
LEVEL 1   Every question has a regal connection

1 Who had a hit with the song 'Stand by Me' in 1961 and 1987?

2 Which controversial song by The Sex Pistols was banned by the BBC in 1977?

3 Was Duke Ellington a famous pianist, saxophonist or guitarist?

4 Mercury, Taylor and May. Who is missing from the line-up of the pop group Queen?

5 Who, despite suffering from cancer at the time, sang his way through the film *Cat Ballou*?

6 Which 1965 hit opens with the line: 'Trailer for sale or rent'?

7 Who was nicknamed 'the king of swing'?

8 What was the title of the first hit single for Dire Straits?

9 Which song from the film *Robin Hood, Prince of Thieves* was a worldwide smash for Bryan Adams?

10 Which American-born vocalist had a 1965 hit with the song 'Princess in Rags'?

481 Can we talk?
LEVEL 2   It's all in the words

1 Which song contains the line 'I'm never going to dance again, guilty feet have got no rhythm'?

2 Who was the lead singer of Talking Heads?

3 Which one-word song title has been a hit for Lulu and Tears for Fears?

4 Which New Romantic group, with lead vocals by Tony Hadley, enjoyed a 1983 hit with the song 'Communication'?

5 Who had his first UK No. 1 hit for 11 years with the 1979 song 'We Don't Talk Anymore'?

6 Which larger-than-life vocalist sang 'You Took the Words Right out of my Mouth' in 1978?

7 Who let out a 'Rebel Yell' in 1985?

8 The song 'Happy Talk' featured in which 1958 musical?

9 According to Elton John in 1976, what seemed to be the hardest word?

10 Who, born in 1915, was nicknamed 'the voice'?

482 Family affairs
LEVEL 3   Keeping it in the family

1 The singer Dionne Warwick has an equally famous singing cousin. Who is she?

2 When the three brothers were performing in The Bee Gees which one was the youngest?

3 What is the name of Loretta Lynn's singing sister?

4 Siblings Jim, Caroline, Andrea and Sharon make up which group?

5 Which son of a Beatle sang the song 'Saltwater'?

6 Sisters Nancy and Ann Wilson were founder members of which rock band?

7 The Sister Sledge hit 'Frankie' was a tribute to who?

8 Who sang about a 'mother and child reunion' in 1972?

9 Which song contains the line 'I've made up my mind, I'm keeping my baby'?

10 Which 1973 hit for The Temptations could possibly have been sung by Jade Jagger?

Sweet music

 **483**

LEVEL 2   Who recorded these 'sweet songs' in the given years?

1 'Sweet Caroline', 1981.

2 'I Get the Sweetest Feeling', 1972.

3 'Sweet Dreams (are Made of This)', 1983.

4 'Sweet Little Mystery', 1987.

5 'Sweets for my Sweet', 1994.

6 'Sweets for my Sweet', 1963.

7 'Sweet Nothings', 1960.

8 'Sweet Child O' Mine', 1988.

9 'Sweet Soul Music', 1967.

10 'Sweet Little Sixteen', 1958.

Echoes of the eighties

 **484**

LEVEL 2   A decade of memories

1 Which Australian band had a worldwide hit in 1983 with the song 'Down Under'?

2 What was the title of the song that Whitney Houston recorded for the 1988 Olympics?

3 Which 1980 hit for Blondie was the theme song for the film *American Gigolo*?

4 In which year was the USA for Africa charity single 'We are the World' released?

5 Which 1980s song contained the line: 'Some people might say my life is in a rut'?

6 Which song, originally a hit for Bread, was covered by Boy George in 1987?

7 Which film director had a 1984 hit with 'The Hitler Rap'?

8 Which 1986 hit for Diana Ross was written by The Bee Gees?

9 What was the title of the 1985 hit which saw David Bowie harmonising with Mick Jagger?

10 What was the title of the John Lennon album that was in the charts at the time of his death?

Backing groups

 **485**

LEVEL 3   Which singers performed with the following backing bands?

1 The Attractions.

2 The Vagabonds.

3 The Famous Flames.

4 The Dreamers.

5 The Union Gap.

6 The E Street Band.

7 The Plastic Population.

8 The Spiders from Mars.

9 The Heartbreakers.

10 The Blackhearts.

Music

Sing a rainbow
486
LEVEL 1 Find the links between questions and colours

1 Which Manchester group were 'Holding Back the Years' in 1986?

2 Which thoroughfare provided Elton John with a 1973 hit album title?

3 Which rock band released the albums *Machine Head* and *Burn*?

4 Name the vocalist who charted with the song 'Never Let Her Slip Away' in 1978.

5 Syd Barratt left which rock band in 1968?

6 What kind of vehicle did Natalie Cole drive up the charts in 1988?

7 What nationality are the members of the rock band Tangerine Dream?

8 In which song did The Rolling Stones ask the question: 'How come you taste so good'?

9 What was blue in the title of the 1961 hit for The Marcels?

10 According to Eddie Cochran, 'there ain't no cure for. . .' what?

Ten steps to heaven
487
LEVEL 1 An angelic chorus

1 According to the song 'Three Steps to Heaven', what is step one?

2 Who, according to The Eurythmics, 'was playing with my heart'?

3 Which American disco group charted with the song 'Heaven Must be Missing an Angel' in 1976?

4 Which song, a hit for Maria McKee, was the theme for the film *Days of Thunder*?

5 Which band was founded by Glenn Gregory after he left The Human League?

6 Who was the father of Paula Yates' child Heavenly Hirani Tiger Lily?

7 Which British band released the song 'Heaven Knows I'm Miserable Now' in 1984?

8 The Gabrielle hit song 'Rise' sampled which Bob Dylan classic?

9 Which former Go-Go had a solo hit with the song 'Heaven is a Place on Earth'?

10 Which Led Zeppelin classic was covered by The Far Corporation and Rolf Harris?

The sailing set
488
LEVEL 2 Don't be all at sea in this musical round

1 Which Gilbert and Sullivan opera was subtitled 'The Lass that Loved a Sailor'?

2 Which 1959 hit for Marty Wilde shared its title with a 1989 film starring Al Pacino?

3 What was the title of the theme song sung by Celine Dion for the film *Titanic*?

4 What was the name of the sailing vessel that provided The Beach Boys with a 1966 hit?

5 Which British rocker released the album *Atlantic Crossing* in 1975?

6 The seafaring opera *Billy Budd* was based on a story by which author?

7 Which song-writing duo wrote the song 'Trains, Boats and Planes'?

8 Which European port provided the title of a 1996 hit for The Beautiful South?

9 Which group caught a 'Night Boat to Cairo' in 1980?

10 Which 1951 musical starring Howard Keel was set on the Mississippi River?

Name that musical

489

Can you identify the musicals shown here?

Music

490 Love songs
LEVEL 2   Name the artists or groups with hits in these years

1 'Love to Love You Baby', 1975.

2 'Love of the Common People', 1983.

3 'Love is the Drug', 1975.

4 'Love Shack', 1990.

5 'Love on the Rocks', 1980.

6 'Love Me For a Reason', 1974.

7 'Love Letters in the Sand', 1957.

8 'Love Don't Live Here Anymore', 1978.

9 'Love is all Around', 1967.

10 'Love Shine a Light', 1997.

491 Albums
LEVEL 2   Classics on vinyl – or CD

1 Name George Michael's debut solo album.

2 The album cover for the The Velvet Underground and Nico featured a banana image by which popular artist?

3 Which band's logo was a stuck-out tongue?

4 Name the two albums by Queen that were named after Marx Brothers films.

5 What was the title of the greatest hits collection released by Madonna in 1990?

6 Which trio's greatest hits collection features the songs, 'Run to Me', 'Nights on Broadway' and 'You Should be Dancing'?

7 Who received a Grammy for the 1979 album *52nd Street*?

8 What is the title of the 1995 album by Oasis that featured the song 'Wonderwall'?

9 Which album cover features Michael Jackson leaning on a wall wearing a tuxedo?

10 'Hello' and 'All Night Long' were singles taken from which Lionel Richie album?

492 Marriage lines
LEVEL 3   When you might hear the 'Wedding March'

1 Which band featured the husband and wife, John and Christine McVie (née Perfect)?

2 Which star of the film *Absolute Beginners* married and split from Liam Gallagher?

3 Renate Blauel married which pop singer on Valentine's Day 1984?

4 The actress Carrie Fisher is the ex-wife of which singer, one half of a famous duo?

5 Who did Michael Jackson marry in 1996?

6 In 2001, Michael Jackson was best man at the wedding of which illusionist?

7 Which member of Bananarama married Dave Stewart?

8 Which pop singer married the actor Emilio Estevez in 1992?

9 Who left her husband Bob Geldof for Michael Hutchence?

10 Which model became Rod Stewart's second wife?

Elton enigmas

493 **LEVEL 1 Questions about one of pop music's greats**

1 Which single overtook Bing Crosby's 'White Christmas' as the biggest-selling single in 1997?

2 Which female singer collaborated with Elton on the 1999 hit 'Written in the Stars'?

3 For which film did Elton perform the song 'Can you Feel the Love Tonight'?

4 Which song contains the line: 'If I was a sculptor, but then again no'?

5 Which operatic tenor collaborated with Elton John on the 1996 hit 'Live Like Horses'?

6 Who did Elton want to kiss, according to the title of a 1983 hit?

7 What was the full title of Elton John's third album that began 'Don't shoot me'?

8 Which song, released in 1974, was re-released by Elton John with George Michael in 1991?

9 With which football club has Elton John had a long association?

10 Who accompanied 'The Jets' in the title of a 1976 Elton John hit?

Stars on celluloid

494 **LEVEL 1 Name the film stars who sang the following songs in these films**

1 'If I Were a Rich Man', *Fiddler On The Roof.*

2 'Wandrin' Star', *Paint Your Wagon.*

3 'Getting to Know You', *The King and I.*

4 'Edelweiss', *The Sound of Music.*

5 'I'm Every Woman', *The Bodyguard.*

6 'You've got to Pick a Pocket or Two', *Oliver.*

7 'Moon River', *Breakfast at Tiffany's.*

8 'Spread a Little Happiness', *Brimstone and Treacle.*

9 'Maybe this Time', *Cabaret.*

10 'Sandy', *Grease.*

Madonna mania

495 **LEVEL 1 How much do you know about the queen of pop?**

1 The video for which Madonna hit featured her writhing on a Venetian gondola?

2 Who married Madonna on her 26th birthday?

3 What was the title of the controversial book, released in 1992, that featured naked photographs of Madonna?

4 What was Madonna's surname at birth?

5 Name the 1998 album on which Madonna collaborated with William Orbit.

6 In which country did Madonna marry film director Guy Ritchie?

7 Which song, a hit for Madonna in 1996, was originally a hit for Julie Covington in 1976?

8 Was Madonna born in Michigan, Maryland or Mississippi?

9 For which 2002 James Bond film did Madonna sing the title track?

10 Mike Myers featured in the video for which 1999 Madonna hit?

Music

496 Banging the drum
LEVEL 2   A percussion round

1 Who played the drums for the pop group Queen?

2 Which famous pop star drummer played an underworld leader in the film *The Running Man*?

3 Which drummer pursued a solo career while still a member of *Genesis*?

4 The timpani is another name for what type of drum?

5 Did Karen or Richard Carpenter play the drums?

6 The song 'Distant Drums' was a 1966 posthumous hit for whom?

7 Which member of the rock trio Emerson, Lake and Palmer played the drums?

8 What is a paradiddle?

9 Which drummer died on September 8, 1978?

10 Name the singing siblings who released a version of the song 'Little Drummer Boy' in 1959?

497 Uncle Sam
LEVEL 1   Sing your way round the USA

1 Which Alaskan city provided the title of a hit record for Michelle Shocked in 1988?

2 Which American group enjoyed a worldwide hit in 1976 with the song 'If you Leave me Now'?

3 How many hours from Tulsa was Gene Pitney in 1963?

4 What was the French title of the 1977 hit for Manhattan Transfer?

5 What was the title of the 1994 hit for Bruce Springsteen, also a Tom Hanks film?

6 Which American state featured in the title of a 1971 hit for Olivia Newton John?

7 Where was Tony Christie asking directions to in 1971?

8 According to Frank Sinatra, which is the 'city that never sleeps'?

9 Which song opens with the line 'All the leaves are brown and the sky is gray'?

10 Who had a 1974 hit with 'Annie's Song', a song that he wrote for his wife?

498 Heavy metals
LEVEL 3   Find the mineral connections

1 Richie Sambora is the lead guitarist with which New Jersey rock group?

2 James Hetfield provides the lead vocals for which heavy metal band?

3 Which one-word song title has been a hit record for Prince, Spandau Ballet and East 17?

4 Which rock band was formed by David Bowie in 1989?

5 Which actor sang about a silver lady in 1977?

6 'An Ordinary Copper' was the title of the theme music to which long-running British TV series?

7 Which heavy metal band, led by John Bush, shares its name with a disease that affects cattle and sheep?

8 Which song contains the line 'Gonna use my arms, gonna use my legs'?

9 Which singer and actor was born Thomas Hicks?

10 Which Goon had a hit with the song 'Any Old Iron' in 1957?

Match the letters

499 LEVEL 1 All 10 questions require two-word answers beginning with the same letter

1 Who had hits with the songs 'I Will Survive' and 'I am What I am'?

2 Which singer played the role of Aunt Entity in the film *Mad Max beyond Thunderdome*?

3 Which British composer wrote *The Young Person's Guide to the Orchestra*?

4 Who sang barefoot at the Eurovision Song Contest in 1967?

5 Who recorded the song 'The Best that You Can Do', the theme for the film *Arthur*?

6 Which singer and actress played the title role in the 1953 film *Calamity Jane*?

7 Under what name did the Philadelphia siblings Kathy, Debra and Joni record numerous hits?

8 Who was 'Doin' the Do' in 1990?

9 In 1989, who released the album *Rhythm Nation 1814*?

10 What was the name of the adolescent rap duo who had a huge hit with the song 'Jump' in 1992?

On the dark side

500 LEVEL 1 Questions with night-time associations

1 Who composed *Serenade No. 13 for Strings in G major*, also known as *Eine Kleine Nachtmusik*?

2 Who duetted with Roberta Flack on the 1983 hit 'Tonight I Celebrate my Love'?

3 According to Elton John, which night is all right for fighting?

4 How did The Beatles sleep in 'A Hard Day's Night'?

5 Who recorded the album *A Night at the Opera*?

6 Which 1977 film featured John Travolta as a Brooklyn disco dancer?

7 The song 'One Night in Bangkok' featured in which stage musical?

8 In 1982, which American group charted with the song 'A Night to Remember'?

9 Which group had a hit with the song 'Nights in White Satin' in 1967, 1972 and 1979?

10 Who composed the score for the musical *A Little Night Music*?

World affairs

501 LEVEL 3 Music around the globe

1 Which Rochdale lass charted with the song 'All Around the World' in 1989?

2 What musical featured the song 'If I Ruled the World'?

3 Who became the oldest singer to reach No. 1 with his song 'What a Wonderful World'?

4 Which Australian harmony group had a hit with the song 'A World of our Own' in 1965?

5 With which song did Status Quo open the 1985 Live Aid concert?

6 According to a Mark Wynter lyric, who is the eighth wonder of the world?

7 Which Birmingham band released the album *A New World Record* in 1976?

8 From which orchestral piece does the music that accompanies the cancan dance derive?

9 Which group claimed that they would like to teach the world to sing in 1971?

10 Which Disney animated film featured the song 'Part of Your World'?

Music

502 Musical roots

LEVEL 2 From which countries do the following singers and groups originate?

1 AC/DC

2 Julio Iglesias

3 Vanessa Paradis

4 Ace of Base

5 Boomtown Rats

6 Kiri Ti Kanawa

7 Simple Minds

8 Shaggy

9 A-Ha

10 Gloria Estefan

503 I feel like dancing

LEVEL 2 Foot-tapping time

1 Which group wanted to 'dance the night away' in 1998?

2 Which Little Eva hit began with the words: 'Everybody's doing a brand new dance now'?

3 Which actress is known for singing: 'I could have danced all night' in the film *My Fair Lady*?

4 Who was known as 'the waltz king'?

5 According to the lyrics, how old was Abba's dancing queen?

6 Which song has been a hit for The Isley Brothers, Salt-n-Pepa, The Tremeloes and Chaka Demus and Pliers?

7 Who sang 'You Make me Feel Like Dancing' in 1976?

8 Which American disco kings were in a 'Boogie Wonderland' in 1979?

9 What was the title of the album released by Michael Jackson in 1997?

10 Who backed Martha Reeves when she was 'Dancing in the Street' in 1964?

504 Keyboard clues

LEVEL 3 All these questions have a link with the piano

1 Which Motown legend charted with the song 'My Old Piano' in 1980?

2 Who is credited with playing the keyboards in The Beatles hit 'Get Back'?

3 Who invented the piano?

4 Who was nicknamed 'the king of ragtime'?

5 Which 1973 album by Elton John included the songs 'Daniel' and 'Crocodile Rock'?

6 Which pianist, who was a favourite of the Queen Mother, enjoyed 1950s hits with 'Side Saddle' and 'Roulette'?

7 Which 1982 hit record contained the line: 'Side by side on my piano keyboard'?

8 Which former boxer released the album *Piano Man* in 1973?

9 Which famous pianist played the part of a pianist in the 1949 film *East of Java*?

10 How is Beethoven's *Piano Sonata No. 14 in C Sharp Minor* more commonly known?

505 Music quest

Can you identify the songs that contain these lines?

1 'Mr Brown goes up to town on the 8:21.'

2 'They call her Natasha when she looks like Elsie ...'

3 'If you can't find a partner use a wooden chair.'

4 'They sprinkled moondust in your hair.'

5 'Just like the old man in that book by Nabokov.'

6 'Wim-o-weh, a-wim-o-weh, a-wim-o-weh, a-wim-o-weh, a-wim-o-weh, a-wim-o-weh, a-wim-o-weh.'

7 'Where can you learn to fly, play in sports or skindive, study oceanography?'

8 'My name is Sue. How do you do?'

9 'Told me love was too plebeian, Told me you were through with me and...'

10 'My parents treat me rough. With all their marijuana, they won't give me a puff.'

11 'Wir betreten feuertrunken himmlische dein Heiligtum.'

12 'The answer was here all the time: I love you and hope you love me.'

13 'Check out Guitar George, he knows all the chords.'

14 'It's the truth, it's actual! Everything is satisfactual.'

15 'One day maybe Fred will win the fight. Then that cat will stay out for the night.'

A clue to question 3

Music

The swinging sixties
506
LEVEL 2   Turn on, tune in and drop out

1   Who wrote the song 'I'm a Believer'?

2   Which rocker was found dead in a swimming pool on July 3, 1969?

3   Name the female lead vocalist of The Seekers.

4   Which 1963 hit written by Rodgers and Hammerstein and featured in the film *Carousel*, was unofficially adopted by Liverpool FC?

5   What was the name of Laura's lover in the song 'Tell Laura I Love Her'?

6   Which backing group for Cliff Richard had instrumental hits with 'Wonderful Land' and 'Foot Tapper'?

7   Who began life as The Quarrymen?

8   Which musical instrument was played by Acker Bilk on the hit 'Stranger on the Shore'?

9   In 1968, the Hugo Montenegro Orchestra had a hit with a film theme from which spaghetti western?

10 In 1968, who charted with the film theme from *Bonnie and Clyde*?

A concert of questions
507
LEVEL 2   A classical lucky dip

1   Which classical composer is buried in the same Parisian cemetery as rock star Jim Morrison?

2   How old was Amadeus Mozart when he gave his first performance, at Salzburg University?

3   What nationality was Georges Bizet, the composer of *Carmen*?

4   Who was George Gershwin's lyricist brother?

5   In which Wagner opera is a Dutch sea captain condemned by the devil to sail the seas forever?

6   By what five-letter name is the classical composer Giuseppe Uttini better known?

7   Who composed 'Land of Hope and Glory' and was appointed Master of the King's Music in 1924?

8   True or false: Johann Sebastian Bach fathered 30 children?

9   *Fingal's Cave Overture* was written by which 19th-century German composer?

10 In 1857, who founded a renowned orchestra based in Manchester?

Body beautiful
508
LEVEL 3   Songs about being human

1   Which song was a hit for Buddy Holly, Showaddywaddy and Nick Berry?

2   Which British female vocalist had a 1978 hit with the song 'Man With the Child in his Eyes'?

3   Who asked 'What Becomes of the Broken Hearted?' in 1966?

4   Who enquired 'Don't It Make Your Brown Eyes Blue'?

5   Where did The Sutherland Brothers wish they were lying in 1975?

6   Who helped to popularise line dancing with his 1992 hit 'Achy Breaky Heart'?

7   'The First Time Ever I Saw Your Face' was the debut hit for which female vocalist?

8   'Take that Look off Your Face' featured in which Andrew Lloyd Webber musical?

9   What was the title of Elvis Presley's first UK hit single?

10 Which Canadian-born singer had a 1950s hit with 'Put Your Head on my Shoulder'?

A musical mystery tour

509

LEVEL 1   Questions to keep you on the move

1 In which Mexican holiday resort were The Four Tops 'going loco' in 1988?

2 According to Gerard Kenny which American city was 'so good they named it twice'?

3 Which crooner won a Grammy for his rendition of 'I Left my Heart in San Francisco'?

4 Benny, Bjorn and Agnetha of Abba were all born in Sweden. In which neighbouring country was the fourth member, Frida, born?

5 Which controversial 1980s group had Holly Johnson as its front man?

6 The groups Oasis, The Smiths and The Hollies were all formed in which English city?

7 Which Beach Boys hit starts with the line: 'Well, East coast girls are hip, I really dig those styles they wear'?

8 Which daughter of a 1950s singing star had a hit with the song 'Kids in America' in 1981?

9 Who was 'Only 24 Hours from Tulsa'?

10 In which city is the musical *Oliver* set?

T Time

510

LEVEL 1   All the answers begin with the letter T

1 In which American state is Elvis Presley's Gracelands mansion?

2 What is the surname of the singer who had a 1999 hit with 'Man I Feel Like a Woman'?

3 Which five-letter word, derived from the Italian for 'time', indicates the speed at which a piece of music should be played?

4 Which five-letter word describes the singing voice of opera star Placido Domingo?

5 Which 1960s group had a hit with the song 'Silence is Golden' in 1967?

6 Which rock musical told the story of a pinball wizard?

7 What surname links the drummers of Duran, Duran and Queen?

8 How many Degrees sang 'When Will I See You Again'?

9 In which No. 1 hit did Spandau Ballet: 'Listen to Marvin all night long'?

10 In the name of the 1970s rock group T. Rex, what did the T originally stand for?

Back to the 1950s

511

LEVEL 3   Early days of rock and pop

1 Name the ex-wife of Roger Moore who sang 'I'm Walking Behind You' in 1953.

2 Name the leather-wearing rock and roller who was backed by The Blue Caps.

3 In 1952, who recorded the song 'Here in My Heart', recognised as the first No. 1 hit single?

4 Which actress played the title role in the 1958 film musical *Gigi*?

5 Which rocker was nicknamed 'the killer'?

6 What weight provided the title of a 1956 hit for Tennessee Ernie Ford?

7 Who as a teenager wrote and had a 1957 hit with the song 'Diana'?

8 Name the American vocalist who enjoyed 1950s hits with the songs 'Singing the Blues' and 'Heartaches by the Number'.

9 Under what name did Walden Robert Cassotto enjoy several hits in the 1950s and 1960s?

10 Who portrayed 1950s rocker Ritchie Valens in the 1987 film *La Bamba*?

Music

512 Cats and dogs
LEVEL 2   Find your pet subject

1 Which painter was the subject of 'Matchstalk Men and Matchstalk Cats and Dogs'?

2 Which female singer provided the vocals for an animated dog when singing 'He's a Tramp' in the film *Lady and the Tramp*?

3 Which song, originally a hit for Cat Stevens, was covered by Boyzone in 1995?

4 Which duo released the song 'The Boxer' in 1969?

5 Which female group had hits with the songs 'I'm so Excited' and 'Slowhand'?

6 Who sang the theme for the 1965 film *What's New Pussycat?*

7 What was the four-letter name of the American vocalist who sang 'Me and You and a Dog Named Boo' in 1971?

8 Who composed *The Pink Panther* theme?

9 Which Bangles hit was covered by the girl band Atomic Kitten?

10 Which fresh-faced teen pop star sang 'Puppy Love'?

513 Musical months
LEVEL 2   Airs for every season

1 Which Scottish singer had a hit with the song 'January, February' in 1980?

2 Which famous composer wrote *The Wedding March*?

3 What was the title of Rod Stewart's first UK No. 1 hit single?

4 The song 'June is Busting Out all Over' is featured in which musical?

5 What did August Darnell change his name to when he was playing with his coconuts?

6 Which disco group boogied their way up the charts with the song 'September' in 1978?

7 Who wrote and recorded the song 'It Might as Well Rain Until September'?

8 In 1981, which rock group released an album called *October*?

9 Which American rockers charted with the song 'November Rain' in 1992?

10 Which group, led by Frankie Valli, released a single entitled 'December 63' in 1976?

514 A dolly mixture
LEVEL 2   Dolls and dames

1 Which quartet had a hit with 'Rag Doll' in 1964?

2 Who was born Damon Vincent Furnier and became notorious for chopping up dolls in his stage act?

3 Which 1969 musical starring Barbra Streisand was based on a play called *The Matchmaker*?

4 Who had a hit with the film theme from *Valley of the Dolls* in 1968?

5 Who represented the UK in the Eurovision Song Contest singing 'Making Your Mind Up'?

6 David Johansen was the lead vocalist with which Manhattan-based rock group in the 1970s?

7 Name Cliff Richard's first UK No. 1 hit single.

8 Which group sang 'Barbie Girl' in 1997?

9 Which song contains the line: 'My momma told me if I was goody that she would buy me a rubber dolly'?

10 Frank Sinatra co-starred with Marlon Brando in which 1955 musical?

515 Name that year

LEVEL 2   Can you identify the year these No. 1 hits reached the top?

1 '(Everything I do) I do it For You', Bryan Adams.

2 'You're the One that I Want', John Travolta and Olivia Newton John.

3 'Wannabe', Spice Girls.

4 'Green Green Grass Of Home', Tom Jones.

5 'Stand and Deliver', Adam and the Ants.

6 'You'll Never Walk Alone', Gerry and the Pacemakers.

7 'Only You', Flying Pickets.

8 'These Boots are Made for Walking', Nancy Sinatra.

9 'Men in Black', Will Smith.

10 'Are Friends Electric?', Gary Numan.

516 The hills are alive

LEVEL 1   Ten questions on The Sound of Music

1 In which country was *The Sound of Music* set?

2 In the song 'Do-Re-Mi', what five words follow Mi?

3 What institution did Julie Andrews leave to become the nanny to the Von Trapp children?

4 What is the first name of the character played by Julie Andrews?

5 What naval rank did Baron Von Trapp, as played by Christopher Plummer, hold?

6 In what year was the film released?

7 According to a song in the film, how old was the oldest Von Trapp daughter?

8 Of the seven Von Trapp children, how many were boys?

9 In the song 'My Favourite Things', what colour are the paper packages that are tied up with string?

10 Christopher Plummer was quoted as saying: 'Working with Julie Andrews is like being hit over the head with' what sort of a card?

517 Building blocks

LEVEL 3   There are buildings in every question or answer

1 Name George Clooney's aunt who had a 1954 hit with the song 'This Ole House'.

2 The American female pop group The Dixie Cups sang about which romantic building in 1964?

3 Which musical featured the song 'Get me to the Church on Time'?

4 Which Swedish group assisted Tom Jones on the 1999 hit 'Burning Down the House'?

5 Tunde Baiyewu is the lead vocalist with which 'family'?

6 Which group sang about 'our house' in 1982?

7 According to The Eagles, where can you: 'check out anytime you like but you can never leave'?

8 Which bestselling 1970 album included the tracks 'El Condor Pasa' and 'Cecilia'?

9 How are Neil Tennant and Chris Lowe collectively known?

10 Which pop star played the character of Pink in the Pink Floyd film *The Wall*?

Music

518 Mothers and fathers
LEVEL 2   Meet the parents

1 Which song opens with the line 'When I find myself in times of trouble, Mother Mary comes to me'?

2 Who did Jimmy Boyd see Mommy kissing in a 1953 hit?

3 Who sang about 'Mother Nature and Father Time' in 1953?

4 What is the title of the West End musical featuring a variety of Abba songs?

5 What was the Spice Girls first hit in 1997?

6 Who had an instrumental hit in 1953 with 'Oh Mein Papa'?

7 What is the name of the priest in The Beatles hit 'Eleanor Rigby'?

8 Which group assisted Tom Jones on his 2000 hit 'Mama Told me not to Come'?

9 Who is the famous mother of the singer Lorna Luft?

10 Which children's characters from Belgium were assisted by Father Abraham in their early hits?

519 Elvis lives!
LEVEL 3   The one and only king of rock and roll

1 True or false, Elvis Presley was a twin?

2 What was the name of Elvis' tyrannical manager?

3 In which film did Elvis sing 'Return to Sender'?

4 What was the name of the record label on which Elvis first recorded in 1954?

5 What song did Elvis sing to the tune of 'O Sole Mio'?

6 What was the title of Elvis Presley's first UK hit single?

7 In which state was Elvis born?

8 Elvis joined the US Army in 1958 as Private 53310761. What rank was he when he left in 1960?

9 What was the title of the first film in which Presley starred?

10 What was the title of Elvis Presley's last UK No. 1 hit whilst he was still alive?

520 What's in a name?
LEVEL 3   Identify the groups from these clues

1 Which 'parental' group originally performed under the name of The New Journeymen?

2 Which pop group took their name from a character played by Robert de Niro in the film *Taxi Driver*?

3 Which rock group named themselves after an American spy plane?

4 Which pop group took their name from the title of a 1950 film starring Bette Davis?

5 To what did The New Yardbirds change their name after an observation by Keith Moon?

6 Who named themselves after the inventor of the seed drill?

7 Which Scottish group took their name from the Greek meaning 'From the womb'?

8 Which group, formed in 1965, took their name from a quote from the poet William Blake?

9 Which villain from the film *Barbarella* provided the name for a new romantic pop group?

10 Which group took their name from a 1984 film directed by Wim Wenders?

All that jazz

521

LEVEL 2   A round for cool cats

1 In which US city was jazz said to have originated in the 1890s?

2 What was the last name of the jazz great, known as 'duke', who died in 1974?

3 Which young cornet and trumpet player was discovered by King Oliver and went on to have chart hits such as 'What a Wonderful World'?

4 What was the name of the most famous jazz club in Harlem, and the title of a 1984 film?

5 Which band made the first jazz recording, in 1917?

6 Under what name did Mack Rebennack perform?

7 Of which instrument was the jazz great, Dizzy Gillespie, a virtuoso?

8 Which of the following is the name of a famous jazz musician: Pork Pie Hardy, Apple Pie Richards or Jelly Roll Morton?

9 What three-letter first name was given to the jazz legend whose last name was Beiderbecke?

10 What connects the jazz legend William Basie with the vampire novel by Bram Stoker?

Ol' blue eyes

522

LEVEL 1   How well do you know Sinatra?

1 Name the band of entertainers that included Sinatra, Dean Martin and Sammy Davis Jr.

2 Which Sinatra song has been covered by Dorothy Squires, Elvis Presley, Shane McGowan and The Sex Pistols?

3 Which Illinois town did Sinatra sing of in 1957?

4 Which daughter of Sinatra's went on to have four UK No. 1 hits between 1966 and 1971?

5 In what year did Sinatra die?

6 Which Hollywood actress released a version of the Sinatra song 'Somethin' Stupid' with Robbie Williams?

7 Which Irish rock singer performed a duet, 'I've Got you Under my Skin', with Sinatra?

8 In which 1988 animated film did Sinatra provide the voice for a singing sword picked up by Bob Hoskins?

9 Sinatra was married four times. To which wife was he married for the shortest time?

10 In which 1956 film did Sinatra star alongside Bing Crosby and Grace Kelly?

Question time

523

LEVEL 3   Who had hits asking the following questions in these years?

1 'Where do you go to my Lovely?', 1969.

2 'Why do Fools Fall in Love?', 1956.

3 'What's the Frequency, Kenneth?', 1994.

4 'What's Up?', 1993.

5 'When Will I be Loved?', 1960.

6 'Do you Really Want to Hurt Me?', 1982.

7 'Does Your Mother Know?', 1979.

8 'Who's Sorry Now?', 1958.

9 'What Have I Done to Deserve This?', 1987.

10 'When Will I be Famous?', 1987.

Quiz night out

Holding a quiz night as a big social event can be great fun and an excellent way of raising funds for a club, school or church: everyone loves the challenge of hauling some half-remembered fact to the front of their mind, and quizzes are always popular events. Follow this advice to give your quiz night a professional touch.

Running a formal quiz night — for fundraising or fun — requires more preparation and organisation than a casual affair for family or friends. Your first step is to find a venue. School halls, village halls and social clubs are all ideal. Pubs tend to be noisy and busy, and are less suitable, unless they have a separate room or you are planning an open-to-all-comers pub quiz.

To some people, the social element of a quiz night is as important as the competition, and players are more likely to want to enter as teams, than individuals. Once you have chosen a venue, consider how big the tables are and how many people will comfortably be able to sit around each one. This will help you to set a recommended or maximum team size: between four and eight people is a good number. You also need to know how many people your venue can hold, so that you can set a limit on the total number of entrants you allow.

Challenge the pub bore

Pubs are popular quiz venues, but require a different approach from the organiser. Publicise the start time, but be prepared for people to turn up on the night and want to join in, so copy plenty of answer sheets.

The key difference when organising a pub quiz is to keep it really simple. You will not be able to regulate the number of people in a team, so pitch the questions to make them suitable for single players or large groups. Avoid complicated questions — pub quizzers are notoriously argumentative — and remember that you will be competing with the noise of people who are not playing. Lastly, keep it short: five rounds, plus a music round and a table round should be plenty.

Get it all right on the night

You can help to create a sense of excitement on the evening by introducing bonus points, jokers, and high-scoring table rounds.

Fun and names

Encourage teams to choose names when they enter and use these to set up a scoresheet. It is also fun to try to invent a misleading or cryptic title for each round: *Short cuts* for a round about film quotes, say, or *Your round*, for questions all about drinks. Write the round titles on a set of answer sheets and put them on each table before the quiz starts, so that the teams can plan their strategy and try to pick a good round for playing their joker.

Double or drop

Jokers are a good way of adding an element of chance to a quiz. You can use the one supplied at the front of this book and photocopy it for each team, or ask teams to bring their own and give a prize for the best. Playing a joker doubles a team's score on that round, so teams need to plan their joker round carefully. The quizmaster should call for jokers to be played at the start of each round – before announcing what the round is about – and accept no late entries.

Take a break

If you are planning an evening quiz, you will need to provide some refreshment. Plan an interval half way through the evening to give people chance to stretch their legs and eat – it will also give the quizmaster a welcome break and allow his helpers to catch up with the marking if necessary.

Table rounds (see pages 344–345) are a good way to keep the quiz momentum going. Collect them at the end of the break, but don't mark the scores on the board until near the end of the quiz to keep teams guessing who is in the lead.

Timetable for a ten-round quiz

Organisation is the key to a successful event. Use this timetable as a guide to lead you up to and through the big day.

Three weeks before
- Book venue
- Check for availability of PA system
- Find out if the venue has a music licence. If not, contact licensing authorities (see page 248)
- Prepare and display posters
- Advertise in local papers

Two weeks before
- Start to write questions

One week before
- Organise answer sheets, score board and jokers
- Photocopy table rounds
- Ensure assistants are available and can help
- Check any special needs with the venue
- Review and start checking questions

On the night: one hour before
- Arrive at venue
- Check PA and sound equipment
- Organise tables and distribute answer sheets and table rounds

7:30
- Round 1: General knowledge
- Rounds 2–4: Themed rounds
- Round 5: Music round

9:00
- Break with picture round

9:20
- Rounds 6–10

10:30
- Announce winner

Music

Motown magic
524 LEVEL 3 Hitsville USA

1 Who founded Motown Records?

2 Which Motown superstar was shot dead by his father in 1984?

3 In which group did Cindy Birdsong replace Florence Ballard?

4 Levi Stubbs provides the lead vocals for which quartet?

5 In 1963 who was billed as 'the 12-year-old genius'?

6 By what name was the group of largely uncredited studio musicians, who recorded the instrumental tracks for many of Motown's biggest hits, known?

7 In which year did the Jackson Five sign for Motown Records?

8 Which was the first Motown male group to have a No. 1 hit in the USA?

9 Which Motown singer was backed by The Pips?

10 Who was the first artist to have a chart record on the Motown label?

Musical monuments
525 LEVEL 2 Questions and answers linked to constructions

1 Which Noel Harrison song was the theme for the 1968 film *The Thomas Crown Affair*?

2 What song, previously a hit for The Drifters, was a top ten hit for actor Bruce Willis?

3 Where did the singer meet the leader of the pack?

4 Which group's only top 30 hit came courtesy of the song 'Love Grows Where my Rosemary Goes' in 1970?

5 According to the B-52's, where is: 'a little place where we can get together'?

6 Which place of worship provided the New Vaudeville Band with a 1966 hit?

7 Which song was a hit for The Red Hot Chili Peppers in 1992 and All Saints in 1998?

8 The song 'Oh What a Circus' featured in which Andrew Lloyd Webber musical?

9 The video for which song featured Michael Jackson gyrating atop the Statue of Liberty?

10 Which pop group from New Zealand was founded by Neil Finn?

Knock on heaven's door
526 LEVEL 3 Gone to the concert in the sky

1 Which rocker, who died aged 36 in 1986, wrote a song called 'Sarah' for his daughter?

2 Which 'pearl' died on October 4, 1970?

3 Buddy Holly, Ritchie Valens and who else died on the same flight in February 1959?

4 Which famous country and western singer died on April 6, 1998?

5 Who died on September 18, 1970 shortly after saying on the phone: 'I need help bad man'?

6 Which singer, backed by The Mothers of Invention, died on December 4, 1993?

7 Which country rock legend was found dead at the Joshua Tree Inn on September 19, 1973?

8 Who died in London on July 29, 1974 from a heart attack, misreported as choking on a sandwich?

9 Name the founder member of Chicago who died on January 23, 1978 after accidentally shooting himself playing Russian roulette?

10 Who died on April 17, 1960 in a Ford Consul car in which he was a passenger?

American pie

527

LEVEL 1   Ten questions on famous US recording artists

1 Which little girl did the Everly Brothers attempt to wake up in the 1957 charts?

2 Justin Timberlake originally found fame in which American boyband?

3 Which black quintet first charted in 1970 with the song 'I Want You Back'?

4 Which rock group formed by Gene Simmons and Ace Frehley were renowned for their outrageous stage act and garish make-up?

5 Who provides lead vocals for Blondie?

6 What request was made by Foreigner in the title of a 1985 UK and USA No. 1 hit?

7 Who partnered John Oates on the hit records 'Maneater' and 'I Can't Go For That'?

8 Which rocker's greatest hits album includes the songs 'School's Out' and 'Elected'?

9 What word follows Sister and Percy to give the names of a female vocal group and a soul singer?

10 Which controversial rap artist appeared on stage wielding a chain saw?

All the world's a stage

528

LEVEL 2   The following songs feature in which stage musicals?

1 'On the Street Where You Live'.

2 'All I Ask of You'.

3 'The Movie in my Mind'.

4 'I Don't Know How to Love Him'.

5 'I Am What I Am'.

6 'It Ain't Necessarily So'.

7 'Love Changes Everything'.

8 'Aquarius'.

9 'Day by Day'.

10 'It's a Hard Knock Life'.

A night at the opera

529

LEVEL 3   Find the operatic greats

1 Which opera character was stabbed to death by Don José?

2 Don Alfonso was a character in which Mozart opera?

3 Mimi, Marcello and Musetta are all characters from which opera?

4 Which pop singer took his name from the man who composed the opera *Hansel and Gretel*?

5 What is the name of the Barber of Seville?

6 The highwayman Macheath is the hero in which opera?

7 Which opera was based on the Alexandre Dumas novel *The Lady of Camelias*?

8 Lieutenant Pinkerton is a character from which opera?

9 Which British composer wrote the opera *Peter Grimes*?

10 Baron Scarpia is a character from which Puccini opera?

Music

Rockin' Robin

530

LEVEL 3   How much do you know about Michael Jackson?

1 Who duetted with Michael Jackson on the track 'The Girl is Mine'?

2 Which singer had a 1982 hit with the song 'Muscles' written by Michael Jackson?

3 Which Michael Jackson hit of 1972 was a theme for a film about a pet rat?

4 Who played the solo guitar on 'Beat It'?

5 Who collaborated with Michael Jackson in writing the charity hit 'We are the World'?

6 On which record label did Michael Jackson record *Thriller*?

7 Who invaded the stage at the 1996 Brit Awards when Michael Jackson was performing 'Earth Song'?

8 Which trio, the nephews of Michael Jackson, charted with the song 'Anything' in 1996?

9 What is the title of Michael Jackson's autobiography?

10 On which 1995 hit did Michael Jackson sing with his sister Janet?

Weather report

531

LEVEL 2   The clues are in the climate

1 Who assisted the comedy duo Baddiel and Skinner on their hit record 'Three Lions'?

2 Which song starts with the words: 'Goodbye Norma Jean'?

3 Which group did Ritchie Blackmore form, following the demise of Deep Purple?

4 Which sibling duo had a hit with the song 'Rainy Days and Mondays'?

5 Where is the answer according to the title of a 1963 hit for Bob Dylan?

6 The song 'Walking in the Air' featured in which animated film?

7 Which song contains the line: 'Someone left a cake out in the rain'?

8 The song 'Raindrops Keep Falling on my Head' featured in which film starring Paul Newman?

9 Which Boogie Nights group was founded by Johnny and Keith Wilder?

10 'Catch the Wind' was a hit for which singer, who was known as Britain's Bob Dylan?

Sugar and spice

532

LEVEL 3   And all questions nice

1 Which band had a 1963 hit with the song 'Sugar and Spice'?

2 Who left The Sugarcubes to forge a successful solo career?

3 By what collective name are Heidi, Keisha and Mutya better known?

4 Which duo charted with the song 'Sugar Candy Kisses' in 1975?

5 Who composed 'The Dance of the Sugar Plum Fairy' from the ballet *The Nutcracker*?

6 Anthony Kiedis is the lead singer with which American band?

7 Which cartoon group topped the charts with the song 'Sugar Sugar' in 1969?

8 How are rappers Cheryl James and Sandra Denton otherwise known?

9 Who did the Spice Girls sack as their manager in 1997?

10 Which song opens with the line 'I'm just mad about Saffron'?

533 Rock on
LEVEL 1   On a roll . . .

1 What colour did rock and roller Gene Vincent always wear on stage?

2 Of the operatic partnership of Gilbert and Sullivan, who lived the longer?

3 Who said 'I'm the originator, the emancipator and the architect of rock and roll'. Was it Bill Haley or Little Richard?

4 'Moonlight Serenade' was the signature tune for which band leader and his orchestra?

5 According to the Erasure song, what colour is the 'savannah'?

6 John Williams composed the film score for which series of shark films?

7 What type of patterned cloth were the Bay City Rollers famous for wearing?

8 Who was the elder: Don or Phil Everly?

9 Which sport featured in the video for the Robbie Williams hit, 'She's the One'?

10 In which city was the Cavern Club, where The Beatles played in their early days?

534 Remember this?
LEVEL 1   A musical mixed bag

1 True or false, Tina Turner was born within the Nutbush city limits?

2 Was Tom Jones born in Scotland, Wales or Ireland?

3 What does the A stand for in the record label RCA?

4 Which 'regal' group collaborated with David Bowie on the song 'Under Pressure'?

5 Which punk rock group's notorious career began with their 1976 release of the song 'Anarchy in the UK'?

6 In which city were the Irish rock group U2 formed?

7 In which decade was the CD single introduced?

8 Which stage musical features the feline characters of Shimbleshanks and Mungo Jerry?

9 Which Ben E. King classic made the charts 25 years after it was recorded?

10 How many of the Walker Brothers trio were related?

535 From the music box
LEVEL 1   All kinds of easy questions

1 Who is Julian Lennon's step-mother?

2 Adrian Boult, André Previn, James Levine and Sir Simon Rattle are all famous for what in the world of music?

3 Which board game shares its name with the stage musical that features the songs 'One Night in Bangkok' and 'I Know him so Well'?

4 Who left The Jam to form The Style Council?

5 What does the letter E stand for in an EP musical disc?

6 In which decade did Elvis Presley have his first chart success?

7 For which musical instrument was George Formby famous?

8 The title of which 1975 hit for Abba is also a distress signal?

9 In the group S Club 7, were there more boys or more girls?

10 Which group, led by Bryan Ferry, had hits with 'Virginia Plain', 'Dance Away' and 'Angel Eyes'?

Music

536 Going for a song
LEVEL 2   Some semi-hard music questions

1 Name the 'queen of soul', who performed the song 'Think' in the film *The Blues Brothers*.

2 Who was the youngest of The Beatles?

3 What was the title of Paul Simon's 1986 Grammy-winning album?

4 Which girl's name provided Barry Manilow with the title of his first UK hit single?

5 Which New York band shouted 'You've Got to Fight for Your Right to Party' in 1987?

6 Who was born Concetta Franconero in 1938 and 20 years later made her chart debut with the song 'Who's Sorry Now'?

7 Which rocker was born in the Canadian province of Ontario on November 5, 1959?

8 What is the title of the song that starts with the line: 'Isn't it rich, aren't we a pair'?

9 Who sold his A&M Record label for US $300 million in 1989?

10 Which hit record by the group D-Ream did the Labour Party use for their 1997 General Election campaign?

537 Heavenly music
LEVEL 1   Questions out of this world

1 Which video for a 1989 Madonna hit, was condemned by the Vatican?

2 What is the name of the garden memorial to John Lennon in New York's Central Park?

3 In which band would you find The Edge and Bono?

4 Which female singer sang 'Unbreak my Heart', one of the biggest hits of 1996?

5 Who was Lisa Marie Presley's second husband?

6 Name the song that was a hit for Roberta Flack in 1973 and The Fugees in 1996.

7 Which song about a famous painter was a hit for Don McLean in 1972?

8 Who left the rock group Genesis in 1975 to pursue a solo career?

9 What does the R stand for in R. Kelly: Richard, Rudy or Robert?

10 Which female singer released a compilation album in 1994 entitled *Twelve Deadly Cyns. . . and then Some*?

538 Expert's choice
LEVEL 3   A tough round of assorted music questions

1 What was the first Beatles record to be No. 1 in America?

2 The Joe Cocker song 'Delta Lady' was a tribute to which female singer?

3 Who wrote the Tina Turner hit 'Private Dancer'?

4 Who said: 'rock journalism is people who can't write, interviewing people who can't speak, for people who can't read'?

5 What is the name of the American DJ who first coined the phrase 'rock-and-roll'?

6 In 1973, who recorded the song 'I Can Hear Music' under the name of Larry Lurex?

7 By what five-letter name is rock guitarist Saul Hudson better known?

8 Who has made hits with Diana Ross, Paul McCartney and Julio Iglesias?

9 What did the American band REO Speedwagon name themselves after?

10 Which song performed by Carly Simon from the film *Working Girl* won a best song Oscar?

Name that tunesmith

539

Can you match the song title to the face of these musical talents?

 1

 2

 3

 4

 5

 6

 7

 8

 9

 10

The Trout Quintet • Wuthering Heights
Layla • Spiders from Mars • Moonlight Serenade
Bitches Brew • Anarchy in the UK
Old Man River • Jet Song • The Firebird

Music

Blue is the colour
540   LEVEL 2   Blues clues

1 Which legendary blues singer was nicknamed Lady Day?

2 Which bluesman had a 1964 hit with 'Smokestack Lightning'. Was it Running Bear, Sly Fox or Howlin' Wolf?

3 The Dexy's Midnight Runners hit 'Geno' was a tribute to which blues legend?

4 Which guitarist was a founder member of Blind Faith, Cream, and Derek and the Dominoes?

5 Clint Eastwood directed the film *Bird*, that told the story of which blues musician?

6 What does R&B stand for?

7 Name the blues rocker who had hits with 'No Particular Place to Go' and 'My Ding-A-Ling'?

8 What was the common surname of the female singer nicknamed 'the empress of the blues'?

9 Which blues musician, who named his guitar Lucille, had a surname preceded by the initials BB?

10 What was the dirty-sounding stage name of bluesman McKinley Morganfield?

Four-letter words   A–J
541   LEVEL 1   Alphabetical clues

1 A – Which group had their last No. 1 with 'Super Trouper'?

2 B – What is the surname of the singer who released the album *The Kick Inside*?

3 C – What is the surname of the Irish family group who had hits with 'So Young' and 'Runaway'?

4 D – Which group, led by Tony Orlando, sang 'Tie a Yellow Ribbon Round the Old Oak Tree'?

5 E – Who left Clannad to have a solo hit with 'Orinoco Flow'?

6 F – What word comes before Young Cannibals to complete the name of a group?

7 G – What percussion instrument was banged by Billy Wells at the beginning of Rank movies?

8 H – What was the title of The Beatles second film?

9 I – Michael Hutchence fronted which Australian rock band?

10 J – What is the last name of Jon Bon, who sang the theme for the film *Young Guns II*?

Golden greats
542   LEVEL 2   Those you have loved

1 Which instrument was played by Dave Clark in the Dave Clark Five?

2 Which crooner had hits with 'Magic Moments' and 'Catch a Falling Star'?

3 Which 1960s quartet included husband and wife John and Michelle Phillips in their line-up?

4 Which New Jersey born singer had a hit with the song 'Hello Mary Lou' in 1961?

5 Which Lennon and McCartney song was a transatlantic hit for Peter and Gordon in 1964?

6 Who, in 1956, hit the charts with the song 'Just Walking in the Rain'?

7 Which country and western legend was nicknamed 'gentleman Jim'?

8 Which river was a hit for Danny Williams?

9 Which 1960s duo with the surnames of Moore and Prater had a hit with the song 'Soul Man'?

10 What was the French title of Jane Birkin and Serge Gainsbourg's banned hit?

543 Fond farewells
LEVEL 2   Parting is such sweet sorrow

1 To what did The Carpenters say goodbye in a 1972 hit single?

2 Which Scottish group sang 'Bye Bye Baby' in 1975?

3 Name the soul star who in 1970 charted with the song 'Farewell is a Lonely Sound'?

4 Who left the message in Paul Evans' 1978 hit, known as the 'Telephone Answering Machine Song'?

5 Which duo had a hit with the song 'Bye Bye Love' in 1957?

6 'Say Hello Wave Goodbye' was a hit for which duo fronted by Marc Almond?

7 Who did Michael Jackson bid farewell to in a 1984 hit?

8 Which song was a hit for Harold Melvin in 1977 and for the Communards in 1986?

9 In a Don McClean song, what five words precede: 'Drove my Chevy to the levee'?

10 Which Forces sweetheart sang 'Auf Wiedersehen Sweetheart' in 1952?

544 Tuned to the classics
LEVEL 2   Questions on the serious side

1 Who founded the Proms Concerts, first held in London in 1895?

2 Which female cellist was married to the pianist Daniel Barenboim and died tragically young of multiple sclerosis?

3 Who conducted his first concert as music director of Berliner Philharmoniker in 2002?

4 In *The Beggar's Opera*, is the hero Macheath: a judge, a doctor or a highwayman?

5 Who founded The London Philharmonic Orchestra in 1932 and The Royal Philharmonic in 1946?

6 How many crotchets are there in a minim?

7 What instrument accompanies a piano, a violin and a viola in a piano quartet?

8 Which opera singer appeared in an Italian court in 2001, charged with tax evasion?

9 What is the name of the opera house in Milan that was built in 1778 on the site of a church?

10 Which American composer wrote *Fanfare for the Common Man*?

545 Three of a kind
LEVEL 3   Ten questions on trios

1 Sheila Ferguson fronted which female trio?

2 Which rock trio had a hit in 1977 with the instrumental 'Fanfare for the Common Man'?

3 Which trio sang 'It ain't What you Do, it's the Way that you Do it' when The Specials split?

4 Which mod trio had their first UK No. 1 with the song 'Going Underground'?

5 Frank Sinatra had a hit singing about three what in 1954?

6 Which trio comprising Fast, Huey and Steve had a 1996 hit with the song 'Scooby Snacks'?

7 Which trio comprised Paul McCartney, his wife Linda and Denny Laine?

8 The pop trio, Yarrow, Stookey and Travers, was better known by their first names. Who are they?

9 Frank Beard was the only member without a beard of which Texan rock trio?

10 Which hit for the pop trio The Police shared its name with a 1987 film starring Steve Martin?

Music

546 Beauty and the best
LEVEL 2   Great looks link to every question

1 Who was walking down the street according to a 1964 Roy Orbison hit?

2 Which brotherly duo asked: 'If I said you had a beautiful body would you hold it against me?'

3 Which British group had a hit with the song 'You're Gorgeous' in 1996?

4 What do the initials PYT stand for in the Michael Jackson hit song?

5 Who asked 'Do Ya Think I'm Sexy' in 1978?

6 Which song about a good-looking male provided Buddy Holly with a 1963 posthumous hit?

7 Which Beatle sang the line 'You're sixteen, you're beautiful and you're mine'?

8 Which 'medical' band charted with the song 'When You're in Love with a Beautiful Woman' in 1979?

9 What was the title of the song that provided Prince with his first No. 1 hit single in the UK?

10 Which film opens with the song 'Oh What a Beautiful Morning'?

547 Brotherly love
LEVEL 2   All these questions are about brothers

1 Which British group had a hit in 1969 and 1988 with 'He Ain't Heavy he's my Brother'?

2 Despite being unrelated, under what name did Scott Engel, John Maus and Gary Leeds perform?

3 Name the brother of Robin, Barry and Maurice Gibb who died in 1988.

4 Who won the Eurovision Song Contest for the UK in 1976?

5 Who was the oldest member of The Osmond Brothers group?

6 Which of Michael Jackson's brothers had a hit with the song 'Let's Get Serious' in 1980?

7 Name the bespectacled Scottish siblings who sang 'Letter to America'.

8 With which Righteous Brothers hit did Tom Cruise serenade Kelly McGillis in *Top Gun*?

9 Which American group reaped a 'Harvest for the World' in 1976?

10 Name the group who recorded the album *Brothers in Arms*.

548 Animal magic
LEVEL 3   A round of questions from the natural world

1 According to the song, what kind of birds flew over the white cliffs of Dover?

2 What sort of creature was Muscles, Michael Jackson's pet?

3 Which 1970s heart-throb sang 'Puppy Love'?

4 Which German rock band had a 1991 hit with the song 'Wind of Change'?

5 Which group had a hit with 'Albatross'?

6 Which band enjoyed a 1960s hit with the song 'Pretty Flamingo'?

7 Which Australian entertainer jumped up the charts with the song 'Tie me Kangaroo Down Sport'?

8 Which member of The Animals went on to manage Jimi Hendrix?

9 Who won a Grammy award in 1995 for the song 'Kiss From a Rose'?

10 Which farm bird provided the Rolling Stones with a 1964 hit?

549 Music quest

Can you identify the songs that contain these lines?

1 'Let's move before they raise the parking rate.'

2 'Ils viennent jusque dans nos bras.'

3 'Other arms reach out to me, other eyes smile tenderly, still in peaceful dreams I see … the road leads back to you.'

4 'And she feeds you tea and oranges that come all the way from China.'

5 'When love congeals it soon reveals the faint aroma of performing seals.'

6 'Glücklich zu sehen, je suis enchanté, happy to see you, bleibe, reste, stay.'

7 'I hate men, I can't abide them – even now and then.'

8 'I know how Columbus felt finding another world.'

9 'Here's to you, raise a glass for everyone…'

10 'Maybe I'm a lonely man who's in the middle of something that he doesn't really understand…'

11 'We got no class; and we got no principles. We got no innocence. Can't even think of a word that rhymes…'

12 'They say that looks don't count for much – if so there goes your proof.'

13 'Ain't nothin' in the world like a big-eyed girl – make me act so funny; make me spend my money.'

14 'So just try and relax, yeah cool it, Fall apart in my backyard.'

15 'You can dance! You can jive – having the time of your life.'

A clue to question 2

Music

The Beatles
550   LEVEL 1   The greatest band of all time

1 What was The Beatles first UK No. 1 hit, in April 1963?

2 Which Beatles album holds the record for being the biggest-ever seller in the UK?

3 What song was a double A-side single with 'Strawberry Fields Forever'?

4 What was the name of the 2000 compendium release of Beatles singles that became the fastest-selling album of all time at that point?

5 What was the name of the record label set up by the band?

6 What was the Beatles first film called?

7 Which track from *Magical Mystery Tour* had the line: 'There's nothing you can do that can't be done. Nothing you can sing that can't be sung'?

8 Which ex-Beatle's debut album was *All things Must Pass*?

9 Richard Starkey is the real name of which one of the Fab Four?

10 How many times was 'Yellow Submarine' performed live by the band?

Jazz it up
551   LEVEL 2   All that jazz

1 Born in 1917 and died in 1996, who recorded the Songbook series of albums?

2 Who was the jazz pianist famous for singing songs like 'Mona Lisa' and 'Rambling Rose'?

3 Courtney Pine is most associated with the playing of which instrument?

4 Which song with a weather connection was a hit for Johnny Mathis and was written by jazz musician Erroll Garner?

5 Name the British female jazz singer who married her band leader husband Johnny Dankworth in 1958?

6 Was Buddy Rich a drummer or a trumpeter?

7 Which trumpet-playing jazz great was nicknamed 'Satchmo'?

8 Acker Bilk was the first UK musician to have a US No. 1 hit with what tune?

9 Who, backed by The Jazz Men, had chart hits with 'The Green Leaves of Summer' and 'Midnight in Moscow'?

10 What is the real name of Duke Ellington?

In sheep's clothing
552   LEVEL 3   All connected with wolves or sheep

1 Which group performed the song 'Born to be Wild' that featured in the film *Easy Rider*?

2 The song 'Bad Moon Rising' featured in which 1981 film directed by John Landis?

3 Which group from Hull charted with a song entitled 'Sheep' in 1986?

4 Who backed Sam the Sham on 'Wooly Bully'?

5 In 1974 which group released the album *The Lamb Lies Down on Broadway*?

6 By what name was the DJ Robert Smith better known?

7 Which new romantic band had a 1982 hit with the song 'Hungry Like the Wolf'?

8 Peter Wolf provides the lead vocals for which American band?

9 Which song contains the line: 'I was the black sheep of the family, you tried to teach me right from wrong'?

10 Who composed the musical work *Peter and the Wolf*?

553 Pop trivia
LEVEL 1 A mixed bag of easy questions

1 What was the name of the duo formed by Siobhan Fahey and Marcella Detroit?

2 Who wrote the lyrics for *Jesus Christ Superstar*?

3 Which Motley Crue drummer married Pamela Anderson?

4 The Kemp brothers from Spandau Ballet played which twins in a 1990 film?

5 By what name was Ernest Evans known when he acquired the nickname of 'the king of twist'?

6 What was the bestselling classical album of the 20th century?

7 Who is the high-pitched lead vocalist with The Four Seasons?

8 Which song was released by Paul McCartney in 1977 because he felt that Scotland needed a new anthem?

9 What was the surname of Gerry of Gerry and the Pacemakers fame?

10 Which song provided the first UK No. 1 hit single for Whitney Houston in 1985?

554 What a classic
LEVEL 1 A round of easy classical questions

1 Handel composed the music to accompany what kind of royal entertainment that went with a bang in 1749?

2 How many reeds does an oboe have?

3 In which capital city is the Bolshoi Theatre?

4 Does the musical term *allegro* signify a slow tempo or a quick tempo?

5 In which century did Tchaikovsky live?

6 From where do Gilbert and Sullivan's pirates hail, according to the title of an 1879 operetta?

7 What musical instrument connects Isaac Stern, Vanessa Mae and Yehudi Menuhin?

8 What instrument was named after its inventor, John Sousa?

9 On which river does the Manaus Opera House in Brazil stand?

10 By what name is *Beethoven's 9th Symphony* more commonly known?

555 Oscar songs
LEVEL 2 In which films did the following Oscar-winning songs feature?

1 'Up Where we Belong', 1982.

2 'Secret Love', 1953.

3 'Over the Rainbow', 1939.

4 'Evergreen', 1976.

5 'You Must Love me', 1996.

6 'Say you Say me', 1985.

7 'Chim Chim Cheree', 1964.

8 'Sooner or Later', 1990.

9 'Zip-a-dee-doo-dah', 1946.

10 'Colours of the Wind', 1995.

Music

Children's choice
556 Kids 7–11 Lucky dip

1 Which Disney character sang the song 'I've got no Strings'?

2 Barbie danced in a famous ballet by Tchaikovsky. What is its name?

3 In which of the following instruments would you find a reed: clarinet, French horn, flute or harp?

4 How many strings are there on a violin: 4, 5 or 6?

5 Which H word is the name given to a song of praise traditionally sung in a church?

6 Which Disney film features the song *The Circle of Life*?

7 Which singer and film actress is known as J.Lo?

8 Was John Lennon a member of The Beatles or of the Rolling Stones?

9 Which instrument does Lisa Simpson play?

10 Which instrument beginning with P is the smallest member of the flute family?

Musical dip
557 Kids 12–14 How well do you know the charts?

1 Which country's national anthem is called 'La Marseillaise'?

2 What nationality is Natalie Imbruglia?

3 Which female singer with a four-letter name had a hit with the song 'White Flag' in 2003?

4 Gareth Gates' single 'Spirit in the Sky' featured which TV family?

5 Who is older: Christine Aguilera or Britney Spears?

6 Which singer enjoyed success with an album called *Dangerously in Love*?

7 Which band had a hit with a song containing the line 'Though I hate to fly'?

8 When should you sing, according to the title of Robbie Williams' third album?

9 Who had a hit with 'Left Outside Alone'?

10 Kylie Minogue first became famous as an actress in which Australian soap?

Take your pick
558 Kids 7–11 All kinds of music

1 Is Luciano Pavarotti a rap artist, an opera singer or a classical composer?

2 Is a tambourine a percussion instrument or a woodwind instrument?

3 Who is older: Michael Jackson or Madonna?

4 Is Alice Cooper a man or a woman?

5 By which part of the body is a cello held: between the legs or under the chin?

6 Who married Whitney Houston: Barry Blue, Bobby Brown or Billy Black?

7 Which of the following instruments is not played by blowing: harmonica, euphonium or harpsichord?

8 The footballer Jamie Redknapp is married to which singer?

9 What has 46 strings: a zither or a harp?

10 Which of the following is not a type of singing voice: baritone, sombrero or soprano?

An easy ABC

559 Kids 12–14 All 10 answers begin with A, B or C

1 Which Danish pop group took their name from the Latin for water?

2 Which Scandinavian pop group sang 'Dancing Queen'?

3 By what name is the band Busted known in Holland (where there is already a band with that name)?

4 Which band's hits include 'The Last Goodbye' and 'Seeya'?

5 Which Mediterranean island does Peter Andre hail from?

6 Which band recorded 'We Wanna Thank You (The Things You Do)'?

7 Which British singer, winner of the best male solo artist at the 2004 Brit Awards, was injured in a car accident?

8 What is the first name of the Westlife member who quit the band in 2004?

9 Which country does Avril Lavigne come from?

10 Which singer married a schoolfriend and divorced the same week in 2004?

A scale of ten

560 Kids 7–11 Lucky dip

1 What name is given to a person who stands at the front of an orchestra and directs the musicians?

2 How many strings are there on a standard guitar?

3 Ant, Sy, Lee and Dynk make up which band?

4 For how many people is a quintet composed?

5 What is the first name of the front man for Maroon 5?

6 By what name is Alecia Moore better known?

7 What is the first name of Ozzy Osbourne's popstar daughter?

8 What is the first name of Daniel Bedingfield's singer sister?

9 Which member of the boy band N'Sync began dating Britney Spears in 1999?

10 To what note, played by the orchestra leader, does the rest of the orchestra tune itself?

Topical tunes

561 Kids 12–14 Pop in the news

1 Which town do the band The Darkness come from?

2 Steve Tyler is the lead singer with which American rock band?

3 What is Madonna's middle name?

4 Which three-digit figure completes the name of a pop group called Blink?

5 How are Danny, Dougie, Harry and Tom collectively known?

6 Who had a hit with a song called 'Dirrty'?

7 Which pop idol thought he had 'Better Leave Right Now'?

8 Which singer-songwriter called her baby Nevis?

9 Which student at Fame Academy sang Britain's entry in the 2004 Eurovision Song Contest?

10 What Scandinavian country do the band Rasmus come from?

562 In tune
Kids 7–11   **Lucky dip**

1 What was in a bottle in a 1999 hit for Christine Aguilera?

2 Which of the following does not have strings: viola, piano or oboe?

3 How many musicians play in a duet?

4 Which TV talent show featured judges Simon Cowell and Pete Waterman?

5 Which film character sings 'Supercalafragalisticexpialadocious'?

6 In which film will you hear the song 'You Got a Friend in Me'?

7 Is Charlotte Church a pianist, a singer or a violinist?

8 Which boy band consists of Aaron, Kevin, Anthony, Leon and Mark?

9 By what name are Romanian twins Gabriela and Monica better known?

10 Which ex-boyfriend of Britney Spears had a huge hit with 'Cry Me a River'?

563 Mixing decks
Kids 12–14   **Lucky dip**

1 Which seven-letter L word is the name given to a soothing song for a baby?

2 Who had a number one hit with 'Yeah' in 2004?

3 Which long-running TV programme was presented by Sophie Ellis Bextor's mother?

4 Which girl band sang 'In the Middle'?

5 Which Queen song was recorded by Robbie Williams for the film *A Knight's Tale*?

6 Which former children's TV presenter married Fat Boy Slim in August 1999?

7 What is the first name of the composer Beethoven?

8 Which singer appears in *Charlies Angels: Full Throttle* as a motorcycle club owner?

9 How many instruments accompany a choir singing a cappella?

10 What is Beyonce's surname?

564 A, B or C
Kids 7–11   **All 10 answers begin with one of these three letters**

1 In which European country was the composer Mozart born?

2 Which of the following is not the name of a musical instrument: accordion, beluga or clavichord?

3 In which song did Robbie Williams sing the line: 'and through it all she offers me protection'?

4 What is the first name of the singer who sang the theme for the film *Titanic*?

5 Which singer married Chris Evans?

6 What name is given to the implement that is used to play a violin?

7 What is the name of the largest wind instrument in a standard orchestra?

8 What type of song traditionally sung at Christmas shares its name with a girl's first name?

9 What are the round metal discs found on a drum kit called?

10 Which German composer is also the name of a St Bernard dog on screen?

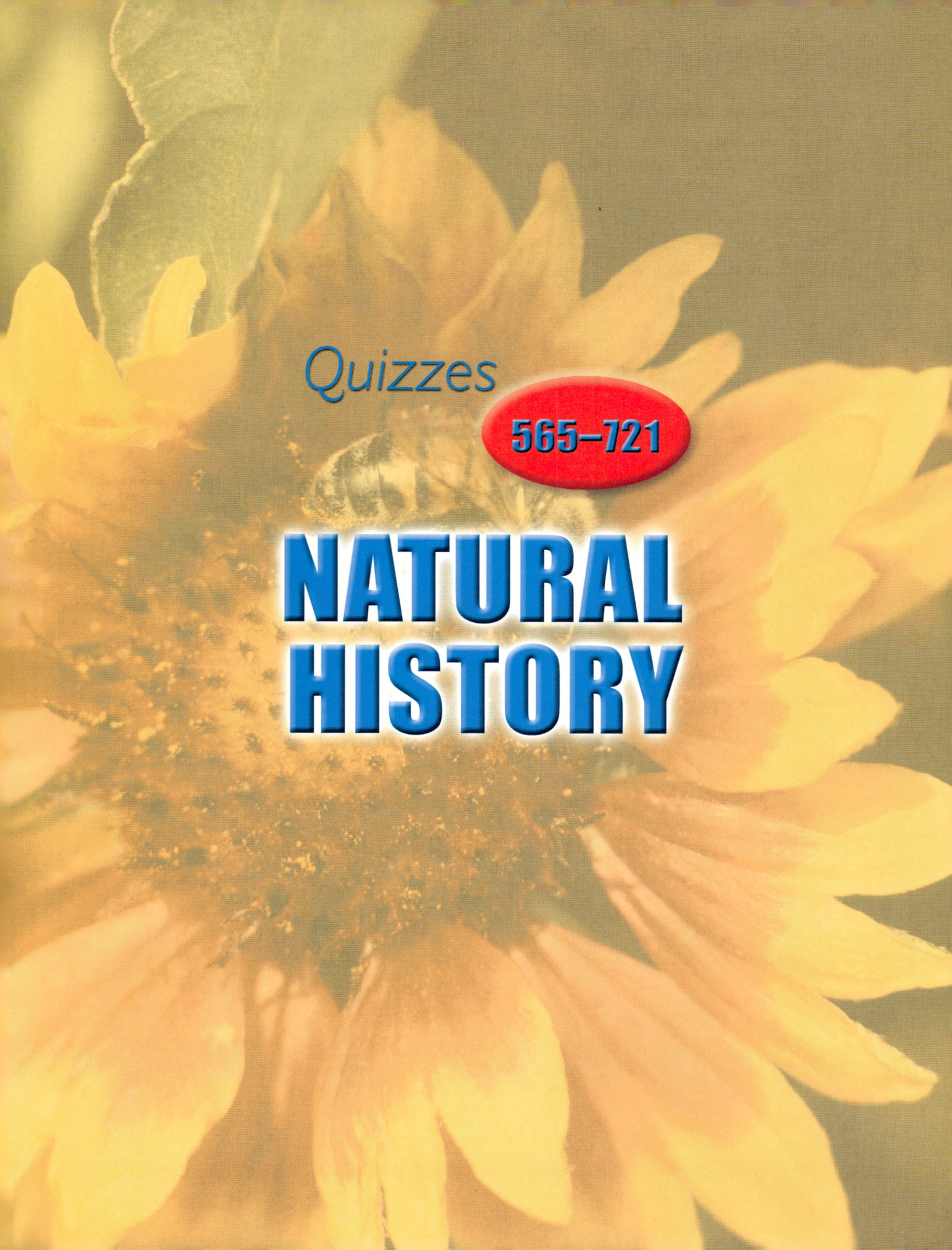

Quizzes

565–721

NATURAL HISTORY

Natural history

Pot pourri

565

LEVEL 1   A round of easy nature questions

1 How do boas kill their prey?

2 What is a bolete?

3 What disease might you catch from an anopheline?

4 What type of creature is a gecko?

5 What Southeast Asian pig is sometimes kept as a household pet?

6 What distant relative of the earthworm was once used by doctors to draw blood from their patients?

7 What plant do you associate with oast houses?

8 What large rodent has a dense mass of long and very sharp black-and-white spines on its back?

9 How many legs has a tarantula?

10 How are the seeds of the burdock dispersed?

Nature's way

566

LEVEL 1   A round of easy mixed natural history questions

1 What is a puffball?

2 From which part of the cinnamon tree is the spice obtained?

3 What is the staple food of the panda?

4 Do African or Indian elephants have the bigger ears?

5 Dover and lemon are types of which fish?

6 What would you find lots of in an arboretum?

7 What is a male bee called?

8 What type of tree has varieties called osier and sallow?

9 Where do polar bears go to hibernate in winter?

10 Which flying animal uses echolocation to navigate through the night?

Nature trail

567

LEVEL 1   A jumble of animal and plant questions

1 The seed of which plant is a major constituent of chocolate?

2 What colour are the fleshy seeds of the yew tree?

3 Where would you find a stonecrop growing?

4 Where are you most likely to find a great crested newt?

5 What mollusc gives its name to a type of explosive mine?

6 Which big cat has large ears with prominent tufts of hair?

7 According to the story, which bird did the ancient mariner kill and then hang around his neck as penance?

8 Which tree's sap is used to produce an edible syrup?

9 What are horsetails and lamb's ears?

10 What name is given to the poison a snake injects through its fangs?

Odds and ends
568

LEVEL 2   A miscellany of tricky posers

1 What kind of organism causes athlete's foot?

2 In which country would you find a dingo?

3 Which is the only great ape not native to Africa?

4 What small bird of prey shares a name with an Arthurian wizard?

5 On which continent would you find a marmoset?

6 What, in animals, is a tarsus?

7 Name the reptile with a very long tongue, mobile eyes and skin that can change colour.

8 What is stored in a camel's hump?

9 What was an australopithecine?

10 What is the main food of koalas?

Take your pick
569

LEVEL 2   Test your knowledge of plants and animals

1 Which group of exotic plants has the smallest seeds?

2 'Gardener's delight', 'delicious', and 'moneymaker' are all varieties of what plant?

3 What tree is associated with the Lebanon?

4 Which creatures have sensory organs called lateral lines?

5 Which one of these is not a true bear: koala, grizzly, kodiak, spectacled or black?

6 The giant eland is the largest of what type of animal?

7 What sort of mammal is a slow loris?

8 Socrates committed suicide by drinking a poison derived from what plant?

9 In which country do budgerigars live in the wild?

10 According to legend, which plant screams when it is pulled from the ground?

Troublesome tests
570

LEVEL 3   Hard questions for the keen biologist

1 Name the large, poisonous lizard that is only found on a few islands in Indonesia.

2 From what is the pigment sepia derived?

3 What is a 'mermaid's purse'?

4 The heaviest living thing is the giant sequoia tree. In which American state is it found?

5 What plant-like organism grows as a thin crust on rocks, walls and tree trunks?

6 What is an aye-aye?

7 On which continent would you find the baobab tree?

8 Which threatened world habitat contains more animal species than all the other land habitats combined?

9 What is a mouflon?

10 What name is given to mammals that possess four stomachs to allow them to digest grass?

Natural history

571 Peas and parakeets
LEVEL 2   All answers begin with the letter P

1 Emperor, king and marconi are all species of what animal?

2 What name is given to dark-skinned leopards with black coats?

3 What family of brightly coloured birds includes parakeets, lorikeets, cockatoos and cockatiels?

4 What black sea bird, said to be one of the world's most numerous, has a distinctive white rump?

5 What South American fish is notorious for being an aggressive and voracious carnivore?

6 What adjective describes a black and white spotted or patched horse?

7 What Arctic animal is the world's largest carnivore?

8 What monkey is characterised by its very large, pendulous nose?

9 Which game bird, with a dark green head and red facial wattles, is hunted from October 1?

10 What bird was used to carry messages from the front during the First World War?

572 Flower arranging
LEVEL 2   Can you identify the flowers from these cryptic clues?

1 Part of an eye.

2 Woman's footwear.

3 An easy way to get a fortune.

4 A flower between hills.

5 What the shepherds were watching while seated on the ground.

6 Buddy gets followed by this.

7 The results from Cupid's arrow.

8 A lover's request.

9 What's the story …

10 Neat ranks.

573 Identity parade
LEVEL 3   Pick the right answers from these lists of imposters

1 Is a tup: a ram, a tit or a hen?

2 Is a gemsbok: an antelope, an Asian shrew or a yellow wildflower found in Corsica?

3 Is ambergris: a semi-precious stone, a substance produced in the sperm whale's gut or a butterfly found in Papua New Guinea?

4 Are gentoos: whales, sharks or penguins?

5 Is a potto: an Asian wild pig, a Scottish heather related to cassiope or a West African lemur?

6 Is a smelt: a fish, a cat related to the jaguar and leopard or a young eel?

7 Is a belemnite: fossilised animal dung, the fossil of a squid-like animal or the scientific name for a stalactite made of limestone?

8 Is a nestling the young of: a polecat, a snake, a rabbit or a Siberian husky?

9 Is a stolon: a horizontal plant stem, the name given to the sexual organs of the fruitbat or an African wasp?

10 Is a beech hanger: a woodland butterfly, a bat native to the forests of New England or a steeply sloping wood of beech trees?

574 Four of a kind
LEVEL 2   All the answers are four-letter words

1 What name is given to the smallest creature in a litter?

2 Common, grey, monk, harp and hooded are all types of what?

3 What is the colour of speedwell?

4 Name a type of animal that is said to rut?

5 What is the name given to the state of dangerous frenzy in male elephants?

6 What is a baby whale called?

7 Royal, male, lady and buckler are all types of what?

8 What 'C', in biology, is composed of cytoplasm and a nucleus?

9 Hercules carried the skin of which fearsome animal?

10 What common herb has a name that also means a wise man?

575 Something fishy
LEVEL 2   A round of things under, on, in or about the water

1 From which fish does caviar come?

2 Which unusual fish can climb trees?

3 What is krill?

4 What is the largest species of ray fish?

5 What does a male sea horse have that makes it unique among male sea creatures and helps it to rear its young?

6 How does an archer fish catch its insect prey?

7 For what do whales use baleen?

8 What does a fish use to extract oxygen from water?

9 Under what name is dogfish usually sold for human consumption?

10 What snake-like fish migrates from Europe to the Sargasso Sea?

576 Natural-born killers
LEVEL 2   Be afraid, be very afraid

1 What, described as the world's most dangerous stinging fish, is easily trodden on?

2 Which is Britain's most poisonous mushroom?

3 Drop for drop, black widow venom is more potent than rattlesnake venom. True or false?

4 Australia is home to one of the world's two most venomous spiders. Name it.

5 What awesome snake, up to 14ft (5m) long, is the largest venomous snake in the world?

6 What name is given to venoms that attack the nervous system, cause muscle paralysis and shut down the respiratory system?

7 Which part of the common tomato plant is poisonous?

8 According to Kipling what is 'more deadly than the male'?

9 The inland taipan (formerly known as the western taipan) is the world's most venomous snake. In which country is it found?

10 What fatal poison can be found in the stones and pips of apricots, plums, cherries, peaches, apples and pears?

Natural history

Easy tiger
577

LEVEL 1   A round for the simpletons

1 On what do the newborn of all mammals feed?

2 What kind of animal is a caribou?

3 Which wild cat has the loudest roar?

4 What colour are laburnum flowers?

5 What connects Charles Darwin to the cartoon-dog Snoopy?

6 What British children's programme about zoos and natural history was presented for many years by Johnny Morris?

7 Kyoto and other Japanese cities are famous for which tree that flowers profusely in March and April?

8 What colour are juniper berries?

9 Koi is a variety of which freshwater fish, much prized in Japan?

10 In prehistoric times how did pterosaurs get around?

Biology test
578

LEVEL 3   A challenging round of general biological knowledge

1 What body part is lacking in agnathan fish?

2 What name is given to the single landmass that, geologists believe, divided to form the modern continents?

3 What name is given to animals that do not migrate?

4 Where does a female bitterling, a fish, lay her eggs?

5 Alpacas are domesticated breeds of which wild South American animal?

6 What is the most characteristic feature of a spawning sockeye salmon?

7 Which is the only order of mammals that can fly?

8 What is a water moccasin?

9 A Maine coon is a large and very furry variety of which domesticated animal?

10 What is a bullace?

Top of the food chain
579

LEVEL 3   Strictly for the well-informed

1 What is the main food of the basking shark?

2 From the wood of what tree are matchsticks most often made?

3 Botanically, what is a petiole?

4 What is a saguaro?

5 What is an olm?

6 Into how many chambers is a cow's stomach divided?

7 What huge long-lived reptiles are found mostly on the Galapagos Islands?

8 What plant is grown to provide linseed oil and fibre for linen?

9 How is a James Bond film linked to a breed of duck?

10 To which domestic pet is the hyena most closely related?

580 57 varieties
LEVEL 2   A round of random questions

1 Where would you find lugs or lugworms?

2 In America they are called chickadees, but what are they called in England?

3 What is a breeding colony of penguins called?

4 What is Yorkshire fog?

5 Dwarf, silver, paper-bark and downy are types of what tree?

6 Why was whalebone, derived from the whale's mouth, so valued in the 19th century?

7 What name, derived from an Afrikaans word, is given to the animal tracks that hunters follow?

8 A hinny is a cross between a horse and what other animal?

9 What kind of plant is quaking aspen?

10 What name is given to the geological period during which most coal deposits were laid down?

581 Flower power
LEVEL 2   Every question is related to flowers

1 In what type of habitat does the edelweiss grow?

2 For how many flowering seasons does a biennial plant live?

3 What plant is often nicknamed granny's bonnet?

4 From what family do the group of plants known as chamomile come, many of which have medicinal and herbal uses?

5 Why are day lilies so called?

6 'Peace' is a yellowish gold variety of what common garden plant?

7 How did the corpse flower get its name?

8 By what romantic name is the amaranth or tassel flower known; so called for its long tassels of crimson-purple flowers?

9 Which TV sitcom of the 1990s featured a character called Hyacinth?

10 What is the national flower of the Netherlands?

582 Speak the language
LEVEL 3   Can you understand these biological terms?

1 What name is given to the characteristic of an animal that never grows up, but reproduces while still in a juvenile stage?

2 Where in a tree would you find the cambium?

3 Why do animals and insects emit chemicals called pheromones at certain times of year?

4 What does pinnate mean?

5 What is a herbarium?

6 What are lamellibranchs and brachiopods?

7 If an animal is said to have raptorial legs, what does this mean?

8 When are trees described as fastigiate?

9 What is a rhizome?

10 Polychaetes are worms, related to earthworms, but what does 'polychaete' literally mean?

Natural history

583 Continental divide
LEVEL 1 On which of the six continents are these found?

1 Gibbon

2 Mandrill

3 Lawson cypress

4 Spiny anteater

5 Harpy eagle

6 Clouded leopard

7 Giant otter

8 Sulphur-crested cockatoo

9 Snowshoe hare

10 Okapi

584 Teeing off
LEVEL 1 The answers to all these questions begin with the letter T

1 Which tropical animal, related to the rhinoceros, has an elongated, flexible nose?

2 To which bird family do the blackbird and nightingale belong?

3 Which flower bulb was the cause of mass speculation, particularly in Holland, in the 17th century?

4 What venomous spider has a body up to 12cm (5in) long, and a leg span of up to 28cm (11in)?

5 Which common freshwater fish is found in rainbow and brown varieties?

6 Which small duck includes the varieties green-winged, blue-winged and cinnamon?

7 What name is given to the treeless and featureless landscape of the Arctic?

8 Which human disease, caused by a bacterium, used to be known as consumption?

9 Which social insects, in the order Isoptera, build large mounds?

10 A fairy ring is a ring of what sort of fungi?

585 Gone, but not forgotten
LEVEL 3 A round about animals now as dead as the dodo

1 On which island did the dodo live?

2 Which fish, from a group thought to be extinct, was discovered in the 1930s?

3 Which large flightless bird, once native to New Zealand, became extinct before the arrival of western settlers in the 18th century?

4 What is the large, flightless seabird that lived in Arctic waters and became extinct in 1844?

5 Extinct in Britain from 1800, what creatures were the large blue and the large copper?

6 Sometimes known as the Tasmanian tiger, what marsupial became extinct in the 20th century?

7 What do some scientists believe became extinct due to a climate change after a meteorite?

8 The fossilised *archaeopteryx* was a creature intermediate between a bird and a what?

9 What lion, an inhabitant of north Africa, became extinct in Morocco in 1922?

10 Which species of North American bird became extinct on September 1, 1914, at 1pm?

Colour me beautiful
586 **LEVEL 2   A round of many colours**

1 What colour is the cap of the fly agaric mushroom?

2 Greenshank, redshank and yellowshank are types of what?

3 What colour is the bill of a chough?

4 How many legs has a silverfish?

5 What is the world's tallest tree?

6 What two colours would you see on a European avocet?

7 What are female blackcock called?

8 What is a clouded yellow?

9 What is the normal colour of Scots pine bark?

10 What colour are the flowers of agrimony?

Famous animals
587 **LEVEL 1   Pets of the rich and famous**

1 At what address did Humphrey the cat live?

2 What was Guy, a famous inhabitant of London Zoo, who died in 1978?

3 Who owned a dog called Checkers?

4 In which city will you find a statue of a dog called Greyfriar's Bobby?

5 Shep the dog was a TV pet on which children's programme?

6 What sort of animal was Chi-Chi, a gift from the Chinese to London Zoo in 1958?

7 What did Churchill call his bouts of depression?

8 What sort of animal was Socks, an inhabitant of the White House?

9 Lucy was the working dog of which Labour politician until her retirement?

10 Burmese, a black mare, was a favoured mount of Queen Elizabeth II at which annual state event?

Unnatural habitats
588 **LEVEL 2   Can you spot the odd ones out?**

1 Which of these only visits Britain in winter: chiffchaff, fieldfare, swallow, spotted flycatcher?

2 Why are you unlikely to catch a turbot with a perch, pike, bream or tench?

3 Why would it be better to walk into a nest of pythons, than of vipers, cobras or mambas?

4 Why would you be unlikely to be able to pick dog's mercury along with dog violet, dog's tooth violet or flowering dogwood?

5 Why would a kiwi not share a forest with a tree-kangaroo, wombat or duck-billed platypus?

6 Why would you not find stonechat where there are newts, dragonflies and dippers?

7 Why would you not see a swallowtail with a red underwing, noctule, tawny owl or pipistrelle?

8 Why would you not see a purple emperor where there were crested tits, pine martins, Scots pines and red squirrels?

9 Why are jackals not eaten by jaguars?

10 Why are angler fish not found with limpets, sea-squirts, eel-grass or bladder wrack?

Natural history

I can see the sea
589

LEVEL 1   Questions for the ocean lover

1 Blue and humpback are types of what animal?

2 What is a Portuguese man-o-war?

3 In winter, what is the colour of the Arctic bird, the ptarmigan's plumage?

4 Name an arthropod that moves sideways?

5 What is the largest type of seaweed?

6 What shark has a bizarre head with eyes at the end of wing-like flaps?

7 Are sea cucumbers animals or plants?

8 What sea-going animal, with a small trunk-like nose, shows the greatest difference in size between the male and female?

9 What fish is called a kipper when it is filleted and dried?

10 What name is given to the thick layer of fat that insulates a whale's body?

Red for danger
590

LEVEL 1   These questions are associated with the colour red

1 What is a redwing?

2 What British butterfly might describe a senior Soviet sailor?

3 What large British mammal was famously painted by Landseer?

4 Name the wading bird with a piping call and red legs found around British coasts?

5 What is the best thing to do with ruby chard?

6 One of the rarest birds in America is the red-cockaded woodpecker – what is a cockade?

7 What is a red underwing?

8 In Britain, what bird is associated with the date August 12?

9 What is a red-hot poker?

10 Which rare British mammal, most common now in Scotland, was largely displaced from the rest of the country by its North American cousin?

Fruit salad
591

LEVEL 1   A sweet round with a fruity flavour

1 Which fruit is the base of the drink perry?

2 What is the major ingredient of guacamole?

3 What fruit shares its name with a high-ranking Chinese civil servant?

4 The juice of what fruit is mixed with coconut and rum to make a piña colada?

5 Of what fruit are laxton's superb and cox's orange pippin varieties?

6 A plantain is a variety of what type of fruit?

7 A loganberry is a cross between a blackberry and what other fruit?

8 Morello is a variety of what type of fruit?

9 A greengage is a green type of which fruit?

10 The name of what fruit is used to mean an unwelcome third person on a romantic occasion for two?

Literary leaves

592

LEVEL 3   A round about the book about the plant or animal

1 What plant of the primrose family was the codename of Baroness Orczy's spy character?

2 What is the only insectivorous mammal to appear in the title of a Shakespeare play?

3 The title of what John Steinbeck novel includes the name of a rodent and a primate?

4 What group of insects appear in the title of William Golding's reworking of *Coral Island*?

5 Who wrote *The Scarlet Letter*?

6 Alfred Noyes wrote a poem in which he told people to go down to Kew at the time of year when what plant was in flower?

7 In a film about Henry II and his wife Eleanor of Aquitaine, Henry was referred to as what large carnivore at what time of year?

8 What type of whale was Moby Dick in Herman Melville's novel?

9 Which tree appears in the title of a wintry novel by David Guterson?

10 Which bird appears in a poem by Edgar Allan Poe where it says, repeatedly, 'nevermore'?

Utter nonsense

593

LEVEL 2   Flights of fictional flora and fauna

1 The unicorn is a mythical creature. But which sea animal does have a single horn?

2 Sightings of which animal are alleged to have led to the mermaid myth?

3 What bird, according to Edward Lear, 'lays its eggs inside a paper bag'?

4 The Norwegian blue is a variety of what bird?

5 Who had trouble with tribbles?

6 By what is *Nessiteras rhombopteryx* better known?

7 In the poem in *Alice in Wonderland*, who said to the snail: 'There's a porpoise close behind us, and he's treading on my tail'?

8 'Is it weakness of intellect, birdie?' I cried, 'Or a rather tough worm in your little inside?' What bird is being addressed in Gilbert and Sullivan's *Mikado*?

9 What large ape took a fancy to Fay Wray?

10 According to a John Wyndham novel, what terrible mobile plant took over the world?

Great naturalists

594

LEVEL 3   A challenging round on some of the great natural scientists

1 With what type of animal do you associate John James Audubon?

2 Who lived at Downe House between 1842 and 1882?

3 Which famous TV naturalist's brother played Pinky in the film of Graham Greene's *Brighton Rock*?

4 Which TV bird-watcher was once chased by an enormous white kitten?

5 Who devoted her life to studying the mountain gorilla, and was the subject of the 1988 film *Gorillas in the Mist*?

6 Which world-famous environmentalist stood for election in 1997 against John Major?

7 Who wrote *The Naked Ape*?

8 Which botanist accompanied Captain Cook on his voyages?

9 With which animal is Jane Goodall associated?

10 What bird links Cetti, Savi, Radde, Upcher, Blyth, Bonelli, Hume, Ménétries, Pallas, Rüppell and Tristram?

Natural history

Cool for cats
595
LEVEL 1   From pussy cats to lions

1 What feature does a Manx cat lack?

2 Which member of the big cat family is the world's fastest animal on land?

3 Which is the largest of the big cats?

4 What is the feline equivalent of the dog world's Cruft's?

5 Which of the big cats can be found in both cold and warm climates?

6 What is distinctive about the sphinx cat?

7 Which big cat is unique in not being able to retract its claws?

8 Which spotted cat of the New World, found in lowland areas from Texas to northern Argentina, has short, smooth fur patterned with black-edged spots?

9 What breed of domestic cat can be fully coloured blue, brown, chocolate, lilac, red or tortoiseshell?

10 Which modern breed of domestic cat is considered to be closest to the cats of ancient Egypt?

Dinosaur dilemmas
596
LEVEL 3   Hard questions on the giants of the past

1 Which was the first dinosaur to be named, in 1824?

2 What is the small distinction of the *compsognathus*, a carnivorous dinosaur from the Jurassic period?

3 What important contribution did Sir Richard Owen make to the study of dinosaurs in 1841?

4 Which dinosaur had a large club tail?

5 To the nearest 10 million years, when did dinosaurs become extinct?

6 Which was the largest raptor: the velociraptor, the utahraptor, or the megaraptor?

7 Which dinosaur had the largest brain?

8 What unique feature did the iguanadon possess?

9 How is the brontosaurus also known?

10 What distinction was shared in the 1820s by William Buckland, a clergyman, and Gideon Mantell, a physician?

Animal in vegetable
597
LEVEL 3   Can you identify the plant with an animal or insect in its name?

1 Which annual or perennial flower of purple, pale, Jersey, common, alpine and ivy-leagued varieties has an amphibian connection?

2 Which pink or white flower, with over 300 species, could be linked to an insect?

3 Which old-fashioned geranium shares part of its name with a large bird?

4 Which yellow-flowered weed, often found in the lawn, sounds like a dapper large cat?

5 Which small flower shares the first part of its name with a domestic pet?

6 Which member of the daisy family has a reptile connection?

7 Which predominantly yellow flower, with over 260 varieties, could be linked to a bird of prey?

8 Which member of the primrose family is linked to an agricultural beast of burden?

9 Which common European herb's name has a connection with a domestic pet?

10 Which low-growing perennial with furry leaves sounds like part of a farm animal?

598 Nature quest

These questions are tougher than the others and you may need to do some research

1 Double-beam, wing-finger, three-horn-face are all types of what?

2 In Russian, the name of this dog means 'swift'. What is it?

3 Which fish takes its name from a heavyweight boxer?

4 What connects the aurora borealis, a comforting liqueur from Louisiana, cowboy movies and (very nearly) Sheena?

5 What is the largest single animal cell to be found in nature?

6 Which develops first in a tadpole – its front legs or its hind legs?

7 Split the following into three groups of three, primarily: stocking, fever, eye, hammer, neck, belly, tit, blood, breast.

8 Etymologically, which breed of dog unearths its quarry.

9 What colour is the beak of a Bombay duck?

10 What phrase, much misunderstood, is Herbert Spencer's main contribution to the theory of evolution?

11 Who said: 'I will not eat oysters. I want my food dead. Not sick, not wounded, dead.'

12 Kingdom, phylum, class, ?, family, genus, species. What is the missing word?

13 'Nor dread nor hope attend a dying animal.' Says who?

14 What is the common name of *Hippocampus hippocampus*?

15 What is the peculiar skill of the Jesus Christ lizard?

A clue to question 7

Natural history

Mammal mania
599

LEVEL 1   Can you identify these warm-blooded animals?

1 Which mammal has the longest neck?

2 Which is the largest living mammal?

3 Which mammal of the African savannah is so named because its call sounds like maniacal giggling?

4 Which mammal is said never to forget?

5 What name is given to mammals that give birth at a very early stage and nourish the newborn with milk rather than a placenta?

6 In what region of the world would you find springboks in the wild?

7 What is the only blood-sucking mammal?

8 Which huge mammal has black, white and Sumatran varieties?

9 Which animal gave its name to an organisation seeking rights for black people in America?

10 What is the only striped equine animal?

Birds of a feather
600

LEVEL 1   Get off to a flying start with these easy questions

1 One brings sorrow, two bring joy. Name the bird.

2 How do drinks link toucans and red grouse?

3 What bird gave its name to a jet fighter that can take off vertically?

4 The bald eagle is not actually bald, so how did it get its name?

5 Brent, Canada, and barnacle are types of what bird?

6 What brightly coloured garden bird has a red, white and black striped head and characteristic jet black wings with a broad yellow stripe?

7 Where would you find the kittiwake, a variety of gull, nesting?

8 On which continents would you find wild turkeys?

9 What type of animal is a Rhode Island red?

10 Shoveler, wigeon, pintail and mallard are types of what?

Mein host
601

LEVEL 2   This round is about animals and other organisms that feed on them

1 What parasitical insect transmits bubonic plague?

2 What parasite can live in your guts and has a long body made of flattened segments?

3 What simple public health measure was responsible for ridding London of cholera?

4 What disease does the tsetse fly carry?

5 The martin bug sucks the blood of house martins, but it has a close relative that feeds on man; what is it called?

6 Of what are crab, head and body varieties?

7 The skin condition ringworm is not caused by worms; what is it caused by?

8 What disease occurs when roundworms block the lymphatic system and organs are enlarged?

9 What desert fly is responsible for spreading the often fatal infection *leishmaniasis*?

10 The bite of what insect can lead to Lyme's disease?

602 Lucky dip
LEVEL 2 A mixed round from the living world

1 For what is an egg tooth, found in birds and some reptiles, used?

2 Chinstrap, jackass and Adelie are types of which bird?

3 What African mammal, which feeds on termites and ants, is also known as the ant bear?

4 What tiny plant floats on water and may have only one or two leaves?

5 What is a brambling?

6 From what animal does cashmere wool come?

7 A lodge is the home of what North American animal?

8 What sea creature has eight arms and a beak?

9 A jay has a small patch of bright feathers on its wing; of what colour?

10 The young of which animal are known as 'joeys' in Australia?

603 Literary creatures
LEVEL 1 The much-loved animal characters from children's fiction

1 What kind of animal is the tailor of Gloucester?

2 What are Flopsy, Mopsy and Peter?

3 Which type of creature is Beatrix Potter's Mrs Tiggywinkle?

4 In *Alice in Wonderland*, who is having tea with the Mad Hatter and the dormouse when Alice arrives?

5 What sort of animal is Winnie the Pooh's friend, Eeyore?

6 According to the nursery-rhyme, what did Mary have?

7 What is the name of Doctor Dolittle's parrot?

8 Which character is surprisingly cowardly in *The Wizard of Oz*?

9 What is the name of the Darling family's dog in *Peter Pan*?

10 In *The Jungle Book*, what kind of animal is Bagheera?

604 Flower it up
LEVEL 2 A veritable bouquet of questions

1 By what other name is traveller's joy, a type of wild clematis found in hedgerows, known?

2 How does the plant fleabane get its name?

3 What is the more common name for the windflower?

4 What colour are the ragwort flowers?

5 What links Van Gogh and *Helianthus annus*?

6 If a flower is described as campanulate, what shape would it be?

7 What is the plant *Nicotiana tabacum* more commonly known as?

8 What are the flower clusters of willow trees called?

9 What colour are most forget-me-not species?

10 Dog, burnet and briar are varieties of which thorny wild flower?

Natural history

Creepy-crawlies

605

LEVEL 1 A round about bugs and other nasties

1 What freshwater insect lives in portable cases made of stones, leaf fragments and other material?

2 A woolly bear isn't a bear at all; what is it?

3 What is the proper name of the often threadlike sense organs on insects' heads?

4 What car manufacturer makes a model nicknamed 'the beetle'?

5 What is the common name for the insects that have the shortest adult lifespan (some as short as five minutes)?

6 In the nursery-rhyme, which insect's house is on fire?

7 To the nearest 50,000, how many species of insect have so far been identified?

8 How many legs has a brown recluse?

9 What distinction does the goliath beetle hold?

10 The firefly isn't a fly. What sort of insect is it?

Bird brains

606

LEVEL 2 A test for the twitchers

1 Pied, yellow and grey are types of what long-tailed bird?

2 What is the smallest British bird?

3 Macaws are large types of which bird?

4 The wryneck is a relative of what common woodland bird?

5 What farmyard animal is a descendant of the wild jungle fowl?

6 What are the dominant colours of the magpie?

7 Bewick, whooper and mute are types of which animal?

8 What common domesticated bird evolved from the rock dove?

9 What colour is a male chaffinch's breast?

10 What is another name for a chiffchaff?

Vets out of practice

607

LEVEL 2 A round about animal illness

1 What pen name did the vet James Alfred Wight adopt?

2 Why do farmers fear the FMD virus?

3 If a vet was asked to examine a horse's fetlock, where would he look?

4 Rinderpest is a disease of which farm animals?

5 Which viral disease of the dog shares its name with a type of paint?

6 From which disease was a vaccine for human smallpox developed in 1796?

7 Psittacosis is a disease of which type of animal?

8 What is the more common name for bovine spongiform encephalopathy?

9 What type of parasite causes mange?

10 What animal suffers from scrapie?

608

A breed apart
Match the skin type to the list of species' skin

Bear fur • Snake skin • Tortoise shell
Cowhide • Fish scales • Elephant skin
Giraffe skin • Jaguar fur • Siberian tiger fur • Zebra skin

Natural history

609 What's in a name
LEVEL 2 A round with animal or plant connections?

1 What sort of plant is a ginkgo biloba?

2 What is the literal translation of rhinoceros?

3 What is the destroying angel?

4 Apart from being part of a horse, what is a coltsfoot?

5 What kind of animal is a corncrake?

6 Apart from being a missile, what is a sidewinder?

7 A domesticated animal that reverts to the wild is said to be what?

8 What flower name did Sir Percy Blakeney use to keep his identity secret?

9 Which U2 album is named after the desert plant *Yucca brevifolia*?

10 By what other name is the gnu known?

610 Boys brigade
LEVEL 3 All the answers in this round are plants containing boys' names

1 What wild flower, also known as golden rod, is named after the brother of Moses?

2 Jacob's youngest son gives his name to which tree that yields benzoin?

3 What popular spiky house plant is named after Eve's husband?

4 Which common garden weed shares a name with the founder of the London police force?

5 By what other name is the goat's beard known?

6 What family of yellow-flowered plants takes its name from the man who baptised Christ?

7 Which son of Isaac and father of the Jewish nation gave his name to a small white or blue flower found in stony, Arctic or alpine soils?

8 Which lily, also known as the paradise lily, shares its name with a make of tobacco?

9 The owner of Winnie-the-Pooh shares a name with which perennial white-flowered garden plant?

10 Which biblical figure, a byword for poverty and patience, gives his name to loosely tufted annual grass?

611 Plan B
LEVEL 3 All about a plant or animal beginning with the letter B

1 What is the more common name of flowerless plants called bryophytes?

2 What are bonitos?

3 Blewits are edible types of what?

4 Brinjal is the Indian name for what vegetable, often used in pickles?

5 What is a bustard?

6 What colour is the borage flower?

7 What type of animal is a Bombay duck?

8 A bonobo is a close relative of which other ape?

9 Boysenberries are hybrids between raspberries and what other fruit?

10 What species of bird is the bateleur?

612 Creature clues

LEVEL 1   Can you identify these plants or animals?

1 What is the world's largest bird of prey?

2 *Ring of Bright Water* by Gavin Maxwell is the story of what species of animal?

3 What is the more common name for the plant ling?

4 What are reindeer known as in North America?

5 Spadefoot, natterjack, clawed and midwife are all types of what?

6 What large South American cat gave its name to a luxury British car?

7 A flying fox is not a fox but what type of animal?

8 Which dog is named after an English Stuart king?

9 What breed of dog takes its name from the capital of China?

10 What is the camel's nautical nickname?

613 Take wing

LEVEL 1   A round on butterflies and moths

1 What is the name of the silken sheath that protects the chrysalis or pupa of certain moths?

2 How do carpet moths get their name?

3 How many functional legs has a red admiral?

4 Black veined, large, Bath, orange tip and wood are all species of which British butterfly?

5 Which group of butterflies shares its name with a species of flower?

6 What distinction does the Queen Alexandra's birdwing butterfly hold?

7 Common, silver studded, holly, long-tailed, Chalkhill and Adonis are species of which butterfly?

8 Why do many naturalists grow buddleia in their garden?

9 Which British butterfly shares its name with a punctuation mark?

10 In which book and film did a murderer leave a death's head hawk moth in the mouth of each of his victims?

614 Planted evidence

LEVEL 1   Questions about plants

1 Which plant flavours gin?

2 What is a perennial plant?

3 Sitka and Norway are types of which coniferous tree?

4 Who saw: '. . . a crowd, a host, of golden daffodils'?

5 What colour are gorse flowers?

6 What does a deciduous tree do with its leaves in winter?

7 From what plant is opium extracted?

8 By what more common name is the flower *impatiens* known?

9 What colour are fresh coconuts?

10 What plant is the national flower of Ireland?

Natural history

Animal magic
615   **LEVEL 2**   **A mixed menagerie**

1 What is the most colourful part of a male mandril?

2 Langurs and colobuses are types of what animal?

3 Name the American marine mammal that lies on its back, cracking shells with a stone?

4 Which large animal of the North American plains was hunted almost to extinction in the 20th century?

5 Which African animal has species named Burchell, Chapman and Grant?

6 From which country does the yak come?

7 Which is the largest of the great apes?

8 The rag doll is a breed of what domestic animal?

9 Gibbons and other primates move through the forest using a type of locomotion called brachiation; what does this mean?

10 Horses have four gaits: walking, trotting, galloping and which other?

Bird man
616   **LEVEL 3**   **A tough bird-related round**

1 Purple-crested, great-spotted, middle-spotted, lesser-spotted and black are all woodpeckers except for one. Which one?

2 Mother Carey's chicken is not a chicken but what type of bird?

3 How did the harlequin duck get its name?

4 What British night-flying bird has a 'churring' call?

5 Why are you unlikely to see bluebirds over the white cliffs of Dover?

6 Supply the bird to complete the English translation of Rossini's opera *La Gazza Ladra* or the thieving … what?

7 What is a flock of snipe called?

8 Where was the extinct ivory-billed woodpecker found?

9 Great northern, red-necked, and black-necked are varieties of what type of bird?

10 Garden, dartford, willow and wood are varieties of what small bird?

Feather-brained
617   **LEVEL 1**   **A round about the language of birds**

Different birds have enriched the English language by providing symbols and figures of speech. What birds are described by the following?

1 Someone who hoards objects.

2 A coward.

3 In cricket, scoring no runs.

4 In golf, two under par.

5 In golf, three under par.

6 Someone who ignores danger, hoping it will go away.

7 Giving up alcohol or drugs you go through cold … what?

8 Someone who stays up all night is a night … what?

9 A greedy person who gulps his food might be accused of being which large white seabird?

10 Someone who is especially vain, and dresses in over-elaborate clothes.

618 Supermarket exotica

LEVEL 1   These once-exotic fruits are now available everywhere

1 What K is a brown furry fruit, that used to be called the Chinese gooseberry?

2 What G is a strongly smelling egg-sized fruit, whose flesh surrounds a pulp of many seeds?

3 What K is a tiny orange-like (but not citrus) oval fruit eaten whole?

4 What L, whose knobbly skin can be peeled away to reveal sweet white flesh surrounding a black stone, is much used in Chinese cooking?

5 What M, common throughout Southeast Asia, is a large fruit with orange flesh?

6 What P is a dark crinkled-skin fruit, with a rich tangy flesh and crunchy seeds?

7 What P is an orange-coloured, cherry-sized fruit sometimes known as a Chinese lantern?

8 Which R is a plum-sized fruit, with white flesh and curved spines that are red when ripe?

9 What S is a waxy fluted fruit with a characteristic five-pointed cross section?

10 What P, sometimes known as Indian fig, is covered in small groups of tiny barbed spines?

619 Dog geography

LEVEL 1   Identify these dog breeds, named after places

1 A hound from a war-torn Asian country.

2 A terrier from a valley in Yorkshire, England.

3 A spotty dog from the Yugoslav coast.

4 A terrier from a north-eastern county of England.

5 A tiny dog from a Mexican province.

6 A very large Scandinavian dog.

7 A pointer from a large European country.

8 A terrier from Cumbria, England.

9 A terrier from the Midlands, England.

10 A retriever from the Canadian east coast.

620 What's in a name?

LEVEL 2   All these names have associations with flowers

1 That which 'by any other name would smell as sweet'.

2 A flowering shrub and the authoress of *Jamaica Inn*.

3 Her surname was Langtree, she was the mistress of Edward VII.

4 The Greek goddess of the rainbow.

5 A characteristic plant of Scottish moorlands.

6 The heroine of Verdi's *La Traviata*.

7 Surname Potter, a comic-book tomboy.

8 A small red fruit with a stone.

9 A fragrant herb used with lamb.

10 The collective name for all the plants in a region.

Natural history

Dem dry bones
621

LEVEL 2   Where in the body are the following bones?

1 Carpals

2 Humerus

3 Tibia

4 Scapula

5 Phalanges

6 Clavicle

7 Ilium and ischium

8 Malleus and incus

9 Sternum

10 Femur

Ologies
622

LEVEL 3   What do the following scientists study?

1 Lepidopterists

2 Palaeontologists

3 Ornithologists

4 Coleopterists

5 Arachnologists

6 Herpetologists

7 Embryologists

8 Hymenopterists

9 Ichthyologists

10 Bryologists

Names in nature
623

LEVEL 1   Test your natural vocabulary

1 What is a cotoneaster?

2 Which well-named toad carries its eggs on the back of the male until they hatch?

3 What familiar hoofed animal is descended from the tarpan (*Equus ferus*)?

4 A Gloucester old spot is what sort of an animal?

5 What mythical bird shares a name with the largest town in Arizona?

6 Barn, tawny and short-eared are types of what bird?

7 A cantaloupe is a type of what sort of fruit?

8 What name is given to the art of trimming hedges and shrubs into ornamental shapes?

9 Spotted, sike-shelled, and alligator snapping are all types of what shelled animal?

10 Highland and Hereford are types of which farmyard animal?

Mixed bag

624

LEVEL 1 A chance round of mixed biology

1 The cayman is closely related to which ferocious river animals?

2 What animals build dams across rivers?

3 What links the Orthoptera to a British national sport?

4 What is the national flower of Scotland?

5 What is furze more commonly called?

6 In the treeless deserts of southwest North America, where do gila woodpeckers nest?

7 What are eyries?

8 What is a cowry?

9 What family of poisonous snakes has a threat display that involves dilating its neck?

10 There are two types of tropical forest; seasonal or monsoon forest is one. What name is given to the other?

Tricky teasers

625

LEVEL 3 Tough questions from across the plant and animal kingdoms

1 What was the real first name of the landscape gardener and architect known as 'Capability' Brown?

2 What type of plants have flowers composed of ray and disc florets?

3 Norfolk Island pines are planted in warmer countries and are ancient plants related to monkey puzzle trees; but where is Norfolk Island?

4 What name describes plants that grow on other plants and survive by collecting rainwater?

5 What is spraint?

6 What is a vegetable sheep?

7 How does the honeyguide bird get its name?

8 What is the world's smallest bird?

9 A tarantula is a spider, but what is a tarantella?

10 From which plant is the Italian drink sambuca made?

Zoo illogical

626

LEVEL 2 Tricky animalistic questions

1 What is the Lone Ranger's horse called?

2 Which species of land mammal has the longest tongue?

3 Forests are divided into four layers: emergents, canopy, understorey and forest floor. Which layer harbours most life?

4 What sort of creatures are babblers and screamers?

5 What is the main diet of the mole?

6 What is a kernel?

7 Which is the only bird that can fly backwards?

8 What, zoologically, is a knot?

9 In what play did Shakespeare write: 'Where the bee sucks, there suck I'?

10 What is the gestation period of a rabbit?

Natural history

Odds and ends
627   **LEVEL 2**   **A round of random questions**

1 With which part of their body do snakes and lizards smell?

2 What do pangolins eat?

3 The loofah is used to wash your back in the bath, but what is it?

4 As well as stunning their prey, for what else do electric eels use their unique attribute?

5 Can you name one type of animal that has a spinneret?

6 During the mating season, what colour are male stickleback breasts?

7 What is a ring ouzel?

8 Where do you find phloem and xylem?

9 What, zoologically, is a monitor?

10 What is odd about the swimming posture of the shrimpfish?

Tough test
628   **LEVEL 3**   **A round of hard questions**

1 What is a leveret?

2 What substance in a flamingo's main food of shrimp gives the bird its characteristic pink colour?

3 What are langoustines?

4 What bright yellow crucifer (member of the cabbage family) is grown as a crop and called canola in the United States of America?

5 Who wrote *The Natural History of Selborne*?

6 What is the world's fastest fish?

7 What is mountain avens?

8 Anthrophobia or anthophobia is the morbid fear of what?

9 Which plant has the largest leaves?

10 By what novel method does the fish called the remora travel around the ocean?

Assorted set
629   **LEVEL 1**   **Some simple questions from the natural world**

1 The wolverine is related to which animals?

2 Which bird, a relative of the cuckoo, is found in dry areas of North America and seldom flies, but runs rapidly across the desert floor looking for prey?

3 What colour is squids' blood?

4 When do peacocks raise their tails?

5 What are elk?

6 Which is bigger, a stoat or a weasel?

7 What name is given to a scientist who studies plants?

8 Mistle and eye-browed are types of which bird?

9 What is a mamba?

10 Which freshwater fish shares a name with a long-shafted weapon?

Simple set
LEVEL 1 Easy if you know the answers

1 Which gastropods are commonly found, to the annoyance of plant lovers, in gardens?

2 What, according to legend, happens if the ravens at the Tower of London leave?

3 What does a pig's skin lack that means it needs to wallow in mud to keep cool?

4 In France, what are known as grenouilles?

5 What popular horticultural radio show was first broadcast in 1947?

6 What name is given to a segment of a garlic bulb?

7 In what habitat do hippopotamuses live?

8 What is the only species of eagle that breeds in England?

9 What do cuckoos and cowbirds have in common?

10 What kind of plant is the Devil's stinkpot?

Nature's way
LEVEL 2 Can you answer these random nature questions?

1 The severed head of what animal featured in the film *The Godfather*?

2 What bird record does the Arctic tern hold?

3 Of which animal does Britain have more than 44 million, while America has fewer than five million?

4 Which is the largest member of the crow family in Europe?

5 How do mantises catch their prey?

6 What is the flower narcissus more commonly called?

7 To which plant family does bamboo belong?

8 What shellfish is reputed to be an aphrodisiac?

9 What name is given to plants that have leaves modified to hold water and acquire nutrients from matter decomposing in the water?

10 What are rudd and tench?

Mixed miscellany
LEVEL 2 Questions to challenge the confident

1 Which word is applied to wheat in Britain but maize in the United States?

2 What is a trilobite?

3 Which lizard has pads on its feet that allow it to walk on ceilings and is often found indoors in warm climates?

4 Which dog breed was named after the saintly 12th-century abbot of Clairvaux?

5 What bird is used by fishermen in the Far East to catch fish?

6 What are the Cambrian, Silurian and Ordovician?

7 Which animal lives in a sett?

8 Botanically, what is timothy?

9 Of what farm animal is the merino a variety?

10 Which tree was frequently planted in churchyards in the Middle Ages, and its wood used to make longbows?

Organising a music quiz

A music round is a good way to liven up a quiz, and there are lots of ways you can use music as the basis of an intriguing set of questions. But there are two things you must bear in mind if you want your music round to go well: firstly, keep the questions brief and straightforward; secondly, make quite sure all your equipment works.

When it comes to music quizzes, the simplest ideas are often the best. You cannot go far wrong if you just record 10 five-second snippets of well-known songs and ask the teams to identify them. But even with an idea this uncomplicated there are things that can go amiss: make sure your extract does not give the game away by including the name of the song; and be sure to make it very clear what the task for the teams is: to get the points do they have to name the song, or the singer, or both?

Plan ahead

It pays to rehearse a music round, testing it on someone before the quiz. The reaction of your 'guinea pig' will help you to decide such things as how many times you are going to play each track.

One good approach is to record each track twice. Leave a short gap (say fifteen seconds) between the two identical recordings, and a gap of five seconds between questions. Players hear each track twice and only twice – and the quizmaster controls the pace of the round by pausing the music between each question. This technique works well if you are recording on tape.

CDs are easier to use because you can jump directly to any track. But to record a CD you need a CD burner on your computer and some specialist knowledge. Whatever system you use, don't record the whole track: 20 seconds is ample – and the shorter the snippet the harder it is to guess.

Check ... and check again

Get to the venue early and run through everything. Be quite certain the hi-fi system works, and that it does not distort music at a high volume. Have a back-up plan in case the PA system breaks down. A portable hi-fi may suit a small venue. If all else fails, have a replacement round ready to substitute for the music round.

Music copyright

It is against the law to copy music and play it in public without the proper authority. Strictly speaking, you need a licence to record music even if you are holding a quiz in your own front room. If you are planning a quiz in a public place, such as a club or a pub, you should certainly ask the venue organiser for advice on the use of music. For more information contact the Mechanical Copyright Protection Society (MCPS). Tel: 020 7306 5544. Or visit their web site on http://**www.mcps.co.uk**

Musical themes

There are lots of ways to give a twist to your music round. Here are some ideas:

Spot the intro

Identify the song title from the opening bars or the introduction of the song (stop the music just before the vocals come in). Name the song from the backing track: karaoke versions are now available without the words, making identification harder. Or use classical music: name the composer or the piece from the opening bars.

Name that film

Make up a quick-fire medley of songs from musicals. It might include *Consider Yourself* (Oliver), *Sandy* (Grease), *A Spoonful of Sugar* (Mary Poppins).

Alphabet songs

Identify the band or composer, all of which begin with the same letter of the alphabet. Get in a good mix of styles: Beatles, Blur, Burt Bacharach, Beach Boys, Bizet, Bananarama, Beethoven.

Version control

Play versions of the same song, and identify the artists. *My Way*, for example, has been recorded by Frank Sinatra, Dorothy Squires, Elvis Presley, Sex Pistols and Shane MacGowan – among others.

Other ideas

- Who's talking? – Identify the voices of famous people recorded from the radio.
- Many tongues – Get contestants to identify foreign languages from short spoken recordings.

American tunes

A music round might make use of a theme such as 'Around the USA'. Players need to name the American city or state, which may be contained either in the title of the song or in the name of the artist.

1 *I Left my Heart in San Francisco*, Tony Bennett
2 *If you Leave me Now*, Chicago
3 *I don't want a Lover,* Texas
4 *Midnight Train to Georgia,* Gladys Knight and the Pips
5 *More than a Feeling,* Boston
6 *New York, New York,* Frank Sinatra
7 *Do you Know the Way to San Jose,* Dionne Warwick
8 *California Dreaming,* Mamas and Papas
9 *24 Hours from Tulsa,* Gene Pitney
10 *Walking in Memphis,* Cher

Equipment checklist

Ideally, the quiz organiser will delegate the technical side of the music round to someone who is familiar with the equipment. That person should be on hand on the night to solve technical hitches. But if something goes wrong, don't spend long fixing it: the patience of an audience can evaporate surprisingly fast.

Here is the basic equipment you will need:

To record your music round

- A tape deck and/or CD burner – most modern computers are now fitted with them.
- Blank tapes/CDs.
- Connectors and leads.

To play it back

- A PA system with a microphone.
  - For tapes: some PA systems have built-in tape machines; otherwise you will need a separate deck.
  - For CDs: a stand-alone CD player. Some personal CDs have an output to allow them to be connected to an amplifier.
    - Connectors and leads.

Natural history

General knowledge
633

LEVEL 2   Tough questions about plants and animals

1 What is the technical name for a group of individual animals that belong to the same species, live in one area and interbreed?

2 Which bird, sometimes called the tickbird, clings to the hide of cattle and big-game animals to remove ticks, flies and maggots?

3 What is the world's fastest-moving animal?

4 What is the name of the muscular second stomach of birds?

5 The crumbly structure of surface soil is known as what?

6 May or may-blossom is a very common shrub and tree more commonly known as what?

7 What colour of dye was obtained from woad?

8 Where is the home of the Royal Horticultural Society?

9 What common foodstuff is known as a love apple?

10 On which continent would you find the poisonous snake the fer-de-lance?

Talking tongues
634

LEVEL 3   Can you understand these scientific terms?

1 To what does the adjective alar (or alary) refer?

2 If an animal is arboreal, where does it live?

3 What are arthropods?

4 What is meant by bioluminescence?

5 What does it mean if a young bird becomes imprinted on you?

6 What are animal horns and nails composed of?

7 What is the function of a plant's stamen?

8 What is the name of the substance that makes plants green?

9 What does parthenogenesis mean?

10 If an animal or insect is said to be oviparous, how does it reproduce?

Sundry sequence
635

LEVEL 1   A miscellaneous round of easier questions

1 What is a taproot?

2 What word describes a plant that can withstand frost and the cold?

3 When would a nocturnal animal hunt?

4 What colour is an Arctic fox in summertime?

5 What is the favourite food of leopard seals?

6 What is the term for an organism that is simultaneously male and female?

7 What is the grated rind of a lemon, orange or other citrus fruit called?

8 What word is used to describe the cutting of a tree so as to produce a close rounded head of young branches?

9 What is a quince?

10 What common bird provided the nickname of the French singer Edith Piaf?

Bright and beautiful

636

LEVEL 1 As simple as a single-celled amoeba

1 From which animals is St Patrick said to have freed Ireland?

2 Where would you find stigma, styles and stamens?

3 Rock, stock, turtle and collared are types of which bird?

4 What does the name of the dinosaur 'triceratops' mean?

5 What word means both an animal's hide and to bombard with stones and other missiles?

6 What domestic pet is also a kind of whip?

7 Why is the horseshoe bat so called?

8 Which fruit produces a kind of oil that can be 'virgin' or 'extra virgin'?

9 Which Asian country has the world's largest number of cattle?

10 Did the extinct reptile known as the plesiosaurus live in forests or in the sea?

The stuff of life

637

LEVEL 2 Challenging biological questions

1 What is the scientific name for the grating or chirping sound which crickets make?

2 Where are you most likely to find a tamarisk tree – in a desert or by the sea?

3 What colour are the flowers of thrift?

4 What is a halibut?

5 How do sea anemones catch their prey?

6 In gardening, what name is given to propagation by burying a plant's stem underground to encourage it to root?

7 Where would you find a butterbur plant? In a marsh or on a rock?

8 What kind of animal is a drongo?

9 Sika and fallow are types of what mammal?

10 If an animal is described as an albino what does it lack?

Lucky dip

638

LEVEL 2 Noah's ark had a less varied collection of animals

1 Roseate, Arctic and black are species of which sea bird?

2 What is an ammonite?

3 What is a male falcon called?

4 Which bird is falsely blamed for the spittle that is actually the protective environment for the larvae of the froghopper?

5 What plant provides the central ingredient for risotto?

6 If an animal is said to be ungulate, what does it have?

7 What name is given to the body off which a parasite lives?

8 A tall tree with upswept branches, the lombardy, is a species of which group of trees?

9 There are three species of snake in Britain: the grass snake, the adder, and what is the third?

10 What distinguishes a mole cricket from other crickets?

Natural history

639 · Odds and ends
LEVEL 3   As tough as a rhino's rear

1 Which religion prohibits the consumption of the pig, the camel, the hare and the prawn?

2 What word beginning with 'e' describes a natural habitat along with all its flora and fauna?

3 What is the name for the long rope-like plants that Tarzan uses to swing from tree to tree?

4 How are willowherb seeds dispersed?

5 In which country will you find pandas in the wild?

6 What is a springtail?

7 Cuckoo-pint, wild arum, or *Arum maculatum* are all names for which common plant?

8 What type of animal is a sambar?

9 In the forests of which continent would you find a bushbaby?

10 Chives, leeks, garlic, onions, radishes. Taxonomically, which is the odd-one-out?

640 · Wild wordpower?
LEVEL 3   If you get fewer than four out of ten, you have been guessing

1 Is a hamadryad a poisonous Indian snake, a bird of prey, or a sub-Saharan flowering bush?

2 Is brooklime the name of a slug's trail, a water-plant related to the speedwells, or the seedpod of a spotted rock rose?

3 Is a cardoon a plant, the ancestor of the horse or a species of pygmy antelope?

4 What type of animal is an onager: a Russian bird, an American shrew or an Asian wild ass?

5 Where on a duck would you find its speculum: on its beak, its underbelly, or wing?

6 From what is Jojoba derived: sperm whale, a desert shrub or avocado pear?

7 What is a crested caracara: a colobus monkey, a European newt or an American bird of prey?

8 What are genets and civets: mammals related to mongooses, song birds or squirrels?

9 What is a wartbiter: a leech, a bush-cricket or an African wading bird?

10 What is an amethyst deceiver: a migratory butterfly, a lizard or a type of fungus?

641 · The place where you live
LEVEL 2   10 questions on habitats and locations

1 The fynbos is famous for its diverse and wonderful flora. On which continent is it?

2 What name is given to the areas of dry scrubland and short trees in North America?

3 Which site in Gloucestershire, created by Peter Scott, is famous as a wildfowl sanctuary?

4 In which country is Amboseli national park?

5 In what state of the USA are the Everglades wetlands?

6 The Camargue is a famous bird-watching site in which country?

7 Grassland with scattered acacia trees is characteristic of what type of African habitat?

8 What national park in the USA is famous for bears, bison and geysers?

9 In which European country would you find a bird called the Andalusian hemipode?

10 Minsmere is a renowned RSPB site in which English county?

642

Anyone here speak Latin?
LEVEL 3 These botanical names are for some well-known wild flowers

What are the common names for these?

1 *Primula vulgaris*

2 *Viola odorata*

3 *Taraxacum officinale*

4 *Ophrys apifera*

5 *Ranunculus repens*

6 *Alchemilla vulgaris*

7 *Papaver rhoeas*

8 *Armeria maritima*

9 *Calluna vulgaris*

10 *Rumex acetosa*

643

Three of a kind
LEVEL 3 Also two of a kind, and four of a kind

1 Man, lady, soldier, frog and monkey are all types of what flowering plant?

2 What is the surprising thing lacking in female winter moths, mottled umber moths and vapourer moths?

3 What are motmots, trogons, guans and chachalacas?

4 Snake-bark and paper-bark are types of which tree?

5 Arabica and robusta are the two major types of which tropical crop?

6 Rock, royal and reticulate are all types of which snake?

7 Adonis, chalkhill, silver-studded, small and common are species of which type of insect?

8 New Forest, Connemaran, Andalucian and Percheon are all types of what animal?

9 Blue rock, rock, song and mistle are all types of which bird?

10 Impala, Grant's and Thomson's are all types of which African mammal?

644

Hart to heart
LEVEL 2 Questions on the deer and the seat of love

1 What is a hart?

2 What is a hart-and-dart?

3 What is a hart's tongue?

4 Which English king fought under the banner of the white hart?

5 On which continent would you find a hartebeest?

6 What is the name of the branch of medicine concerning diseases of the heart?

7 What spiny sea creature often has a heart-shaped external skeleton?

8 How many chambers has a human heart?

9 The pulmonary artery carries blood from the heart to which other organ?

10 In which book of the Bible would you find the words: 'As the hart panteth after the water brooks, so panteth my soul after thee'?

Natural history

Adjectivally yours

645

LEVEL 2   To what animal do these adjectives refer?

1 Bovine

2 Caprine

3 Aquiline

4 Simian

5 Ursine

6 Porcine

7 Ovine

8 Murine

9 Equine

10 Leonine

Nature's chemistry set

646

LEVEL 3   Potent potions for plants and people

1 What disease is quinine used to treat?

2 What plant leaf is used to soothe nettle stings?

3 Digitalis, a drug found in foxgloves, is used to treat which condition?

4 What colour is the pigment carotene?

5 Which flower produces the painkilling drug morphine?

6 Tannin is extracted from bark and other plant material; what was its main traditional commercial use?

7 Which flower's traditional name is 'piss-a-bed', and was used for centuries as a diuretic?

8 Taxol is extracted from American yew trees and is the source of a valuable drug for treating which disease?

9 Which popular drug is derived from willow bark?

10 Belladonna is an alternative name for which poisonous plant?

Talking to the trees

647

LEVEL 1   Tree names often have other meanings, or sound like other words

1 This tree's name also means to long for something.

2 This tree sounds like a coating of hairs.

3 This tree's name also means burnt wood.

4 This tree sounds like an old respected person.

5 This tree's name is also another very poisonous plant.

6 This tree sounds like a Mediterranean island.

7 Take one letter away from this tree and it sounds sacred.

8 This tree's name also means smart or dapper.

9 This tree sounds like the second person (singular or plural).

10 This tree's name is also an ingredient of margaritas.

Hickory dickory dock
LEVEL 1   Mice and their cousins

1 Which rodent can store food in its cheeks?

2 Which rodents are reputed (wrongly) to throw themselves off cliffs in huge herds?

3 Which rodent lives in a drey?

4 Which large aquatic rodent can fell trees?

5 Which hibernating rodent is proverbially sleepy?

6 What was the rodent-like nickname of the British Eighth Army, which fought in North Africa in the Second World War?

7 Which North American rodent digs tunnels in river banks and is noted for its strong musky smell?

8 Bank and field are types of which rodent?

9 Which common rodent is known scientifically as *rattus rattus*?

10 Which rodent, now a popular pet, is sometimes called the sand rat?

Plant life
LEVEL 2   Questions for people who are keen on green

1 Vanilla pods come from what type of flowering plant?

2 Fescue, twitch, brome and pampas are types of what?

3 Why is the pasque flower so called?

4 What type of plant is a prickly pear?

5 What is a filbert?

6 Saffron is obtained from a variety of which spring bulb?

7 What type of flower is a flag?

8 The young shoots of which plant are called crosiers because they look like a bishop's staff?

9 Which daisy-like flower gets its name from the Greek word for star?

10 From which country do the garden plants hebes and phormium (giant flax) come?

Talk to the trees
LEVEL 3   Can you decipher their botanical names?

1 *Populus niger*

2 *Salix alba*

3 *Fraxinus excelsior*

4 *Taxus baccata*

5 *Ilex aquifolium*

6 *Sorbus aucuparia*

7 *Abies alba*

8 *Laurus nobilis*

9 *Fagus sylvatica*

10 *Corylus avellana*

Natural history

Leggy

651

LEVEL 2 Insects, spiders and other crawly things

1 Who claimed to 'float like a butterfly, sting like a bee'?

2 How many sides does each cell of a honeycomb have?

3 Which biblical patriarch unleashed a plague of locusts on the Egyptians?

4 The Colorado beetle is a pest of which crop?

5 Name the multi-faceted sight organs of insects, spiders, crustaceans and their relatives.

6 What is the name for the middle section of an insect's body?

7 Which Russian composer wrote *The Flight of the Bumble Bee*?

8 Blackfly and greenfly are more properly called what?

9 Which carnivorous plant has leaves that spring shut to capture small insects?

10 What is the name of the substance which is fed to certain bees to make them become queens?

Crazy names

652

LEVEL 3 Oddly named plants or animals

1 Which sea urchin is named for its resemblance to a coin?

2 Which ant has a name that would strike a chord with Winnie-the-Pooh?

3 Which fungus has a name that might be rendered 'terrestrial celestial bodies'?

4 What kind of animal is an 'oo'?

5 Which breed of dog shares its name with a Chinese rebellion?

6 Which aptly named wasp builds a nest out of mud that bakes hard in the sun?

7 What is a Jersey tiger?

8 Which bird acquired its name because the feathers at the back of its head were said to look like quill pens?

9 The longest-known worm has the Latin name *Lineus Longissimus* – what is its common name?

10 Which deep-sea fish has a lure attached to the tip of its snout to attract prey?

Buzz off

653

LEVEL 1 Can you solve the fly connections in this round?

1 What is the common name for the large flies with very long thin legs, sometimes known as 'crane flies'?

2 Which biting fly carries the diseases yellow fever and malaria?

3 Which fly has a name that is also a disrespectful word for a police officer?

4 Which fly is responsible for transmitting sleeping sickness?

5 What large, thick-bodied, biting insects might particularly trouble equestrians?

6 Which fly, which is striped like a wasp, can remain suspended in flight above a flower?

7 What is the common name of the fly *Musca domestica*?

8 What phrase containing 'fly' means something that spoils an otherwise happy situation?

9 Which minute biting flies occur in huge numbers in Scotland during summer?

10 Complete this line from *Dumbo*: 'But I'd been done seen about everything when I see an...'

 **654**

Nature's medicine chest
LEVEL 3 Cures and potions that grow in the ground

1 Which plant was used by early herbalists as a cure for toothache?

2 The oil from which Australian tree is used as a natural antiseptic and for treating skin conditions?

3 What word beginning with E is an extract of the purple coneflower used to treat colds?

4 Which yellow flowering plant is often used to treat depression?

5 What is the common name for *Vitex agnus-castus*, a herb, that eases menstrual problems?

6 Oil from the seeds of which evening-flowering yellow plant can treat hormonal imbalance?

7 The juice of which spiky African plant is used as an ingredient in cosmetics and to treat burns?

8 Extracts from which Chinese tree are used to boost mental capacity?

9 Which flower is used to produce calendula creams, ointments and teas?

10 The roots of which plant are used to produce a sedative?

 **655**

Amphibians and reptiles
LEVEL 2 Questions on animals which are at home on land and water

1 What amphibian was once believed to be able to live in fire?

2 What is the common name for the larvae of frogs and toads?

3 What word beginning with C is given to the bony shell of reptiles such as tortoises, turtles and terrapins?

4 Palmate, smooth and great-crested are types of what?

5 Tree, marsh and edible are types of what animal?

6 The Galapagos Islands have the world's only sea-going lizard, what is its name?

7 Which mythical-sounding creature is the world's largest lizard?

8 What is the name of the hypnotic snake in the Disney film *The Jungle Book*?

9 A testudo was a wheeled shelter used by Roman soldiers besieging walled cities; from which reptile did it take its name?

10 Which colourful South American frog secretes a deadly venom?

 **656**

Astronomical animals
LEVEL 2 The stars of the animal world

1 What animal is associated with the constellation Taurus?

2 What animal is associated with the constellation Delphinus?

3 What animal is associated with the constellations Ursa Major and Ursa Minor?

4 What animal is associated with the constellation Lacerta?

5 What animal is associated with the constellation Capricorn?

6 What animal is associated with the constellation Vulpecula?

7 What is the other name for the star Sirius?

8 What type of animal was Pegasus, after which a constellation is named?

9 What animal is associated with the constellation Aquila?

10 What animal is associated with the constellation Cygnus?

Natural history

657 Bodily parts
LEVEL 2   Where in the body are the following?

1 Alveola

2 Cerebellum

3 Fovea centralis

4 Ventricles

5 Diaphragm

6 Cervical vertebrae

7 Sternum

8 Patella and cruciate ligaments

9 Aorta

10 Semi-circular canals

658 Zoo time
LEVEL 3   A round about books on the shelf marked 'Nature'

1 Who wrote *Dinosaur in a Haystack*?

2 What is the name of the theory, developed by James Lovelock, that the Earth is a self-regulating organism?

3 What is the name of Rachel Carson's crusading book about the dangers of pesticides?

4 Who wrote *My Family and other Animals*?

5 Who wrote and illustrated *Birds from Britannia*?

6 Jacob Bronowski produced a classic 1970s TV series and an accompanying book shared its name. What is it called?

7 Who wrote a book about chimpanzees entitled *In the Shadow of Man*?

8 Paul Gallico's *The Snow Goose* is set during which war?

9 Who wrote the novel *Great Apes*?

10 What is the title of Charles Darwin's revolutionary book on evolution, published in 1859?

659 British beasts
LEVEL 1   To which animals found in Britain do these descriptions apply?

1 A spiny insectivore that can roll itself into a ball.

2 The smallest British bat.

3 A beetle with a red shell and black spots.

4 Originally an American animal farmed for its fur, which escaped and has become naturalised.

5 A small insectivorous mammal with a long nose, with two species called common and pygmy.

6 An ancestor of a farm animal, with tusks and bristly hair.

7 In folklore this animal is often named Reynard.

8 A primarily fish-eating animal related to the stoat.

9 Common and grey are the only two species of this aquatic animal regularly seen in British waters.

10 A black-and-white animal sometimes called a brock.

660 Mountain high

LEVEL 3   All these plants and animals live on British moors or mountains

1 Which bird's breeding call is a rapid shrill 'kek-kek-kek'?

2 What is a large wall brown?

3 Is a bee fly a bee or a fly?

4 What is the yellow Xanthoria aureola?

5 What is the name for the mating season of red deer?

6 Which upland shrub bears green berries that ripen to black the following year and are used as a culinary flavouring?

7 What is the cinnamon cortinarius?

8 What type of animal might be whitefaced, blackfaced, rough fell or Cheviot?

9 What is the name for a domesticated polecat?

10 What is the name for the place where black grouse perform their courtship dance?

661 Giants and titans

LEVEL 2   A round on some of nature's gargantuan marvels

1 Which large dinosaur had a series of bony plates that formed a crest along its back?

2 Lodgepole, Scots and bristlecone are all types of which tall organism?

3 What is the fastest animal on two legs?

4 What is the biggest living animal – and probably the largest animal ever?

5 Which is the heaviest terrestrial mammal?

6 Which bird has the largest wingspan?

7 What is the fastest animal on land?

8 In which American state are you most likely (if you are unlucky) to encounter a Kodiak bear, the largest land carnivore?

9 Which is the world's largest fish?

10 What kind of flying insect is an African giant swallowtail?

662 Order! Order!

LEVEL 2   Can you identify the animals which belong to the following orders?

1 Chas and Dave kept on talking about this fast breeding lagomoph.

2 This pinnipede (meaning 'feather feet') had a long chat to the carpenter?

3 These chiropterans (meaning 'hand wings') are maddeningly often found in the belfry.

4 This edentate (meaning 'toothless') could leave Dec without a partner.

5 This cetacea, the largest creature ever to have lived on Earth, is sad having a great time.

6 This artiodactyl (meaning even number of toes), horse of the river, is all Greek to us.

7 You could put a monkey on this perissodactyl's (meaning odd number of toes) nose.

8 A barrel-load of these primates (the highest order of mammals) would keep you busy.

9 This proboscidea (meaning 'nose animal') wouldn't forget you.

10 This prickly insectivora (meaning 'insect-eating') is a privet creature and a bit greedy.

Natural history

It's in the genes

663

LEVEL 2   Questions on the nuts and bolts of biology (and other things)

1 Who discovered the structure of DNA?

2 Who wrote *The Selfish Gene*?

3 Who sang 'Sweet Gene Vincent'?

4 How many copies of each gene does a woman carry?

5 Which is the 'universal' blood group?

6 Who was born first, Gene Kelly or Fred Astaire?

7 What was the name of the Austrian monk who discovered the fundamental laws of genetics by experimenting with plants?

8 What is the name of the undertaking to 'map' all the genes in the human body?

9 How many pairs of chromosomes are there in a normal human cell?

10 What name is given to conditions inherited through the genes of parents?

Death and the devil

664

LEVEL 3   Ghoulish things in the natural world

1 What is a Satan's bolete?

2 Why is the death's head hawk moth so called?

3 What was the distinctive feature of Cerberus, the dog that in Greek mythology guarded the gates of Hades?

4 What is a devil's coach-horse?

5 What, in the sea, are dead man's fingers?

6 What colour is the flower of the Devil's-bit scabious?

7 Why are the fungi death's caps and destroying angels so called?

8 How does the death-watch beetle betray its presence?

9 What fruit is a central ingredient of the dish called 'devils on horseback'.

10 According to Meatloaf, what flying animal emerged from hell?

Slippery as a snake

665

LEVEL 2   All the answers begin with the letter S

1 What name is given to the species of willow with broad leaves?

2 In heraldry what word means black, and is also a species of antelope?

3 Which rodent can be grey, red or flying?

4 Which bird beginning with S is a close relative of the cormorant?

5 From which shrub can an anti-constipation preparation be made?

6 What small, sour fruit of the blackthorn is used to flavour a type of gin?

7 What S is a kind of sedimentary rock, red outcrops of which are particularly prominent in Devon?

8 Name the spotted bird that roosts in enormous flocks in trees and in city buildings.

9 Which North American mammal is characterised by its ability to produce an overpowering stench?

10 Which plant is named after the mark of the wisest king of Israel?

A bug's life

666

LEVEL 1   Questions about creepy crawlies

1 What name is given to the process by which an insect sheds its skin?

2 What is the name for a scientist who studies insects?

3 By what common name are headlice known?

4 Red, black and army are all types of which insect?

5 Common, American, German and Australian are types of what unpleasant insect?

6 What insect has pincers at the end of its body, and got its name because it was once believed to crawl into one of your sense organs?

7 What bug gets its name because it is shaped like a piece of defensive armour?

8 Which insect is known to perform a dance that leads others of its species to pollen sources?

9 What large bug has a very loud chirping call, a characteristic sound of the tropics and sub-tropics?

10 The *bombyx mori* produces in its cocoon a fine, lustrous fibre used to make a certain high-quality cloth. Which cloth?

For the bookworms

667

LEVEL 3   Animals and plants in myth and fiction

1 What is Kipling's Rikki Tikki Tavi?

2 In Greek mythology, what fruit did Persephone eat and so condemn herself to spend six months in the Underworld?

3 The opera singer, Jenny Lind, was known as the Swedish what?

4 In Old Possum's *Book of Practical Cats*, which gravity-defying mystery cat is called the 'hidden claw'?

5 In the Bible, who slew a thousand men with the jawbone of an ass?

6 Which witty writer was much upset by the death of his favourite cat, Hodge?

7 Which large African herbivore did the humourists Flanders and Swann write a song about?

8 What sort of animal was Hercules required to bring from Crete to Mycenae?

9 In Greek mythology, what form did the god Zeus take to seduce Leda?

10 In which novel does the pig Napoleon appear?

Pond life

668

LEVEL 2   Is there something fishy going on in this watery round?

1 How does a sergeant fish get its name?

2 What type of fish is a wobbegong?

3 Does a coconut sink or float on salt water?

4 To which class of mammal does the duck-billed platypus belong?

5 Which appropriately named fish is entirely transparent?

6 Which flightless bird of the Southern Hemisphere lives in rookeries?

7 Who wrote *Moby Dick*?

8 Which sea animal moves through the water by a form of jet propulsion?

9 Who wrote *The Little Mermaid*?

10 Which fish has species known as three-spined and ten-spined?

Natural history

American beasties
669 LEVEL 3   Fauna of the New World

1 What are colonies of prairie dogs called?

2 What kind of animal is a fisher?

3 What is the name of the armoured animal found in the southern states of the US?

4 What animal makes domed 'houses' of vegetation in marshlands?

5 What kind of mammal is a peccary?

6 What is the largest North American deer?

7 What is the name of the only North American antelope?

8 What kind of animal is a jaguarundi?

9 What animals featured in the 1972 horror film *The Night of the Lepus*?

10 What kind of animal is a chickaree?

Biodiversity
670 LEVEL 3   A round as varied as the plumage of a rainbow lorikeet

1 Which European tree lives longest?

2 How many species of domestic dog are found today?

3 What are the young of bats called?

4 Which leaves are the preferred food of the silkworm?

5 At which end of a rattlesnake is its rattle?

6 The word chivalry derives from the Old French for which animal?

7 In which country would you find the bird known as a kookaburra?

8 What kind of living thing is yeast?

9 What is the hardest mineral?

10 The Hindu god Ganesh has the head of which animal?

Insect orders
671 LEVEL 3   Which insects belong to the following orders?

1 *Lepidoptera* (scale-winged; many brightly coloured).

2 *Trichoptera* (hair-winged; aquatic insects with portable homes).

3 *Coleoptera* (sheath-winged; with hard protective wing cases, the largest insect order).

4 *Homoptera* (same-winged; contains major pests of roses and other plants).

5 *Siphonaptera* (wingless with sucking mouth parts).

6 *Ephemeroptera* (on the wing for a very brief period of time).

7 *Hymenoptera* (membrane-winged; includes very active insects with complex societies).

8 *Orthoptera* (firm wings; many make chirping sounds).

9 *Zygoptera* (two sets of similar wings; large predatory insects with aquatic larvae).

10 *Dictyoptera* (net-winged; contains pests that live in kitchens and other warm places).

Hello petal

672

LEVEL 3   Give the scientific name for these flower parts

1 The organ that receives the pollen.

2 The structure that supports the stigma.

3 The stalk of the stamen.

4 The part of the stamen that produces the pollen.

5 The ring of green leafy organs behind the petals.

6 A flower head composed of many flowers on stalks arising from a single point.

7 Flower stalk.

8 The organ producing the nectar.

9 A multi-branched flower head.

10 A flower that is in fact composed of many flowers in a tight head.

Strictly lepidopterous

673

LEVEL 3   Which butterflies fit the following descriptions?

1 Large, black and yellow, with tails on the wing.

2 Pure yellow, one of the first butterflies to fly in spring.

3 Single bold eyespots on each wing.

4 Wings with a very jagged outline, underside dark with a silver, semi-circular mark.

5 A large, rare migrant; orange with strong black veining.

6 A spring butterfly, predominantly white but the male with orange markings.

7 A woodland butterfly, flying in sunspots, dark brown with lighter spots.

8 A white and black checkerboard patterned butterfly.

9 A small butterfly, upper wings bright orange with darker spots, lower wings dark except for an orange margin.

10 A large, fast-flying butterfly, wings metallic purple-black with a broken line of white markings.

Monochrome

674

LEVEL 1   All the answers are animals with black or white colouring

1 Which large North American mammal of the *ursidae* family is known to hunt fawns and fish, though it is mostly vegetarian?

2 Which is the largest and most numerous rhinoceros?

3 Which venomous snake is probably the fastest in the world?

4 Which shark is blamed for more attacks on humans than any other?

5 What are black in Australia, black-necked in South America and white elsewhere?

6 Which fish is also known as the common jollytail?

7 What kind of insect is sometimes known as a buffalo gnat or turkey gnat?

8 Which owl nests on the tundra and feeds on lemmings, rabbits and hares?

9 Which common Eurasian bird is noted for its 'chak-chak' call as it goes to roost?

10 Which big cat, an endangered species, is found in central, south and east Asia?

Natural history

675 A dog's life

LEVEL 1   A not very natural history quiz on man's best friend

1 Which dog was the first animal movie star, featuring in 22 films from 1925?

2 Velma, Daphne, Fred and Shaggy. Who is the missing member of the gang?

3 What is the name of the dog in Tom and Jerry?

4 Which dog has a name that in German means 'badger hound'?

5 What dog breed takes its name from an area of eastern France famous for its perfumed white wines?

6 Which country has the largest population of pet dogs, with approximately 59 million?

7 In the Charles M. Schultz comic strip, what kind of dog is Snoopy?

8 What was the name of President Clinton's dog?

9 What is the domesticated dog's closest wild relative?

10 How many puppies featured in the film *101 Dalmatians*?

676 No shrinking violets

LEVEL 3   Every answer is a flower named after a girl

1 What wild flowering plant is linked to the lead actress in the 1985 film *Prizzi's Honor*?

2 What golden and red-leaved plant shares its name with a British Wimbledon champion?

3 What wild flower, also known as Aaron's beard, shares its name with an Israeli prime minister?

4 A wild growing perennial herb is linked to which late British musical actress?

5 Which herb of the mustard family shares its name with the Pulitzer prize-winning author of *Foreign Affairs*?

6 Which plant, sometimes known as giant buckwheat, is linked to Michael Douglas' wife?

7 What flower, known as melancholy gentleman, shares its name with a matron-playing actress?

8 Which dramatic climber, also known as morning glory, is linked to French and Saunders?

9 Which autumnal plant takes its name from 'the face that launched a thousand ships'?

10 Named after the daughter of King Priam, which marsh plant is also called the leatherleaf?

677 Articulate animals

LEVEL 3   What is the scientific name for these insect parts?

1 Balancing organs in flies.

2 The first leg segment.

3 The organ through which air enters the breathing tubes.

4 The cheek.

5 The units of the compound eye.

6 Hairs on a wing.

7 The organ with which eggs are laid.

8 A dark mark on the leading edge of the wing.

9 Segmented taste organs around the mouth.

10 The hardened forewings of beetles.

 **Nature quest**

These questions are tougher than the others and you may need to do some research

1 What do the following animals have in common: the blue antelope, the Falklands fox, the Bali tiger, the Badlands bighorn sheep?

2 In Malay this animal's name means 'man of the forest'. What is it?

3 In Old Afrikaans this animal is 'earth pig'. What is it?

4 Which animal would you associate with a 'Nantucket sleighride'?

5 Where the bee sucks, there sucks who?

6 What is the link between the glowworm, the koala bear and the Tasmanian tiger?

7 Cambrian, Ordovician, Silurian: what next?

8 Which Wilde animal is uneatable?

9 'The unicorn is a passing ugly beast to look upon,' wrote a disappointed Marco Polo in the 14th century, ''Tis altogether different from what we imagined.' What was it he had seen, in fact?

10 Hibernation means sleeping through the winter – but what is the word for sleeping through the summer?

11 Collared, dusky, superb fruit. Which bird?

12 Sea, tumble, giant hog. All types of what?

13 'In their queer, inimitable, vegetative gracefulness … a family of rare, long-stemmed speckled gigantic flowers slowly advancing.' Which animals are being described here?

14 Rumen, abomasum, omasum, reticulum. The four parts of what?

15 After what animal are the Canary Isles named?

 A clue to question 6

Natural history

679 Gardener's question time
LEVEL 2 Questions on backyards, potting sheds and allotments

1 Which garden vegetable is a symbol of Wales?

2 What is the name for a tree that does not shed its leaves in winter?

3 What is the name for the transparent glass or plastic cover used for growing delicate plants?

4 What is the name for the practice of cutting-off spent blooms to encourage new ones?

5 Which plant bulbs, associated with Holland, were sold for fortunes in the 16th century?

6 In the Beatrix Potter stories, which garden vegetable sends the Flopsy Bunnies to sleep?

7 What drink would you make from the leaves of the *Camellia sinensis* plant?

8 For what purpose are fans, cordons and espaliers used?

9 What name is given to the process of growing a plant cutting on a different rootstock?

10 With which English county would you associate a red rose?

680 Who's coming to dinner?
LEVEL 3 Can you give the scientific name for animals that obtain nourishment in the following ways?

1 Obtains its energy from sunlight.

2 Eats seeds.

3 Feeds on animals, but without killing them.

4 Eats fragments of plant material.

5 Eats plants.

6 Feeds on the meat of other animals.

7 Feeds on grass.

8 A plant that feeds on decaying matter.

9 Eats fish.

10 Literally means eats everything, but used for an animal with a very broad diet.

681 M is for Moo
LEVEL 1 All the answers begin with the letter M

1 Tiny relatives of spiders.

2 The commonest wild duck.

3 A member of the cabbage family, its seeds are used to make a hot condiment.

4 An insect resembling someone at prayer.

5 Field, sugar, and Norway are varieties of this tree.

6 A dangerous type of eel, brightly coloured and found in tropical waters.

7 An evolutionary strategy whereby an animal protects itself by having the same markings as a more dangerous species.

8 A relative of the starling that can copy human voices.

9 A mythical Cretan creature, half bull, half human.

10 Sand, house and crag are varieties of this bird.

682 The ABC of biology
LEVEL 1 Every answer begins with the letter A, B or C

1 What A is a bony growth on the head of a deer?

2 What A is the only poisonous British snake?

3 What A is the mountain range where you might find an edelweiss?

4 What Bs live in an apiary?

5 What B is another name for a blackberry?

6 What B is a British spring-flowering wildflower, found in woodlands in huge numbers?

7 What B is the name given to the cabbage family, which includes cabbage, sprouts, cauliflower and broccoli?

8 What C is the rubbery substance that forms part of the vertebrae?

9 What C is a vegetable known as zucchini in the USA?

10 What C is another name for a puma?

683 Hello weed
LEVEL 2 Questions about the gatecrashers in your garden

1 What eastern-sounding creeper grows so fast it can smother other plants and even buildings?

2 What is the common name of convolvulus?

3 What common weed is a source of food for butterflies and can be made into soup?

4 What common weed is extremely poisonous to horses and cattle but not sheep?

5 What is glyphosate?

6 What common lawn weed, with white and yellow flowers, gives its name to the largest plant family?

7 The weed herb robert is a relative of which common garden plant?

8 What name is given to the layer of compost, peat, manure or other organic matter applied to smother weeds?

9 What weed is a traditional remedy for nettle stings?

10 What colour are the flowers of willowherb?

684 Noah's Ark
LEVEL 2 You will find all kinds of animals in here

1 What is the largest species of penguin?

2 What is the name of the shelter a hedgehog builds to live in through the winter?

3 What is the name of the fungal delicacy sought out by pigs?

4 According to folklore, what does it mean when swallows are flying high?

5 Is a thorny devil a reptile or an insect?

6 What is the name of the repellent acid produced by ants?

7 What is the main food of salmon, which gives them their pink-tinted flesh?

8 What is the common name for the egg-cases of skates and rays, which are often found washed up on beaches?

9 Which ancient people actually ate the edible dormouse and considered it a delicacy?

10 What colour is the skin of a polar bear?

Natural history

685 Habits

LEVEL 3 What do these descriptions of the habits and habitats of plants and animals refer to?

1 Riparian

2 Fluvial

3 Littoral

4 Abyssal

5 Benthic

6 Boreal

7 Lacustrine

8 Pelagic

9 Halophile

10 Xerophile

686 Over a new leaf

LEVEL 3 Questions on plants and trees

1 Which Southeast Asian plant has the biggest flowers, which give off a rotten smell?

2 What is the most troublesome water weed, which has clogged up many lakes in Africa and rivers in the Far East?

3 Where can you find the largest water lilies in the world, which measure 2m (7ft) across?

4 How does the North American pitcher plant attract its prey?

5 Which tree has more than 1000 trunks?

6 In which country were Wollemi pines first discovered in 1994?

7 What North American plant, with small green flowers and whitish berries, is highly toxic?

8 What plant, with a university association, is found alongside railway lines in Britain?

9 What does the Mexican jumping bean contain that enables it to hop?

10 Which rare palm tree, found in the Seychelles, has the biggest seeds in the world, each one weighing up to 20kg (44lb)?

687 Herbal rides again

LEVEL 1 Questions on spices and herbs

1 What herb is used to make pesto?

2 What part of the ginseng plant is used in herbalism?

3 Pennyroyal is a type of what herb?

4 What herb is commonly mixed with onion in stuffings?

5 What herb is used in the making of the salmon dish gravadlax?

6 'Parsley, sage, rosemary and thyme' is a line from which song by Simon and Garfunkel?

7 The lacy outer covering of the nutmeg is ground to make which spice?

8 With which spice is the Colman family most closely associated?

9 Which herb, frequently used as a garnish, comes in flat-leaved and curly forms?

10 Which pungent plant allegedly keeps vampires away?

688

Flying high
Can you identify these birds using the list below?

Cap white eye • White pelican • Barn swallow
Bearded vulture • Arctic tern • Canada goose
Great egret • Snowy owl
Cardinal • Guinea fowl

Natural history

Trees

689

LEVEL 2 Plucking from the tree of knowledge

1 Which plangent tree grows in damp places and has long drooping branches?

2 Which tree would you most closely associate with the Lebanon?

3 Which country has a maple leaf as its national emblem?

4 Which rock band produced an album called *The Joshua Tree*?

5 Copper, silver and common are all types of what tree?

6 Which native European tree is the tallest?

7 In which country is Aleppo, from which Aleppo pine takes its name?

8 What is the more common name of the Linden tree?

9 Why is *Picea abies* in demand at Christmas?

10 According to the carol, of all the trees in the wood which one bears the crown?

Kids' stuff

690

LEVEL 1 What name is given to the young of the following creatures

1 Giraffe

2 Ostrich

3 Goat

4 Swan

5 Owl

6 Turkey

7 Zebra

8 Duck

9 Goose

10 Fish

Pots and pansies

691

LEVEL 2 Flowers you might have around the house

1 Who wrote the novel *Keep the Aspidistra Flying*?

2 What is the name of the Japanese art of growing miniature trees?

3 What is the name for the Japanese art of flower-arranging?

4 What colour are the flowers of the bottlebrush?

5 *Echinocereus*, *Opuntia* and *Mammillaria* are types of what prickly houseplant?

6 What is the general name for plants with fleshy leaves that grow in dry places?

7 What is the more common name for *Philodendron pertusum*, noted for its glossy, perforated leaves slashed to the margins?

8 What colour are the upper leaves of poinsettia?

9 According to his poem, what common flower did Wordsworth encounter when he 'wandered lonely as a cloud'?

10 What is the name for a small posy of flowers, as pinned to a woman's dress on a special occasion?

Roses by other names
LEVEL 2   Some of these questions are thorny

1 What type of rose is named after a French royal house?

2 What type of rose takes its name from the capital of Syria?

3 Rose hips are a rich source of which vitamin?

4 What characteristic of tea roses gave them their popular name?

5 How many petals does the flower of a simple wild rose have?

6 Which English king adopted the Tudor rose as his official emblem?

7 Which poet coined the phrase 'unofficial English rose'?

8 What colour is the Queen Elizabeth rose?

9 According to the song, what colour is the rose of Texas?

10 In which Shakespeare play will you find the famous line: 'That which we call a rose by any other name would smell as sweet'?

What shape is a leaf?
LEVEL 3   Botanists have a long list of terms to describe leaf shapes; what do the following terms mean?

1 Palmate

2 Sagittate

3 Cordate

4 Spatulate

5 Capitate

6 Dentate

7 Hastate

8 Serrate

9 Linear

10 Crenulate

Deadlier than the male
LEVEL 1   What is the word for the female of these generic animal names or male terms?

1 Boar

2 Ass

3 Giraffe

4 Hare

5 Zebra

6 Sheep

7 Rooster

8 Fox

9 Gander

10 Tomcat

Natural history

Eat your greens
695
LEVEL 1   A greengrocer's banquet of a round

1 What colour is the skin of a sweet potato?

2 If you have an 'iceberg' in your salad, what is it?

3 Globe, Jerusalem and Chinese are all types of which vegetable?

4 Which vegetable is traditionally eaten with haggis on Burns' night?

5 What fruit is associated with October 31?

6 Of what is King Edward a variety?

7 Which salad ingredient is traditionally known as the 'love apple'?

8 Lima, French and runner are types of which vegetable?

9 What purple-skinned vegetable used to be known as 'poor man's meat'?

10 What is is the main ingredient of hummous?

South American animals
696
LEVEL 3   How well do you know the animals south of Mexico?

1 What is the only South American marsupial?

2 Which South American comes in two-toed and three-toed varieties?

3 What kind of animal is the tamarin?

4 The world's largest rodent lives in South America. What is it called?

5 What are margays and oncillas?

6 In addition to manatees, what other normally marine mammal is found in the Amazon?

7 Which is the biggest cat in the rain forest?

8 Which appropriately named monkeys indulge in long choruses of roaring, especially at dawn?

9 Which South American snake has a name derived from the Sinhalese words for 'lightning stem'?

10 What kind of animal is the tamandua?

World tour
697
LEVEL 2   Questions from all four corners of the Earth

1 Which ocean is larger, the Pacific or the Atlantic?

2 At which pole would you find polar bears?

3 Which plant is traditionally used for scaffolding in China?

4 Angel Falls is the tallest waterfall in the world. Which country is it in?

5 Which mountain range contains 96 of the world's 100 tallest mountains?

6 In Greek mythology, what was the name of the hunter turned into a stag by the goddess Diana?

7 Which breed of cat was traditionally used to guard temples in Thailand?

8 On which continent might you encounter a prairie chicken?

9 What seeds are chewed in parts of Asia to aid digestion and freshen breath?

10 On which continent would you be if you saw a galah bird?

British birds of prey
698

LEVEL 3 Questions on the hunters of the skies

1 What rare bird of prey has a name that reflects its love of feeding on bees and wasps?

2 What bird of prey was until recently restricted to Wales, but is now successfully reintroduced to the Chilterns and elsewhere in England?

3 What bird of prey famously nests at Loch Garten?

4 Hobbys, kestrels and merlins are varieties of which bird of prey?

5 The female hen harrier is brown, but what colour is the male?

6 Which harrier is specialised to reed beds and similar habitats?

7 What large eagle has been recently reintroduced to the Scottish Islands, where it is sometimes seen flying with golden eagles?

8 Which British owl looks ghostly white in flight?

9 How many species of owl breed in Britain?

10 What British owl is most likely to be seen hunting by day?

Smoke gets in your eyes
699

LEVEL 2 Questions on how pollution is affecting the natural world

1 What name is given to the gases that are said to be causing global warming?

2 What is the name of the layer of the atmosphere which is being eroded by CFC gases?

3 Name the Soviet nuclear plant which exploded with devastating effects in 1986.

4 What was the purpose of the damaging chemical DDT?

5 Who operated a ship named *Rainbow Warrior*?

6 The Kyoto protocol on climate change was signed in 1997. In which country is Kyoto?

7 Which country uses the most nuclear energy for its domestic electricity supply?

8 What was Agent Orange used for in the Vietnam War?

9 What was the name of the ship which ran aground in Alaska in 1989, causing an immense oil spill?

10 Which British moth evolved from speckled to black when its habitat became dark and sooty?

Ticklish allsorts
700

LEVEL 2 A mixed bag of nature questions

1 What feminine name is sometimes given to the vegetable called okra or bindi?

2 With what spice do Mexicans traditionally flavour their coffee?

3 The orca is another name for which species of whale?

4 Is it the male or the female mosquito which buzzes?

5 Only one of the big cats has claws that do not retract. Which one?

6 What is the more prosaic name for the rock dove?

7 Which animal has varieties known as red, Arctic and bat-eared?

8 Orb, hammock and scaffold are three types of what natural phenomenon?

9 What kind of animal is a sidewinder?

10 What name is used for the 'radar' system by which bats fly in the dark?

Natural history

701 Gone tomorrow

LEVEL 2 On which continent might you have seen or hope to see these extinct or endangered species?

1 Tasmanian wolf

2 Passenger pigeon

3 Golden bamboo lemur

4 Lar gibbon

5 Andean tapir

6 Barbary lion

7 Short-tailed chinchilla

8 Javan rhino

9 Kemp's Ridley sea turtle

10 Amur leopard

702 Brain teasers

LEVEL 3 Tough tests from the living world

1 What does a dendrologist study?

2 What is the more common name for nacre, found in oysters and other shellfish?

3 What name is given to the cotton-like fibre derived from the seeds of tropical trees and often used as padding or stuffing?

4 What is the milky, sticky sap that is derived from rubber trees?

5 What word is used to describe the production of light by animals such as glow-worms and fireflies?

6 What colour are the flowers of centaury?

7 By what other name is the scarab known?

8 Salsify is a plant that is sometimes cultivated for food; what part of it do you eat?

9 What does tomentose mean (used, for example, to describe a leaf)?

10 Shrimp, prawn, mussel, lobster. Mollusc or crutacean? How many of each?

703 Three's company

LEVEL 1 The answer to every question is a three-letter word

1 What small shrub is often used as a decorative border, especially in formal gardens?

2 What large flightless bird is Australia's largest native bird?

3 What name is given to a male cat?

4 By what more common name is an animal's bone called the mandible known?

5 What word is a type of snake and also a lady's long fur or feather throat wrap?

6 What name is given to a young bear?

7 What is a female pig called?

8 What name is given to the vital juice in the stem of a plant?

9 Great, blue, and azure are all types of what bird?

10 What is the name for the habitat of oysters?

Birds on the wing
704 LEVEL 3 Some recently introduced species

1 What duck-like goose, common on the Nile, has become naturalised in Britain?

2 What is the only British breeding owl to have been artificially introduced?

3 What reddish, American stiff-tailed duck has become naturalised in Britain?

4 What birds are Golden and Lady Amherst?

5 What large North American water bird is a very common, introduced species in Britain?

6 What now common species of partridge was introduced to Britain in the 18th century?

7 What beautiful orange duck, originally from China, has become established in Britain?

8 What species of parrot has established itself in the London area?

9 What South American duck, with a name derived from a Russian city, is encountered in the wild in Britain?

10 On which continent did the wood duck originate?

Them bones
705 LEVEL 2 Questions about the inner workings of the human body

1 What is the scientific name for the collar bone?

2 In which organ of the body would you find alveoli?

3 Where in your body is the pituitary gland?

4 To within ten, how many bones are there in the adult human body?

5 Where in the body is the aorta?

6 Sucrose and glucose are types of what substance?

7 Hinge, pivot and ball-and-socket are all types of what?

8 Which organ of the body produces bile?

9 A, B_5, B_{12}, C and K are all types of what?

10 What feature of the body is classified using the terms whorl, arch and loop?

C here
706 LEVEL 2 The answers all begin with the letter C

1 What C is one of the four humours, also known as yellow bile?

2 Which early spring bulbs, often yellow and purple, are sometimes planted in drifts below trees?

3 What C is the only cat with non-retractable claws?

4 What name is given to a small wood of small trees grown for periodical cutting?

5 Which bird is associated with miners' safety?

6 Crowned and demoiselle are types of which bird?

7 What is another name for hemp, and also an illegal drug?

8 What is the first geological period from which fossils are commonly collected?

9 What alcoholic drink, used to make kir, is made from blackcurrant?

10 What C is a spring wild flower, closely related to the primrose?

Natural history

Lucky dip

707

LEVEL 2 A miscellany of questions from the natural world

1 Which land animal has the longest gestation period?

2 What do the initials RSPB stand for?

3 What is distinctive about the flower of Moschatel (also called Town-hall Clock)?

4 In which botanical gardens is the Princess of Wales conservatory?

5 On which continent would you find a marsh mongoose in the wild?

6 What sort of animal is a Weimaraner?

7 What happens to a flatworm if you cut its head off?

8 What, zoologically, is a true-lovers' knot?

9 Which gem derives its green colour from the presence of copper?

10 What is a dik-dik?

African birds

708

LEVEL 3 From the 'dark continent'

1 Wattled, hadada, sacred and glossy are types of which African bird?

2 One of the most beautiful African birds is the malachite kingfisher. What is malachite?

3 Which eagle, found perching high on branches over rivers, is known as the 'voice of Africa'?

4 How do weaver birds get their name?

5 What large pink bird is found in huge numbers in the most alkaline of the Rift Valley lakes?

6 What are the South American equivalents of the small, brightly coloured sunbirds that feed on flower nectar in Africa?

7 How do widowbirds get their name?

8 In casqued hornbills, what is a casque?

9 How did the 'go-away-bird' get its name?

10 What general name is given to the food source of, among others, the African white-backed vulture?

Bulbs

709

LEVEL 2 Enlighten yourself on this plant round

1 Which bulb, with delicate white and green flowers, is among the first to flower in January?

2 What term is used for a bulb that produces leaves but no flowers?

3 To what plant family do cyclamen belong?

4 How do grape hyacinths get their name?

5 What is the title of Deborah Moggach's romantic thriller set in 17th-century Amsterdam?

6 Which bulb has a name which means 'little sword' in Latin?

7 Turk's cap is a variety of which bulbous plant?

8 Which French author, who wrote *The Man in the Iron Mask*, also wrote *The Black Tulip*?

9 What is the name of the dry scaly layers that protect the inner bulb?

10 What word is used to describe the process of making a bulb flower out of season?

British bird triplets

710

LEVEL 2   Of what type of bird are the following triplets species?

1 Arctic, great and long-tailed

2 Meadow, tree, and rock

3 Long-tailed, crested and coal

4 Sandwich, caspian and little

5 Slavonian, black-necked and little

6 Common, black-backed and little

7 Long-eared, tawny and little

8 Manx, cory and little

9 Garden, marsh and wood

10 Sky, wood and shore

Lucky dip

711

LEVEL 3   A set of general questions to challenge even the best

1 Which porous rock is made from the fossilised shells of tiny animals?

2 The Latin name for wrens is *Troglodytes*, but what is a human troglodyte?

3 What is the name of the huge, iridescent blue butterflies, found in the forests of South America?

4 The nest of which bird is used to make the Chinese delicacy bird's-nest soup?

5 What is the name for the spectacular sight of a whale leaping clear of the water and plunging back in?

6 Which reptile often lives a century, and has been known to reach the age of 152?

7 Is Dutch Elm disease caused by a parasite, a fungus or a virus?

8 Which mythical animal was the symbol of the Russian tsars?

9 What kind of animal is the resplendent quetzal?

10 What, zoologically, is an ounce?

Mother Earth

712

LEVEL 1   A round of questions on the workings of the planet

1 What is measured on the Beaufort scale: storm damage, wind strength or ocean currents?

2 What element are both diamonds and graphite made from?

3 Which of these planets orbits closest to the Sun: Pluto, Mercury or Earth?

4 What is measured with the Modified Mercalli scale: humidity, hardness of minerals, or earthquake intensity?

5 Shoemaker-Levy, Halley and Hale-Bopp are all examples of what astronomical phenomenon?

6 Which gas is most plentiful in the Earth's atmosphere?

7 Is magma a kind of seaweed, a form of radiation or molten rock?

8 Where would you find the Marianas Trench?

9 Which river is longest: the Amazon, the Ob or the Amur?

10 What is the name for the large, slow-moving masses of compacted ice and snow that occur in mountainous and polar regions?

Lucky dip

713 **Kids 7–11** **Some mixed questions about the living world**

1 Where does a mother kangaroo keep her baby?

2 In films and cartoons, what type of animal was Godzilla?

3 If you plant an acorn in the ground, what will grow from it?

4 What is a female fox called?

5 What is frog spawn?

6 What do you call the tortoise-like animals which live in the sea?

7 What is the largest ape in the world?

8 What is the name given to an elephant's long pointed teeth?

9 Which country is the natural home of the Tasmanian devil?

10 If you added together all the legs on a spider, a fly, and a robin, what number would you get?

General knowledge

714 **Kids 12–14** **A mixture of questions**

1 What animal did the poet William Blake describe as 'burning bright, in the forest of the night'?

2 What bird of prey shares its name with a flying toy?

3 Is a ling a fish, a bird or a breed of dog?

4 What type of noise is a hyena said to make?

5 Why would you not be frightened of a garden tiger?

6 Is a fly agaric an insect, a fungus or a fly-eating plant?

7 The equus is an extinct ancestor of which animal?

8 What type of animal is an iguana?

9 Which part of a rhubarb plant is poisonous?

10 2-spot, 7-spot, 22-spot and 24-spot are varieties of what insect?

Odds and ends

715 **Kids 7–11** **Some troublesome tests**

1 What are bluebottles and greenbottles?

2 In the book by Anne Sewell, Black Beauty is what type of animal?

3 Nemo lives in what sort of large underwater habitat?

4 What important daily food is made using yeast?

5 What bird is often nicknamed the redbreast?

6 Koala bears prefer to eat the leaves of varieties of which particular tree ?

7 Which is the only continent in which penguins are found in their natural habitat?

8 In German, this animal's name means 'flying mouse'; what is it called in English?

9 Is a spruce a rodent, a duck or a tree?

10 From which part of the coffee bush is the drink made?

716 Sundry set
Kids 12-14 A round of miscellaneous questions

1 Which mammal produces the largest offspring?

2 Andean and Californian are the two types of which large bird of prey?

3 What unit of measurement is used only for determining the height of horses?

4 Centipede means 'a hundred feet'; what does 'millipede' mean?

5 Which British bird of prey hovers?

6 The waggle dance is performed by which animal to communicate where food is?

7 What sort of animal is a rottweiler?

8 What type of vegetable is a King Edward?

9 In which country is Lake Baikal, the largest freshwater lake in the world?

10 Which is the largest of the five Great Lakes in North America?

717 Random round
Kids 7-11 Questions from right across the natural world

1 A foal is the offspring of what type of animal?

2 In the Winnie-the-Pooh stories, what type of animal was Eeyore?

3 Which bird completes the saying 'One . . . does not make a summer'?

4 What is the seed of a horse chestnut popularly called?

5 Siamese, Burmese and Persian are all types of what pet animal?

6 What animal completes the title of the book: *The . . . , the Witch and the Wardrobe*'?

7 What type of bird delivers letters to Harry Potter?

8 What breed of dog has black spots on a white background?

9 Bramleys, coxes and Granny Smiths are types of which common fruit?

10 What is the name of Bart Simpson's dog?

718 You're a star!
Kids 12-14 What type of animal were the following?

1 Tarka

2 Hazel and Big-Ears

3 Jerry

4 Red Rum

5 Baloo

6 Pluto

7 Skippy

8 Minnie

9 Babar

10 Tom

Says who?

719

Kids 12–14 Fill in the missing animal in these well-known phrases

1 Throwing pearls before … ?

2 A red rag to a … ?

3 No room to swing a … ?

4 Itsy-bitsy … climbing up the spout?

5 To have a … in your bonnet?

6 Four and twenty … baked in a pie?

7 Mad as a March … ?

8 If you pay peanuts you get … ?

9 To have … in your pants?

10 Like a … in a china shop?

Colour me a rainbow

720

Kids 7–11 A round of bright and colourful questions?

1 What colour are daffodils?

2 Which red-berried plant is traditionally associated with Christmas?

3 Richard Of York Gave Battle In Vain helps you to remember the colours of what?

4 A piebald pony is coloured black and which other colour?

5 What is the colour of the biggest whale?

6 If you mixed red paint with yellow paint, what colour would you get?

7 Which planet is known as the red planet?

8 Which colourful island would you find in the Arctic?

9 What bright blue bird lives by rivers in Britain and dives into the water to catch fish?

10 What colour is a ruby?

National mascots

721

Kids 12–14 Can you identify the plants and animals from these clues?

1 Which spring flower is associated with the patron saint of Wales?

2 Which country has a kiwi bird as its mascot?

3 What kind of leaf is on the Canadian flag?

4 Which animal – now popular as a pet – did the Ancient Egyptians worship?

5 Which Scottish loch is said to contain a legendary monster?

6 What kind of bird is often associated with the United States of America?

7 Which plant – the Irish emblem – is said to bring good luck?

8 The South African rugby team takes its nickname from what kind of antelope?

9 In what kind of tree, often associated with England, did Charles I hide from his enemies during the Civil War?

10 What is regarded as the national flower of the Netherlands?

Quizzes

722–774

SCIENCE

Science

Weird science
722
LEVEL 1   A random round of questions

1 What sex is a person with XX chromosomes?

2 If you sprinkle sodium chloride on your chips, what are you putting on them?

3 What does a solar cell produce?

4 What is the body's biggest organ?

5 Who was the first man to walk on the Moon?

6 What name is given to the 0° line of longitude?

7 Who 'discovered' gravity?

8 In which country is it believed that gunpowder was invented?

9 What travels at approximately 186,000 miles (299,000km) a second?

10 What Cold War-era academic system now connects millions of computers across the world?

Brain box
723
LEVEL 2   See how scientific you are with these questions

1 What waste gas, a product of animal life, and a major contributor to the greenhouse effect, is vital for green plants to survive?

2 Which famous French underwater explorer was the co-inventor of the aqualung?

3 What name is given to the process that breaks crude oil into its constituent parts?

4 From what are Saturn's rings made?

5 Where in Britain is the Windscale nuclear plant?

6 North of the Equator, which way does water swirl as it goes down the plughole?

7 What name is given to the soft patch on a new-born baby's skull?

8 Vitamin C prevents which disease historically prevalent among sailors?

9 Which metal forms part of a black-and-white photograph?

10 Who gave his name to a widely used road-surfacing material?

Random round
724
LEVEL 1   Easy science questions

1 The medical condition caused by a malfunctioning pancreas, and treated with insulin injections, is known as what?

2 What is the hardest substance in your body?

3 How many yards make a mile?

4 What is 'dry ice'?

5 What gas is needed for iron to rust?

6 What metal covers a galvanised bucket?

7 What is the scientific name for frozen soil that never thaws?

8 Within 5 per cent what percentage of the body is made from muscle?

9 What chemical in the skin is responsible for its colour?

10 What is measured on the Richter scale?

The appliance of science
LEVEL 2   Open your mind

1 In medicine, what do the initials CAT stand for?

2 What device allows a car's driving wheels to turn at different speeds from each other?

3 Which celestial object, once seen as a harbinger of doom, will be seen again in 2062?

4 What was special about the Stockton and Darlington Railway?

5 What is it called when a rocket can overcome the force of the Earth's gravity?

6 What name is given to the simple paint mark that stops ships from being overloaded?

7 What popular name is given to muscles that cannot be consciously controlled, such as the heart?

8 What aid to motoring safety was invented in 1934 by Percy Shaw?

9 What is the connection between soot, pencil leads and diamonds?

10 Which was the first commonly used plastic?

Are you scientific?
LEVEL 2   A test for the best

1 Who, from observations made on his voyage on the *Beagle*, caused a scientific uproar?

2 Which North Sea oil rig was destroyed in a fire in 1988?

3 What do the initials FRS after a scientist's name mean?

4 Where in your body does hydrochloric acid occur naturally?

5 Which world-famous scientist declined the presidency of Israel?

6 In shipping terms, what does P&O stand for?

7 The bubbling of which gas in the blood of a diver causes 'the bends'?

8 What do bird-dogs, chipmunks and eagles have in common?

9 What unit of area was originally defined as the area of land that a pair of oxen could plough in a day?

10 What is a U-bahn?

Lucky dip
LEVEL 3   Questions for the technologically minded

1 Where can you experience 'the Spirit of Ecstasy'?

2 Which people-carrier was introduced to the UK by Harrods in 1898?

3 Which ship, designed by Brunel, laid the first transatlantic telephone cable?

4 What does an odometer measure?

5 What sort of triangle has two equal sides?

6 What might a psephologist predict?

7 Which scientist was tried for heresy by the Inquisition in 1633?

8 How did the *Breitling Orbiter 3* earn its place in history?

9 What name is normally given to the process of parturition?

10 What might you measure with a Bourdon gauge?

Science

General knowledge
728

LEVEL 1   Some basic science questions

1 What does a barometer measure?

2 What is the name for the strongest type of wind that is measured on the Beaufort scale?

3 What type of car engine, excluding electric, has no spark plugs?

4 What is the ratio of a circle's circumference to its diameter called?

5 Which layer of the Earth's atmosphere is thinning over the South Pole?

6 The purity of what metal is measured in carats?

7 What do the letters EPNS on cutlery stand for?

8 Which is the world's largest hot desert, where evaporation exceeds precipitation?

9 What is the lightest gas?

10 What metal is the main constituent of steel?

Simple science
729

LEVEL 1   Don't be a simpleton

1 What does a wind farm do?

2 Iron pyrites is better known as what?

3 Where in your body would you find the small bones called hammer, anvil and stirrup?

4 In which direction does a concave lens bend light?

5 Which waves are shorter: television or radio?

6 How do speed cameras measure a car's speed?

7 What common name is given to the cocktail of polluting gases that hangs over several major cities?

8 If your doctor tells you that you have a 'strep throat', what sort of infection is causing it?

9 What happens when the power sent to the wheels of a car is greater than the forces of friction?

10 In electrical terms, what do the initials DC stand for?

Chance testers
730

LEVEL 2   A round for the brainier few

1 What scientific principle makes sounds rise and fall as a vehicle passes by?

2 In radio, what does the abbreviation FM stand for?

3 What do Cora, Ruth, Anne, Andrew and Brent have in common?

4 Who gave his name to the first mass-produced ball-point pen?

5 Who might get pneumoconiosis?

6 What is the name for the bowl-like, silvered part of a lamp reflector?

7 Which polluting metal was used to help car engines run more smoothly?

8 In which part of the body would you find your thyroid gland?

9 Ozone is a pungent form of which life-giving substance?

10 Diamorphine is the scientific name for which illegal street drug?

Selective approach

731

LEVEL 3   The harder the questions, the brainier you need to be

1 At what point of its orbit is the Earth when it is at 'perihelion'?

2 Where would you find your sartorius muscle?

3 Which mother of nine was responsible for popularising the use of anaesthesia during childbirth?

4 How is deuterium oxide commonly known?

5 What very hard substance is used in light bulbs, bullets and ball-point pens?

6 What is a synapse?

7 Which green deposit gradually develops on copper?

8 Plasmodium causes which often fatal disease?

9 Someone who suffers from nyctophobia is scared of what?

10 Whose 'last theorem' has recently been solved?

On the rack

732

LEVEL 2   Science puzzlers to stretch you

1 What killer disease was controlled by Jonas Salk's vaccine?

2 What is the term for the total destruction of a nuclear reactor?

3 What sort of things are weighed in Troy measurements?

4 What nationality was the inventor of the metric system?

5 The lacrimal glands produce what bodily fluid?

6 What was special about Dolly the sheep?

7 Where in your body would you find your pericardium?

8 Studying dreams and early childhood experiences led Freud to develop which branch of psychiatry?

9 What sheep disease is thought to have led to BSE?

10 Which building is popularly believed to be the one from which Galileo carried out the first practical research on gravity?

Step up the pace

733

LEVEL 3   Science questions for the boffins

1 What did the American Electric Boat Company build?

2 How many sides are there in a dodecahedron?

3 The discoverer of the modern battery shares his name with a dance. Who is he?

4 Who invented the device used to measure radioactivity?

5 What would you call an alloy of copper, tin and zinc?

6 What briefly put new life into Louis Washkansky in 1967?

7 What measurement describes the speed with which you can download material from the internet?

8 What are chemicals with the same formulae, but different properties, called?

9 Who, together with Ada, Countess Lovelace, is credited with designing the first computer?

10 What product of cinchona bark is used both to flavour tonic water and as a medicine?

Science

734 Noises off
LEVEL 2   This round is all about sound

1 Alexander Graham Bell is generally credited with inventing what essential piece of office and home equipment?

2 What device, introduced from Japan in 1979 with the product number WM-1, changed how people listened to music?

3 Sounds were first recorded onto what shaped objects?

4 Which company developed the audio cassette?

5 Where would you find tweeters and woofers?

6 What sort of sounds would you hear in space?

7 On October 14, 1947, flying the *Bell XS-1*, Captain Charles 'Chuck' Yeager became the first man to do what?

8 What was the earliest primitive type of radio that operated without any electrical power supply called?

9 How does a bat find its food?

10 Who connected Poldhu, Cornwall in England with Newfoundland in 1901?

735 Doctor, doctor
LEVEL 1   A round dedicated to medicine

1 What pain-killer is related to the cricket bat?

2 Who might use a nebuliser?

3 What is the ancient Chinese practice of sticking fine needles into a person called?

4 What poisonous garden plant is used in the production of a powerful heart medicine?

5 What invention of Wilhelm Roentgen revolutionised modern medicine by allowing doctors to see inside the human body?

6 Alexander Fleming is credited with discovering which antibiotic after studying the growth of mould?

7 In alternative medicine, what name is given to the practice of exposing the body to ultra-dilute solutions?

8 Warfarin, once used as a rat poison, is used to treat what medical condition?

9 For what surgical procedure is Dr Magdi Yacoub famous?

10 By what name is nitrous oxide more commonly known?

736 Taking wing
LEVEL 3   All about flight

1 What is the largest aeroplane ever built?

2 At more than US$2 billion each, what is the world's most expensive aircraft?

3 What name is given to the design of aircraft with the tail-wing in front of the main wing?

4 At the 1973 Paris Air Show, the spectacular crash of the Soviet version of Concorde put paid to its ambitions. By what name was the plane better known?

5 Britain was the first country to introduce a jet passenger liner. What was its name?

6 Name the first aircraft capable of vertical take-off.

7 Apart from being the fastest aircraft, when built, what is the other unique claim to fame of the rocket-powered *X-15*?

8 What 1960s vintage aircraft still holds the record for the fastest manned flight?

9 How, in the Second World War, did one join the 'caterpillar club'?

10 Which US bomber, used in Vietnam, the Persian Gulf and Afghanistan is still on active service?

Do you compute?

737

LEVEL 2 How much do you know about floppy disks?

1 Name the German codes broken by the computer *Colossus*, during the Second World War.

2 What do the letters of the acronym WYSIWYG (wizzywig) stand for?

3 What was the name of the disobedient computer in the film *2001*?

4 In 1988, the film *Tin Toy*, made by Pixar, won an Oscar. What made that award unique?

5 What computing revolution was heralded by the introduction, in 1981, of the *Osborne 1* computer, which weighed nearly 25lb (11kg)?

6 Which colourful computer, invented by Clive Sinclair, began the home computer revolution?

7 Which blue-chip company launched the first PC in 1981?

8 How many megabytes are there in a gigabyte?

9 What is a malicious computer program, designed to damage other computers, called?

10 What did Nolan Bushnell invent that changed the way a generation spent their spare time?

Underground Earth

738

LEVEL 2 Going down…

1 In which direction does a stalagmite grow?

2 What name is given to the liquid rock beneath the Earth's surface that is violently ejected from volcanoes as lava?

3 What natural phenomenon gave rise to the city of Bath and other spa towns?

4 What name is given to the study of volcanoes?

5 Earth movement causes cracks in underground rock. What are these cracks called?

6 In Yellowstone National Park what is referred to as 'old faithful'?

7 What blasts out of a fumarole?

8 There is a traditional way to locate underground water so wells can be dug. What is it called?

9 What is the common name for the gas that can cause explosions in coal mines?

10 What volcanic eruption, in 1883, was the most violent ever recorded?

Why, it's elementary

739

LEVEL 3 A round all about the elements

1 Which is the only radioactive element that is a gas at normal room temperature and pressure?

2 What name was given to the fruitless search for a process by which base metals could be converted to gold?

3 According to Oriental philosophy, how many elements are there?

4 Which common element evolved from a rare commodity into metal due to the Bayer process?

5 Name the smallest particle of an element.

6 Which is the most reactive gas, so reactive that even water will burn in it?

7 Which element has close to 10 million known compounds?

8 Name the title of the semi-autobiographical work written by Primo Levi.

9 What is the only metal that is liquid at room temperature?

10 Which is the most common element in the Earth's crust?

What's the score?

Keeping track of the scores is probably the hardest job on quiz night. The eyes of the whole room will be on the person at the blackboard (or on the laptop) as the results are updated. So the scorer needs to be someone with a head for figures and an ability to stay cool under pressure – because no mistakes are allowed.

The scorer should stick close to the scoreboard throughout the quiz, and should have an assistant, whose job it is to deliver the marked answer sheets as soon as they are ready. The work of the scorer proceeds quietly in the background while the hubbub of the quiz goes on. The results of Round One should be written up on the board while Round Two is being played, and so on through the evening.

Markers should write the total for each round in big letters on the marked sheets. This will help the scorer fill in the scoreboard quickly and correctly. It goes without saying that the scorer, as well as being good at arithmetic, needs to have reasonably legible handwriting.

Scoring quickfire rounds

For quickfire quizzes you need a way to show the score totting up with every correctly answered question. There is an easy-to-make and infallible solution. Use an A4 ring binder file and a box of punched plastic A4 wallets. Number sheets of paper or card in large numerals 1 to 50, insert one into each wallet, and fix them into the ring binder. Fix the binders firmly to the table upright so that the numbers can be clearly seen. Every time a correct answer is given, flip to the next card and so add a point to the total.

Consistent marking

Markers should be briefed on what constitutes a right answer. If, for example, players are asked to name a historical character, do they have to give the full name? If it is important that the full name is given, the quiz master must make this clear in the question. Many players, after all, would answer the question 'Who wrote the 1812 Overture?' with the single word 'Tchaikovsky'. So if someone ventured to give the composer's first name and got it wrong, most quizsetters would be inclined to give the point. By the same token, most quizzers would think it harsh to penalise players for bad spelling. Knowing the answer is enough to earn the points.

Running the scoreboard

Venues such as schools will have everything you need to hand. A black or white board and some chalks or markers may be all that is needed. If not, you can use sheets of marked up A1 paper pinned to a wall. Whichever method you use, make sure the board is big enough for the teams to see.

The scoreboard itself will take the form of a simple grid. List the team names down one side, and write the round numbers along the top. Leave a column at the end for the final score.

Now put a diagonal line through each cell from one corner to the other. As the quiz proceeds, write the score for each round in the upper triangle, and the running total in the lower one. It will be easier for players to read the scoreboard if you use different coloured pens for these two sets

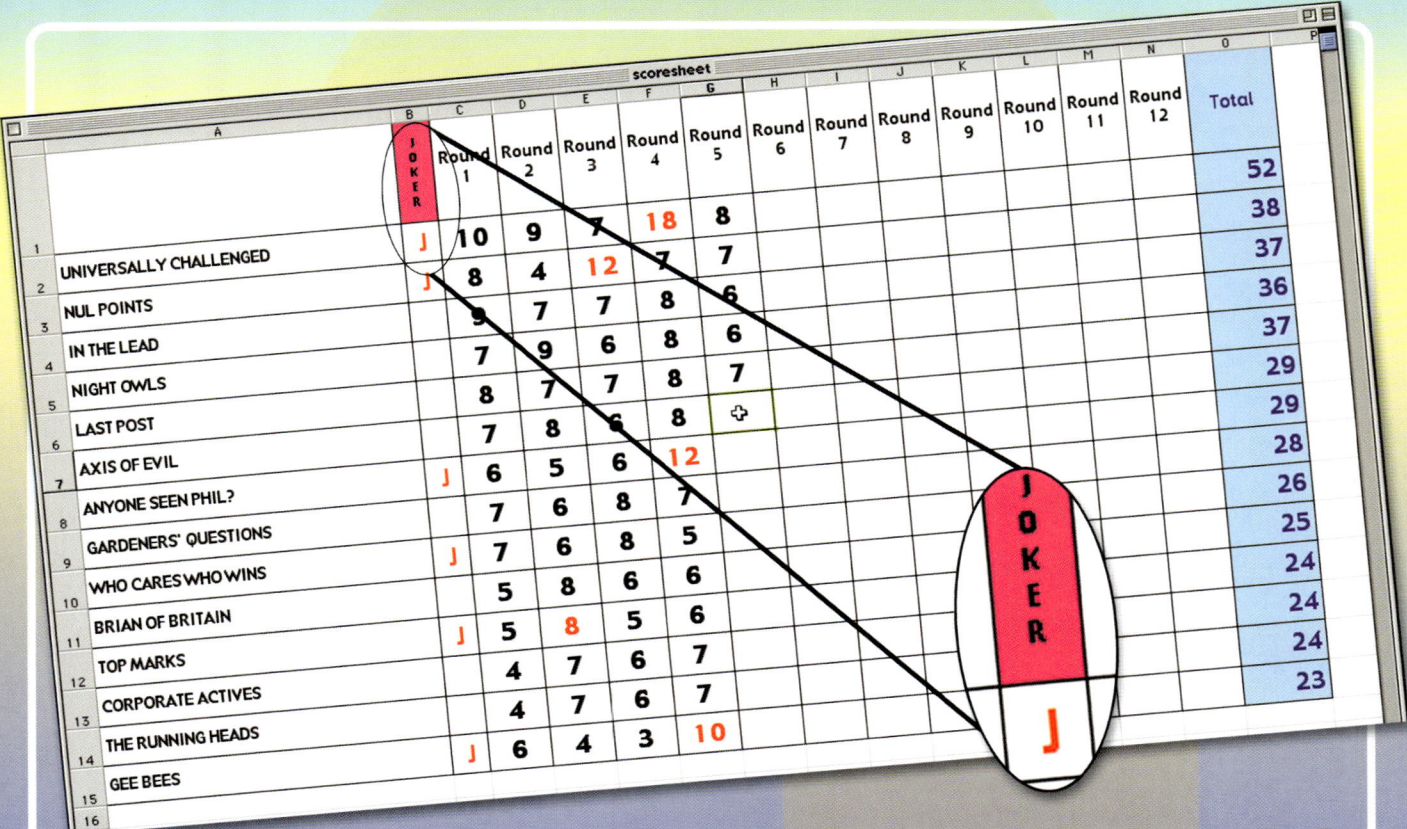

Setting up an Excel scoresheet

An Excel scoresheet adds a professional touch to your quiz. It allows you to display the leaders in descending order – in the time-honoured manner of the Eurovision Song Contest.

When you know how many rounds your quiz will have and how many teams will be playing, enter the information into a spreadsheet: teams down the side and round titles across the top. Include a column next to the team names where you will be able to indicate with a letter 'J' whether a team has played its joker.

Make the last column in the spreadsheet a 'Total' column and input an equation to automatically sum the figures in each row – click the 'autosum' button and specify the relevant cells, such as 'C2:N2', then click and drag down the total column to apply the same formula to each row. As you enter the scores for each round, the totals will automatically be updated.

To show who is in the lead after each round, use the 'sort descending' function. This moves the leaders to the top. To keep track of which team has played its joker and when, it is a good idea to format the cell for their joker score so that the text appears in a different colour from the rest of the scores.

of figures. It helps maintain excitement if after each round the scorer asterisks the top three scores – maybe in a third colour. Teams will then be able to see at a glance if they are in line for the trophy.

We have a tie for first place

Announce at the start of the quiz what will happen if the quiz ends in a tie. There are two simple options: have another round of questions prepared and use them to separate the tied teams, or choose one of the tie-breaker questions listed on page 396 of this book, which ask you to list as many items in a category as you can in a fixed time.

If you prefer to think up your own tie-breaker, then be sure that your category is a genuine closed set. If, for example, you ask people to list Beatles albums they might write down all manner of imports, bootlegs and compilations. Quiz people are by nature disputatious, and a good quiz is one that gives no-one any grounds for argument.

Science

Tools of the trade
740   **LEVEL 1**   **Who uses what?**

1 Traditionally, what was the main constituent of solder?

2 You might sharpen a chisel on a stone but what is the proper name for this process?

3 Who might use a theodolite?

4 An ophthalmoscope is used to examine which part of the body?

5 Limestone, clay and gypsum are ground together to make which building material?

6 What laboratory aid was invented by German chemist Robert Bunsen?

7 What kind of telescope might a radio astronomer use?

8 What would a doctor use a sphygmomanometer to measure?

9 Who might use a dibber?

10 What would a curry comb be used for?

Domestic science
741   **LEVEL 1**   **Everyday objects around the home**

1 Where might you find a tungsten filament?

2 Magnetrons are devices used in radar transmitters. Where would you find one in the kitchen?

3 What do the initials VCR stand for?

4 What role does sodium hydrogen carbonate have in the making of cakes?

5 Which 1967 invention made use of bacteria to help brighten the washing of clothes?

6 In what form might you have live bacteria lactobaccilli in your refrigerator?

7 Which form of abbreviation tells you which additives have been added to prepared food?

8 Alva Fisher's 1906 invention changed Mondays in the home forever. What was the invention?

9 What product, first used by the ancient Egyptians, is still used by women today to enhance their eyes?

10 What name is given to the process by which yeast converts sugar to alcohol?

Space, the final frontier
742   **LEVEL 2**   **How spaced out are you?**

1 What was the American astronaut Alan B. Shepard's unique achievement?

2 Christa McAuliffe died when the *Challenger* spaceship exploded. What kind of spaceship was it?

3 Around 1900, astronomer Percival Lowell thought he saw what on the surface of Mars?

4 What rocket was used to launch the *Apollo* Moon missions in the 1960s and 1970s?

5 Which country launched the first-ever satellite?

6 What was the first living creature sent into space?

7 What name is given to the course of an object circling a planet or the Sun?

8 Soviet cosmonaut Valentina Tereshkova achieved what first for her country on June 16, 1963?

9 What was the name of the first space shuttle?

10 Which *Apollo* mission went disastrously wrong, resulting in the famous radio transmission: 'Houston, we have a problem'?

Dry bones

743

LEVEL 2   How well do you know your skeleton?

1   What is another name for your sternum?

2   Which rubbery material is found at the ends of bones and prevents them from grinding against each other?

3   What sort of joint connects your femur with your hip bone?

4   If you knock your hallux, what would hurt?

5   Where in your body is there a bone that does not touch any other bones?

6   Which is the longest bone in the body?

7   Does a baby have more or fewer bones than an adult?

8   What is the proper name for the rounded part of your skull?

9   If a person is suffering from a 'dowager's hump' what part of them would be afflicted?

10 Which actor, best known for playing Superman, fractured his spine in a riding accident in May 1995?

Building big

744

LEVEL 2   Tallest or biggest buildings

1   What was distinct about the ten-storey Home Insurance building in Chicago in 1885?

2   Where in Asia is the tallest pair of tower blocks?

3   What is the tallest office building in Britain?

4   Which river in Britain does the world's first iron bridge span?

5   Which British landmark finished up in the Arizona Desert?

6   Which is the world's largest office building?

7   What invention by Elisha Otis, in 1853, allowed the skyscraper to become a reality?

8   Until it fell down in 1991, what record did the Warsaw TV-mast hold?

9   On May 1, 1931, President Herbert Hoover pressed a button in Washington DC to turn on the lights of which American landmark?

10 Which Paris landmark was supposed to have been torn down only ten years after it was built?

Wheels on fire

745

LEVEL 3   Some motoring questions

1   The 1878 Locomotive Amendment Act made life a little easier for Britain's fledgling motorists by cutting what encumbrance?

2   Which car was the first to include air conditioning as standard?

3   What was unusual about the American Stanley car, made between 1905 and 1916?

4   In 1952, which company built the world's first jet-powered car?

5   In which car did Sir Malcolm Campbell break the world land speed record?

6   Which famous sports car manufacturer was founded by Colin Chapman?

7   What distinction is held by the Bugatti Type 41 Royale, of which only six were ever made?

8   What family car was designed by Ferdinand Porsche?

9   In 1900, what was the speed limit in Britain?

10 Which country switched to driving on the right in 1967?

Science

Whither the weather

746

LEVEL 2   A national obsession but do you pay attention?

1 Which country has the highest average annual temperature?

2 Would cirrus clouds be described as: wispy, horse's tails; rounded, fluffy and billowing; or low and overcast?

3 On the 12-point Beaufort Scale, what number is given to a storm?

4 What instrument is used to measure wind force and speed?

5 Complete the saying: 'Rain before seven, fine after…'?

6 What shape do the individual ice crystals in snowflakes form?

7 What name is given to the lines connecting points of equal pressure on a weather map?

8 Which agency is responsible for producing weather forecasts?

9 The daughter of which famous footballer became a TV weather presenter?

10 In the Earth's atmosphere, which is higher: the thermosphere or the stratosphere?

Testing time

747

LEVEL 3   A round of scientific puzzlers for egg heads

1 Where will you find the islets of Langerhans?

2 Skin, hair and nails are all toughened by one substance. What is it?

3 Where would you find the Nuclear Island of Stability?

4 Iodine, bromine and chlorine are all very active halogens. Name the next element in this series.

5 How did Patrick Steptoe and Robert Edwards give Louise Brown a unique start in life in 1978?

6 Mixed together, nitric and hydrochloric acids make which royal liquid?

7 *Alvin* and *Trieste* went down in the dark. What were they?

8 Frenchman Dubois de Chemant's 1789 invention transformed the way many people ate their food. How?

9 Who invented revolutionary geodesic domes used for building, and gave his name to a new form of carbon called 'buckyballs'?

10 What links the elements helium, selenium and uranium?

Brain drain

748

LEVEL 3   A round of challenging problems

1 Which Class A drug was once included in a popular soft drink as a pick-me-up?

2 What is the link between Irish author James Joyce and high-energy physics?

3 What octogenarian sang 'I wish I was 18 again'?

4 After diamond, which is the next hardest stone found in nature?

5 What hormone does your body produce when you are ready for fight or flight?

6 What is the name of double star systems in which two stars revolve around one another?

7 A, C, T are three of the four different DNA bases. What is the missing fouth letter?

8 According to Archbishop Ussher, what happened on Sunday 23 October, 4004 BC?

9 What was British naturalist Philip Henry Gosse's controversial fossil theory?

10 Which is the only planet to spin from east to west?

749 **Science quest**

These questions are tougher than the others and you may need to do some research

1 Water freezes at 32°F. What is significant about 0°F?

2 Up, down, top, bottom, strange and charm are all characteristics of what?

3 Who said: 'Science without religion is lame, religion without science is blind'?

4 Which branch of knowledge is called 'the dismal science'?

5 At what temperature (in Fahrenheit) does paper spontaneously combust?

6 Which science-fiction writer invented the Tramalfadores?

7 If you were to put some of Schrodinger's animals with some of Pavlov's animals, what kind of weather would you be looking at?

8 What connects the engraving tool, the octant, the pair of compasses and the air pump?

9 Microwave infrared, visible, ultraviolet … what comes next?

10 If Einstein is 99, Curie is 96 and Fermi is at 100 – what number is Mendeleyev?

11 Adaptation, growth, metabolism, reproduction, responsiveness … and one other. What is it?

12 What single word was the first ever to be reproduced on a photocopier?

13 How many bits in a byte?

14 Name an eight-letter word that contains the first six letters of the alphabet?

15 What causes passing planets to change colour and passing sirens to change pitch?

A clue to question 7

Science

Chemical compounds

750

LEVEL 2 These chemicals can be found around the home

Can you give the more common household name for these substances?

1 Di-hydrogen oxide

2 Calcium sulphate

3 Sodium hydroxide

4 Acetic acid

5 Magnesium sulphate

6 Sodium hypochlorite

7 Magnesium hydroxide

8 Acetylsalicylic acid

9 Ascorbic acid

10 Methyl alcohol

Science fact

751

LEVEL 3 Identify the scientists by their contribution to understanding

1 Which pair of Cambridge scientists unravelled the secrets of DNA?

2 Which 19th-century chemist uncovered the principles of electromagnetism?

3 What former patent office clerk invented the theory of relativity?

4 Which ancient Greek philosopher and mathematician discovered the mathematical constant 'pi'?

5 What amateur chemist, born in 1733, is credited with the discovery of oxygen?

6 Which Polish-born French scientist discovered radium, which led to the harnessing of X-rays?

7 Which British scientist is recognised as inventing the World Wide Web?

8 Which British doctor introduced antiseptics?

9 Which American polymath invented the lightning conductor?

10 Which prodigious American inventor, who held 1093 patents, is credited with inventing the phonograph?

Off the rails

752

LEVEL 3 Gauge your knowledge of railways

1 What is the popular name for the Hikari Super Express in Japan?

2 Where is the world's shortest railway?

3 Which British locomotive still holds the world speed record for steam-powered trains at 201km (125 miles) per hour?

4 In 1904, what linked Europe with the Pacific?

5 What do the initials TGV stand for?

6 Which was the first London Underground line?

7 Which longest railway bridge in the UK was also responsible in 1879 for one of the worst rail disasters?

8 How was power supplied in the first mine railways?

9 Where is the world's biggest railway station?

10 What was special about the Union Pacific Big Boy class of locomotives?

Partial postcards

753

**Can you name these world-famous monuments?
Some of them are shown from an unusual angle**

1

2

3

4

5

6

7

8

9

10

Science

The heart of the matter
754   LEVEL 2   Questions about your blood and heart

1 What is the name given to the constituent of blood that is responsible for getting oxygen to your muscles?

2 Lipids are one of the constituents of blood. What are they?

3 How many chambers does your heart have?

4 Which is the only living part of the body without a blood supply?

5 If you have AB blood, whose blood could you safely receive in a transfusion?

6 Which is the only muscle in the body that never tires?

7 What blood-sucking parasites were widely used to treat numerous medical conditions?

8 Which pioneering South African surgeon conducted the world's first heart transplant in 1967?

9 Which is the largest blood vessel in your body?

10 If a patient had a myocardial infarction, what would have happened to them?

Food and fitness
755   LEVEL 2   You are what you eat

1 What process, beginning in your mouth, is finally completed in your colon?

2 Cows have four and humans have one. What?

3 Apart from bones, what other part of the body uses most of the calcium in your diet?

4 What causes the uncomfortable condition of a 'stitch' during exercise?

5 Which mineral is the main constituent of red blood cells?

6 The illegal use of which type of banned substance caused Ben Johnson to be stripped of his 1988 Olympic gold medal?

7 Which brown-green secretion helps you to digest fat?

8 The eating of which vegetable was used as a cover story to hide the development of radar in the Second World War?

9 Rickets is caused by a lack of which vitamin?

10 A high level of what naturally occurring substance in the bloodstream is an important cause of the hardening of the arteries?

Sailing the seas
756   LEVEL 3   Ship ahoy

1 How might you win the Blue Riband?

2 What was the biggest sailing vessel ever built?

3 Which clipper broke records regularly between 1885 and 1895 on the Australia-England route?

4 What distinction does the *Carnival Destiny* hold?

5 This giant liner was supposed to have been called *Queen Victoria*, but had to be renamed due to a misunderstanding. What was it called?

6 What was the first-ever nuclear-powered surface ship called?

7 *Titanic's* sister ship also sank tragically and mysteriously during the First World War. What was she called?

8 Laid down in 1914, the *Argus* was the first ship of its type. What was it?

9 What do sailors keep in a binnacle?

10 Which was the fastest-ever clipper ship on the China tea route?

Body bits
LEVEL 2   A round on your insides

1 What are you suffering from if you have spasms of your diaphragm, technically called singultus?

2 Where and when does air from your body reach hurricane speed?

3 Where on the male body does human hair grow the fastest?

4 Where would you find your umbilicus?

5 Borborygmus is the scientific name for which embarrassing bodily function?

6 Which bony rings surround and protect your spinal cord?

7 What is the common name for your trachea?

8 How heavy is an average human brain?

9 Approximately how fast in mph does a signal travel through the nervous system?

10 If you can see your epidermis, what are you looking at?

The planet suite
LEVEL 1   Questions about our planetary neighbours

1 The orbit of which planet takes it farthest from the Sun?

2 Which planet is named after the Roman god of the sea?

3 In which year did man land on the Moon?

4 What name is given to the group of planets that orbit the Sun?

5 Which planet has prominent rings around it?

6 Which planet is known as the Red Planet?

7 Which planet is the brightest object in the sky after the Sun and Moon?

8 Which is the third planet from the Sun?

9 Rocks that fall from space and collide with Earth are known as what?

10 What name is given to the dark patches that are seen on the surface of the Sun?

Disease!
LEVEL 2   We all fall down

1 Which disease killed more people in 1918 than died in the First World War?

2 What do the initials BSE stand for?

3 What common insect helped to spread the 'black death' throughout the Middle Ages?

4 What is commonly called 'the kissing disease'?

5 What sort of virus causes cold sores and shingles?

6 What is the only disease, that affects humans, to have been completely eradicated from the population?

7 What disease, introduced during the Second World War, made the Scottish island of Gruinard uninhabitable?

8 Which viral disease is characterised by a violent fear of water?

9 If an epidemic is a disease prevalent among humankind, what is an epizootic?

10 What is the oldest known infection?

Science

760 Stars in their eyes
LEVEL 1 Questions for the stars

1 By what name is the Polaris Star better known?

2 What super-telescope orbiting in space went embarrassingly wrong in 1990?

3 What is a light year?

4 What name is given to a star that has collapsed so far in on itself that nothing, not even light, can escape its gravitational pull?

5 Which wheelchair-bound scientist wrote the bestselling science book *A Brief History of Time*?

6 The American space programme is run by NASA. What do the initials stand for?

7 What name is given to the stars that are grouped together to form an imaginary outline?

8 What are the 12 astrological signs collectively known as?

9 Which British astronomer has presented *The Sky at Night* since its inception in 1957?

10 Approximately (to the nearest billion years) how old is the Solar System?

761 Wet and wild
LEVEL 2 A watery round

1 What natural force produces an invisible skin on the surface of water?

2 Water forms approximately what percentage of the mass of a human body?

3 Name the science of flowing liquids.

4 Why does a frozen water pipe split?

5 What is the oldest known method of harnessing power from water?

6 What is the energy that is created by water flowing through turbines in a dam called?

7 On average, how many centimetres of snow make one centimetre of water?

8 What name is given to a whirlwind that occurs over water and results in a spiralling column of spray and mist?

9 What entry in the *Guinness Book of World Records* makes the North Fork Roe River in Montana unique?

10 What percentage of the world's water is not salt water (within 1 per cent)?

762 Great inventions
LEVEL 3 Who's the inventors? What's the invention?

1 What was invented between 1935 and 1939 by Robert Watson-Watt?

2 What did Werner von Braun first launch in 1944?

3 Nicolaus Otto's invention helps your car to run smoothly. What is it?

4 Which process invented by Charles Goodyear toughened up rubber enough to make motor tyres?

5 Which company patented the first microprocessor in 1971?

6 What was George Eastman's invention?

7 Chester Carlson's 1937 invention transformed the modern office. What is it?

8 What invention, first conceived by Da Vinci around 1500, was not realised until 1936?

9 What new form of transport did Sir Christopher Cockerell invent in 1959?

10 James Hargreaves' invention of the 1760s caused a riot in Blackburn when it went on sale, but transformed an industry. What was it?

Pleasing puzzlers

763

LEVEL 1   Random science questions to please everyone

1 What is thought to have been created in the Big Bang?

2 What name is given to lines of equal pressure on a meteorological map?

3 What was Count Zeppelin's great invention?

4 What name is given to a robot that has a human-like appearance?

5 What was the popular name for the Model T Ford?

6 In northern Europe, which is the shortest day?

7 Who founded the software giant Microsoft?

8 Into how many continents is the Earth's land surface divided?

9 What name is given to the flexible joints that connect bone together?

10 The heart of a computer is a CPU. What do the initials stand for?

Lucky dip

764

LEVEL 1   How scientific is your mind?

1 What name is given to a number that is divisible only by itself and one?

2 What is the study and treatment of diseases and conditions of the mind called?

3 What does the acronym AIDS stand for?

4 What name is given to the blood vessels that carry blood to the heart?

5 How many faces has a tetrahedron?

6 Which Norwegian word describes a flooded glacial valley?

7 How long does it take for the Earth to orbit the Sun?

8 What would you call a triangle with three equal sides?

9 What is defined as the length of a path travelled by light in a vacuum during a time interval of 1/299,792,458 seconds?

10 What is ornithology?

A scientific assortment

765

LEVEL 1   These questions will sort the men from the boys

1 By what modern name is the disease consumption now known?

2 Who developed the theorem $E=mc^2$?

3 What does a Bessemer Converter produce?

4 Which of your abilities is impaired if you have laryngitis?

5 What is the name for the 3-D image used as a security device on credit cards?

6 Which wild flower is the first stage in heroin production?

7 Which is the world's deepest ocean?

8 How old must an embryo be before it is classed as a foetus?

9 Which type of boat engine hangs over the back of the craft?

10 What is the name for a ring-shaped island formed by coral growth?

Science

766 All sorts
Kids 7–11   Science solutions

1 What do you have tested when you visit an optician?
2 What are the primary colours of paint?
3 What gas do you need to breathe in order to live?
4 What is a thermometer used to measure?
5 What shape is the flat base of a cone?
6 Of what are hailstones made?
7 What name is given to the three-dimensional object that has six equal square faces?
8 Can sound travel through liquids?
9 What are your first set of teeth called?
10 From what metal are most soft drink cans made?

767 Lucky dip
Kids 12–14   The appliance of science

1 Are warts contagious?
2 What do the Roman numerals MCLXIII stand for?
3 Is splitting the atom called fusion or fission?
4 What lets a boat climb to a higher water level in a canal or river?
5 What process is thought to cause animals and plants to change over many millions of years?
6 An early version of what machine was known as a 'bone shaker'?
7 What is generally accepted to be a billion?
8 Which type of watercraft skims along just over the surface?
9 What name is given to people who break into computers without permission?
10 What river, that flows from the heart of Africa to Egypt, is the longest in the world?

768 Out and about
Kids 7–11   Sort it out

1 What are the bones around your chest called?
2 What name is given to the device that allows you to move the cursor around the computer screen?
3 What fruit, according to legend, fell on Isaac Newton's head that led him to form The Law of Gravitation?
4 What do divers use to breathe underwater?
5 What unit of measurement is used for sound?
6 What sort of bridge could be pulled up to prevent enemies from entering a castle?
7 What does invisible mean?
8 What happens to your voice if you speak after inhaling helium?
9 What is pumped by the heart?
10 Where would you find your incisors?

Pay attention

769

Kids 12–14   You'll wish you'd taken more notice of your science teacher

1 What is the corrosion of iron and steel more commonly known as?

2 What method of food preservation did Clarence Birdseye invent?

3 Which is the lightest metal?

4 What covers more than two-thirds of the world's surface?

5 In which country was the atom bomb invented?

6 What name is given to the alphabet made of raised dots which blind people read by touching?

7 Where in the home would you find a cathode ray tube?

8 What is the science that deals with the study of sound?

9 Which vitamin are oranges rich in?

10 Why can't you see ultraviolet light?

Worldly-wise

770

Kids 7–11   Know-it-all

1 Which Japanese company invented the Walkman?

2 What organs in your chest are used for breathing?

3 What name is given to the temperature when a liquid becomes a solid?

4 When it is summer in Australia, what season is it in Europe?

5 Are all metals magnetic?

6 What word is used to describe the process when a solid changes to a liquid?

7 What sort of code uses dots and dashes to spell out words?

8 What is the proper name for spit?

9 What is the effect of too much sun on your skin?

10 What name is given to objects too small to be seen by the human eye?

Mixed up science

771

Kids 12–14   Test your skills

1 What name is given to the combination of dead skin cells, dirt and oil found on the head?

2 Approximately what percentage of our DNA do we share with chimps (within 2 per cent)?

3 Where is the 'Sea of Tranquillity'?

4 How long from cutting yourself does it take the body to begin the healing process?

5 What substance is used to make computer chips?

6 What invention stops buildings from being damaged by lightning?

7 Where in your body are the organs that control your balance?

8 What name is given to the imaginary line that divides the Earth into the northern and southern hemispheres?

9 Is it more appropriate to treat viral infections, such as chicken pox, influenza, and the common cold, with antibiotics or with aspirin?

10 What is it called when the Sun is obscured by the Moon passing in front of it?

Science

772 Science facts
Kids 7–11   Know your facts

1 What does UFO stand for?

2 What is put in a torch to give it power to work?

3 What alcoholic drink is made from crushed grapes?

4 Where in your body might you find plaque?

5 Why does the Moon look the same size as the Sun in the sky, even though it is much smaller?

6 How long does it take for the Earth to make a complete turn on its axis?

7 What is another name for your pelvis?

8 What is a galaxy?

9 What forms over a wound after you have cut yourself?

10 If you mix red and blue paint, what colour is produced?

773 Tougher ones
Kids 12–14   Put your brain to the test

1 What name is given to the Earth's insulating blanket of gases that protect it from the light and heat of the Sun?

2 What sort of boat has two hulls joined together?

3 Why is the air inside a balloon under pressure?

4 When yeast is used to make bread rise, what gas is produced?

5 What makes the Moon shine?

6 Which is the largest planet in the Solar System?

7 What is the hardest mineral?

8 What is the Base 2 number system more commonly known as?

9 What is the name for the coloured light you see when ordinary light shines through a prism?

10 What gas, used as a weapon in the First World War, is used to kill bacteria in swimming pools?

774 Knowledgeable?
Kids 7–11   How much do you know?

1 What type of boat can travel underwater?

2 In computing terms, what does PC mean?

3 What happens (at sea level) to water at 100°C (212°F)?

4 Do magnets with the same poles facing each other repel or attract?

5 How many sides does a normal dice have?

6 How many senses does the body have?

7 Where in your mouth do you taste things?

8 What lifts a kite into the air?

9 Where in a bone is the marrow?

10 What force causes things to fall to the ground when dropped?

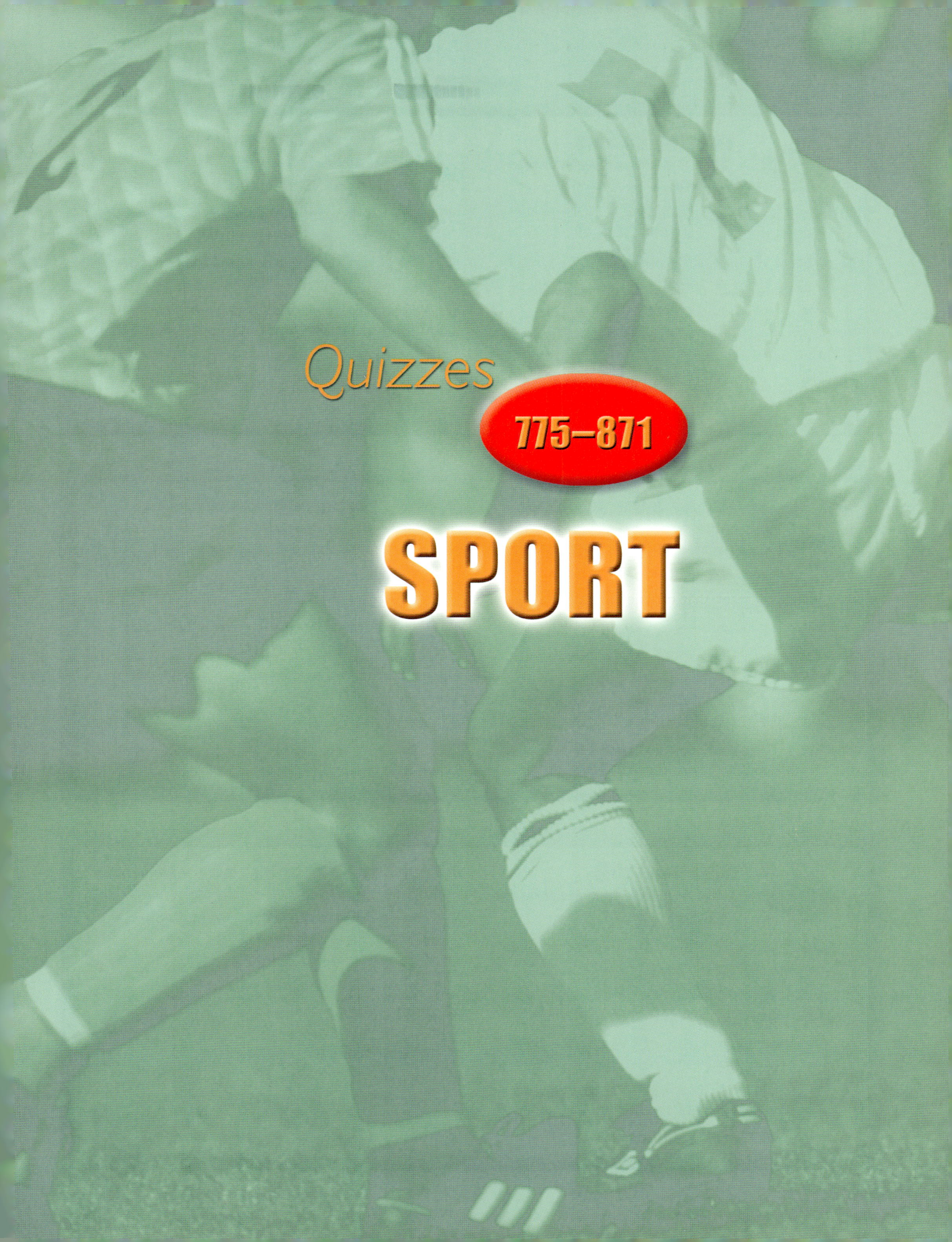

Quizzes

775–871

SPORT

Sport

Winning colours

775

LEVEL 1   A colourful round of sports questions

1 In snooker, how many points is the green ball worth?

2 What is the nickname of Manchester United?

3 In which branch of sport did Carl Lewis win nine Olympic gold medals?

4 In which sport do red and yellow balls oppose black and blue balls?

5 Who is the manager who resigned as boss of Scotland's national football team in 2001?

6 What name is given to the white ball in snooker?

7 In which sport do the All-Blacks play?

8 In which Canadian city do the baseball team the Blue Jays play their home games?

9 What colour links the home shirts of Glasgow Rangers, Everton and Millwall?

10 Which English football team are nicknamed 'the black cats' and play their home games at the Stadium of Light?

On the fairway

776

LEVEL 1   Be a sporting hero by answering these questions

1 Is a spoon, a knife or a fork a type of golf club?

2 In what capacity was Harold 'Dickie' Bird a leading figure in the game of cricket?

3 What colour belt does a first Dan wear in judo?

4 In which English city was the boxer Prince Naseem Hamed born?

5 Which German tennis star won his first Wimbledon singles title in 1985?

6 Which cricketing nation was captained by Clive Lloyd?

7 Alpine and Nordic are types of which sport?

8 How many football World Cups were contested in the 1940s?

9 Which British driver was crowned Formula 1 World Champion in 1992?

10 For how many minutes does a 'chukka' last in the game of polo?

Take your pick

777

LEVEL 1   Choose from these sporting challenges

1 Which former British Prime Minister named his competition yacht *Morning Cloud*?

2 Which former English cricket captain also played football for Scunthorpe United?

3 What is the nationality of Formula 1 racing driver Jacques Villeneuve?

4 What colour is the name given to the centre of an archery target?

5 In canoeing, what is category K?

6 What does the B stand for in the initials, IBF, WBC and WBA?

7 In tennis what is the score in games when a tie-break comes into operation?

8 What is the Gaelic word for pole, the type that is thrown in the Highland Games?

9 Other than Munich, what is the only other German city to host the Summer Olympics in the 20th century?

10 What mechanical animal does a greyhound chase in greyhound races?

Mixed bag
778 LEVEL 2 Step up the pace with these sporty teasers

1 Name the actor, famous for playing Tarzan, who was the first man to swim 100m in under 1 minute.

2 In which sport is the All-Ireland final contested annually on the first Sunday in September?

3 Which female tennis player married fellow player Roger Cawley in 1975?

4 At which famous racing course do horses turn around Tattenham Corner?

5 What three-letter word is the name given to a forward sail on a yacht?

6 In which sport did Jahangir Khan win the British Open in consecutive years from 1982 to 1991?

7 In darts, what is the lowest possible score that cannot be attained with one dart?

8 What is always the final event in a decathlon?

9 Which former darts world champion was nicknamed 'the crafty cockney'?

10 What do the letters WD stand for on a netball bib?

Troublesome teasers
779 LEVEL 2 Gold, silver and bronze questions

1 How many players make up a beach volleyball team?

2 Which former England football team manager died on April 28, 1999 aged 79?

3 In which sport is the Canadian pairs race?

4 Which Irish player scored three tries against France in the 2000 Six Nations Championship?

5 Which American won the most men's singles titles at Wimbledon in the 20th century?

6 Which Suffolk town is home to the headquarters of the Jockey Club?

7 According to the song 'Where do you go to my Lovely?', who bought 'my lovely' a racehorse for Christmas?

8 In which sport did Ivan Mauger win six world titles?

9 In gymnastics, which piece of apparatus is 5m long?

10 Which Asian city hosted the Olympics at which Ben Johnson tested positive for illegal substances?

Freestyle
780 LEVEL 2 A medley of questions

1 Which Australian golfer carried the Olympic torch over Sydney Harbour Bridge at the opening ceremony of the 2000 Olympics?

2 At which cricket venue are the W.G. Grace Gates found?

3 What nationality is the tennis player Michael Stich?

4 Which colour is representative of the most difficult ski runs?

5 Which horse is buried at the winning post at Aintree?

6 Which city won the right to host the 2008 Summer Olympics?

7 What is the name of Venus Williams' tennis playing sister?

8 What do the initials NFL stand for in American sport?

9 What is the second fastest swimming stroke?

10 Who scored 375 runs for the West Indies in a 1994 Test match against England?

Sport

781 Sport around the world
LEVEL 1   International games or players

1 Brothers Scott and Gavin Hastings have both played international rugby for which country?

2 What is Canada's national sport?

3 Who won more Ryder Cups in the 20th century: the USA or Europe?

4 In which country was tennis star Anna Kournikova born?

5 The football club Feyenoord play their home matches in which city?

6 In which country is the cricket trophy, the Sheffield Shield, contested annually?

7 In which country were the Olympic Games held in 776 BC?

8 In which country did the sport of sumo wrestling originate?

9 The Harlem Globetrotters basketball team was founded in which city?

10 Which country has won football's World Cup on five occasions?

782 Either or...
LEVEL 1   Take a gamble on the right answer

1 In 1984, which water event was introduced to the Olympics?

2 Which of these playing cards is known as 'the black lady': Queen of Spades or the Queen of Clubs?

3 In the 20th century, did Oxford or Cambridge win more Varsity rugby union matches?

4 In hurling, what name is given to the hurling stick: a hurl or a ling?

5 What was Nick Skelton sitting on when he won the 1995 Volvo World Cup?

6 The Grand National was staged at an airport during the First World War: was it Gatwick or Heathrow?

7 In rounders, is the ball made of wood or leather?

8 Can ice-hockey players kick the puck?

9 Is an archery target divided into five or ten zones?

10 Does Everton play its home matches in Leeds or Liverpool?

783 Mixed bag
LEVEL 2   Do you know your Marathon from your Wimbledon?

1 With Holland, which country jointly hosted the 2000 European football championships?

2 In which year was the first London Marathon held?

3 Who partnered Billie Jean King at doubles in 1979, when she won her 20th Wimbledon title?

4 At which boxing weight did Floyd Patterson win an Olympic gold medal in 1952?

5 Which English county side plays at the Oval cricket ground?

6 Which sport is played by the Philadelphia Flyers?

7 Who was the first boxer to beat Sugar Ray Leonard professionally?

8 Alongside Norway, which other country pioneered orienteering?

9 Who was the first American cyclist to win the Tour de France?

10 In which British town is the National Hockey Stadium to be found?

784 Putting you to the test
LEVEL 2   Can you score a perfect 10 on this round?

1 In 1999 who smashed the men's 100m world record at a meeting in Athens?

2 In 1986, who became the youngest ever World Heavyweight Boxing Champion?

3 Which showjumper's autobiography is entitled *V is for Victory*?

4 Which sport is played by the New York Knicks?

5 In horse racing, what is the maximum age for a filly?

6 Who was the last Englishman of the 20th century to score a Test triple century?

7 How many events are there in a pentathlon?

8 What is the name of the target ball in a game of bowls?

9 Which famous car rally is held annually in Monaco?

10 Which 1927 invention enabled sprinters to start faster?

785 Grand slam
LEVEL 2   Sporting selection

1 In which country was the tennis star Greg Rusedski born?

2 What do the rings on the Olympic flag represent?

3 Who was the cricketer that appeared on the cover of the 140th edition of Wisden's Cricketers' Almanack?

4 Which country's rugby union team is known as The Springboks?

5 Which racket sport is the national sport of Malaysia?

6 Which is the only Grand Slam tennis title that Bjorn Borg did not win?

7 What is the highest possible score that can be made by throwing just one dart?

8 Which two English counties contest a 'roses' cricket match?

9 How many sailing hulls has a trimaran got?

10 In a 110m hurdles race, how many hurdles are negotiated?

786 In the rough
LEVEL 3   A seriously sporting challenge

1 Which duo did Barber and Slater succeed as British champions?

2 Traditionally, which country leads the parade at the opening ceremony of the Olympics?

3 On which course is the Kentucky Derby run?

4 Who was John McEnroe's doubles partner in four of his five Wimbledon doubles titles?

5 In 1990, which boxer was charged with the attempted murder of promoter Frank Warren?

6 Who was the first driver to register 50 Grand Prix wins on four wheels?

7 Which colourful horse won the 2001 Grand National?

8 At which sport did Prince William co-captain the Eton school team?

9 In which country were the first-ever Commonwealth Games held?

10 How many Wimbledon singles titles did Martina Navratilova win?

Sport

787 The sporting nineties
LEVEL 1   It seems like only yesterday

1 Which Spanish city hosted the 1992 Summer Olympics?

2 In 1998, did Mark O'Meara win golf's British Open or the US Open?

3 In 1997 who became the youngest-ever woman to win a Grand Slam tennis title?

4 In 1996, which legendary ice-hockey player moved from the St Louis Blues to play for the New York Rangers?

5 In which year of the 1990s was the Grand National postponed due to a bomb scare?

6 Who resigned as England's football manager in 1993?

7 In 1993, which tennis player was stabbed on court by Gunther Parche?

8 In 1996, which baseball team won their first world series for 18 years?

9 Name the sports commentator, nicknamed 'the voice of tennis', who died in 1992 aged 84.

10 What was the American venue of the 1996 Summer Olympics?

788 Ball sports
LEVEL 1   Kick them, hit them, or bounce them

1 Trevor Brooking became caretaker manager of which football club in 2002/03 season?

2 Which is the only English football league team with a day of the week in their name?

3 What name is given to a cricket fielder who stands closest to, but not behind, the wicket?

4 What colour shirts are worn by the French rugby union national team?

5 What is the duration of a netball game?

6 In golf, which B word is a depression in the ground usually covered with sand?

7 What is the minimum number of players in a softball team?

8 When Arthur Ashe won his only Wimbledon singles title, which fellow American did he beat in the final?

9 In American Football, what phrase means that a team has prevented another from registering any points?

10 Which American sport was invented by Abner Doubleday?

789 The Olympic Games
LEVEL 2   The world's greatest sporting spectacle

1 What name is given to the Olympic yachting event for a crew of three people?

2 In which sport was Irish competitor Michell de Bruin (née Smith) banned for four years in 1998, after a positive drug test?

3 What colour of medal was presented to the winners in the first modern Olympics in 1896?

4 Which famous American won his second Olympic title in the 400m hurdles in 1984?

5 How many laps of the track are run for a 400m outdoor race?

6 Who won the Heavyweight Boxing gold medal at the 1964 Olympics?

7 Who won a gold medal for the 100m in 1924 and featured in the film *Chariots of Fire*?

8 Which member of the British royal family opened the 1956 Melbourne Olympics?

9 In which year did Japan first compete in the Summer Olympics: 1912, 1952 or 1972?

10 At the 1992 Olympics, which country won seven gold medals in boxing?

A round of golf

790 LEVEL 1 Can you unravel this golfing terminology

1 What nickname is given to the clubhouse on a golf course?

2 How many shots under par is a birdie?

3 On a golf course, what do the initials GUR stand for?

4 What name is given to the closely mown section of a golf hole between the green and the tee?

5 What is the American term for a bunker?

6 What is affected if a golfer is suffering from 'the yips'?

7 What is the alternative name for a No. 3 wood?

8 Which form of golf is based on holes won, lost and halved, as opposed to the total strokes taken?

9 What name is given to a stroke when the head of the club fails to make any contact with the ball?

10 Which playing card is the alternative name for a hole in one?

A trophy test

791 LEVEL 2 Prize questions

1 In the Orient, in which sport is the Emperor's Cup contested?

2 What do the initials TT stand for in the Isle of Man TT Races?

3 Which golfing trophy is named after an American president?

4 Which sporting trophy was held by the USA for 132 consecutive years?

5 In which sport is the Thomas Cup contested?

6 The Solheim Cup is the female version of which contest?

7 What do the initials FA stand for in the FA Cup?

8 The Fastnet Race is one of the events originally contested in which cup competition?

9 In which sport is the North Sea Cup contested: canoeing, long-distance swimming or windsurfing?

10 In which event is the Lugano Trophy contested: ballooning, archery or walking?

Girl power

792 LEVEL 3 Great women in sport

1 In which year were women's track and field events first included in the Summer Olympics?

2 Which female boxer is nicknamed 'the Fleetwood assassin'?

3 Who was the first woman to ride in the Epsom Derby?

4 In which sport does Laura Davies compete?

5 Which American tennis star won the women's singles gold medal at the 1992 Olympics?

6 Who was the only female competitor not to be given a sex test at the 1976 Olympics?

7 In which sport does the Lady Paramount act as an official?

8 Heather McKay and Michelle Martin are both famous names in which sport?

9 Who was the first woman to run a sub-5 minute mile?

10 Which male tennis player did Billie Jean King play in a 1973 match billed as 'the battle of the sexes'?

Sport

Games and pastimes
793   **LEVEL 1**   **Board games for the bored**

1 How many black squares are there on a chess board?

2 How many different colours are there on a Rubik's cube?

3 Which pastime involves descending sheer cliffs using ropes and tackle?

4 What name is given to a hand in poker in which all the cards are of the same suit?

5 What is the name of the man of the cloth in the board game Cluedo?

6 In which 1973 film did Paul Newman play poker aboard a train?

7 What does a philatelist collect?

8 What is the game of draughts called in America?

9 Which is the only chess piece that cannot move backwards?

10 How many cards does each player receive in a game of gin rummy?

Football World Cup
794   **LEVEL 1**   **Football's ultimate trophy**

1 Which Frenchman gave his name to the original World Cup trophy?

2 In 1982, which nation became the second to win the World Cup for the third time?

3 Gerd Muller was the leading scorer in the 1970 World Cup finals. Which country did he represent?

4 Which nation lost consecutive World Cup finals in 1974 and 1978?

5 How many years separated the third and fourth World Cups?

6 Who scored the first-ever hat-trick in a World Cup final?

7 Which nation qualified for the 2002 World Cup as holders?

8 What was the nickname of Zaire, the first African nation to qualify for the World Cup?

9 What sort of animal was 'World Cup Willie', England's 1966 mascot?

10 Who managed the England team in the 1998 World Cup finals?

You wear it well
795   **LEVEL 3**   **A well-cut round about sporting fashion**

1 Which American jockey was nicknamed 'the shoe'?

2 Who wore the No. 1 bib at the 2003 London Marathon?

3 In the USA, what is the name of the premier boxing tournament for amateur boxers?

4 In rugby union, which nation wears shirts displaying a silver fern emblem?

5 Which item of a footballer's kit was made compulsory by a law passed by FIFA in 1990?

6 In the 20th century, which goalkeeper won the most international caps for England at football?

7 What name is given to a skier's quilted trousers?

8 Who did Rocky Marciano beat to become World Heavyweight Boxing Champion?

9 What number is traditionally worn on a full back's shirt in rugby union?

10 In which sport do participants wear an outfit called a 'keikogi'?

Formula 1 facts

796

LEVEL 1   Can you keep up with the fastest sport on Earth

1 Which famous track hosted the British Grand Prix in 1985?

2 The tyres of which company have been used for the majority of world championship cars?

3 Which son of a Brazilian diplomat won the first of his three world titles in 1981?

4 Who was the first Frenchman to become Formula 1 World Champion?

5 Which famous name in the world of Grand Prix racing became confined to a wheelchair after a road crash in 1986?

6 Who was Damon Hill's father?

7 Which Grand Prix is contested around the streets of Monte Carlo?

8 What nationality is Keke Rosberg?

9 In which year was the 300th motor racing Grand Prix staged: 1968, 1978 or 1988?

10 Which horse-racing course staged five British Grand Prix races?

A rugby round

797

LEVEL 2   Keep in touch with these questions

1 What was the name of the student who is credited with originally 'picking up the ball and running with it', thus creating rugby?

2 In rugby union, which nation was the 1999 World Champion?

3 Which former England rugby union captain was born in 1965 in Bradford upon Avon?

4 What is the nickname of Leeds' rugby league side?

5 What is the name of the ceremonial dance performed by the New Zealand rugby union team before each game?

6 In rugby union, where in England is 'HQ'?

7 What colour shirt does Jonah Lomu wear when playing rugby union at international level?

8 Who kicked England's 24 points beating Scotland on their way to a 1995 Grand Slam?

9 Which country joined the Five Nations Championships in 2000 to make it six nations?

10 Which RAF pilot scored 49 tries for England between 1984 and 1996?

Football frolics

798

LEVEL 3   How well do you know your soccer?

1 In the 1990s, which English football team was managed by Ossie Ardiles, Kevin Keegan, Kenny Dalglish and Ruud Gullit?

2 In what colour do the New Zealand football international team play?

3 Who was the first Dutch footballer to be named European Footballer of the Year?

4 In 1956, who kept goal in the FA Cup final with a broken neck?

5 Who was sacked as manager of the Scottish football club Celtic in February 2000?

6 Which was the first club to win the European Cup for three consecutive years?

7 Founded by two clergymen, what is London's oldest football club?

8 Which footballer's autobiography, *Head to Head*, was published in 2001?

9 Linfield are the most successful football club in which country?

10 In which decade was the FA Cup first contested?

Sport

Nice move
799
LEVEL 1 Weave your way round these questions

1 In baseball, what do the initials NL stand for?

2 How many minutes does a round last in a boxing bout under the Queensberry Rules?

3 Which country won the football World Cup in 1986?

4 At what type of sporting contest are bullriding and calf roping two of the six disciplines?

5 What is the least number of darts required to score 501?

6 In which country was the sport of croquet invented?

7 Over what distance is the longest track event in the women's heptathlon?

8 Which organisation makes the rules for flat horse racing in England?

9 In fencing, which is heavier: a foil or an épée?

10 How many rings are depicted on the Olympic flag?

Place your bets
800
LEVEL 1 Take your chance with this easy sporting round

1 What kind of sporting animal was 'Mick the Miller'?

2 Grand Master Bowman is the name given to the highest standard of competitor in which sport?

3 Which sport featured in the films *When we were Kings*, *The Main Event* and *The Hurricane*?

4 What does the letter C signify on a hockey shirt?

5 Which sport featured in the Chevy Chase film *Caddyshack*?

6 Which member of the royal family competed in three-day eventing at the 1976 Olympics?

7 In which event did Great Britain win gold at the 2002 Winter Olympics?

8 What kind of sporting projectile was thrown by Geoff Capes in the Olympic Games?

9 Henley-on-Thames is associated with which sport?

10 What name is given to the obedience section of an equestrian event?

Keep on your toes
801
LEVEL 1 Some easily defended questions for the sports fan

1 What ball game is played on an area measuring 9 x 5ft (2.7 x 1.5m)?

2 In rugby union, in what colour shirts do the Welsh team play?

3 Who was the manager of Manchester United before Sir Alex Ferguson?

4 Which actor played a golfer in the film *Tin Cup* and a baseball player in the film *Field of Dreams*?

5 In which country are 'serie A' football games played?

6 How many lanes are there on an Olympic running track?

7 What was the nationality of the Grand Prix driver Jack Brabham?

8 What age are all the horses that contest the Epsom Derby?

9 In which sport did Robin Cousins win a 1980 Winter Olympic gold medal?

10 The name of which watch company adorns the scoreboard of Wimbledon's centre court?

802

A sporting chance
Correctly identify these sporting heroes

1

2

3

4

5

6

7

8

9

10

Sport

803 Jumpers
LEVEL 2   How high can you go?

1 Which horse jumped into the history books by winning a third Grand National in 1977?

2 Who recorded a leap of 18.29m to win a triple jump gold medal at the 1995 World Athletics Championships?

3 Who wrote a book called *The Perfect Jump* after breaking the world record in 1968?

4 What nickname was given to the British ski jumper Eddie Edwards?

5 Which sport featured in the film *White Men Can't Jump*?

6 Who took his tally of Olympic gold medals to nine when winning the long jump in Atlanta?

7 Which Welshman won the 1964 Olympic gold medal for the long jump?

8 Who was the first pole-vaulter to clear a height of over 20ft (6m)?

9 Which American gold medal winner of 1968 gave his name to a style of high jumping?

10 In which athletics track event is the water jump negotiated seven times?

804 Birds of a feather
LEVEL 2   All the questions are about birds, in one way or another

1 Which cricket umpire wrote the book *White Cap and Bails*?

2 In which year did Robin Cousins win a gold medal in the Winter Olympics?

3 What name is given to a score of three under par on a golf hole?

4 What is the nickname of Newcastle United?

5 What was the name of the vessel in which Donald Campbell was killed?

6 What football team are nicknamed 'the owls'?

7 What is the alternative name for trap or skeet shooting?

8 For what sport is John Parrott famous?

9 Which world-famous cricket star was out for a duck in his last ever Test innings to give him a Test average score of 99.14?

10 Which was the first non-American team to win the World Series in baseball?

805 On the attack
LEVEL 3   A tough challenge for sporting heroes

1 Which famous sporting contest acquired its name after Charles Bunbury lost on the toss of a coin?

2 Which sport employs the Stableford scoring system?

3 In sumo wrestling, what name is given to a wrestler who has attained the rank of Grand Champion?

4 What is Bulgaria's national sport?

5 *The Glory Game*, a book about Tottenham Hotspur, was written by which author?

6 What is a more common name for a natatorium?

7 The rules for which sport is governed by the IRF?

8 Octopush is an underwater version of which sport?

9 In which sport could a player serve an underarm twist service or a giraffe service?

10 The Hawaii Ironman competition, first held at Waikiki Beach in 1978, is what type of event?

The Olympic Games
806

LEVEL 2   Those great Olympians

1 In which year were Israeli Olympic athletes murdered by terrorists?

2 In which decade were the games first televised?

3 What record did the Soviet gymnast Nikolai Andrianov achieve between 1972 and 1980?

4 Which is the only swimming event to have been held in every Olympics?

5 Which sport featured only at the 1900 Olympics, between France and Britain?

6 To what position in the Olympic hierarchy was Juan Antonio Samaranch elected in 1980?

7 How many Olympic Games have been missed due to war?

8 Which member of the Royal Family is a British representative on the International Olympic Committee?

9 Which city, that played host to the 1984 Winter Games, was devastated by civil war in the 1990s?

10 Hans Gunnar Liljenwall was the first athlete to test positive for drug use at an Olympic Games. Which country did he represent?

The FA Cup
807

LEVEL 2   The high point of the footballing calendar

1 In 1923, which stadium hosted the FA Cup for the first time?

2 Which was the losing side in consecutive finals in 1998 and 1999?

3 Who was the youngest-ever goalkeeper to play in an FA Cup final?

4 Who was the first Frenchman to captain an FA Cup-winning side?

5 Morton Peto Betts won what FA Cup honour?

6 The fastest FA Cup final goal on record is 43 seconds scored by Chelsea in 1997, against which side?

7 Only two sides won consecutive FA Cup finals in the 20th century. Newcastle was one team, which was the other?

8 Which is the only non-English team to have won the FA Cup?

9 Which team achieved the biggest victory in an FA Cup final in the 1990s?

10 Chelsea's Peter Osgood was the last player of the 20th century to achieve what feat in the FA Cup?

First in line
808

LEVEL 3   Can you place these memorable firsts?

1 Which Welshman became the first-ever darts World Champion in 1978?

2 In 1994 Colin McRae became the first British driver in 16 years to win which race?

3 Who was the first cricketer to score 10,000 Test runs?

4 In 1959 who became the first driver to win a Formula 1 World Championship in a car bearing his own name?

5 Which footballer scored the first goal in Premiership history?

6 At which venue was the first British Grand Prix held in 1926?

7 Which famous name in the world of cricket was also the first-ever president of the England Bowls Association?

8 Which colour moves first in the game of chess?

9 What was the nationality of the first-ever gymnast to score a perfect ten?

10 On what date do all racehorses celebrate their birthday?

Sport

809 Number crunching
LEVEL 1 A round number of questions on sports statistics

1 How many players are there in a volleyball team?

2 How many people participate each year in the Oxford and Cambridge boatrace?

3 How many points is a bullseye worth in darts?

4 Over how many holes are major golf tournaments contested: 36, 54 or 72?

5 How many hoops are used in a game of croquet?

6 How many faults are incurred if a fence is knocked down in showjumping?

7 How many members are there in a tug-of-war team: 8, 9 or 10?

8 How many holes are there in a ten-pin bowling ball?

9 How many reds are there on the table at the start of a snooker game?

10 On each side of a Ryder Cup team, are there 10, 12 or 14 players?

810 A sporting chance
LEVEL 1 Take a chance on these puzzlers

1 Who won the 1980 Wimbledon mixed doubles title with her brother John Austin?

2 Over how many metres is a metric mile run in a track race?

3 Which member of the British royal family owns the Oval cricket ground?

4 How long is the interval between boxing rounds?

5 In sailing, how many masts does a sloop have: one, two or three?

6 Is the WBA or the WBO the oldest governing body in boxing?

7 In rugby, if the ball is 'in touch' is it in or out of play?

8 Who won the first-ever cricket Test match?

9 In which sport is a technique called herringboning used to travel up a hill?

10 How many Olympics of the 20th century were held in Africa?

811 Random relay
LEVEL 2 Dig in as the going gets tough

1 Why did the USA boycott the 1980 Moscow Olympics?

2 Which colour is associated with the baseball teams of Boston and Cincinnati?

3 Which number on a dartboard is sandwiched between 20 and 12?

4 What is an illegal delivery in cricket called?

5 Swimming, running and which other discipline comprise a triathlon?

6 Which fence at Aintree's Grand National course was named after a captain who fell there?

7 How old was Boris Becker when he won his first Wimbledon title?

8 Which swimming stroke begins the first leg of a 4 x 100m medley relay?

9 What has a length of 35 yards: an ice-hockey rink, a croquet lawn or a bowling green?

10 Who was crowned Formula 1 World Champion in 1997?

 **812** ## Sport quest

These questions are tougher than the others and you may need to do some research

1 What is 28in (71cm) high and 9in (22cm) wide?

2 In which game does a player shoot from a line called a taw?

3 Who was the first person to captain, coach and manage England at cricket?

4 What first did Bunny Austin achieve on Centre Court at Wimbledon in 1933?

5 Which Scottish soccer team shares its name with a novel by Sir Walter Scott?

6 In which sport is a string applied to a nock?

7 In the 1998 soccer World Cup, which nation's squad of players contained 11 members with names ending in the letter U?

8 A Morgan, a small dog, a liner, an iron. Where will you find them together?

9 Who said: 'The English are not very spiritual people, so they invented cricket to give them some idea of eternity.'

10 If Sunderland did it in 1979 and Villa did it in 1981, who did what in 1982?

11 What connects a boxer named Larry and a golfer named Tom with the creator of Holmes?

12 What connects Newcastle United, Norwich City, Brighton and Hove Albion, and Crystal Palace?

13 If red is one; blue is two; and white, black and yellow are three, four and five respectively – what's the sport and what is six?

14 If the fool has no number and the world is XXI, what is the hanged man?

15 Which was the only Olympics to feature the killing of animals, and what was the event?

A clue to question 4

Sport

Sporting trivia
813

LEVEL 2   Pit your wits against these sporting trials

1 When was Donald Campbell killed while attempting to break the water speed record?

2 In golf, the first-ever US Open was played in 1895 at the Newport Club, in which state?

3 What was said to have been invented by Brian Gamlin: roller skates, a two-piece snooker cue or the numbering system on a dartboard?

4 The upper limit for which weight division in boxing is 54kg (118lb)?

5 Under what name did Robert Craig perform motorcycle stunts?

6 Which horse that contested the 2001 Prix de L'Arc de Triomphe, shares its name with the state capital of Arkansas?

7 Which cyclist won Britain's first gold medal at the 2000 Sydney Olympics?

8 Which actress married golfer Sam Torrance?

9 In 2001, tennis star Goran Ivanisevic was called up for national service for which country?

10 What is the name of the annual yachting festival that is held on the Isle of Wight?

On your marks
814

LEVEL 2   You'll have to use some random reasoning here

1 In Formula 1 Grand Prix racing how many points are awarded to a driver who finishes second in a race?

2 What is the shortest distance over which races are run in major indoor athletics events?

3 In which animated film of 2003 was the Tour de France depicted?

4 With which baseball team did Babe Ruth begin his major league career?

5 Was Dennis Lillee banned from using a glass, aluminium or stainless-steel cricket bat?

6 Which word is an acknowledgment spoken when a hit is scored in fencing?

7 Cumberland and Westmorland are both what?

8 Which of the following sportsmen might be disciplined for excessive use of the whip: Jensen Button, Pat Eddery or Hanse Cronje?

9 Which Spanish football team play their home matches at the Nou Camp Stadium?

10 What bats can have a maximum of 50 pimples per cm²?

Be a sport
815

LEVEL 3   Tough questions for even the most dedicated sports fan

1 Who captained the US Ryder Cup team in 1999?

2 In which throwing event are competitors referred to as either shifters or spinners?

3 What does the word real signify in Real Madrid?

4 What sport is divided into eight 'chukkas', each of 7 minutes duration?

5 In which card game is the Bermuda Bowl contested?

6 In which European country was the boxer Joe Bugner born?

7 Name the sport that can begin with a beach start or a dock start.

8 In which European country is the Zandvoort Grand Prix race track?

9 How high is a table-tennis net?

10 Which nation was expelled from the 1992 European Football Championships, following sanctions imposed by the UN?

Give us a cue

816

LEVEL 2   A round of questions about snooker and billiards

1 Which snooker star is nicknamed 'rocket Ronnie'?

2 In snooker how many points are conceded when committing a foul on the green ball?

3 How many balls are used in a game of billiards?

4 In 1982, who cradled the World Championship trophy in one arm and his daughter in the other?

5 Which former snooker champion shares his surname with a sign of the Zodiac?

6 How many successive pots must a snooker player make to score a 147 break?

7 Which Canadian World Champion was nicknamed 'the grinder'?

8 What is the nationality of snooker star James Wattana?

9 Which letter of the alphabet can be seen on the baulk line of a snooker table?

10 At the start of a game of snooker into what shape are the red balls placed?

Connections

817

LEVEL 2   Can you find the missing connections?

1 What connects the nicknames of Jimmy White, Barry McGuigan and Alex Higgins?

2 What word can follow real, table or lawn?

3 What is the connection between Joe Frazier, Ian Botham, Graham Hill and Brian Clough?

4 Find the connection between the numbers 17, 3, 19, 7 and 16, and name the next one?

5 What is the connection between the World Snooker Champions of 1926, 1949 and 1981?

6 What connects the American football team from Miami, the golfer Greg Norman and the swimmer Eric Moussambani?

7 What is the sporting connection between the years 1916, 1940 and 1944?

8 What connects the football World Cup years 1958, 1962 and 1970?

9 Which sport connects the Dunhill Cup and the Curtis Cup trophies?

10 Which country connects the 1968 Olympic Games with the 1986 Football World Cup?

Sporting symphonies

818

LEVEL 3   Music from the terraces – and other places

1 The song 'Sweet Georgia Brown' is the theme song for which sporting team?

2 Which hit for the pop group 10 CC contains the line: 'I don't like cricket, I love it'?

3 'I'm Forever Blowing Bubbles' is the signature tune for which football team?

4 Which song, a hit for Eric Clapton in 1975, was adopted as England's anthem by rugby union supporters?

5 To the strains of which Tina Turner hit did Chris Eubank make his ring entrances?

6 With John McEnroe, who was the other half of a pop group called The Full Metal Rackets?

7 Which hymn was traditionally sung before the start of Wembley FA Cup finals?

8 The Elton John hit 'Philadelphia Freedom' was a tribute to which American female sports star?

9 Who recorded the song 'Burning Heart' the 1985 theme for the film *Rocky IV*?

10 Who composed 'Nessum Dorma' sung by Luciano Pavarotti for 'Italia 90' in the World Cup?

Quick off the mark

It is one thing to know the answer, quite another to be able to bring it to mind instantly. A buzzer quiz is harder to set than an ordinary one, but it can be worth the effort if you have the time and the expertise. This kind of quiz favours quick-witted risk-takers, and it is almost as exciting to watch as it is to take part.

Buzzer quizzes are mainly used for tournaments or knock-out contests. The idea is that teams or players are eliminated over a number of rounds leading to a final. This differs from the more traditional quiz night where all the teams or players take part in every round, and the winner is the person or team with the highest score.

In a tournament, teams should be kept small. Two or three to a side is manageable; four or more is unwieldy. You need at least eight teams for a knockout tournament to work; sixteen is better. If you have more than eight but less than sixteen, you need a way of deciding which teams get a bye through to the next round.

Fingers on buzzers

There are two kinds of quick-fire quiz — those that are played head-to-head and those that are played against the clock. Head-to-head rounds pit two teams against each other, as TV quizzes such as *University Challenge*. Against-the-clock rounds require teams to buzz in with their answers and score the maximum number of points in a fixed time, as in shows such as *Mastermind*.

As quiz master you will need an assistant in

Choosing your buzzers

If you haven't the time to make a buzzer how about collecting together different bicycle bells or air horns. You could use ready-made toys with different squeaks, klaxon horns, or even party blowers. If you have a number of teams it will be easier to have easily distinguishable noises so that there is no mistake about which team gets in first. Make sure your adjudicator is someone who can make decisive lightning judgments.

quick-fire rounds – someone to keep a close eye on the time and to keep score. Don't try to do this yourself: you will have your hands full reading the questions.

I've started so I'll finish

Against-the-clock quizzes work best with small numbers. More than three or four teams and the process becomes tedious for the teams waiting their turn – imagine *Mastermind* with 15 contestants.

The questions can be addressed either to the team as a whole or to individuals in turn, but do not allow team members to confer or this will slow the pace. If you allow five seconds for answering each question you will need some 24 questions in a two-minute round. But prepare at least 40 per round – you don't want to run out. (This is a big consideration in a quick-fire quiz: you need far more questions than in the traditional pub-quiz format.)

Make a show of shuffling the questions before you start. That way you can't be accused of rigging.

Pose the questions in a clear, even and paced voice. As soon as a competitor interrupts, stop. If they are wrong, give the correct answer then move on. If you get to the end of a question allow no more than five seconds for an answer. They can either pass or take a stab at it.

In this kind of quiz there is no penalty for a wrong answer or a pass. If you have started a question when the two minutes are up, carry on and allow the competitor to answer. Otherwise stop, give the answers to any questions that were passed on, and tell the competitor their score.

Your starter for ten

Head-to-head rounds are classic buzzer quizzes. Decide on a scoring system, such as two points for a correct answer, one for a bonus – and one lost point for a wrong answer (to discourage wild guesses). You should also penalise teams that buzz and then can't answer. If an incorrect answer is given, you can offer it to the other side – but it is often faster not to.

If you decide not to allow bonus questions, score one point for a correct answer and one lost point for a wrong answer. If no-one buzzes, wait a few seconds before giving the answer and moving on to the next question.

Writing buzzer questions

Writing for the buzzer requires a specific approach. The fact that the players can interrupt means that you have to phrase the questions so that they 'unfold'. Here is a good buzzer question:

'Which composer, born in Bonn in 1770, wrote nine symphonies, and by the time of his death in Vienna in 1827 was profoundly deaf?'

A good player could jump in after only the seventh word, more would pick up on the nine symphonies, and most people could get it by the end. The same question rewritten – *'Which famously deaf composer . . .'* – would produce a very different response. Most would get it right at the outset and the scoring would come down to speed, rather than knowledge.

It is worth throwing in the odd trick question with a real clue at the end such as:

'Who was the first actor to play Doctor Who on film?'

Many will jump in and say that it was William Hartnell (the first Doctor Who on screen). But the first to play Doctor Who on film was Peter Cushing in *Dr Who and the Daleks*.

Not every question need be a cascade of facts. Vary the pace with some quick, straightforward questions such as:

'How many old pence in an old pound.'

Sport

819   The sporting eighties
LEVEL 2   Can you remember the highs and lows of this decade?

1 Name the American hurdler who was beaten in June 1987 by Danny Harris, after 122 consecutive wins.

2 Which Austrian driver won his third Formula 1 World Championships in 1984?

3 Which European nation won its first Davis Cup in 1984 beating the USA 4–1 in the final?

4 In which year did 96 football spectators die in the Hillsborough tragedy?

5 At the 1980 Olympics, Pietro Mennea won the gold medal and Alan Wells the silver in what?

6 In 1981, Sue Brown became the first woman to take part in which race?

7 What was won by a catamaran called *Stars and Stripes* in 1988?

8 On which horse did Bob Champion jump to Grand National victory in 1981?

9 What did Bernard Hinault win for the fifth time in 1985?

10 Which football team, led by Alex Ferguson, won the European Cup Winners Cup in 1983?

820   Formula 1 facts
LEVEL 2   Trackside teasers for speed demons

1 Who was the first British driver to become Formula 1 World Champion?

2 Which motor-racing entrepreneur donated £1 million to the British Labour Party in 1997?

3 The Formula 1 World Championship was inaugurated at which British track?

4 Which former World Motor-racing Champion died of a heart attack in 1993?

5 Which Argentinian-born driver was a five-times World Champion in the 1950s?

6 What nationality was Jim Clark?

7 In what year did Michael Schumacher win his first world title?

8 Which former motor-racing World Champion appeared in the video for the Robbie Williams hit record *Supreme*?

9 Who was killed at Imola in 1994 when leading the field into the Tamburello corner?

10 Which son of a postmaster became America's first Formula 1 World Champion?

821   Well equipped
LEVEL 3   Can you identify the sports or sporting equipment?

1 In which sport does the net stand at a height of 8ft (2.4m)?

2 In 1863 the 'Cambridge Rules' became the first commonly accepted rules for which sport?

3 In which sport and pastime would a silver Wilkinson be used?

4 What is the stick used in lacrosse called?

5 What does a stimpmeter measure on a golf course?

6 What stands 10ft high (3m) and has a diameter of 18in (45cm)?

7 What name is given to the ropes on a yacht for hoisting the sails?

8 The basic equipment of what competition includes cross-country skis, poles, boots and a bolt-action (non-automatic) rifle?

9 Which sport, popular in Latin America, is played with a 'cesta in a cancha'?

10 What was Jack Broughton's pugilistic invention?

The sporting seventies
LEVEL 1   The decade of the footballers' perm

1 Who won her 20th Wimbledon title in 1979?

2 In the 1970s, who did Bob Paisley succeed as the manager of Liverpool?

3 Which media mogul organised the breakaway World Series Cricket Tournament in 1977?

4 How many football World Cups were held during the 1970s?

5 Which World Championships were staged for the first time at the Sheffield Crucible in 1977?

6 Which famous horse race was 100 years old in 1975?

7 Which tennis player got engaged to Jimmy Connors in 1974?

8 In which sport did the Whitbread Round the World Race begin in 1973?

9 Which Swede won the greatest number of men's singles Wimbledon titles in the 1970s?

10 Which West Indian cricketer was knighted on New Year's Day 1975?

Cricket clues
LEVEL 1   The gentleman's game

1 Which Y word is the name given to a bowling delivery that passes under the bat?

2 How many bowls comprise one over in cricket?

3 Which Test cricket ground is in Nottingham?

4 A figure of whom appears on the weathervane at Lord's?

5 Name the Australian fast bowler, born in Perth in 1949, with a career total of 355 Test wickets.

6 Which famous cricket ground has a pavilion end and a nursery end?

7 In which decade was England's infamous 'bodyline tour' of Australia?

8 Who was the first Australian cricketer to receive a knighthood?

9 Against which nation does England play for the Wisden Trophy?

10 Which famous cricket trophy is derived from a mock obituary of 1882?

Ice and snow
LEVEL 2   Don't get frozen out by this round

1 In which sport do competitors change lanes after every lap?

2 Which was the first Asian country to host the Winter Olympics?

3 Which famous Austrian skier was World Downhill Champion four times in the 1970s?

4 Which country won 29 gold medals at the 1998 Winter Olympics?

5 Which city hosted the 2002 Winter Olympics?

6 What nationality is alpine skier Ingemar Stenmark: Finnish, Norwegian or Swedish?

7 What piece of equipment takes its name from the Norwegian for snowshoe?

8 Which East German skater received a special Olympic award from the IOC president in 1988?

9 Who composed 'Bolero' to which Torvill and Dean skated and won a gold medal?

10 In mountaineering, what C word is the name of the metal plates with spikes that are fixed to the feet when climbing on ice?

Sport

Money matters
825
LEVEL 2   Place your bets for a round about the green stuff

1 At which English horse-racing course is the 2000 Guineas run?

2 Who won the 1987 Wimbledon Men's Singles Championship?

3 In betting parlance, how much is a monkey worth in pounds sterling?

4 What P word is the name given to the prize money for a boxing bout?

5 For what was the jockey Lester Piggott jailed?

6 Which Argentinean footballer did Manchester United sign for £28 million in 2001?

7 Which defender transferred to Manchester United from Leeds United for £29.1 million in 2002?

8 For which Brazilian superstar did Barcelona pay £13.2 million in July 1996?

9 Which sporting trophy was made from melted-down rupees?

10 In which film did Cuba Gooding Junior play an American footballer whose catchphrase was: 'Sho' me the money'?

How many?
826
LEVEL 2   Statistical challenge

1 Under NBA rules, a basketball player is removed from the game after committing how many fouls?

2 How many consecutive strikes would a ten-pin bowler have to make in order to achieve a perfect score of 300?

3 How many players form a Gaelic football team?

4 A marathon is run over 26 miles (42km) and how many yards?

5 How many consecutive fights did Rocky Marciano win, 43 by knockouts: 49, 50 or 51?

6 In Olympic archery, how many points do you get for hitting the inner red ring of a target?

7 Over how many laps is a standard speedway race contested?

8 What is the duration in minutes of a hockey game: 60, 70 or 80?

9 How many players comprise an Australian rules football team?

10 How many points are required to win a game of squash?

Horse play
827
LEVEL 3   A day at the races

1 In 1996, which super-rich horse race was won in its inaugural year by *Cigar*?

2 Which race forms the US Triple Crown with the Preakness Stakes and the Kentucky Derby?

3 Who was the first woman to train a Grand National winner?

4 What are Yankees, Canadians and Trixies?

5 Which famous jockey has the middle names of Hunter Fisher?

6 What was the appropriately named winning horse in the Grand National in the 1992 election year?

7 Which is the shortest of the following races: the French Derby, the Irish Derby, the Epsom Derby or the Kentucky Derby?

8 If a horse was to race a distance of 3km (2 miles), how many furlongs would it have travelled?

9 What name is given to a matador on horseback?

10 On which course is the Prix de l'Arc de Triomph run?

Stumped!
828

LEVEL 2 Questions from the crease

1 Which New Zealander was the first bowler to take 400 Test wickets?

2 In which country was England cricket captain Nasser Hussain born?

3 In which city was the first-ever cricket Test match played?

4 Which Yorkshireman was the first English cricketer to take 300 Test wickets?

5 Which island country played their first-ever Test match in 1982?

6 With which county did Ian Botham end his professional playing career?

7 In 1975, which country won cricket's first World Cup?

8 Which famous cricketer, nicknamed 'the Brylcreem boy', died in 1997 aged 78?

9 In Australia, they are called sundries. What is the English equivalent?

10 How many different ways are there of being out at cricket?

Sporting venues
829

LEVEL 2 Are you playing at home or away?

1 Which Scottish city hosted the Commonwealth Games in 1970?

2 Which football stadium was famed for its twin towers?

3 Which sporting team's stadium is known as 'the house that Ruth built'?

4 Which was the first Australian city to host the Summer Olympics?

5 In which city does the Tour de France finish?

6 On which course is the Irish Derby run?

7 Name the royal and ancient club that is known as 'the home of golf'.

8 At which famous racing course do horses cross the Melling Road?

9 Which French venue played host to the 2003 World Athletics Championships?

10 In which Australian city is the Ballymore Oval cricket ground?

Football World Cup
830

LEVEL 2 Kick off for football's greatest spectacle

1 In October 2001, who scored a last minute free kick to clinch England's qualification for the 2002 World Cup?

2 Which German legend is the only person to lift the World Cup as a team captain and manager?

3 How old was Pele when he first won the World Cup in 1958: 17, 18 or 19?

4 Against which country did Michael Owen score his first World Cup goal?

5 Which group recorded 'World in Motion', the World Cup song for England in 1990?

6 Which South American country played host to the inaugural World Cup finals in 1930?

7 In the 1986 World Cup finals, who was sent off while captaining England?

8 Which Asian country shocked the world by beating Italy in the World Cup finals of 1966?

9 Which goalkeeper captained Italy to World Cup glory in 1982?

10 In which American city was the 1994 World Cup final played?

Sport

Football superstars
831 LEVEL 1 The greats of football

1 Which country did Pele represent?

2 Which English striker was voted European Footballer of the Year in 2001?

3 With which country did Diego Maradona win a World Cup medal?

4 Which former France and Manchester United star appeared in the 1998 film *Elizabeth*?

5 In 1973, who won his 108th International Cap for England?

6 Which French star was voted 'World Footballer of the Year' in 2003?

7 Who wrote of his historic hat-trick in his book *1966 and all That*?

8 Which knighted footballer scored 49 goals for England?

9 What colour jersey did goalkeeper Lev Yashin always wear when playing for Russia?

10 Which Manchester United player was best man at David Beckham's wedding to Victoria Adams?

It's just cricket
832 LEVEL 1 You won't be out for a duck in this round

1 In which city is the Edgbaston Test Ground?

2 Which former Pakistan cricket captain married Jemima Goldsmith?

3 If the initials RO are next to a batsman's name on the scoreboard, how has he been dismissed?

4 Which famous cricket venue staged the first three cricket World Cup finals?

5 Which former England cricket captain became a team captain on TV's *They Think it's All Over*?

6 For which cricketing nation did Sir Richard Hadlee play Test cricket?

7 How many wickets need to have fallen for the batting side to be given 'all out'?

8 Brothers Greg, Ian and Trevor all played Test cricket for Australia. What is their surname?

9 Which wood is traditionally used to make cricket stumps?

10 What is the name of the Test cricket ground in the city of Leeds?

Rugby round
833 LEVEL 1 A round for those who try

1 Do the British Lions play rugby league or rugby union?

2 Who won the Six Nations Championships in 2003?

3 How many points is a try worth in rugby union?

4 Which New Zealand rugby star is known as 'the man mountain'?

5 Who was sacked as England's rugby union captain in 1995 but reinstated in 1996?

6 Which South African player scored a record 34 points, all from drop goals, against England in the 1999 World Cup?

7 Which former Supremes singer opened the 1995 rugby league World Cup?

8 What kind of animal stands atop rugby union's Calcutta Cup?

9 Which ground is the home of the headquarters of Scottish rugby union?

10 In the 20th century, which rugby league club played in the most Challenge Cup finals?

General knowledge
834

LEVEL 2   A sports lover's dream

1 The words Citius, Altius, Fortius can be seen on which flag?

2 Which singer enjoyed a disco hit in 1974 with the song 'Kung Fu Fighting'?

3 Carlton Blues, Geelong Cats and Sydney Swans are all names of teams in which sport?

4 On what make of motorcycle did Barry Sheene win the 500cc world title in 1977?

5 In which South American country was the tennis player Gabriella Sabatini born?

6 What is the lower age limit for horses competing in the Aintree Grand National?

7 Which boxer's left hook was known as 'Enery's 'Ammer'?

8 In the game of fives, what is used to hit the ball?

9 According to the history books, what game was played by the crew on board the *Mayflower*: darts, polo or table tennis?

10 Who won Britain's only gold medal at the 2001 World Athletics Championships?

Early bath
835

LEVEL 2   Can you go the distance or will you be sent off?

1 In 1998, the actor Micky Rourke starred in a film about which famous racehorse?

2 Why were all sporting events cancelled in Britain on September 6, 1997?

3 In the world of sport, what is 19m (62ft 10in) long and 1.07m (3ft 6in) wide?

4 Which former Heavyweight Boxing World Champion was nicknamed 'the easton assassin'?

5 Which Malaysian city hosted the 1998 Commonwealth Games?

6 The eruption of which mountain prevented the 1908 Olympics from being held in Rome?

7 Which Italian footballer acquired the nickname, 'the divine ponytail'?

8 What type of event is a Canadian pairs race?

9 Which king officially opened Wimbledon in 1922?

10 Which Colombian driver won his first Formula 1 race at the 2001 Italian Grand Prix?

Testing teasers
836

LEVEL 2   How many of these sports challenges can you take on?

1 Which baseball star was nicknamed 'the yankee clipper'?

2 How many Olympic gold medals for gymnastics did Britain win in the 20th century?

3 Which is the only chess piece that can jump over another piece?

4 In which park does the New York marathon finish?

5 In which country is the Royal Troon golf course?

6 Which bald sports star won Britain's only swimming gold medal in the 1980 Olympics?

7 Including intervals what would be the full duration of a 12-round boxing bout?

8 In the USA what do the initials NBA stand for?

9 Which 2002 film, set in Hounslow, West London, and Hamburg, explores the world of women's football?

10 In athletics, by what name is the British Empire Games now known?

Sport

Take your pick
837

LEVEL 1   Pick your way through these posers

1 What old-fashioned article of clothing is associated with New York's basketball team?

2 What kind of pass was legalised in American football in 1906 to revolutionise the game?

3 Why were women forbidden from watching the ancient Olympic Games?

4 Which sport features a jump called an axel, named after Axel Rudolph Paulsen?

5 In yachting, what shape is a spinnaker sail?

6 In what year did Bjorn Borg win his last Wimbledon singles title?

7 The classic horse race the Epsom Oaks is limited to horses of which sex?

8 How many points are required to win a table-tennis game?

9 What colour flag indicates a foul throw in a javelin competition?

10 Who won her first tennis US Open in 1991?

Feeling lucky
838

LEVEL 1   Take your chances with these random questions

1 How many blades does a kayak paddle have?

2 In the game of softball is the ball pitched underarm or overarm?

3 In which 1945 film did *Velvet Brown* win the Grand National?

4 In what decade was the first-ever London Marathon run?

5 In which sport is a puck stopper a term for a goaltender?

6 Which is the only Grand Slam tennis tournament that is played in the Southern Hemisphere?

7 What is the duration of a basketball match?

8 What word follows the names of the soccer teams Oldham, Wigan and Charlton?

9 In amateur sports, what do the initials IAAF stand for?

10 Who was the last British athlete of the 20th century to win an Olympic gold medal for the 100 metres?

The B team
839

LEVEL 2   Every answer begins with the letter B

1 What sport would you be watching if the Detroit Pistons beat the Washington Bullets?

2 What animal provides Chicago's American Football team name?

3 In which sport are shots called 'long jenny' and 'short jenny' played?

4 Which Briton won the WBC heavyweight title against Oliver McCall in 1995?

5 In cricket, was Bob Willis a bowler or batsman?

6 In tennis, what is the line at the back of the court called?

7 What name is given to the score of one over par on a golf hole?

8 In which English city could you watch a Derby football match between the Pirates and the Robins?

9 Which of the following is a style of high jump: a boom bounce, a brill bend or a button bound?

10 Which American city do the Orioles baseball team come from?

840 Olympic cities

Identify these Olympic cities using the clue, the last date the Olympics were held in each

1 1896

2 1996

3 1936

4 1952

5 1948

6 1972

7 1960

8 1964

9 1988

10 2000

Sport

841 Sporting jargon
LEVEL 1 Can you speak sports?

1 In which sport do competitors employ 'snatch' or 'clean and jerk' methods?

2 If a cricket batsman scored a pair of spectacles what would his total score be: zero, 100 or 200?

3 In motor racing which C word is the name given to a series of bends or obstacles?

4 What is used to hit the ball in a game of croquet?

5 What name is given to double one in darts: the asylum, the madhouse or the daft double?

6 In which sport would a competitor employ the penholder grip trying to win the Corbillon Cup?

7 In which board game would the Sicilian defence be used?

8 In which sport could a competitor suffer a wipe out on a Malibu board?

9 Which sport features holds and moves called half nelson and a flying mare?

10 In which sport could you face a Chinaman or a googly?

842 Sporting superstars
LEVEL 1 The greats of the game

1 In 1996, which Canadian athlete ran the 100m in 9.84 seconds?

2 Which sweet name was adopted by the boxer who was born Walker Smith Junior?

3 For which country did goalkeeper Pat Jennings win 119 International Caps?

4 Which tennis player is nicknamed 'pistol Pete'?

5 Which cricketing nation was captained by Imran Khan?

6 Which England striker was the leading goal scorer at the 1986 World Cup finals?

7 In March 1999, who drew with Lennox Lewis in a world title fight?

8 In 1977, who left Liverpool FC to join SV Hamburg?

9 In 1999, which golfer had a hip replacement operation that caused him to miss the Masters for the first time in 40 years?

10 Which legendary British tennis player died on February 2, 1995 aged 85?

843 You cannot be serious!
LEVEL 3 Tennis: it's not all strawberries and cream

1 What is John McEnroe's middle name?

2 In 1953, who became the first female to complete the tennis Grand Slam?

3 Who was John Lloyd's doubles partner when he won the mixed doubles title at Wimbledon in 1983?

4 What collective nickname was given to the French tennis stars, Henri Cochet, Jacques Brugnon, Rene Lacoste and Jean Borotra?

5 At which venue was the US tennis Open held between 1967 and 1977?

6 Wimbledon was what type of sports club when it first opened?

7 What is the name of the women's team tennis championships contested between the UK and the USA?

8 When the world rankings were first instigated in 1973, who was ranked as the men's No. 1?

9 Which Australian tennis star born in 1934 was nicknamed Muscles?

10 How long, in feet, is a tennis court?

Meet the teams

844

LEVEL 2 A round for the team players

1 In which ball sport team event did Britain's men win a 1988 Olympic gold?

2 How many players are there in a rugby league team?

3 Which Scottish football team took their name from the Roman name for Ireland?

4 Which sport is played by the London Monarchs?

5 Who has managed both England and Australia's national football teams?

6 In which team sport is the game started with a tip-off?

7 David Campese is a famous former captain for which rugby union nation?

8 What name is given to a wrestling team comprising two people?

9 In which Italian city do Lazio play their home matches?

10 In which sport would the Pirates face the Phillies?

Anyone for tennis?

845

LEVEL 2 A racket round all about tennis

1 Which female tennis star won the Grand Slam in 1988?

2 Which former British champion had a set of gates at Wimbledon named after him in 1984?

3 What name is given to a point-winning serve that is not touched by the opponent?

4 What was the surname of the brother and sister mixed doubles partnership who won Wimbledon in 1980?

5 How high in feet is the middle of a tennis net?

6 What do the initials LTA stand for?

7 How many consecutive Men's Singles Wimbledon titles did Bjorn Borg win?

8 In which country was Martina Navratilova born?

9 On what kind of surface is the French Open played?

10 Which American tennis champion married the skier Andy Mill in July 1988?

Football crazy

846

LEVEL 3 Questions for the serious football fan

1 Who was the first footballer to be capped 100 times for England?

2 Which was the first European country to host football's World Cup?

3 What is a football referee signalling when raising the left arm vertically?

4 Who was the youngest member of England's 1966 World Cup winning team?

5 Which was the only non-English team to win the FA Cup in the 20th century?

6 What is the name of the only Scottish league football team based in England?

7 At the 1998 World Cup what colour did the Nigerian squad dye their hair to match their shirts?

8 Who was the first British football team to win a European trophy?

9 Which pop star was caught crying on TV cameras at the 1984 FA Cup final?

10 In 2000, who was World Footballer of the Year?

Sport

847 Colour codes
LEVEL 1 An easy round to brighten things up

1 What medal did Fatima Whitbread win in the 1988 Olympics?

2 What colour of card is shown to a footballer when he is cautioned?

3 How many points is the brown ball worth in snooker?

4 Which team won the Superbowl in 1997?

5 What is the name of the home ground of Tottenham Hotspur FC?

6 What colour of flag indicates a legal throw in a javelin competition?

7 In judo, what colour of belt follows a yellow?

8 What colour is the cap worn by a goalkeeper in water polo?

9 In Grand Prix racing, what does a black flag signify?

10 What colour balls were used at Wimbledon for the first time in 1986?

848 Football fanatics
LEVEL 1 How well do you know the great game?

1 Supporters of which English football team are known as 'the toon army'?

2 Which of the following footballers has not been knighted: Stanley Matthews, Geoff Hurst, Bobby Charlton or George Best?

3 What is the four-letter acronym of football's governing body, established in 1904?

4 The name of which football team is sometimes abbreviated to WBA?

5 What do the initials OG stand for in football?

6 Who managed Manchester United when they won their 1999 treble?

7 Which former owner of the *Daily Mirror* was chairman at both Oxford United and Derby County?

8 Who has managed Watford, Aston Villa, Wolves, Lincoln and England?

9 What colour shirts did England wear in their 1966 World Cup victory over West Germany?

10 In which British city do the Auld Firm Derby matches take place?

849 Try hard
LEVEL 3 A mauling round of rugby teasers

1 Who scored 64 tries in 101 rugby union internationals for Australia?

2 How many players from each side form a rugby union scrum?

3 In 2001, which rugby union nation did England defeat 134–0?

4 Which country plays their home matches at a stadium called Ellis Park?

5 Who played in 111 internationals for France between 1982 and 1995?

6 Which rugby league team are nicknamed 'the chemics'?

7 What is the name of the stadium at which France plays their home rugby union matches?

8 Which Australian rugby champions did Wigan beat 20–18 to win the 2001 World Club Challenge?

9 What colour are the jerseys of Ireland's rugby union team?

10 Who captained the 1997 British Lions?

What's my name

850

LEVEL 1   The missing link is easier than you think

Complete the team names of these well-known football clubs.

1 Raith …

2 Preston …

3 Queen of the …

4 Nottingham …

5 Plymouth …

6 Hamilton …

7 Bolton …

8 Charlton …

9 Blackburn …

10 Crystal …

Crash, bang, wallop

851

LEVEL 2   Some unforeseen contact sports

1 In the 1993 world title fight between Evander Holyfield and Riddick Bowe who or what unexpectedly crashed into the ring?

2 What is a martial arts school called?

3 In which sport do five hits win a bout?

4 Why was the 1993 Grand National declared null and void?

5 In which sport would a 'forearm smash' be administered?

6 Greg Louganis won a gold medal in the 1988 Olympic springboard diving competition – despite what accident?

7 Who was the first male tennis player to achieve the tennis Grand Slam?

8 Who collided with Mary Decker in the 1984 Olympic final for the 3000 metres?

9 Which English cricketer had his nose broken during the 1986 tour of the West Indies?

10 Which Chicago Bulls basketball player was fined $20,000 for head-butting a referee in 1996?

US sports

852

LEVEL 3   How well do you know your North American sports?

1 Which baseball team plays at Wrigley Field?

2 What name is given to the action of tackling a quarterback before he can throw a pass?

3 Complete this NFL team name. Dallas …?

4 What shirt number was worn by Edmonton Oilers star player Wayne Gretzky?

5 Which basketball player achieved the highest points average in the 20th century?

6 Paul Hornung holds the record for the most number of points scored in an NFL season, with 176. For which team did he play?

7 In baseball, what is a 'dinger'?

8 Denver Broncos lost to which team in the 1990 Superbowl by a record 45 points?

9 Which basketball team plays in the Palace of Auburn Hills?

10 What is the name of Vancouver's NHL ice-hockey team?

Sport

Cricket clues
853

LEVEL 1 When the man in is out, he goes off

1 Father and son, Colin and Chris, both captained England at cricket. What is their surname?

2 Is the maximum length of a cricket bat: 28, 38 or 48 inches?

3 Who captained the West Indies from 1965 to 1974?

4 Which former English wicket-keeper shares his nickname with a breed of small dog?

5 Which county cricket team did Ian Botham leave following Viv Richards and Joel Garner's departure?

6 What kind of flower is depicted on the badge of county cricket club Glamorgan?

7 In March 2001, which West Indian fast bowler became the first to take 500 Test wickets?

8 How many runs do the batting side record if the ball hits a helmet?

9 Who was appointed England cricket captain in July, 2003?

10 In cricket, what does the c stand for in c and b?

Football facts
854

LEVEL 1 He shoots, he scores! Can you score with this round?

1 Which former Liverpool goalkeeper also played for Zimbabwe?

2 Which English football team play their home matches at Elland Road?

3 How many yards is the penalty spot from the goal?

4 What trophy is contested prior to the English football season, when the reigning league champions play the current FA Cup holders?

5 How many FA Cups were cancelled in the 20th century due to war?

6 Who scored the winning goal for Arsenal in the 2003 FA Cup Final?

7 Which football stadium is situated in Sir Matt Busby Way?

8 In which country does the team Rapid Vienna play its home matches?

9 Which Italian club signed Paul Gascoigne from Tottenham Hotspur?

10 Who was the first footballer to score 100 goals in England's premiership?

Gymnastics
855

LEVEL 2 A mind-bending round of questions

1 On which piece of equipment would a male gymnast perform a double leg circle?

2 Who scored the first perfect ten?

3 Which form of gymnastics involves the use of hoops, streamers and balls?

4 On which apparatus would a male gymnast perform a crucifix?

5 Which Russian gymnast won a gold medal for her floor exercise at the 1972 Olympics?

6 Which D word describes the final movement of a gymnast when descending from the apparatus?

7 What name is given to the handles on a gymnastic horse?

8 In gymnastics, what is a *tsukahara*?

9 What name is given to the bars on which female gymnasts compete?

10 Which of the following is not a discipline in a women's Olympic event: floor, rings or vault?

856 Sports quest

These questions are tougher than the others and you may need to do some research

1 The Venus Rosewater Dish is presented to the winner of which sporting event?

2 What is the sporting connection between the jazz drummer Buddy Rich, the racing driver Nigel Mansell and the actress Sharon Stone?

3 Who in his early life kept goal for the amateur football team Wotsyla and went on to make world news headlines in 1978?

4 Southland Greyhound Park, the largest greyhound stadium in the USA, is located in which city?

5 In which sport is a manoeuvre called a barani performed?

6 Which footballing nation won its first-ever competitive game in 1990 when it recorded a surprise victory over Austria?

7 Which sport has a name that means, 'The way of the sword'?

8 In 1894 A.G Spalding & Brothers, a company based in Massachusetts, invented the first official what?

9 What piece of sporting equipment has a crossbar, nose wires, a keel, a kingpost and a sail?

10 In which sport do the Hamburg Crocodiles play in the German Bundesliga?

11 In the TV series *Magnum PI*, Tom Selleck when playing Magnum was often seen wearing a baseball cap of which team?

12 Which sport was invented by YMCA director William Morgan in 1895?

13 The rules of badminton state that a shuttlecock must have exactly how many feathers?

14 Which famous sporting course is 3977ft (1212m) long and has two start points called The Junction and The Top?

15 Which sport was formerly known by the names of Baggataway and Tewaarathon?

A clue to question 3

Sport

857 Sporting birthdays
LEVEL 2   Who was born on these days?

1 Who was born in London on July 30, 1958 and won his first Olympic title in 1980?

2 Who was born on November 3, 1949 and was World Heavyweight Boxing Champion in 1978?

3 Who was born in the USSR on July 29, 1957 and became the second-ever female gymnast to score a perfect ten?

4 Who was born in Ontario on January 26, 1961 and was known as 'the great one' in ice hockey?

5 Who was born in Maryland on July 4, 1962 and won 20 doubles titles with Martina Navratilova?

6 Born in Kansas City on September 4, 1949, who captained the US Ryder Cup team in 1993?

7 Which swimmer was born on June 2, 1904 and appeared in six films with Maureen O'Sullivan?

8 Born in Paris on July 2, 1904, who used an embroidered crocodile as his sports gear logo?

9 Born on March 21, 1935, whose 2002 autobiography, was called: *Walking on Water*?

10 Born on May 1, 1960, who was the first jockey to win the Epsom Derby and Kentucky Derby?

858 A losing streak
LEVEL 2   Some you win, some you lose

1 Who lost on the black ball to Dennis Taylor in the 1985 World Snooker Championship final?

2 Which nation lost in the final of football's World Cup in 1974 and 1978?

3 Which nation suffered the most defeats in the final stages of the FIFA World Cup in the 20th century?

4 Who were defeated 34–7 by the Baltimore Ravens in Superbowl XXXV in 2001?

5 How many strokes over par are taken if a golfer makes a snowman?

6 Which British boxer lost his World Heavyweight title to Hasim Rahman in 2001?

7 In 1993, which tennis player was consoled by the Duchess of Kent after losing Wimbledon?

8 Who lost the 1991 Superbowl final when the New York Giants beat them 20–19?

9 In 1991 who were the losers in the Ryder Cup?

10 Which Spanish team lost the 2001 Champions League final to Bayern Munich on penalties?

859 Obituaries
LEVEL 3   A tough round about late great sports stars

1 Who died on April 12, 1981, having been boxing champion between 1937 and 1948?

2 Who died on April 23, 1986 and once took 19 wickets in the fourth Test of a series in 1956?

3 Which Formula 1 World Champion died in 1975 in a plane crash?

4 Which famous tennis star died of an AIDS-related illness on February 6, 1993?

5 Nicknamed 'the brockton bomber', who perished in a plane crash on August 31, 1969?

6 Name the famous 19th-century jockey who committed suicide on November 8, 1886.

7 Who died on July 10, 1978 and won 15 World Snooker titles between 1926 and 1946?

8 Who was born in Dudley on October 1, 1936 and died in the Munich air crash in 1958?

9 Which swimmer, who died on April 23, 1983, played Buck Rogers and Flash Gordon on film?

10 In which sport was Malcolm Marshall, who was born in 1958 and died in 1999, famous?

Troublesome tests

860

LEVEL 2 A round of sports challenges

1 Name the American superstar athlete who won gold medals at the 1996 Olympics at both 200m and 400m.

2 What item of clothing was introduced into the Tour de France in 1919?

3 If a snooker player compiles a 147 break, how many points will the black ball have scored?

4 Michael Jordan won six NBA basketball titles with which team?

5 Over how many kilometres is the cycling section of a triathlon raced?

6 Which country was granted cricket Test status in 2000?

7 Which track sport has categories called individual, pairs, team and long track?

8 What type of court has a short line, a sidewall line and a service line?

9 Which was the second-ever German city to host the Summer Olympics?

10 Which boxer, beaten by Lennox Lewis in 1995, starred in the film *Rocky V*?

Selective sequence

861

LEVEL 2 A selection of questions from all sports

1 Which sport is played by the Philadelphia Flyers?

2 In 1997, who became the youngest-ever winner of the US Masters in golf?

3 What is the longest distance over which swimming events are contested at the Olympic Games?

4 Which British driver competed in his first Grand Prix in 1980, driving for the Lotus team?

5 Which New Zealand runner won a 1976 Olympic gold medal for the 1500m?

6 What do the initials NO signify next to the score of a batsman in cricket?

7 At which stadium does Scotland's rugby union national team play its home matches?

8 What nationality is 1980 Olympic gold medallist Mirtus Yifter, nicknamed 'yifter the shifter'?

9 How many substitutes are allowed in the game of water polo?

10 What is the name of Leon Spinx's boxing brother?

Lucky for some

862

LEVEL 3 A tough round of questions from across the board

1 Which Spanish football club was managed by Bobby Robson?

2 Which American basketball team are known as 'the nuggets'?

3 In which sport do competitors attempt to win the Giro D'Italia?

4 In 1975, which New Zealand athlete became the first man to run the mile in under 3 minutes 50 seconds?

5 In Australian Rules Football, in which city is the AFL Grand Final played?

6 Which sporting trophy did the Montréal Canadiens win 24 times in the 20th century?

7 By what five-letter name is the female WWF wrestler Joanie Laurer better known?

8 Who, in 1998, won a fifth consecutive world title on a 500cc motorcycle?

9 In golf, what name is given to a shot that misses the ball completely but counts as a shot?

10 How many players comprise a Gaelic football team?

Sporting people

863

KIDS 12–14 Famous faces from sporting arenas

In which sports are these sportsmen famous?

1 Dennis Rodman

2 Frankie Dettori

3 David Coulthard

4 Shane Warne

5 Prince Naseem

6 Steve Austin

7 Eric Cantona

8 Stephen Hendry

9 Steve Redgrave

10 Colin McRae

Sports fans' dream

864

KIDS 7–11 Call yourself a real fan?

1 How many events make up a biathlon?

2 In horse racing, what name is given to the rider of a horse?

3 The Oxford and Cambridge boat race takes place on which famous river?

4 In athletics, which projectile is shaped like a spear?

5 What colour ball is worth the most points in snooker?

6 What is used in the game of hockey: clubs, rackets, or sticks?

7 In cricket, which is the only member of the fielding team allowed to wear large gloves?

8 How many different colours are there on a Rubik's Cube?

9 How many runs has a cricket batsman scored if he has made a half-century?

10 How many pockets are there on a snooker table?

Bits and pieces

865

KIDS 12–14 A round to test your winning streak

1 How heavy, in pounds, is the men's shot putt: 16, 18 or 20?

2 How many squares are there on a Monopoly board?

3 In the world of athletics what does the ringing of a bell signify in a track race?

4 How many bishops are on a chess board at the beginning of a game?

5 Is a pole vaulter's pole made from silicon, glass fibre or platinum?

6 What nationality is the England football manager Sven Goran Eriksson?

7 Would you expect to see Chris Boardman riding a horse, a go-kart or a bicycle?

8 What kind of sportsman might use a wedge or a niblick?

9 How many lanes are there in an Olympic-sized swimming pool?

10 When a sports coach forms a letter T with his hands what does this signify?

Sporty allsorts

866

KIDS 7–11   A round for the sports lovers

1 The name of which bird signifies a score of zero in cricket?

2 In the sport of kendo what are the fencing swords made from?

3 What number is at the top of a dartboard?

4 What last name is shared by football teams from Manchester, Cambridge, Newcastle and Leeds?

5 In which sport might competitors perform the butterfly and the crawl?

6 In which American sport are the players known as quarterbacks?

7 How many events make up a decathlon?

8 How many goals has a footballer scored if completing a hat trick?

9 How many yards wide is a football goal: six, eight or ten?

10 In which sport are 'fine leg' and 'silly mid-off' fielding positions?

Take your pick

867

KIDS 12–14   Questions for the true sports fanatic

1 Which sport is represented by the BFA (the F is the clue)?

2 Which sport has more players in a team: a rugby league or rugby union?

3 What colour shares its name with the area surrounding a golf hole?

4 What clothing accessory is traditionally presented to winners of boxing titles?

5 Which sport is played with a puck?

6 In which sport might a player receive an 'assist' and 'slam dunk' the ball to score two points?

7 The home end at the ground of which football team is known as 'the kop'?

8 What is a 'luge'?

9 Are racehorses released from traps, blocks or stalls?

10 In which sport do teams compete for the Ryder Cup?

All sports

868

KIDS 7–11   Are you a real sports fan? Put yourself to the test

1 At the Olympics, which is usually thrown further: a javelin or a shot putt?

2 What sport is sometimes called ping-pong?

3 What shape is a boxing ring?

4 How many women play in the Ryder Cup?

5 Is the front of a skateboard called the nose or the eye?

6 Which football club play their home matches at Anfield?

7 At which sport does Lindsay Davenport excel?

8 Is a speedway race contested on a motorbike or in a motorcar?

9 How many numbers does a referee count up to for a boxer to be knocked out?

10 What is higher: a badminton net or a volleyball net?

869 Play to win

KIDS 12–14 Apply yourself to this round of random questions

1 On which racecourse is the Grand National run?

2 How long is a marathon: 16 miles, 26 miles or 36 miles?

3 In which sport might a player be sent into the 'sin bin' for 'slashing'?

4 In which country was Diego Maradona born?

5 What colour jersey is worn by the leader of the Tour de France?

6 In tennis, what comes in to play when the game score in a set is 6–6?

7 What is passed between the athletes in a track relay race?

8 How many attempts is a high jumper allowed at each separate height?

9 What do the initials LBW stand for in cricket?

10 How many red balls are used in a frame in a game of snooker?

870 Sporting medley

KIDS 7–11 How much do you know about sport?

1 If golfers use clubs, what do table-tennis players use?

2 From which country does the football club Real Madrid originate?

3 What sport is played by teams of four who try to score goals on horseback?

4 What shape is a rugby ball?

5 In a greyhound race, what kind of mechanical animal do the dogs chase?

6 What kind of flag ends a Grand Prix race?

7 How many runs are scored in cricket if the ball passes the boundary without touching the ground?

8 Where were the 2002 Winter Olympics held?

9 With how many pawns does each player start in a game of chess?

10 In which sport do competitors use a foil, a sabre or an épée?

871 Sporting terms

KIDS 12–14 Do you know these sporting phrases?

1 What name is given to a return in tennis when the ball is hit before it touches the ground?

2 What scores six points in a game of American football?

3 In which sport is a 'Boston crab' a painful position?

4 In ten-pin bowling, what name is given to a bowl that knocks down all the pins in one go?

5 What is the white ball in a game of snooker called?

6 In which sport can a birdie or an eagle be scored?

7 What does a Formula 1 car drive into when in need of fuel or repairs?

8 In baseball, what is the equivalent to a cricket bowler?

9 Which sport is played with a shuttlecock?

10 Which three-letter word is the name given to a replayed point in tennis?

THE ARTS

The Arts

Fantasy and horror
872
LEVEL 1   A round for those with a strong disposition

1 Which bestselling author's first novel was *Carrie*, the story of a tormented teenager?

2 Which jungle hero, created by Edgar Rice Burroughs in 1912, was the son of Lord Greystoke?

3 Who wrote the *Discworld* series of fantasy novels?

4 Whose chilling work includes the *Rats* and *The Fog*?

5 Who is the dark, other side of Dr Jekyll?

6 Which English playwright wrote *Titus Andronicus*, a play in which a girl is raped and has her hands cut off?

7 Which horror writer wrote books including *To the Devil a Daughter* and *The Devil Rides*?

8 What is the English title of the book by Victor Hugo, featuring Quasimodo and a Paris church?

9 Which monster, the brainchild of Mary Shelley, was immortalised on screen by Boris Karloff?

10 Which sailor's fantastic adventures are told in the *Arabian Nights* tales?

William Shakespeare
873
LEVEL 1   How well do you know your bard?

1 In which English town was Shakespeare born?

2 What relation was Mary Arden to Shakespeare?

3 Which Anne did Shakespeare marry?

4 Which Shakespeare play begins with a Danish prince meeting his father's ghost?

5 In which Shakespeare play does a character begin a funeral speech with the words: 'Friends, Romans, countrymen, lend me your ears'?

6 In which play does the Moor of Venice kill his wife in a fit of jealousy?

7 Which London theatre, where many of Shakespeare's plays were staged, burnt down in 1613 and has now been re-created?

8 What do the initials RSC stand for in the theatre world?

9 Which Shakespeare play is never supposed to be named inside a theatre for fear of bad luck?

10 In which Shakespeare comedy does a fairy queen fall for a weaver named Bottom?

Adventure stories
874
LEVEL 1   Some ripping yarns to test you

1 In which John Grisham novel does the hero discover he is working for the Mafia?

2 In which children's story by Robert Louis Stevenson does cabin-boy Jim Hawkins sail in search of pirate gold?

3 In Tom Clancy's novel *The Hunt for Red October*, what is Red October?

4 Which bestselling author wrote *The Scarlatti Inheritance*?

5 In John le Carré's *Tinker Tailor Soldier Spy*, which character was played on TV by Sir Alec Guinness?

6 Which former SAS soldier wrote the action thrillers *Bravo Two Zero* and *Remote Control*?

7 What kind of prehistoric creatures feature in Michael Crichton's *The Lost World*?

8 In which multinational army are the characters in P.C. Wren's novel *Beau Geste* serving?

9 Which continent is the setting for *A Time to Die* and other stories by Wilbur Smith?

10 Which king's mines are the object of the quest in an adventure story by H. Rider Haggard?

 **875**

Myth and fable
LEVEL 2   Questions about the classics, and others

1 If the Elysian Fields were heaven to ancient Greeks, where was heaven to Norsemen?

2 Which king unwittingly married his mother?

3 Which legendary warrior pulled a sword from a stone to demonstrate his kingly aptitude?

4 In which country's mythology are dragons usually friendly and bearers of good fortune?

5 From which continent do the stories of Hiawatha and Paul Bunyan originate?

6 Which Greek hero's weak spot was his heel – the only part not protected when his mother dipped him in the River Styx?

7 In the fable, how did the wolf trick the shepherd in order to get a meal?

8 According to legend, who were the twins, suckled by a wolf, who founded Rome?

9 On which European river is the cliff Lorelei, where legend says a river nymph's songs lured sailors to their deaths?

10 Who flew too close to the Sun, causing the wax in his wings to melt and him to fall to his death?

 **876**

Women
LEVEL 2   A round on female authors and painters

1 What did Dorothea Lange use to portray the sufferings of poor Americans during the Great Depression of the 1930s?

2 Who is Celia, the author of *The Prince*?

3 Who wrote the Pulitzer prize-winning *To Kill a Mocking Bird*, her only novel?

4 Which Japanese-born artist became world famous after meeting her future husband at her avant garde show at the Indica gallery in 1966?

5 Wife to a former England cricketer, who wrote *Another Bloody Tour* and novels such as *Games*?

6 Which American biologist's book *Silent Spring* alerted readers to the dangers of pesticides?

7 To which British poet was the American writer Sylvia Plath married?

8 Which British writer wrote *The Passion of New Eve* and *Wise Children*, published in 1992?

9 *Kate Hannigan's Girl* was whose 100th novel?

10 Which American writer and wit, who died in 1967, declared: 'Men seldom make passes at girls who wear glasses'?

 **877**

Crime-busters
LEVEL 3   Arresting questions about crime and crooks

1 In which precinct does American writer Ed McBain set most of his police stories?

2 In which 1930s crime stories, filmed with William Powell and Myrna Loy, do the clue-solvers Nick and Nora Charles appear?

3 Which amateur sleuth was pictured on book jackets as a 'matchstick man' wearing a halo?

4 Which 1989 novel by E.L. Doctorow explores life growing up among New York mobsters?

5 In which play by Terence Rattigan is a schoolboy accused of stealing a postal order?

6 Which French writer wrote *J'accuse* (I accuse) which won a new trial for Captain Dreyfus?

7 Which private investigator, created by Sara Paretsky, first appeared in *Indemnity Only*?

8 Which Victorian author created Sergeant Cuff, in his 1868 novel *The Moonstone*?

9 Why was Henry Fielding, author of *Tom Jones*, often found in Bow Street Court in London?

10 Which Irish playwright wrote *Lord Arthur Savile's Crime*, and ended up in Reading jail?

Table rounds

Table rounds are the warm-up rounds of your quiz – something to help the players limber up and get their brains in gear before the serious puzzling begins. Prepare a few picture puzzles or word teasers for teams to work on when they arrive, in the interval, and in the lulls between rounds: they can make or break the final score.

There is always a good deal of milling around at the beginning of a quiz night, as teams arrive and get settled, and table rounds are a great way to keep people occupied and get quizzers in the mood. To be successful, these rounds should provoke discussion and, ideally, include an element of lateral thinking, where enough pondering might eventually winkle out the correct answer.

Can you see at the back?
Picture rounds work well as table questions, because unless you are running a small family quiz, it is logistically very difficult to make sure that everyone can see the pictures clearly as you hold them up. You may need access to a colour photocopier to make a round like identifying countries from their flags possible, but many pictures will work just as well in black and white. Try asking teams to identify sports by their equipment used or give the meaning of road signs.

A high-tech alternative to sticking and copying is to scan images into a computer, arrange them on a page and simply print out as many copies as you need.

Words, not pictures
You can easily make entertaining table rounds without any pictures. A round of ditloids (see box) will keep people guessing at the answers all night. Picking out song lines and asking players to identify the song, challenging teams to name products from their advertising slogans, or drawing a map of your local high street and setting the task of naming all the shops along it: all these work well.

Ditloid dilemmas
If you can guess why these quizzes are called 'ditloids', then you'll know how to solve them. Using a combination of numbers and initial letters, the clue 'I ditloid' leads to the answer: *One Day in the Life of Ivan Denisovich*. Look on the Internet for more examples.

1760 Y in a M (yards in a mile)
12 SOTZ (signs of the Zodiac)
2 G of V (Gentlemen of Verona)
50 WTLYL (ways to leave your lover)
366 D in a LY (days in a leap year)
90 D in a RA (degrees in a right angle)
57 HV (Heinz varieties)
7 B for SB (Brides for Seven Brothers)
64 S on a CB (squares on a chessboard)
206 B in the HB (bones in the human body)

Round 5
FLAGS
Name the country

A chance to get creative

The suggestions listed below will all make good table rounds, but let your imagination run wild and look out for other good picture opportunities in the run up to your quiz.

Spot the link

Try to trace the link between seemingly unconnected pictures. For example, pictures of Brian May (lead guitarist of Queen), Grace Kelly (actress) and Jackie Stewart (racing driver) contain the hidden connection: England cricket captains (Peter May, W.G. Grace, Alec Stewart).

Who or what?

Taking familiar objects out of context or showing just a portion of a well-known face can make identifying the subject a tricky task. Get teams to identify counties or countries from their outlines, or try removing or covering up the words on book jackets, album covers or film posters and asking players to name them.

Finding pictures

Pictures for simple 'Who is it?' or 'What is it?' quizzes are easy to find. Simply cut out celebrity shots from magazines or snip obscure objects from catalogues. But more complicated picture quizzes may need some picture research.

The internet is a rich source of images and, as they are electronic, pictures can be easily manipulated: try cutting out one half of a couple. There are many picture collections on line that will provide images for free on a variety of subjects – try the image search at www.google.co.uk

Remember that picture use is covered by copyright law. It is against the law to copy an image without the permission of the owner. If in any doubt you must contact the owner of the copyright.

Odd one out

Put together four pictures, three of which have something in common, and ask the players to identify the odd one out. For example, Johnny Vaughan, Lord Archer, Lester Piggot and Ronnie Barker. In this case, Ronnie Barker is the odd one out. He played the prisoner Fletcher in *Porridge*, but the others have all actually served time in prison.

Fill in the gaps

Follow the *Have I Got News For You* model, and compile a topical news quiz. Cut out headlines from a variety of newspapers on the morning of the quiz, blank out a key word in each and ask players to fill in the gaps. Try to keep it light-hearted by spotting the witty headlines and make sure you know the stories so that you can explain them when you give the answers.

The Arts

878 Country matters

LEVEL 2 Every answer is a country, or contains the name of a country

1 Hans Christian Andersen was which country's most famous writer and collector of fairytales for children?

2 What is the home country of writer, scholar and feminist Germaine Greer?

3 Novelist Henry James lived in England, but from which country did he originate?

4 Which John le Carré novel features a book publisher travelling to Moscow?

5 Name the Ira Levin novel about fugitive Nazis plotting in a South American country.

6 What was the title of E.M. Forster's novel set around an incident at the Marabar Caves?

7 Which European country produced the painters Giotto, Raphael and Canaletto?

8 In which European country did Molière write his plays and David paint his pictures?

9 Which Caribbean island is the birthplace of 2001 Nobel prize-winner V.S. Naipaul?

10 In which country's capital city could you visit the Abbey Theatre and Marsh's Library?

879 Ships and the sea

LEVEL 2 A round all at sea

1 Who is the British naval officer-hero of C.S. Forester's popular novels?

2 Which writer's nautical novels feature Jack Aubrey as a British naval officer?

3 Which famous hard-drinking author wrote *The Old Man and the Sea*?

4 In John Winton's naval thriller *HMS Leviathan*, what kind of warship is *Leviathan*?

5 What was Captain Ahab hunting?

6 Name the fictional liner which capsizes after being hit by a giant wave?

7 Herman Wouk wrote a 1951 novel about a mutiny on board a US destroyer. What was the ship's name?

8 The phrase: 'Ships that pass in the night' was coined by which 19th-century American poet, whose first names were Henry Wadsworth?

9 What was the title of Nicholas Monsarrat's wartime novel that was made into a film starring Jack Hawkins?

10 In what sort of leaky vessel did Edward Lear's Jumblies go to sea?

880 Once a knight

LEVEL 3 A round on courtly matters and knights of the realm

1 Who was the Knight of La Mancha?

2 Which Shakespearean knight finally gets the regal brush-off from his companion Prince Hal?

3 Which pair of Jacobean playwrights wrote *The Knight of the Burning Pestle*?

4 According to Malory, how many Knights of the Round table were there?

5 In which Shakespeare play do Sir Andrew Aguecheek and Sir Toby Belch appear?

6 For which knight did the Lady of Shalott fall, when she saw him riding by?

7 Which queen awarded the first-ever knighthood to an English actor?

8 Which English author wrote about a 'verray parfit gentil knight' who told tales?

9 Which African-American poet and activist of the 1960s wrote *Poems from Prison*, a long narrative poem recited in street slang?

10 Whose autobiography entitled *Living Dangerously*, tells of his life with actress Barbara Windsor?

881 Literary dogs
LEVEL 1 Doggedly hard questions

1 Which mischievous schoolboy takes his dog Jumble to play with the Outlaws?

2 Who hunted the hound of the Baskervilles?

3 Bull's Eye belonged to a burglar, Bill. In which Charles Dickens book does Bull's Eye appear?

4 In which of Enid Blyton's fictional groups did Timmy the dog make up the numbers?

5 What sort of dogs featured in a much-loved children's novel by Dodie Smith?

6 Nana the Newfoundland, pet and nurse to the little Darlings, is left grounded as they fly away – in which book?

7 Punch and Judy had a dog. What was its name?

8 In whose house would you find 'the dog tossed by the cow with the crumpled horn'?

9 Who wrote *The Dogs of War* about a group of mercenaries in Africa?

10 Which very famous screen dog made her first appearance in a novel written by Eric Knight?

882 Get a job
LEVEL 1 What occupations do these questions reveal?

1 Who are Jack Ryan's secretive employers in *Clear and Present Danger*?

2 In Judith Krantz's *Dazzle*, what kind of business goes on at Dazzle?

3 For whom does Jeeves work in the novels by P.G. Wodehouse?

4 In the bestselling 2001 biography *Jack: Straight From the Gut*, what job does Jack hold?

5 James Herriott wrote about what profession?

6 Round which sport are John Francome's novels, such as *Dead Ringer,* set?

7 John Grisham's *The Pelican Brief* is not about animals. Which profession is featured?

8 In Tannochbrae, the Scottish setting for the novels of A.J. Cronin, what profession do Cameron and Finlay practise?

9 What is Lovejoy's line of work in the books by Jonathan Gash, made into a popular TV series?

10 What is Mr Dolittle's job in Shaw's play, *Pygmalion*?

883 What's in a name?
LEVEL 3 Authors hiding behind other names

1 Which sisters hid their literary identities under the names Currer, Ellis and Acton Bell?

2 By what name was the wife of archaeologist Max Mallowan known to her reading public?

3 By what name was Eric Blair celebrated as the writer who warned us of Big Brother?

4 What was George Eliot's real name?

5 Which writer and TV arts presenter nodded to his Cumbrian roots in *The Maid of Buttermere*?

6 Which bestselling author has written about the Harte family, in novels such as *To be the Best*?

7 *Primary Colors*, published as Anonymous, was actually written by which US journalist?

8 Which Irish-sounding name connects an American novelist who wrote about the 'Jazz Age' with a 19th-century writer who translated *The Rubaiyat of Omar Khayyam*?

9 By what other name is the crime writer Barbara Vine known?

10 Which famous author of detective stories published romance novels under the name of Mary Westmacott?

The Arts

884 Colours

LEVEL 1   Every answer contains a colour

1 What was clockwork in the title of the 1962 novel by Anthony Burgess?

2 What colour were the gables in the house where Anne lived?

3 What colour was the boy painted by Gainsborough?

4 What colour is the badge of courage in Stephen Crane's novel about the American Civil War?

5 Which colour connects the author of *The Sword and the Stone*, and the girl in the fairy story who meets seven dwarfs?

6 Name Alice Walker's 1982 bestseller.

7 What colour was the horse in Anna Sewell's children's classic?

8 Which Ian Fleming novel featured a plot to rob Fort Knox?

9 Which 20th century artist is particularly admired for his 'Blue Period'?

10 Whose schooldays did Thomas Hughes write about?

885 Detective work

LEVEL 2   A round on famous sleuths

1 Which aristocratic sleuth features in *The Nine Tailors* by Dorothy L. Sayers?

2 Which fictional detective potters about the English village of St Mary Mead?

3 Which literary detective, created by P.D. James, was a policeman, as well as an amateur poet?

4 Who are detectives Andy and Peter, created by Reginald Hill in *A Clubbable Woman*?

5 Which American crime writer created the character of Dr Kay Scarpetta?

6 Which priest-detective did G.K. Chesterton create?

7 Which American writer wrote about Philip Marlowe in mysteries such as *The Big Sleep*?

8 Which lawyer in the crime stories by Erle Stanley Gardner is assisted by Della Street?

9 Name France's best-known fictional detective created by Belgian author, Georges Simenon.

10 Which who-dun-it by Dashiell Hammett features the sleuth Sam Spade?

886 Architects with style

LEVEL 3   Great builders and buildings

1 Which English architect, noted for his London churches, features in a Peter Ackroyd novel?

2 Which British architect designed Paris's Centre Pompidou and London's Millennium Dome?

3 Where did Italian architect Filippo Brunelleschi see his great new dome rise over a city cathedral in the early 1400s?

4 Which Chinese architect designed the East Wing of Washington's National Gallery?

5 Which planner designed Regent Street and Regent's Park in 19th-century London?

6 Which architect founded the Bauhaus School of Modern Design in Germany in 1919?

7 Which 19th-century Scottish architect designed the Glasgow School of Art?

8 Which famous British architect went on to be founder of the Royal Society?

9 Which American architect designed the New York Guggenheim Museum?

10 Which Indian city was designed and built by Sir Edwin Lutyens?

Haven't read it but I've seen the film

Ever seen a film and wished you'd read the book first? Test your knowledge by matching the titles listed below to the film scenes shown

Little Women • Moby Dick • Chocolat
The Great Gatsby •The Mirror Cracked
Doctor Zhivago
The Beach • Death in Venice
A Christmas Carol • Treasure Island

The Arts

Mixed library
888
LEVEL 3   How much do you know about literature?

1 Which European capital crops up in titles by Christopher Isherwood and Len Deighton?

2 What, according to American writer Anita Loos, is a gentleman's preference?

3 In which classic novel do Heathcliff and Catherine Earnshaw yearn for each other across the moors?

4 In which Jane Austen classic does Miss Bennet rea ise the merits of Mr Darcy?

5 In which American novel does Hawkeye battle the Huron with the aid of Uncas and Chingachgook?

6 In which novel of the American Civil War do Rhett Butler and Ashley Wilkes appear?

7 In which fictional cathedral city do Dr Proudie and Mr Slope make their rounds?

8 What job does Mr Stevens hold in Kazuo Ishiguro's novel *The Remains of the Day*?

9 In which story does Man Friday leave a footprint in the sand?

10 Who does Mr Rochester hire as a governess in a classic novel by Charlotte Brontë?

Open and shut
889
LEVEL 2   Some opening and closing lines. Identify the book

1 'It is a truth universally acknowledged, that a single man in possession of a good fortune, must be in want of a wife.'

2 'All happy families resemble one another, but each unhappy family is unhappy in its own way.'

3 'The past is a foreign country: they do things differently there.'

4 'And out again, upon the unplumb'd salt, estranging sea.'

5 'If you really want to hear about it, the first thing you'll probably want to know is where I was born, and what my lousy childhood was like.'

6 'As Gregor Samsa awoke one morning from uneasy dreams he found himself transformed in his bed into a gigantic insect.'

7 'After all, tomorrow is another day.'

8 'The flowers formed a wavering garland around the coffin.'

9 'I'm so glad to be at home again!'

10 'He wrested the world's whereabouts from the stars, and locked the secret in a pocket watch.'

Famous buildings
890
LEVEL 3   You know the building, but who was the architect?

1 Bank of China Tower, Hong Kong, China

2 The Chrysler Building, New York, USA

3 The White House, Washington DC, USA

4 Guggenheim Museum, Bilbao, Spain

5 Sydney Opera House, Australia

6 Chek Lap Kok Airport, Hong Kong, China

7 Eiffel Tower, Paris, France

8 Petronas Towers, Kuala Lumpur, Malaysia

9 Greenwich Hospital, Greenwich, England

10 United Nations Headquarters, New York, USA

891 Book quest

These questions are tougher than the others and you may need to do some research

1 What connects Steppenwolf, Bruce Springsteen, Elsa, Oliver Stone and Bruce Springsteen again?

2 What connects Huxley's *Brave New World*, Forsyth's *The Dogs of War* and Bradbury's *Something Wicked This Way Comes*?

3 Which book begins with the words, 'Call me Ishmael'?

4 Which writer and man of authority said: 'This is the sort of English up with which I will not put'?

5 What is the more common word for a fylfot?

6 What connects Fyodor Dostoyevsky, Oscar Wilde, Primo Levi and Brendan Behan (apart from the fact that they are all writers)?

7 What's the connection: Charles Lutwidge Dodgson, Nevil Shute and *The Color Purple*?

8 Which literary character lived at 7 Savile Row, Burlington Gardens?

9 What connects Rudyard Kipling poem, a Malcolm McDowell film, and a song by Bread?

10 What connects *A Tale of Two Cities*, *The Prince and The Pauper* and *The Prisoner of Zenda*?

11 Crossword clue: Upset hams in a mobile hospital (4)

12 What connects John Steinbeck's *The Grapes of Wrath*, Brett Easton Ellis's *Less Than Zero*, and the movie *Chariots of Fire*?

13 Who started his career writing under the name 'Boz'?

14 What does the PG stand for in P.G. Wodehouse?

15 What connects *The Death of a Salesman*, *The Tropic of Cancer* and a renowned series of collectible guides?

He's in question 1

The Arts

892 Odd locations

LEVEL 1 Location, location, location. But where?

1 Where is Roddy Doyle's *The Commitments* set?

2 Which family of writers has put Haworth, in Yorkshire, on the tourist map?

3 Which are the two cities in Dickens' novel *A Tale of Two Cities*?

4 Which English county is the setting for Susan Howatch's *Penmarric* novels?

5 In which city is Gorky Park, in the crime story by Martin Cruz Smith?

6 Which English pot-making city was the model for Arnold Bennett's *Anna of the Five Towns*?

7 In which European city was agent Harry Palmer sent to a funeral, in a thriller by Len Deighton?

8 Which African river features in the title of an Agatha Christie mystery?

9 Dr Kay Scarpetta is the chief medical examiner for which US state?

10 In which county were the bridges in the title of a novel by Robert James Waller?

893 The art of plants

LEVEL 1 All questions relate somehow to plants

1 Who wrote *The Grapes of Wrath*?

2 For painting which pond plants is the French artist Monet famous?

3 What pot plant, a favourite in Victorian parlours, is kept flying in the title of a novel by George Orwell?

4 Who was Walt the American poet, whose poems are collected under the title *Leaves of Grass*?

5 Apart from irises, which other flowers are associated with the artist Vincent van Gogh?

6 Which novel by Umberto Eco featured a series of murders in a monastery?

7 Which agony aunt turned novelist wrote *The Poppy Chronicles*, inspired by Flanders poppies?

8 In which musical film does Seymour nurture a carnivorous plant?

9 Which Russian dramatist wrote the play *The Cherry Orchard*?

10 Which Romantic poet wrote *Daffodils*?

894 Modern times

LEVEL 3 A hard round on modern literature

1 Which Irish poet produced an award-winning adaptation of the epic *Beowulf* in 1999?

2 Which Irish teacher-turned-novelist wrote *Paddy Clarke Ha Ha Ha*?

3 Can you name the author of *Trainspotting*?

4 Who won the Booker Prize in 2003 for his novel *Vernon God Little*?

5 Which Calcutta-born writer is the author of *A Suitable Boy* and *An Equal Music*?

6 Edmund Morris' book *Dutch* was a biography of a famous 20th-century American politician. Who was the politician?

7 Who wrote *Captain Corelli's Mandolin*?

8 What sport features in Don DeLillo's *Underworld*?

9 For what kind of artistic achievement is the Orange Prize awarded?

10 Which 2002 novel featured a young Indian boy adrift in a boat with a Bengal tiger called Richard Parker as his companion?

Everyday things
895
LEVEL 2   The art and literature of the common place

1 Which Suffolk-born artist painted *The Haywain*?

2 Who's associated with the artwork featuring repeated prints of a Campbell's soup tin?

3 What name describes paintings of fruit, flowers, food, dead birds and other inanimate things?

4 Who wrote *Old Possum's Book of Practical Cats*?

5 Which tiny people created by Mary Norton live on everyday things 'loaned' unwittingly by the big people whose homes they share?

6 In Evelyn Waugh's novel of wartime, *Men at Arms*, what was Apthorpe's 'thunder-box', which blew up when its owner sat on it?

7 What did St Paul say was the root of all evil?

8 Which couple dined on mince and slices of quince, which they ate with a runcible spoon?

9 Which surrealist artist often featured strange and twisted clocks in his paintings?

10 Whose controversial artwork featuring an unmade bed was shortlisted for the 1999 Turner Prize?

Biographies
896
LEVEL 2   Can you identify the famous subject?

1 Which famous golfer's biography is called *How I Play Golf*?

2 *Stroll On* is about an actor who has a British politician as a son-in-law. Who is the actor?

3 Which comedian's life-story was called *Arias and Raspberries*?

4 *Daddy We Hardly Knew You* is which Australian feminist academic's account of her upbringing?

5 Who is the songwriter subject of Barry Miles' book *Many Years from Now*?

6 *In for a Penny* was a book about a writer who made millions, but lost his freedom. Who was the subject of this book by Jonathan Mantle?

7 Which comedian's biography is *The Big Yin*?

8 *A Soldier's Way* tells of which US general who later became US Secretary of State?

9 Which actor published an autobiography curiously entitled *A Postillion Struck by Lightning*?

10 What was the second volume of David Niven's autobiography after *The Moon's a Balloon*?

It makes you laugh
897
LEVEL 3   Books to giggle about

1 What was the name of Helen Fielding's sequel to *Bridget Jones' Diary*?

2 In which guide to the future do Zaphod Beeblebrox and Ford Prefect bemuse and confuse Arthur Dent?

3 Sherman McCoy was the main character in which black comedy novel by Tom Wolfe?

4 Name Bill Bryson's comic travelogue about his trek in the Appalachian Mountains of America.

5 Which dramatist wrote *The Norman Conquests*?

6 Which academic's novels such as *The History Man* involve academic anguish, lust and apathy?

7 Who was E.F. Benson's pair of formidable females, who vied for supremacy in Tilling?

8 Which US writer wrote a book subtitled *The Lighter Side of Overpopulation, Famine, Ecological Disaster, Ethnic Hatred, Plague, and Poverty*?

9 In Don Marquis' poem *Archy and Mehitabel*, what sort of insect was Mehitabel?

10 In which Richard Brinsley Sheridan comedy does Mrs Malaprop get into verbal twists?

The Arts

Numbers
898

LEVEL 1 Every question has a numerical angle

1 In the poem *Charge of the Light Brigade*, how many 'rode into the valley of death'?

2 How many gospels are there in the New Testament of the Bible?

3 What was the numerical catch in Joseph Heller's satirical novel about US aircrew in the Second World War?

4 How many steps did John Buchan's hero, Richard Hannay, have to watch for?

5 According to Ray Bradbury, in his novel, at what temperature do books burn?

6 How were Peter, Jack, Barbara, George, Pam, Colin and Janet better known?

7 How many agents precede James Bond on the 'licensed to kill' list?

8 According to Jerome K. Jerome, how many men in a boat were there?

9 How many days did it take Phileas Fogg to travel around the world?

10 How many gentlemen of Verona were there?

Books and pictures
899

LEVEL 1 A picture is worth a thousand words

1 In which country was the *Book of the Dead* written on papyrus?

2 At which end of a book is the preface?

3 Baskerville, Times, Helvetica and Arial are all forms of what?

4 Which bird first appeared on a paperback in 1935?

5 What is the first book of the Bible?

6 Which comic book hero, with help from his assistant, protects Gotham City?

7 Which famous humorous magazine took its name from a puppet character fond of wife-beating?

8 For what were Vicky, Low, Giles and Herblock all famous in their own style?

9 Of what type of book are *Poor Richard's* and *Old Moore's* examples?

10 What would you expect to see written on a bookplate?

Greeks and Romans
900

LEVEL 3 How well do you know Italy and Greece?

1 Which mystery writer created the toga-clad detective Marcus Didius Falco?

2 Who coined the phrase: 'It was Greek to me'?

3 Which writer, who lived for a time on Corfu, wrote *The Alexandria Quartet*?

4 Who wrote *The Decline and Fall of the Roman Empire*?

5 How was the painter Domenikos Theotokopoulos known in the art world?

6 Which author created Aurelio Zen, a detective in modern Rome?

7 In which book by James Joyce, set within the span of a single day in Dublin, does Molly Bloom become a modern-day Penelope?

8 In an ancient Greek theatre, what did actors do in the 'skene' or stage house?

9 Which ancient Greek philosopher wrote *The Republic*?

10 Which English poet wrote an ode on a Greek pot?

The grand tour

901

LEVEL 1   A round of European art

1 In which European city is the Uffizi art gallery?

2 The novel *Anna Karenina* was written in which language?

3 The adventure story *Kidnapped* by Robert Louis Stevenson is set in which country?

4 In which country did Impressionist painters first show their work in the 19th century?

5 What nationality was the writer Henrik Ibsen, author of the plays *Hedda Gabler* and *Ghosts*?

6 Where is Britain's biggest annual festival of the arts held every autumn?

7 In which country do bards win prizes at the annual Royal National Eisteddfod?

8 Which European country is generally regarded as the home of opera?

9 In which country did Diaghilev start his famous ballet company in 1909?

10 Goethe, Karl Marx, Brecht and Thomas Mann all wrote in the same language. Which one?

Bestsellers

902

LEVEL 1   They made it to the top of the list. Can you remember them?

1 The Lucasian Professor of Mathematics at Cambridge University wrote one of the most unlikely bestselling books. Who is he?

2 Which Alistair Maclean book was filmed with Clint Eastwood and Richard Burton?

3 Garrison Keillor wrote a series of short stories centred around which US small town?

4 Which writer of family sagas wrote *Bill Bailey's Daughter* and many other bestsellers?

5 In which French town, much visited by pilgrims, is Irving Wallace's *The Miracle* set?

6 Who wrote the bestselling books set in the Far East that include *Noble House* and *Saipan*?

7 Name the jockey-turned-author whose horse-racing mysteries include *Dead Cert*?

8 Which Second World War thriller by Jack Higgins is about a German plot to kidnap Winston Churchill?

9 Which book, exploring grammar and punctuation, was the surprise hit of 2003?

10 Who is the author of *A Woman of Substance*?

Out of this world

903

LEVEL 3   Science-fiction classics

1 In a book by Jules Verne, how were the 19th-century voyagers *From the Earth to the Moon* sent on their way into space?

2 Which two worlds fought in *The War of the Worlds*?

3 Whose *Brave New World* of 1932 made readers think the future wasn't so bright?

4 In which 18th-century satire does the hero, previously bemused by being a giant among midgets, encounter a flying island?

5 In which 20th-century trilogy do the imaginary lands of Mordor, Gondor and Rohan feature?

6 Which story by Arthur C. Clarke was a basis for Stanley Kubrik's *2001: A Space Odyssey*?

7 Which English novelist, wrote *Lucky Jim* and a science-fiction survey called *New Maps of Hell*?

8 Which planet's Chronicles were published by Ray Bradbury in 1950?

9 Whose 1950 novel *I, Robot* established the 'three laws' of robotics?

10 Who wrote *Dune*, a novel of imperial intrigue and ecology on a desert world?

The Arts

Family values

904 **Kids 7–11** **A round about homes and families**

1 Who is Annie Rose's big brother?

2 How many Wise Men came to see the baby Jesus in the stable?

3 Who jumps out of the oven and runs away from home?

4 Whom did James meet on that magical day when it started to snow?

5 Who was King Mufasa and Queen Sarabi's son?

6 Which schoolboy goes home in the holidays to 4 Privet Drive?

7 In *Peter Pan*, where did the 'lost boys' find a new home?

8 In which land does Noddy drive his car round the streets, usually with Big Ears as passenger?

9 In the *Winnie the Pooh* stories, who lives in a gloomy place 'rather boggy and sad'?

10 Who lives in Nutwood with Mr and Mrs Bear?

A good read

905 **Kids 12–14** **Ten questions for bookworms**

1 In a famous book (and film) who did Dorothy hope to find at home in the Emerald City?

2 Who is the hated boss of school created by author Gillian Cross?

3 In which snowy land does a child come across the faun Mr Tumnus under a lamp-post?

4 Who was spring-cleaning in the dark before he heard the 'wind in the willows'?

5 In which book does Gollum seek his 'precious'?

6 In K.M. Peyton's book *Flambards*, what or who is Flambards?

7 As which broomstick-riding character does Mildred Hubble get into all kinds of trouble?

8 Who joined the Pussycat on a voyage in a pea-green boat?

9 'Five and twenty ponies, trotting through the dark'. What were they bringing for the Parson?

10 Which teenager's Second World War diaries, written in hiding in Nazi-occupied Amsterdam, became a modern classic?

Can you remember?

906 **Kids 7–11** **Questions from the classics**

1 Which puppet-turned-boy finds his nose starts to grow when he tells lies?

2 What kind of animal is Jeremy Fisher in the Beatrix Potter story?

3 In a famous fable by Aesop, which animal beats the hare in a race?

4 Which member of the big cat family did the poet William Blake write was 'burning bright in the forests of the night'?

5 The Bad Baby forgot his manners. What did it not say, in *The Elephant and the Bad Baby*?

6 In which pantomime does a girl run home without her glass slipper?

7 Which tank engine has to watch out for The Fat Controller?

8 How many bears did Goldilocks meet?

9 Which animal in the Dr Dolittle books has a head at each end?

10 What kind of animals are Dumbo and Babar?

907 Showing off

Kids 12–14 A round about artists, craftsmen and performers

1 What kind of artist would use a palette?

2 What do we call a painting of an artist done by himself or herself?

3 Sheraton and Chippendale are names for different styles of what?

4 What might someone make on a spinning wheel that had nothing to with thread?

5 To which performance art do Robert de Niro, Kenneth Branagh and Julia Roberts belong?

6 What did Rudolf Nureyev and Margot Fonteyn do on stage that held audiences spellbound?

7 In what kind of stage performance do the performers sing arias?

8 Wedgwood, Meissen and Ming are all names for types of what?

9 In which city is Britain's Royal National Theatre?

10 What do we call a piece of sculpture showing only the head and shoulders of a person?

908 Bookish baddies

Kids 7–11 Everyone loves a villain really

1 What is the name of the horrible headteacher who makes Matilda's life a misery?

2 Who tries to make fur coats out of cuddly spotted pups?

3 What kind of creature is Sher Khan in *The Jungle Book*?

4 Whose school life does Draco Malfoy try to make unpleasant?

5 Who makes it always winter, never Christmas, in Narnia?

6 Which croquet-playing queen keeps ordering her guards to chop off people's heads?

7 Whose house do the weasels and stoats take over, until evicted by Badger and his friends?

8 What fruit did the Wicked Queen give Snow White to eat?

9 In which story does Jafar try to get hold of a magical lamp?

10 What lurks under the bridge waiting for the Three Billy Goats Gruff?

909 Wizard wheezes

Kids 12–14 How well do you know your Harry Potter?

1 Which hooded creatures guard the prison at Azkaban?

2 In *Harry Potter and the Goblet of Fire*, who is the Minister of Magic?

3 In *Harry Potter and the Prisoner of Azkaban*, Dobby is the house elf of which family?

4 What creature does Harry defeat inside the chamber of secrets?

5 Who is Harry Potter's godfather?

6 Which Hogwart's teacher leaves after he is revealed as a werewolf?

7 In *Harry Potter and the Goblet of Fire*, what does Mad Eye Moody teach?

8 Gryffindor, Slytherin and Ravenclaw are three of the four houses at Hogwarts. What is the fourth?

9 What is the name of the non-muggle village near to Hogwarts?

10 Who is the Hogwart pupil to die in *Harry Potter and the Goblet of Fire*?

The Arts

910 Lucky dip
Kids 7–11 Questions from books everyone knows

1 In *The Lion, the Witch, and the Wardrobe*, what kind of creature is Aslan?

2 What kind of factory does Willy Wonka give to Charlie Bucket?

3 In *James and the Giant Peach*, to which city does the Giant Peach sail?

4 Who gets stuck in Rabbit's doorway?

5 What is Paddington Bear's favourite food?

6 Who was Vicky's best friend in *Vicky Angel*?

7 What kind of creature is Mrs Tiggywinkle?

8 In which book does the Headteacher control his school with his scary eyes?

9 What is the name of the bogeyman in the Raymond Briggs book?

10 What fruit turned into a carriage for Cinderella?

911 Under the covers
Kids 12–14 How much do you know about books?

1 Who wrote *The Hobbit*?

2 In Arthur Ransome's *Swallows and Amazons*, what are *Swallow* and *Amazon*?

3 How old was Adrian Mole when he wrote his secret diary?

4 Who lived at 221B Baker Street?

5 Who wrote *Anne of Green Gables*?

6 Who was the creator of agent 007?

7 What is the name of Lyra's daemon in *The Northern Lights*?

8 Which female author wrote *Malory Towers* and the stories of the Famous Five?

9 Who wrote *Emma* and *Sense and Sensibility*?

10 What was the title of Sir Alex Ferguson's bestselling autobiography?

912 Bedtime reading
Kids 7–11 A round of your favourite stories

1 What kind of animals are featured in *Watership Down*?

2 In Jon Scieszka's *The Stinky Cheese Man and other Fairly Stupid Tales*, what does the ugly duckling grow up to be?

3 What do the initials BFG stand for in the book *The BFG*?

4 In the book by Quentin Blake, how many boots does Mister Magnolia have?

5 According to Roald Dahl, to witches what do children smell of?

6 Who wrote *The Diary of a Killer Cat*, *Goggle Eyes*, *Madame Doubtfire* and *Charm School*?

7 What is the password for Ali Baba's cave?

8 What scary series of books, also adapted for TV, are written by R.L. Stine?

9 What was the name of the woman in the Alf Proysen stories who would suddenly shrink very small?

10 What brothers are famous for writing fables and tales?

QUICK QUIZZES

To play the Quick Quizzes in this section, first pick a number from 1 to 36 and turn to the corresponding quiz. You can answer all the questions on the page if you wish, or throw a dice to pick one of the six panels on the page. Then you can either answer all the questions in the panel or throw the dice again to choose random questions – it's up to you.

Quick quizzes 1

1 Building bridges

1 Which duo sang 'Bridge over Troubled Water' in 1970?

2 The Bosphorus Bridge connects Europe with which other continent?

3 In which American city is the Golden Gate Bridge?

4 Name the acting father of Jeff and Beau Bridges.

5 In which Italian city is the Bridge of Sighs?

6 Who directed the film *The Bridge on the River Kwai*?

2 Who said that?

1 'Dr Livingstone, I presume?'

2 'You can have any colour as long as it's black.'

3 'We're more popular than Jesus now.'

4 'A horse, a horse, my kingdom for a horse.'

5 'I have nothing to offer but blood, toil, tears and sweat.'

6 'Ask not what your country can do for you, but what you can do for your country.'

3 Animal magic

1 When does a nocturnal creature hunt for prey?

2 Which S word is the name given to a group of bees?

3 How many legs does a shrimp have?

4 Russian Blue and Havana Brown are both breeds of what?

5 Which screen cowboy rode a horse called Trigger?

6 In the Herman Melville novel, what type of creature was Moby Dick?

4 General knowledge

1 In the Bible, who was swallowed by a whale?

2 Who did Sid James play in the film *Carry On Cleo*?

3 In Greek mythology, which Titan carried the world on his shoulders?

4 Which famous American stage-coach company was founded in 1852?

5 With which other island does Trinidad form a republic?

6 What colour accompanies red on the Spanish flag?

5 Literary logic

1 What nationality is the novelist Maeve Binchy?

2 Who owned the factory in *Charlie and the Chocolate Factory*?

3 Which detective solved the murder on the *Orient Express*?

4 What school did Tom Brown attend in *Tom Brown's Schooldays*?

5 Which autobiography written by a former African president is called *Long Walk to Freedom*?

6 *Stark* was which TV comedian's first novel?

6 Waterworld

1 Which Great Lake on the American–Canadian border has the shortest name?

2 Which river flows from the Black Forest to the Black Sea?

3 How many states does the Mississippi River flow through?

4 Which waterfall is divided into two cataracts by Goat Island?

5 In which sea, an arm of the Mediterranean, does the island of Crete lie?

6 Which of the world's capital cities stands on the Potomac River?

Quick quizzes 2

1 Around the USA

1 What is the USA's smallest state?

2 In which state is Disney, Orlando?

3 What is the most highly populated city in Illinois?

4 In 1969, what was the first city to be mentioned in a broadcast from the Moon?

5 What city was originally called New Amsterdam?

6 What is the name of the highest concrete dam in the USA?

2 General knowledge

1 Which female first name is also the capital of the Italian region of Tuscany?

2 Which former American President acquired the nickname 'the comeback kid'?

3 Which 1974 film spawned four sequels and starred Charles Bronson as a vigilante?

4 In 1982, General Galtieri of Argentina ordered the invasion of which islands?

5 Who was Canada's Prime Minister from 1968 to 1979 and again from 1980 to 1984?

6 In *Thunderbirds*, what is the surname shared by Virgil, Scott, Alan, Gordon and John?

3 Around Europe

1 In which London building is the tomb of the Duke of Wellington?

2 *La Stampa* is a newspaper published in which country?

3 To which country does the island of Corfu belong?

4 What is the capital city of Austria?

5 On which Spanish costa does Benidorm stand?

6 In which French city is Interpol's headquarters?

4 Words

1 What word can be the bottom part of a shoe and the name of a flat fish?

2 Of what are there 360 in a circle?

3 Which S word is the name of a platform on which executions took place?

4 Which F word is the name given to the body of an aircraft?

5 Which three-letter word is the name of a long wooden seat in a church?

6 What name is given to a quantity of paper comprising 500 sheets?

5 Films

1 Which flying car was driven on screen by Dick van Dyke?

2 Who played Rhett Butler in the film *Gone with the Wind*?

3 Which Susan won an Oscar for *Dead Man Walking*?

4 In which musical did Liza Minnelli play Sally Bowles?

5 In which 1997 film did Gene Hackman play President Richmond?

6 Who played the butler, Hobson, in the 1981 film *Arthur*?

6 Instruments

1 Who wrote the song 'Mr Tambourine Man'?

2 For playing which musical instrument was Liberace famous?

3 What instrument does Jack Lemmon play in the 1959 film comedy *Some Like it Hot*?

4 What instrument shares its name with a kitchen device used for slicing vegetables?

5 What instrument was played by the 'boogie woogie boy from Company B'?

6 What is the smallest woodwind instrument in a symphony orchestra?

Quick quizzes 3

1 TV greats

1 In which decade was the TV series *M*A*S*H** set?

2 Which actor played Dr Who and Worzel Gummidge?

3 Which policeman was continually at loggerheads with Top Cat?

4 Who played Pamela Ewing in *Dallas*?

5 Dr Sam Beckett is the lead character in which time-travelling adventure series?

6 In *Star Trek*, what colour is Klingon blood?

2 Music

1 Which surfing group had hits with 'Good Vibrations' and 'I Get Around'?

2 Which band had a 1974 hit with 'This Town ain't Big Enough for the Both of Us'?

3 Which Irish rock band recorded the album *The Joshua Tree*?

4 Sir Edward Elgar composed which piece of music most commonly associated with the last night of the Proms?

5 Which country singer's autobiography was entitled *Take me Home*?

6 How many strings does a balalaika have?

3 Famous people

1 Who founded *Playboy* magazine?

2 Who created *Thunderbirds* and *Stingray*?

3 Who was President of the USA when the first man landed on the Moon?

4 Which Scottish poet was nicknamed 'the bard of Ayrshire'?

5 Who rode naked through the streets of Coventry to persuade her husband to reduce taxation?

6 Which of Queen Elizabeth II's children was born in 1950?

4 General knowledge

1 The annual Promenade Concerts are performed in which famous British building?

2 What nationality is racing driver Michael Schumacher?

3 What is studied by a linguist?

4 What is Wimpy's favourite food in the *Popeye* cartoons?

5 Which pantomime character married Alice Fitzwarren and became Lord Mayor of London?

6 What did Jesus turn into wine at a wedding in the village of Cana?

5 Around the world

1 Mount Everest lies in which mountain range?

2 In which country was the author Rudyard Kipling born?

3 Cairo is the capital of which African country?

4 What is the official language of Cuba?

5 What is the name of the southernmost tip of South America?

6 Which capital city is an anagram of the word mail?

6 Think of a number

1 How many sides has a heptagon?

2 Which number is associated with the phrase: 'the key of the door'?

3 In Roman numerals, what number is represented by the letter M?

4 How many states of the USA are there?

5 What emergency number is the American equivalent of Britain's 999?

6 What Beverly Hills zip code was the title of a TV series?

Quick quizzes 4

1 Crime and punishment

1 Which notorious doctor was Britain's worst serial killer?

2 Which is Britain's infamous prison for the criminally insane?

3 Which of the Kray twins died first?

4 DA is the abbreviation for which legal office in the USA?

5 Which gangster couple were shot dead in an ambush on May 23, 1934?

6 Which of the 'great train robbers' returned to Britain from exile in 2001?

2 General knowledge

1 What is the smallest mammal after which a year is named in the Chinese calendar?

2 Who, in 1995, left the boy band Take That?

3 *The Slipper and the Rose* was a film version of which fairy story?

4 Which series of horror films chronicled the life of the devilish Damien Thorn?

5 What gas propels the cork from a champagne bottle?

6 With which sport do you associate Sharron Davies?

3 Title roles

Who played the title roles in the following films?

1 *Beetlejuice*

2 *Citizen Kane*

3 *Spartacus*

4 *Shakespeare in Love*

5 *Lawrence of Arabia*

6 *Annie Hall*

4 You wear it well

1 Which fashion designer invented the mini skirt?

2 Who said: 'The only thing I wear in bed is Chanel No. 5'?

3 On which part of the body are epaulettes worn?

4 What colour of jacket does the winner of golf's US Masters receive?

5 Was a cardigan named after an Earl, a battle or a bay?

6 In which country was the wearing of pigtails outlawed in 1911?

5 Child's play

1 Singer Natalie Cole is the daughter of which famous singer?

2 Who wrote the novel *The Children of the New Forest*?

3 Which pop star released the single 'From Jesus to a Child' in 1996?

4 Who said: 'Any man who hates dogs and children can't be all bad'?

5 Which 'little orphan' has a dog called Sandy and a guardian called Daddy Warbucks?

6 What is the name of Tony Curtis and Janet Leigh's actress daughter?

6 Kids' TV

1 In which city is Grange Hill school?

2 What colour is Dipsy, the teletubby?

3 Tommy, Chuckie, Angelica, Lil and Phil are the stars of which successful animated series?

4 Who sailed to sea in the *Black Pig*?

5 What was the name of the baby elephant that had an unfortunate accident on *Blue Peter* in 1969?

6 PAT 1 is the number plate on which TV character's van?

Quick quizzes 5

1 Nursery rhymes

1 Which trio of musicians accompanied Old King Cole?

2 Which nursery-rhyme character mislaid a flock of sheep?

3 Which medical man got wet in Gloucester?

4 Which nursery rhyme is linked to the Black Death?

5 Which nursery-rhyme character suffered from arachnophobia?

6 Who had a small creature that followed her to an institution for the education of children?

2 Body matters

1 What colour are the blood cells that combat infection?

2 What are biceps, lumbricals and triceps?

3 Which bearded Texan trio had a hit with a song called 'Legs' in 1985?

4 What facial feature is missing from the painting *Mona Lisa*?

5 Of what are there 33 in the human body?

6 Which internal organ produces bile?

3 Flower power

1 The film *The Rose* starring Bette Midler was based on whose life?

2 Which flower is Scotland's national symbol?

3 Dame Edna Everage extols the virtues of which flower?

4 Who directed the film *Broadway Danny Rose*?

5 Hyacinth Bucket is the lead character in which British sitcom?

6 What colour of rose represented Lancaster in the War of the Roses?

4 A veggie table

1 Which vegetable is the main ingredient of the Russian soup borscht?

2 Which bestselling dolls of the 1980s came complete with their own adoption papers?

3 Which 1995 animated film introduced us to the character of Mr Potato Head?

4 Broad, green and butter are all types of what?

5 What is the proper name for a pepper?

6 What is Baldrick's favourite vegetable in the *Blackadder* comedy series?

5 General knowledge

1 Who wrote the novel *Our Man in Havana*?

2 Who was the Emperor of Rome immediately after Caligula?

3 Which country was runner-up in the 2002 football World Cup?

4 What bird is the symbol of peace?

5 What name is given to the principal church in a district controlled by a bishop?

6 What is the name of the largest railway station in the city of New York?

6 Transport trivia

1 What is the USA's largest airport?

2 What does the A stand for in the abbreviation RAC?

3 What is the name of the famous road that runs from Chicago to Los Angeles?

4 From what word is bus a shortened form?

5 Which car company has made models called the Elite and the Esprit?

6 In which English city is the National Railway Museum?

Quick quizzes 6

1 Superman

1 Who plays Superman in the TV series *The New Adventures of Superman*?

2 What is the everyday identity of Superman?

3 Who did Margot Kidder play in the *Superman* films?

4 In which tiny town did Superman live as a young boy?

5 On screen, which Oscar-winning actor played the natural father of Superman?

6 In the 1978 film, which actor played Otis, Lex Luthor's sidekick?

2 Sport

1 In which sport could a 16lb projectile score a strike?

2 Which Londoner won his first World Snooker title in 1981?

3 How long is a basketball match?

4 How many failed attempts is a pole vaulter allowed before elimination?

5 Which Asian country won the 1983 Cricket World Cup?

6 How many players are there in a volleyball team?

3 General knowledge

1 What is a male sheep called?

2 Which continent has no capital cities?

3 In New York, which island is sandwiched between the East and Hudson Rivers?

4 How many lines are there in a limerick?

5 What is the main ingredient of coq au vin?

6 Kabul is the capital city of which country?

4 Fictional characters

1 Which of the three musketeers is noted for his strength?

2 Winston Smith is the lead character in which George Orwell novel?

3 Sam Cayhall is a racist bomber on death row in which John Grisham novel?

4 Who is the eponymous heroine in the novel by R.D. Blackmore?

5 Which detective, created by Chester Gould, was played on screen by Warren Beatty?

6 Which seafaring captain first appeared in a novel called *The Happy Return*?

5 Furniture facts

1 What is the name of the highest fence in the Aintree Grand National?

2 In a nursery rhyme, whose cupboard was bare, to the dismay of her dog?

3 What type of furniture is a chesterfield?

4 From what did Jesus tell the beggar Lazarus that he should 'get up and walk'?

5 What is the body of ministers that attend councils with the British Prime Minister?

6 In a well-known children's story, what item of furniture provided a gateway to the mythical land of Narnia?

6 Under the sea

1 Humpbacked, killer and sperm are species of what?

2 In monetary terms, what does the acronym COD stand for?

3 Suffered by deep-sea divers, by what shorter name is decompression sickness also known?

4 Which bestselling author wrote the short story *Twelve Red Herrings*?

5 Which is the world's largest predatory shark?

6 What colour is a lobster before it is cooked?

Quick quizzes 7

1 General knowledge

1 What type of cigar did the capital of Cuba give its name to?
2 Which is the largest of the Scandinavian countries?
3 From which meat is pastrami made?
4 The name of Henry Steinway is associated with which musical instrument?
5 What is the name of the woven cloth on which artists apply their paint?
6 According to the proverb, what keeps the doctor away?

2 Colourful questions

1 What is the more common name for an aeroplane's flight recorder?
2 Which Scottish town is a popular destination for eloping couples?
3 What type of drink is Earl Grey?
4 Who played Ena Sharples in TV's *Coronation Street*?
5 How many years of marriage are celebrated on a golden anniversary?
6 What name is given to the scarlet coat worn by huntsmen?

3 Kings

1 Who wrote the horror novels *Carrie* and *Misery*?
2 The Authorised Version of the Bible, published in the 15th century, is also known by what other name?
3 Which rock idol was nicknamed 'the king'?
4 In which TV series was John Steed assisted by Tara King?
5 Who was the first English king to be divorced?
6 Who was the king of the swingers in the Disney film *The Jungle Book*?

4 The name's the same

1 What is the official language of China and also a variety of orange?
2 Which drink is also the name for one side of a ship?
3 Which writing instrument can also be an animal enclosure?
4 What short word can apply to a water barrier and a foal's mother?
5 Which G word means a narrow opening between hills and to eat greedily?
6 What bird, a member of the falcon family, is also a flying toy?

5 Star Wars

1 What spaceship does Han Solo fly?
2 Who played Senator Padme Amidala in *Episode II: Attack of the Clones*?
3 In which year was the original *Star Wars* film released?
4 What name is given to the group of fighters ranged against the Empire?
5 What is the name of the floppy-eared alien who befriends the Jedi knights in *Episode I: Phantom Menace*?
6 What massive weapon system is destroyed at the end of the original *Star Wars* film?

6 Days like these

1 What is the name of the high school in the sitcom *Happy Days*?
2 After which Norse God was Thursday named?
3 What name is given to the day before the beginning of Lent?
4 By what name did the press call the day Britain was forced to leave the Exchange Rate Mechanism in 1992?
5 Which saint's day is celebrated on March 17?
6 Who wrote the song 'Perfect Day'?

Quick quizzes 8

1 Tree trivia

1 The leaf of which tree is the national symbol of Canada?

2 What E word is the opposite of deciduous?

3 What was the second David Bowie song to feature Major Tom?

4 Who was the lead singer of T. Rex who was killed when his car hit a tree?

5 The name of which kind of tree also means 'to long for'?

6 What kind of tree would a genealogist study?

2 T time

All six answers begin with the letter T.

1 What character did Julia Roberts play in the film *Hook*?

2 What name is given to an elephant's upper incisor?

3 Which six-letter word is the name given to a cruel, oppressive leader?

4 Which daily newspaper is nicknamed 'the thunderer'?

5 What is the larva of a frog called?

6 From which language does the word *kiosk* originate?

3 General knowledge

1 Which Shakespeare play featured the feuding Capulet and Montague families?

2 From 1924 to 1972 who was the director of the FBI?

3 In which 1986 film did Jeff Goldblum turn into an insect?

4 Which metal is represented by the chemical symbol Ba?

5 From which animal is mohair obtained?

6 Which mystical sign was incorporated into the German flag in 1933?

4 Superstar marriages

1 Which US senator, who died in 1998, was married to Cher?

2 Which super model was married to Hollywood star Richard Gere?

3 How many years of marriage are celebrated by a coral anniversary?

4 Which Hollywood actress married a trucker called Larry Fortensky?

5 Who has walked down the aisle with Brooke Shields and Steffi Graf?

6 Who wrote the novel *The World is Full of Married Men*?

5 Nationalities

1 What is the common name for the disease *rubella*?

2 What was the nationality of the painter Vincent van Gogh?

3 Which actress plays TV's Vicar of Dibley?

4 Which fleet did Francis Drake defeat after finishing his game of bowls?

5 Which all-girl group recorded the song 'Walk Like an Egyptian'?

6 Which 1951 film co-starred Katharine Hepburn and Humphrey Bogart?

6 Novel locations

In which countries were the following novels set?

1 *The Three Musketeers*

2 *Dr Zhivago*

3 *The Prime of Miss Jean Brodie*

4 *Heidi*

5 *The Jungle Book*

6 *Anne of Green Gables*

Quick quizzes 9

1 General knowledge

1 What is the official language of Fiji?

2 In which decade was the Empire State Building completed?

3 Which part of the body is contorted if a person is gurning?

4 What is the hardest gemstone after a diamond?

5 Does a supernova signify the birth or death of a star?

6 Of what are there 225 on a Scrabble board?

2 The size of it

1 By area, what is the second largest state of the USA?

2 Which popular holiday destination is the largest of the Balearic Islands?

3 What is the world's smallest bird?

4 Which singer had 1960s hits with 'Let the Heartaches Begin' and 'Mexico'?

5 Honshu is the largest island of which country?

6 Which is the heaviest land animal?

3 Twins

1 Carol and Mark are twin children of which former British Prime Minister?

2 Which star sign does the twins represent?

3 Matt and Luke Goss were twin brothers in which 1980s pop group?

4 Chang and Eng were the first recorded case of what?

5 In which cartoon series did the Thompson Twins appear?

6 What are the names of the mythological heavenly twins?

4 Take a letter

1 Which letter is associated with the late Desmond Llewelyn in the James Bond films?

2 Which letter of the alphabet represents 100 in Roman numerals?

3 Who directed the 1954 thriller *Dial M for Murder*?

4 What does the U stand for in the classification of films?

5 What is the most common blood group?

6 Which American TV series starred Marc Singer battling against alien invaders?

5 All-rounders

1 Which film company's logo is a snow-capped mountain surrounded by stars?

2 Alexandria is the second largest city in which country?

3 Chanter and bellows are parts of which Scottish musical instrument?

4 Sirocco, simoom and mistral are the names of types of what?

5 Which element, used in atom bombs, has the symbol Pu?

6 Which American group recorded the albums *Desperado* and *Hotel California*?

6 Clockwise

1 Who was backed by The Comets when singing *Rock Around the Clock*?

2 Do Olympic athletes run clockwise or anti-clockwise in track races?

3 In the poem *Hickory Dickory Dock*, what time was it when the mouse ran down the clock?

4 Which 1952 film featured Gary Cooper, Grace Kelly and a clock?

5 What D word is given to the face of a clock?

6 Who played a headmaster called Mr Stimpson in the film *Clockwise*?

Quick quizzes 10

1 Singers

1 Which singer was addicted to love in 1986?

2 Who is the oldest of the Bee Gees?

3 Who, inspired by his wife, recorded the song 'The Lady in Red' in 1986?

4 In the 1960s what was the name of Gerry Marsden's backing group?

5 Who provided lead vocals for Wet, Wet, Wet?

6 Who accompanied her brother Donny singing 'I'm Leaving it all up to You'?

2 Initials

1 What does the H stand for in H.G. Wells?

2 What does the P stand for in ESP?

3 What does the C stand for in Washington DC?

4 The letter D is the international car registration plate for which country?

5 What does the I stand for in IQ test?

6 With regards to the Internet, what do the initials AOL stand for?

3 General knowledge

1 Which American city is home to Candlestick Park?

2 What was used to behead Anne Boleyn?

3 Which 1979 Monty Python film was accused of blasphemy?

4 Which part of the body is affected by tinnitus?

5 On which river does the city of Amsterdam stand?

6 Which former Cambodian dictator died in 1998?

4 TV comedy

1 Which American sitcom featured a shop called 'Buy the Book'?

2 Who plays the bad-tempered Doctor Becker in the American sitcom *Becker*?

3 What is the first name of Matt le Blanc's character in *Friends*?

4 Which British sitcom was set in Slade Prison?

5 On which thoroughfare did the Muppets make their TV debut?

6 Which seedy landlord lusted after Miss Jones in *Rising Damp*?

5 Creepy crawlies

1 Is it the male or female firefly that glows in the dark?

2 Who left The Crickets and had a solo hit with 'Peggy Sue'?

3 Which sweet liquid is gathered by bees from flowers?

4 Deathwatch and Goliath are both species of what?

5 Who was transformed into Spiderman after being bitten by a radioactive spider?

6 How many wings does a common housefly have?

6 Rocking all over the world

1 From where did Little Jimmy Osmond's 'long haired lover' hail?

2 Which duo had hits with 'America' and 'Scarborough Fair'?

3 Randy Crawford sang about a rainy night in which American state?

4 Which of the world's continents provided the title of a hit record for Toto?

5 Peter Cetera provided the lead vocals for which group named after their home city?

6 According to a famous song, what is the city that never sleeps?

Quick quizzes 11

1 Stones

1 Which actress starred in the films *Casino* and *Total Recall*?

2 What is the most common colour of topaz gemstones?

3 Which pop group took their name from a Muddy Waters song?

4 How many pounds are there in a stone?

5 Complete the biblical saying: 'Let he who is without sin…'.

6 Which cartoon family live next door to the Flintstones?

2 G force

The answers to all these questions begin with the letter G

1 What is the world's largest island?

2 What is the world's most northerly desert?

3 Accra is the capital of which African country?

4 Which Scottish city stands on the River Clyde?

5 Olympic Airways is the national airline of which country?

6 What does the G stand for in GMT?

3 Prefixes

What word can go before the three words in each group?

1 Bank, brother and group

2 Cake, suit and card

3 Stroke, glasses and spot

4 Chocolate, bottle and teeth

5 Dress, axe and ship

6 Wheel, pistol and fall

4 Beastly books

1 Who wrote *The Giraffe, The Pelly and Me*?

2 Which Jack London novel featured a dog called Buck?

3 *Moon Tiger* was a 1987 Booker Prize winner for whom?

4 Who wrote the novel *Of Mice and Men*?

5 Which 1995 film was adapted from a novel called *Sheep Pig*?

6 What type of creature was Winston Smith terrified of in the novel *1984*?

5 General knowledge

1 Which European country has been ruled by 18 kings named Louis?

2 Which part of the body does a chiropodist treat?

3 In which country is the River Marne?

4 What name is given to the spiritual leader of a Jewish congregation?

5 Which American city's nickname is The Big D?

6 Who played Private Ryan in the film *Saving Private Ryan*?

6 All Davids

1 Who played James Bond in the film *Casino Royale*?

2 Who created Ziggy Stardust?

3 Which magician was engaged to the super-model Claudia Schiffer?

4 Which heart-throb had hits with 'Daydreamer' and 'Cherish' in the 1970s?

5 In the Bible, which giant was slain by David with a slingshot?

6 Who took over as British Home Secretary in 2001?

Quick quizzes 12

1 Initial queries

What do the following sets of initials stand for?

1 HGV

2 MSP

3 ICBM

4 OBE

5 ITN

6 AIDS

2 Baby talk

1 Which 1987 film co-starred Diane Keaton and Sam Shepard?

2 Which all-girl group recorded the 1960s smash hit 'Baby Love'?

3 What name is given to a young goose?

4 Who provided the voice of the baby Mikey in the film *Look Who's Talking*?

5 Tom the chimney sweep is the central character in which Charles Kingsley novel?

6 What was the surname of the 1930s gangster who was nicknamed 'baby face'?

3 General knowledge

1 What is the drink *sake* distilled from?

2 Who directed the films *Spartacus* and *The Shining*?

3 Which vowel of the alphabet is represented in Morse Code by two dots?

4 Of what are deed, pop, bib and pip all examples?

5 Which country has the international car registration plate EC?

6 Whose Tubular Bells music featured in the film *The Exorcist*?

4 Who's who?

1 Who packed her trunk and said goodbye to the circus?

2 Who won a best actress Oscar for *The Silence of the Lambs*?

3 Who wrote *The Canterbury Tales*?

4 Who was the first Hollywood actress to command US$10 million for a film?

5 Who captained England in their 5–1 victory over Germany in 2001?

6 Who was Ronald Reagan's first wife?

5 Pie posers

1 Which comic strip strongman eats cow pie in Cactusville?

2 What kind of bird is the cartoon character Tweetie Pie?

3 With which 1971 hit did Madonna top the charts in 2000?

4 What is the Italian word for pie?

5 Which nursery-rhyme character met a pie man?

6 In clothing terms, what is a pork pie?

6 C here?

1 Which coarse cloth of hemp or flax is used to make tents?

2 What collective name is given to soldiers who go to war on horseback?

3 Which musical instrument is associated with Acker Bilk?

4 What is the opposite of discord?

5 What name is given to the ceremony for the crowning of a monarch?

6 What is the transparent covering of the eyeball in front of the iris called?

Quick quizzes 13

1 General knowledge

1 What was the first book that Joy Adamson wrote about Elsa the lioness?

2 Which Sicilian volcano erupted in 1669?

3 How many stars feature on New Zealand's flag?

4 Who did Charlton Heston play in the film *The Ten Commandments*?

5 What is the first name of the Leslie Charteris literary character *The Saint*?

6 Which TV drama is set in County General Hospital in Chicago?

2 Countries

1 What is the largest South American country through which the Equator passes?

2 Maoris are the indigenous people of which country?

3 The lotus flower is the national symbol of which Asian country?

4 The Republic of San Marino lies within which other country?

5 Budapest is the capital of which country?

6 In which country is the Aswan Dam?

3 On the march

1 Where was Helen Shapiro walking back to in the title of her 1961 song?

2 Which TV comedy series featured a sketch about the Ministry of Funny Walks?

3 The Long March was an epic trek made by communists in which country?

4 Which *Railway Children* actress starred in the 1971 film *Walkabout*?

5 Which group of 'brothers' had a 1966 No. 1 hit with 'The sun ain't gonna shine anymore'?

6 Which Roman emperor was warned, according to Shakespeare, to 'beware the ides of March'?

4 Mammal mania

1 Which is the only mammal capable of true flight?

2 Which animal is a cross between a male donkey and a female horse?

3 Which animal makes its home in a form?

4 What name is given to both a male bear and a male pig?

5 By what three-letter name is a wildebeest also known?

6 What boy's name is also the name of a young kangaroo?

5 Soccer nicknames

The following are nicknames of English football teams. What are their real team names?

1 The Owls

2 The Hammers

3 The Sky Blues

4 The Rams

5 The Dons

6 The Saints

6 The state of things

1 In which American state is the John F. Kennedy Space Center?

2 Which is the only American state that begins with A, but does not end in A?

3 What D is the state capital of Colorado?

4 What became the 50th American state in 1959?

5 Which American state founded in 1907 became the title of a film musical in 1955?

6 What is the only American state beginning with the letter L?

Quick quizzes 14

1 Lessons in love

1 Who wrote the novel *Love Story*?

2 For which film did Wet, Wet, Wet perform the song 'Love Is All Around'?

3 'Saving All My Love For You' was the debut hit for which singing star?

4 Complete the following saying. 'It is better to have loved and lost than...'.

5 Who is the patron saint of lovers?

6 Which Beatles song began with a snatch of the French national anthem?

2 House and home

1 Which government building is the British monarch forbidden to enter?

2 According to the title of a Dickens novel, at which unappealing address did John Jarndyce live?

3 Which eager creature's home is called a lodge?

4 Which children's TV characters live in a grassy knoll called Home Hill?

5 In which 1953 horror film did Vincent Price play a murderous sculptor?

6 Which pop group had 1980s hits with 'Our House' and 'House of Fun'?

3 General knowledge

1 What is a male fox called?

2 In which building did Prince Charles and Lady Diana Spencer get married?

3 Who played the lead guitar for the pop group Queen?

4 The title of which well-known novel is cockney-rhyming slang for fist?

5 What flavours the drinks ouzo and pernod?

6 How was Ginger Rogers related to Rita Hayworth?

4 Songs

1 Which famous song begins with the line: 'Start spreading the news'?

2 Which soul and disco icon had a 1974 hit with 'You're the first, the last, my everything'?

3 Which Spanish city name provided a hit for Freddie Mercury and Montserrat Caballé?

4 Which Kate Bush hit was also the title of a novel by Emily Brontë?

5 In which film did Barbra Streisand sing 'Second Hand Rose'?

6 Which song was a hit for Harry Nilsson and Mariah Carey?

5 The female of the species

What are the female names of these animals?

1 Goat

2 Sheep

3 Rabbit

4 Tiger

5 Elephant

6 Donkey

6 Movie men

1 Who played the title role in the film *The Horse Whisperer*?

2 Which actor was singing in the rain as Don Lockwood?

3 Who played the title role in the 1986 film *Highlander*?

4 What were Abbot and Costello's first names?

5 On film, who played the lead roles in *American Gigolo* and *An Officer and a Gentleman*?

6 Name the actor who played Sonny Corleone in *The Godfather*.

Quick quizzes 15

1 Heavy metal

1 Bronze is an alloy of tin and which other metal?

2 Which pop group had a 1979 hit with 'Brass in Pocket'?

3 In which Indian city would you find the Golden Temple?

4 What kind of creature is a small copper?

5 Who had a 1980 hit with 'Silver Dream Machine'?

6 Who wrote the novel *The Tin Drum*?

2 Leading ladies

1 When Warren Beatty played Clyde who played Bonnie?

2 Who played the title role in the film *Miss Congeniality*?

3 Who was Julie Andrews playing when she sang: 'A spoonful of sugar makes the medicine go down'?

4 Who portrayed the estranged wife of Dustin Hoffman in *Kramer Versus Kramer*?

5 Who played Rita in the film *Educating Rita*?

6 With which actress did Michael Douglas suffer a fatal attraction?

3 How many?

1 How many points has the Star of David?

2 How many labours did Hercules perform in Greek mythology?

3 How many plagues of Egypt were there in the Bible?

4 How many different Popes were there in 1978?

5 In the game of Scrabble how many points is the letter X worth?

6 How many girls were members of Enid Blyton's Famous Five?

4 Fraction facts

1 In American currency how many cents are there in a quarter?

2 Is the numerator the top or bottom number of a fraction?

3 The Muppets were how far down the stairs in their 1977 top 10 record?

4 What is one-twelfth of a foot?

5 How is three-quarters expressed as a percentage?

6 Which 1948 film was introduced by the Harry Lime theme?

5 General knowledge

1 Which part of the human body is affected by a condition called glaucoma?

2 Which river ran alongside the Hanging Gardens of Babylon?

3 What sport is played by the Texas Rangers?

4 What is agoraphobia a fear of?

5 Phil Collins and Peter Gabriel have both provided lead vocals for which group?

6 In 1991 which city was replaced by Abuja as the capital of Nigeria?

6 Musical instruments

1 Is a spinet a keyboard or a woodwind instrument?

2 Which is the only stringed instrument of a symphony orchestra not played with a bow?

3 What instrument can be Spanish, acoustic or electric?

4 Vanessa Mae and Nigel Kennedy are both famous for playing which instrument?

5 Which musical instrument was invented by John Sousa?

6 Did the zither originate in China, Cuba or Canada?

Quick quizzes 16

1 Shared names

What surname is shared by...

1 A singer named Tasmin and the author of the novel *First Among Equals*?

2 An actor and a fashion designer?

3 A British Prime Minister and an American President?

4 A singer named Johnny and a Wimbledon champion called Pat?

5 An American author named Mark and a Canadian singer called Shania?

6 A snooker player named Alex and the professor in *Pygmalion*?

2 Doggy dilemmas

1 What breed of dog is named after the city of Peking?

2 French, toy and standard are all types of which dog breed?

3 What is the name of the dog in *The Magic Roundabout*?

4 From which North American country did the Chihuahua originate?

5 Cocker and King Charles are both types of which breed of dog?

6 What sort of dog was Lassie?

3 General knowledge

1 Who sang 'The Power of Love' when backed by a band called The News?

2 What word can follow pill, letter and toy?

3 Which musical featured the song '76 Trombones'?

4 Mallard and merganser are both species of which bird?

5 Which city is known as Canada's gateway to the Pacific?

6 In which TV drama series does James Gandolfini play New Jersey Mafia boss Tony?

4 Three-letter words

1 In Pontoon, what card can be worth one or eleven?

2 Which drink is flavoured with juniper berries?

3 Which cooking vessel is also the name of the pipe-playing Greek god of shepherds?

4 What name is given to grass-cuttings that are dried to make animal fodder?

5 What is the principal monetary unit of Japan?

6 What sort of bird can be blue, great, crested or long-tailed?

5 Stevens and Stephens

1 On what date is St Stephen's Day?

2 Who wrote the music for the musical *A Little Night Music*?

3 Which Steven fronted the band, The Smiths?

4 Which Stephen King novel told the story of a haunted hotel called *The Overlook*?

5 Who directed the films *Jaws* and *Jurassic Park*?

6 Whose hit 'I Just Called to say I Love You' became Motown's best ever seller?

6 Lords and ladies

1 Gamekeeper Oliver Mellors was the lover of which literary Lady?

2 Who played Steve McGarrett in *Hawaii Five-O*?

3 In which musical was the character Tracy Lord played by Grace Kelly?

4 Sir Ian McKellen plays which on-screen wizard in the *Lord of the Rings* trilogy?

5 The song 'Lady Marmalade' features in which film starring Ewan McGregor and Nicole Kidman?

6 Which Gilbert and Sullivan operetta featured The Lord High Executioner?

Quick quizzes 17

1 General knowledge

1 How many horns does a Sumatran rhinoceros have?

2 By what name is the Welsh singer Thomas Woodward better known?

3 Named after a British scientist, what is the capital of the Northern Territory of Australia?

4 What colour connects Bobby Vinton's velvet and Carl Perkins' shoes?

5 In which European country was the actress Audrey Hepburn born?

6 In the Bible, who lived for 969 years?

2 To cap it all

All six answers begin with the letters 'cap'.

1 What word can be a small cloak or a headland?

2 What word means to overturn, especially when applied to a boat?

3 Which star sign does a goat represent?

4 What name is given to the detachable compartment of a space craft?

5 What name is given to a domestic cock that is castrated and fattened for eating?

6 What name is given to a revolving barrel for winding in cable?

3 Author, author

1 Who created the characters of Tigger and Eeyore?

2 Who wrote the poem *Paradise Lost*?

3 Which Washington Irving character fell asleep for 20 years?

4 Which writer created the character Uncle Remus?

5 Whose comic diary did Helen Fielding write?

6 What does the D stand for in D.H. Lawrence?

4 Classic TV

1 Which adversaries of Doctor Who had the menacing catchphrase: 'Exterminate, exterminate'?

2 In which TV series did Robert Wagner and Stefanie Powers star as husband and wife?

3 What type of animal was the talking Mr Ed?

4 Which large family lived in the Blue Ridge mountains of Virginia in the 1930s?

5 Who played Kid Curry in *Alias Smith and Jones*?

6 What was the name of Samantha's daughter in the sitcom *Bewitched*?

5 Who said it?

1 'I don't care to belong to any club that will have me as a member.'

2 'If Hitler invaded hell I would make at least a favourable reference to the devil. . . .'

3 'If there were no bad people there would be no good lawyers.'

4 'A classic: something that everybody wants to have read and nobody wants to read.'

5 'Being powerful is like being a lady. If you have to tell people you are, you aren't.'

6 'That woman speaks 18 languages and can't say "no" in any of them.'

6 Capital punishment

1 What is the capital city of Uruguay?

2 The Acropolis looks over which Greek city?

3 What is the nearest capital city to the site of the Battle of Waterloo?

4 On which river does Cairo stand?

5 Which Bolivian city is the world's highest capital city?

6 What city was the capital of West Germany?

Quick quizzes 18

1 Body wise

1 Which side of the brain is more concerned with rational thought?

2 In which African city was the first successful heart transplant carried out?

3 If your skin was jaundiced what colour would it be?

4 What is the non-technical name for the cranium?

5 Which flower shares its name with the coloured part of the eye?

6 What grows from a sheath called a follicle?

2 TV duos

1 In *The Dukes of Hazzard*, how were Bo and Luke related?

2 Huggy Bear was the flamboyant informant of which TV crime-fighting duo?

3 In which city was *Cagney and Lacey* set?

4 What were the first names of the comedy duo Morecambe and Wise?

5 What kind of business did Steptoe and Son run?

6 Which violent cartoons were produced by Fred Quimby and featured a dog called Spike?

3 General knowledge

1 In the film *Jaws* who played the character of Matt Hooper?

2 Who wrote the novel on which the musical *Les Misérables* is based?

3 In the USA which nuts are commonly known as filberts?

4 King Edward and Maris Piper are both varieties of which vegetable?

5 What can be found at the mouth of a river, and is the fourth letter of the Greek alphabet?

6 What colour are the hottest stars: yellow, white or blue?

4 Sporting personalities

1 Who captained the Australian cricket team to World Cup glory in 1987?

2 Which snooker champion gained fame as much for his attire as for his talent?

3 Who managed the 1966 England World Cup winning football team?

4 What is the name of Michael Schumacher's racing brother?

5 What nationality are the tennis stars Stefan Edberg and Mats Wilander?

6 Which Welshman won golf's US Masters in 1991?

5 Worldly wisdom

1 On which sea does the Bulgarian port of Varna stand?

2 Which Red Indian tribe shares its name with the state capital of Wyoming?

3 Which famous Parisian nightspot celebrated its 100th birthday in 1989?

4 In which ocean are the Canary Islands?

5 In 1965 which group of people in Australia were given the vote for the first time?

6 Which is the largest bay in the world?

6 What's the word?

1 What is a reading desk in a church called?

2 What M word is the name given to a change in a gene?

3 Madam I'm Adam. What is the sequence of letters in that sentence called?

4 What name is given to the male equivalent to a mermaid?

5 What are trams called in the USA?

6 What word meaning to pressgang people into becoming sailors is also the name of a Chinese city?

Quick quizzes 19

1 The sixties

1 Whose first thriller was *Cover Her Face*?

2 In 1964 where was Nelson Mandela imprisoned?

3 Which London Tube line opened in 1969?

4 Who was lead singer with Herman and the Hermits?

5 Which English football legend retired from the game in 1965, aged 50?

6 Which book by D.H. Lawrence featured in a notorious obscenity trial in 1960?

2 Tasty trivia

1 What type of pasta literally means 'little tongues' in Italian?

2 A savoy is a variety of which vegetable?

3 With which period in the Christian calendar are simnel cakes associated?

4 What colour is cayenne pepper?

5 In which country did chutney originate?

6 What is the only vitamin that is not present in eggs?

3 As easy as ABC

1 What A is the study of celestial bodies and the Universe?

2 What A is the flavour of fennel leaves?

3 What B is the name of a horse's head harness?

4 What B is the name given to whale fat?

5 What C is a breed of dog that can be bearded and border?

6 What C changes petrol into vapour in a car engine?

4 Model questions

1 Which slender 1960s model starred in the film *The Boyfriend*?

2 Which supermodel fell over on the catwalk while modelling a pair of Vivienne Westwood platform shoes?

3 Which supermodel is known as 'the body'?

4 Which car company made models called Polo and Golf?

5 Which Texan model married Mick Jagger?

6 Camel, Hurricane, Lancaster and Stirling are all models of what?

5 General knowledge

1 What do the initials HB stand for on a pencil?

2 In which sea does the Isle of Man lie?

3 What is the only animal used as a playing piece in Monopoly?

4 Who became President of South Africa in 1994?

5 On which major African river does the Kariba Dam stand?

6 Which internal organs of the body remove waste products from the blood?

6 The phonetic alphabet

1 What boy's name represents the letter V?

2 Which capital city represents the letter L?

3 Which Canadian province represents the letter Q?

4 Which sport represents the letter G?

5 Which drink represents the letter W?

6 What type of building represents the letter H?

Quick quizzes 20

1 Art for art's sake

1 What nationality was the painter Salvador Dali?

2 Which famous sculpture was found on the island of Melos minus its arms?

3 Who painted five of the ten most expensive paintings sold at auction in the 20th century?

4 The National Gallery is situated in which London square?

5 In which city is the Louvre?

6 Who painted the ceiling of the Sistine Chapel?

2 Film roles

1 Who played Maverick in the film *Top Gun*?

2 When Madonna played Eva Peron in *Evita*, who played Che Guevara?

3 Which musical instrument was played by Dooley Wilson in the film *Casablanca*?

4 Who played Zorba the Greek in the 1964 film?

5 In which 1995 box-office flop did Kevin Costner play the Mariner?

6 Who played Dustin Hoffman's wife in the 1971 film *Straw Dogs*?

3 General knowledge

1 What was the first item that Old King Cole called for?

2 What day, celebrated on February 2 in the USA, became the title of a Bill Murray film?

3 Who was Sir Lancelot's son?

4 What does the F stand for in FBI?

5 How many teeth has a sloth?

6 What is added to orange juice to make a Buck's Fizz?

4 Playing the game

1 How many pawns are on a chessboard at the start of a game of chess?

2 Which card game uses the terms yarborough, dummy and grand slam?

3 In charades, what is signified by a person placing two fingers on their arm?

4 What colour are the hotel pieces in Monopoly?

5 How many spots are on the domino that is nicknamed 'snake eyes'?

6 What does double top score in a game of darts?

5 Real names

1 Which *Carry On* film actress was born Barbara Deeks?

2 What is the actress Bette Davis' first real name: Rebecca, Ruby or Ruth?

3 Under what name did George Booth gain fame with the help of a ukulele?

4 Which actress was born Shirley Beaty?

5 Who was born Harvey Lee Yeary and went on to play a bionic man?

6 Which actress, born Mary Cathleen Collins, was given a mark of ten by Dudley Moore?

6 C creatures

1 What is the name of a young swan?

2 Which is the only wild cat that possesses non-retractable claws?

3 Which butterfly shares its name with an area of London?

4 What powerful freshwater reptile has remained largely unchanged for approximately 65 million years?

5 Plymouth Rock and Leghorn are both breeds of what?

6 What land creature is able to change colour to blend into the background?

Quick quizzes 21

1 Sporting chance

1 Who wore the No. 7 shirt for Manchester United in the 2002–2003 season?

2 Who captained England's cricket team in 54 tests between 1993 and 1998?

3 Which English rugby union captain led the team to Grand Slam victories in 1991 and 1992?

4 For which Formula 1 team did Michael Schumacher win the 1995 Constructor's title?

5 Vinny Jones played football at international level for which country?

6 What sport do the New York Yankees play?

2 TV drama

1 In which crime drama did Robert Stack play Eliot Ness?

2 Inspector Morse was set in which city?

3 Who plays the character of Ling Woo in Ally McBeal?

4 In which popular British TV series did Robson and Jerome play Tucker and Garvey?

5 Who played the character of Ricardo Tubbs in Miami Vice?

6 What was the name of the detective agency in Moonlighting?

3 Colourful songs

1 Who starred in the film, and sang the theme for, Men in Black?

2 What colour wine did UB40 sing about?

3 Which group recorded the 1960s smash hit 'A Whiter Shade of Pale'?

4 What colour of eyes did Van Morrison's girl have?

5 Who sang 'Purple Rain' and 'Little Red Corvette'?

6 Who had a UK No. 1 hit in 1981 with 'Green Door'?

4 Puddings and pies

1 What kind of pie is traditionally eaten on Thanksgiving Day in America?

2 From which country did the savoury tart called quiche lorraine originate?

3 What fruit is the main ingredient of Eve's pudding?

4 In the nursery rhyme, how many blackbirds were baked in a pie?

5 What amphibious name is given to a dish of sausages in Yorkshire pudding?

6 Which farm animal's blood is dried to make black pudding?

5 General knowledge

1 What V word was the name of the American equivalent of the British music hall?

2 What three-letter word can go before wax, wig and ring?

3 How many lines are in a sonnet?

4 In which country is the opera Madame Butterfly set?

5 What is the highest mountain in the Grampians range?

6 What is the name of the fault line on which San Francisco lies?

6 Languages

1 What is the French word for three?

2 Which group of people speak a language called Romany?

3 If you are bilingual how many languages can you speak?

4 What do Americans call curtains?

5 What is the second letter of the Greek alphabet?

6 What is Brazil's official language?

Quick quizzes 22

1 V is for . . . ?

1 What does a virologist study?

2 Stromboli and Krakatoa are both names of what?

3 What name is given to calfskin, dressed and prepared for writing on?

4 Which Scandinavian people worshipped Odin and travelled in longboats?

5 What name is given to the movable front part of a helmet?

6 In which country is the Orinoco River?

2 Planet Earth

1 Borneo is the largest island in which ocean?

2 In which country is the source of the River Amazon?

3 Which of America's Great Lakes boasts the largest volume of water?

4 On which continent is the Sahara Desert?

5 Which river forms a natural border between the USA and Mexico?

6 Is the Red Sea or the Dead Sea the saltiest sea in the world?

3 General knowledge

1 In which country was the great lover Casanova born?

2 What is the only rank above general in the British Army?

3 What is the name of the bone that extends from the shoulder to the elbow?

4 What is the smallest of the world's oceans?

5 In an opera, when is an overture played?

6 What is the name of the oldest university in Scotland?

4 Wildlife

1 Bushmaster, black mamba and taipan are all species of what?

2 How many toes does an African elephant have on its hind feet?

3 What is the biggest fish?

4 From what is the horn of a rhinoceros made?

5 What is the largest species of mammal?

6 What is the most abundant class of animal on Earth: birds, insects or fish?

5 Alphabetically

1 Alphabetically, which is the first of the seven dwarfs?

2 Alphabetically, what is the last planet in our Solar System?

3 How many American states have a Q in their name?

4 What letter is sited next to Q on a computer keyboard?

5 Alphabetically, which British university comes first?

6 What do the initials PG stand for with regard to film classification?

6 Partners

1 Neil Tennant and Chris Lowe formed which pop duo?

2 Who assisted Burke in stealing bodies for Dr Knox?

3 Which pop brothers had hits with 'Cathy's Clown' and 'Bye Bye Love'?

4 On TV, did Sharon Gless play Cagney or Lacey?

5 Who was the larger, Stan Laurel or Oliver Hardy?

6 Contrasting partners are said to be like chalk and what?

Quick quizzes 23

1 General knowledge

1 The organisation CND campaigns for what?

2 Jade is a shade of which colour?

3 Which musical duo wrote *HMS Pinafore*?

4 What does the Statue of Liberty hold in her left hand?

5 What title was given to the wife of a tsar?

6 What is the name of the Flintstones' pet dinosaur?

2 An Asian experience

1 What colour provides the alternative name for the Huang He River?

2 Which pass connects Pakistan and Afghanistan?

3 What is the capital of India?

4 Which country is known as 'the land of the rising sun'?

5 Peking, the Chinese capital, is more commonly called what?

6 Which group hit the charts in 1987 with the song 'China in your Hand'?

3 From head to toe

1 Which part of the head is also the name for a place of worship?

2 With which organ is a cardiologist concerned?

3 Which part of Adam's body did God use to create Eve?

4 Which mammal features on Australia's coat of arms?

5 Shin Bet is the counter-intelligence agency for which country?

6 What is the game of noughts and crosses called in America?

4 TV jobs

1 In *Frasier*, what occupation does Niles Crane follow?

2 In *Coronation Street*, what is Kevin Webster's trade?

3 What is the name of the president in *The West Wing*?

4 What occupation do Perry Mason and Ally McBeal share on TV?

5 On TV, who played Dr Kildare and an amorous priest in *The Thorn Birds*?

6 Who played the part of Nurse Carol Hathaway in *ER*?

5 Oscar round

1 Marlon Brando has won two best actor Oscars. One for *The Godfather*. Name the other.

2 What city was Nicolas Cage leaving, in the film, for which he won best actor Oscar in 1995?

3 Who won best actor for his role in *The Kiss of the Spiderwoman*?

4 Jason Robards has won two best supporting actor Oscars. One for *Julia*. Name the other.

5 In 1996 Cuba Gooding Jr won best supporting actor for his role as a sportsman in which film?

6 In 2001, Michael Caine won a best supporting actor Oscar, but in which film?

6 Opening lines

1 Which song from a famous film starts with the line: 'I got chills; they're multiplying'?

2 Which Michael Jackson hit starts with: 'It's close to midnight'?

3 Which Abba hit begins: 'I work all night, I work all day'?

4 Which song by The Police opens with the line: 'Giant steps are what you take'?

5 Which duet starts with Cher singing: 'They say we're young and we don't know'?

6 Which song begins with: 'And now the end is near, and so I face the final curtain'?

Quick quizzes 24

1 Screen greats

1 Which rebel without a cause died in a 1955 car crash?

2 Who did Vivien Leigh play in *Gone with the Wind*?

3 Who directed the films *Psycho*, *The Birds* and *Vertigo*?

4 Who played the part of Rick in the film *Casablanca*?

5 Who played the gangster Rocky Sullivan in *Angels with Dirty Faces*?

6 Which screen siblings starred in the film *Duck Soup*?

2 Let's dance

1 Which energetic dance was popularised by Chubby Checker in the 1950s?

2 Which British dancer, often partnered with Nureyev, became president of the Royal Academy of Dancing in 1954 and died in 1991?

3 The Lambeth walk was named after a street in which city?

4 How many dancers perform a *pas de deux*?

5 Which dance craze was a hit record for Little Eva and Kylie Minogue?

6 Which dance represents the letter F in the phonetic alphabet?

3 General knowledge

1 A hirsute person has an abundance of what?

2 In which American state is Anchorage?

3 Which soul singer was backed by The Bluenotes?

4 What name is shared by a female trout and a female chicken?

5 Which instrument is played by the leader of the orchestra?

6 Which queen was executed in Fotheringay Castle in 1587?

4 Space

1 What name is given to a space from which all air has been removed?

2 Who made a historic journey in a spaceship called *Vostock 1*?

3 Is Mars smaller or larger than Earth?

4 Which known planet has the most moons?

5 Is Jupiter's red spot made up of solids, liquids or gases?

6 *Dark Side of the Moon* was a bestselling album for which rock band?

5 A call to arms

All six answers begin with the letters 'arm'.

1 Of which European country is Yerevan the capital?

2 What South American burrowing animal has a body encased in bony plates?

3 In the Bible, what battle will take place at the end of the world?

4 What name is given to an agreement to stop fighting and negotiate peace?

5 In the human body, how is the axilla known?

6 What is the name for defensive clothing worn during battle?

6 A cookery lesson

1 What is gazpacho?

2 Which traditional Scottish dish comprises of a sheep's stomach filled with offal?

3 From which farm bird is *paté de fois gras* obtained?

4 Bath, Chelsea and hot cross are all types of what?

5 From which country does Edam cheese originate?

6 What colour is the German bread pumpernickel?

Quick quizzes 25

1 General knowledge

1 In which country was Bob Hope born?

2 How many points are scored for potting the brown in a game of snooker?

3 The intensity of what is measured by a photometer?

4 Which role did Michael Jackson play in the film *The Wiz*?

5 Which large black birds are associated with the Tower of London?

6 In which American city is the Guggenheim Museum?

2 Who wrote it?

1 Who wrote the first gospel of the New Testament?

2 Who wrote the lyrics for the song 'Yesterday'?

3 Who wrote the novel *A Clockwork Orange*?

4 Who wrote the play *Death of a Salesman* and was married to Marilyn Monroe?

5 Who wrote stories about *Noddy* and *The Secret Seven*?

6 Who wrote *The Ballad of Reading Gaol* while imprisoned there?

3 Pen and ink

1 Pen and ink is cockney-rhyming slang for what?

2 The female for which bird is called a pen?

3 Which London street is nicknamed 'the street of ink'?

4 What word completes the following saying: 'the pen is mightier than the…'?

5 What Q word is the name given to the hollow stem of a feather used as a writing implement?

6 Who or what is a *nom de plume*?

4 The Jacksons

1 Who played Mr Hudson in *Upstairs, Downstairs*?

2 What was the name of Michael Jackson's pet chimpanzee?

3 Which Jackson was devoured by a shark in the 1999 film *Deep Blue Sea*?

4 Which British athlete held the 110m hurdles world record in 1999?

5 Jackson is the state capital of which American state beginning with M?

6 Which Jackson was a modern artist who painted vast, abstract, challenging works of art?

5 Sporting chance

1 In 1999, who became the fifth man to have won all four Grand Slam tennis titles?

2 Who scored Scotland's only goal in Euro 1996?

3 How many hurdles are there in the 400m hurdles?

4 What is the surname of the former England Rugby Test wingers Rory and Tony?

5 With which sport do you associate Dennis Rodman?

6 Who captained the 1999 European Ryder Cup winning side?

6 Religion and belief

1 According to the proverb, what is next to godliness?

2 Which Hindu god is the god of creation and destruction?

3 In which 1981 film did Laurence Olivier play Zeus?

4 In which mythology is Odin the leader of the gods?

5 In Christianity, how many days did it take for God to create the Earth?

6 The Talmud is one of the sacred texts of which religion?

Quick quizzes 26

1 Trees

1 From which trees do conkers come?

2 Cobnuts and filberts come from what species of tree?

3 *The Maple-leaf Rag* was composed by which famous American?

4 What is another name for a gum tree?

5 Which tree is often associated with graveyards?

6 Around which bush do children dance in the well-known nursery rhyme?

2 Around the year

1 Which precious stone is the birthstone for September?

2 Which astrological sign does the archer represent?

3 The 1973 Arab–Israeli War took its name from the Jewish Day of Atonement. By what name is the festival known?

4 When is St George's day?

5 Which R word is the name of the ninth month of the Muslim year?

6 What connects St George and the Chinese year of 2000?

3 General knowledge

1 Is a condor an eagle or a vulture?

2 From which political party did American President Gerald Ford come?

3 Which metal has the chemical symbol Ni?

4 The River Jordan flows into which sea?

5 Where does velvet grow on a deer?

6 In which decade was the first Austin Mini sold?

4 Three-letter words

1 What was the title of Michael Jackson's follow-up album to *Thriller*?

2 Which part of the body is examined with an otoscope?

3 What creature provides the symbol for the Aries star sign?

4 According to the rhyme, Wednesday's child is full of what?

5 What is a female bear called?

6 Other than humans, what is the only mammal that suffers from sunburn?

5 Four-letter words

1 Which pop group was founded by George Michael and Andrew Ridgeley?

2 What flower is England's national symbol?

3 Which Andrew Lloyd Webber musical features the song 'Memory'?

4 In Scotland, what name is given to a lake?

5 Pb is the chemical symbol for what?

6 In imperial measurements, 1760 yards is equivalent to one what?

6 Firsts

1 Launched in 1971, what was the name of the first space station?

2 In a game of chess, who moves first: white or black?

3 Who met Sherlock Holmes for the first time in 1881 at the Criterion Bar?

4 Who was the first woman to win the Grand Slam in tennis?

5 Which singer called Ella was known as 'the first lady of song'?

6 Alphabetically, what is the first American state?

Quick quizzes 27

1 Plants and gardening

1 Iceberg, Peace, Ena Harkness and New Dawn are all well-known varieties of what?

2 John Innes No.1 is a favourite brand of what?

3 Which popular gardener died in 1996 and is remembered for his work on BBC's *Gardener's World* and on his own garden at Barnsdale?

4 Who had a celebrated and much copied white garden at Sissinghurst in Kent?

5 What world-famous gardening event is held every May in central London?

6 Beer and eggshells are frequently used to trap which common garden pests?

2 Five-letter words

1 What is the capital of Japan?

2 What is the largest internal organ in the human body?

3 What kind of fruit is a muscat?

4 What name is given to a group of lions?

5 What was the name of The Who's pinball wizard?

6 According to the Bible, who received the Ten Commandments on Mount Sinai?

3 Six-letter words

1 In which film was Janet Leigh murdered by Anthony Perkins while taking a shower?

2 Of which musical instrument was Yehudi Menuhin a virtuoso?

3 By what name is Bruce Wayne known when he dons a mask and cape?

4 What is the most southerly of the Channel Islands?

5 According to legend, what metal must a bullet be made of if it is to kill a werewolf?

6 In what part of a flower, beginning with A, is pollen contained?

4 L of a film

1 In which film did Lou Diamond Philips play rock and roller Ritchie Valance?

2 What film featured Jim Carrey as a lawyer who had to tell the truth?

3 Which 1962 film featured Peter O'Toole riding a camel?

4 Which film saw the James Bond debut of Roger Moore?

5 In which film did David Bowie play the king of the goblins?

6 What was the title of the 1972 sequel to *Born Free*?

5 General knowledge

1 Which beach in Rio was the subject of a Barry Manilow hit?

2 In which century did Washington become the capital of the USA?

3 Whose singing voice did Bill Lee dub in the film *The Sound of Music*?

4 What type of fork did trumpeter John Shore invent in 1711?

5 Which country has the world's longest coastline?

6 In which ocean are The Bahamas?

6 Husbands and wives

1 Which *Baywatch* star married rock drummer Tommy Lee?

2 Commander Tim Laurence became the second husband of which member of the royal family?

3 What did Linda Eastman's name become when she married a famous pop star?

4 Name the Charlie's Angel who married a bionic man?

5 Aristotle Onassis was the second husband of which former First Lady?

6 What was the first name of President Richard Nixon's wife?

Quick quizzes 28

1 Fashion facts

1 Is a boa a skirt, a scarf or a shawl?

2 What M is a name given to soft leather shoes or slippers?

3 Who designed the conical basque worn by Madonna?

4 In which country did the Benetton fashion house originate?

5 What article of attire was named after John Stetson?

6 Around which part of the body would you wear a cummerbund?

2 The A list

1 What traffic-light colour is also the name of a fossil resin?

2 What does the A stand for in NATO?

3 What measurement of land is equivalent to 4840 square yards?

4 Which beautiful youth of Greek mythology was loved by the goddess Venus?

5 What does the chemical symbol As stand for?

6 Which language, derived from Dutch, is spoken in South Africa?

3 General knowledge

1 In astrology is Scorpio a fire or a water sign?

2 Which planet shares its name with a type of carnivorous plant?

3 Which creator of *The Muppets* died in 1990?

4 Who presented the TV series *Life on Earth*?

5 What is the name of the Disney deer created by Felix Salten?

6 Which member of the onion family is said to repel vampires?

4 Creature comforts

1 Which wild dog, native to Australia, is incapable of barking?

2 What name is given to a group of locusts?

3 Earth, slow and blood are all types of what?

4 What name is given to a male bee?

5 What is Europe's most common gull?

6 Which bird builds a nest called an eyrie?

5 T time

1 Ankara is the capital of which country?

2 Which English royal house or dynasty began with Henry VII and ended with Elizabeth I?

3 What name is given to the three-pronged spear brandished by Britannia?

4 Which gland in the human body lies near the larynx?

5 What name is given to a group of soldiers and a group of monkeys?

6 Which 1960s group recorded 'Hole in my Shoe'?

6 Water, water

1 What famous children's story was written by Charles Kingsley?

2 Who composed the *Water Music*?

3 Who played the part of Terry McCann in the TV series *Minder*?

4 At what temperature does water boil on the Fahrenheit scale?

5 How many people play in a water polo team?

6 What 1884 invention by Lewis Waterman changed people's writing habits?

Quick quizzes 29

1 Cities

1 By what name was the city of St Petersburg known between 1924 and 1991?

2 What is the name of Edinburgh's main shopping street?

3 What was the capital city of East Germany?

4 Is the city of Wellington on the North or South Island of New Zealand?

5 In which American state is the city of Tucson?

6 In the centre of which city will you find the so-called Forbidden City?

2 Science

1 Which two elements combine to make water?

2 How many centimetres are there in a decimetre?

3 How many decimetres are there in a decametre?

4 Which bird lays the largest egg?

5 What weapon of war was produced by the Manhattan Project?

6 Who wrote the controversial scientific work, *On the Origin of Species*?

3 People

1 What was Franklin D. Roosevelt's middle name?

2 Of what nationality was the psychologist Carl Jung?

3 Which former James Bond actor received a knighthood?

4 Which country did Augusto Pinochet rule from 1973 to 1990?

5 Who invented the characters Wallace and Gromit?

6 In which of the arts was Emeric Pressburger a leading figure?

4 History

1 Who said: 'There can be no whitewash at the White House'?

2 In which century was the Crimean War?

3 The eastern part of which country became the independent nation of Bangladesh?

4 Who succeeded John Paul I as Pope?

5 Where was cricket's first World Cup held in 1975?

6 Which Briton won his only Formula 1 title in a McLaren in 1975?

5 General knowledge

1 What nationality was the painter Rembrandt?

2 What is made when milk is artificially curdled by bacteria?

3 Through which capital city does the River Liffey flow?

4 In American football, from where do the Dolphins come?

5 Which English football team's name is also a place where weapons are stored?

6 What kind of a creature is a gecko?

6 A to F

1 What A is the name given to a large cage or building where birds are kept?

2 Sofia is the capital of which country?

3 Which C is one hundredth of a Euro?

4 What is the name of the line that cuts a circle in half?

5 What seven-letter word is the name given to a territory surrounded by a foreign dominion?

6 From which plant is linseed obtained?

Quick quizzes 30

1 G to L

1 What G is the name of an armoured glove thrown down as a challenge?

2 What does the H stand for in the medical treatment HRT?

3 What I word can precede curtain, lady and lung?

4 In what sport does an ippon score ten points?

5 In which American state is Fort Knox?

6 Which EU country has the smallest population of all the EU states?

2 M to R

1 On which Mediterranean island did the British actor Oliver Reed die?

2 What three-letter word precedes the names of four American states?

3 What name is given to a musical composition for eight singers or players?

4 Andorra lies in which mountain range?

5 What word is given to a porcupine's sharp spines?

6 Which Alex Haley novel featured the character Chicken George?

3 S to X

1 Which British river beginning with S was named Sabrina by the Romans?

2 What is the capital city of Albania?

3 Which African country borders the north shore of Lake Victoria?

4 What has a person lost if suffering from aphonia?

5 What name is given to a native North American Indian's tent?

6 How is 19 written in Roman numerals?

4 Sporting terms

1 What boy's name is also a grade of proficiency in judo?

2 In which sport would a competitor call 'en garde' to an opponent?

3 In ten-pin bowling, how many bowls are delivered to score a spare?

4 In which sport might one encounter a full nelson and a flying mare?

5 The 'Fosbury flop' is a technique employed in which athletics event?

6 What type of racing event uses a parachute called a 'laundry' to slow down the cars?

5 Places

1 Seoul is the capital of which Asian country?

2 What is 466km (290 miles) long and is found in Arizona?

3 What colour is the disc on the Japanese flag?

4 BKK is the airport code for which capital city?

5 At 2012km (1250 miles) in length, what is the world's longest reef, found off Australia?

6 Which of the seven continents has the largest population?

6 Plant posers

1 Which tree has pink flowers and edible nuts that are used to flavour marzipan?

2 Which root, used to flavour cooking, is also a term for red hair?

3 Which North American shrub shares its name with Tom Sawyer's best friend?

4 What plant is traditionally worn in buttonholes on St Patrick's Day?

5 In *Citizen Kane*, Kane's last word was 'Rosebud'. What was Rosebud?

6 Which flower is also the last colour of the rainbow?

Quick quizzes 31

1 Film females

1 Who connects the films *Alien* and *Ghostbusters*?

2 Which actress has married Don Johnson and Antonio Banderas?

3 For which 1998 film did Gwyneth Paltrow win best actress Oscar?

4 Which chart-topping singer has starred in the films *Mermaids* and *Moonstruck*?

5 Whose voice was provided by Minnie Driver in Disney's film adaptation of *Tarzan*?

6 Who connects the films *The First Wives Club* and *Big Business*?

2 Feathered friends

1 Which member of the crow family is also the name of a chess piece?

2 Which flightless bird is the fastest-running creature on two legs?

3 What colour are budgerigars in the wild?

4 What bird is traditionally used as a symbol of wisdom?

5 What bird is known for laying its eggs in other birds' nests?

6 John Parrot is a professional player in which sport?

3 United Kingdom

1 Where in London does the London Marathon finish?

2 Which is Britain's oldest university?

3 In which British city did Henry Bessemer invent a process for manufacturing steel?

4 Which English county shares its name with a four-wheeled horse-drawn carriage, that, in the song, 'had a fringe on top'?

5 In which month is the *Last Night of the Proms* held?

6 On which island did Queen Victoria die?

4 Music

1 Which much-loved TV personality was also an accomplished pianist, who deliberately played wrong notes for comic effect?

2 With what part of your body do you play the Jew's Harp?

3 Who devised *Desert Island Discs*?

4 'Catgut' is used to make the strings of violins, violas, cellos and other string instruments. But which animals' guts are actually used?

5 What does *pizzicato* mean?

6 Which celebrated 'it girl' is also a pianist who gives recitals for charity?

5 General knowledge

1 What is the most frequent name for popes?

2 Which German city is served by Templehof Airport?

3 In 1994, which car company took over Rover?

4 Which member of The Rolling Stones died in 1969?

5 The Azores island group belong to which European country?

6 What piece of sporting equipment is traditionally made with 16 feathers and a cork base?

6 Cooking

1 What is a *bain-marie*?

2 When do we traditionally eat pancakes?

3 What is a *roux*?

4 Who advised us to: 'first catch your hare'?

5 What is TVP?

6 What gives Worcestershire Sauce its distinctive flavour?

Quick quizzes 32

1 Saints

1 With which sport is Ian St John associated?

2 Who succeeded Roger Moore in the title role of the TV programme *The Saint*?

3 Which football team is nicknamed 'The Saints'?

4 Who had a 1980 hit with 'There's no one quite like Grandma'?

5 Which Scottish singer was a host on the BBC's *The Generation Game*?

6 Which university admitted Prince William as an undergraduate in 2001?

2 On wine

1 Which South American country is known for its good value red wine?

2 In wine-making, what is marc?

3 What is Patsy and Edina's favourite fizzy tipple in *Absolutely Fabulous*?

4 Which veteran TV cook is notorious for swigging a glass of wine on his shows?

5 For which French wine is there an annual race?

6 Which famous auction house is known for its wine courses?

3 Oscar round

1 Which actress won a best actress Oscar in 1966 for her role in *Who's Afraid of Virginia Woolf*?

2 For which film did Holly Hunter win best actress Oscar in 1993?

3 Who was the first deaf actress to win an Oscar for her role in *Children of a Lesser God*?

4 Which actress got the most nominations in the 20th century for best supporting actress?

5 Which legendary actress won her only Oscar for her role in the 1954 *The Country Girl*?

6 For what 8-minute role did Judi Dench win a best supporting actress Oscar?

4 Which month?

1 In which month does Libra's star sign end?

2 In which month was the Gunpowder Plot exposed?

3 What name was given to the 300 mile (483km) trek made by northern English workers during the great depression?

4 Carole King wrote and sang 'It might as well rain until...' when?

5 What was the first name of the girl from uncle, as played by Stephanie Powers?

6 What other name is given to the large beetle sometimes called a cockchafer?

5 General knowledge

1 Which Italian city gave its name to a type of cheese and ham?

2 Which London landmark was named after Sir Benjamin Hall?

3 What game played on a lawn involves the use of six hoops?

4 What name is given to a group of geese?

5 In which country is Shakespeare's *Hamlet* set?

6 Which British airport has the airport code LHR?

6 Collective nouns

What collective names are given to the following groups of things?

1 Crows

2 Gulls

3 Flies

4 Monkeys

5 Angels

6 Sheep

Quick quizzes 33

1 Cities

1 Which New Zealand city has the largest population?

2 What is the capital city of Finland?

3 In which American state is Honolulu?

4 A statue of who overlooks Rio de Janeiro?

5 Which European capital city is known as 'the city of light'?

6 In which African country is the city of Khartoum?

2 Fact or fiction?

1 Chop suey was invented in the USA.

2 The Tin Man in *The Wizard of Oz* was called Chicory.

3 The stethoscope was invented by Pierre de Girond.

4 A dorgi is a cross between a dachshund and a corgi.

5 The father of Matt Groenig, the creator of *The Simpsons,* is called Homer.

6 Walt Disney's middle name was Donald.

3 Mountain mania

1 What is the highest mountain in western Europe?

2 In which country is Table Mountain?

3 What is the second highest mountain in the world?

4 Which musical featured the song 'Climb Every Mountain'?

5 The Colorado River flows through which mountain range?

6 What is the world's longest mountain range?

4 General knowledge

1 In a 1988 film, who was Jessica Rabbit's husband?

2 In what do marsupials carry their young?

3 'Plates of meat' is cockney-rhyming slang for what part of the human body?

4 Which of the seven deadly sins is said to come before a fall?

5 In geography, what is the name of the world's largest gulf?

6 What does J stand for in the name of *Dallas* villain J.R. Ewing?

5 Rodent round

1 Which large rodent is Canada's national animal?

2 Which common household pet is descended from the cavy?

3 Which front man for the Boomtown Rats organised the Live Aid concerts?

4 Which cartoon mouse is assisted by Penfold?

5 Who, later Director General of the BBC, was responsible for introducing Roland Rat to the screen?

6 Timothy the mouse was which Disney character's best friend?

6 Island info

1 What is the official language of the island of Jersey?

2 Which island hosts motorcycle's TT races?

3 In which ocean are the Maldives?

4 Hobart is the capital of which Australian island state?

5 On which isle is Canary Wharf?

6 Which island is separated from the African mainland by the Mozambique straits?

Quick quizzes 34

1 Books

1 Becky Thatcher is the girlfriend of which Mark Twain character?

2 Which Russian heroine committed suicide by throwing herself under a train?

3 With which gypsy girl did the hunchback of Notre Dame fall in love?

4 On what day of the week did Robinson Crusoe find his manservant?

5 Which of the Brontë sisters wrote *Jane Eyre*?

6 Which literary character rode his horse *Rosinante* at windmills?

2 General knowledge

1 Ganymede is which moon's largest planet?

2 Which is the only American state whose name begins with the letter G?

3 In the nursery rhyme, whose wife did the three blind mice chase?

4 Aer Lingus is which country's national airline?

5 According to popular legend, what type of bird delivers babies to their mothers?

6 If you are suffering from amnesia, what have you lost?

3 TV sitcoms

1 What job did Gladys Emmanuel have in *Open All Hours*?

2 Which *Friends* actress also starred in the *Scream* films?

3 Which award-winning comedy starred Caroline Aherne as Denise?

4 Which actor portrays Frasier Crane?

5 Which American sitcom featured the antics of the Sunshine Cab Company?

6 Who plays Patsy Stone in *Absolutely Fabulous*?

4 Religion

1 What name is given to the period of 40 days that precedes Easter?

2 What profession was followed by Peter, Jesus' disciple?

3 In Judaism, what day of the week is the Sabbath?

4 In which river was Jesus baptised?

5 What is the name of the main religion in Japan?

6 How many pillars of Islam are there?

5 For the bird brains

1 Are penguins native to the North Pole or the South Pole?

2 What food traditionally has the saliva of a swiftlet as its main ingredient?

3 Elf, tawny, snowy and barn are all species of which bird?

4 On the sixth day of Christmas what did my true love give to me?

5 What is a female peacock called?

6 For what is a bluebird a traditional symbol?

6 Selective knowledge

1 What is the third book of the New Testament?

2 Which tunnel was officially opened on May 6, 1994?

3 Which sporting contest was formerly called the Liverpool and National Steeplechase?

4 What colour is traditionally associated with envy?

5 What is the star sign of a person born on Valentine's Day?

6 In a French hotel which letter would indicate the cold water tap?

Quick quizzes 35

1 Down by the riverside

1 On which river does the city of Paris stand?

2 What three-letter word is the Spanish for river?

3 What is the longest river in South America?

4 In 1980 which American singer released an album called *The River*?

5 Which chat-show host claimed that Mick Jagger had child-bearing lips?

6 Which pop group recorded the 1978 hit 'Rivers of Babylon'?

2 Nicknames

1 Which singer, nicknamed 'little miss dynamite', sang 'Sweet Nuthings'?

2 Which US President was nicknamed 'tricky dicky'?

3 Which silent movie star was nicknamed 'the great stone face' because he rarely smiled?

4 What is the full name of the athlete who was nicknamed 'Flo-Jo'?

5 Who was responsible for the murder of Jack 'the Hat' McVitie in November 1996?

6 Who is known as 'the crafty cockney'?

3 General knowledge

1 Who wrote the novel *The Shining*?

2 In which country is Jan Smuts airport?

3 Moving clockwise round a dartboard, which number comes after nine?

4 What name is given to a group of rhinoceroses?

5 Which sign of the Zodiac is represented by a pair of scales?

6 Which of these metals is most dense: lead, gold or platinum?

4 Fruity facts

1 Which fruit is grown in a vineyard?

2 What kind of fruit did Little Jack Horner pull out of a pie?

3 Which Israeli port is also the name of a variety of orange?

4 On which record label did The Beatles record 'Hey Jude'?

5 Who wrote the novel *Oranges are not the Only Fruit*?

6 Cantaloupe and honeydew are varieties of which fruit?

5 TV cooks

1 Which TV cook's bestselling book was called *How to be a Domestic Goddess*?

2 Which TV cook is also a director of Norwich City Football Club?

3 Which 'pukka' young TV chef also plays drums in a band?

4 Who famously said: 'Life is too short to stuff a mushroom'?

5 Which of the two fat ladies rode a motorcycle?

6 Which couple, attired in evening dress, showed us how to cook in the 1950s and 1960s?

6 Star trekking

1 Which enemy of the Federation had starships fitted with 'cloaking devices'?

2 Who created the *Star Trek* series?

3 What nationality was the *Star Trek* character Chekov?

4 What crystal was essential for enabling the *Starship Enterprise* to travel at 'warp drive'?

5 What is Mr Spock's home planet?

6 In which decade did *Star Trek* first appear on TV?

Quick quizzes 36

1 Falling down

1 Which Hollywood star played the male lead role in the 1993 film *Falling Down*?

2 In which country are the Angel Falls?

3 Which song was a hit for Nat King Cole, Donny Osmond and Rick Astley?

4 Which singer couldn't stand up for falling down in the 1980s?

5 Who played the title role in the TV series *The Fall Guy*?

6 Which waterfall provided the title of a 1952 Marilyn Monroe film?

2 Movie music

1 Which film starring Madonna featured the song 'Into the Groove'?

2 Which film featured the song 'Anything You can do, I can do Better'?

3 The national flower of Austria inspired which song in *The Sound of Music*?

4 'Food Glorious Food' is the opening song in which musical?

5 The musical *Camelot* was based on the life of which legendary king?

6 Which 1982 film featured 'Eye of the Tiger' by Survivor?

3 General knowledge

1 What was the title of the western TV series in which Lorne Greene played Ben Cartwright?

2 How many rooms are there on a Cluedo game board?

3 The Order of Lenin is which country's highest decoration?

4 What type of snake appeared on the crowns of Egyptian pharaohs?

5 What is the name of London's largest park?

6 What species of crab is known for occupying empty shells?

4 Yellow perils

1 What is the name of the oldest National Park in the USA?

2 What could a person described as 'yellow bellied' be accused of?

3 What word can follow scarlet, night and yellow?

4 Which animated film featured the song 'All You Need is Love'?

5 What colour follows yellow in a rainbow?

6 What song, associated with the American Civil War, was a hit for Mitch Miller in 1955?

5 First names

1 What was the first name of Constable who painted *The Haywain*?

2 What was Kojak's first name as played by Telly Savalas?

3 What was the first name of Morse, a detective played on television by John Thor?

4 What was the first name of Bill Sikes' girlfriend in *Oliver Twist*?

5 Which name, more common for girls, was John Wayne's real first name?

6 What is the first name of the Agatha Christie character Miss Marple?

6 Vegetable mix

1 In *The Sun*, which England football manager had a turnip superimposed over his head ?

2 Yosemite Sam is the arch-enemy of which carrot-munching cartoon character?

3 Which explorer is credited with introducing the potato to Britain?

4 According to the saying, what butters no parsnips?

5 Which of these is not a vegetable: cabbage, cucumber or cauliflower?

6 Which Greek island is also the name of a type of lettuce?

Tie-breakers

If your quiz ends in a tie, choose a question from this list and give each player or team two minutes to write down as many answers as they can. Whoever has most correct, wins. If you want to give players something to aim for, the numbers in brackets refer to the total number of correct answers in each instance. Some of the bigger categories might also make good table rounds (see page 345).

1 James Bond films based on Ian Fleming novels (15)

2 Ten sports of the decathlon (10)

3 The Seven Dwarfs (7)

4 Number one Spice Girls hits of the 20th century (8)

5 Streets on a Monopoly board (22)

6 Gifts given on the 12 days of Christmas (12)

7 Books of the Old Testament (39)

8 London Underground stations beginning with S (31)

9 Seven Wonders of the ancient world (7)

10 20th-century presidents of the United States of America (18)

11 Formula 1 championship winners (27)

12 Countries that were formed on the break up of the USSR (15)

13 Members of the *Monty Python* team (6)

14 Christmas number ones of the 20th century from 1970 (31)

15 *Blue Peter* presenters of the 20th century (28)

16 Capital cities of Europe (45)

17 The Beatles' number one singles (17)

18 Winners of the best motion picture/best picture Oscar (75)

19 *Carry On* films (30)

20 Post-war British prime ministers (11)

21 Titles of Shakespeare's plays (37)

22 Winners of the FIFA World Cup (8)

23 Nine planets of the Solar System (9)

24 Signs of the Zodiac (12)

25 Wacky Races starting grid (11)

26 Actors who have played Doctor Who on TV (7)

27 Complete operas of Gilbert and Sullivan (14)

28 Children's novels by Roald Dahl (17)

29 The 10 plagues of Egypt (10)

30 Officer ranks of the British Army (11)

Answers

General knowledge

001
1 Bridge 2 H_2O (water) 3 Prince Andrew 4 Michael J. Fox 5 Danish 6 Votes for women 7 *The King and I* 8 Nitrogen 9 Spain 10 They both have the surname Fleming: Alexander and Ian respectively

002
1 Coven 2 *Macbeth* 3 Witch hazel 4 Salem 5 Warlock 6 Narnia 7 *The Wizard of Oz* 8 Eastwick 9 By twitching her nose 10 *The Blair Witch Project*

003
1 The Rolling Stones 2 At the bottom of the sea 3 Mel Smith 4 Tom Jones 5 Ian Smith 6 Grace Jones 7 Will Smith 8 Indiana Jones 9 Maggie Smith. In the *Sister Act* films she played Mother Superior; she played Harry Potter's Deputy Headmistress Minerva McGonagall; and in the film *The Clash of The Titans* she played Thetis a shape-changing sea goddess 10 Jim Jones

004
1 A rollmop 2 Frank 3 The Pope 4 Kevin Kline 5 A frog 6 A whale 7 Two 8 Robert Shaw 9 Billy Liar 10 Fish was the lead singer of Marillion. His real name is Derek Dick and his ex-landlady nicknamed him Fish because of the amount of time he spent in the bath

005
1 HMS *Victory* 2 *The Little Mermaid* 3 Kissing in the back row of the movies 4 Rodin 5 Georgie Porgie 6 Mistletoe 7 Sealed With A Loving Kiss 8 The Duchess of York 9 *The Taming of the Shrew* 10 Tony Curtis was reported as saying those words after starring with Marilyn Monroe in the film *Some Like It Hot*

006
1 The Guardian Angels 2 Woodrow Wilson 3 Margaret Thatcher, who married Dennis Thatcher, who had been previously married to Margaret Kempson. 4 Chicago 5 Rabbi 6 Oswald Moseley 7 General Leopoldo Galtieri 8 James Buchanan 9 Egyptian 10 Alec Guinness

007
1 *Sleepless in Seattle* 2 A sleepwalker 3 Rapid Eye Movement 4 A dormouse 5 Doris Day 6 Crystal Gayle 7 Dance 8 Freddy Krueger 9 Philip Marlowe, created by Raymond Chandler 10 Zebedee

008
1 Origami 2 Old Kent Road (£60) 3 Five 4 Poker 5 Fifteen 6 Checkers 7 Barcelona 8 Bridge 9 Happy Families 10 Plumber

009
1 Iris 2 The Foundations 3 A rose 4 Narcissus 5 Umberto Eco 6 The Cherry Blossom 7 'Flowers in the Rain' by The Move, the first song to be played on BBC Radio 1 8 Anther 9 Tiger Lily 10 Daisy

010
1 Joan of Arc 2 The Sorbonne, the common name for the University of Paris 3 The Moulin Rouge 4 The Palace of Versailles 5 Bonnie Tyler 6 Laurent Blanc 7 Marseilles 8 The Tricolour 9 Vichy France 10 The Pyrenees

011
1 Cathedral 2 Sousaphone 3 Viscount 4 *Starlight Express* 5 Italy 6 Lambada, which became popular in 1989 following a hit film *Lambada*, performed by a French group called Kaoma 7 Florence 8 Christian Dior 9 Putty 10 Oslo

012
1 Wyatt Earp 2 Lee Harvey Oswald was shot and killed by Jack Ruby 3 Chester Gould created the character of Dick Tracy who was played on film in 1990 by Warren Beatty 4 A strawberry 5 Benjamin Franklin 6 A list of books banned by the Roman Catholic church 7 A long-distance swimming race 8 Hypnus (Hypnos) 9 The age of a horse 10 Sweden

013
1 Aquarius 2 Atom 3 Alsatian 4 Allah 5 Abstain 6 Adultery 7 Antidote 8 Aswan 9 Andalucia 10 Apollo

014
1 Alva 2 Alpenstock 3 Aniseed 4 Acrophobia 5 The Alamo 6 *Alien* 7 Abraham 8 Army 9 Argentina 10 Afghanistan

015
1 Artichoke 2 Archdeacon 3 Ambergris 4 Aquamarine 5 Arkansas 6 Astor 7 Adonis 8 Atacama, located in Chile 9 Armpit 10 Aurora

016
1 Bantamweight 2 Bigamy 3 Beethoven 4 Brussels 5 Bamboo 6 *Baywatch* 7 Billingsgate 8 Buck 9 Boer 10 Botany

017
1 Badminton 2 Bill Beaumont 3 Bloodhound 4 Bandicoot 5 Bellamy 6 Bile 7 B-17 8 Beefeaters 9 Baritone 10 Buddleia

018
1 *Cheers* 2 Caber 3 California 4 Chequers 5 Colt, from the age of one to four a young horse is known as a colt and from then it is known as a stallion 6 Capitol 7 Centaur 8 Coyote 9 Cougar 10 Chameleon

019
1 Sporran 2 'My Favourite Things' 3 Bugs Bunny 4 Dido 5 Vests 6 Periscope 7 The Pentagon 8 Wellington 9 Photosynthesis 10 Downhill skiing

020
1 Brighton 2 Quentin Crisp 3 John Lennon and Yoko Ono 4 Sheffield 5 *Women In Love* 6 Belinda Carlisle 7 Erica Roe 8 Ray Stevens 9 Gymnophobia 10 Marcel Duchamp

021
1 Edgar Rice Burroughs 2 Rhesus 3 Terry Gilliam, who first found fame as the animator for Monty Python 4 Troop 5 Monkey Puzzle tree 6 *The Wizard of Oz* 7 Marx Brothers 8 £500 9 A brass rack used to store cannon balls. When it contracted in

cold weather it would eject the cannon balls, hence the expression 'cold enough to freeze the balls off a brass monkey' **10** A monkey wrench, named after the inventor

022

1 Shirley Bassey **2** Eire **3** 40 **4** The bombing of Pearl Harbor **5** South Africa **6** *The Jazz Singer* **7** Topaz **8** Ruby Murray **9** *The Jewel of the Nile* **10** Among the Crown Jewels. It is the centrepiece of the crown worn by Queen Elizabeth, the Queen Mother, at her 1937 coronation

023

1 Colonel Gadaffi **2** Billie Jean Moffit **3** Jamaica **4** Clark Gable **5** Rudyard Kipling **6** *King Lear* **7** BB King **8** *The King and I* **9** H. Rider Haggard **10** George III who reigned for 59 years

024

1 The retina **2** Oklahoma, the song being 'Oh What A Beautiful Morning' **3** Cats eyes **4** Double vision **5** Aldous Huxley **6** *Mickey Blue Eyes* **7** 'Bright Eyes' by Art Garfunkel **8** Cataract **9** Eye patches. The singer of 'Dreams', Gabrielle, wore one as did the lead character Rooster Cogburn in the film *True Grit*. HMS *Victory* was the flagship of eye patch wearer Admiral Nelson **10** The giant squid, their eyes can measure up to 500mm (20in) across

025

1 Biscuit **2** Barbican **3** Balthazar **4** Billiards **5** Binnacle **6** *Buster*, which saw Phil Collins star as the Great Train Robber, Buster Edwards **7** Borak **8** Bromine **9** Bigglesworth **10** Bastinado

026

1 Crozier **2** Concave **3** Czechoslovakia **4** Cairn **5** Churchyard **6** Candlemas **7** Cutler **8** Columbia **9** Catamaran **10** Chewbacca

027

1 Codes **2** *Cyborg* **3** Calyx **4** Croquet **5** Cochineal **6** Canopy **7** Cacography **8** Crete, the largest of the Greek islands **9** Cornet **10** *Calypso*

028

1 They were all teachers before they became rock stars **2** Red **3** Lord of Flies **4** Magic **5** S – they are the first letters of the French numbers: Un, deux, trois, quatre, cinq, six, sept… **6** Whisky: Johnnie Walker; Jack Daniels; Jim Beam **7** They all turned down or returned awards: Olympic medal, OBE, Nobel prize **8** Popeye: Crystal City is a centre of spinach production **9** £20 note (Edward Elgar replaced Michael Faraday) **10** Champagne bottles: the gardens were commissioned by Nebuchadnezzar, which is a 20 size bottle of champagne, Tom Selleck played Magnum a two size bottle and one of the three wise men was called Balthazar, a 16 size bottle **11** They were all parents of twins **12** Canada **13** Sunday ('Tuesday Morning', 'Wednesday Week', 'Sunday Girl') **14** By winning the Eurovision Song Contest for Israel as a transsexual named Dana International **15** A 2CV

029

1 *Dixon of Dock Green* **2** He named Greenland, which is actually predominantly snowy white, not green. He wanted to make it sound attractive to Viking colonists **3** Arsenal **4** Greg Dyke **5** Yes **6** *2001: A Space Odyssey* **7** 300 **8** Madonna **9** Desperate Dan **10** Doctors (Author of *Doctor Zhivago*, *Portrait of Doctor Gachet*, Beatles song 'Dr Robert', Doctor Dolittle)

030

1 Dallas **2** Domesday Book **3** Déjà vu **4** Dublin **5** Doris Day **6** Dante **7** Danish pastry **8** Democracy **9** Demerara **10** Dundee

031

1 Apple **2** Pick me up **3** A banana ice cream, made by Ben and Jerry's **4** Blackberry **5** Eggs **6** Choux **7** Scotland **8** No **9** (Finger of) fudge **10** Ice cream, meringue, sponge

032

1 Arnold Schwarzenegger **2** Madonna **3** Princess Diana **4** Mikhail Gorbachev **5** Hugh Grant **6** Paul McCartney **7** Bill Clinton **8** Elvis Presley **9** Paul Newman **10** Michael Jackson

033

1 Dutch **2** Darling **3** Denver **4** Daddy-long-legs **5** Deerstalker **6** Drone **7** *Death Wish* **8** Dromedary **9** Deuce **10** Duke

034

1 Dice **2** Don **3** Dorsal **4** Dyslexia **5** D-Day **6** *Disclosure* **7** Delaware **8** Desdemona **9** Dawn, and the k stands for Kathryn **10** Diana

035

1 Dancing **2** Daiquiri **3** Dirt **4** Dzo. The female is called a dzomo **5** Dhoti **6** Dam, standing at 335m (1099ft) tall **7** *Diminuendo* **8** Dangerman **9** Dewlap **10** Dendrochronology

036

1 Joe Frazier **2** Burt Reynolds **3** White smoke from the Vatican means a new Pope has been elected. The smoke is caused by the burning of the ballot papers **4** The Platters **5** 1965 **6** Frankfurter **7** Pipe Smoker of the Year **8** Smokey Robinson **9** Rudyard Kipling **10** Steve McQueen, as Fire Chief Michael O'Hallorhan

037

1 Ned Kelly **2** Hobart **3** Koala – the koala does not actually drink but obtains the necessary fluids it needs from the juices of eucalyptus leaves **4** Uluru **5** *Strictly Ballroom* **6** Sydney Opera House **7** Rod Laver **8** Ramsey Street **9** 18 **10** The Seekers

038

1 Foxhunting **2** Joan Rivers **3** Babel fish **4** Soliloquy **5** Nancy Astor, who in 1919 became the first female MP to take a seat in the British Parliament **6** St Paul's Cathedral **7** Edvard Münch **8** Belize **9** Nicholas Evans **10** Wilbur Post

039

1 Otters **2** The Boomtown Rats **3** *The Postman Always Rings Twice* **4** Phalanges **5** Richard Wagner, the four operas being *Gotterdammerung*, *Das Rheingold*, *Siegfried* and *Die Valkyrie* **6** Anne Boleyn **7** *Lord of the Rings* **8** *Rowan and Martin's Laugh In* **9** Anita Ward **10** Tom Thumb

040

1 Rip Van Winkle in the story by Washington Irving 2 Mount McKinley 3 The Eiger 4 'Over the Hills and Far Away' 5 *Cliffhanger* 6 Mount Sinai 7 Scafell Pike, Cumbria 978m (3210ft) 8 Salzburg 9 Turkey 10 In the Blue Ridge Mountains of Virginia

041

1 ElectroPlated Nickel Silver 2 Jeff Beck 3 John Cleese 4 Bob Seger 5 *The Silver Chair*, in order the seven books that make up the Chronicles of Narnia are, *The Magician's Nephew*; *The Lion, the Witch, and the Wardrobe*; *The Horse and his Boy*; *Prince Caspian*; *The Voyage of the Dawn Treader*; *The Silver Chair* and *The Last Battle* 6 Goldfinger, the eponymous villain in the Bond film 7 Fool's gold 8 Miami 9 Nine 10 Ghana

042

1 George Washington 2 Photographs of: 'Every head he has had the pleasure to know' 3 Dire Straits 4 30 pieces of silver 5 Johnny Cash 6 *The Hustler* 7 Rouble (100 kopek = 1 rouble) 8 Clint Eastwood 9 Threadneedle Street, founded by William III 10 *Who Wants to be a Millionaire?*

043

1 Peaches 2 Cha 3 Handel 4 Portugal 5 Bill Owen 6 Laurie Lee 7 Fosters 8 Mexico 9 Pears 10 *The Rime of the Ancient Mariner* by Samuel Taylor Coleridge

044

1 The Panama Canal 2 Moriarty, enemy of Sherlock Holmes 3 A tidal wave 4 Jack Hawkins 5 Thailand 6 Enya 7 The Baltic Sea 8 'Bridge Over Troubled Water' by Simon and Garfunkel 9 The Solent 10 The Amazon, the flow of the Amazon is 60 times greater than that of the Nile and at its deepest point it is 124m (407ft) deep

045

1 Gary Oldman 2 Capillaries 3 Embolism 4 The Salvation Army 5 Plasma 6 Alice Cooper 7 Green 8 General Patton 9 Errol Flynn 10 Prince Charles in 1985

046

1 Ra 2 *Hair* 3 Jabba the Hut 4 12, the last of which was in 1972 5 Argentina 6 Icarus 7 Somerset Maugham 8 'Vincent' by Don McLean 9 The Who 10 Reverend Sun Myung Moon

047

1 Sadler's Wells. The Royal Ballet is the title under which the British Sadler's Wells Ballet (at Covent Garden), Sadler's Wells Theatre Ballet, and the Sadler's Wells Ballet school were incorporated in 1956 2 Tony Manero 3 A Haka 4 *Dances with Wolves* 5 Anna Pavlova 6 Mazurka 7 Cyd Charisse 8 *Me and My Gal* 9 Salome 10 Gavotte

048

1 Purple 2 Sultana 3 John Wayne 4 Princess Leia 5 Charles II referring to his mistress Nell Gwynn on his deathbed 6 A Viscount. Barons are the lowest rank of the Aristocracy 7 The Dukes of Hazzard 8 Lord Lucan 9 Humphrey Bogart 10 The British armed forces

049

1 Alex Higgins 2 Tintin 3 *Bambi* 4 Vivien Leigh 5 Geri Halliwell 6 Peter Snow 7 Tom Cruise 8 R.D. Wingfield 9 H. Norman Schwarzkopf, the US Commander 10 *Camberwick Green*

050

1 The tank 2 The Battle of Balaclava, part of the Crimean campaign 3 A lieutenant general 4 The Soviet Union 5 The Warsaw Pact 6 The Cenotaph 7 The Salvation Army 8 Dad's Army 9 Airborne troops such as parachutists 10 The Medal of Honor

051

1 'Hotel California' 2 Squab 3 Walter Lantz 4 Ibis 5 Albatross, the wandering albatross has a wingspan about 4m (between 11 and 12ft) 6 Green 7 Shrike 8 Arthur Ransome 9 Alfred Hitchcock 10 The bee hummingbird, males of this species measure only 2¹/₄in (57mm) in length, and half of that length is taken up by the bill and the tail

052

1 Gauchos 2 Ponderosa 3 Hiawatha 4 Pocahontas 5 *Young Guns* 6 Scout 7 Chuck Connors 8 *The Last of the Mohicans* 9 The Hole in the Wall Gang 10 *Little Big Man*

053

1 Blind Pew 2 *The Grapes of Wrath* 3 Matt Busby. He was knighted in 1968 4 St Luke 5 George Kennedy 6 Mark Fowler in *EastEnders* 7 Luke Skywalker played by Mark Hamill 8 Richard Thomas, although in the final series he was played by Robert Wightman 9 A simple, US made free-flight rocket capable of delivering a nuclear warhead 10 Matthew Modine

054

1 Ebony 2 Epsom 3 Edelweiss 4 Ear 5 Epiphany 6 Exodus 7 Earthquakes 8 Elgin Marbles 9 ET 10 Euro

055

1 Euphrates 2 Eucalyptus 3 Epilepsy 4 *Emma* 5 Ernesto 6 Executor 7 ERNIE – Electronic Random Number Indicator Equipment 8 Elbe 9 Edinburgh 10 Edward II, murdered in Berkeley Castle

056

1 Embrasure 2 Esau, the brother of Jacob 3 Earwax 4 Eurydice 5 Exhaltation 6 *Eroica* 7 Extreme 8 Endymion 9 Echinoderms 10 The Equals

057

1 Furlong 2 Fez 3 Foreman 4 Ferrari 5 Flower 6 Flush 7 Fetlock 8 Fester 9 Fulcrum 10 Fat, which is converted into food and water

058

1 Fossils 2 *Fortissimo*, not *forte* which means loud 3 Forum 4 Fiji 5 Fallopian 6 Florence 7 Femur 8 Fingal's 9 Farthingale 10 Flatford

059

1 *Flatliners* 2 Florentine 3 Flies, as used by anglers in fly fishing 4 Firkin 5 Flotsam, as opposed to jetsam which are goods thrown overboard 6 Forget-me-not 7 Fratricide 8 Frankfurt, signed in 1871 9 Farad, named after Michael Faraday 10 *Frenzy*

060

1 Lucy Lockett 2 Nick Leeson
3 General George Custer 4 Bayern
Munich 5 *Lost in Space* 6 Tokyo
7 Shangri La 8 Gordon Banks 9 Skin
10 The Righteous Brothers, namely
Bobby Hatfield and Bill Medley

061

1 Chelsea FC 2 Red Crescent
3 China 4 Black 5 The Orange
Order 6 Purple Heart 7 White
8 Redcaps on account of their bright
red headgear 9 Captain Black 10 *Just
William*

062

1 Rowan Atkinson 2 Kidney beans
3 Buttercup 4 A la bretonne 5 Paul
Newman 6 *Goldeneye* 7 Beanie
Babies 8 Biffo 9 Hannibal Lecter,
played by Sir Anthony Hopkins in *The
Silence of the Lambs* 10 A funny
machine

063

1 Tanzania 2 Jellystone Park
3 Wallace and Gromit 4 Serpentine
5 Dinosaurs 6 *Barefoot in the Park*
7 Richard Harris. It was also
re-recorded ten years later by Donna
Summer and became a hit again
8 Gatcombe Park 9 Isaac Hayes
10 Yellowstone National Park

064

1 Chlorophyll 2 L.M. Montgomery
3 A plum 4 The Ecology Party
5 Booker T and the MG's 6 Cape
Farewell 7 *The Green Mile* 8 The
Falklands in 1982 9 'Spirit in the Sky'
10 Wales, set in a Welsh mining village

065

1 Dodecanese, its name means 12
islands 2 *Papillon* 3 Richard Branson,
appropriately Neckar Island is one of
the Virgin Islands 4 Martinique
5 Lucy Irvine 6 Barbados
7 R.M. Ballantyne 8 Grenada 9 Chris
Blackwell 10 'I am a Rock' by Simon
and Garfunkel

066

1 Anne Frank 2 Nancy Reagan née
Davis 3 Nelson Mandela 4 101
5 Brooklyn Beckham, son of Victoria
and David 6 Diana, Princess of Wales
7 Rocco, son of Madonna and Guy
Ritchie 8 Ronnie Biggs 9 Adolf Hitler

10 David Duchovny who plays Fox
Mulder in *The X Files*

067

1 Bruce Springsteen 2 Whitney
Houston 3 Carly Simon 4 Roy
Orbison 5 Tina Turner 6 George
Harrison 7 Gloria Estefan 8 Will
Young 9 Cyndi Lauper 10 Janet
Jackson

068

1 Angela Lansbury 2 Harold
Macmillan 3 Jane Austen 4 Tony Blair
5 Beatrix Potter 6 Chairman Mao
Tse-tung 7 Desmond Tutu 8 Elvis
Presley 9 James Dean, who died
driving a Porsche 550 Spyder 10 John
Cleese

069

1 Mother Teresa 2 Bobby Robson
3 Andy Warhol 4 Michael Bentine
5 Abraham Lincoln 6 Elton John
7 Barbra Streisand 8 Yuri Gagarin,
who orbited the earth in 1961
9 A.A. Milne, the creator of Winnie
the Pooh 10 Pele

070

1 Charlie Chaplin 2 Daniel Radcliffe.
He shares a birthday with J K Rowling,
author of the *Harry Potter* books
3 Raymond Burr who played the San
Francisco detective Ironside 4 Roger
Moore 5 Phil Silvers who played
Sergeant Bilko 6 Denzel Washington
7 Tommy Lee Jones 8 Desi Arnaz
9 Kevin Spacey 10 Doris Day

071

1 Rudyard Kipling 2 Martin Luther
King 3 Robert Runcie 4 Sir Thomas
More 5 Benito Mussolini 6 Sigmund
Freud 7 Richard III 8 Marilyn
Monroe would have celebrated her
74th birthday. She was born on June, 1
1926 9 Pablo Picasso 10 Thomas
Telford

072

1 Bangkok 2 A dog 3 Cain and Abel
4 Mary Whitehouse 5 A synagogue
6 'Into the groove' 7 George Orwell
in the novel *1984* 8 Malta 9 Special
Air Service 10 John le Carré

073

1 Prince Otto von Bismarck
2 A smoked herring 3 New York
4 *Notting Hill* 5 Vienna 6 Six, and

two mainland territories 7 One who
practises in, and deals with, ailments of
the feet 8 Microsoft 9 Pale blue
10 A shortening of BInary digiT

074

1 Adam Ant 2 The Flying Flea
3 Entomology 4 Peter Parker, who
became Spiderman after being bitten
by a radioactive spider
5 Arachnophobia 6 Formic acid
7 The Goliath beetle which on average
weighs between 70 and 100 grams
8 Michael Keaton 9 *Kung Fu*
10 Termite

075

1 Arnold Schwarzenegger 2 'Never
Ever' 3 Green 4 'For Valour'
5 Tokyo 6 *Oxford English Dictionary*
7 Killer whale 8 Cabbage 9 MI6
10 Leeds

076

1 *The Financial Times* 2 Boxing
3 Hair 4 A boat 5 Edward VII
6 One 7 Rovers 8 Ten 9 Los
Angeles 10 Israel

077

1 Seven (A to G) 2 Sir Stanley
Matthews 3 1980 4 Five 5 Anthony
Trollope 6 Physics 7 Chris Patten
8 Saturn 9 Severe Acute Respiratory
Syndrome 10 Polo

078

1 In Mary Shelley's Frankenstein
2 The venue for the FA Cup Final
3 *Butch Cassidy and the Sundance Kid*,
Henry Longbaugh being the Kid's real
name 4 Blair: Dr Kildare worked at
Blair General Hospital, Eric Blair is the
real name of George Orwell the
author of *1984* and Prime Minister
Tony Blair was once a member of a
pop group called The Ugly Rumours
5 All are mentioned in the lyrics of
the song 'Where do you go to my
Lovely' by Peter Sarstedt 6 They have
all competed in the Olympic Games,
Princess Anne in equestrian events, Dr
Spock in rowing and Errol Flynn in
boxing 7 Amsterdam. These places
are mentioned in that order in the
lyrics of 'The Ballad of John and Yoko'.
8 Norman Bates played by Anthony
Perkins in the *Psycho* films 9 Lemuel
10 First film to win a Best Picture
Oscar 11 Juliet – it is NATO's

phonetic alphabet: Echo, Foxtrot, Golf, Hotel, India... **12** They are all works based on Shakespeare's *Romeo and Juliet* **13** The Brady Bunch **14** *War of the Worlds*. H.G. Wells wrote the novel; Gene Barry played the lead male role in the 1953 film version; Orson Welles produced a radio version; Jeff Wayne wrote and produced a concept album inspired by the novel **15** Peach Melba (Helen Mitchell is the real name of Dame Nellie Melba)

079

1 Rupert the Bear **2** Sow **3** Baloo **4** Theodore (Teddy) Roosevelt **5** Cindy **6** A bearskin **7** Michael Bond **8** Kodiak bears **9** Danny DeVito **10** A.A. Milne

080

1 Carlsberg lager **2** William Hurt **3** His second best bed **4** George Best **5** *To a Mouse* by Robert Burns **6** 'The Summer of '69' **7** *The Best Little Whorehouse in Texas* **8** Gladys Knight and the Pips **9** Basketball **10** Supporter

081

1 Garlic **2** Garnet **3** Gypsies **4** Gallon **5** Gruel **6** Ganges **7** Goat **8** Guillotine **9** Gizzard **10** Gridiron

082

1 Geisha **2** Genocide **3** Galvanization **4** Geriatrics **5** Griffin **6** Ghana **7** Gyroscope **8** Genetically and the M stands for modified **9** Gnu **10** Guilder

083

1 Galileo **2** Gallifrey **3** Gerrymandering **4** Gout **5** Greenfly **6** Gallipoli **7** George II, in the Battle of Dettingen of 1743 **8** Gendarme **9** Gnomon **10** Guinevere

084

1 Hercules **2** *Heidi* **3** Halo **4** Hammer **5** Henry V **6** Hungarian, his name was Laszlo Biro **7** Harvard **8** Hogmanay **9** Havana **10** Haggis

085

1 Hobbit **2** Handmade **3** Hen **4** Hemlock **5** Hippocrates **6** Hitler's **7** *Hamlet* **8** Harare **9** Henna **10** Hectare

086

1 Harpy **2** Humidity **3** Hippodrome **4** Husky **5** Homer the Greek poet acquired his nickname because he lived by the River Meander **6** Hamilton **7** Hypochondriac **8** Herbert and the D stands for David **9** Hale-Bopp **10** Hassock

087

1 10cc **2** Telly Savalas **3** David Beckham **4** Errol Brown **5** 'Help me Make it through the Night', written by Kris Kristofferson **6** Nik Kershaw **7** Blackbeard **8** A breed of dog **9** Bo Derek **10** Samson

088

1 Merlin **2** Barry Manilow **3** Claudia Schiffer **4** Professor Albus Dumbledore **5** Magic Johnson **6** *Highlander* **7** George Lucas **8** Puff the Magic Dragon **9** Ermintrude **10** 1967

089

1 Damascus **2** Albert De Salvo **3** John Sousa **4** Jack Dempsey **5** Andrew Jackson **6** Bryan Adams **7** Kookaburra **8** Doris Day **9** Babe Ruth **10** James I

090

1 *The Sting* **2** King of hearts **3** American Express **4** These are the two divisions in a pack of Tarot cards, which are then divided into the four suits of cups, swords, pentacles and wands **5** Omar Sharif **6** The Knave of Hearts **7** Ian Richardson **8** Ten **9** The Queen of Hearts **10** Motorhead

091

1 The Mr Men **2** The Merry Wives of Windsor **3** Mr Benn **4** *Mrs Brown* **5** David Copperfield **6** Joe DiMaggio **7** J. P. Marquand **8** Mr Magoo **9** Mrs Goggins **10** Sally Field

092

1 Alfred Nobel **2** J. Robert Oppenheimer, inventor of the atom bomb **3** A roulette wheel **4** Nylon **5** Spencer Tracy **6** Mickey Rooney **7** Kaleidoscope **8** Hungarian **9** Michael Redgrave **10** Hedy Lamarr. She devised a system of frequency changing to prevent remote control missiles and torpedos being jammed.

093

1 Ellis Peters **2** Shirley Maclaine **3** Utah **4** A grandmother **5** Humphrey Bogart **6** Harriet Beecher Stowe **7** Mycroft **8** Adam Sandler **9** Gerald Durrell **10** Sister Sledge

094

1 The sword Excalibur **2** *Loch Ness* **3** Lake Victoria **4** 'I Believe In Father Christmas' **5** The Caspian Sea (A lake is any body of water surrounded by land and very large lakes are sometimes called seas.) **6** The Sea of Galilee **7** Coniston Water **8** Lake Ontario **9** The Winter Olympics **10** Crocodile

095

1 Pepper Anderson **2** *The Mona Lisa* **3** Stuart Copeland **4** David Niven **5** *The Remorseful Day* **6** Procrastination **7** Jan Hammer **8** *The Blue Lamp* **9** Danny Glover **10** Sam Bass

096

1 Karen Blixen (her real name was Isak Dinesen) played in the film by Meryl Streep **2** Sudan **3** Mali **4** C. S. Forester **5** Toto **6** Abyssinia, which is now called Ethiopia **7** Zanzibar **8** Cairo, the capital of Egypt **9** Nigeria **10** Botswana

097

1 Earl of Wessex **2** Switzerland **3** Libya **4** Lee Marvin **5** Public limited company **6** The Smiths **7** Chief superintendent **8** April 23rd (St George's Day) **9** Germany **10** Ostrich

098

1 The hippopotamus **2** Grand Slam **3** Group Captain **4** 12 **5** :) [colon, closed bracket] **6** Federal Republic of Yugoslavia **7** A single dot **8** Autumn **9** Abu Dhabi **10** The face

099

1 Michael Knighton, chairman of Carlisle after narrowly avoiding relegation **2** Kosovo **3** Senator Bob Dole **4** Charon **5** On British coinage. It is short for '*Dei Gratia Regina Fidei Defensor*' (By the Grace of God, Queen, Defender of the Faith)

6 Albania 7 She would be an Honourable 8 Hot Chocolate 9 Straw weight 10 She was the oldest female competitor to date in an Olympic games

100
1 Lulu 2 SNOW (if you run together the chemical symbols Sn, O, W) 3 Route 66 4 Points of the compass: *Westworld*, Southfork, Clint Eastwood, Oliver North 5 JFK 6 It means 'quickly' – the word was picked up by French soldiers in Russian taverns during the Napoleonic wars. 7 They were all brought up by people other than their true parents 8 The novel *1984* 9 The Moon: *Au Clair de Lune*, *Moonlight Sonata* and *Bad Moon Rising* 10 They all have a bun or cake named after them 11 Green 12 Citrus fruits: Harry Lime, Jack Lemmon, the House of Orange, Satsuma ware 13 *Sesame Street* 14 F – (as in the musical scale Do, Re Mi, Fa, Sol, La, Ti, Do) 15 Gustave (first name of Mahler, Holst – composer of *The Planets*, and M. Eiffel)

101
1 Napoleon Bonaparte 2 Yorick 3 Rickets 4 206 5 He-Man 6 Scapula 7 King Kong 8 'Bohemian Rhapsody' 9 DeForest Kelley 10 Collar bone

102
1 Scalene 2 Twenty 3 Gandalf 4 Belinda Carlisle 5 John Nash 6 *Gentlemen Prefer Blondes* 7 Atoll 8 Brasilia 9 Iman, the wife of David Bowie 10 Colorado

103
1 Incisors 2 Indigo 3 Ice hockey 4 Insomnia 5 Islam 6 Ireland 7 India 8 Insulin 9 Illinois 10 Ivan

104
1 Indigestion 2 Iberia 3 Imperial, ICI stands for Imperial Chemical Industries 4 Incubator 5 Islamabad 6 'If' 7 Ivanhoe 8 Incas 9 Indonesia, behind China, India and the US 10 Incubus

105
1 Ichthyologist 2 *Ishtar* 3 Insects 4 Ishmael 5 Ivory, the 14th wedding anniversary 6 Irises by Vincent Van

Gogh 7 Irrawaddy 8 Ileum 9 Iran 10 Ikebana

106
1 Javelin 2 James 3 Jeans 4 Juliet 5 Jodhpurs 6 Jericho 7 Jaundice 8 Job 9 Jack 10 Jabberwocky

107
1 Kidneys 2 Kaiser 3 Korean War 4 Kindergarten (*Kindergarten Cop*) 5 Kneecap 6 Kama 7 Korky 8 Kamikaze 9 Keystone Kops 10 Kremlin

108
1 Kedgeree 2 Kibbutz 3 *Kismet* 4 Kappa 5 Kosher 6 Kenneth 7 Kentucky 8 Kashmir 9 *Klute* 10 Kitten

109
1 President John F. Kennedy 2 Dorothy Parker 3 Winston Churchill 4 Groucho Marx 5 Mao Tse-tung 6 Edmund Burke 7 Ralph Waldo Emerson 8 Albert Einstein 9 Oscar Wilde 10 Benjamin Franklin

110
1 New Zealand 2 Brazil 3 France 4 Greece 5 Mexico 6 Madagascar 7 Sri Lanka 8 Portugal 9 Norway 10 Vietnam

111
1 Luftwaffe 2 The Pope 3 The Village People 4 *GI Jane* 5 *Carry On Sergeant* 6 Napoleon Bonaparte 7 Who Dares Wins 8 19 9 The French Foreign Legion 10 The Royal Navy

112
1 W.C. Fields 2 Thomas Gainsborough 3 Johnny Mathis 4 The Great Ormond Street Hospital 5 Paediatrician 6 Captain Marryat 7 Loving and giving 8 Dr Benjamin Spock 9 Richard III 10 Anna Paquin

113
1 Philadelphia 2 Charleston 3 Detroit 4 Rhode Island 5 Phoenix 6 The President of the United States. It is the address of The White House 7 Pittsburgh, named after William Pitt 8 Jamestown 9 Hawaii 10 Nashville

114
1 Oxford 2 Stephen King 3 Snickers 4 Sebastian Coe. He was William Hague's chief of staff 5 Runaround Sue 6 Alan Sillitoe 7 Kevin Rowlands 8 Harold Abrahams 9 111 10 Jesse Owens

115
1 King Duncan 2 Jack the Ripper 3 John George Haigh 4 Aldo Moro 5 Sharon Tate 6 Nancy Spungen 7 The Land of Nod 8 The Democratic Republic of Congo 9 Gianni Versace 10 John Gotti

116
1 John Hurt 2 Stevie Wonder 3 Bull 4 Timothy 5 The Republican Party 6 Howdah 7 Babar the Elephant 8 Jumbo 9 Rudyard Kipling 10 Denmark

117
1 Jack Nicholson 2 Jackie Charlton 3 Jack Jones 4 Jack Dawkins 5 Jack Nicklaus 6 Jackie Chan 7 Jackie Stewart 8 Jackie Wilson 9 Jack London 10 Jack Palance

118
1 Christopher Lee 2 Arrows 3 Axl Rose 4 The Battle of the Somme 5 Dum Dum 6 *The Threepenny Opera* 7 Samuel Colt 8 Magnum 44 9 Alistair MacLean 10 A type of spear used by Zulu warriors

119
1 Neptune 2 Mercury 3 Duran Duran 4 Metropolis 5 Uranus (Miranda, Oberon, Titania, Ariel and Umbriel. The last is from Pope's *Rape of the Lock*) 6 Mars 7 *The Tempest* 8 Holst 9 Tim Burton 10 Saturn

120
1 *One Million Years BC* 2 Bobby Vee 3 911 4 Vinnie Jones 5 40 6 35 7 The number 13 8 Cecil B de Mille 9 Vivaldi 10 *The Wild One*

121
1 A tangelo 2 A flavour-enhancing mould (Botrytis cinerea) used in the production of wines 3 Arabic 4 Sarsaparilla 5 Cheshire cheese 6 Jerez de la Frontera 7 Alimentary canal 8 Candlemas 9 Fugu fish. If not prepared properly the chef can release a deadly poison from the fish's internal

organs (tetrodotoxin, a powerful neurotoxin) that can cause death in approximately 60 per cent of persons who ingest it **10** India

122

1 Lair **2** Lucifer **3** Lemur **4** Lasso **5** Lama **6** Lectern **7** Lion **8** Litter **9** Lloyd's **10** Lilliput

123

1 Latex **2** Lurcher **3** Liffey **4** Lactic acid **5** Lazarus **6** Librarian **7** Legion **8** London **9** Litmus paper **10** 'Layla'

124

1 Lymph **2** Lepidopterist **3** Laburnum **4** Lammas **5** Lyre **6** Luanda **7** *Lolita* **8** Lyonnaise **9** Lakes **10** Libretto

125

1 Manhattan **2** Marathon **3** Mars **4** Marsupial **5** Muesli **6** Merman **7** Mecca **8** Mallet **9** Mead **10** Mac

126

1 Magma **2** Mah-jongg **3** Miracles **4** Mace **5** Mercer **6** Metronome **7** Mandarin **8** Myxomatosis **9** Manifesto **10** 'Michelle'

127

1 Meridian **2** Midshipman **3** Mandible **4** Minaret **5** Marchioness **6** Mantilla **7** Meerschaum **8** Mezzo-soprano **9** Minotaur **10** Methodist

128

1 Nike **2** *Neighbours* **3** Nairobi **4** Nectar **5** Nicholas **6** Never Never Land **7** National Guard **8** Nile **9** Nagasaki **10** Newton, after Sir Isaac Newton who discovered gravity

129

1 Naples **2** Nave **3** Nicaragua **4** *Nautilus* **5** Nutmeg **6** Noah **7** Nutria **8** Needles **9** Nuncio **10** Nirvana

130

1 Nagano, Japan **2** Newspeak **3** Numismatist **4** Narwhal **5** Nubian **6** Naphthalene **7** Nyctophobia **8** Numerator **9** Nesta **10** Necrotizing fasciitis

131

1 Oasis **2** Old Bailey **3** Oscars **4** Ostrich **5** Olive **6** Orbit **7** Obtuse **8** Onyx **9** Obituary **10** Ohm

132

1 Obverse **2** Olympus **3** Opaque **4** Orienteering **5** Ornithology **6** Overture **7** Orang-utan **8** Opossum **9** Omega **10** Oast

133

1 *Opus* **2** Octopussy **3** Otitis **4** Ombudsman **5** Oology **6** Ottoman **7** Oubliette **8** Oxonian **9** Ophthalmologist **10** Oedipus

134

1 Meatloaf **2** Fifteen **3** Gotham City **4** Alan Ball **5** Table tennis bat **6** Pawnbroker **7** Sir Garfield (Gary) Sobers **8** A batman **9** *Last of the Summer Wine* **10** Casey Jones

135

1 Mad Max **2** Lex Luthor **3** Black box **4** Texas **5** Flax **6** Roxanne **7** T. Rex **8** Alexandre Dumas **9** *Taxi Driver* **10** Chickenpox

136

1 'My Generation' **2** Dean Cain **3** Little Nell **4** *The Blue Max* **5** New Edition **6** Prince Charles **7** Franklin D. Roosevelt **8** Green **9** The New Seekers **10** Lend-Lease programme

137

1 Cape of Good Hope **2** Walter Matthau **3** *Little Women* **4** Donna Summer **5** Sergio Leone **6** Bad Manners **7** Bob Hoskins **8** 1987 **9** James Hilton **10** Mae West

138

1 German **2** Scotland **3** A bull **4** Venice **5** Finland **6** The monarchy **7** Hungary **8** Switzerland **9** Genoa **10** Turkey

139

1 Mount Ararat **2** The feeding of the five thousand **3** Ruth and Esther **4** Mary Magdalene **5** Matthias **6** Pentateuch **7** 'Jesus wept' (John 11:35) **8** The Ten Commandments **9** Book of Revelation **10** The Garden of Gethsemane

140

1 George Lucas **2** On the front of the *Starship Enterprise* in *Star Trek* **3** Buck Rogers **4** Arthur C. Clarke **5** The Jetsons **6** Dirk Benedict **7** Douglas Adams **8** Ridley Scott **9** Patrick Stewart **10** Frank Herbert

141

1 Loretta Swit **2** Cryogenics **3** Billy Wilder **4** Pluto **5** *Cat On A Hot Tin Roof* **6** Cold sore **7** Rod Steiger **8** Gazpacho **9** Montgolfier **10** Dry ice

142

1 The Tsar Kolokol is the world's largest bell weighing 180 tonnes and was cast in 1735 but broke before it ever rang **2** *For Whom the Bell Tolls* **3** Alastair Sim **4** Erasure **5** Campanology **6** Quasimodo, the Hunchback of Notre Dame **7** Anita Ward **8** Julia Roberts **9** Vietnam **10** Alexander Graham Bell

143

1 Like a horse and carriage **2** Andre Agassi **3** Erich Segal **4** Andie MacDowell **5** Ten years **6** The Beatles **7** Mick Jagger **8** Aristotle Onassis **9** D.H. Lawrence **10** Tomato

144

1 *A Tale of Two Cities* **2** Boz **3** Fagin **4** Marshalsea Prison **5** *Great Expectations* **6** *Bleak House* **7** *A Christmas Carol* **8** Nicholas Nickleby **9** *Barnaby Rudge* **10** *The Mystery of Edwin Drood*

145

1 Komodo Dragon **2** Odin, the King of the Viking Gods **3** Captain Flint **4** Hearts **5** Guinea Pig **6** The Unicorn. It was a 'supporter' of the coat of arms of James VI of Scotland and was incorporated into the Royal Coat of arms on his accession to the throne. It has remained ever since. **7** Jill **8** King cobra **9** Whelp **10** Bats

146

1 Croatia **2** Chile **3** Colombia **4** Costa Rica **5** Republic of Chad **6** Canada **7** Cuba **8** Cyprus **9** Cambodia **10** Cameroon

147

1 Canterbury Cathedral **2** Libel **3** Charles Lindbergh **4** Los Angeles **5** 1964 **6** Salim Malik **7** Abraham Lincoln who was shot whilst watching a play called *Our American Cousin* in Ford's Theatre, Washington **8** O.J. Simpson **9** Moscow **10** Son of Sam

148

1 Thomas Hardy 2 Oliver Goldsmith 3 Robert Louis Stevenson 4 John le Carré 5 Yukio Mishima 6 Thomas Mann 7 Leslie Thomas 8 James M. Cain 9 Henry James 10 James Joyce

149

1 Sweden 2 Metro 3 Vaporetti 4 Georgia 5 Amoco Cadiz 6 The Ford Edsel 7 Bristol Brabazon, built in 1948 with a 180 passenger capacity 8 Mumbai 9 The *Mary Rose*, the flagship of Henry VIII 10 The Chattanooga Choo Choo. This was also the title of the first ever song to receive a gold disc

150

1 Arabic 2 Chinese 3 Hebrew 4 Russian 5 Greek 6 Vietnamese 7 Potuguese 8 Irish Gaelic 9 Hindi 10 Icelandic

151

1 Sidney Poitier, for the 1963 film *Lilies of the Field* 2 Windsurfing 3 Carlos Santana 4 Children's literature, specifically for book illustrations 5 Winston Churchill 6 Ruud Gullit 7 Barbra Streisand 8 Marlon Brando 9 Peter Finch, for the 1976 film *Network* 10 The Palme d'Or

152

1 Chile 2 Venezuela 3 Suriname 4 Montevideo 5 Argentina 6 Rio de Janeiro 7 Paraguay 8 Lake Titicaca 9 The sucre 10 Colombia

153

1 Advent 2 The Grinch 3 Jacob Marley 4 Capricorn 5 Holly 6 Hollywood 7 *Twelfth Night* 8 Indian Ocean 9 Cupid 10 Sir Isaac Newton

154

1 Midge Ure 2 Bing Crosby 3 'Happy Christmas War is Over' by John Lennon 4 Wizzard 5 Cliff Richard 6 Eight maids a-milking 7 Irving Berlin 8 Dickie Valentine 9 'Away in a Manger' 10 Harry Belafonte

155

1 Coca-Cola featured Santa in an advertisement as a plump humorous person rather than an elf in a green suit 2 Os o 3 Ptarmigan 4 The Ugly Sisters 5 Raymond Briggs 6 'Winter Wonderland' 7 Dick Whittington 8 St Stephen 9 George V, in a radio broadcast of a speech that was written by Rudyard Kipling 10 Tibet

156

1 Little Jack Horner 2 Caribou 3 The Goons 4 The Three Wise Men 5 Shepherds 6 Rubik's Cube 7 A football match took place in No Man's Land 8 Prague 9 Dana 10 Mikhail Gorbachev

157

1 Bill Murray 2 Richard Attenborough 3 *It's a Wonderful Life* 4 *The World is Not Enough* 5 *Jingle all the Way* 6 Michael Caine 7 Jack Frost 8 Aled Jones 9 Hulk Hogan 10 Tom Conti

158

1 Poult 2 Swedish 3 Clement Moore 4 Melbourne in 1956 5 Dora Bryan 6 Bohemia 7 The Seychelles 8 Santa Claus 9 *Holiday Inn* 10 J.S. Bach

159

1 Paddy 2 Panama 3 Pelican 4 Philatelist 5 Phoenix 6 Patrick 7 Pasteurisation 8 Pistachio 9 Paprika 10 Palindrome

160

1 Pompeii 2 Pirouette 3 Pampas 4 Parable 5 Pentecost 6 Pharmacology 7 Piebald 8 Pistil 9 Plaintiff 10 Plutonium

161

1 Polaris 2 Pedometer 3 Plover 4 *Pianissimo* 5 Pinniped 6 Palaeontology 7 Pan 8 Pyx 9 Pulmonary 10 Pinion

162

1 Quaver 2 Quidditch, in the Harry Potter books 3 Quire 4 Quakers 5 Quiver 6 Quoits 7 Queen 8 Quartermaster 9 Quebec 10 Quecha

163

1 Rowan 2 Regatta 3 Rookery 4 Rayon 5 Rabies 6 Renaissance 7 Rutland 8 Rye 9 Radiography 10 Rouble

164

1 Rowel 2 Ruminant 3 Regicide 4 Raisa 5 Rowlock 6 Ruritania 7 Roxette 8 Ribbentrop 9 Rampant 10 *Rebecca*

165

1 Swarm 2 *Showboat* 3 Sonnet 4 Shamrock 5 Scrabble 6 Screwdriver 7 Scalpel 8 Seven 9 Shark 10 SS, an abbreviation of Schutzstaffel, German for 'Protective Echelon'

166

1 Senne 2 Sanskrit 3 Sarajevo 4 *Spartacus* 5 Symphony 6 Senlac 7 Semibreve 8 Stromboli 9 Sternum 10 Stenographer

167

1 Sacramento 2 Scree 3 Sable 4 Stupa 5 Sharia 6 Semantics 7 Sulky 8 Spy Wednesday 9 Snowman 10 Staples, and the C stands for Clive

168

1 Touchline 2 *Thriller* 3 Tunisia 4 Theology 5 Tutu 6 Trident 7 Troggs 8 Tudor 9 Triads 10 Tsetse

169

1 Teenagers 2 Tetanus 3 Topiary 4 *The Terminator* 5 Tapioca 6 *Tommy* 7 Tequila 8 Terrestrial 9 Thoroughbred 10 Trinitrotoluene

170

1 Titania 2 Troon 3 Turmeric 4 Troposphere 5 Trichology 6 Troika 7 Turkish 8 Trilby 9 Trampolining 10 Taffrail

171

1 Mrs Robinson in *The Graduate* 2 George and Ira Gershwin 3 They have all played Joseph in *Joseph and the Technicolor Dreamcoat* 4 *The King and I* 5 *Macbeth* 6 T.S. Eliot 7 Vietnam 8 Broadway 9 *Camelot* 10 Manchester United

172

1 Citrus 2 Stairs 3 Kiwi fruit 4 Idaho 5 Anton Chekhov 6 Parsnips 7 'Strawberry Fields Forever' 8 Vincent van Gogh 9 Mange tout 10 Loganberry

7 Ken Russell 8 Austin Powers 9 *My Best Friend's Wedding* 10 *Enemy at the Gates*

269
1 Walnut Grove 2 *Independence Day* 3 *Shirley Valentine* 4 John Belushi 5 *Brideshead Revisited* 6 *Gone with the Wind* 7 *The Apartment* 8 *House of Cards* 9 *Man about the House* 10 *Bless this House*. It ran from 1971–1976

270
1 Michael Ondaatje 2 William Friedkin 3 *The Italian Job* 4 Switzerland 5 Cycling 6 *The Maltese Falcon* 7 Hugh Grant 8 *French Kiss* 9 Michael Douglas 10 *For Your Eyes Only*, the actor being Topol

271
1 *Cleopatra* 2 *Natural Born Killers* 3 Tony Robinson 4 Indiana Jones 5 *Anaconda* 6 *Snake Eyes* 7 Kaa 8 *Cobra* 9 *Monty Python and the Holy Grail* 10 *Live and Let Die*

272
1 *Beauty and the Beast* 2 Monstro 3 *Fantasia* 4 *The Aristocats* 5 Pongo and Perdita 6 A bear 7 Flower 8 *Pocahontas* 9 *The Lion King* 10 *The Rescuers*, the sequel being *The Rescuers Down Under*

273
1 Talia Shire 2 Anne Archer 3 *The War of the Roses* 4 Tony Curtis and Janet Leigh 5 Mel Brooks 6 Peter Sellers 7 Rita Hayworth 8 Melanie Griffith and Antonio Banderas 9 Carole Lombard 10 Hattie Jacques

274
1 Ice hockey 2 *Jerry Maguire* 3 *Escape to Victory* 4 Baseball 5 Hugh Hudson 6 *Rollerball* 7 Nick Hornby 8 Paul Newman 9 *Rocky* 10 *The Legend of Bagger Vance*

275
1 Derek Jacobi 2 Uncle Buck 3 George Clooney 4 James Caan 5 Morticia 6 Kim Basinger 7 Napoleon Solo 8 *Sister Act* 9 *Father Ted* 10 They both have plots that revolve around twins

276
1 Leslie Nielsen 2 Tom Cruise 3 Bram Stoker 4 Klaus Kinski 5 Sarah Michelle Gellar 6 Anthony Hopkins 7 *From Dusk till Dawn* 8 Christopher Lee 9 George Hamilton 10 Bela Lugosi

277
1 Rosanna Arquette 2 Richard Attenborough 3 Julie Andrews 4 Jean Alexander 5 Don Ameche 6 Dan Aykroyd 7 Gillian Anderson 8 Alan Alda 9 Woody Allen 10 Jenny Agutter

278
1 John Mortimer 2 Raymond Burr 3 *A Few Good Men* 4 Martin Shaw 5 *Presumed Innocent* 6 *LA Law* 7 *Kavanagh QC* 8 *Twelve Angry Men* 9 *Jagged Edge* 10 Kelly McGillis

279
1 *One Million Years BC* 2 *1984* 3 Anne Boleyn 4 *48 Hours* 5 *Brewster's Millions* 6 666 7 *9 to 5* 8 The Three Stooges 9 *Nine and a half weeks* 10 *The Ten Commandments*

280
1 Demi Moore 2 *You've Got Mail*. They also starred in *Sleepless in Seattle* and *Joe Versus the Volcano* 3 Emma Thompson 4 Sally Field 5 Julie Walters 6 Katharine Hepburn 7 Shelley Duval 8 Goldie Hawn 9 Faye Dunaway 10 Gwyneth Paltrow

281
1 *Who Wants to be a Millionaire* 2 *And Now For Something Completely Different* 3 Dame Edna Everage 4 Jack Lord 5 *The Price is Right* 6 Porky Pig 7 *Terminator* 8 Kojak 9 Dick Dastardly 10 Anne Robinson

282
1 *The Towering Inferno* 2 *The Poseidon Adventure* 3 Morgan Freeman 4 Kate Winslett 5 *Armageddon* 6 *The Hindenberg* 7 *The Perfect Storm* 8 Pierce Brosnan 9 *The China Syndrome* 10 Jeff Goldblum

283
1 *Seven* 2 Yul Brynner 3 *Seven* 4 Sherlock Holmes 5 *Seven Brides for Seven Brothers* 6 *The Seven Year Itch* 7 Frank Sinatra 8 1937 9 *Seven Years in Tibet* 10 Akira Kurosawa

284
1 *Angel* 2 *The Virginian* 3 *Happy Days* 4 *A Different World* 5 *Star Trek: Voyager* 6 *Upstairs Downstairs* 7 *Softly, Softly*. It was a spin-off from *Z Cars* 8 *Wacky Races* 9 *The Rockford Files* 10 They were spin-offs from *The Mary Tyler Moore Show*

285
1 *As Good as it Gets* 2 Ray Milland 3 *Endless Love* 4 Bonnie and Clyde 5 Kate Capshaw 6 Milford 7 *Lady and The Tramp* 8 Jane Wyman 9 *To Have and Have Not* 10 *Woman of the Year*, made in 1942

286
1 Helicopter 2 Robin Reliant van 3 Tardis (stands for Time and Relative Dimensions in Space) 4 Motorcycle with sidecar 5 Reverend Awdry 6 *Airwolf* 7 Ford Torino 8 Peter Perfect 9 Erik Estrada 10 Pike was the captain of the USS *Enterprise* in the pilot episode of *Star Trek*

287
1 Judy Garland 2 John Wayne 3 Robert Shaw 4 Alan Ladd 5 Natalie Wood 6 Dean Martin 7 Richard Harris 8 Steve McQueen 9 Bette Davis 10 Edward G. Robinson

288
1 *How Green was my Valley* 2 Stanley Kubrick 3 Quasimodo. The Sunday after Easter Sunday is called Low Sunday, or Quasimodo Sunday. Salvatore Quasimodo, an Italian poet, won 1959 Nobel prize for literature, and Anthony Quinn played Quasimodo in the 1956 film *Notre Dame de Paris* 4 *The Usual Suspects* 5 Hopalong Cassidy 6 Joel Schumacher 7 The French actor Yves Montand whose screen character died of a cardiac arrest in the film *IP5* 8 Richard Gere (*Breathless*) 9 Anthony Hopkins (*Silence of the Lambs*) 10 Roger Moore

289
1 Endeavour 2 Shirley Temple 3 Katherine Hepburn 4 Liza Minnelli, who won a best actress Oscar for the 1972 film *Cabaret*. Her mother Judy Garland won a special Academy award in 1939 and her father Vincente

Minnelli won a best director Oscar for the 1958 film *Gigi* **5** United Network Command for Law Enforcement **6** Oscar Hammerstein **7** Casey Jean **8** The dialogue is spoken entirely in Esperanto **9** *It Happened One Night.* Vest sales plummeted when the film star Clark Gable removed his shirt to reveal he was not wearing one **10** They were R2D2 and C3PO in the Star Wars films **11** Wayne (Bruce Wayne, Wayne Fontana, John Wayne) **12** They are the Warner Brothers, who owned the rights to Bugs **13** *Jemima* **14** *Field of Dreams* **15** Vienna (in *Rising Damp*)

290

1 New Zealand **2** Mick Jagger **3** Erinsborough High **4** *Home and Away* **5** *The Flying Doctors* **6** *The Sullivans* **7** *Walkabout* **8** Sir Les Patterson **9** Russell Crowe **10** Abba

291

1 The Borg **2** Alan Rickman **3** Darth Vader **4** Professor Moriarty **5** Oliver Reed **6** Emperor Zurg **7** Rosa Klebb **8** Psychiatry **9** *Apocalypse Now* **10** Gene Hackman

292

1 *The Fisher King* **2** C.S. Lewis **3** Umberto Eco **4** Mario Puzo **5** *The Dam Busters* **6** Lucy Irvine **7** Irwin Shaw **8** Charles Webb **9** *Remains of the Day* **10** Tess of the D'Urbervilles

293

1 Mick Jagger **2** Val Kilmer **3** David Bowie **4** Ritchie Valens **5** Madonna **6** Jennifer Lopez **7** Ike Turner, the husband of Tina who was played by Angela Bassett **8** Kurt Russell **9** Phil Collins **10** Huey Lewis

294

1 Sylvester Stallone **2** *Austin Powers: International Man of Mystery* **3** Seven **4** Terence Stamp **5** *Grease II* **6** *The Wrath of Khan* **7** Friday the 13th. The first film was made in 1980, the last, *Freddy vs Jason*, was made in 2003 **8** Danny deVito **9** *The Omen* **10** *The Return of the Jedi*

295

1 Richard Burton **2** Robert Culp **3** Sam Neill **4** Paul McCartney **5** *The Ipcress File* **6** *The Spy who Loved Me*,

the character being Jaws played by Richard Kiel **7** Robert Redford **8** *Carry on Spying*, STENCH stood for Society For the Total Extinction Of Non-Conforming Humans **9** *Harriet the Spy* **10** A bulldog

296

1 Toad Hall **2** Bullseye **3** A duck **4** Batmobile **5** *Fantasia* **6** Tweety Pie **7** Cruella de Vil **8** Red **9** The Queen Vic (or Victoria) **10** A cat

297

1 Gimli **2** Vulcan **3** Pebbles **4** Scar **5** TARDIS **6** Lurch **7** *The Lion King* **8** Sunnydale High **9** Ross **10** Tom Cruise

298

1 Four **2** Kim **3** Goblin **4** Brandybuck **5** Bruce Banner **6** Pickles **7** Eliza Thornberry **8** Thing One and Thing Two **9** Three **10** Velma

299

1 Mr C. Montgomery Burns **2** Scottish **3** Moe's Bar **4** Millhouse **5** Principal Skinner **6** *The Itchy and Scratchy Show* **7** Gumble **8** A blackboard **9** Krusty the Clown **10** Sideshow Bob

300

1 A brain **2** Green **3** Sticky spider's webs **4** A spoonful of sugar **5** Jane **6** Mike **7** Carrots **8** Balloo **9** Casper **10** Cocker spaniel

301

1 Robbie Coltrane **2** Professor Slatero Quirrell **3** Slytherin **4** Professor Severus Snape **5** Hedwig **6** A cat **7** His pet dragon sets it alight **8** A harp **9** It contains the tail feather of a phoenix **10** In the Mirror of Erised

302

1 Spinach **2** Pizza Planet **3** A cat **4** Red **5** *A Bug's Life* **6** A penguin **7** Merlin **8** Jessie **9** A crocodile **10** In the laboratory

303

1 Luke Skywalker **2** *Episode V: The Empire Strikes Back* **3** Light sabres **4** Ewoks **5** Stormtroopers **6** Chewbacca **7** Darth Maul **8** Yoda **9** Ben Kenobi, also known as Obi-Wan

Kenobi **10** Harrison Ford

304

1 His nose **2** Dumbo **3** The Seven Dwarves **4** Honey **5** Pegasus **6** Pluto **7** The genie **8** Emperor Zurg **9** Ariel **10** Mice

History

305

1 Alfred **2** Acropolis **3** Roald Amundsen **4** Attila **5** African National Congress **6** Alexandria **7** Argentina **8** Edwin E ('Buzz') Aldrin **9** Afghanistan **10** Ataturk

306

1 The collapse of the Berlin Wall **2** Glorious Revolution **3** Spartacus **4** The Stars and Stripes flag of the United States **5** Paris **6** Dublin **7** The Normans, who had conquered England **8** The Maoris **9** The Peasants' Revolt **10** Lenin

307

1 Field Marshal Erwin Rommel **2** Pol Pot **3** Viet Cong **4** Kaiser Wilhelm II **5** Argentina **6** France **7** Leonid Ilych Brezhnev **8** George Washington **9** Slobodan Milosevic **10** Reichsmarschall Hermann Göring

308

1 France **2** The Armistice came into effect, bringing the First World War to its end **3** The Declaration of Independence on 4 July **4** The Romans **5** Christopher Columbus **6** Russia **7** Kuwait **8** John F. Kennedy **9** On the surface of the Moon, by Neil Armstrong **10** Two atom bombs were dropped on Japan

309

1 London's first public flushing lavatory for men was opened **2** Cyprus **3** Waco **4** It was blown up, provoking war between Spain and the USA **5** Charles II **6** 1971 **7** The Portland Vase **8** Captain James Cook **9** The Glencoe massacre **10** Spain

310

1 Singapore **2** The Doolittle raid, after General James Doolittle who led the planes **3** Colombo **4** Bomb-carrying balloons **5** Orde Wingate

6 Leyte Gulf 7 They were code names for Japanese bombers 8 The Enola Gay, the plane that dropped the Hiroshima atom bomb 9 Okinawa 10 USS *Indianapolis*

311

1 The Spanish Armada 2 *Graf Spee* 3 *Canberra* 4 A passenger liner, the *Lusitania* was sunk by a German submarine in 1915 5 Galleys with oars 6 The surrender of Japan at the end of the Second World War 7 HMS *Victory* 8 The battle of Jutland, 1916 9 The battle of the Coral Sea 10 Guided missiles

312

1 St Patrick 2 Bloody Sunday 3 David Trimble 4 Mary Robinson 5 Leprechauns 6 Oliver Cromwell 7 The Battle of the Boyne 8 Bobby Sands 9 Trinity College 10 Eamon de Valera – the term came into use with the Constitution of 1937

313

1 Paris 2 Giant pandas 3 Emperor Hirohito of Japan 4 *The Washington Post* 5 Jimmy Carter, he was taken ill while running 6 Ayatollah Khomeini 7 Chess – Nigel Short was a juvenile master 8 Pakistan 9 In space. Astronauts Deke Slayton (US) and Alexei Leonov (USSR) were taking part in the first joint Soviet-American space mission 10 Princess Anne, who married Captain Mark Phillips

314

1 Paperclip, Johan Vaaler, 1899 2 Telephone, Alexander Graham Bell, 1876 3 Parking meter, Carl Magee, 1932 4 Difference engine (computer), Charles Babbage, 1822 5 Dishwasher, Josephine Garis Cochran, 1886 6 Bicycle, Baron Karl von Sauerbronn, 1817 7 Hovercraft, Christopher Cockerell, 1956 8 Electric iron, Henry Seeley, 1882 9 Lava lamp, Craven Walker, 1963 10 Electric chair, Edwin R. Davis, 1890

315

1 F. W. Woolworth 2 Foyle's 3 McDonald's 4 It was the first US self-service supermarket 5 The Netherlands 6 Sochiro Honda 7 Cabs – he laid on four coaches to carry passengers, charging by the hour

8 Steel 9 William Henry Hoover 10 The Salvation Army

316

1 Athens 2 Russia 3 England in the 1600s, under Charles I and Cromwell 4 Iceland's Althing 5 Fidel Castro of Cuba 6 England and Portugal 7 Tonga 8 The United States 9 One day 10 The European Commission

317

1 Dean Acheson, US Secretary of State, 1962 2 Sir Winston Churchill, British Prime Minister, 1942 3 Martin Luther King, civil rights leader, 1963 4 Harold Macmillan, British Prime Minister, 1958 5 Arthur Wellesley, Duke of Wellington, 1809 6 Harry S Truman, US President, 1958 7 Horatio Nelson, Admiral, 1798 8 Abraham Lincoln, US President, 1862 9 Margaret Thatcher, British Prime Minister, 1980 10 Richard Nixon, US President, 1973

318

1 Germany in 1885 2 Greece 3 They were the first men to reach the summit of Mt Everest 4 Cornflakes 5 Queen Victoria 6 Matthew Webb, in 1875 7 The Maoris 8 Rugby football – he was a student at Rugby School in England 9 Thomas Cook 10 'the Terrible'

319

1 Charles II 2 Charlie Chaplin 3 Prince Charles 4 Charles the Greedy 5 Karl Marx 6 Charles Darwin 7 De Gaulle 8 Ireland (he was prime minister) 9 Culloden 10 Charlemagne

320

1 Lord Shaftesbury 2 Canada 3 The City of London; kings had to ask the mayor for permission to enter the City 4 Grub Street 5 Phoenix Park 6 Pennsylvania Avenue in Washington DC 7 Red Square in Moscow 8 Yonge Street in Toronto 9 Bow Street 10 Manchester

321

1 Nell Gwynn 2 Emma Hamilton 3 Wallis Simpson 4 Eva Braun 5 Mark Antony 6 Giovanni Giacomo Casanova 7 Abelard (he was castrated) 8 Edward, Prince of Wales

(later King Edward VII) 9 King David (the lover was Bathsheba) 10 Dante

322

1 Genghis Khan 2 Alexander the Great 3 Islam 4 Alaric the Visigoth 5 The Inca empire 6 'General' Winter (i.e. the weather) 7 Czechoslovakia 8 Africa (West Africa) 9 Zulus, led by Dingiswayo 10 Japan

323

1 George Washington 2 It was the first bomb dropped on British soil in wartime 3 The Stone of Scone (now back in Scotland permanently) 4 The Japanese army 5 Winter bathing in the lake 6 Vasco da Gama 7 Isaac Newton 8 Lew Grade 9 Clara Barton 10 'White Christmas' sung by Bing Crosby

324

1 Israel 2 The Arc de Triomphe 3 Nelson 4 Egypt 5 Washington DC 6 Mount Rushmore in the Black Hills of South Dakota 7 John Kennedy 8 Edinburgh 9 First World War 10 The Great Fire of London, 1666

325

1 Buffalo Bill Cody 2 William Jefferson Clinton 3 William Boeing, founder of the aerospace corporation 4 William Wilberforce 5 William Hague 6 Germany, he was emperor during the First World War 7 William Whitelaw 8 William I, the Conqueror 9 William Pitt (the Younger) at the age of 24 10 One of the first steam locomotives, built by William Hedley to pull coal wagons

326

1 Rudolf Valentino 2 The Duke of York (later King George VI) 3 The first Winter Olympics were held in the French Alps 4 Mussolini 5 It was the first commercial film with sound 6 Isadora Duncan 7 The Charleston 8 Malcolm Campbell 9 Wall Street 10 Inside Tutankhamun's tomb, opened in 1922

327

1 A type of beer 2 Coffee 3 They drank toasts from it 4 Asparagus 5 Lampreys, he died from eating too many 6 Rabbits 7 'Sour krout' or

pickled cabbage (along with orange and lemon juice) helped ward off the disease scurvy on long voyages **8** Coca-Cola **9** Milk chocolate **10** Thanksgiving Day in the USA

328

1 Papyrus **2** Valley of the Kings **3** Abu Simbel **4** The Sphynx **5** Osiris **6** A jackal **7** The mummy of the deceased **8** Two **9** A pyramid **10** 1972

329

1 He was a polygamous Mormon **2** Winston Churchill **3** At Monza in Italy **4** The FA Cup Final was staged there **5** The new Central Underground rail line, which ran from Shepherds Bush to the Bank **6** A dance **7** Mafeking **8** New legislation raised the age limit for work in coal mines from 12 to 13 **9** The people of Ireland **10** Across the Atlantic Ocean, it was a Hamburg American liner

330

1 The Jews. The Maccabees were a family of Jewish patriots in the 2nd and 1st centuries BC **2** Joe McCarthy **3** Rob Roy **4** Niccolo Machiavelli **5** John McCarthy **6** William McKinley (Mount McKinley) **7** Harold Macmillan **8** Robert MacNamara **9** Douglas MacArthur **10** McGill

331

1 Votes for women (women's suffrage); both were leading suffragettes in the UK **2** Queen Victoria **3** Queen Elizabeth II **4** Boudicca (Boadicea) **5** Marie Curie **6** Barbara Cartland **7** Mary Shelley **8** Margaret Thatcher **9** Hillary Clinton **10** Indira Gandhi (her married name)

332

1 Chariots **2** Plebeians (plebs) **3** Julius Caesar **4** He was the first Christian emperor **5** A legion **6** The town hall **7** Jupiter, also known as Jove **8** A large catapult for throwing boulders **9** Central heating, using a fire to send warm air under floors and between walls **10** A dome – the largest in the ancient world

333

1 Pitt the Elder (The Earl of Chatham) and Pitt the Younger **2** James Callaghan

(1.87m or 6ft 1in) **3** Marquis of Salisbury (1895–1902) **4** He was a Scot, the first Scottish-born premier **5** Tony Blair **6** Ramsay Macdonald **7** Sir Anthony Eden **8** First Lord of the Treasury **9** Arthur James Balfour **10** Sir Robert Walpole

334

1 Lizzie Borden **2** Lucrezia Borgia **3** Annie Oakley **4** Lord Byron **5** She was a pirate **6** Burma (now called Myanmar) **7** Eleanor of Aquitaine **8** Egypt **9** Ancient Rome **10** Israel

335

1 Henry Ford **2** President Clinton on smoking marijuana **3** Dorothy Parker **4** George IV on meeting Caroline of Brunswick **5** Winston Churchill, in 1947 **6** Herbert Hoover **7** Queen Elizabeth I **8** Warren G Harding **9** Napoleon Bonaparte **10** David Lloyd George

336

1 Oliver (Cromwell) **2** Evita **3** Charles **4** Australia (Whitlam, Hawke, Keating) **5** France (the last Louis was only king for a day, in 1830) **6** Dwight **7** Augustus (August) **8** Anwar (Sadat) **9** Samuel (Morse and Johnson) **10** Boris (Yeltsin)

337

1 Qing Dynasty **2** Philip II **3** The Punic Wars **4** Passchendaele **5** William Pitt, the Elder **6** Kim Philby **7** Pharaoh **8** Pakistan **9** Qantas **10** Mary Quant

338

1 Pyrrhus, King of Epirus **2** Durham Cathedral **3** Philadelphia **4** Germany **5** The obelisks known as Cleopatra's Needles **6** Coventry **7** George and Martha Washington **8** Rio de Janeiro **9** Athena **10** China

339

1 First licensed woman pilot **2** Rudolf Hess **3** Paris, heading for New York **4** Charles II, who was restored as Britain's king in 1660 **5** Iran **6** They were daredevil stunt flyers, performing aerobatics and wing-walking displays **7** The North Pole **8** She was the first woman pilot to break the sound barrier **9** A parachute **10** Moses

340

1 Richard I, the Lionheart **2** King Harald V of Norway **3** The Empress Josephine, wife of Napoleon I **4** Charles I **5** Queen Isabella of Spain **6** Queen Adelaide **7** She married (1962) Juan Carlos, who became king of Spain in 1975 **8** Henry V **9** Grace Kelly, who married Prince Rainier of Monaco **10** Prince Albert, Duke of York, later King George VI

341

1 The Spartans **2** Leonidas **3** Plato **4** Columns in buildings **5** A foot soldier – it was a very long spear **6** Athens **7** Herodotus **8** Thucydides **9** Delphi **10** Socrates

342

1 Soccer's World Cup **2** King John **3** Gold – triggering the great Californian gold rush **4** Theseus **5** The remains of an ancient burial ship **6** General George Custer **7** One of his artificial legs – a replacement leg was dropped by parachute **8** George Mallory **9** Anastasia, daughter of Czar Nicholas II **10** Submarines

343

1 The USSR **2** Prince Andrew and Sarah Ferguson, The Duke and Duchess of York **3** Poland **4** Beirut, in the Lebanon **5** J.R. Ewing of the *Dallas* TV series **6** Lockerbie in Scotland **7** Edwina Currie **8** Grenada **9** The Grand Hotel in Brighton, when it was bombed by the IRA **10** Sweden

344

1 Rudolf Hess **2** Cardinal Thomas Wolsey **3** The Taj Mahal **4** Central African Republic **5** It was made of ice **6** Nero **7** The Crystal Palace **8** Brunei **9** William Randolph Hearst **10** St Petersburg

345

1 F.W. (Frederik Willem) de Klerk **2** Walker **3** Spencer **4** Lyndon Baines Johnson **5** Edward **6** James. Wilson was followed as prime minister by James Callaghan **7** Fitzgerald (after his mother's family name) **8** R.A. (Richard Austen) Butler **9** Milhous **10** Nothing. He only had an initial

346

1 He was the last person executed

there **2** London Bridge **3** Mary, Queen of Scots **4** The guillotine **5** Charles I **6** Two **7** She refused to put her head on the block **8** King Louis XVI and Queen Marie Antoinette of France **9** Oliver Cromwell, after the restoration of Charles II **10** William I, the Conqueror

347

1 William Tell **2** Mae West **3** Al Capone **4** Dr Hawley Harvey Crippen, arrested as a result of a radio message to the ship carrying him and Ethel Le Neve to Canada **5** Idi Amin **6** Robert Maxwell **7** Adolf Eichmann, executed in 1962 **8** Patty Hearst **9** Lord Lucan, who vanished and was then sought for the alleged murder of his child's nanny **10** The Gang of Four

348

1 The Falklands War of 1982 **2** El Alamein **3** Stalingrad **4** Balaklava **5** The American Revolutionary War **6** Battle of Jutland **7** Waterloo **8** The Pacific **9** The Battle of Gettysburg **10** The First World War

349

1 Margaret Thatcher **2** Joseph Stalin **3** Henry VIII **4** Germany's **5** Ronald Reagan and Bill Clinton **6** Aircraft carriers **7** Erwin Rommel, German commander of the Afrika Corps in the Second World War **8** British prime minister Harold Macmillan **9** Winston Churchill **10** Napoleon Bonaparte

350

1 Samuel de Champlain **2** New France **3** United Empire Loyalists **4** Pierre Elliot Trudeau **5** Upper and Lower Canada **6** The Canadian Pacific railway **7** 1931 **8** W L Mackenzie King **9** The maple leaf **10** Kim Campbell

351

1 Simon Bolivar (Bolivia) **2** The Incas **3** Haiti **4** The USA after Spain's defeat in the war of 1898 **5** Peru **6** Jamaica **7** Spain and Portugal **8** Chile **9** Brazil **10** Nicaragua

352

1 The Royal Flying Doctor Service **2** Lindy Chamberlain **3** The Ned Kelly outlaw gang **4** Sir Robert Menzies

5 Australia won the America's Cup yacht races **6** Gold **7** 'Waltzing Matilda' **8** Sir Henry Parkes (1815-96) **9** Malcolm Fraser **10** Joseph Banks

353

1 Theodore Roosevelt, later US President **2** P.V. Narasimha Rao **3** Ramses II **4** Sir Stamford Raffles **5** Paul Robeson **6** Rasputin **7** Roanoke Island **8** Richelieu **9** Rhineland **10** The Red Cross

354

1 China **2** The Egyptians **3** The Vikings **4** Sir Walter Raleigh **5** Captain James T. Kirk and the Starship Enterprise **6** Australia **7** The Cape of Good Hope **8** Lake Victoria **9** America **10** Ferdinand Magellan

355

1 Animals for their skin and fur **2** It carried their food **3** Wild Bill Hickok **4** Crazy Horse, co-leader of the Indians at the battle of the Little Big Horn **5** On his legs. Chaps were leather guards to protect him from thorny brush **6** Chiricahua Apaches **7** Buffalo hides **8** Texas **9** Jim Bowie **10** The Derringer pocket pistol (1855)

356

1 Jamestown **2** William Penn **3** Alaska **4** People accused of witchcraft **5** Plymouth Colony **6** Harvard **7** The Boston Massacre **8** Georgia **9** France **10** It was America's first continuously published newspaper

357

1 Charles Lindbergh **2** Around the world **3** North Carolina (at Kill Devil Hills, Kitty Hawk) **4** Captain John Alcock and Lt Arthur Whitten Brown **5** Australia **6** Croydon **7** An airship **8** First flight of a jet-powered fighter **9** London's Heathrow **10** It began the first regular trans-Atlantic airmail service

358

1 Field Marshal Edmund Henry Hynman Allenby, 1st Viscount Allenby of Megiddo and of Felixstowe **2** General Sir Peter de la Billiere **3** General Bernard Law Montgomery **4** Field Marshal Horatio Herbert Kitchener, 1st Earl Kitchener of

Khartoum **5** Gen William Tecumseh Sherman **6** General Ulysses S. Grant **7** General George Catlett Marshall **8** The Duke of Cumberland **9** He was the first enlisted man to reach the highest rank in the British Army **10** General Ferdinand Foch

359

1 PAYE (Pay As You Earn) **2** The Duke of Kent **3** Monte Cassino **4** Glenn Miller **5** The Arab-Israeli war **6** India, when it became independent of Britain **7** The forming of the National Health Service **8** Jane, who was always losing her clothes **9** Sir Henry Wood, founder of the Proms **10** Fashion

360

1 John Profumo **2** The South Sea Bubble **3** Mohammed al Fayed **4** New York City **5** Eisenhower **6** Lord Byron **7** Sir Richard Burton **8** Jeremy Thorpe **9** 1979 **10** Monica Lewinsky

361

1 The Zulus **2** The French, who were beaten by the Viet Minh in 1954 **3** Dunkirk **4** Bangladesh **5** Pudding Lane **6** Halifax **7** Aberfan **8** Singapore, taken by the Japanese **9** An earthquake **10** The Exxon Valdez

362

1 Mithras **2** The Freemasons **3** India **4** China **5** Naples **6** Mau Mau **7** Ku Klux Klan **8** Triads **9** The Hell-Fire Club **10** The Fenians

363

1 Both were the first people to be the official deputy to their country's elected leader **2** They are all the official residences of Vice Presidents, in Indonesia, Taiwan and the US respectively **3** They have all won the Nobel Prize for Peace **4** No one. The office was vacant **5** Martin van Buren **6** They were all once Vice President and some time in their lives, earned a nomination for President – and then lost the election **7** Geraldine Ferraro **8** Richard Nixon **9** They were Vice Presidents that missed being president because they died, were replaced, or resigned from office **10** John Nance Garner, 32nd Vice President

364

1 Charles I: he was from the House of Stuart, the others were Tudor monarchs 2 John F. Kennedy: he was a Democrat, the others were Republicans 3 Alaska 4 Kinnock, who lost a general election while in opposition. All the rest lost while in government 5 Nelson, the others were born in Scotland 6 Lincoln was the only one with a beard 7 Childers was shot (by the British), the others were hanged 8 Chiang Kai-shek, who led Nationalist China until his death in 1975 – the others were all Communist Chinese leaders 9 Cardiff – the others were all names of British Second World War bomber planes 10 Sidney – the others are the names of HRH the Prince of Wales

365

1 1963 – the spacewoman was Valentina Tereshkova, the shooting that of President Kennedy 2 1932 3 1910 4 1580 5 1783 6 1837 7 1984 8 1959 – the architect was Frank Lloyd Wright 9 1972 – the Munich Games were hit by terrorists who attacked Israeli athletes in the Olympic village. 10 It was 1939, the year the Second World War began

366

1 Norfolk: all the others were British prime ministers 2 The Pock-marked 3 Louis XV, according to the French revolutionary calendar 4 The printing press 5 They were all wives of English kings named George 6 Harold Macmillan (to the House of Lords) 7 1963 – years in which US presidents were assassinated 8 They all died as a result of riding accidents 9 The Argonauts 10 Lord Kitchener ('Your country needs YOU') 11 The Charge of the Light Brigade 12 On the new 1963 £5 note, Britannia's helmet was missing 13 Harry, Dick, John, Harry – Norman kings of England 14 Ulysses: Ulysses S Grant (pictured) was a general in the Civil War; Joyce wrote the novel Ulysses; and Ulysses himself killed the Cyclops. 15 Black: Friars, Country, Horse

367

1 Owen Glendower 2 Caratacus 3 Colchester 4 Saxon warriors, invited to help the Britons fight their enemies after the Romans left 5 Lindisfarne 6 York 7 King Arthur 8 Glamorgan 9 Offa (Offa's Dyke) 10 Scotland

368

1 HMS *Sheffield*, during the 1982 Falklands Conflict 2 HMS *Ark Royal* 3 USS *Missouri* 4 Greek oared galleys 5 USS *Constitution* 6 The Japanese battleship *Yamato* 7 It was the first armoured warship 8 Patrol boat Torpedo 9 *Tirpitz* 10 She is the world's first nuclear powered aircraft carrier

369

1 The Nile, in Egypt 2 The St Lawrence in Canada 3 The Thames 4 Julius Caesar 5 The Styx 6 The Tiber 7 The Yangtze (Change Jiang) 8 The Thames, in London 9 The Rhine 10 Alexander the Great

370

1 The Bush family 2 Oil 3 Banking 4 The Kennedys 5 Mountbatten 6 The Tudors 7 Persia (Iran) 8 The Hapsburg dynasty 9 Dame Shirley Porter 10 China

371

1 It was a covered wagon, named after a valley in Pennsylvania 2 Wild Bill Hickok 3 Horses 4 The Oregon Trail 5 They chewed it – it was dried meat 6 A travelling preacher 7 The Black Hills 8 Pony Express 9 Tombstone, Arizona 10 Tough, half-wild cattle, roaming the unfenced ranches

372

1 To go to sea. Knorrs were heavy cargo and passenger ships 2 Normandy – the Normans were of Viking origin 3 The king's council 4 Ethelred II, known as the Unready – he was trying to buy off the Vikings 5 Eric the Red 6 Forkbeard 7 Godwin 8 Alfred the Great 9 He was archbishop of Canterbury 10 The battle of Maldon

373

1 William III 2 James I of England/ James VI of Scotland 3 John 4 Edward VII 5 Harold I 6 Edward VII 7 George I 8 George V 9 William I, the Conqueror 10 George III

374

1 Portugal 2 The electric motor 3 Sir Henry Bessemer 4 Henry II (the priest was Thomas Becket) 5 Harry Houdini 6 William the Conqueror 7 Henry VIII (Wolsey, More and Cromwell) 8 Harry S Truman 9 Patrick Henry (1736–99) 10 Henry Heinz (1844–1919)

375

1 Woden (Odin) 2 Zeus 3 Artemis (Diana) 4 Horus 5 Loki 6 The Aztecs 7 Korea 8 Ancient Hinduism 9 Venus 10 Janus

376

1 The D-Day landings 2 William Wallace 3 The American Civil War 4 George Armstrong Custer 5 David Lean 6 James Stewart 7 Rod Steiger 8 *Schindler's List* 9 Richard Harris 10 Winston Churchill

377

1 The Suez Canal 2 The coronation ceremony of Elizabeth II 3 Hungary 4 Teddy boys 5 The first US hydrogen bomb 6 Mount Everest 7 The *Boeing 707* 8 Roger Bannister 9 It was the world's first fullscale nuclear power plant 10 It was the first man-made object to reach the moon

378

1 Hadrian 2 Augustus (formerly known as Octavian) 3 Claudius, after the Roman invasion of 43 4 Tiberius 5 Nero 6 Cassius 7 Caligula 8 Livy 9 Vespasian 10 He was the last Roman emperor (AD 475–476)

379

1 The Chinese Communist Party 2 The silver jubilee of Queen Elizabeth II 3 Liberal Party 4 Spain 5 Adolf Hitler 6 Ireland 7 Liberal 8 Boston Tea Party 9 The Communist Party of the Soviet Union 10 Labour

380

1 1580 2 Lisbon in Portugal 3 Kristallnacht 4 The Great Fire of London 5 Chile 6 Chicago 7 China 8 Earthquake and then fire 9 Boston 10 Rome

381

1 Shogun (meaning 'general') 2 The legendary first emperor of Japan

(about 660 BC) **3** Holland **4** Aum Supreme Truth cult **5** The US Navy led by Commodore Matthew Perry **6** Meiji **7** The Russian fleet **8** Manchuria **9** An earthquake **10** Akihito

382

1 Slobodan Milosevic **2** Ken Livingstone **3** Failed US presidential hopeful Al Gore's **4** NATO, as supreme commander **5** To mark the 60th anniversary of the Dunkirk evacuation during the Second World War **6** The Millennium Bridge over the Thames in London **7** The world's newest and largest roller coaster **8** The Space Shuttle **9** Russia, which voted to restore the old Soviet anthem **10** Airbus Industries

383

1 Mary II of England **2** George V of Great Britain **3** She was the first star of the ballet to dance on the points of her toes **4** Queen Marie Antoinette of France **5** Marie Tussaud **6** Mary Wollstonecraft **7** Marie de' Medici **8** The Austrian **9** Mary, Queen of Scots **10** King James II of Great Britain

384

1 Thomas Paine **2** King John of England **3** A black woman, she refused to give up her seat to a white passenger. The arrest led to a boycott of buses, and a repeal of the law **4** She attempted to catch the reins of the King's horse but was fatally wounded **5** Set up a new state in Africa **6** Little Rock, Arkansas **7** Britain **8** He became the first black member of the Supreme Court **9** The Million Man March **10** Martin Luther King

385

1 Stockholm harbour – the warship had been built only the year previously **2** It was a French submarine **3** Henry VIII – the ship was the *Mary Rose* **4** *The Royal Oak* **5** *The General Belgrano* **6** Gold bullion **7** *Kursk* **8** She explored the Marianas Trench, the deepest point in the oceans (10,912m/35,802 ft) **9** It was the first by a nuclear-powered submarine **10** She was the largest ship ever sunk by a submarine

386

1 Quebec, in Canada **2** They were the first iron warships to exchange shots in anger **3** To knock them down. Bombards were cannon used to fire stones at the walls **4** China **5** Horatio Nelson at Trafalgar **6** The Bay of Pigs invasion **7** Balloons **8** The *Repulse* and *Prince of Wales*, both sunk **9** Guns **10** Richard III of England

387

1 Saint Augustine, founded by Spanish explorer Pedro Menendez de Aviles in 1565 **2** Paris **3** The British and Spanish fought a naval battle **4** Yves Saint Laurent **5** She was shot by the Germans for helping Allied soldiers escape from a hospital where she worked as a nurse **6** President Reagan **7** John Paul II **8** St Augustine of Hippo **9** Dr John Barnardo **10** Lord Shaftesbury

388

1 Cuba, when the USA demanded the removal of Soviet missiles installed there **2** Wallis Simpson. Edward VIII abdicated when she was ruled unacceptable as queen **3** Berlin **4** The Falklands issue between Argentina and Britain **5** Poland. Britain and France declared war on Germany two days later **6** The Soviet Union moved in to repress the democracy movement **7** Boris Yeltsin **8** James Callaghan **9** The Indian Mutiny – Indian soldiers protested at the use of the cartridges and then revolted **10** Sarajevo

389

1 King Harold II (Harold Godwinsson) **2** Stamford Bridge, home of Chelsea FC and the site in Yorkshire of the English victory over an invading Norwegian army in 1066 **3** The Bayeux Tapestry **4** W.C. Sellar and R.B. Yeatman **5** A destrier was a warhorse **6** A battle axe, held in both hands **7** Westminster Abbey **8** Battle Abbey in East Sussex **9** It was kite-shaped **10** They fought on horseback; the English fought on foot

390

1 Gary Gilmore **2** William Joyce, 'Lord Haw Haw' **3** Judge Jeffreys (George Jeffreys, Baron Wem

1645–1689) **4** Judge Roy Bean (about 1825–1904), presiding in Langtry, Texas **5** Roger Tichborne, heir to a large English fortune who was presumed lost at sea in 1854 **6** 105 **7** South Korea **8** Transylvania (modern Romania) **9** He was Britain's last official hangman **10** Fred and Rosemary West

391

1 Wood **2** Bletchley Park **3** US fighter planes, the P-38 and P-47 respectively **4** Artificial harbour used by the Allies after D-Day 1944 to land troops and supplies in France **5** German V-1 flying bombs **6** It was Hitler's plan to invade Britain **7** Iwo Jima **8** Italy **9** Burma **10** Battle of the Bulge

392

1 The red cross **2** That it sold wine **3** Barbers, who were originally surgeons as well **4** King Richard II **5** Black **6** The Roman (it's a flag) **7** Ireland **8** The crescent moon **9** Their eagle standard **10** Sweden

393

1 President Gerald Ford **2** Jesse James **3** She mistakenly shot down an Iranian commercial airliner **4** German Nazi propaganda chief Joseph Goebbels **5** Gandhi **6** John Stalker **7** Manfred von Richthofen, the Red Baron **8** President Kennedy's death in Dallas – Zapruder was a bystander **9** Richard I **10** Robert Stewart, Viscount Castlereagh

394

1 Arrows **2** Salisbury (the spire is 123 m/404 ft) **3** Geoffrey Chaucer **4** Oxen **5** The sheep (there were more than 15 million sheep in England) **6** Singing and making music **7** Venice **8** The Crusades **9** Squires **10** Highly decorative illustrations

395

1 William Hague **2** Into space aboard a Russian spaceship **3** Timothy McVeigh **4** Queens **5** He threw an egg at Mr Prescott, who then punched him **6** Jeffrey Archer **7** It caused the Foot and Mouth outbreak **8** Prince Charles **9** Afghan armed opposition **10** The 1988 Lockerbie bombing

1 Black slaves escaping to the North in the 1850s **2** Brooklyn Dodgers baseball star Jackie Robinson **3** The Boston Massacre of 1770 **4** Matthew Henson **5** Marian Anderson **6** Andrew Young **7** Arthur Ashe **8** The Black Panthers **9** *La Amistad* **10** *Uncle Tom's Cabin*

397

1 Sir Francis Drake, after his round-the-world voyage **2** Queen Mary **3** He was stripped of his peerage **4** A musical instrument played by a keyboard **5** Sir Philip Sidney **6** He was the Pope **7** Sir Francis Walsingham **8** Robert Dudley, Earl of Leicester **9** It was an acting troupe, of which Shakespeare was a member **10** London Bridge

398

1 The Duke of Wellington **2** Oliver Cromwell **3** Abraham Darby **4** Toledo **5** David Steel **6** The Iron Age **7** Joseph Stalin **8** The Iron Cross **9** Winston Churchill **10** Romania

399

1 David Livingstone **2** Franklin D. Roosevelt **3** Anwar Sadat **4** Iceland, scene of a summit meeting between Ronald Reagan and Mikhail Gorbachev **5** Captain James Cook **6** British prime minister Neville Chamberlain **7** Henry VIII, who met Francis I of France **8** Aristotle **9** Marco Polo **10** Montezuma II, leader of the Aztecs

400

1 Edward **2** Six **3** France – Louis XIV **4** King Juan Carlos **5** Thailand **6** Edward VIII **7** Catherine Parr **8** Edward **9** Mary I (Bloody Mary) **10** Belgium

401

1 Waterloo **2** Balaclava **3** The Battle of Kursk between the Soviet Union and Germany **4** Joan of Arc **5** The Little Big Horn **6** The American Civil War **7** Battle of Trafalgar **8** The Gulf War **9** Battle of Britain **10** Dubrovnik

402

1 Vikings or Varangians **2** Catherine the Great **3** Mikhail Gorbachev **4** Ivan the Terrible **5** Romanov **6** 15 **7** The Crimean War **8** Boris Godunov **9** St Petersburg **10** Nikita Khrushchev

403

1 John F. Kennedy **2** John Young **3** Brigham Young **4** Turkey **5** Tony Blair **6** The Young Men's Christian Association (YMCA) **7** He was 12 **8** 23 **9** The Rosetta Stone **10** Blondie

404

1 The Crimean War **2** Selfridges **3** Malta **4** A weather chart **5** The Royal Air Force **6** A US communications satellite **7** William Wordsworth **8** The Empire State Building was completed **9** The Great Exhibition **10** Alan Shepard, the first US astronaut

405

1 Tariq Aziz **2** Brigadier Patrick Cordingley **3** Marlin Fitzwater (White House Press Secretary) **4** John Major **5** Peter Arnett **6** A short-range tactical missile **7** Farzad Bazoft **8** *Bravo Two Zero* **9** The Republican Guard **10** The Stealth Fighter

406

1 Ronald Reagan **2** Israel **3** Ross McWhirter **4** Indira Gandhi **5** Gianni Versace **6** William McKinley **7** Lee Harvey Oswald **8** Abraham Lincoln **9** 1968 **10** Earl Mountbatten

407

1 1979 **2** 1 AD, there was no year 0 **3** The 17th century **4** 1984 **5** 116 years **6** Five years, J.F.K. in 1963 and Robert in 1968 **7** 1850s **8** 1914 **9** Italy **10** 1988

408

1 Betty Ford **2** Texas **3** Billy the Kid **4** The *Mayflower* **5** John F. Kennedy **6** George Washington. He approved the act that led to its construction **7** Buffalo, as his nickname was Buffalo Bill **8** Franklin D. Roosevelt **9** X **10** Shirley Temple

409

1 Thomas Jefferson **2** Edinburgh **3** Treetops Hotel, in Kenya's Aberdare National Park **4** Christopher Wren **5** Adolf Hitler **6** A mixture of clay and straw (wattle was made from woven sticks) **7** Hatfield House **8** The Foreign Secretary **9** Sandringham **10** The Palace of Versailles

410

1 France – the same coach at Compiegne had been used in 1918 to seal Germany's surrender **2** Richard Trevithick **3** The Atlantic and Pacific coasts of the USA – the first railroad link across the United States **4** The first commercial journey by Eurostar **5** It was the first railway to carry fare-paying passengers, in 1807 **6** The gauge of 4ft 8in was the same as the width of most wagon axles (the distance between the wheels) **7** Thomas Edison **8** The Trans-Siberian Railway **9** The first true locomotive sleeping carriages **10** *Mallard,* set in 1938 (126mph/201.16km/h)

411

1 Blenheim. Blenheim Palace was Churchill's birthplace **2** An Iron Curtain **3** The Duke of Marlborough, the victor at Blenheim **4** Harrow **5** South Africa, during the Boer War **6** Neville Chamberlain **7** The United States **8** He was awarded the Nobel prize for literature **9** The United States **10** He became the first non-American to have a warship named after him

412

1 Beethoven 1770–1827, composed *Für Elise* **2** Christopher Columbus 1451–1506, sailed to America in 1492 **3** Charles Dickens 1812–1870, wrote under pen name Boz **4** Pocahontas 1595–1617, married an English settler **5** Henry VIII 1491–1547, established the Church of England **6** Shakespeare 1564–1616, staged plays at the Globe Theatre **7** Wyatt Earp 1848–1929, fought the gunfight at the OK Corral **8** Galileo 1564–1642. Angered Church with views of Universe **9** Marie Curie 1867–1934, physicist who studied radio activity **10** Rembrandt 1606–1669, painted 60 self portraits

413

1 Joan of Arc **2** Anne Frank **3** She was the first female cabinet minister (Minister of Labour) **4** Eva Peron **5** Roberts **6** Calamity Jane **7** Eva Braun **8** Jackie Kennedy, wife of President Kennedy **9** Grace Kelly **10** Coco

414

1 *Butch Cassidy and the Sundance Kid*
2 Mark Antony 3 Sir Ben Kingsley
4 Sid James 5 Al Capone 6 Samson
7 T.E. Lawrence (Lawrence of
Arabia) 8 Douglas Bader 9 El Cid
10 George III

415

1 Khartoum 2 China 3 Cecil Rhodes
4 Aztecs 5 Iran 6 Japan 7 India
8 Venice 9 Saigon 10 Normandy

416

1 Nicolaus Copernicus 2 A court,
used by English kings but abolished in
1641 3 The *Titanic* 4 Star Wars
5 The Royal Greenwich Observatory
6 The Star of David 7 The Star of
India diamond 8 England (Yorkshire)
9 13 10 Texas

417

1 UN Secretary General 2 Harold
Wilson 3 Rhodesia 4 Rod Laver of
Australia 5 Nigeria 6 Sir Winston
Churchill 7 Senator Edward
Kennedy's 8 The *Torrey Canyon*
9 Yassir Arafat 10 A polar bear cub,
born in London Zoo, December 1967

418

1 Florida 2 New Zealand in 1893
3 1918 4 Rhodesia (now Zimbabwe)
5 The Liberal/Social Democrat Alliance
6 Franklin D. Roosevelt 7 Richard M.
Nixon 8 Gough Whitlam 9 India
10 The Philippines

419

1 Jimmy Carter 2 Ronald Reagan
3 North Korea – Kim il-Sung was
known as the Dear Leader. His son,
Kim Jong-il is the Great Leader
4 Lech Walesa 5 Colonel Oliver
North 6 Imran Khan 7 Margaret
Thatcher 8 Haiti 9 Al Gore 10 The
Labour Party

420

1 China 2 The American War of
Independence 3 The Trojan War
4 American troops in the First World
War 5 Guy Gibson 6 France 7 The
1991 Gulf War 8 The bombing of
Pearl Harbor 9 The International Red
Cross 10 Turkey

421

1 Helmut Kohl 2 They have all been
Popes 3 Pablo Picasso 4 St

Valentine's Day 5 Libya 6 South
Africa 7 Genghis Khan 8 Robert
Peel 9 General Charles de Gaulle
10 Pierre

422

1 India 2 Australia 3 Canada
4 Queen Victoria 5 Slavery 6 China
7 Mafeking 8 The North West
Mounted Police (The Mounties) 9 The
Indian Muntiny of 1857–1859
10 Australia (Lake Eyre)

423

1 John Calvin 2 Christian Science
3 John Wesley 4 Abraham 5 Salt
Lake City 6 Guru Nanak 7 Sunni
8 St Patrick 9 Hinduism
10 Siddhartha Gautama, the Buddha

424

1 Near the top of Mount Everest
2 None 3 'Flying saucers' 4 A lost
continent, sunk beneath the ocean
5 Bigfoot or Saskwatch 6 The
Bermuda triangle 7 America
8 A UFO 9 The Loch Ness Monster
10 King Arthur

425

1 Richard Crossman 2 Conscription
3 Cyprus 4 Campaign for Nuclear
Disarmament (CND) 5 William
Caxton 6 Chester 7 Crystal Palace
8 Conscientious objectors
9 Crusades 10 Cold War

426

1 Egyptians 2 Greeks 3 The Romans
4 The Italians 5 India 6 Germany
7 The Phoenicians 8 China 9 The
USA 10 France

427

1 Africa 2 Kilometres of rail track
3 Hungary, Spain, Poland 4 Franklin:
Benjamin (publisher) and Sir John
(explorer) 5 Ottoman 6 Hatshepsut
7 Thomas – the first three presidents
of the USA: George Washington, John
Adams, Thomas Jefferson 8 They were
all volunteer Nazi Waffen SS units
during the Second World War (British,
French, Flemish) 9 Sir Isaac Newton
10 Brown

428

1 (War of Jenkin's) Ear, Nose and
(Deep) Throat 2 These are the
colours of the four horsemen of the
Apocalypse 3 George Bernard Shaw

4 Peter, Susan, Edmund and Lucy (in
The Lion, The Witch and the Wardrobe)
5 Butler (RAB, Samuel, the bus driver
in the sitcom, the occupation of
Jeeves) 6 Carrie Fisher. She sent
Postcards from the Edge; the others
sent letters (to Churches, from
America; to a trainee demon – in CS
Lewis's edifying book) 7 Hill: (Fanny,
Rowland, Blueberry) 8 Milou
9 McDonald's: he bought the
hamburger stand belonging to Mac
and Dick McDonald and turned it into
an empire 10 The coronation of
Queen Elizabeth II, at which all these
pieces were performed 11 There was
no such day. In 1752, when Britain
switched from the Julian to the
Gregorian calendar, September 3 was
followed the next day by September
13 12 On the cover of The Beatles
album *Sgt Pepper's Lonely Hearts Club
Band* 13 Fingerprints 14 The
Marathon – when he ran 150 miles in
2 days to bring news of a Greek
victory at the Battle of Marathon
15 Their bodies were all preserved:
Alexander's, according to legend, in
honey; Nelson's in a butt of brandy;
Lenin's to a secret Soviet recipe

429

1 Mars 2 Laundrette 3 London
4 Colin Powell 5 Appendix operation
6 Baseball 7 Smallpox
8 Hippopotamus 9 The first
Supermarket, opened in New York
10 Telephone directory

430

1 Pontius Pilate 2 Genesis 3 Cain
4 Philistines 5 To name the animals
6 Gabriel 7 13 8 Good Friday
9 Abraham 10 Thomas

431

1 George Washington 2 Ronald
Reagan 3 Children 4 Bill Clinton
5 Lyndon Johnson 6 Theodore
Roosevelt 7 They were all
assassinated 8 Franklin D. Roosevelt
9 Bill Clinton 10 Gerald Ford. He
was appointed Vice President by
Richard Nixon, and took over as 38th
President of the United States

432

1 Malawi 2 Ghana 3 Kush 4 Benin
5 South Africa 6 Zambia 7 Germany
8 Liberia 9 Algeria 10 Zanzibar

433
1 A railway station 2 The French Revolution 3 The Marseillaise 4 Cardinal 5 The fleur-de-lis 6 Charles de Gaulle 7 Calais 8 The Maginot Line was a defence system designed, but failed to keep out the Germans in 1940 9 The Channel Tunnel 10 She was France's first woman prime minister

434
1 Moses 2 Queen Elizabeth I of England 3 Portland 4 A Lockheed U-2 spy plane 5 Holland 6 The Gunpowder Plot, for which Guy Fawkes was 'front man' 7 The US Central Intelligence Agency (CIA) 8 Julius and Ethel Rosenberg, who passed A-bomb secrets to the Russians 9 Kim Philby 10 The USA – he was a British officer acting as a messenger to the spy Benedict Arnold

435
1 Bakelite 2 Basketball, invented by James Naismith 3 Karl Benz 4 Robert Baden-Powell 5 The Bolsheviks 6 Boston 7 Stanley Baldwin 8 George Bush 9 Betty Boothroyd 10 Dr Richard Beeching

436
1 Hong Kong 2 Los Angeles 3 NATO 4 Russia 5 Elizabeth II 6 Canada 7 Hillary Clinton 8 Tony Blair 9 Belgium 10 Windsor Castle

437
1 St Francis of Assisi 2 Robert F. Kennedy, brother of John 3 Uncle Sam 4 Jimmy Carter 5 Mary I – her sister became Elizabeth I 6 Ronnie and Reggie Kray 7 Orville and Wilbur Wright 8 Prime minister of India – Gandhi was the family name 9 Henry VIII – the bride was Catherine of Aragon 10 Queen Elizabeth II

438
1 The Moon – it was the first unmanned US spacecraft to soft-land there 2 It was the first pedal-powered plane to cross the English Channel 3 Christopher Columbus 4 Captain Cook, on his first visit to Australia 5 Louis Blériot, after flying from France to England 6 The Korean War (1950–53) 7 Charles Lindbergh 8 Allied paratroops, during the Arnhem landings 9 Julius Caesar 10 Orville Wright

439
1 Queen Elizabeth I of England 2 Queen Victoria 3 She was executed 4 Princess Grace of Monaco 5 She was the last woman hanged for murder in Britain 6 The liner *Queen Elizabeth* 7 Empress Josephine, wife of Napoleon Bonaparte 8 Margaret Thatcher 9 Amelia Earhart 10 Diana, Princess of Wales

440
1 Ostriches 2 Russia 3 Wolf 4 Ravens 5 The giraffe 6 A wild ox 7 The lion and the unicorn 8 An asp, a venomous snake 9 An elephant 10 A spaniel dog

441
1 The Rock of Gibraltar 2 Furniture 3 Calcutta 4 Halley's Comet 5 Spain 6 England and Scotland 7 Tartan 8 George I 9 Convicts 10 Scurvy

442
1 Slavery 2 Canada 3 Can Can 4 *Oxford English Dictionary* 5 The revolver 6 The Irish potato famine 7 Eiffel Tower 8 The Reform Acts (1832, 1867, and 1884–85) 9 Frank 10 Luddites

443
1 Columbia 2 Prince William 3 AC Milan 4 Serena Williams 5 Zimbabwe 6 Phil Spector 7 Liberia 8 Concorde 9 Mars 10 Saddam Hussein

444
1 The first British crematorium opened 2 The Pony Express 3 Samuel Pepys 4 The first moving electric sign 5 The Middle Ages 6 Television advertising 7 Wheel-clamping 8 The Tudors, with Henry VII 9 The Olympic flame, carried by torch 10 The breathalyser.

445
1 Spanish Civil War 2 The Commonwealth of Nations 3 Egypt 4 Herbert Hoover, beaten in the race to be US President 5 The Great Depression 6 Czechoslovakia 7 Adolf Hitler 8 Cricket 9 A champion Australian racehorse which died mysteriously in 1932 10 He was the BBC's first TV announcer

446
1 Cyril Smith 2 They were pioneer long-distance aviators 3 English architect and designer Inigo Jones 4 Jack Jones 5 Adam Smith 6 Captain John Smith 7 Casey Jones 8 He became Britain's Astronomer Royal 9 The Rocky Mountains 10 John Smith

447
1 London 2 The Moon 3 The Second World War 4 The attempt to blow up the Houses of Parliament 5 Normandy, part of modern France 6 The *Titanic* 7 The destruction of the World Trade Center 8 The Black Death 9 The First World War 10 India

448
1 True 2 False. It was St Helena 3 False. It was Lord Nelson 4 False. It was the Diet of Worms 5 True 6 True 7 False. It is a Roman warship 8 True 9 False. It was President Lincoln 10 True

449
1 Elizabeth I 2 Henry VIII 3 Victoria 4 Elizabeth II 5 King Harold 6 Richard I, known as Richard the Lionheart 7 France 8 Boudicca 9 Prince Philip, Duke of Edinburgh 10 Buckingham Palace

450
1 A Prison 2 Pacific and Atlantic 3 The first steam locomotive 4 Russia 5 Ireland 6 Puritans 7 Peasants' Revolt 8 1066 9 Magna Carta 10 Roundheads

451
1 A highwayman 2 Australia 3 Robin Hood 4 Horses and cattle 5 Guy Fawkes 6 The dead. It was the nickname for the town cemetery 7 The Skull and Crossbones, or Jolly Roger 8 The United States of America 9 The Crown Jewels 10 Chicago

452
1 James II 2 Charles I 3 Oliver Cromwell 4 Henry VIII 5 Edward VIII 6 Bayeux 7 Lady Jane Grey 8 James I

of England, VI of Scotland **9** George I
10 Elizabeth I

453

1 Legionnaires **2** Julius Caesar
3 Latin **4** In northern England **5** 10
6 1000 **7** Carthage **8** A shield
9 Britannia **10** Farming

454

1 Suez **2** Tank **3** Iran **4** Atom
5 Boer **6** Gaul **7** Zulu **8** King
9 East **10** Euro

455

1 Elephants **2** A dragon **3** Egyptians
4 The Black Rat **5** Kangaroo **6** The
United States of America **7** Ostriches
8 Deer **9** Horses **10** Husky

456

1 America **2** Vietnam War **3** White
4 The Phoney War **5** Archduke
Ferdinand **6** Boer War **7** The Second
World War **8** America **9** The A-
Bomb (or Atom Bomb) **10** The First
World War

457

1 The First World War **2** Adolf Hitler
3 John Major **4** Argentina
5 Television **6** The Blitz **7** Queen
Elizabeth II **8** Saddam Hussein
9 One, Margaret Thatcher
10 The Second World War

458

1 Admiralty **2** Archaeology **3** Armada
4 Robert Baden-Powell **5** Black
Death **6** Bloody Sunday **7** Battle of
Britain **8** Canada **9** Coronation
10 Charles I

459

1 The Bronze Age **2** The Tiber
3 King Harold **4** The First World War
5 Prince Albert **6** None **7** The
President of the United States of
America **8** A postage stamp **9** Mount
Vesuvius **10** Alfred Nobel (of Nobel
prize fame)

460

1 Benito Mussolini **2** Robert Mugabe
3 China **4** Stalin **5** Churchill
6 Nelson Mandela **7** George Bush.
His son became President after
Clinton **8** George Washington
9 Germany **10** Vladimir Putin

461

1 Florence Nightingale **2** Henry VIII
3 Sir Walter Raleigh **4** Isambard
Kingdom Brunel **5** Saint Bede
6 Japan **7** King Alfred **8** Papyrus
9 Tanks **10** King Arthur

Music

462

1 *The Full Monty* **2** Ike **3** Wham!
4 Davy Jones **5** Annie Lennox
6 Ernie **7** Culture Club **8** Cilla Black
9 Tim Rice **10** Glen Campbell

463

1 Sting **2** *Wuthering Heights* **3** Cat
Stevens **4** Jim Morrison **5** Hot
Chocolate **6** *Tubular Bells* **7** Slade
8 Andrew Lloyd Webber **9** France
10 Crying, so much so he acquired
the nicknames of 'The Sultan of Sob'
and 'The Prince of Wails'

464

1 The Osmonds **2** Hayley Mills
3 Red **4** Electric Light Orchestra
5 Four **6** Shirley Bassey **7** 'On the
Dock of the Bay' **8** 'Space Oddity'
9 Jones **10** Ronnie Wood

465

1 Stockholm **2** The Commodores
3 New Kids on the Block **4** Dire
Straits **5** Kenny Rogers **6** Michael
Stipe **7** Aerosmith **8** Johnny Rotten
also known as John Lydon **9** The
Bangles **10** FBI

466

1 Christie Brinkley **2** Carl Perkins
3 Carole King **4** Jerry Lee Lewis
5 Prince **6** Don Henley **7** Lou Reed
8 *Jagged Little Pill* **9** All these groups
contained band members with the
surname of Jones. Davy, Mick and
Brian respectively **10** The Village
People, each member of the band
dressed in one of the outfits

467

1 'Baby I Love You' **2** Lonnie Donegan
3 Electric and Musical Industries
4 'Any Dream Will Do' **5** Courtney
Love **6** The Supremes **7** 'Angie'
8 'Daniel' **9** 1991 **10** Simple Minds

468

1 The Bangles **2** Greek **3** The 1960s
4 Bing Crosby **5** Roger Daltrey
6 Eddy Grant **7** Horse **8** The
Simpsons **9** 'Sailing' **10** Roy

469

1 Swans **2** Ireland **3** Fred **4** Three
5 Led Zeppelin **6** Fagin **7** Semi-
quaver **8** Ian Dury **9** Mersey
10 Rex Harrison

470

1 Jean-Michel Jarre **2** The name
Woodward, this being Tom Jones's
real surname and that of the star of
The Equaliser, Edward Woodward
3 Andy Kaufman **4** 'Dancing Queen'
5 'I Can't Stop Loving You' **6** Quentin
Crisp **7** Buddy Holly, with the song
'It Doesn't Matter Any More' in 1959
8 Clannad **9** Jackie Wilson **10** Cliff
Richard

471

1 Prince **2** Black Sabbath **3** *Dark Side
of the Moon* **4** Cilla Black **5** 'White
Lines (Don't do it)' **6** Jimi Hendrix
7 Guy Mitchell **8** Barry White
9 Cream **10** 'Lily the Pink'

472

1 Dolly Parton **2** Jim Reeves **3** Sissy
Spacek **4** Tammy Wynette **5** Johnny
Cash **6** Kenny Rogers **7** Shania Twain
8 Willie Nelson **9** Glen Campbell
10 John Denver

473

1 Diana Ross **2** Kiki Dee **3** 'Lucille'
4 Billy Connolly **5** The Police **6** Terry
Jacks **7** Malcolm McClaren
8 'Amazing Grace' by The Band
of the Royal Scots Dragoon Guards
9 Sweet **10** Charles Aznavour

474

1 Dusty Springfield **2** Donna Summer
3 Chrissie Hynde **4** Joan Armatrading
5 Dolly Parton **6** Mel C (Melanie
Chisholm) **7** Gracie Fields
8 Catatonia **9** Dionne Warwick
10 Dannii Minogue

475

1 'The Sabre Dance' **2** Johann Strauss
3 1812 **4** Loud **5** *5th Symphony*
6 Salzburg **7** Violin **8** Soprano
9 New York Philharmonic Orchestra
10 Prima Donna

476
1 Don Johnson 2 The Everly Brothers 3 Simon and Garfunkel 4 Beavis and Butthead 5 George Michael 6 Frank and Nancy Sinatra 7 Israeli 8 Tammi Terrell 9 'Endless Love' 10 'Up Where We Belong'

477
1 'House of the Rising Sun' 2 'Another Brick in the Wall' 3 'Staying Alive' 4 'Kissing In The Back Row Of The Movies' 5 'American Pie' 6 'Suspicious Minds' 7 'Close To You' 8 'Yellow Submarine' 9 'Love Is All Around' 10 'Big Spender'

478
1 Ringo Starr 2 Parlophone 3 George Harrison with the song 'My Sweet Lord' 4 Miami – the line is 'Flew in from Miami beach BOAC' 5 *Please Please Me* 6 'Lucy In The Sky With Diamonds' 7 *Abbey Road* 8 Cynthia 9 Pete Best 10 1967

479
1 Mozart 2 *From the New World* 3 J.S. Bach 4 *Rigoletto* 5 *Billy Budd* 6 Edvard Grieg 7 *Fidelio* 8 Johann Strauss 9 *Air on a G String* 10 That the music should get slower

480
1 Ben E King 2 'God Save The Queen' 3 Pianist 4 Deacon 5 Nat King Cole 6 'King of the Road' 7 Benny Goodman 8 'Sultans of Swing' 9 'Everything I do I do it for You' 10 Gene Pitney

481
1 'Careless Whisper' by George Michael 2 David Byrne 3 'Shout' 4 Spandau Ballet 5 Cliff Richard 6 Meatloaf 7 Billy Idol 8 *South Pacific* 9 Sorry 10 Frank Sinatra

482
1 Whitney Houston 2 Maurice Gibb 3 Crystal Gayle 4 The Corrs 5 Julian Lennon 6 Heart 7 Frank Sinatra 8 Paul Simon 9 'Papa Don't Preach' by Madonna 10 'Papa Was a Rollin' Stone'

483
1 Neil Diamond 2 Jackie Wilson 3 Eurythmics 4 Wet Wet Wet 5 C.J. Lewis 6 The Searchers 7 Brenda Lee 8 Guns n' Roses 9 Arthur Conley 10 Chuck Berry

484
1 Men At Work 2 'One Moment In Time' 3 'Call Me' 4 1985 5 'Going Underground' by The Jam 6 'Everything I Own' 7 Mel Brooks 8 'Chain Reaction' 9 'Dancing in the Street' 10 *Double Fantasy*

485
1 Elvis Costello 2 Jimmy James 3 James Brown 4 Freddie (Garrity) 5 Gary Puckett 6 Bruce Springsteen 7 Yazz (Yasmin Summers) 8 Ziggy Stardust (David Bowie) 9 Tom Petty 10 Joan Jett

486
1 Simply Red 2 'Goodbye Yellow Brick Road' 3 Deep Purple 4 Andrew Gold 5 Pink Floyd 6 Pink Cadillac 7 German 8 Brown Sugar 9 'Blue Moon' 10 'The Summertime Blues'

487
1 Step one, you find a girl to love 2 An angel ('There must be an angel (playing with my heart)') 3 Tavares 4 'Show Me Heaven' 5 Heaven 17 6 Michael Hutchence 7 The Smiths 8 'Knockin' On Heaven's Door' 9 Belinda Carlisle 10 'Stairway To Heaven'

488
1 HMS *Pinafore* 2 'Sea of Love' 3 'My Heart Will Go On' 4 *Sloop John B* 5 Rod Stewart 6 Herman Melville 7 Burt Bacharach and Hal David 8 Rotterdam 9 Madness 10 *Showboat*

489
1 *Rocky Horror Picture Show* 2 *Oliver* 3 *West Side Story* 4 *My Fair Lady* 5 *The Wizard of Oz* 6 *Cats* 7 *Mary Poppins* 8 *Starlight Express* 9 *Cabaret* 10 *Les Miserables*

490
1 Donna Summer 2 Paul Young 3 Roxy Music 4 B-52s 5 Neil Diamond 6 The Osmonds 7 Pat Boone 8 Rose Royce 9 The Troggs 10 Katrina and The Waves

491
1 *Faith* 2 Andy Warhol 3 The Rolling Stones 4 *Night at the Opera* and *A Day at the Races* 5 *The Immaculate Collection* 6 The Bee Gees 7 Billy Joel 8 *(What's the Story) Morning Glory* 9 *Off the Wall* 10 *Can't Slow Down*

492
1 Fleetwood Mac 2 Patsy Kensit 3 Elton John 4 Paul Simon 5 Debbie Rowe 6 Uri Geller 7 Siobhan Fahey 8 Paula Abdul 9 Paula Yates 10 Rachel Hunter

493
1 'Candle in the Wind' 1997 2 LeAnn Rimes 3 *The Lion King* 4 'Your Song' 5 Luciano Pavarotti 6 The Bride 7 *Don't Shoot Me I'm Only The Piano Player* 8 'Don't let the Sun go down on Me' 9 Watford FC 10 Bennie

494
1 Topol 2 Lee Marvin 3 Deborah Kerr 4 Christopher Plummer 5 Whitney Houston 6 Ron Moody 7 Audrey Hepburn 8 Sting 9 Liza Minnelli 10 John Travolta

495
1 'Like a Virgin' 2 Sean Penn 3 *Sex* 4 Ciccone 5 *Ray of Light* 6 Scotland, in Skibo Castle 7 'Don't Cry For Me Argentina' 8 Michigan 9 *Die Another Day* 10 'Beautiful Stranger'

496
1 Roger Taylor 2 Mick Fleetwood 3 Phil Collins 4 Kettledrum 5 Karen 6 Jim Reeves 7 Carl Palmer 8 A drum roll 9 Keith Moon 10 The Beverley Sisters

497
1 Anchorage 2 Chicago 3 24 4 'Chanson d'Amour' 5 'The Streets of Philadelphia' (the film was *Philadelphia*) 6 Ohio, the song being 'Banks of the Ohio' 7 Amarillo, the song being 'Is this the way to Amarillo?' 8 New York 9 'California Dreaming' 10 John Denver

498
1 Bon Jovi 2 Metallica 3 'Gold' 4 Tin Machine 5 David Soul 6 *Dixon of Dock Green* 7 Anthrax 8 'Brass in Pocket' 9 Tommy Steele 10 Peter Sellers

499
1 Gloria Gaynor 2 Tina Turner
3 Benjamin Britten 4 Sandie Shaw
5 Christopher Cross 6 Doris Day
7 Sister Sledge 8 Betty Boo 9 Janet
Jackson 10 Kris Kross

500
1 Mozart 2 Peabo Bryson 3 Saturday
Night 4 'Sleeping like a log'
5 Queen 6 *Saturday Night Fever*
7 *Chess* 8 Shalamar 9 The Moody
Blues 10 Stephen Sondheim

501
1 Lisa Stansfield 2 *Pickwick* 3 Louis
Armstrong, who topped the charts in
1968 aged 67 4 The Seekers
5 'Rockin' all over the World'
6 'Venus In Blue Jeans' 7 Electric Light
Orchestra 8 *Orpheus In The
Underworld* 9 New Seekers 10 *The
Little Mermaid*

502
1 Australia 2 Spain 3 France
4 Sweden 5 Ireland 6 New Zealand
7 Scotland 8 Jamaica 9 Norway
10 Cuba

503
1 The Mavericks 2 'The Locomotion'
3 Audrey Hepburn 4 Johann Strauss
5 Seventeen 6 'Twist and Shout'
7 Leo Sayer 8 Earth, Wind and Fire
9 *Blood on the Dance Floor* 10 The
Vandellas

504
1 Diana Ross 2 Billy Preston
3 Bartolome Cristofori 4 Scott Joplin
5 *Don't Shoot me I'm only the Piano
Player* 6 Russ Conway 7 'Ebony and
Ivory' 8 Billy Joel 9 Liberace
10 *Moonlight Sonata*

505
1 'Who do you Think you are Kidding
Mister Hitler' (theme tune of *Dad's
Army*) 2 'I Don't want to go to
Chelsea' (Elvis Costello) 3 'Jailhouse
Rock' (Elvis Presley) 4 'Close To You'
(The Carpenters) 5 'Don't Stand so
close to Me' (The Police) 6 'The Lion
Sleeps Tonight' (Tight Fit) 7 'In the
Navy' (Village People) 8 'A Boy
named Sue' (Johnny Cash) 9 'Cry me
a River' (Julie London) 10 'Officer
Krupke' (from *West Side Story*)

11 'Ode To Joy' (from Beethoven's 9th
Symphony) 12 'Don't Cry For Me,
Argentina' (from *Evita*) 13 'Sultans of
Swing' (Dire Straits) 14 'Zippadee
Doo-dah' (from *Song of the South*)
15 'Meet the Flintstones' (*Flintstones*
theme)

506
1 Neil Diamond 2 Brian Jones of the
Rolling Stones 3 Judith Durham
4 'You'll Never Walk Alone' 5 Tommy
6 The Shadows 7 The Quarrymen
became The Silver Beatles who
became The Beatles 8 Clarinet
9 *The Good, the Bad and the Ugly*
10 Georgie Fame

507
1 Chopin 2 Five 3 French 4 Ira
Gershwin 5 *The Flying Dutchman*
6 Verdi 7 Edward Elgar 8 False, he
could only manage twenty 9 Felix
Mendelssohn 10 Charles Hallé

508
1 'Heartbeat' 2 Kate Bush 3 Jimmy
Ruffin 4 Crystal Gayle 5 'In The
Arms of Mary' 6 Billy Ray Cyrus
7 Roberta Flack 8 *Song and Dance* or
Tell me on a Sunday
9 'Heartbreak Hotel' 10 Paul Anka

509
1 Acapulco 2 New York 3 Tony
Bennett 4 Norway 5 Frankie Goes
to Hollywood 6 Manchester
7 'California Girls' 8 Kim Wilde, the
daughter of Marty Wilde 9 Gene
Pitney 10 London

510
1 Tennessee 2 Twain (Shania)
3 Tempo 4 Tenor 5 Tremeloes
6 *Tommy* 7 Taylor, and coincidentally
both had the first name of Roger
8 Three 9 'True' 10 Tyrannosaurus

511
1 Dorothy Squires 2 Gene Vincent
3 Al Martino 4 Leslie Caron 5 Jerry
Lee Lewis 6 16 Tons 7 Paul Anka
8 Guy Mitchell 9 Bobby Darin
10 Lou Diamond Phillips

512
1 L.S. Lowry 2 Peggy Lee 3 'Father
and Son' 4 Simon and Garfunkel
5 The Pointer Sisters 6 Tom Jones
7 Lobo 8 Henry Mancini 9 'Eternal
Flame' 10 Donny Osmond

513
1 Barbara Dickson 2 Felix
Mendelssohn 3 'Maggie May'
4 *Carousel* 5 Kid Creole 6 Earth,
Wind and Fire 7 Carole King 8 U2
9 Guns n' Roses 10 The Four
Seasons

514
1 The Four Seasons 2 Alice Cooper
3 *Hello Dolly* 4 Dionne Warwick
5 Bucks Fizz 6 New York Dolls
7 'Living Doll' 8 Aqua 9 'The
Clapping Song', originally a hit for
Shirley Ellis 10 *Guys and Dolls*

515
1 1991 2 1978 3 1996 4 1966
5 1981 6 1963 7 1983 8 1966
9 1997 10 1979

516
1 Austria 2 A name I call myself
3 A convent 4 Maria 5 Captain
6 1965 7 Sixteen going on seventeen
8 Two 9 Brown 10 Valentine's

517
1 Rosemary Clooney 2 'Chapel of
Love' 3 *My Fair Lady* 4 The Cardigans
5 The Lighthouse Family 6 Madness
7 'Hotel California' 8 *Bridge over
Troubled Water* 9 Pet Shop Boys
10 Bob Geldof

518
1 'Let it Be' 2 Santa Claus 3 Nat
King Cole 4 *Mamma Mia* 5 'Mama'
6 Eddie Calvert 7 Father McKenzie
8 The Stereophonics 9 Judy Garland
10 The Smurfs

519
1 True, Elvis's twin, Jesse, was stillborn
2 Colonel Tom Parker 3 *Girls, Girls,
Girls* 4 Sun Records 5 'It's now or
Never' 6 'Heartbreak Hotel'
7 Mississippi 8 Sergeant 9 *Love Me
Tender* 10 'The Wonder of You' in
1970, 'Way Down' a No. 1 hit in 1977
was a posthumous release

520
1 The Mamas and the Papas 2 Travis,
the character was called Travis Bickle
3 U2 4 All About Eve 5 Led
Zeppelin. Keith Moon, on hearing
them play, said that they would go
down like a lead balloon 6 Jethro Tull
7 Del Amitri 8 The Doors, the quote
read 'If the doors of perception were

fully cleansed we should see life as it really is' **9** Duran Duran **10** Texas, the film was called *Paris, Texas*

521
1 New Orleans **2** Ellington **3** Louis Armstrong **4** *The Cotton Club* **5** The Original Dixieland Jazz Band **6** Dr John **7** Trumpet **8** Jelly Roll Morton **9** Bix **10** They were both known as counts: Basie and *Dracula*

522
1 The Rat Pack **2** 'My Way' **3** 'Chicago' **4** Nancy **5** 1998 **6** Nicole Kidman **7** Bono **8** *Who Framed Roger Rabbit?* **9** Mia Farrow **10** *High Society*

523
1 Peter Sarstedt **2** Frankie Lymon and the Teenagers **3** REM **4** Four Non Blondes **5** Everly Brothers **6** Culture Club **7** Abba **8** Connie Francis **9** Pet Shop Boys with Dusty Springfield **10** Bros

524
1 Berry Gordy Jr **2** Marvin Gaye **3** The Supremes **4** The Four Tops **5** Stevie Wonder **6** The Funk Brothers **7** 1969 **8** The Temptations in 1965 with the song 'My Girl' **9** Gladys Knight **10** Smokey Robinson with the song 'Shop Around' in 1961

525
1 'Windmills of your Mind' **2** 'Under the Boardwalk' **3** At the candy store **4** Edison Lighthouse **5** 'The Love Shack' **6** Winchester Cathedral **7** 'Under The Bridge' **8** *Evita* **9** 'Black or White' **10** Crowded House

526
1 Phil Lynott of Thin Lizzy **2** Janis Joplin **3** The Big Bopper (J.P. Richardson) **4** Tammy Wynette **5** Jimi Hendrix, the phone call he made was to his manager Chas Chandler **6** Frank Zappa **7** Gram Parsons **8** Mama Cass Elliot **9** Terry Kath **10** Eddie Cochran

527
1 Suzie **2** N'Sync **3** The Jackson Five **4** Kiss **5** Debbie Harry **6** 'I want to know what love is' **7** Daryl Hall **8** Alice Cooper **9** Sledge **10** Eminem

528
1 *My Fair Lady* **2** *Phantom of the Opera* **3** *Miss Saigon* **4** *Jesus Christ Superstar* **5** *La Cage Aux Folles* **6** *Porgy and Bess* **7** *Aspects of Love* **8** *Hair* **9** *Godspell* **10** *Annie*

529
1 *Carmen* **2** *Cosi Fan Tutte* **3** *La Bohème* **4** Engelbert Humperdinck **5** *Figaro* **6** *The Beggar's Opera* **7** *La Traviata* **8** *Madame Butterfly* **9** Benjamin Britten **10** *Tosca*

530
1 Paul McCartney **2** Diana Ross **3** 'Ben' **4** Eddie Van Halen **5** Lionel Richie **6** Epic **7** Jarvis Cocker **8** 3T **9** *Moonwalk* **10** 'Scream'

531
1 Lightning Seeds **2** 'Candle In The Wind' **3** Rainbow **4** The Carpenters **5** 'Blowin' in the Wind' **6** *The Snowman* **7** 'Macarthur Park' **8** *Butch Cassidy and the Sundance Kid* **9** Heatwave **10** Donovan

532
1 The Searchers **2** Björk **3** Sugababes **4** Mac and Katie Kissoon **5** Tchaikovsky **6** Red Hot Chili Peppers **7** The Archies **8** Salt-n-Pepa **9** Simon Fuller **10** 'Mellow Yellow'

533
1 Black **2** Gilbert, who was born 1836 and died 1911. Sullivan was born 1842 and died 1900 **3** Little Richard **4** Glenn Miller **5** Blue **6** *Jaws* **7** Tartan **8** Don, who was born in 1937 whilst Phil was born two years later **9** Ice skating **10** Liverpool

534
1 True **2** Wales **3** America, Radio Corporation of America **4** Queen **5** Sex Pistols **6** Dublin **7** 1980s (1988) **8** *Cats* **9** 'Stand By Me' **10** None. The line up consisted of Scott Engel, Gary Leeds and John Maus

535
1 Yoko Ono **2** Conducting **3** Chess **4** Paul Weller **5** Extended (extended play) **6** 1950s **7** Ukulele **8** 'S.O.S.' **9** The girls outnumber the boys by 4 to 3 **10** Roxy Music

536
1 Aretha Franklin **2** George Harrison **3** *Graceland* **4** Mandy **5** The Beastie Boys **6** Connie Francis **7** Bryan Adams **8** 'Send In The Clowns' **9** Herb Alpert **10** 'Things Can Only Get Better'

537
1 'Like a Prayer' **2** Strawberry Fields **3** U2 **4** Toni Braxton **5** Michael Jackson **6** 'Killing me softly with his song' **7** 'Vincent', inspired by Vincent van Gogh **8** Peter Gabriel **9** Robert **10** Cyndi Lauper

538
1 'I wanna hold your hand' **2** Rita Coolidge **3** Mark Knopfler **4** Frank Zappa **5** Alan Freed **6** Freddie Mercury **7** Slash of Guns 'N' Roses fame **8** Stevie Wonder **9** A vintage fire engine **10** 'Let the River Run'

539
1 Spiders from Mars (David Bowie) **2** The Trout Quintet (Schubert) **3** The Firebird (Stravinsky) **4** Old Man River (Paul Robeson) **5** Wuthering Heights (Kate Bush) **6** Moonlight Serenade (Glen Miller) **7** Layla (Eric Clapton) **8** Bitches Brew (Miles Davis) **9** Anarchy in the UK (Johnny Rotten) **10** Jet Song (Leonard Bernstein)

540
1 Billie Holliday **2** Howlin' Wolf **3** Geno Washington **4** Eric Clapton **5** Charlie Parker **6** Rhythm and Blues **7** Chuck Berry **8** Smith, Bessie Smith **9** BB King, the BB stands for Blues Boy **10** Muddy Waters

541
1 Abba **2** Bush (Kate Bush) **3** Corr **4** Dawn **5** Enya **6** Fine **7** Gong **8** *Help* **9** INXS **10** Jovi

542
1 Drums **2** Perry Como **3** Mamas and the Papas **4** Ricky Nelson **5** 'World Without Love' **6** Johnny Ray **7** Jim Reeves **8** 'Moon River' **9** Sam & Dave **10** 'Je T'Aime...Moi Non Plus'

543
1 'Goodbye To Love' **2** The Bay City Rollers **3** Jimmy Ruffin **4** Joannie **5** Everly Brothers **6** Soft Cell

7 'Farewell My Summer Love'
8 'Don't Leave Me This Way' **9** 'Bye Bye Miss American Pie' **10** Vera Lynn

544
1 Sir Henry Wood **2** Jacqueline du Pré **3** Sir Simon Rattle **4** Highwayman **5** Sir Thomas Beecham **6** Two **7** Cello **8** Luciano Pavarotti **9** La Scala **10** Aaron Copland

545
1 The Three Degrees **2** Emerson, Lake and Palmer **3** Fun Boy Three **4** The Jam **5** 'Three Coins In A Fountain' **6** Fun Lovin' Criminals **7** Wings **8** Peter, Paul and Mary **9** ZZ Top **10** 'Roxanne'

546
1 'Pretty Woman' **2** Bellamy Brothers **3** Baby Bird **4** Pretty Young Thing **5** Rod Stewart **6** Brown Eyed Handsome Man **7** Ringo Starr **8** Dr Hook **9** 'The Most Beautiful Girl In The World' **10** *Oklahoma*

547
1 The Hollies **2** The Walker Brothers **3** Andy Gibb **4** Brotherhood of Man **5** Alan Osmond **6** Jermaine Jackson **7** The Proclaimers **8** 'You've Lost that Loving Feeling' **9** The Isley Brothers **10** Dire Straits

548
1 Bluebirds **2** Snake **3** Donny Osmond **4** The Scorpions **5** Fleetwood Mac **6** Manfred Mann **7** Rolf Harris **8** Chas Chandler **9** Seal **10** Little Red Rooster

549
1 'All Right Now' (Free)
2 'La Marseillaise' (the French national anthem) **3** 'Georgia on my Mind' (Hoagy Carmichael) **4** 'Suzanne' (Leonard Cohen) **5** 'I Wish I Were In Love Again' (from *Babes In Arms*)
6 'Cabaret' (from the film *Cabaret*)
7 'I Hate Men' (from *Kiss Me Kate*)
8 'How Long Has This Been Going On' (from *Rosalie*) **9** 'Feed The World' (Bob Geldof and others) **10** 'Maybe I'm Amazed' (Paul McCartney)
11 'School's Out' (Alice Cooper)
12 'Is She Really Going out with Him' (Joe Jackson) **13** 'Chantilly Lace' (The Big Bopper) **14** 'Bear Necessities' (from *Jungle Book*)

15 'Dancing Queen' (Abba)

550
1 'From me to you' **2** *Sgt. Pepper's Lonely Hearts Club Band* **3** 'Penny Lane' **4** *1* **5** Apple **6** *A Hard Day's Night* (1964) **7** 'All you need is love' **8** George Harrison **9** Ringo Starr **10** Never

551
1 Ella Fitzgerald **2** Nat 'King' Cole **3** Saxophone **4** 'Misty' **5** Cleo Laine **6** Drummer **7** Louis Armstrong **8** 'Stranger on the Shore' **9** Kenny Ball **10** Edward Kennedy

552
1 Steppenwolf **2** *An American Werewolf In London* **3** The Housemartins **4** The Pharaohs **5** Genesis **6** Wolfman Jack **7** Duran Duran **8** J. Geils Band **9** 'Seasons In The Sun' by Terry Jacks **10** Prokofiev

553
1 Shakespear's Sister, which they deliberately spelt incorrectly **2** Tim Rice **3** Tommy Lee **4** The Krays **5** Chubby Checker **6** *The Three Tenors Concert* **7** Frankie Valli **8** 'Mull of Kintyre' **9** Marsden **10** 'Saving All My Love For You'

554
1 A fireworks display **2** One. It is folded into a double reed **3** Moscow **4** Quick tempo **5** 19th century, 1840–1893 **6** Penzance **7** Violin **8** Sousaphone **9** Amazon **10** *The Choral Symphony*

555
1 *An Officer and a Gentleman*
2 *Calamity Jane* **3** *The Wizard of Oz*
4 *A Star is Born* **5** *Evita* **6** *White Nights*
7 *Mary Poppins* **8** *Dick Tracy* **9** *Song of the South* **10** *Pocahontas*

556
1 Pinocchio **2** *The Nutcracker*
3 Clarinet **4** Four **5** Hymn
6 *The Lion King* **7** Jennifer Lopez
8 The Beatles **9** The saxophone
10 Piccolo

557
1 France's **2** Australian **3** Dido
4 The Kumars **5** Britney Spears by one year and 16 days **6** Beyonce
7 Busted **8** Sing when you're winning

9 Anastacia **10** *Neighbours*

558
1 An opera singer **2** Percussion
3 Madonna is older. She was born on August 16, 1958 and Michael Jackson was born 13 days later **4** A man
5 Between the legs **6** Bobby Brown
7 Harpsichord **8** Louise **9** Harp
10 Sombrero – it is a hat

559
1 Aqua **2** Abba **3** Bust **4** Atomic Kitten **5** Cyprus **6** Big Brovaz
7 Daniel Bedingfield **8** Bryan (McFadden) **9** Canada **10** Britney Spears

560
1 Conductor **2** Six **3** Blue **4** Five
5 Adam **6** Pink **7** Kelly **8** Natasha
9 Justin Timberlake **10** A

561
1 Lowestoft **2** Aerosmith **3** Louise
4 182 **5** McFly **6** Christina Aguilera
7 Will Young **8** Nelly Furtado
9 James Fox **10** Finland

562
1 Genie **2** Oboe **3** Two **4** *Pop Idol*
5 Mary Poppins **6** *Toy Story*
7 A singer **8** V **9** The Cheeky Girls
10 Justin Timberlake

563
1 Lullaby **2** Usher **3** Blue Peter
4 Sugababes **5** 'We Are The Champions' **6** Zoë Ball **7** Ludwig
8 Pink **9** None **10** Knowles

564
1 Austria **2** Beluga, which is a type of fish **3** 'Angels' **4** Celine **5** Billie Piper
6 Bow **7** Bassoon **8** Carol
9 Cymbals **10** Beethoven

Natural history

565
1 They curl round them and squeeze them to death **2** A type of toadstool
3 Malaria **4** A type of lizard **5** The Vietnamese pot-bellied pig **6** The leech **7** The hop plant (an oast is a kiln for hops) **8** The porcupine
9 Eight, like other spiders **10** They stick to the fur of animals

566
1 A large, ball-shaped fungus 2 The bark 3 Bamboo 4 African elephants 5 Sole, a sort of flatfish 6 Trees 7 A drone 8 Willow 9 They hibernate in a snow hole 10 The bat

567
1 Cacao 2 Red 3 On rocks and walls 4 In a pond 5 Limpet 6 The lynx 7 An albatross 8 The maple 9 Types of plants 10 Venom

568
1 A fungus 2 Australia 3 Orang-utan 4 The merlin 5 South America 6 It is another name for an animal's 'foot' 7 The chameleon 8 Fat 9 An extinct man-like ape 10 Eucalyptus leaves

569
1 Orchids 2 The tomato 3 The cedar 4 Fish 5 Koala: a koala is a marsupial; the others are true bears 6 Antelope 7 A monkey 8 Hemlock 9 Australia 10 Mandrake

570
1 The Komodo Dragon 2 The cuttlefish (whose Latin name is Sepia) 3 The egg case of the skate 4 California 5 Lichen 6 A small lemur from Madagascar 7 Africa 8 Tropical forest 9 A type of European wild sheep 10 Ruminants

571
1 Penguin 2 Panthers 3 Parrots 4 Storm petrel 5 Piranha 6 Piebald 7 Polar bear 8 Proboscis monkey 9 Pheasant 10 Pigeon

572
1 Iris 2 Lady's slipper 3 Marigold 4 Lily of the valley 5 Phlox 6 Holly 7 Bleeding heart 8 Forget-me-not 9 Morning Glory 10 Primrose

573
1 A ram, a male sheep 2 A large antelope 3 A substance produced in the sperm whale gut 4 Penguins 5 A West African lemur 6 A fish 7 The fossil of a squid-like animal 8 Rabbits 9 A horizontal plant stem 10 A steeply sloping wood of beech trees

574
1 Runt 2 Seal 3 Blue 4 Deer 5 Must 6 Calf 7 Fern 8 Cell 9 Lion 10 Sage

575
1 The sturgeon 2 The mudskipper 3 A small shrimp-like animal, found in vast numbers in the ocean, and fed on by whales and other animals 4 The manta ray 5 A pouch in his abdomen, where the young are hatched 6 It knocks them off overhanging leaves by squirting a jet of water 7 To filter water for small animals on which they feed 8 Gills 9 Rock salmon 10 The eel

576
1 Stonefish 2 The death cap 3 True. About ten times the potency 4 Sydney funnel web 5 King cobra 6 Neurotoxins 7 All of it, except for the fruit 8 'The female of the species' 9 Australia 10 Cyanide

577
1 Milk 2 A large deer 3 Lion 4 Yellow 5 Beagle. Snoopy is a beagle, Darwin sailed in HMS *Beagle* 6 *Animal Magic* 7 Cherry 8 Bluish-black 9 Carp 10 They flew

578
1 Jaws 2 Pangaea 3 Sedentary 4 Into the cavity of freshwater mussels 5 Llamas 6 Its bright red body 7 Bats 8 A poisonous type of North American viper 9 Cat 10 A wild plum tree

579
1 Plankton 2 Poplars 3 A leaf stalk 4 A cactus (A large variety found in the south-west American deserts and often seen in cowboy movies) 5 A blind European salamander 6 Four 7 Giant tortoises 8 The flax plant 9 Goldeneye: a film starring Pierce Brosnan and a variety of duck 10 The cat

580
1 Buried in seaside sand and mud 2 Tits 3 A rookery 4 A type of grass 5 Birch 6 Women's corsets and other undergarments were made from it 7 Spoor 8 A donkey 9 A tree. It has leaves with different coloured upper and lower surfaces which makes the tree look as if it is quivering in the wind 10 Carboniferous

581
1 On alpine slopes 2 Two 3 The columbine or Aquilegia 4 The daisy family 5 Their flowers last one day 6 Rose 7 It smells of rotting flesh 8 Love-lies-bleeding 9 *Keeping up Appearances* 10 The tulip

582
1 Neotony 2 Just under the bark 3 To attract a mate 4 Feather-like 5 A botanist's collection of dried plants 6 Sea creatures with shells 7 The legs are adapted to catch prey 8 When the branches grow vertically, parallel to the trunk 9 A rootstock or underground stem 10 Many bristles: they are very hairy worms

583
1 Asia 2 Africa 3 North America 4 Australasia 5 South America 6 Asia 7 South America 8 Australasia 9 North America 10 Africa

584
1 Tapir 2 Thrush 3 Tulip 4 Tarantula 5 Trout 6 Teal 7 Tundra 8 Tuberculosis 9 Termites 10 Toadstools

585
1 Mauritius, in the Indian Ocean 2 The coelacanth 3 The Moa 4 The Great Auk 5 Butterflies 6 The thylacine 7 Dinosaurs 8 Reptile 9 Barbary lion 10 Passenger pigeon

586
1 Red (with white spots) 2 Wading birds 3 Bright red 4 Six, it is a small wingless insect 5 Redwood 6 Black and white 7 Greyhens 8 A butterfly 9 Pinkish brown 10 Yellow

587
1 10 Downing Street 2 Gorilla 3 President Nixon 4 Edinburgh 5 *Blue Peter* 6 Giant Panda 7 His 'black dog' 8 A cat 9 David Blunkett 10 Trooping the Colour

588
1 Fieldfare 2 All are freshwater fish except the turbot 3 The python is non-venomous, the others are highly venomous 4 Dog's mercury is the only winter-flowering plant of the list 5 The kiwi is restricted to New Zealand, the others live in Australia 6 They are all associated with water except the stonechat 7 The swallowtail is a day-flying butterfly, the

others are nocturnal **8** All are found in Scottish pine forests, except the purple emperor **9** There are no jackals in South America, where jaguars are found **10** All are associated with the sea shore apart from the deep-ocean angler fish

1 Whale **2** A jellyfish **3** White, to camouflage itself against the snow **4** Crab **5** Giant Kelp **6** Hammerhead shark **7** Animals **8** Elephant seals: females are a third the size of the males **9** Herring **10** Blubber

1 Type of bird **2** The red admiral **3** Red deer (Landseer painted the *Monarch of the Glen*) **4** Redshank **5** Cook it; it's a vegetable related to spinach **6** A badge or feather attached to your hat **7** A moth **8** Red grouse **9** A flowering plant, Kniphofia, much grown in gardens **10** The red squirrel

1 Pears **2** Avocado **3** Mandarin **4** Pineapple (piña is Spanish for pineapple) **5** Apple **6** Banana **7** Raspberry **8** Cherry **9** Plum **10** Gooseberry

1 The Scarlet Pimpernel **2** Shrew. *The Taming of the Shrew* **3** *Of Mice and Men* **4** Flies in *Lord of the Flies* **5** Nathaniel Hawthorne **6** 'Go down to Kew in Lilac-time' **7** The Lion in Winter **8** Sperm whale **9** The cedar (*Snow Falling on Cedars*) **10** The Raven

1 The Narwhal **2** The manatee (also called Dugong or Sea Cow) **3** 'The Common Cormorant or Shag' **4** A parrot, according to the Monty Python team **5** The Star Trek crew **6** Nessie, the Loch Ness Monster; this is the Latin name given it by Sir Peter Scott **7** A Whiting **8** A lovesick tom-tit, or titwillow **9** King Kong **10** The Triffid, in *The Day of the Triffids*

1 He was a pioneer in the study of American birds **2** Charles Darwin **3** David Attenborough (his brother is the actor Richard) **4** Bill Oddie

(chased by a giant kitten in *The Goodies*) **5** Dianne Fosse **6** David Bellamy **7** Desmond Morris **8** Sir Joseph Banks **9** Chimpanzees **10** All these naturalists had a Warbler named after them

1 A tail **2** Cheetah **3** Tiger **4** The National Cat Club Show **5** Leopard **6** It is hairless **7** Cheetah **8** Ocelot **9** Burmese **10** The Abyssinian

1 *Megalosaurus* **2** It is the smallest dinosaur yet found. It was about the size of a chicken **3** He coined the term 'dinosaur' – meaning 'terrible lizard' **4** *Ankylosaurus* **5** 65 million years ago **6** *Utahraptor*. The *velociraptor* was about the size of a large poodle **7** *Tyrannosaurus Rex* **8** It had a pointed spike-like thumb **9** *Diplodocus* **10** They are credited with the earliest published announcements of what later would be recognised as dinosaurs

1 Toadflax **2** Catchfly **3** Crane's-bill **4** Dandelion **5** Dog-violet **6** Viper's-grass **7** Hawkweed **8** Oxlip **9** Catmint **10** Lamb's ears

1 Dinosaur (*Diplodocus*, *pteradactyl*, *triceratops*) **2** Borzoi **3** Jack Dempsey **4** The points of the compass: Northern Lights, Southern Comfort, westerns, and Easton **5** An unfertilised ostrich egg **6** Hind legs **7** Red; eye, neck, breast; Yellow: fever, hammer, belly; Blue: stocking, tit, blood **8** Terrier (which means digger in the earth) **9** Trick question: a bombay duck has no beak, it's a fish **10** 'Survival of the fittest' **11** Woody Allen **12** Order **13** W.B. Yeats **14** Seahorse **15** It can walk on water

1 Giraffe **2** Blue whale **3** Laughing hyena **4** The elephant **5** Marsupial **6** Southern Africa **7** The vampire bat **8** Rhinoceros **9** Panther **10** Zebra

1 The Magpie **2** Both have advertised alcohol (Guinness and Famous Grouse whisky) **3** The Harrier **4** It has a

white head that makes it looks bald **5** Goose **6** Goldfinch **7** On sea cliffs **8** The Americas **9** A variety of chicken **10** Duck

1 The flea **2** A tapeworm **3** The provision of universal fresh, uncontaminated water **4** Sleeping sickness **5** The bed bug **6** Louse **7** A fungus **8** Elephantiasis **9** Sandfly **10** A tick

1 Breaking out of eggs **2** Penguins **3** Aardvark **4** Pond weed **5** A type of finch **6** Kashmir goats **7** A beaver **8** An octopus **9** Blue **10** The kangaroo

1 Mouse **2** Rabbits **3** Hedgehog **4** The March hare **5** Donkey **6** A little lamb **7** Polynesia **8** The lion **9** Nana **10** Panther

1 Old man's beard **2** It was thought to deter fleas **3** Wood anemone **4** Yellow **5** Helianthus is the sunflower that Van Gogh painted so often **6** Bell shaped **7** Tobacco plant **8** Catkins **9** Blue **10** Rose

1 Caddis fly larvae **2** A moth **3** Antennae **4** Volkswagen **5** Mayflies **6** Ladybird **7** Approximately 800,000 **8** Eight, it is a poisonous spider **9** It is the largest insect in the world **10** A beetle

1 Wagtail **2** The goldcrest **3** Parrot **4** Woodpecker **5** The farmyard hen and cockerel **6** Black and white **7** Swan **8** The pigeon **9** Reddish **10** A leaf warbler (it gets the name 'chiffchaff' from its characteristic song)

1 James Herriot **2** FMD stands for Foot and Mouth Disease **3** Just above the hoof **4** Cattle **5** Distemper **6** Cow pox **7** Birds (especially parrots) **8** Mad cow disease (or BSE) **9** A mite **10** Sheep

1 Fish scales **2** Bear fur **3** Cowhide **4** Elephant skin **5** Giraffe skin

6 Tortoise shell 7 Jaguar fur 8 Zebra skin 9 Snake skin 10 Siberian tiger fur

609
1 A tree; also called the Maidenhair tree, a native of China 2 Nose horn 3 A poisonous toadstool 4 A perennial weed from the daisy family 5 A bird 6 A type of rattlesnake that moves by a sideways looping motion 7 Feral 8 The Scarlet Pimpernel 9 *The Joshua Tree* 10 Wildebeest

610
1 Aaron's rod 2 Benjamin bush or tree 3 Adam's needle 4 Herb Robert 5 Jack-go-to-bed-at-noon 6 St John's wort 7 Jacob (Jacob's ladder) 8 St Bruno's lily 9 Herb Christopher 10 Job's tear

611
1 Mosses 2 Mackerel-like fish 3 Wild mushroom 4 The aubergine 5 A large bird 6 Blue 7 A fish 8 Chimpanzee 9 Blackberries 10 Eagle

612
1 The Andean condor 2 An otter 3 Heather 4 Caribou 5 Toad 6 The Jaguar 7 Fruitbat 8 King Charles Spaniel 9 Pekinese 10 The ship of the desert

613
1 Cocoon 2 They have wing patterns that look like patterned carpets 3 Four (plus two that are not used) 4 Whites 5 Fritillary 6 It is the world's largest butterfly 7 Blues 8 To attract butterflies, the plant is also called the butterfly bush 9 Comma 10 *Silence of the Lambs*

614
1 Juniper 2 One that lives for more than one season 3 Spruce 4 William Wordsworth 5 Yellow 6 It sheds them 7 The poppy 8 Busy lizzie 9 Green 10 The Shamrock

615
1 Its bottom 2 Monkeys 3 The sea otter 4 The bison 5 Zebra 6 Tibet, they are a type of shaggy ox adapted to high altitudes 7 The gorilla 8 Cat: it often goes limp when picked up 9 Movement using the arms, such as swinging from branch to branch 10 Cantering

616
1 The Purple-crested 2 A small seabird 3 It has brightly coloured, patchwork markings 4 The Nightjar 5 There is no British bird called a Bluebird 6 Magpie 7 A wisp 8 In the swamps of Louisiana and adjacent states 9 Divers 10 Warbler

617
1 Magpie 2 Chicken 3 Duck 4 Eagle 5 Albatross 6 Ostrich (which is said to stick its head in the sand when danger approaches) 7 Turkey 8 Owl 9 Gannet 10 Peacock

618
1 Kiwi fruit 2 Guava 3 Kumquat 4 Lychee 5 Mango 6 Passion fruit 7 Physalis 8 Rambutan 9 Star fruit 10 Prickly pear

619
1 Afghan hound 2 Airedale terrier 3 Dalmatian 4 Yorkshire terrier 5 Chihuahua 6 Great Dane 7 German pointer 8 Lakeland terrier 9 Staffordshire pit bull terrier 10 Labrador

620
1 Rose 2 Daphne 3 Lily 4 Iris 5 Heather 6 Violetta 7 Pansy 8 Cherry 9 Rosemary 10 Flora

621
1 Hand 2 Arm 3 Lower leg 4 Shoulder 5 Fingers 6 Collar 7 Hip 8 Ear 9 Breast 10 Thigh

622
1 Butterflies and moths 2 Fossils 3 Birds 4 Beetles 5 Spiders 6 Reptiles and amphibians 7 The development of plants and animals 8 Wasps, bees and ants 9 Fish 10 Mosses

623
1 A type of shrub 2 Midwife toad 3 The horse 4 A pig 5 The Phoenix 6 Owl 7 Melon 8 Topiary 9 Turtle 10 Cow

624
1 The alligator and crocodile 2 Beavers 3 A cricket is a type of orthopteran 4 The thistle 5 Gorse 6 In holes in giant (saguaro) cacti 7 The nests of eagles and other big birds of prey 8 A type of seashell 9 The cobras 10 Rain forest

625
1 Lancelot 2 Members of the daisy family (Compositae or Asteraceae) 3 Between Australia and New Zealand 4 Epiphytes 5 Otter dung 6 An alpine New Zealand plant, that forms a large hairy mound that looks like a sheep 7 It leads honey badgers to bees' nests 8 The bee hummingbird 9 A lively Italian dance; a spider bite was once thought to cause manic dancing 10 The Elder plant (Sambucus)

626
1 Silver 2 Giraffe 3 Canopy 4 Types of bird 5 The earthworm 6 The seed inside a hard nut 7 The hummingbird 8 A small, wading bird 9 *The Tempest* 10 30 days

627
1 Their tongues 2 Ants and termites 3 The fibrous fruit of a tropical marrow 4 For navigation in much the same way a bat uses sound 5 Spiders or silkworms 6 Red 7 A thrush-like bird, typically found in moorland 8 In plant stems and trunks; they are the vessels that carry water and food 9 A type of large lizard 10 It swims head-down

628
1 A juvenile hare 2 Carotene 3 Edible crustaceans, related to lobsters and prawns 4 Oil-seed rape 5 Gilbert White 6 The sailfish 7 A type of mountain plant (Dryas) 8 Flowers 9 The giant water lily 10 By attaching itself to sharks, other big fish and even ships

629
1 The otter and weasel 2 Roadrunner 3 Blue 4 During courtship 5 A type of large deer 6 A stoat 7 Botanist 8 Thrush 9 A snake: a species of large, dangerous, poisonous snake belonging to the cobra family 10 Pike

630
1 Slugs and snails 2 England will be invaded 3 Sweat glands 4 Frogs 5 *Gardeners' Question Time* 6 Clove

7 In and around freshwater lakes and rivers **8** The Golden Eagle **9** They lay their eggs in the nests of other birds **10** A fungus (the common stinkhorn fungus)

631
1 Horse **2** Longest bird migration **3** Sheep **4** Raven **5** They grab them with their predatory forelegs **6** Daffodils **7** The grass family **8** The oyster **9** Pitcher plants **10** Types of freshwater fish

632
1 Corn **2** A fossil animal, distantly related to crustaceans, spiders and insects **3** Gecko **4** The St Bernard **5** Cormorant. They fit a ring round its neck to prevent it swallowing its catch **6** Geological periods **7** A badger **8** A type of grass **9** Sheep **10** Yew

633
1 Population **2** Oxpecker **3** The peregrine falcon (in a dive it can reach 155mph/250 km/h) **4** Gizzard **5** Tilth **6** Hawthorn **7** Indigo **8** Wisley **9** Tomato **10** South America

634
1 A wing **2** Fully or partly in trees **3** Animals which have jointed bodies and limbs (such as spiders, crustaceans, insects and centipedes) **4** The production of light by living things (e.g. fireflies) **5** It thinks you are its mother (typically because you were the first thing it saw on hatching) **6** The protein keratin **7** It produces pollen **8** Chlorophyll **9** Producing offspring without mating **10** By laying eggs

635
1 A large root that grows vertically down below the stem **2** Hardy **3** At night **4** Brown **5** Penguins **6** Hermaphrodite **7** Zest **8** Pollarding **9** A type of fruit **10** Sparrow

636
1 Snakes **2** In flowers **3** Dove **4** Triceratops means three-horned-face: the dinosaur has horns above its eyes and on its nose **5** Pelt **6** Cat **7** It has a lobe of skin shaped like a horseshoe on its nose **8** The olive **9** India **10** In the sea

637
1 Stridulation **2** By the sea **3** Pink **4** A sea fish **5** They sting and paralyse them with their tentacles **6** Layering **7** In a marsh **8** A tropical bird **9** Deer **10** Pigmentation

638
1 Terns **2** A fossil **3** A tiercel **4** The cuckoo **5** Rice **6** Hooves **7** Host **8** Poplar **9** The smooth snake **10** It has strong front legs for digging

639
1 Judaism **2** Ecosystem **3** Lianas **4** They have feathery seeds and are dispersed by the wind **5** China **6** A tiny jumping insect **7** Lords-and-Ladies **8** A type of deer **9** Africa **10** Radishes, which are related to the cabbage: all the others are related to each other in the genus Allium

640
1 An Indian snake **2** A water plant **3** A plant related to the artichoke **4** An Asian wild ass **5** It is a bright patch of feathers on the wing **6** A desert shrub **7** A bird of prey **8** Carnivorous mammals related to mongooses **9** A bush-cricket **10** A type of fungus

641
1 South Africa **2** Chaparral **3** Slimbridge **4** Kenya **5** Florida **6** France **7** Savannah **8** Yellowstone, in Wyoming **9** Spain **10** Suffolk

642
1 Primrose **2** Sweet violet **3** Dandelion **4** Bee orchid **5** Creeping buttercup **6** Lady's mantle **7** Field poppy **8** Thrift **9** Heather **10** Sorrel

643
1 Orchids **2** None of them has wings **3** Tropical birds **4** Maple **5** Coffee **6** Python **7** Blue butterflies **8** Pony **9** Thrush **10** Gazelle

644
1 A male deer **2** A moth with heart and dart shaped markings **3** A fern **4** Richard II **5** In Africa, it is a type of antelope **6** Cardiology **7** Sea urchins **8** Four, two atriums and two ventricles **9** The lung **10** Psalms

645
1 Cow **2** Goat **3** Eagle **4** Ape **5** Bear **6** Pig **7** Sheep **8** Mouse **9** Horse **10** Lion

646
1 Malaria **2** Dock **3** Heart disease **4** Orange **5** Poppy **6** Making leather (tanning) **7** Dandelion **8** Breast cancer **9** Aspirin **10** Deadly nightshade

647
1 Pine **2** Fir **3** Ash **4** Elder **5** Hemlock **6** Cypress **7** Holly **8** Spruce **9** Yew **10** Lime

648
1 Hamster **2** Lemmings **3** Squirrel **4** Beaver **5** Dormouse **6** The desert rats **7** Muskrat **8** Vole **9** Black rat **10** Gerbil

649
1 Orchids **2** Grass **3** It flowers at Easter (Pasque in Old French) **4** It's a variety of cactus (Opuntia) **5** A hazel nut **6** Crocus **7** An iris **8** Bracken **9** Aster **10** New Zealand

650
1 Black poplar **2** White willow **3** Common ash **4** Yew **5** Holly **6** Rowan or mountain ash **7** Silver fir **8** Sweet bay **9** Common beech **10** Hazel

651
1 Muhammad Ali **2** 6 – they are hexagons **3** Moses **4** Potato **5** Compound eyes **6** Thorax **7** Nikolai Rimsky-Korsakov **8** Aphids **9** The Venus Flytrap **10** Royal Jelly

652
1 Sand dollar **2** Honey-pot ants **3** Earthstars **4** A bird **5** Boxer **6** Potter wasps **7** A moth **8** The secretary bird **9** The bootlace worm **10** The angler fish

653
1 Daddy-long-legs **2** Mosquito **3** Bluebottle **4** Tsetse **5** Horse flies **6** Hover fly **7** House fly **8** Fly in the ointment **9** Midges **10** Elephant fly

654
1 Toothwort **2** The tea tree **3** Echinacea **4** St John's wort **5** Chaste-berry **6** Evening primrose

7 Aloe vera **8** Ginkgo biloba
9 Marigold **10** Valerian

655

1 Salamander **2** Tadpoles **3** Carapace
4 Newt **5** Frog **6** Marine iguana
7 Komodo dragon **8** Kaa **9** Tortoise
(testudo in Latin) **10** Arrow-poison
frog

656

1 Bull **2** Dolphin **3** Bear **4** Lizard
5 Goat **6** Fox **7** The Dog Star
8 Horse **9** Eagle **10** Swan

657

1 Lungs **2** Brain **3** Eye **4** Heart
5 Thorax **6** Base of the spine
7 Chest **8** Knee **9** Leading from the
heart **10** Ear

658

1 Stephen Jay Gould **2** The Gaia
hypothesis **3** *Silent Spring* **4** Gerald
Durrell **5** The Duke of Edinburgh
6 *The Ascent of Man* **7** Jane Goodall
8 Second World War **9** Will Self
10 *On the Origin of Species*

659

1 Hedgehog **2** Pipistrelle **3** Ladybird
4 Mink **5** Shrew **6** Wild Boar **7** Fox
8 Otter **9** Seal **10** Badger

660

1 Sparrowhawk **2** A butterfly **3** A fly
4 A lichen **5** Rut **6** Juniper
7 A toadstool **8** A sheep **9** A ferret
10 Lek

661

1 The *Stegosaurus* **2** Pine trees
3 The ostrich **4** The Blue whale
5 The African Elephant **6** Great White
Pelican **7** The cheetah **8** Alaska
9 The whale shark **10** Butterfly

662

1 Rabbit **2** Walrus **3** Bats
4 Ant-eater **5** Blue whale
6 Hippopotamus **7** Horse
8 Monkeys **9** Elephant
10 Hedgehog

663

1 Crick and Watson **2** Richard
Dawkins **3** Ian Dury **4** Two
5 The O group **6** Fred Astaire – in
1899 (Gene Kelly was born in 1912)
7 Gregor Mendel **8** The Genome
Project **9** 23 **10** Hereditary

664

1 A type of poisonous fungus **2** It has
a skull-shaped mark on its thorax **3** It
had three heads **4** A type of beetle
5 A type of soft coral **6** Purple
7 They are deadly poisonous
8 It makes an audible tapping sound
9 Plums – they are prunes wrapped in
bacon. **10** A bat

665

1 Sallow **2** Sable **3** Squirrel **4** Shag
5 Senna **6** Sloe **7** Sandstone
8 Starling **9** Skunk **10** Solomon's seal

666

1 Moulting **2** Entomologist **3** Nits
4 Ant **5** Cockroach **6** Earwig
7 Shieldbug **8** Bee **9** Cicada **10** Silk
– the *bombyx mori* is the silkworm

667

1 A mongoose **2** The pomegranate
3 Nightingale **4** Macavity **5** Samson
6 Dr Johnson **7** The gnu **8** A bull
9 A swan **10** *Animal Farm*

668

1 It has chevron markings like a
sergeant's stripes **2** A shark **3** Float,
as a form of seed dispersal
4 Monotremes **5** The glassfish
6 Penguins **7** Herman Melville **8** The
octopus **9** Hans Christian Andersen
10 Stickleback

669

1 Towns **2** A large martin, a relative
of stoats and weasels **3** Armadillo
4 Muskrat **5** A type of wild pig
6 Moose **7** Pronghorn **8** A type of
wild cat **9** Rabbits (giant mutated
ones) **10** A type of squirrel

670

1 The yew **2** One – all domestic dogs
are the same species **3** Pups
4 Mulberry **5** The tail end **6** The
horse **7** Australia. It is a type of
cockatoo **8** A fungus **9** Diamond
10 An elephant

671

1 Butterflies and moths **2** Caddis flies
3 Beetles **4** Aphids, planthoppers and
relatives **5** Fleas **6** Mayflies **7** Ants,
bees and wasps **8** Grasshoppers,
crickets and relatives **9** Dragonflies
10 Cockroaches (and mantids)

672

1 Stigma **2** Style **3** Anther
4 Filament **5** Calyx **6** Umbel
7 Pedicel **8** Nectary **9** Panicle
10 Composite flower

673

1 Swallowtail **2** Brimstone **3** Peacock
4 Comma **5** Monarch (Milkweed)
6 Orange Tip **7** Speckled Wood
8 Marbled White **9** Small Copper
10 Purple Emperor

674

1 Black bear **2** White rhinoceros
3 Black mamba **4** Great White Shark
5 Swans **6** Whitebait **7** Black fly
8 Snowy owl **9** Blackbird **10** Snow
leopard

675

1 Rin Tin Tin **2** Scooby-doo **3** Spike
4 Dachshund **5** Alsatian **6** The USA
7 Beagle **8** Buddy **9** The wolf **10** 99
– the other two were the parent
Dalmatians

676

1 Wild Angelica. Anjelica Houston
starred in the film **2** Virginia creeper.
Virginia Wade won the women's title
in 1977 **3** Rose of Sharon. Ariel
Sharon was elected prime minister in
February 2001 **4** Cicely. Dame
Cicely Courtneidge was made a DBE
in 1972 **5** Sweet Alison. Alison Lurie
won the Pulitzer in 1985 **6** St
Catherine's lace. Catherine Zeta Jones
married in November 2000
7 Hattie's pincushion. Hattie Jacques
played Matron in *Carry On Matron*
8 Blue dawn flower. Dawn French and
Jennifer Saunders form the duo
9 Helen's flower. Helen of Troy
was reputedly the most beautiful
woman in the ancient world
10 Cassandra. She was doomed to
make prophecies no one believed

677

1 Haltere **2** Coxa **3** Spiracle
4 Gena **5** Ommatidium **6** Cilia
7 Ovipositor **8** Stigma **9** Palpi
10 Elytra

678

1 They are all extinct **2** Orang-utan
3 Aardvark **4** A whale: a Nantucket
sleigh ride is the name sailors gave to
the experience of being dragged along

in their ship by a harpooned whale
5 Ariel (who speaks this line in *The Tempest*) **6** None of them is what it's name claims: a glowworm is not a worm, it is a beetle; a koala is not a bear, it is a marsupial; and a Tasmanian tiger is not a tiger, it is an extinct striped wolf **7** Devonian (Geological eras) **8** The fox (according to Oscar Wilde) **9** A rhinoceros **10** Estivation **11** Dove **12** Weed **13** Giraffes (in Karen Blixen's *Out of Africa*) **14** A cow's stomach **15** Dogs (the word canary comes from the Latin canis)

679

1 The leek **2** An evergreen **3** Cloche **4** Dead heading **5** Tulips **6** Lettuce **7** Tea **8** Training trees **9** Grafting **10** Lancashire

680

1 Phototroph **2** Granivore **3** Parasite **4** Detritivore **5** Herbivore **6** Carnivore **7** Graminivore **8** Saprophyte **9** Piscivore **10** Omnivore

681

1 Mites **2** Mallard **3** Mustard **4** Mantis **5** Maple **6** Moray **7** Mimicry **8** Myna **9** Minotaur **10** Martin

682

1 Antler **2** Adder **3** Alps **4** Bees **5** Bramble **6** Bluebell **7** Brassica **8** Cartilage **9** Courgette **10** Cougar

683

1 Russian vine **2** Bindweed **3** Nettles **4** Common ragwort **5** A weedkiller **6** Daisy **7** Geranium **8** Mulch **9** Dock **10** Pink

684

1 Emperor **2** Hibernaculum **3** Truffles **4** It means that good weather is on the way **5** A reptile. It is an Australian lizard **6** Formic acid **7** Shrimps **8** Mermaids' purses **9** The Romans **10** Black

685

1 River banks **2** Rivers **3** Sea shore **4** Ocean depths **5** Sea bottom **6** Northern and mountain regions **7** Lakes **8** Open Ocean **9** Salt tolerance **10** Tolerance of dry habitats

686

1 Rafflesia **2** Water hyacinth **3** The Amazon river **4** By its strong, rotting smell **5** The banyan tree **6** Australia **7** Poison ivy **8** Oxford ragwort **9** A caterpillar **10** The coco-de-mer

687

1 Basil **2** The root **3** Mint **4** Sage **5** Dill **6** Scarborough Fair **7** Mace **8** Mustard **9** Parsley **10** Garlic

688

1 Arctic Tern **2** Bearded Vulture **3** Canada Goose **4** Great Egret **5** Cap White Eye **6** Snowy Owl **7** Cardinal **8** White Pelican **9** Guinea Fowl **10** Barn Swallow

689

1 Weeping willow **2** Cedar **3** Canada **4** U2 **5** Birch **6** Silver fir **7** Syria **8** Lime **9** It is the most common species of Christmas tree **10** The holly

690

1 Calf **2** Chick **3** Kid **4** Cygnet **5** Owlet **6** Poult **7** Foal **8** Duckling **9** Gosling **10** Fry

691

1 George Orwell **2** Bonsai **3** Ikebana **4** Orange-red **5** Cacti **6** Succulents **7** Swiss cheese plant **8** Red **9** Daffodil **10** A corsage

692

1 Bourbon **2** Damask (from Damascus) **3** Vitamin C **4** Their scent (which is said to be like fresh-packed tea) **5** Five **6** Henry VII (Henry Tudor) **7** Rupert Brooke **8** Pink **9** Yellow **10** *Romeo and Juliet*

693

1 Hand-shaped **2** Arrow-shaped **3** Heart-shaped **4** Spoon-shaped **5** Head-shaped **6** Tooth-shaped **7** Spear-shaped (triangular) **8** Notched like a saw **9** Long and straight-sided **10** With a wavy edge

694

1 Sow **2** Jenny **3** Cow **4** Doe **5** Mare **6** Ewe **7** Hen **8** Vixen **9** Goose **10** Queen

695

1 Red **2** Lettuce **3** Artichoke **4** Turnips (known as 'neeps' in Scotland) **5** Pumpkin **6** Potato **7** Tomato **8** Bean **9** Aubergine **10** Chick pea

696

1 Opossum **2** Sloth **3** A monkey **4** Capybara **5** Cats **6** River dolphins **7** Jaguar **8** Howler monkeys **9** Anaconda **10** A species of anteater

697

1 The Pacific – it occupies a third of the world's surface and contains more than half the water on the planet **2** The North Pole (Arctic) **3** Bamboo **4** Venezuela **5** The Himalayas (including the Karakorams) **6** Actaeon **7** Siamese **8** North America **9** Cardamom **10** Australia

698

1 Honey buzzard **2** Red kite **3** Osprey **4** Falcons **5** Blue-grey **6** Marsh harrier **7** White-tailed eagle **8** Barn owl **9** Five **10** Short-eared owl

699

1 Greenhouse gases **2** The ozone layer **3** Chernobyl **4** It was an insecticide **5** Greenpeace **6** Japan **7** France, at 77 per cent **8** To defoliate forests **9** *The Exxon Valdez* **10** The peppered moth

700

1 Lady's fingers **2** Chilli **3** Killer whale **4** Female **5** The cheetah **6** Common pigeon **7** The fox **8** Spiders' webs **9** A snake **10** Echolocation

701

1 Australia **2** North America **3** Africa (Madagascar) **4** Asia **5** South America **6** Africa **7** South America **8** Asia **9** North America (Mexico) **10** Asia (Siberia)

702

1 Trees **2** Mother-of-pearl **3** Kapok **4** Latex **5** Bioluminescence **6** Pink **7** Dung beetle **8** The root **9** Covered in a thick, felty layer of hair **10** The mussel is a mollusc, and the others are crustaceans

703

1 Box 2 Emu 3 Tom 4 Jaw 5 Boa
6 Cub 7 Sow 8 Sap 9 Tit 10 Bed

704

1 Egyptian Goose 2 Little Owl
3 Ruddy Duck 4 Pheasant 5 Canada
Goose 6 Red-legged (or French)
Partridge 7 Mandarin duck 8 Ring-
necked parakeet 9 Muscovy duck
10 North America

705

1 Clavicle 2 Lungs 3 In the brain
4 206 (any number from 196 to 216
will do) 5 In the heart 6 Sugar
7 Joint 8 Liver 9 Vitamin
10 Fingerprints

706

1 Choler 2 Crocuses 3 Cheetah
4 Coppice 5 Canary 6 Crane
7 Cannabis 8 Cambrian 9 Cassis
10 Cowslip

707

1 Elephant (20-22 months) 2 Royal
Society for the Protection of Birds
3 It has four flowers pointing in
different directions like the faces of a
church clock, and a fifth pointing up to
the sky 4 Kew Gardens 5 Africa
6 A dog 7 It grows another one
8 A moth 9 Malachite 10 A small
forest antelope

708

1 Ibis 2 A green mineral (copper
carbonate) 3 African fish eagle 4
They weave their nest 5 Flamingo
6 Hummingbird 7 Most species are
predominantly dark coloured like a
widow's mourning dress 8 A helmet
like extension to the upper part of
the beak 9 Its call sounds like the
phrase 'go away' 10 Carrion

709

1 Snowdrop 2 Blind 3 Primrose
4 Their flowers resemble a bunch of
grapes 5 *Tulip Fever* 6 Gladiolus
7 Lily 8 Alexandre Dumas 9 The
tunic 10 Forcing

710

1 Skua 2 Pipit 3 Tit 4 Tern
5 Grebe 6 Gull 7 Owl
8 Shearwater 9 Warbler 10 Lark

711

1 Limestone 2 A cave dweller
3 Morphos 4 The cave swiftlet
5 Breaching 6 The giant tortoise
7 A fungus 8 The two-headed eagle
9 A bird 10 A kind of leopard

712

1 Wind strength 2 Carbon
3 Mercury 4 Earthquake intensity
5 Comets 6 Nitrogen 7 Molten rock
8 The Pacific Ocean 9 The Amazon
10 Glaciers

713

1 In her pouch 2 A dinosaur 3 An
oak tree 4 A vixen 5 Frog eggs
6 Turtles 7 The gorilla 8 Tusks
9 Australia 10 16 (8 + 6 + 2)

714

1 The tiger 2 Kite 3 A fish
4 Hyenas are said to laugh 5 It is a
harmless moth 6 A fungus 7 The
horse 8 A lizard 9 The leaves
10 Ladybirds

715

1 Types of fly 2 A horse 3 A coral
reef 4 Bread 5 The robin
6 Eucalyptus 7 Antarctica 8 A bat
9 A tree 10 The beans

716

1 The blue whale 2 Condor 3 Hands
4 A thousand feet 5 The kestrel
6 The honeybee 7 A dog 8 A potato
9 Russia 10 Superior

717

1 A horse 2 A donkey 3 Swallow
4 A conker 5 Cat 6 Lion 7 An owl
8 Dalmatian 9 Apple 10 Santa's Little
Helper

718

1 Otter 2 Rabbits 3 Mouse
4 Horse 5 Bear 6 Dog 7 Kangaroo
8 Mouse 9 Elephant 10 Cat

719

1 Swine 2 Bull 3 Cat 4 Spider
5 Bee 6 Blackbirds 7 Hare
8 Monkeys 9 Ants 10 Bull

720

1 Yellow 2 Holly 3 A rainbow
4 White 5 Blue 6 Orange 7 Mars
8 Greenland 9 Kingfisher 10 Red

721

1 Daffodil 2 New Zealand 3 Maple
4 Cat 5 Loch Ness 6 Eagle
7 Shamrock 8 Springbok 9 Oak
10 Tulip

Science

722

1 Female 2 Table salt 3 Electricity
from light 4 Skin 5 Neil Armstrong
on the Apollo 11 mission 6 The
Greenwich Meridian 7 Sir Isaac
Newton 8 China 9 Light 10 The
Internet or World Wide Web

723

1 Carbon dioxide (or CO_2)
2 Jacques Cousteau 3 Cracking
4 Primarily water ice 5 At Sellafield
in Cumbria. It changed its name
6 Anticlockwise 7 Fontanelle
8 Scurvy 9 Silver 10 John McAdam
(tarmac)

724

1 Diabetes 2 Tooth enamel 3 1760
4 Solid carbon dioxide (CO_2)
5 Oxygen 6 Zinc 7 Permafrost
8 About 30 per cent in a normal adult
9 Melanin 10 The strength of an
earthquake

725

1 Computerised Axial Tomography
2 Differential 3 Halley's comet 4 It
was the first public railway 5 Escape
velocity 6 Plimsoll Line 7 Involuntary
muscle 8 Cats-eyes 9 They are all
forms of carbon 10 Bakelite

726

1 Charles Darwin 2 Piper Alpha
3 Fellow of the Royal Society 4 In
your stomach 5 Albert Einstein
6 Peninsula and Oriental 7 Nitrogen
8 They are all names of aircraft 9 An
acre 10 A German underground
railway

727

1 On the bonnet of a Rolls Royce –
it's the radiator mascot 2 An
escalator 3 *Great Eastern* 4 Distance
5 Isosceles 6 The results of an
election 7 Galileo 8 It was the first
balloon to travel round the world
9 Birth 10 Pressure, it was invented
in 1849 by Eugène Bourdon

728

1 Pressure – specifically atmospheric pressure as an indicator of weather 2 Hurricane 3 Diesel engine 4 pi (approx 3.14159) 5 The Ozone layer 6 Gold 7 Electro Plated Nickel Silver 8 The Sahara 9 Hydrogen 10 Iron

729

1 Generates electricity from wind 2 Fool's gold 3 In the ear 4 Outwards 5 Television 6 It uses radar 7 Smog 8 Bacteria, typically Streptococcus 9 Wheel spin 10 Direct current

730

1 The Doppler effect 2 Frequency Modulation 3 They are all North Sea oil fields 4 Lazlo Biro 5 Miners. It is a chronic disease of the lungs as a result of repeated inhalation of dust 6 Parabola 7 Lead 8 In your neck 9 Oxygen 10 Heroin

731

1 Closest to the Sun 2 In your leg – it's the longest muscle in the body 3 Queen Victoria 4 Heavy water 5 Tungsten 6 The gap between nerve cells 7 Verdigris 8 Malaria 9 They are scared of the dark or of the night 10 The mathematician Pierre de Fermat, whose theory resisted proof for more than 350 years, until finally solved in 1995

732

1 Polio 2 Meltdown 3 Precious metals 4 French 5 Tears 6 She was the first large cloned animal 7 It is the tissue surrounding your heart 8 Psychoanalysis 9 Scrapie 10 The leaning Tower of Pisa

733

1 Submarines 2 Twelve 3 Count Alessandro Volta 4 Hans Geiger 5 Gun metal 6 First heart transplant 7 Baud rate 8 Isomers 9 Charles Babbage 10 Quinine

734

1 The telephone 2 The Sony Walkman 3 Cylinders 4 Philips in 1964 5 Inside a speaker 6 None. Sound waves do not travel through space 7 Fly faster than sound 8 Crystal set 9 By echolocation 10 Guglielmo Marconi, with the first transatlantic radio transmission

735

1 Aspirin, which is derived from substances found in willow bark. Cricket Bats are traditionally made of willow 2 Someone with asthma 3 Acupuncture 4 Foxglove (digitalis) 5 X-rays 6 Penicillin 7 Homeopathy 8 It is an anti-coagulant used in the treatment of a stroke and thrombosis 9 Heart and lung transplants 10 Laughing gas – a painkiller

736

1 *HK-1*, later changed to *H-4 Hughes* Flying Boat commonly called the 'Spruce Goose' 2 The *B2 Spirit* Stealth Bomber 3 Canard 4 *Concordski* 5 The Comet 6 The Harrier Jump Jet 7 It was the first aircraft ever to fly into space, in 1967 8 The SR-71 Blackbird spyplane 9 By escaping from an aeroplane by parachute. The club was named after the silk worm (caterpillar) that provided the parachute silk 10 B52

737

1 Enigma codes 2 Acronym of: What You See Is What You Get 3 HAL 9000 4 It was the first computer animated film to win an Oscar 5 It was the first 'portable' computer 6 The Sinclair Spectrum 7 IBM, known as Big Blue 8 A gigabyte is 1000 megabytes (actually, it's 1024 megabytes, rounded to 1000) 9 A computer virus 10 He released Pong in 1972, the first commercially successful video arcade game

738

1 Straight up 2 Magma 3 Hot springs 4 Vulcanology 5 Faults 6 A Geyser 7 Volcanic vapours, particularly steam 8 Dowsing 9 Fire damp 10 The eruption of Krakatoa

739

1 Radon 2 Alchemy 3 Five; wood, fire, metal, earth and water 4 Aluminium 5 An atom 6 Fluorine 7 Carbon 8 *The Periodic Table* 9 Mercury 10 Oxygen. Most of it is bound in compounds with other elements, not free in the air

740

1 Lead 2 Whetting 3 A surveyor 4 The eye 5 Cement 6 The Bunsen burner 7 Radio telescope 8 Blood pressure 9 A gardener. It is used for planting 10 For grooming animals

741

1 In a light bulb 2 Microwave cooker 3 Video cassette recorder 4 It is the chemical name for baking soda, a raising agent 5 Biological washing powder 6 Yoghurt 7 E numbers 8 The washing machine 9 Kohl, an eyeliner consisting of salts of heavy metals, such as antimony and lead 10 Fermentation

742

1 He was the First American in space 2 Space shuttle 3 Canals 4 *Saturn V* 5 The USSR launched *Sputnik* in 1957 6 The dog Laika, in 1957 7 Orbit 8 She was the first woman in space 9 *Enterprise* 10 *Apollo 13*

743

1 Breastbone 2 Cartilage 3 Ball and socket joint 4 Your big toe 5 In your throat (hyoid bone) 6 The thigh bone, or femur 7 More (330 in a new born: 206 in a fully grown adult) 8 Cranium 9 Their spine. It would curve, causing them to stoop 10 Christopher Reeve

744

1 It was the world's first skyscraper 2 Kuala Lumpur, the Petronas Twin Towers. They are 451.9m (1483ft) from pavement to tip 3 Canary Wharf 4 The Severn 5 London Bridge 6 The US Department of Defense, known as the Pentagon 7 He invented a safety device that allowed electric lifts to be built 8 It was the world's tallest structure at 645m (2115ft) 9 The Empire State Building in New York. The lights were switched on from Washington DC 10 The Eiffel Tower, built in 1889

745

1 The requirement for all motor vehicles to be preceded by a man 60 yards in front carrying a red flag. The distance was cut to 20 yards and made optional 2 The first car with a refrigeration system was the 1940 model Packard 3 It was steam-powered 4 Rover 5 Bluebird 6 Lotus 7 It is the world's most expensive car. One was sold, in

1987, for £5.5 million **8** Volkswagen 'Beetle' **9** 12 mph **10** Sweden

746
1 Ethiopia **2** Wispy, mare's tails **3** 10
4 Anemometer **5** 11 **6** Hexagon
7 Isobar **8** The Meteorological Office
9 Sir Bobby Charlton. His daughter is Suzanne **10** Thermosphere

747
1 They are a small clusters of cells inside the pancreas **2** Keratin **3** In Periodic Table beyond element 114
4 Fluorine **5** They developed the technique which made her the first test-tube baby **6** Aqua Regia, an acid that will dissolve gold **7** Bathyscaphes. Deep-diving submarines that went into the deepest ocean trenches
8 He patented hard-baked, rot-proof porcelain dentures **9** Buckminster Fuller **10** They are named after astronomical bodies. Helium is named after the Sun, selenium after the Moon, uranium after Uranus

748
1 Cocaine. In Coca-Cola in the 1880s
2 Quarks. Nobel laureate Murray Gell-Mann introduced the concept of quarks as a type of fundamental particle, adopting the term from a passage in James Joyce's novel *Finnegans Wake* **3** George Burns
4 Sapphire **5** Adrenaline **6** Binary stars **7** G. They are the four different DNA bases – adenine, cytosine, thymine and guanine – from which all DNA is made **8** He calculated it to be the exact day the world was created. Modern geologists consider he was out by approximately 4.6 billion years **9** He claimed that fossils were put on Earth by God to deceive geologists **10** Venus

749
1 It is the freezing point of salt water, the coldest substance that Daniel Gabriel Fahrenheit could produce
2 Quarks, one of the fundamental sub-atomic particles **3** Albert Einstein
4 Economics **5** 451°F **6** Kurt Vonnegut **7** Rain (Schrödinger's cat and Pavlov's dogs) **8** They are all constellations in the Southern Hemisphere **9** X-ray, on the electromagnetic spectrum **10** 101 – these are the atomic numbers of the

elements named after these scientists
11 Movement: these are the six characteristics of living things
12 Astoria – which was the name of the hotel where Charles Carlson, inventor of the xerox, carried out his earliest experiments **13** Eight
14 Feedback **15** The Doppler effect

750
1 Water **2** Plaster of Paris **3** Caustic Soda **4** Vinegar **5** Epsom salts
6 Bleach **7** Milk of Magnesia
8 Aspirin **9** Vitamin C **10** Methylated spirits

751
1 Crick and Watson **2** Michael Faraday **3** Albert Einstein
4 Archimedes **5** Joseph Priestley
6 Marie Curie **7** Tim Berners-Lee
8 Joseph Lister **9** Benjamin Franklin
10 Thomas Alva Edison

752
1 Bullet train **2** The Angel's Flight Railway in Los Angeles **3** Mallard
4 The Trans-Siberian railway **5** Train à Grande Vitesse **6** Metropolitan (1863)
7 Tay bridge **8** Horses **9** Beijing West Railway station. It is 58.8 hectares in size **10** They were the heaviest land vehicle ever constructed (540 tons)

753
1 Statue of Liberty **2** Empire State Building **3** St Basil's Cathedral, Moscow **4** Golden Gate Bridge
5 Sphinx **6** Sydney Opera House
7 Taj Mahal **8** Tower Bridge **9** Eiffel Tower **10** Reichstag

754
1 Haemoglobin **2** Fats **3** Four (left and right ventricle, left and right atrium) **4** The cornea (part of the eye) **5** Anyone's. AB is known as the universal receiver **6** The heart. It beats about 100,000 times a day
7 Leeches **8** Christiaan Barnard
9 The aorta **10** They would have had a heart attack

755
1 Digestion **2** Stomachs **3** Teeth
4 A stitch is a cramp of the diaphragm muscle **5** Iron **6** He used steroids
7 Bile **8** Carrots. The British let it be known that pilots were eating carrots that allowed them to see in the dark.

In fact their night time successes against the Germans was due to the development of radar **9** Vitamin D
10 Cholesterol

756
1 Fastest transatlantic passenger ship crossing **2** *France II*, built in 1911. She weighed 5909 tonnes **3** *Cutty Sark* **4** She is the largest passenger vessel ever built **5** *Queen Mary*
6 *Lenin*. It was a Soviet icebreaker built in 1957 **7** *Britannic* **8** An aircraft carrier **9** Compass
10 *Flying Cloud*

757
1 Hiccoughs **2** In your nose, when you sneeze **3** The beard **4** On your belly. It is your belly button **5** Tummy rumbling **6** Vertebrae **7** Windpipe
8 About 3lb (1.4kg) **9** approx 100m/sec or about 225mph **10** Skin

758
1 Pluto **2** Neptune **3** 1969 **4** The Solar System **5** Saturn **6** Mars
7 Venus **8** The Earth **9** Meteorites
10 Sun spots

759
1 Influenza **2** Bovine Spongiform Encephalopathy **3** The flea
4 Glandular Fever, or Infectious Mononucleosis **5** Herpes **6** Smallpox
7 Anthrax **8** Rabies **9** A disease prevalent among animals **10** Leprosy. It was first described in ancient Egypt in 1350 BC

760
1 The Pole Star **2** The Hubble telescope **3** The distance light travels in a year (9461 billion km/5880 billion miles) **4** A black hole **5** Stephen Hawking **6** National Aeronautical and Space Administration **7** Constellation
8 The Zodiac **9** Sir Patrick Moore
10 4.6 billion years old

761
1 Surface tension **2** 55 per cent
3 Hydraulics **4** Because water expands as it freezes **5** Water wheel
6 Hydroelectric power **7** About 10cm **8** A waterspout **9** At 200ft (61m) long it is the world's shortest river **10** About 3 per cent

762
1 Radar **2** The V-2 rocket **3** The

4-stroke motor **4** Vulcanisation
5 Intel **6** The Kodak camera **7** The photocopier **8** The helicopter **9** The hovercraft **10** The spinning jenny – a device for spinning thread

763

1 Everything. It was the moment when the Universe began **2** Isobars **3** An airship **4** An android **5** Tin Lizzie
6 December, 21 **7** Bill Gates **8** Seven: Europe, Asia, Africa, North America, South America, Oceania/Australasia and Antarctica **9** Ligaments
10 Central Processing Unit

764

1 A prime number **2** Psychiatry
3 Acquired Immune Deficiency Syndrome **4** Veins **5** Four **6** Fjord
7 One year **8** Equilateral triangle
9 A metre **10** The study of birds

765

1 Tuberculosis **2** Albert Einstein
3 Steel **4** Speech **5** Hologram
6 Opium poppy **7** The Pacific **8** Seven weeks **9** Outboard motor **10** Atoll

766

1 Your eyes **2** Red, Yellow and Blue
3 Oxygen **4** Temperature **5** A circle
6 Ice **7** Cube **8** Yes. Faster than in air
9 Milk teeth **10** Aluminium

767

1 Yes, because they are caused by a virus **2** 1163 **3** Fission **4** Locks
5 Evolution **6** The bicycle **7** A thousand million **8** Hovercraft
9 Hackers **10** The Nile It is 4160 miles (6694km) long

768

1 Ribs **2** A mouse **3** Apple
4 Aqualung **5** Decibel **6** Drawbridge
7 You cannot see it **8** It goes much higher and squeakier **9** Blood **10** In your mouth. They are the sharp teeth at the front of the jaw

769

1 Rust **2** Deep freezing **3** Lithium
4 Water **5** America **6** Braille
7 In your TV or computer. It creates the picture on the screen **8** Acoustics
9 Vitamin C **10** The wavelength of ultraviolet light is too short

770

1 Sony **2** Lungs **3** Its freezing point

4 Winter **5** No **6** Melting **7** Morse Code **8** Saliva **9** Sunburn
10 Microscopic

771

1 Dandruff **2** 98 per cent **3** On the Moon **4** Healing begins within 10 seconds **5** Silicon **6** The lightning conductor, a copper strip running down to the ground **7** The inner part of your ears **8** The Equator **9** With aspirin. They are caused by viruses which are not treatable by antibiotics
10 An eclipse

772

1 Unidentified Flying Object **2** A battery **3** Wine **4** On your teeth
5 Because the Moon is much nearer to Earth **6** 24 hours/one day **7** Hip bone **8** A giant group of millions of stars in space **9** Scab **10** Purple

773

1 The atmosphere **2** Catamaran
3 Because the stretched rubber is trying to squeeze the balloon down to its original size **4** Carbon dioxide
5 Light reflected from the sun
6 Jupiter **7** Diamond **8** Binary
9 Spectrum **10** Chlorine

774

1 Submarine **2** Personal Computer
3 It boils and becomes steam **4** They repel each other **5** Six **6** Five: seeing, hearing, smelling, tasting and touching
7 Tongue **8** Wind **9** In the centre
10 Gravity

Sport

775

1 Three **2** The Red Devils **3** Athletics (or Track and Field) **4** Croquet
5 Craig Brown **6** Cue ball **7** Rugby Union. New Zealand's national team
8 Toronto **9** Blue **10** Sunderland

776

1 Spoon **2** Umpire **3** Black
4 Sheffield **5** Boris Becker **6** West Indies **7** Skiing **8** None due to the Second World War **9** Nigel Mansell
10 Seven minutes

777

1 Edward Heath **2** Ian Botham
3 Canadian **4** Gold **5** Kayak

6 Boxing **7** 6-6 **8** Caber **9** Berlin
10 Hare

778

1 Johnny Weissmuller **2** Hurling
3 Evonne Goolagong **4** Epsom **5** Jib
6 Squash **7** 23 **8** 1500 metres **9** Eric Bristow **10** Wing defence

779

1 Two **2** Sir Alf Ramsey **3** Canoeing
4 Brian O'Driscoll **5** Pete Sampras
6 Newmarket **7** The Agha Khan
8 Speedway **9** The beam **10** Seoul

780

1 Greg Norman **2** Lord's **3** German
4 Black **5** Red Rum **6** Beijing
7 Serena **8** National Football League
9 Butterfly **10** Brian Lara

781

1 Scotland **2** Ice hockey **3** USA, who won it 24 times **4** Russia
5 Rotterdam **6** Australia **7** Greece
8 Japan **9** New York **10** Brazil

782

1 Synchronised swimming **2** Queen of Spades **3** Cambridge **4** Hurl
5 A horse, he is a show jumper
6 Gatwick **7** Leather **8** Yes **9** Ten
10 Liverpool

783

1 Belgium **2** 1981 **3** Martina Navratilova **4** Middleweight **5** Surrey
6 Ice hockey **7** Roberto Duran
8 Sweden **9** Greg LeMond **10** Milton Keynes

784

1 Maurice Greene **2** Mike Tyson
3 Harvey Smith **4** Basketball **5** Four
6 Graham Gooch **7** Five **8** Jack
9 Monte Carlo Rally **10** Starting blocks

785

1 Canada **2** The five continents of the world **3** Michael Vaughan **4** South Africa **5** Badminton **6** US Open
7 60 **8** Lancashire and Yorkshire
9 Three **10** Ten

786

1 Torvill & Dean **2** Greece, where the Olympics originated **3** Churchill Downs **4** Peter Fleming **5** Terry Marsh **6** Alain Prost **7** Red Marauder
8 Swimming **9** Canada **10** Nine

787

1 Barcelona 2 British Open
3 Martina Hingis 4 Wayne Gretzky
5 1997 6 Graham Taylor 7 Monica
Seles 8 New York Yankees 9 Dan
Maskell 10 Atlanta

788

1 West Ham 2 Sheffield Wednesday
3 Slip 4 Blue 5 60 minutes 6 Bunker
7 Nine 8 Jimmy Connors 9 Shutout
10 Baseball

789

1 Soling 2 Swimming 3 A silver
medal was awarded to winning
athletes in the first modern Olympics
and they also received a certificate
and an olive branch 4 Ed Moses
5 One 6 Joe Frazier 7 Harold
Abrahams 8 The Duke of Edinburgh/
Prince Philip 9 1912 10 Cuba

790

1 The 19th Hole 2 One under par
3 Ground under repair 4 Fairway
5 Sand trap 6 The yips is a nervous
condition affecting a golfer's putting
7 A spoon 8 Matchplay 9 Air shot
10 An ace

791

1 Sumo wrestling 2 Tourist Trophy
3 The Eisenhower Trophy 4 The
America's Cup 5 Badminton 6 The
Ryder Cup 7 Football Association
8 The Admiral's Cup in yachting
9 Wind surfing 10 Walking

792

1 1928 2 Jane Couch 3 Alex Greaves
4 Golf 5 Jennifer Capriati 6 Princess
Anne (or The Princess Royal)
7 Archery 8 Squash 9 Diane Leather
in 1955 10 Bobby Riggs

793

1 32 2 Six 3 Abseiling 4 Flush
5 Reverend Green 6 *The Sting*
7 Stamps 8 Checkers 9 Pawn
10 Ten

794

1 Jules Rimet 2 Italy 3 West
Germany 4 Netherlands 5 12 years,
the third being held in 1938 and the
fourth, due to the Second World War,
being held in 1950 6 Geoff Hurst
7 France 8 The Leopards 9 Lion
10 Glenn Hoddle

795

1 Willie Shoemaker 2 G. Abera
3 Golden Gloves 4 New Zealand
5 Shin pads 6 Peter Shilton
7 Salopettes 8 Jersey Joe Walcott
9 15 10 Kendo

796

1 Silverstone 2 Goodyear 3 Nelson
Piquet 4 Alain Prost 5 Frank
Williams 6 Graham 7 Monaco
Grand Prix 8 Finnish 9 1978
10 Aintree

797

1 William Webb Ellis 2 Australia
3 Will Carling 4 Rhinos 5 Haka
6 Twickenham 7 Black 8 Rob
Andrew 9 Italy 10 Rory Underwood

798

1 Newcastle United 2 All white
3 Johann Cryuff 4 Bert Trautmann
5 John Barnes 6 Real Madrid
7 Fulham 8 Jaap Stam 9 Northern
Ireland 10 1870s

799

1 National League 2 Three minutes
3 Argentina 4 Rodeo 5 Nine
6 France 7 800 metres 8 The Jockey
Club 9 Epée. Types of sword 10 Five

800

1 Greyhound 2 Archery 3 Boxing
4 Captain 5 Golf 6 Princess Anne
(or The Princess Royal) 7 Curling
8 Shot putt 9 Rowing 10 Dressage

801

1 Table tennis 2 Red 3 Ron Atkinson
4 Kevin Costner 5 Italy 6 Eight
7 Australian 8 Three years old
9 Figure skating 10 Rolex

802

1 Ayrton Senna 2 Babe Ruth 3 Billie
Jean King 4 Mark Spitz 5 Pele
6 Muhammad Ali 7 Carl Lewis
8 Magic Johnson 9 Nadia Comaneci
10 Steve Redgrave

803

1 Red Rum 2 Jonathan Edwards
3 Bob Beamon 4 Eddie the Eagle
5 Basketball 6 Carl Lewis 7 Lynn
Davies 8 Sergei Bubka 9 Dick
Fosbury 10 3000m steeplechase

804

1 Dickie Bird 2 1980 3 Albatross
4 Magpies 5 *Bluebird* 6 Sheffield
Wednesday 7 Clay pigeon shooting
8 Snooker 9 Don Bradman
10 Toronto Blue Jays

805

1 The Epsom Derby. The toss of the
coin was called correctly by the 12th
Earl of Derby. If Sir Charles had won,
the race would have been called The
Bunbury Cup. He did gain some
consolation as the owner of Diomed,
the winner of the first-ever Epsom
Derby in 1780 2 Golf 3 Yokozuna
4 Weightlifting 5 Hunter Davies
6 A swimming pool 7 Racquetball
8 Hockey 9 Real tennis 10 Triathlon

806

1 1972, in Munich 2 1960s (the 1960
Rome games) 3 Most number of
medals (15) 4 1500m freestyle
5 Cricket 6 President 7 Five. 1916
Summer Games and the 1940 and
1944 Summer and Winter games
8 Princess Anne (or The Princess
Royal) 9 Sarajevo 10 Sweden

807

1 Wembley 2 Newcastle United
3 Peter Shilton 4 Eric Cantona 5 He
scored the first goal in an FA Cup final
6 Middlesbrough. The scorer was
Roberto di Matteo 7 Tottenham
Hotspur 8 Cardiff City 9 Manchester
United: beat Chelsea 4-0 10 Score a
goal in every round

808

1 Leighton Rees 2 RAC Rally 3 Sunil
Gavaskar 4 Jack Brabham 5 Brian
Deane 6 Brooklands 7 W.G. Grace
8 White 9 Romanian 10 January 1

809

1 Six 2 18, eight rowers plus a cox in
each boat 3 50 4 72 5 Six 6 Four
7 Eight 8 Three 9 15 10 12

810

1 Tracy Austin 2 1500 3 Prince
Charles 4 One minute 5 One
6 WBA, which was founded in 1921,
the WBO was founded in 1988 7 Out
of play 8 Australia 9 Skiing 10 None

811

1 In protest at the Soviet Union's
invasion of Afghanistan 2 Both teams

are known as the Reds **3** Five **4** No ball **5** Cycling **6** Becher's Brook **7** Seventeen **8** Backstroke **9** A croquet lawn **10** Jacques Villeneuve

812

1 Cricket stumps **2** Marbles **3** Ray Illingworth **4** Wearing shorts **5** Heart of Midlothian **6** Archery, the nock is a notch at the end of a bow to run the string through. The nocking point is the point of the bow string which is applied to the notch **7** Romania **8** In a Monopoly box **9** George Bernard Shaw **10** Glenn Hoddle – who scored the winner for Tottenham Hotspur in the FA Cup Final. Alan Sunderland did it for Arsenal in 1979, and Ricky Villa for Tottenham in 1981 **11** The surname Doyle (Arthur Conan Doyle created Sherlock Holmes) **12** They all have nicknames which are species of bird: magpies, canaries, seagulls, eagles. **13** Black and white – they are the colours of the jackets worn by the dogs in greyhound racing. **14** 12 – in a set of Tarot cards. **15** It was the 1904 Olympics in St Louis, which featured live pigeon shooting.

813

1 1967 **2** Rhode Island **3** Dartboard numbers **4** Bantamweight **5** Evel Knievel **6** Little Rock **7** Jason Queally **8** Suzanne Danielle **9** Croatia **10** Cowes

814

1 Eight **2** 60 metres **3** *Belleville Rendezous* **4** Boston Red Sox **5** Aluminium **6** *Touché* **7** Types of wrestling **8** Pat Eddery, the horseracing jockey **9** Barcelona **10** Table tennis bats

815

1 Ben Crenshaw **2** Shot Putt **3** Real means Royal **4** Polo **5** Bridge **6** Hungary **7** Water skiing **8** Netherlands **9** 6in (15.25cm) **10** Yugoslavia

816

1 Ronnie O'Sullivan **2** 4 points **3** Three **4** Alex Higgins **5** John Virgo **6** 36 **7** Cliff Thorburn **8** Thai **9** The letter D **10** Triangle

817

1 All have nicknames with a wind connection, Jimmy Whirlwind White, The Clones Cyclone and Alex Hurricane Higgins **2** All can be followed by the word tennis **3** All had sons who followed them in to the sport which made them famous. Marvis Frazier, Liam Botham, Damon Hill and Nigel Clough **4** The numbers in the given sequence can be seen on a dart board; the next is 8 **5** All have the surname of Davis, Joe, Fred and Steve respectively **6** All have nicknames of marine creatures, Miami Dolphins, The Great White Shark and Eric the Eel **7** Olympic Games were cancelled in those years due to World Wars **8** All were won by Brazil **9** Golf **10** Both were hosted by Mexico

818

1 Harlem Globetrotters **2** 'Dreadlock Holiday' **3** West Ham United **4** 'Swing Low Sweet Chariot' **5** 'Simply the Best' **6** Pat Cash **7** 'Abide With Me' **8** Billie Jean King **9** Survivor **10** Puccini

819

1 Ed Moses **2** Niki Lauda **3** Sweden **4** 1989 **5** Men's 200m **6** Oxford & Cambridge boat race **7** America's Cup **8** Aldaniti **9** Tour de France **10** Aberdeen

820

1 Mike Hawthorn **2** Bernie Ecclestone **3** Silverstone **4** James Hunt **5** Juan Miguel Fangio **6** Scottish **7** 1994 **8** Jackie Stewart **9** Ayrton Senna **10** Phil Hill

821

1 Volleyball **2** Football **3** Angling, it is a type of fly used in salmon fishing **4** Crosse **5** The pace of the green **6** A basketball hoop **7** Halyards **8** Biathalon **9** Pelota **10** Boxing gloves

822

1 Billie Jean King **2** Bill Shankly **3** Kerry Packer **4** Three **5** Snooker **6** Kentucky Derby **7** Chris Evert **8** Yachting or sailing **9** Bjorn Borg **10** Gary Sobers

823

1 Yorker **2** Six **3** Trent Bridge **4** Old Father Time **5** Dennis Lillee **6** Lord's **7** The 1930s **8** Don Bradman **9** West Indies **10** The Ashes, which was named after a newspaper report published in the *Sporting Times* after England's first-ever defeat by Australia. The obituary read 'In affectionate remembrance of English cricket which died at the Oval on August 29, 1882. The body will be cremated and the ashes taken to Australia'

824

1 Speed skating **2** Japan **3** Franz Klammer **4** Germany **5** Salt Lake City **6** Swedish **7** Ski **8** Katarina Witt **9** Ravel **10** Crampons

825

1 Newmarket **2** Pat Cash **3** £500 **4** Purse **5** Tax evasion **6** Juan Sebastian Veron **7** Rio Ferdinand **8** Ronaldo **9** Calcutta Cup **10** *Jerry Maguire*

826

1 Six **2** 12 **3** 15 **4** 385 **5** 49 **6** Eight **7** Four **8** 70 **9** 18 **10** Nine

827

1 Dubai World Cup **2** Belmont Stakes **3** Jenny Pitman **4** Types of accumulator bets **5** Willie Carson **6** Party Politics **7** The Kentucky Derby is run over 1 mile 2 furlongs, the others are raced over 1 mile 4 furlongs **8** 16 furlongs **9** Picador **10** Longchamps

828

1 Richard Hadlee **2** India **3** Melbourne **4** Freddie Trueman **5** Sri Lanka **6** Durham **7** West Indies **8** Dennis Compton **9** Extras **10** Ten

829

1 Edinburgh **2** Wembley **3** New York Yankees **4** Melbourne **5** Paris **6** The Curragh **7** St Andrews **8** Aintree **9** Paris **10** Brisbane

830

1 David Beckham **2** Franz Beckenbauer **3** 17 **4** Romania in 1998 **5** New Order **6** Uruguay **7** Ray Wilkins **8** North Korea **9** Dino Zoff **10** Pasadena

835

831
1 Brazil 2 Michael Owen 3 Argentina
4 Eric Cantona 5 Bobby Moore
6 Zinedine Zidane 7 Geoff Hurst
8 Sir Bobby Charlton 9 Black
10 Gary Neville

832
1 Birmingham 2 Imran Khan 3 Run
out 4 Lord's 5 David Gower 6 New
Zealand 7 Ten 8 Chappell 9 Ash
10 Headingley

833
1 Rugby union 2 England 3 Five
4 Jonah Lomu 5 Will Carling 6 Jannie
de Beer 7 Diana Ross 8 Elephant
9 Murrayfield 10 Wigan

834
1 The Olympic Flag 2 Carl Douglas
3 Australian Rules Football 4 Suzuki
5 Argentina 6 Seven 7 Henry
Cooper 8 The hand 9 Darts
10 Jonathan Edwards

835
1 Shergar 2 Due to the funeral of
Princess Diana 3 Ten pin bowling alley
4 Larry Holmes 5 Kuala Lumpur
6 Vesuvius 7 Roberto Baggio
8 Canoeing 9 George V 10 Juan
Pablo Montoya

836
1 Joe di Maggio 2 None 3 Knight
4 Central Park 5 Scotland 6 Duncan
Goodhew 7 Forty-seven minutes, 12 x
3 minute rounds and 11 one minute
breaks 8 National Basketball
Association 9 Bend It Like Beckham
10 The Commonwealth Games

837
1 Knickerbockers, from their name
NY Knickerbockers, sometimes
shortened to the NY Knicks
2 Forward pass 3 Because the male
athletes competed naked 4 Ice
skating 5 Triangular 6 1980
7 Female, the race is for fillies only
8 21 9 Red 10 Monica Seles

838
1 Two 2 Underarm 3 *National Velvet*
4 The 1980s, first run in 1981 5 Ice
hockey 6 The Australian Open
7 Sixty minutes 8 Athletic
9 International Amateur Athletics
Federation 10 Linford Christie

839
1 Basketball 2 Bears 3 Billiards
4 Frank Bruno 5 Bowler 6 Baseline
7 Bogey 8 Bristol, Bristol Rovers v
Bristol City 9 A Brill bend named
after female high jumper Debbie Brill
10 Baltimore

840
1 Athens 1896 2 Atlanta 1996
3 Berlin 1936 4 Helsinki 1952
5 London 1948 6 Munich 1972
7 Rome 1960 8 Tokyo 1964
9 Seoul 1988 10 Sydney 2000

841
1 Weightlifting 2 Zero 3 Chicane
4 Mallet 5 Madhouse 6 Table tennis
7 Chess 8 Surfing 9 Wrestling
10 Cricket, they are styles of delivery
by a cricket bowler

842
1 Donovan Bailey 2 Sugar Ray
Robinson 3 Northern Ireland 4 Pete
Sampras 5 Pakistan 6 Gary Lineker
7 Evander Holyfield 8 Kevin Keegan
9 Jack Nicklaus 10 Fred Perry

843
1 Patrick 2 Maureen Connolly
3 Wendy Turnbull 4 The Four
Musketeers 5 Forest Hills 6 Croquet
7 Wightman Cup 8 Ilie Nastase
9 Ken Rosewall 10 78ft

844
1 Hockey 2 13 3 Hibernians
4 American Football 5 Terry Venables
6 Basketball 7 Australia 8 Tag team
9 Rome 10 Baseball, Pittsburgh
versus Philadelphia

845
1 Steffi Graf 2 Fred Perry (The Perry
Gates) 3 Ace 4 Austin, Tracy and
Roger 5 Three feet 6 Lawn Tennis
Association 7 Five 8 Czechoslovakia
9 Clay 10 Chris Evert-Lloyd

846
1 Billy Wright 2 Italy in 1934 3 An
indirect free kick 4 Alan Ball
5 Cardiff City 6 Berwick Rangers
7 Green 8 Tottenham Hotspur, who
won the European Cup Winners Cup
in 1963 9 Elton John, who was
chairman of Watford, beaten 2-0 in the
1984 final by Everton 10 Zinedine
Zidane

847
1 Silver 2 Yellow 3 Four points
4 Green Bay Packers 5 White Hart
Lane 6 White flag 7 Orange belt
8 Red cap 9 That a driver has been
disqualified 10 Yellow balls

848
1 Newcastle United 2 George Best
3 FIFA 4 West Bromwich Albion
5 Own goal 6 Alex Ferguson
7 Robert Maxwell 8 Graham Taylor
9 Red 10 Glasgow, Celtic v Rangers

849
1 David Campese 2 Eight 3 Romania
4 South Africa 5 Philippe Sella
6 Widnes 7 Stade de France
8 Brisbane Broncos 9 Green
10 Martin Johnson

850
1 Rovers 2 North End 3 South
4 Forest 5 Argyle 6 Academicals
7 Wanderers 8 Athletic 9 Rovers
10 Palace

851
1 A parachutist 2 Dojo 3 Fencing
4 Due to a false start 5 Wrestling
6 He banged his head on the board
during one of his dives 7 Don Budge
8 Zola Budd 9 Mike Gatting
10 Dennis Rodman

852
1 Chicago Cubs 2 Sacking
3 Cowboys 4 99 5 Michael Jordan
6 Green Bay Packers 7 A home run
8 San Francisco 49ers 9 Detroit
Pistons 10 Vancouver Canucks

853
1 Cowdrey 2 38in 3 Garfield Sobers
4 Jack Russell 5 Somerset 6 Daffodil
7 Courtenay Walsh 8 Five 9 Michael
Vaughan 10 Caught

854
1 Bruce Grobbelaar 2 Leeds Utd
3 12 yards 4 The FA Charity Shield
5 Ten, 1916-1919 inclusive and 1940-
1945 6 Robert Pires 7 Old Trafford,
the home of Manchester Utd
8 Austria 9 Lazio 10 Alan Shearer

855
1 Pommel horse 2 Nadia Comaneci
3 Rhythmic gymnastics 4 The rings
5 Olga Korbut 6 Dismount
7 Pommels 8 A type of vault

9 Asymmetric **10** Rings

856

1 The Women's Wimbledon Singles
2 Judo black belts **3** John Paul II who was appointed Pope in 1978
4 Memphis **5** Trampolining, it is a front somersault with a half twist
6 Faroe Islands **7** Kendo
8 Basketball, the first of which comprised of panels of leather that were stitched together over a bladder made of rubber **9** Hang glider
10 Ice hockey **11** Detroit Tigers
12 Volleyball **13** 16 feathers, the best shuttlecocks are made from the feathers of the left wing of a goose
14 The Cresta Run at St Moritz in Switzerland **15** Lacrosse

857

1 Daley Thompson **2** Larry Holmes
3 Nelli Kim **4** Wayne Gretzky **5** Pam Shriver **6** Tom Watson **7** Johnny Weissmuller, Maureen O'Sullivan played Jane in six Tarzan films **8** Rene Lacoste **9** Brian Clough **10** Steve Cauthen

858

1 Steve Davis **2** Netherlands
3 Mexico **4** New York Giants
5 Three strokes, a snowman is a score of three over par **6** Lennox Lewis
7 Jana Novotna **8** Buffalo Bills
9 Europe **10** Valencia

859

1 Joe Louis **2** Jim Laker **3** Graham Hill **4** Arthur Ashe **5** Rocky Marciano
6 Fred Archer **7** Joe Davis **8** Duncan Edwards **9** Buster Crabbe
10 Cricket

860

1 Michael Johnson **2** Yellow jersey
3 112 **4** Chicago Bulls **5** 180
6 Bangladesh **7** Speedway **8** Squash court **9** Munich **10** Tommy Morrison

861

1 Ice hockey **2** Tiger Woods **3** 1500 metres **4** Nigel Mansell **5** John Walker **6** Not out **7** Murrayfield
8 Ethiopian **9** Four **10** Michael

862

1 Barcelona **2** Denver Nuggets
3 Cycling **4** John Walker
5 Melbourne **6** The Stanley Cup in ice hockey **7** Chyna **8** Michael

Doohan **9** An air shot **10** 15

863

1 Basketball **2** Horse Racing
3 Motor Racing **4** Cricket **5** Boxing
6 Wrestling **7** Football **8** Snooker
9 Rowing **10** Motor Rally

864

1 Two **2** Jockey **3** London **4** Javelin
5 Black **6** Sticks **7** Wicket Keeper
8 Six **9** 50 **10** Six

865

1 16lb **2** Forty **3** The final lap is starting **4** Four, two for each player
5 Glass fibre **6** Swedish **7** Bicycle
8 Golfer **9** Eight **10** Time out

866

1 Duck **2** Bamboo **3** 20 **4** United
5 Swimming **6** American Football
7 Ten **8** Three **9** 8 yards **10** Cricket

867

1 Fencing **2** Rugby Union. 15 compared to 13 **3** Green **4** Belts
5 Ice hockey **6** Basketball
7 Liverpool **8** A small toboggan
9 Stalls **10** Golf

868

1 Javelin **2** Table tennis **3** Square
4 None **5** Nose **6** Liverpool
7 Tennis **8** Motorbike **9** Ten
10 Volleyball

869

1 Aintree **2** 26 miles **3** Ice hockey
4 Argentina **5** Yellow **6** Tie breaker
7 Baton **8** Three **9** Leg before wicket
10 15

870

1 Bats **2** Spain **3** Polo **4** Oval
5 Hare **6** Chequered flag **7** Six
8 Salt Lake City, Utah, USA **9** Eight
10 Fencing

871

1 Volley **2** Touchdown **3** Wrestling
4 Strike **5** Cue ball **6** Golf **7** The pits **8** Pitcher **9** Badminton **10** Let

The Arts

872

1 Stephen King **2** Tarzan of the Apes
3 Terry Pratchett **4** James Herbert
5 Mr Hyde **6** Shakespeare **7** Denis

Wheatley **8** *The Hunchback of Notre Dame* **9** Frankenstein's monster
10 Sinbad the Sailor

873

1 Stratford-upon-Avon, Warwickshire
2 She was his mother **3** Anne Hathaway **4** *Hamlet* **5** *Julius Caesar* – speech by Mark Antony **6** *Othello*
7 The Globe **8** Royal Shakespeare Company **9** *Macbeth* **10** *A Midsummer Night's Dream*

874

1 *The Firm* **2** *Treasure Island*
3 A Soviet submarine **4** Robert Ludlum **5** George Smiley **6** Andy McNab **7** Dinosaurs **8** The French Foreign Legion **9** Africa **10** King Solomon's Mines

875

1 Valhalla **2** Oedipus **3** King Arthur
4 China **5** North America **6** Achilles
7 It wore a sheepskin – 'a wolf in sheep's clothing' **8** Romulus and Remus **9** The Rhine **10** Icarus, son of Daedalus

876

1 A camera – she was a photographer
2 Celia Brayfield **3** Harper Lee
4 Yoko Ono **5** Frances Edmonds
6 Rachel Carson **7** Ted Hughes
8 Angela Carter **9** Catherine Cookson **10** Dorothy Parker

877

1 The 87th Precinct **2** *The Thin Man*
3 Simon Templar (The Saint), hero of the books by Leslie Charteris
4 Billy Bathgate **5** *The Winslow Boy*
6 Emile Zola (in the Dreyfus case 1898) **7** V. I. Warshawski **8** Wilkie Collins **9** He was a justice of the peace (from 1748) **10** Oscar Wilde

878

1 Denmark **2** Australia **3** USA
4 *The Russia House* **5** *The Boys from Brazil* **6** *A Passage to India* **7** Italy
8 France **9** Trinidad **10** Ireland

879

1 Horatio Hornblower **2** Patrick O'Brian **3** Ernest Hemingway **4** An aircraft carrier **5** Moby Dick, the white whale **6** SS *Poseidon* – filmed as *The Poseidon Adventure* **7** USS *Caine* – *The Caine Muntiny* **8** Longfellow
9 *The Cruel Sea* **10** A sieve

1 Don Quixote 2 Sir John Falstaff in Henry V 3 Beaumont and Fletcher 4 150 5 *Twelfth Night* 6 Sir Lancelot 7 Queen Victoria, knighting Henry Irving in 1895 8 Geoffrey Chaucer in his *Canterbury Tales* 9 Etheridge Knight 10 Ronnie Knight

1 Richmal Crompton's William (Just William) 2 Sherlock Holmes 3 Oliver Twist – the dog belonged to Bill Sikes 4 The Famous Five 5 Dalmatians, 101 of them 6 *Peter Pan* 7 Toby 8 The house that Jack built 9 Frederick Forsyth 10 Lassie

1 The CIA (Central Intelligence Agency) 2 Photography – Dazzle is the name of a photographers' studio in California 3 Bertie Wooster 4 Jack is Jack Welch, CEO of General Electric 5 A vet 6 Horse racing 7 The law 8 Medicine – they're both doctors 9 Antiques 10 He's a dustman

1 Charlotte, Emily and Anne Brontë 2 Agatha Christie 3 George Orwell 4 Mary Ann Evans 5 Melvyn Bragg 6 Barbara Taylor Bradford 7 Joe Klein 8 Fitzgerald – the novelist Scott and the English translator Edward 9 Ruth Rendell 10 Agatha Christie

1 Orange – *Clockwork Orange* 2 Green – *Anne of Green Gables* by L.M. Montgomery 3 Blue 4 Red – *The Red Badge of Courage* 5 White – T.H. White, Snow White 6 *The Color Purple* 7 Black – *Black Beauty* 8 *Goldfinger* 9 Picasso 10 Tom Brown

1 Lord Peter Wimsey 2 Miss Marple 3 Adam Dalgliesh 4 Dalziel and Pascoe 5 Patricia D. Cornwell 6 Father Brown 7 Raymond Chandler 8 Perry Mason 9 Jules Maigret 10 *The Maltese Falcon*

1 Nicholas Hawksmoor (1661–1736) – the novel *Hawksmoor* appeared in 1986 2 Richard Rogers 3 Florence 4 I.M. Pei 5 John Nash (1752–1835) 6 Walter Gropius 7 Charles Rennie Mackintosh (1868–1928) 8 Sir Christopher Wren (1632–1723) 9 Frank Lloyd Wright 10 New Delhi

1 *A Christmas Carol* 2 *Chocolat* 3 *Death in Venice* 4 *Dr Zhivago* 5 *Little Women* 6 *Moby Dick* 7 *The Beach* 8 *The Great Gatsby* 9 *The Mirror Cracked* 10 *Treasure Island*

1 Berlin – Isherwood's *Goodbye to Berlin*, Deighton's *Funeral in Berlin* 2 Blondes 3 *Wuthering Heights* 4 *Pride and Prejudice* 5 *The Last of the Mohicans* 6 *Gone With The Wind* 7 Barchester 8 He is a butler 9 *Robinson Crusoe* 10 Jane Eyre

1 *Pride and Prejudice* by Jane Austen 2 *Anna Karenina* by Leo Tolstoy 3 *The Go-Between* by L.P. Hartley 4 *The French Lieutenant's Woman* by John Fowles 5 *Catcher in the Rye* by J.D. Salinger 6 *The Metamorphosis* by Franz Kafka 7 *Gone with the Wind* by Margaret Mitchell 8 *Empire of the Sun* by J.G. Ballard 9 *The Wonderful Wizard of Oz* by L. Frank Baum 10 *Longitude* by Dava Sobel

1 I.M. Pei 2 William Van Alen 3 James Hoban 4 Frank Gehry 5 Jorn Utzon 6 Norman Foster 7 Gustave Eiffel 8 Cesar Pelli 9 Sir Christopher Wren 10 Le Corbusier

1 Born (Born to be wild; Born to Run; Born Free; Born on the 4th July; Born in the USA) 2 All the titles are quotes from Shakespeare 3 *Moby Dick* 4 Winston Churchill 5 Swastika 6 They all wrote books about prison (*Notes From the Underground*; *De Profundis*; *The Drowned and the Saved*; *Borstal Boy*) 7 Alice (*Alice in Wonderland*; *A Town Like Alice*; Alice Walker) 8 Phileas Fogg (in *Round The World In 80 Days*) 9 If (a poem; a film; a song) 10 They all have plots that involve doubles or twins 11 MASH 12 The titles are all quotes from songs ('Battle Hymn of the Republic'; 'Less Than Zero'; 'Jerusalem') 13 Charles Dickens 14 Pelham Greville 15 Miller. Arthur, Henry and Miller's

1 Dublin 2 The Brontës 3 London and Paris 4 Cornwall 5 Moscow 6 Stoke on Trent 7 Berlin 8 The Nile – *Death on the Nile* 9 Virginia 10 Madison – *The Bridges of Madison County*

1 John Steinbeck 2 Water lilies 3 Aspidistra – *Keep The Aspidistra Flying* 4 Walt Whitman 5 Sunflowers 6 *The Name of the Rose* 7 Clare Rayner 8 *Little Shop of Horrors* 9 Anton Chekhov 10 William Wordsworth

1 Seamus Heaney 2 Roddy Doyle 3 Irvine Welsh 4 DBC Pierre 5 Vikram Seth 6 Ronald Reagan 7 Louis de Bernières 8 Baseball 9 It's a fiction prize for the best novel by a woman 10 *Life of Pi*

1 John Constable 2 Andy Warhol 3 Still life 4 T.S. Eliot 5 The Borrowers 6 A portable toilet 7 The love of money – 1 Timothy 8 The Owl and the Pussy-Cat (in the verse by Edward Lear) 9 Salvador Dali 10 Tracey Emin

1 Tiger Woods 2 Tony Booth (father-in-law of Tony Blair) 3 Sir Harry Secombe 4 Germaine Greer 5 Paul McCartney 6 Jeffrey Archer 7 Billy Connolly 8 Colin Powell 9 Dirk Bogarde 10 *Bring on the Empty Horses*

1 *The Edge of Reason* 2 *The Hitch-Hikers Guide to the Galaxy* 3 *Bonfire Of The Vanities* 4 *A Walk in the Woods* 5 Alan Ayckbourn 6 Malcolm Bradbury 7 Mapp and Lucia 8 P.J. O'Rourke 9 A cockroach 10 *The Rivals*

1 600 2 Four (Matthew, Mark, Luke and John) 3 22 – the novel's title is *Catch 22* 4 Thirty Nine 5 451°F – the book is *Fahrenheit 451* 6 The Secret Seven 7 Six – Bond is 007 8 *Three Men in a Boat* 9 Eighty, in Jules Verne's *Around the World in Eighty*

Days (1873) **10** Two

899

1 Ancient Egypt **2** The front **3** Fonts (or typefaces) **4** The Penguin logo, on the first Penguins **5** Genesis **6** Batman, Bruce Wayne **7** *Punch* **8** All cartoonists **9** Almanacs **10** The owner's name (This book belongs to)

900

1 Lindsey Davis **2** Shakespeare, in *Julius Caesar* (spoken by Casca, Act 1 scene II) **3** Lawrence Durrell **4** Edward Gibbon **5** El Greco – 'The Greek' **6** Michael Dibdin **7** *Ulysses* **8** They got dressed – later it became part of the background or 'scenery' **9** Plato **10** John Keats – *Ode on a Grecian Urn*

901

1 Florence, Italy **2** Russian, by Tolstoy **3** Scotland **4** France **5** Norwegian **6** Edinburgh, Scotland **7** Wales **8** Italy **9** Russia **10** German

902

1 Professor Stephen Hawking. The book is *A Brief History of Time* **2** *Where Eagles Dare* **3** Lake Wobegon **4** Catherine Cookson **5** Lourdes **6** James Clavell **7** Dick Francis **8** *The Eagle Has Landed* **9** *Eats, Shoots & Leaves* **10** Barbara Taylor Bradford

903

1 They were shot from a giant cannon **2** Earth and Mars, in the book by H.G. Wells **3** Aldous Huxley **4** *Gulliver's Travels* – the Island is Laputa **5** *The Lord of the Rings* by J.R.R. Tolkien **6** *The Sentinel* **7** Kingsley Amis **8** Mars – *The Martian Chronicles* **9** Isaac Asimov **10** Frank Herbert

904

1 Alfie, in the books by Shirley Hughes **2** Three **3** The Gingerbread Man **4** *The Snowman* (by Raymond Briggs) **5** Simba, the Lion King **6** Harry Potter **7** The Never-Never Land **8** Toyland **9** Eeyore the donkey **10** Rupert

905

1 *The Wonderful Wizard of Oz* **2** The Demon Headmaster **3** Narnia in C.S. Lewis's *The Lion, The Witch and The Wardrobe* **4** The Mole in *The Wind in the Willows* **5** *The Hobbit* **6** A house **7** The Worst Witch **8** The Owl **9** Brandy (and baccy – tobacco – for the clerk) **10** Anne Frank

906

1 Pinocchio **2** A frog **3** The tortoise **4** The Tiger **5** Please **6** *Cinderella* **7** Thomas the Tank Engine **8** Three **9** The Pushmi-Pullyu **10** They are both elephants

907

1 A painter **2** A self-portrait **3** Furniture **4** A clay pot, on a potter's wheel **5** Acting **6** Dance – they were ballet dancers **7** Opera **8** Types of pottery or porcelain **9** London **10** A bust

908

1 Miss Trunchball, in *Matilda* by Roald Dahl **2** Cruella De Vil in *101 Dalmatians* **3** A tiger, with man-eating tendencies **4** Harry Potter's **5** The White Witch **6** The Red Queen in *Alice in Wonderland* **7** Toad's in *The Wind in the Willows* **8** A poisoned apple **9** *Aladdin* **10** The Big Bad Troll

909

1 Dementors **2** Cornelius Fudge **3** The Malfoys **4** A basilisk **5** Sirius Black **6** Professor Remus Lupin **7** Defence against the Dark Arts **8** Hufflepuff **9** Hogsmead **10** Cedric Diggory

910

1 A lion **2** His chocolate factory **3** New York **4** Winnie The Pooh **5** Marmalade sandwiches **6** Jade **7** A hedgehog **8** The Demon Headmaster **9** Fungus **10** A pumpkin

911

1 J.R.R. Tolkien **2** Sailing boats **3** Thirteen and Three-Quarters **4** Sherlock Holmes **5** L. M. Montgomery **6** Ian Fleming **7** Pantalaimon **8** Enid Blyton **9** Jane Austen **10** Lewis Carroll

912

1 Rabbits **2** A really ugly duck **3** Big Friendly Giant **4** One **5** Dog's droppings **6** Anne Fine **7** Open, Sesame! **8** *Goosebumps* **9** Mrs Pepperpot **10** The Brothers Grimm

Quick Quizzes

Building bridges 1 Simon and Garfunkel **2** Asia **3** San Francisco **4** Lloyd Bridges **5** Venice **6** David Lean
Who said that? 1 Henry Morton Stanley **2** Henry Ford **3** John Lennon **4** Richard III **5** Winston Churchill **6** John F. Kennedy
Animal magic 1 At night **2** Swarm **3** Ten **4** Cats **5** Roy Rogers **6** Whale
General knowledge 1 Jonah **2** Mark Antony **3** Atlas **4** Wells Fargo **5** Tobago **6** Yellow
Literary logic 1 Irish **2** Willy Wonka **3** Hercule Poirot **4** Rugby **5** Nelson Mandela **6** Ben Elton
Waterworld 1 Erie **2** Danube **3** 12 **4** Niagara Falls **5** Aegean Sea **6** Washington DC

Around the USA 1 Rhode Island **2** Florida **3** Chicago **4** Houston **5** New York **6** Hoover Dam (221m)
General knowledge 1 Florence **2** Bill Clinton **3** *Death Wish* **4** Falkland Islands **5** Pierre Trudeau **6** Tracy
Around Europe 1 St Paul's Cathedral **2** Italy **3** Greece **4** Vienna **5** Costa Blanca **6** Lyon
Words 1 Sole **2** Degrees **3** Scaffold **4** Fuselage **5** Pew **6** Ream
Films 1 Chitty Chitty Bang Bang **2** Clark Gable **3** Susan Sarandon **4** *Cabaret* **5** *Absolute Power* **6** Sir John Gielgud
Instruments 1 Bob Dylan **2** Piano **3** Double Bass **4** Mandolin **5** Bugle **6** Piccolo

TV greats 1 1950s **2** Jon Pertwee **3** Officer Dibble **4** Victoria Principal **5** Quantum Leap **6** Purple
Music 1 The Beach Boys **2** Sparks **3** U2 **4** *Pomp and Circumstance March* (Land of Hope and Glory) **5** John Denver **6** Three
Famous people 1 Hugh Hefner **2** Gerry Anderson **3** Richard Nixon **4** Robert Burns **5** Lady Godiva

6 Princess Anne
General knowledge **I** Royal Albert Hall **2** German **3** Languages **4** Hamburgers **5** Dick Whittington **6** Water
Around the world **I** Himalayas **2** India **3** Egypt **4** Spanish **5** Cape Horn **6** Lima
Think of a number **I** Seven **2** 21 **3** 1000 **4** 50 **5** 911 **6** 90210

Crime and punishment
I Dr Harold Shipman **2** Broadmoor **3** Ronnie Kray **4** District Attorney **5** Bonnie and Clyde **6** Ronnie Biggs
General knowledge **I** Rat **2** Robbie Williams **3** *Cinderella* **4** *The Omen* **5** Carbon dioxide **6** Swimming
Title roles **I** Michael Keaton **2** Orson Welles **3** Kirk Douglas **4** Joseph Fiennes **5** Peter O'Toole **6** Diane Keaton
You wear it well **I** Mary Quant **2** Marilyn Monroe **3** Shoulders **4** Green **5** An Earl **6** China – pigtails were seen as a symbol of obedience to the Manchu dynasty
Child's play **I** Nat King Cole **2** Captain Frederick Marryat **3** George Michael **4** W.C. Fields **5** Annie **6** Jamie Lee Curtis
Kids' TV **I** London **2** Green **3** Rugrats **4** Captain Pugwash **5** Lulu **6** Postman Pat

Nursery rhymes **I** Fiddlers three **2** Little Bo Peep **3** Dr Foster **4** *Ring a Ring of Roses* **5** Little Miss Muffet **6** Mary
Body matters **I** White **2** Muscles **3** ZZ Top **4** Eyebrows **5** Vertebrae **6** Liver
Flower power **I** Janis Joplin **2** Thistle **3** Gladiolus **4** Woody Allen **5** *Keeping Up Appearances* **6** Red
A veggie table **I** Beetroot **2** Cabbage Patch Dolls **3** *Toy Story* **4** Bean **5** Capsicum **6** Turnips
General knowledge **I** Graham Greene **2** Claudius **3** Germany **4** Dove **5** Cathedral **6** Grand Central
Transport trivia **I** O'Hare in Chicago **2** Automobile **3** Route 66 **4** Omnibus **5** Lotus **6** York

Superman **I** Dean Cain **2** Clark Kent **3** Lois Lane **4** Smallville **5** Marlon Brando **6** Ned Beatty
Sport **I** Ten pin bowling **2** Steve Davis **3** 60 minutes **4** Three **5** India **6** Six
General knowledge **I** Ram **2** Antarctica **3** Manhattan **4** Five **5** Chicken **6** Afghanistan
Fictional characters **I** Porthos **2** *1984* **3** *The Chamber* **4** Lorna Doone **5** Dick Tracy **6** Horatio Hornblower
Furniture facts **I** The Chair **2** Old Mother Hubbard **3** A settee or a couch **4** Bed **5** The Cabinet **6** Wardrobe
Under the sea **I** Whale **2** Cash On Delivery **3** The bends **4** Jeffrey Archer **5** The Great White **6** Blue

General knowledge **I** Havana **2** Sweden **3** Beef **4** Piano **5** Canvas **6** An apple a day
Colourful questions **I** Black box **2** Gretna Green **3** Tea **4** Violet Carson **5** Fifty **6** Pink coat
Kings **I** Stephen King **2** King James Bible **3** Elvis Presley **4** *The Avengers* **5** Henry VIII **6** King Louie
The name's the same **I** Mandarin **2** Port **3** Pen **4** Dam **5** Gorge **6** Kite
Star wars **I** *The Millennium Falcon* **2** Natalie Portman **3** 1977 **4** Rebel Alliance **5** Jar Jar Binks **6** The Death Star
Days like these **I** Jefferson High School **2** Thor **3** Shrove Tuesday **4** Black Wednesday **5** Patrick **6** Lou Reed

Tree trivia **I** Maple **2** Evergreen **3** 'Ashes to Ashes' **4** Marc Bolan **5** Pine **6** Family tree
T time **I** Tinkerbell **2** Tusk **3** Tyrant **4** *The Times* **5** Tadpole **6** Turkish
General knowledge **I** *Romeo and Juliet* **2** J. Edgar Hoover **3** *The Fly* **4** Barium **5** Goat **6** Swastika
Superstar marriages **I** Sonny Bono **2** Cindy Crawford **3** 35 **4** Elizabeth Taylor **5** Andre Agassi

6 Jackie Collins
Nationalities **I** German measles **2** Dutch **3** Dawn French **4** Spanish Armada **5** The Bangles **6** *The African Queen*
Novel locations **I** France **2** Russia **3** Scotland **4** Switzerland **5** India **6** Canada

General knowledge **I** English **2** 1930s **3** The face **4** Sapphire **5** The death **6** Squares
The size of it **I** Texas **2** Majorca **3** Bee hummingbird **4** Long John Baldry **5** Japan **6** African elephant
Twins **I** Margaret Thatcher **2** Gemini **3** Bros **4** Siamese or conjoined twins **5** *The Adventures of Tintin* **6** Castor and Pollux
Take a letter **I** Q **2** C **3** Alfred Hitchcock **4** Universal **5** O **6** *V*
All-rounders **I** Paramount **2** Egypt **3** Bagpipes **4** Winds **5** Plutonium **6** The Eagles
Clockwise **I** Bill Haley **2** Anti-clockwise **3** One O'Clock **4** *High Noon* **5** Dial **6** John Cleese

Singers **I** Robert Palmer **2** Barry Gibb **3** Chris de Burgh **4** The Pacemakers **5** Marti Pellow **6** Marie Osmond
Initials **I** Herbert **2** Perception **3** Columbia **4** Germany **5** Intelligence **6** America On Line
General knowledge **I** San Francisco **2** A sword **3** *The Life of Brian* **4** The ear **5** Amstel **6** Pol Pot
TV comedy **I** *Ellen* **2** Ted Danson **3** Joey **4** *Porridge* **5** Sesame Street **6** Mr Rigsby
Creepy crawlies **I** Male **2** Buddy Holly **3** Nectar **4** Beetle **5** Peter Parker **6** Four
Rocking all over the world **I** Liverpool **2** Simon & Garfunkel **3** Georgia **4** Africa **5** Chicago **6** New York

Stones **I** Sharon Stone **2** Yellow **3** The Rolling Stones **4** 14 **5** 'Cast the first stone' **6** The Rubbles
G force **I** Greenland **2** Gobi Desert

3 Ghana 4 Glasgow 5 Greece
6 Greenwich (Mean Time)
Prefixes I Blood 2 Birthday
3 Sun 4 Milk 5 Battle 6 Water
Beastly books I Roald Dahl 2 *The Call of the Wild* 3 Penelope Lively
4 John Steinbeck 5 *Babe* 6 Rats
General Knowledge I France
2 The feet 3 France 4 Rabbi
5 Dallas 6 Matt Damon
All Davids I David Niven 2 David Bowie 3 David Copperfield 4 David Cassidy 5 Goliath 6 David Blunkett

Initial queries I Heavy Goods Vehicle 2 Member of the Scottish Parliament 3 Intercontinental Ballistic Missile 4 Officer of the Order of the British Empire 5 Independent Television News 6 Acquired Immune Deficiency Syndrome
Baby talk I *Baby Boom* 2 The Supremes 3 Gosling 4 Bruce Willis
5 *The Water Babies* 6 Nelson
General knowledge I Rice
2 Stanley Kubrick 3 I 4 Palindromes (a word or phrase that reads the same backwards as forwards) 5 Ecuador
6 Mike Oldfield
Who's who? I Nellie the elephant
2 Jodie Foster 3 Geoffrey Chaucer
4 Julia Roberts – for *Mary Reilly*
5 David Beckham 6 Jane Wyman
Pie posers I Desperate Dan
2 Canary 3 'American Pie' 4 Torta
5 Simple Simon 6 A type of hat
C here? I Canvas 2 Cavalry
3 Clarinet 4 Concord 5 Coronation
6 Cornea

General knowledge I *Born Free*
2 Mount Etna 3 Four 4 Moses
5 Simon 6 *ER*
Countries I Brazil 2 New Zealand
3 India 4 Italy 5 Hungary 6 Egypt
On the march I Happiness. The song is 'Walking back to Happiness'
2 Monty Python's Flying Circus
3 China 4 Jenny Agutter 5 Walker Brothers 6 Julius Caesar
Mammal mania I Bat 2 Mule
3 Hare 4 Boar 5 Gnu 6 Joey
Soccer nicknames I Sheffield Wednesday 2 West Ham United
3 Coventry City 4 Derby County
5 Wimbledon 6 Southampton
The state of things I Florida

2 Arkansas 3 Denver 4 Hawaii
5 Oklahoma 6 Louisiana

Lessons in love I Erich Segal
2 *Four Weddings and a Funeral*
3 Whitney Houston 4 'Never to have loved at all' 5 St Valentine 6 'All You Need Is Love'
House and home I House of Commons 2 *Bleak House* 3 Beaver
4 Teletubbies 5 *House of Wax*
6 Madness
General knowledge I Dog
2 St Paul's Cathedral 3 Brian May
4 Oliver Twist 5 Aniseed 6 Cousins
Songs I 'New York, New York'
2 Barry White 3 Barcelona
4 'Wuthering Heights' 5 *Funny Girl*
6 'Without You'
The female of the species
I Nanny 2 Ewe 3 Doe 4 Tigress
5 Cow 6 Jenny
Movie men I Robert Redford
2 Gene Kelly 3 Christopher Lambert
4 Bud and Lou 5 Richard Gere
6 James Caan

Heavy metal I Copper 2 The Pretenders 3 Amritsar 4 A butterfly
5 David Essex 6 Günter Grass
Leading ladies I Faye Dunaway
2 Sandra Bullock 3 Mary Poppins
4 Meryl Streep 5 Julie Walters
6 Glenn Close

How many? I Six 2 12 3 Ten
4 Three 5 Eight 6 Two: Anne and George
Fraction facts I 25 2 Top number
3 Halfway 4 An inch 5 75 per cent
6 *The Third Man*
General knowledge I The eyes
2 Euphrates 3 Baseball 4 Open spaces 5 Genesis 6 Lagos
Musical instruments
I Keyboard 2 Harp 3 Guitar
4 Violin 5 Sousaphone 6 China

Shared names I Archer
2 McQueen 3 Wilson 4 Cash
5 Twain 6 Higgins
Doggy dilemmas I Pekinese

2 Poodle 3 Dougal 4 Mexico
5 Spaniel 6 Collie
General knowledge I Huey Lewis
2 Box 3 *The Music Man* 4 Duck
5 Vancouver 6 *The Sopranos*
Three-letter words I Ace 2 Gin
3 Pan 4 Hay 5 Yen 6 Tit
Stevens and Stephens
I December 26 2 Stephen Sondheim
3 Steven Patrick Morrissey 4 *The Shining* 5 Steven Spielberg 6 Stevie Wonder
Lords and ladies I Lady Chatterley
2 Jack Lord 3 *High Society* 4 Gandalf
5 *Moulin Rouge* 6 *The Mikado*

General knowledge I Two 2 Tom Jones 3 Darwin 4 Blue 5 Belgium
6 Methuselah
To cap it all I Cape 2 Capsize
3 Capricorn 4 Capsule 5 Capon
6 Capstan
Author, author I A.A. Milne
2 John Milton 3 Rip Van Winkle
4 Joel Chandler Harris 5 Bridget Jones 6 David
Classic TV I The Daleks 2 *Hart to Hart* 3 Horse 4 The Waltons 5 Ben Murphy 6 Tabitha
Who said it? I Groucho Marx
2 Winston Churchill 3 Charles Dickens 4 Mark Twain 5 Margaret Thatcher 6 Dorothy Parker
Capital punishment I Montevideo
2 Athens 3 Brussels 4 The Nile
5 La Paz 6 Bonn

Body wise I Left 2 Cape Town
3 Yellow 4 Skull 5 Iris 6 Hair
TV duos I Cousins 2 Starsky and Hutch 3 New York 4 Eric and Ernie
5 Rag and bone 6 *Tom and Jerry*
General knowledge I Richard Dreyfuss 2 Victor Hugo 3 Hazelnuts
4 Potato 5 Delta 6 Blue
Sporting personalities I Allan Border 2 Joe Johnson 3 Alf Ramsey
4 Ralf 5 Swedish 6 Ian Woosnam
Worldly wisdom I Black Sea
2 Cheyenne 3 Moulin Rouge
4 Atlantic Ocean 5 Aborigines
6 Hudson Bay
What's the word? I Lectern
2 Mutation 3 Palindrome 4 Merman
5 Streetcars 6 Shanghai

The sixties 1 P.D. James 2 Robben Island 3 The Victoria Line 4 Peter Noone 5 Stanley Matthews 6 *Lady Chatterley's Lover*

Tasty trivia 1 Linguine 2 Cabbage 3 Lent 4 Red 5 India 6 Vitamin C

As easy as ABC 1 Astronomy 2 Aniseed 3 Bridle 4 Blubber 5 Collie 6 Carburettor

Model questions 1 Twiggy 2 Naomi Campbell 3 Elle MacPherson 4 Volkswagen 5 Jerry Hall 6 Aircraft

General knowledge 1 Hard black 2 The Irish Sea 3 Dog 4 Nelson Mandela 5 Zambezi 6 Kidneys

The phoenetic alphabet 1 Victor 2 Lima 3 Quebec 4 Golf 5 Whisky 6 Hotel

Art for art's sake 1 Spanish 2 Venus de Milo 3 Pablo Picasso 4 Trafalgar Square 5 Paris 6 Michelangelo

Film roles 1 Tom Cruise 2 Antonio Banderas 3 Piano 4 Anthony Quinn 5 *Waterworld* 6 Susan George

General knowledge 1 His pipe 2 Groundhog Day 3 Sir Galahad 4 Federal 5 None 6 Champagne

Playing the game 1 16 2 Bridge 3 That a word has two syllables 4 Red 5 Two, the domino is double one 6 40

Real names 1 Barbara Windsor 2 Ruth 3 George Formby 4 Shirley Maclaine 5 Lee Majors 6 Bo Derek

C creatures 1 Cygnet 2 Cheetah 3 Camberwell Beauty 4 Crocodile 5 Chicken 6 Chameleon

Sporting chance 1 David Beckham 2 Michael Atherton 3 Will Carling 4 Benetton 5 Wales 6 Baseball

TV drama 1 *The Untouchables* 2 Oxford 3 Lucy Liu 4 *Soldier, Soldier* 5 Philip Michael Thomas 6 Blue Moon

Colourful songs 1 Will Smith 2 Red wine 3 Procol Harum 4 Brown 5 Prince 6 Shakin' Stevens

Puddings and pies 1 Pumpkin 2 France 3 Apple 4 24 5 Toad in the hole 6 Pig

General knowledge 1 Vaudeville 2 Ear 3 14 4 Japan 5 Ben Nevis 6 San Andreas Fault

Languages 1 Trois 2 Gypsies 3 Two 4 Drapes 5 Beta 6 Portuguese

V Is for ...? 1 Viruses 2 Volcanoes 3 Vellum 4 Vikings 5 Visor 6 Venezuela

The planet Earth 1 Indian Ocean 2 Peru 3 Lake Superior 4 Africa 5 Rio Grande 6 Dead Sea

General knowledge 1 Italy 2 Field Marshal 3 Humerus 4 Arctic 5 The beginning 6 St Andrews

Wildlife 1 Snake 2 Three 3 Whale Shark 4 Hair 5 Blue Whale 6 Insect

Alphabetically 1 Bashful 2 Uranus 3 None 4 W 5 Aberdeen 6 Parental Guidance

Partners 1 Pet Shop Boys 2 Hare 3 Everly Brothers 4 Cagney 5 Oliver Hardy 6 Cheese

General knowledge 1 Nuclear disarmament 2 Green 3 Gilbert and Sullivan 4 A book 5 Tsarina 6 Dino

An Asian experience 1 Yellow River 2 Khyber Pass 3 New Delhi 4 Japan 5 Beijing 6 T'Pau

From head to toe 1 Temple 2 Heart 3 Rib 4 Kangaroo 5 Israel 6 Tic Tac Toe

TV jobs 1 Psychiatrist 2 Car mechanic 3 Josiah Bartlet 4 Lawyers 5 Richard Chamberlain 6 Julianna Margulies

Oscar round 1 *On the Waterfront* 2 Las Vegas. The film was *Leaving Las Vegas* 3 William Hurt 4 *All the President's Men* 5 *Jerry Maguire* 6 *The Cider House Rules*

Opening lines 1 'You're the One that I Want' 2 'Thriller' 3 'Money, Money, Money' 4 'Walking on the Moon' 5 'I Got You Babe' 6 'My Way'

Screen greats 1 James Dean 2 Scarlett O'Hara 3 Alfred Hitchcock 4 Humphrey Bogart 5 James Cagney 6 The Marx Brothers

Let's dance 1 The twist 2 Dame Margot Fonteyn 3 London 4 Two 5 Locomotion 6 Foxtrot

General knowledge 1 Hair 2 Alaska 3 Harold Melvin 4 Hen 5 Violin 6 Mary, Queen of Scots

Space 1 Vacuum 2 Yuri Gagarin 3 Smaller 4 Saturn 5 Gases 6 Pink Floyd

A call to arms 1 Armenia 2 Armadillo 3 Armageddon 4 Armistice 5 Armpit 6 Armour

A cookery lesson 1 A cold soup 2 Haggis 3 Goose 4 Buns 5 Netherlands 6 Black

General knowledge 1 England 2 Four 3 Light 4 The scarecrow 5 Ravens 6 New York

Who wrote it? 1 Matthew 2 Paul McCartney 3 Anthony Burgess 4 Arthur Miller 5 Enid Blyton 6 Oscar Wilde

Pen and ink 1 Stink 2 Swan 3 Fleet Street 4 Sword 5 Quill 6 It is a pen name; a pseudonym used to disguise an author's true identity

The Jacksons 1 Gordon Jackson 2 Bubbles 3 Samuel L. Jackson 4 Colin Jackson 5 Mississippi 6 Jackson Pollock

Sporting chance 1 Andre Agassi 2 Ally McCoist 3 Ten 4 Underwood 5 Basketball 6 Mark James

Religion and belief 1 Cleanliness 2 Shiva 3 *Clash of the Titans* 4 Norse or Viking 5 Six 6 Judaism

Trees 1 Horse chestnut 2 Hazel 3 Scott Joplin 4 Eucalyptus 5 Yew 6 Mulberry

Around the year 1 Sapphire 2 Sagittarius 3 Yom Kippur 4 April 23 5 Ramadan 6 A dragon

General knowledge 1 Vulture 2 Republican 3 Nickel 4 Dead Sea 5 On the antlers 6 1950s

Three-letter words 1 *Bad* 2 Ear 3 Ram 4 Woe 5 Sow 6 Pig

Four-letter words 1 Wham 2 Rose 3 *Cats* 4 Loch 5 Lead 6 Mile

Firsts 1 Salyut 1 2 White 3 Dr Watson 4 Maureen Connolly 5 Ella Fitzgerald 6 Alabama

Plants and gardening 1 Rose
2 Potting compost 3 Geoff Hamilton
4 Vita Sackville-West 5 Chelsea
Flower Show 6 Slugs and snails
Five-letter words 1 Tokyo 2 Liver
3 Grape 4 Pride 5 Tommy 6 Moses
Six-letter words 1 *Psycho* 2 Violin
3 Batman 4 Jersey 5 Silver 6 Anther
L of a film 1 *La Bamba* 2 *Liar, Liar*
3 *Lawrence of Arabia* 4 *Live and Let Die*
5 *Labyrinth* 6 *Living Free*
General knowledge 1 Copacabana
2 The 18th century 3 Christopher
Plummer 4 Tuning fork 5 Canada
6 Atlantic Ocean
Husbands and wives 1 Pamela
Anderson 2 Princess Anne 3 Linda
McCartney 4 Farrah Fawcett 5 Jackie
Kennedy 6 Patricia

Fashion facts 1 A scarf
2 Moccasins 3 Jean Paul Gaultier
4 Italy 5 A broad brimmed hat
6 Around the waist
The A list 1 Amber 2 Atlantic
3 Acre 4 Adonis 5 Arsenic
6 Afrikaans
General knowledge 1 Water sign
2 Venus 3 Jim Henson 4 David
Attenborough 5 Bambi 6 Garlic
Creature comforts 1 Dingo
2 Swarm 3 Worm 4 Drone
5 Herring Gull 6 Eagle
T time 1 Turkey 2 Tudor 3 Trident
4 Thyroid 5 Troop 6 Traffic
Water, water 1 *The Water Babies*
2 George Frideric Handel 3 Dennis
Waterman 4 212°F 5 Seven 6 The
fountain pen

Cities 1 Leningrad 2 Princes Street
3 Berlin 4 North Island 5 Arizona
6 Beijing (Peking)
Science 1 Hydrogen and oxygen
2 10 (a decimetre is 10cm) 3 100 (a
decametre is 10m) 4 Ostrich 5 The
atom bomb 6 Charles Darwin
People 1 Delano 2 Swiss 3 Sean
Connery 4 Chile 5 Nick Park
6 Cinema
History 1 Richard Nixon 2 The
19th (1853–1856) 3 Pakistan 4 John
Paul II 5 Lord's 6 James Hunt

General knowledge 1 Dutch
2 Yoghurt 3 Dublin 4 Miami
5 Arsenal 6 Lizard
A to F 1 Aviary 2 Bulgaria 3 Cent
4 Diameter 5 Enclave 6 Flax

G to L 1 Gauntlet 2 Hormone
3 Iron 4 Judo 5 Kentucky
6 Luxembourg
M to R 1 Malta 2 New 3 Octet
4 Pyrenees 5 Quills 6 *Roots*
S to X 1 Severn 2 Tirana 3 Uganda
4 Voice 5 Wigwam 6 XIX
Sporting terms 1 Dan 2 Fencing
3 Two 4 Wrestling 5 High jump
6 Drag racing
Places 1 South Korea 2 The Grand
Canyon 3 Red 4 Bangkok 5 The
Great Barrier Reef 6 Asia
Plant posers 1 Almond 2 Ginger
3 Huckleberry 4 Shamrock
5 A toboggan 6 Violet

Film females 1 Sigourney Weaver
2 Melanie Griffith 3 *Shakespeare in
Love* 4 Cher 5 Jane 6 Bette Midler
Feathered friends 1 Rook
2 Ostrich 3 Green 4 Owl
5 Cuckoo 6 Snooker
United Kingdom 1 The Mall
2 Oxford 3 Sheffield 4 Surrey
5 September 6 Isle of Wight
Music 1 Les Dawson 2 Your teeth
3 Roy Plomley 4 Sheep 5 Plucking
the string (not bowing) 6 Tara
Palmer-Tomkinson
General knowledge 1 John
2 Berlin 3 BMW 4 Brian Jones
5 Portugal 6 Shuttlecock
Cooking 1 It is a hot water bath in
which you place a dish to be gently
cooked 2 Shrove Tuesday
3 A thickening made from equal
quantities of flour and butter cooked
together 4 Mrs Beeton 5 Textured
vegetable protein (derived from
Soybeans) 6 Anchovies

Saints 1 Football 2 Ian Ogilvy
3 Southampton 4 St Winifred's
School Choir 5 Isla St Clair
6 St Andrews
On wine 1 Chile 2 The fruit residue

3 Bollinger Champagne 4 Keith Floyd
5 Beaujolais Nouveau 6 Sotheby's
Oscar round 1 Elizabeth Taylor
2 *The Piano* 3 Marlee Matlin
4 Katharine Hepburn, with 12
nominations 5 Grace Kelly 6 Queen
Elizabeth I in *Shakespeare in Love*
Which month? 1 October
2 November 3 Jarrow March
4 September 5 April 6 Maybug
General knowledge 1 Parma
2 Big Ben 3 Croquet 4 Gaggle
5 Denmark 6 London Heathrow
Collective nouns 1 Murder
2 Colony 3 Swarm 4 Troop 5 Host
6 Flock

Cities 1 Auckland 2 Helsinki
3 Hawaii 4 Jesus 5 Paris 6 Sudan
Fact or fiction? 1 Fact 2 Fiction, he
was called Hickory 3 Fiction, Rene
Laennec was the inventor 4 Fact
5 Fact 6 Fiction, his middle name
was Elias
Mountain mania 1 Mont Blanc
2 South Africa 3 K2 4 *The Sound of
Music* 5 The Rockies 6 The Andes
General knowledge 1 Roger
Rabbit 2 A pouch 3 Feet 4 Pride
5 The Gulf of Mexico 6 John
Rodent round 1 Beaver 2 Guinea
pig 3 Bob Geldof 4 Danger Mouse
5 Greg Dyke 6 Dumbo
Island info 1 French 2 Isle of Man
3 Indian 4 Tasmania 5 Isle of Dogs
6 Madagascar

Books 1 Tom Sawyer 2 Anna
Karenina 3 Esmerelda 4 Friday
5 Charlotte 6 Don Quixote
General knowledge 1 Jupiter
2 Georgia 3 The farmer's wife
4 Ireland 5 Stork 6 Memory
TV sitcoms 1 Nurse 2 Courtney
Cox 3 *The Royle Family* 4 Kelsey
Grammar 5 *Taxi* 6 Joanna Lumley
Religion 1 Lent 2 Fisherman
3 Saturday 4 Jordan 5 Shinto 6 Five
For the bird brains 1 South Pole
2 Bird's nest soup 3 Owl 4 Six geese
a-laying 5 Peahen 6 Happiness
Selective knowledge 1 Luke
2 Channel Tunnel 3 The Grand
National 4 Green 5 Aquarius 6 F

35

Down by the riverside I Seine
2 Rio 3 Amazon 4 Bruce Springsteen
5 Joan Rivers 6 Boney M
Nicknames I Brenda Lee
2 Richard Nixon 3 Buster Keaton
4 Florence Griffith-Joyner 5 Reggie
Kray 6 Eric Bristow
General knowledge I Stephen
King 2 South Africa 3 12 4 A crash
5 Libra 6 Lead
Fruity facts I Grapes 2 Plum
3 Jaffa 4 Apple 5 Jeanette Winterton
6 Melon
TV cooks I Nigella Lawson 2 Delia
Smith 3 Jamie Oliver 4 Shirley
Conran 5 Jennifer Patterson 6 Fanny
and Johnny Cradock
Star trekking I Romulans 2 Gene
Roddenberry 3 Russian 4 Dilithium
5 Vulcan 6 1960s

 36

Falling down I Michael Douglas
2 Venezuela 3 'When I Fall In Love'
4 Elvis Costello 5 Lee Majors
6 Niagara
Movie music I *Desperately Seeking
Susan* 2 *Annie get your Gun*
3 'Edelweiss' 4 *Oliver* 5 King Arthur
6 *Rocky III*
General knowledge I *Bonanza*
2 Nine 3 Russia 4 Cobra 5 Hyde
Park 6 Hermit crab
Yellow perils I Yellowstone
National Park 2 Cowardice 3 Fever
4 *Yellow Submarine* 5 Green 6 'Yellow
Rose of Texas'
First names I John 2 Theo
3 Endeavour 4 Nancy 5 Marion
6 Jane
Vegetable mix I Graham Taylor
2 Bugs Bunny 3 Sir Walter Raleigh
4 Smooth words 5 Cucumber, which
is a fruit 6 Kos

Tie Breakers

**1 James Bond films based on Ian
Fleming novels (15)** *Casino Royale*
(1967) • *Diamonds Are Forever* (1971) •
Dr. No (1962) • *For Your Eyes Only* (1981)
• *From Russia with Love* (1963) • *Goldfinger*
(1964) • *Live and Let Die* (1973) • *The
Living Daylights* (1987) • *The Man with the*

Golden Gun (1974) • *Moonraker* (1979) •
Octopussy (1983) • *On Her Majesty's Secret
Service* (1969) • *The Spy Who Loved Me*
(1977) • *Thunderball* (1965) • *You Only
Live Twice* (1967)

2 Sports of the decathlon (10)
100 metres • 110 metres hurdles
• 400 metres • 1500 metres • Discus •
High jump • Javelin • Long jump • Pole
vault • Shot-put

3 The Seven Dwarfs (7) Bashful
• Doc • Dopey • Grumpy • Happy •
Sleepy • Sneezy

**4 Number one Spice Girls hits of
the 20th century (8)** 2 Become 1
• Goodbye • Mama/Who Do You Think
You Are • Say You'll Be There • Spice Up
Your Life • Too Much • Viva Forever
• Wannabee

5 Streets on a Monopoly board (22)
The Angel, Islington • Bond Street • Bow
Street • Coventry Street • Euston Road •
Fleet Street • Leicester Square
• Marlborough Street • Mayfair •
Northumberland Ave • Old Kent Road
• Oxford Street • Pall Mall • Park Lane •
Pentonville Road • Piccadilly • Regent
Street • Strand • Trafalgar Square • Vine
Street • Whitechapel Road • Whitehall

**6 Gifts given on the 12 days of
Christmas (12)** One partridge in a
pear tree • Two turtle doves • Three
French hens • Four calling birds • Five
golden rings • Six geese a-laying • Seven
swans a-swimming • Eight maids a-milking
• Nine ladies dancing • Ten lords
a-leaping • Eleven pipers piping • Twelve
drummers drumming

7 Books of the Old Testament (39)
Amos • 1 Chronicles • 2 Chronicles
• Daniel • Deuteronomy • Ecclesiastes •
Esther • Exodus • Ezekiel • Ezra •
Genesis • Habakkuk • Haggai • Hosea
• Isaiah • Jeremiah • Job • Joel • Jonah •
Joshua • Judges • 1 Kings • 2 Kings
• Lamentations • Leviticus • Malachi •
Micah • Nahum • Nehemiah • Numbers
• Obadiah • Proverbs • Psalms • Ruth •
1 Samuel • 2 Samuel • Song of Solomon
• Zechariah • Zephaniah

8 London Underground stations

beginning with S (31) Seven Sisters
• Shadwell • Shepherds Bush (Central
line) • Shepherds Bush (Hammersmith &
City line) • Shoreditch • Sloane Square
• Snaresbrook • South Ealing • South
Harrow • South Kensington • South
Kenton • South Quay • South Ruislip
• South Wimbledon • South Woodford •
Southfields • Southgate • Southwark • St
James's Park • St John's Wood • St Paul's
• Stamford Brook • Stanmore • Stepney
Green • Stockwell • Stonebridge Park •
Stratford • Sudbury Hill • Sudbury Town
• Surrey Quays • Swiss Cottage

**9 Seven Wonders of the ancient
world (7)** Colossus of Rhodes
• Hanging Gardens of Babylon •
Mausoleum of Halicarnassus • Pharos of
Alexandria • Pyramids of Giza • Statue
of Zeus at Olympia • Temple of
Artemis at Ephesus

**10 20th century Presidents of the
USA (18)** George Bush (1989-93)
• Jimmy Carter (1977-81) • William J.
Clinton (1993-2001) • Calvin Coolidge
(1923-29) • Dwight D. Eisenhower (1953-
61) • Gerald R. Ford (1974-77) • Warren
Harding (1921-23) • Herbert Hoover
(1929-33) • Lyndon B. Johnson (1963-69)
• John F. Kennedy (1961-63) • William
McKinley (1897-1901) • Richard M.
Nixon (1969-74) • Ronald W. Reagan
(1981-89) • Franklin D. Roosevelt (1933-
45) • Theodore Roosevelt (1901-09) •
William H. Taft (1909-13) • Harry S
Truman (1945-53) • Woodrow Wilson
(1913-21)

**11 Formula 1 championship
winners (27)** Mario Andretti • Alberto
Ascari • Jack Brabham • Jim Clark •
Juan Manuel Fangio • Guiseppi Farina
• Emerson Fittipaldi • Mika Hakkinen •
Mike Hawthorn • Damon Hill • Graham
Hill • Phil Hill • Denis Hulme • James
Hunt • Alan Jones • Niki Lauda • Nigel
Mansell • Nelson Piquet • Alain Prost
• Jochen Rindt • Keke Rosberg • Jody
Scheckter • Michael Schumacher • Ayrton
Senna • Jackie Stewart • John Surtees •
Jacques Villeneuve

**12 Countries formed on the break
up of the USSR (15)** Armenia
• Azerbaijan • Byelorussia • Estonia •
Georgia • Kazakhstan • Kyrgyzstan
• Latvia • Lithuania • Moldova • Russia •

444

Tajikistan • Turkmenistan • Ukraine • Uzbekistan

13 Members of the Monty Python team (6) Graham Chapman • John Cleese • Terry Gilliam • Eric Idle • Terry Jones • Michael Palin

14 Christmas number ones, 1970-2000 (31) 2 Become 1 (Spice Girls, 1996) • Always On My Mind (Pet Shop Boys, 1987) • Another Brick in the Wall (Pink Floyd, 1979) • Bohemian Rhapsody (Queen, 1975) • Bohemian Rhapsody (Queen, 1991) • Can We Fix It? (Bob the Builder, 2000) • Do They Know It's Christmas? (Band Aid, 1984) • Do They Know It's Christmas? (Band Aid 2, 1989) • Don't You Want Me? (The Human League, 1981) • Earth Story (Michael Jackson, 1995) • Ernie (The Fastest Milkman In The West) (Benny Hill, 1971) • Goodbye (Spice Girls, 1998) • I Have a Dream / Seasons in the Sun (Westlife, 1999) • I Hear You Knockin' (Dave Edmunds, 1970) • I Will Always Love You (Whitney Houston, 1992) • Lonely This Christmas (Mud, 1974) • Long Haired Lover From Liverpool (Little Jimmy Osmond, 1972) • Mary's Boy Child (Boney M, 1978) • Merry Christmas Everyone (Shakin' Stevens, 1985) • Merry Xmas Everyone (Slade, 1973) • Mistletoe and Wine (Cliff Richard, 1988) • Mr Blobby (Mr Blobby, 1993) • Mull of Kintyre (Wings, 1977) • Only You (The Flying Pickets, 1983) • Reet Petite (Jackie Wilson, 1986) • Save Your Love (Renee and Renato, 1982) • Saviour's Day (Cliff Richard, 1990) • Stay (East 17, 1994) • There's No-one Quite Like Grandma (St Winifred's School Choir, 1980) • Too Much (Spice Girls, 1997) • When a Child is Born (Johnny Mathis, 1976)

15 Blue Peter presenters of the 20th century (28) Richard Bacon (1997-98) • Matt Baker (1999-) • Mark Curry (1986-89) • Romana D'Annunzio (1996-98) • Peter Duncan (1980-84) and (1985-86) • Janet Ellis (1983-87) • Yvette Fielding (1987-92) • Sarah Greene (1980-83) • Simon Groom (1978-86) • Tina Heath (1979-80) • Katy Hill (1995-2000) • Konnie Huq (1997-) • Caron Keating (1986-90) • Diane-Louise Jordan (1990-96) • Lesley Judd (1972-79) • John Leslie (1989-94) • Stuart Miles (1994-99) • John Noakes (1965-78) • Peter Purves (1967-78) • Valerie Singleton (1962-72) • Michael Sundin (1984-85) • Simon Thomas (1999-) • Christopher Trace (1958-67) • Anthea Turner (1992-94) • Tim Vincent (1993-97) • Christopher Wenner (1978-80) • Anita West (1962) • Leila Williams (1958-62)

16 Capital cities of Europe (45) Amsterdam / The Hague (accept either) (Netherlands) • Ankara (Turkey) • Andorra la Vella (Andorra) • Athens (Greece) • Belgrade (Yugoslavia (Serbia)) • Berlin (Germany) • Bern (Switzerland) • Bratislava (Slovakia) • Brussels (Belgium) • Bucharest (Romania) • Budapest (Hungary) • Chisinau (Moldova) • Copenhagen (Denmark) • Dublin (City) (Ireland) • Helsinki (Finland) • Kiev (Ukraine) • Lisbon (Portugal) • Ljubljana (Slovenia) • London (UK) • Luxembourg (Luxembourg) • Madrid (Spain) • Minsk (Belarus) • Monaco (Monaco) • Moscow (Russia) • Nicosia (Lefkosia) (Cyprus) • Oslo (Norway) • Paris (France) • Prague (Czech Republic) • Reykjavik (Iceland) • Riga (Latvia) • Rome (Italy) • San Marino (San Marino) • Sarajevo (Bosnia & Herzegovina) • Skopje (Macedonia) • Sofia (Bulgaria) • Stockholm (Sweden) • Tallinn (Estonia) • Tirana (Albania) • Vaduz (Liechtenstein) • Valletta (Malta) • Vatican City (Holy See) • Vienna (Austria) • Vilnius (Lithuania) • Warsaw (Poland) • Zagreb (Croatia (Hrvatska))

17 The Beatles' number ones (17) A Hard Day's Night • All You Need Is Love • Ballad Of John And Yoko • Can't Buy Me Love • Day Tripper/We Can Work It Out • Eleanor Rigby/Yellow Submarine • From Me To You • Get Back • Hello Goodbye • Help! • Hey Jude • I Feel Fine • I Want To Hold Your Hand • Lady Madonna • Paperback Writer • She Loves You • Ticket To Ride

18 Winners of the best motion picture/best picture Oscar (75) *A Beautiful Mind* (2001) • *A Man for All Seasons* (1966) • *All about Eve* (1950) • *All Quiet on the Western Front* (1930) • *All the King's Men* (1949) • *Amadeus* (1984) • *American Beauty* (1999) • *An American in Paris* (1951) • *Annie Hall* (1977) • *The Apartment* (1960) • *Around the World in 80 Days* (1956) • *Ben Hur* (1959) • *The Best Years of Our Lives* (1946) • *Braveheart* (1995) • *The Bridge on the River Kwai* (1957) • *The Broadway Melody* (1929) • *Casablanca* (1943) • *Cavalcade* (1933) • *Chariots of Fire* (1981) • *Cimarron* (1931) • *Dances With Wolves* (1990) • *The Deer Hunter* (1978) • *Driving Miss Daisy* (1989) • *The English Patient* (1996) • *Forrest Gump* (1994) • *The French Connection* (1971) • *From Here to Eternity* (1953) • *Gandhi* (1982) • *Gentleman's Agreement* (1947) • *Gigi* (1958) • *Gladiator* (2000) • *The Godfather* (1972) • *The Godfather Part II* (1974) • *Going My Way* (1944) • *Gone with the Wind* (1939) • *Grand Hotel* (1932) • *The Great Zeigfeld* (1936) • *The Greatest Show on Earth* (1952) • *Hamlet* (1948) • *How Green was my Valley* (1941) • *In the Heat of the Night* (1967) • *It Happened One Night* (1934) • *Kramer vs. Kramer* (1979) • *The Last Emperor* (1987) • *Lawrence of Arabia* (1962) • *The Life of Emile Zola* (1937) • *The Lost Weekend* (1945) • *Marty* (1955) • *Midnight Cowboy* (1969) • *Mrs Miniver* (1942) • *Mutiny on the Bounty* (1935) • *My Fair Lady* (1964) • *Oliver!* (1968) • *On the Waterfront* (1954) • *One Flew Over the Cuckoo's Nest* (1975) • *Ordinary People* (1980) • *Out of Africa* (1985) • *Patton* (1970) • *The Pianist* (2002) • *Platoon* (1986) • *Rain Man* (1988) • *Rebecca* (1940) • *Rocky* (1976) • *Schindler's List* (1993) • *Shakespeare in Love* (1998) • *The Silence of the Lambs* (1991) • *The Sound of Music* (1965) • *The Sting* (1973) • *Terms of Endearment* (1983) • *Titanic* (1997) • *Tom Jones* (1963) • *Unforgiven* (1992) • *West Side Story* (1961) • *Wings* (1928) • *You Can't Take it With You* (1938)

19 *Carry On* films (30) *Abroad* • *Again Doctor* • *At Your Convenience* • *Behind* • *Cabby* • *Camping* • *Cleo* • *Columbus* • *Constable* • *Cowboy* • *Cruising* • *Dick* • *Doctor* • *Don't Lose Your Head* • *Emmannuelle* • *England* • *Follow That Camel* • *Girls* • *Henry* • *Jack* • *Loving* • *Matron* • *Nurse* • *Regardless* • *Screaming!* • *Sergeant* • *Spying* • *Teacher* • *Up The Jungle* • *Up the Khyber*

20 Post-war British prime ministers (11) Clement Attlee (Labour, 1945-51) • Tony Blair (Labour, 1997-) • James Callaghan (Labour, 1976-79) • Winston Churchill (Conservative, 1951-55) • Alec Douglas-Home (Conservative, 1963-64) • Anthony Eden (Conservative, 1955-57) • Edward Heath (Conservative, 1970-74)

• Harold MacMillan (Conservative, 1957-63) • John Major (Conservative, 1990-97) • Margaret Thatcher (Conservative, 1979-90) • Harold Wilson (Labour, 1964-70 and 1974-76)

21 Shakespeare's plays (37)
All's Well That Ends Well • Antony and Cleopatra • As You Like It • The Comedy of Errors • Coriolanus • Cymbeline • Hamlet • Henry IV part 1 • Henry IV part 2 • Henry V • Henry VI part 1 • Henry VI part 2 • Henry VI part 3 • Henry VIII • Julius Caesar • King John • King Lear • Love's Labour's Lost • Macbeth • Measure for Measure • The Merchant of Venice • The Merry Wives of Windsor • A Midsummer Night's Dream • Much Ado About Nothing • Othello • Pericles Prince of Tyre • Richard II • Richard III • Romeo and Juliet • The Taming of the Shrew • The Tempest • Timon of Athens • Titus Andronicus • Troilus and Cressida • Twelfth Night • The Two Gentlemen of Verona • The Winter's Tale

22 Winners of the FIFA World Cup (8) Argentina (1978, 1986) • Brazil (1958, 1962, 1970, 1994, 2002) • England (1966) • France (1998) • Germany (1990) • Italy (1934, 1938, 1982) • Uruguay (1930, 1950) • West Germany (1954, 1974)

23 Planets of the Solar System (9)
Earth • Jupiter • Mars • Mercury • Neptune • Pluto • Saturn • Uranus • Venus

24 Signs of the Zodiac (12)
Aquarius • Aries • Cancer • Capricorn • Gemini • Leo • Libra • Pisces • Sagittarius • Scorpio • Taurus • Virgo

25 Wacky Races starting grid (11)
00 Dick Dastardly & Mutley in the Mean Machine • 1 The Slagg brothers in the Boulder Mobile • 2 The Gruesome Twosome in the Creepy Coupé • 3 Professor Pat Pending in the Ring-a-Ding Convert-a-Car • 4 Red Max in the Crimson Haybailer • 5 Penelope Pitstop in the Compact Pussycat • 6 Sarge & Private Peevley in The Army Surplus Special • 7 The Ant Hill Mob in the Bullet-proof Bomb • 8 Luke & Blubber Bear in the Arkansas Chugabug • 9 Peter Perfect in the Turbo Terrific • 10 Rufus & Sawtooth in the Buzzwagon

26 Actors who have played Doctor Who on TV (7) Colin Baker • Tom Baker • Peter Davison • William Hartnell • Sylvester McCoy • Jon Pertwee • Patrick Troughton

27 Complete Operas of Gilbert and Sullivan (14) *The Gondoliers • The Grand Duke • HMS Pinafore • Iolanthe • The Mikado • Patience • The Pirates of Penzance • Princess Ida • Ruddigore • The Sorcerer • Thespis • Trial By Jury • The Yeomen of the Guard • Utopia Limited*

28 Children's novels by Roald Dahl (17) *The BFG • Charlie and the Chocolate Factory • Charlie and the Great Glass Elevator • Danny, the Champion of the World • The Enormous Crocodile • Esio Trot • Fantastic Mr Fox • George's Marvelous Medicine • The Giraffe and the Pelly and Me • The Gremlins • James and the Giant Peach • The Magic Finger • Matilda • The Minipins • The Twits • The Vicar of Nibbleswicke • The Witches*

29 The 10 plagues of Egypt (10)
Boils and sores • Cattle die from disease • Darkness • Death of the first born • Frogs • Hail • Lice, sand flies or fleas • Locusts • Swarms of flies • Water turns to blood

30 Officer ranks of the British Army (11) 2nd Lieutenant • Brigadier • Captain • Colonel • Field Marshal • General • Lieutenant • Lieutenant Colonel • Lieutenant General • Major • Major General

Miles Kelly Publishing

Director: Jim Miles
Editorial Director: Anne Marshall
Project Editor: Jenni Rainford
Art Director: Clare Sleven
Copywriter: Ben Rooney
Question-setters: Mark Bastable, Charles Godfray, Richard Hunter, Christopher Rigby, Brian Ward, Brian Williams
Fact checkers: Georgia Cameron-Clarke, Matt Parselle
Design: John Christopher, Dick Skelt
Model-maker: Melanie Williams
Language Consultant: Luke Seaber
Photography: Tony Poole, Alan Roberts
Picture Research: Liberty Newton, Bethany Walker

Reader's Digest

Project Editors: Jonathan Bastable, Alison Candlin
Art Editor: Julie Bennett
Editorial Assistant: Lucy Murray
Proofreaders: Barry Gage, Ken Vickery
Pre-press Accounts Manager: Penny Grose
Senior Production Controller: Sarah Fox

Reader's Digest, General Books, London

Editorial Director: Cortina Butler
Art Director: Nick Clark
Executive Editor: Julian Browne
Development Editor: Ruth Binney
Publishing Projects Manager: Alastair Holmes
Picture Resource Manager: Martin Smith
Style Editor: Ron Pankhurst
Book Production Manager: Fiona McIntosh
Pre-press Manager: Howard Reynolds

Quiz Night was published by The Reader's Digest Association Ltd, London

First edition Copyright © 2002 The Reader's Digest Association Ltd, 11 Westferry Circus, Canary Wharf, London E14 4HE
www.readersdigest.co.uk

We are committed to both the quality of our products and the service we provide to our customers.

We value your comments, so please feel free to contact us on 08705 113366 or via our web site at: www.readersdigest.co.uk

If you have any comments or suggestions about the content of our books, email us at: gbeditorial@readersdigest.co.uk

Copyright © 2002 Reader's Digest Association Far East Ltd
Philippines copyright © 2002 Reader's Digest Association Far East Ltd

Reprinted in hardback with amendments 2004

Quiz Night was edited and produced by Miles Kelly Publishing for the Reader's Digest Association Limited, London

Origination
Colour Systems Ltd

Printing and binding
Everbest Printing Co Ltd, China

CONCEPT CODE UK 1325/G
BOOK CODE 400-224-01
ISBN 0 276 42946 X
ORACLE CODE 250008904H.00.24

Answer card photocopy as needed

Team name:	
Round:	
Question 1	
Question 2	
Question 3	
Question 4	
Question 5	
Question 6	
Question 7	
Question 8	
Question 9	
Question 10	

Scorecard

Team name	Round 1	Round 2	Round 3	Round 4	Round 5